SECOND EDITION

SUPPLY CHAIN MANAGEMENT

Strategy, Planning, and Operations

Sunil Chopra

Kellogg School of Management
Northwestern University

Peter Meindl

Stanford University

PEARSON
Prentice
Hall

Pearson Education International

Executive Editor: Tom Tucker
Editor-in-Chief: P.J. Boardman
Assistant Editor: Erika Rusnak
Editorial Assistant: Dawn Stapleton
Media Project Manager: Nancy Welcher
Marketing Manager: Debbie Clare
Marketing Assistant: Amanda Fisher
Managing Editor (Production): John Roberts
Production Editor: Renata Butera
Production Assistant: Joe DeProspero

Permissions Coordinator: Suzanne Grappi
Associate Director, Manufacturing: Vincent Scelta
Production Manager: Arnold Vila
Manufacturing Buyer: Michelle Klein
Cover Design: Bruce Kenselaar
Composition: Pine Tree Composition, Inc.
Full-Service Project Management: Pine Tree Composition, Inc.
Printer/Binder: Von Hoffmann

If you purchase this book within the United States or Canada you should be aware that it has been wrongfully imported without the approval of the Publisher or the Author.

Credits and acknowledgments borrowed from other sources and reproduced, with permission, in this textbook appear on appropriate page within the text.

Microsoft® and Windows® are registered trademarks of the Microsoft Corporation in the U.S.A. and other countries. Screen shots and icons reprinted with permission from the Microsoft Corporation. This book is not sponsored or endorsed by or affiliated with the Microsoft Corporation.

Pearson Education LTD.
Pearson Education Singapore, Pte. Ltd
Pearson Education Canada, Ltd.
Pearson Education—Japan

Pearson Education Australia PTY, Limited
Pearson Education North Asia Ltd
Pearson Educación de Mexico, S.A. de C.V.
Pearson Education Malaysia, Pte. Ltd
Pearson Education, Upper Saddle River, NJ

1 0 9 8 7 6 5 4
ISBN 0-13-121745-3

I would like to thank my colleagues at Kellogg for all that I have learnt from them about logistics and supply chain management. I am grateful for the love and encouragement my parents Krishan and Pushpa, and sisters, Sudha and Swati, have always provided during every endeavor in my life. I thank my children Ravi and Rajiv for the joy they have brought me. Finally, none of this would have been possible without the constant love, caring, and support of my wife Maria Cristina.

Sunil Chopra

I would like to thank three mentors: Sunil Chopra, my co-author; Hau Lee, my advisor at Stanford and beyond; and Gerry Lieberman—all of whom have taught me a great deal and inspired me even more. I would like to thank my parents and sister for their constant love and support as well as my sons Jamie and Eric for making me smile and teaching me the right perspective on life. And, most importantly, I would like to thank my wife, Sarah, who makes my life wonderful and whom I love with all of my heart.

Pete Meindl

Brief Contents

PART VI: COORDINATION AND TECHNOLOGY IN THE SUPPLY CHAIN   475

Contents

Preface

This book has grown from a course on supply chain management taught to second-year MBA students at the Kellogg School of Management at Northwestern University. The goal of this class was to cover not only high-level supply chain strategy and concepts, but also to give students a solid understanding of the analytical tools necessary to solve supply chain problems. With this class goal in mind, our objective was to create a book that would develop an understanding of the following key areas and their inter-relationships:

- The strategic role of the supply chain
- The key strategic drivers of supply chain performance
- Analytic methodologies for supply chain analysis

Our first objective in this book is for the reader to learn the strategic importance of good supply chain design, planning, and operation for every firm. The reader will be able to understand how good supply chain management can be a competitive advantage while weaknesses in the supply chain hurt the performance of a firm. We use many examples to illustrate this idea and develop a framework for supply chain strategy.

Within the strategic framework, we identify facilities, inventory, transportation, and information as the key drivers of supply chain performance. Our second goal in the book is to convey how these drivers may be used on a conceptual level during supply chain design, planning, and operation to improve performance. For each driver of supply chain performance, our goal is to provide readers with practical managerial levers and concepts that may be used to improve supply chain performance.

Utilizing these managerial levers requires knowledge of analytic methodologies for supply chain analysis. Our third goal is to give the reader an understanding of these methodologies. Every methodological discussion is illustrated with its application in *Excel*. In this discussion, we also stress the managerial context in which they are used and the managerial levers for improvement that they support.

The strategic frameworks and concepts discussed in the book are tied together through a variety of examples that show how a combination of concepts is needed to achieve significant improvement in performance.

CHANGES TO THE NEW EDITION

Although the basic goal of the book remains unchanged, this second edition has several significant changes that we believe improve the book. The first such change is the addition of new chapters on distribution networks (Chapter 4), sourcing (Chapter 13), and price and revenue management (Chapter 15).

Chapter 4 provides a conceptual basis for designing a distribution network. It contains a discussion of different distribution networks and when a firm should prefer one over the other. The chapter provides a framework to answer questions such as: When is it best to structure a direct distribution system with all inventory stored at the manufacturer? When is it better to go through an intermediate distributor? When is it appropriate to stock and sell products at retail stores? Our goal is to provide managers with a logical framework for selecting the appropriate distribution network given product characteristics and the markets being served.

Chapter 13 takes a comprehensive look at various sourcing decisions within a supply chain. We discuss different sourcing activities including supplier assessment, supplier contracts, design collaboration, and procurement. Building on previous chapters, we show how a supplier's performance impacts total supply chain cost and provide a structure for supplier evaluation based on total cost. We describe various forms of supplier contracts and discuss their impact on supply chain profits, information distortion, and supplier behavior. Our goal in this chapter is to provide a framework for evaluating a variety of sourcing decisions.

Chapter 15 discusses how pricing and revenue management may be used to improve profits from a given set of supply chain assets. We discuss various situations where revenue management is applicable. The use of revenue management in supply chains is still in its early stages but is likely to become increasingly important. The goal of this chapter is to allow a manager to identify scenarios where revenue management can be used and then devise appropriate revenue management tactics. We believe that the areas addressed in the three new chapters are important and a significant addition to the first edition.

The second change in this edition is the sequence in which the material is presented. The major change relative to the first edition is that we have moved forward the section on designing the supply chain network (now Chapters 5 and 6). After developing a strategic framework, many will find it a more logical flow to discuss supply chain network design and then move on to demand, supply, inventory, and transportation planning.

In addition, we have completely rewritten Chapter 17 on information technology in the supply chain. Here we develop a new framework for supply chain software that we feel provides a much improved view of where enterprise software is headed. And finally, we have updated all of the remaining chapters, adding new ideas and examples, to keep the book on the forefront of supply chain management.

The book is targeted towards an academic as well as a practitioner audience. On the academic side, it should be appropriate for MBA students, engineering masters students, and senior undergraduate students interested in supply chain management and logistics. It should also serve as a suitable reference for both concepts as well as methodology for practitioners in consulting and industry.

There are many people we would like to thank who helped us throughout this process. We thank the reviewers whose suggestions significantly improved the book: Zhi-Long Chen, University of Maryland; Michael G. Kay, North Carolina State University; Ronald Lau, Hong Kong University of Science and Technology/University of South Dakota; Gregory N. Stack, Northern Illinois University; Dr. Srinivas Talluri, Michigan State University; and Lawrence E. Whitman, Witchita State University. We are grateful to the students at the Kellogg School of Management who suffered through typo-ridden drafts of earlier versions of the book. Specifically, we thank Christoph Roettelle and Vikas Vats for carefully reviewing several chapters and solving problems at the end of the chapters. Our developmental editor, Libby Rubenstein, who read all our writing with a critical eye and raised all the right issues, was instrumental in improving the book. The book is much better because of her involvement. We would also like to thank our editor Tom Tucker and the staff at Prentice Hall for their effort with the book. Finally, we would like to thank you, our readers, for reading and using this book. We hope it contributes to all of your efforts to improve the performance of companies and supply chains throughout the world.

Sunil Chopra
Kellogg School of Management
Northwestern University

Peter Meindl
Stanford University

Building a Strategic Framework to Analyze Supply Chains

C H A P T E R   1

Understanding the Supply Chain

C H A P T E R   2

Supply Chain Performance: Achieving Strategic Fit and Scope

C H A P T E R   3

Supply Chain Drivers and Obstacles

The goal of the three chapters in Part I is to provide a strategic framework to analyze the design, planning, and operational decisions within supply chains. Such a framework helps clarify supply chain goals and identify managerial actions that improve supply chain performance in terms of the desired goals.

Chapter 1 defines a supply chain and establishes the impact that supply chain decisions have on a firm's performance. A variety of examples are used to illustrate supply chain decisions, their influence on performance, and their role in a firm's competitive strategy. Chapter 2 describes the relationship between supply chain strategy and the competitive strategy of a firm and emphasizes the importance of ensuring that strategic fit exists between the two strategies. The chapter also discusses how expanding the scope of strategic fit across all functions and stages within the supply chain improves performance. Chapter 3 describes the four supply chain performance drivers—facilities, inventory, transportation, and information. Key decisions related to each driver are identified and linked to a company's ability to support its competitive strategy.

CHAPTER

1

Understanding the Supply Chain

Learning Objectives

After reading this chapter, you will be able to:

1. Describe the cycle and push/pull views of a supply chain.

2. Classify the supply chain macro processes in a firm.

3. Identify the three key supply chain decision phases and explain the significance of each one.

4. Discuss the goal of a supply chain and explain the impact of supply chain decisions on the success of a firm.

In this chapter, we provide a conceptual understanding of what a supply chain is and the various issues that need to be considered when designing, planning, or operating a supply chain. We discuss the significance of supply chain issues to the success of a firm. We also provide several examples from different industries to emphasize the variety of supply chain issues that companies need to consider at the strategic, planning, and operational levels.

1.1   WHAT IS A SUPPLY CHAIN?

A *supply chain* consists of all parties involved, directly or indirectly, in fulfilling a customer request. The supply chain not only includes the manufacturer and suppliers, but also transporters, warehouses, retailers, and customers themselves. Within each organization, such as a manufacturer, the supply chain includes all functions involved in receiving and filling a customer request. These functions include, but are not limited to, new product development, marketing, operations, distribution, finance, and customer service.

Consider a customer walking into a Wal-Mart store to purchase detergent. The supply chain begins with the customer and their need for detergent. The next stage of this supply chain is the Wal-Mart retail store that the customer visits. Wal-Mart stocks its shelves using inventory that may have been supplied from a finished-goods warehouse that Wal-Mart manages or from a distributor using trucks supplied by a third party. The distributor in turn is stocked by the manufacturer (say Procter & Gamble [P&G] in this case). The P&G manufacturing plant receives raw material from a variety of suppliers who may themselves have been supplied by lower tier suppliers. For example, packaging material may come from Tenneco packaging while Tenneco receives raw materials to manufacture the packaging from other suppliers. This supply chain is illustrated in Figure 1.1.

A supply chain is dynamic and involves the constant flow of information, product, and funds between different stages. In our example, Wal-Mart provides the product, as well as pricing and availability information, to the customer. The customer transfers funds to Wal-Mart. Wal-Mart conveys point-of-sales data as well as replenishment orders to the warehouse or distributor, who transfers the replenishment order via trucks back to the store. Wal-Mart transfers funds to the distributor after the replenishment. The distributor also provides pricing information and sends delivery schedules to Wal-Mart. Similar information, material, and fund flows take place across the entire supply chain.

FIGURE 1.1   Stages of a Detergent Supply Chain

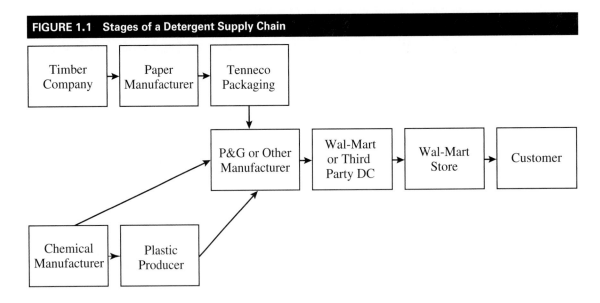

In another example, when a customer purchases online from Dell Computer, the supply chain includes, among others, the customer, Dell's Web site that takes the customer's order, the Dell assembly plant, and all of Dell's suppliers and their suppliers. The Web site provides the customer with information regarding pricing, product variety, and product availability. Having made a product choice, the customer enters the order information and pays for the product. The customer may later return to the Web site to check the status of the order. Stages further up the supply chain use customer order information to fill the order. That process involves an additional flow of information, product, and funds between various stages of the supply chain.

These examples illustrate that the customer is an integral part of the supply chain. The primary purpose for the existence of any supply chain is to satisfy customer needs, in the process generating profits for itself. Supply chain activities begin with a customer order and end when a satisfied customer has paid for his or her purchase. The term *supply chain* conjures up images of product or supply moving from suppliers to manufacturers to distributors to retailers to customers along a chain. It is important to visualize information, funds, and product flows along both directions of this chain. The term supply chain may also imply that only one player is involved at each stage. In reality, a manufacturer may receive material from several suppliers and then supply several distributors. Thus, most supply chains are actually networks. It may be more accurate to use the term *supply network* or *supply web* to describe the structure of most supply chains, as shown in Figure 1.2.

A typical supply chain may involve a variety of stages. These supply chain stages include:

- Customers
- Retailers
- Wholesalers/Distributors
- Manufacturers
- Component/Raw material suppliers

FIGURE 1.2 Supply Chain Stages

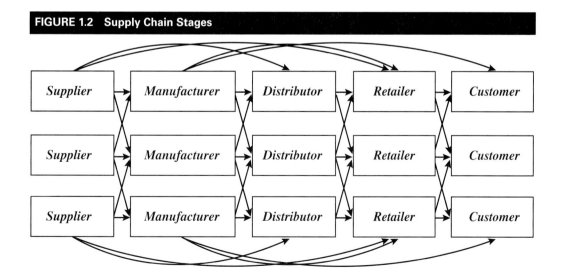

Each stage in Figure 1.2 need not be present in a supply chain. The appropriate design of the supply chain will depend on both the customer's needs and the roles of the stages involved. In some cases, such as Dell, a manufacturer may fill customer orders directly. Dell builds-to-order; that is, a customer order initiates manufacturing at Dell. Dell does not have a retailer, wholesaler, or distributor in its supply chain. In other cases, such as the mail order company L. L. Bean, manufacturers do not respond to customer orders directly. In this case, L. L. Bean maintains an inventory of product from which they fill customer orders. Compared to the Dell supply chain, the L. L. Bean supply chain contains an extra stage (the retailer, L. L. Bean itself) between the customer and the manufacturer. In the case of other retail stores, the supply chain may also contain a wholesaler or distributor between the store and the manufacturer.

The Objective of a Supply Chain

The objective of every supply chain is to maximize the overall value generated. The *value* a supply chain generates is the difference between what the final product is worth to the customer and the effort the supply chain expends in filling the customer's request. For most commercial supply chains, value will be strongly correlated with *supply chain profitability,* the difference between the revenue generated from the customer and the overall cost across the supply chain. For example, a customer purchasing a computer from Dell pays $2,000, which represents the revenue the supply chain receives. Dell and other stages of the supply chain incur costs to convey information, produce components, store them, transport them, transfer funds, and so on. The difference between the $2,000 that the customer paid and the sum of all costs incurred by the supply chain to produce and distribute the computer represents the supply chain profitability. *Supply chain profitability* is the total profit to be shared across all supply chain stages. The higher the supply chain profitability, the more successful the supply chain. Supply chain success should be measured in terms of supply chain profitability and not in terms of the profits at an individual stage. (In subsequent chapters we see that a focus on profitability at individual stages may lead to a reduction in overall supply chain profits.)

Having defined the success of a supply chain in terms of supply chain profitability, the next logical step is to look for sources of revenue and cost. For any supply chain, there is only one source of revenue: the customer. At Wal-Mart, a customer purchasing detergent is the only one providing positive cash flow for the supply chain. All other cash flows are simply fund exchanges that occur within the supply chain given that different stages have different owners. When Wal-Mart pays its supplier, it is taking a portion of the funds the customer provides and passing that money on to the supplier. All flows of information, product, or funds generate costs within the supply chain. Thus, the appropriate management of these flows is a key to supply chain success. *Supply chain management* involves the management of flows between and among stages in a supply chain to maximize total supply chain profitability.

In the next section, we categorize supply chain decision phases based on the frequency with which they are made and the time frame they take into account.

1.2   DECISION PHASES IN A SUPPLY CHAIN

Successful supply chain management requires many decisions relating to the flow of information, product, and funds. These decisions fall into three categories or phases, depending on the frequency of each decision and the time frame over which a decision phase has an impact.

1. *Supply chain strategy or design:* During this phase, a company decides how to structure the supply chain over the next several years. It decides what the chain's configuration will be, how resources will be allocated, and what processes each stage will perform. Strategic decisions made by companies include the location and capacities of production and warehousing facilities, the products to be manufactured or stored at various locations, the modes of transportation to be made available along different shipping legs, and the type of information system to be utilized. A firm must ensure that the supply chain configuration supports its strategic objectives during this phase. Dell's decisions regarding the location and capacity of its manufacturing facilities, warehouses, and supply sources are all supply chain design or strategic decisions. Supply chain design decisions are typically made for the long term (a matter of years) and are very expensive to alter on short notice. Consequently, when companies make these decisions, they must take into account uncertainty in anticipated market conditions over the next few years.

2. *Supply chain planning:* For decisions made during this phase, the time frame considered is a quarter to a year. Therefore, the supply chain's configuration determined in the strategic phase is fixed. This configuration establishes constraints within which planning must be done. Companies start the planning phase with a forecast for the coming year (or a comparable time frame) of demand in different markets. Planning includes decisions regarding which markets will be supplied from which locations, the subcontracting of manufacturing, the inventory policies to be followed, and the timing and size of marketing promotions. Dell's decisions regarding markets a given production facility will supply and target production quantities at different locations are classified as planning decisions. Planning establishes parameters within which a supply chain will function over a specified period of time. In the planning phase, companies must include uncertainty in demand, exchange rates, and competition over this time horizon in their decisions. Given a shorter time horizon and better forecasts than the design phase, companies in the planning phase try to incorporate any flexibility built into the supply chain in the design phase and exploit it to optimize performance. As a result of the planning phase, companies define a set of operating policies that govern short-term operations.

3. *Supply chain operation:* The time horizon here is weekly or daily, and during this phase companies make decisions regarding individual customer orders. At the operational level, supply chain configuration is considered fixed and planning policies are already defined. The goal of supply chain operations is to handle incoming customer orders in the best possible manner. During this phase, firms allocate inventory or production to individual orders, set a date that an order is to be filled, generate pick lists at a warehouse, allocate an order to a particular shipping mode and shipment, set delivery schedules of trucks, and place replenishment orders. Because operational decisions are

being made in the short term (minutes, hours, or days), there is less uncertainty about demand information. Given the constraints established by the configuration and planning policies, the goal during the operation phase is to exploit the reduction of uncertainty and optimize performance.

The design, planning, and operation of a supply chain have a strong impact on overall profitability and success. Continuing with our example, consider Dell Computer. In the early 1990s, Dell management began to focus on improving the design, planning, and operation of the supply chain, with the result of significantly improved performance. Both profitability and the stock price have soared and Dell stock has had outstanding returns over this period.

In later chapters, we develop concepts and present methodologies that can be used at each of the three decision phases described earlier. Most of our discussion addresses the supply chain design and planning phases.

> **Key Point**   Supply chain decision phases may be categorized as design, planning, or operational, depending on the time frame over which the decisions made in a given phase apply.

1.3   PROCESS VIEW OF A SUPPLY CHAIN

A supply chain is a sequence of processes and flows that take place within and between different stages and combine to fill a customer need for a product. There are two different ways to view the processes performed in a supply chain:

1. *Cycle view:* The processes in a supply chain are divided into a series of cycles, each performed at the interface between two successive stages of a supply chain.
2. *Push/pull view:* The processes in a supply chain are divided into two categories depending on whether they are executed in response to a customer order or in anticipation of customer orders. *Pull* processes are initiated by a customer order whereas *push* processes are initiated and performed in anticipation of customer orders.

Cycle View of Supply Chain Processes

Given the five stages of a supply chain shown in Figure 1.2, all supply chain processes can be broken down into the following four process cycles, as shown in Figure 1.3:

- Customer order cycle
- Replenishment cycle
- Manufacturing cycle
- Procurement cycle

Each cycle occurs at the interface between two successive stages of the supply chain. The five stages thus result in four supply chain process cycles. Not every supply chain will have all four cycles clearly separated. For example, a grocery supply chain in which a retailer stocks finished-goods inventories and places replenishment orders

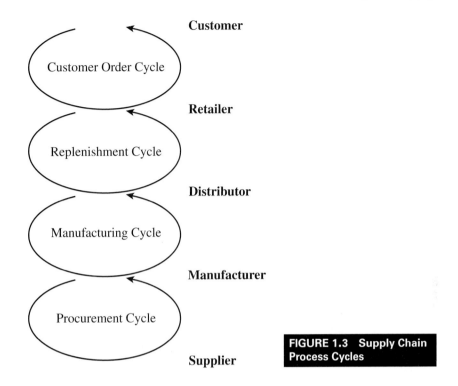

FIGURE 1.3   Supply Chain Process Cycles

with a distributor is likely to have all four cycles separated. Dell, in contrast, sells directly to customers, thus bypassing the retailer and distributor.

A cycle view of the supply chain is very useful when considering operational decisions because it clearly specifies the roles and responsibilities of each member of the supply chain. The detailed process description of a supply chain in the cycle view forces a supply chain designer to consider the infrastructure required to support these processes. The cycle view is useful, for example, when setting up information systems to support supply chain operations, as process ownership and objectives are clearly defined. We now describe the various supply chain cycles in greater detail.

Customer Order Cycle

The *customer order cycle* occurs at the customer/retailer interface and includes all processes directly involved in receiving and filling the customer's order. Typically, the customer initiates this cycle at a retailer site and the cycle primarily involves filling customer demand. The retailer's interaction with the customer starts when the customer arrives or contact is initiated and ends when the customer receives the order. The processes involved in the customer order cycle are shown in Figure 1.4 and include:

- Customer arrival
- Customer order entry
- Customer order fulfillment
- Customer order receiving

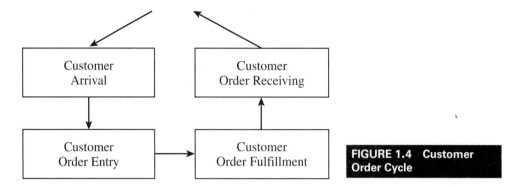

FIGURE 1.4 Customer Order Cycle

Customer Arrival   The term *customer arrival* refers to the customer's arrival at the location where he or she has access to his or her choices and makes a decision regarding a purchase. The starting point for any supply chain is the arrival of a customer. Customer arrival can occur when

- The customer walks into a supermarket to make a purchase
- The customer calls a mail order telemarketing center
- The customer uses the Web or an electronic link to a mail order firm

From the supply chain perspective, the key flow in this process is the customer's arrival. The goal is to facilitate the contact between the customer and the appropriate product so that the customer's arrival turns into a customer order. At a supermarket, facilitating a customer order may involve managing customer flows and product displays. At a telemarketing center, it may mean ensuring that customers do not have to wait on hold for too long. It may also mean having systems in place so that sales representatives can answer customer queries in a way that turns calls into orders. At a Web site, a key system may be search capabilities with tools such as personalization that allow customers to quickly locate and view products that may interest them. The objective of the customer arrival process is to maximize the conversion of customer arrivals to customer orders.

Customer Order Entry   The term *customer order entry* refers to customers informing the retailer what products they want to purchase and the retailer allocating products to customers. At a supermarket, order entry may take the form of customers loading all items that they intend to purchase onto their carts. At a mail order firm's telemarketing center or Web site, order entry may involve customers informing the retailer of the items and quantities they selected. The objective of the customer order entry process is to ensure that the order entry is quick, accurate, and communicated to all other supply chain processes that are affected by it.

Customer Order Fulfillment   During this process, the customer's order is filled and sent to the customer. At a supermarket, the customer performs this process. At a mail order firm this process generally includes picking the order from inventory, packaging it, and shipping it to the customer. All inventories will need to be updated, which may result in the initiation of the replenishment cycle. In general, customer order fulfill-ment takes place from retailer inventory. In a build-to-order scenario, however, order fulfillment takes place directly from the manufacturer's production line. The objective of the customer order fulfillment process is to get the correct orders to customers by the promised due dates at the lowest possible cost.

Customer Order Receiving   During this process, the customer receives the order and takes ownership. Records of this receipt may be updated and payment completed. At a supermarket, receiving occurs at the checkout counter. For a mail order firm, receiving occurs when the product is delivered to the customer.

Replenishment Cycle

The *replenishment cycle* occurs at the retailer/distributor interface and includes all processes involved in replenishing retailer inventory. It is initiated when a retailer places an order to replenish inventories to meet future demand. A replenishment cycle may be triggered at a supermarket that is running out of stock of detergent or at a mail order firm that is low on stock of a particular shirt.

The replenishment cycle is similar to the customer order cycle except that the retailer is now the customer. The objective of the replenishment cycle is to replenish inventories at the retailer at minimum cost while providing high product availability. The processes involved in the replenishment cycle are shown in Figure 1.5 and include:

- Retail order trigger
- Retail order entry
- Retail order fulfillment
- Retail order receiving

Retail Order Trigger   As the retailer fills customer demand, inventory is depleted and must be replenished to meet future demand. A key activity the retailer performs during the replenishment cycle is to devise a replenishment or ordering policy that trig-gers an order from the previous stage. The objective when setting replenishment order triggers is to maximize profitability by ensuring economies of scale and balancing product availability and the cost of holding inventory. The outcome of the retail order

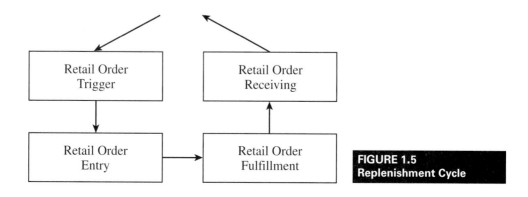

FIGURE 1.5
Replenishment Cycle

trigger process is the generation of a replenishment order that is ready to be passed on to the distributor or manufacturer.

Retail Order Entry   This process is similar to customer order entry at the retailer. The only difference is that the retailer is now the customer placing the order that is conveyed to the distributor. This may be done electronically or by some other medium. Inventory or production is then allocated to the retail order. The objective of the retail order entry process is that an order be entered accurately and conveyed quickly to all supply chain processes affected by the order.

Retail Order Fulfillment   This process is very similar to customer order fulfillment except that it takes place at the distributor. A key difference is the size of each order as customer orders tend to be much smaller than replenishment orders. The objective of the retail order fulfillment is to get the replenishment order to the retailer on time while minimizing costs.

Retail Order Receiving   Once the replenishment order arrives at a retailer, the retailer must receive it physically and update all inventory records. This process involves product flow from the distributor to the retailer as well as information updates at the retailer and the flow of funds from the retailer to the distributor. The objective of the retail order receiving process is to update inventories and displays quickly and accurately at the lowest possible cost.

Manufacturing Cycle

The *manufacturing cycle* typically occurs at the distributor/manufacturer (or retailer/manufacturer) interface and includes all processes involved in replenishing distributor (or retailer) inventory. The manufacturing cycle is triggered by customer orders (as is the case with Dell), replenishment orders from a retailer or distributor (Wal-Mart ordering from P&G), or by the forecast of customer demand and current product availability in the manufacturer's finished-goods warehouse.

One extreme in a manufacturing cycle is an integrated steel mill that collects orders that are similar enough to enable the manufacturer to produce in large quantities. In this case, the manufacturing cycle is reacting to customer demand (referred to as a *pull process*). Another extreme is a consumer products firm that must produce in anticipation of demand. In this case the manufacturing cycle is anticipating customer demand (referred to as a *push process*). The processes involved in the manufacturing cycle are shown in Figure 1.6 and include the following:

- Order arrival from the finished-goods warehouse, distributor, retailer, or customer
- Production scheduling
- Manufacturing and shipping
- Receiving at the distributor, retailer, or customer

Order Arrival   During this process, a finished-goods warehouse or distributor sets a replenishment order trigger based on the forecast of future demand and current product inventories. The resulting order is then conveyed to the manufacturer. In some cases the customer or retailer may be ordering directly from the manufacturer. In

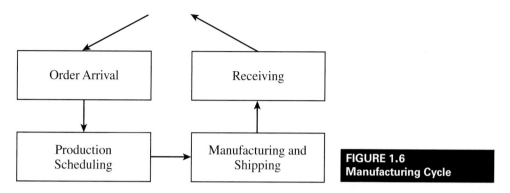

**FIGURE 1.6
Manufacturing Cycle**

other cases a manufacturer may be producing to stock a finished-products warehouse. In the latter situation, the order is triggered based on product availability and a forecast of future demand. This process is similar to the retail order trigger process in the replenishment cycle.

Production Scheduling   This process is similar to the order entry process in the replenishment cycle where inventory is allocated to an order. During the production scheduling process, orders (or forecasted orders) are allocated to a production plan. Given the desired production quantities for each product, the manufacturer must decide on the precise production sequence. If there are multiple lines, the manufacturer must also decide which products to allocate to each line. The objective of the production scheduling process is to maximize the proportion of orders filled on time while keeping costs down.

Manufacturing and Shipping   This process is equivalent to the order fulfillment process described in the replenishment cycle. During the manufacturing phase of the process, the manufacturer produces to the production schedule. During the shipping phase of this process, the product is shipped to the customer, retailer, distributor, or finished-product warehouse. The objective of the manufacturing and shipping process is to create and ship the product by the promised due date while meeting quality requirements and keeping costs down.

Receiving   In this process, the product is received at the distributor, finished-goods warehouse, retailer, or customer and inventory records are updated. Other processes related to storage and fund transfers also take place.

Procurement Cycle

The *procurement cycle* occurs at the manufacturer/supplier interface and includes all processes necessary to ensure that materials are available for manufacturing to occur according to schedule. During the procurement cycle, the manufacturer orders components from suppliers that replenish the component inventories. The relationship is quite similar to that between a distributor and manufacturer with one significant difference. Whereas retailer/distributor orders are triggered by uncertain customer demand, component orders can be determined precisely once the manufacturer has decided what the production schedule will be. Component orders depend on the production schedule. Thus it is important that suppliers be linked to the manufacturer's production schedule. Of course, if a supplier's lead times are long, the supplier has to produce to forecast because the manufacturer's production schedule may not be fixed that far in advance.

In practice, there may be several tiers of suppliers, each producing a component for the next tier. A similar cycle would then flow back from one stage to the next. The processes in the procurement cycle are shown in Figure 1.7.

We do not detail each process here because this cycle has processes similar to those discussed in the context of other cycles.

> **Key Point** A cycle view of the supply chain clearly defines the processes involved and the owners of each process. This view is very useful when considering operational decisions because it specifies the roles and responsibilities of each member of the supply chain and the desired outcome for each process.

Push/Pull View of Supply Chain Processes

All processes in a supply chain fall into one of two categories depending on the timing of their execution relative to end customer demand. With pull processes, execution is initiated in response to a customer order. With push processes, execution is initiated in anticipation of customer orders. Therefore, at the time of execution of a pull process, customer demand is known with certainty whereas at the time of execution of a push process, demand is not known and must be forecast. Pull processes may also be referred to as *reactive processes* because they react to customer demand. Push processes may also be referred to as *speculative processes* because they respond to speculated (or forecasted) rather than actual demand. The *push/pull boundary* in a supply chain separates push processes from pull processes. At Dell, for example, the beginning of PC assembly represents the push/pull boundary. All processes before PC assembly are push processes and all processes after and including assembly are initiated in response to a customer order and are thus pull processes.

A push/pull view of the supply chain is very useful when considering strategic decisions relating to supply chain design. This view forces a more global consideration

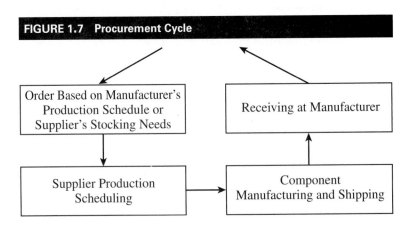

FIGURE 1.7 Procurement Cycle

of supply chain processes as they relate to a customer order. Such a view may, for instance, result in responsibility for certain processes being passed on to a different stage of the supply chain if making this transfer allows a push process to become a pull process.

Let us consider two distinct supply chains that we have discussed and relate them to the push/pull and cycle views. One supply chain is a mail order company like L. L. Bean that receives customer orders through its telemarketing center or Web site. The other is a build-to-order computer manufacturer like Dell.

L. L. Bean executes all processes in the customer order cycle *after* the customer arrives. All processes that are part of the customer order cycle are thus pull processes. Order fulfillment takes place from product in inventory that is built up in anticipation of customer orders. The goal of the replenishment cycle is to ensure product availability when a customer order arrives. All processes in the replenishment cycle are performed in anticipation of demand and are thus push processes. The same holds true for processes in the manufacturing and procurement cycle. In fact, raw material like fabric is often purchased six to nine months before customer demand is expected. Manufacturing itself begins three to six months before the point of sale. All processes in the manufacturing and procurement cycle are thus push processes. The processes in the L. L. Bean supply chain break up into pull and push processes, as shown in Figure 1.8.

The situation is different for a build-to-order computer manufacturer like Dell. Dell does not sell through a reseller or distributor but directly to the consumer. Demand is not filled from finished-product inventory, but from production. The arrival of a customer order triggers production of the product. The manufacturing cycle is thus part of the customer order fulfillment process in the customer order cycle. There are

FIGURE 1.8   Push/Pull Processes for the L. L. Bean Supply Chain

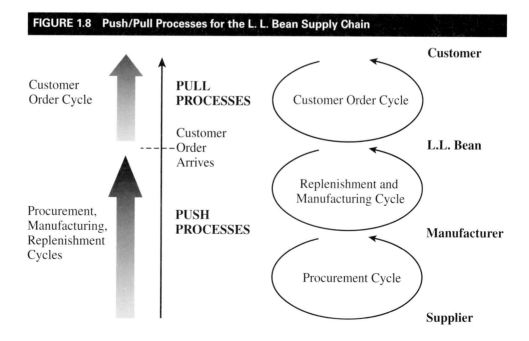

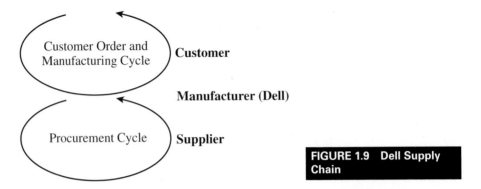

FIGURE 1.9 Dell Supply Chain

effectively only two cycles in the Dell supply chain: (a) a customer order and manufacturing cycle and (b) a procurement cycle, as shown in Figure 1.9.

All processes in the customer order and manufacturing cycle at Dell are thus classified as pull processes because they are initiated by customer arrival. Dell, however, does not place component orders in response to a customer order. Inventory is replenished in anticipation of customer demand. All processes in the procurement cycle for Dell are thus classified as push processes because they are in response to a forecast. The processes in the Dell supply chain break up into pull and push processes as shown in Figure 1.10.

One clear distinction between the two supply chains discussed earlier is that the Dell supply chain has fewer stages and more pull processes than the L. L. Bean supply chain. As we see in the following chapters, this fact has a significant impact on supply chain performance.

FIGURE 1.10 Push/Pull Processes for Dell Supply Chain

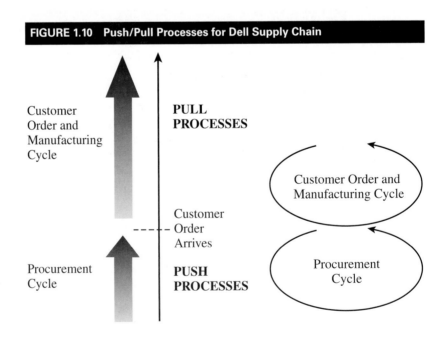

Key Point   A push/pull view of the supply chain categorizes processes based on whether they are initiated in response to a customer order (pull) or in anticipation of a customer order (push). This view is very useful when considering strategic decisions relating to supply chain design.

Supply Chain Macro Processes in a Firm

All supply chain processes in a firm can be classified into the following three macro processes as shown in Figure 1.11:

1. Customer Relationship Management (CRM): All processes that focus on the interface between the firm and its customers.
2. Internal Supply Chain Management (ISCM): All processes that are internal to the firm.
3. Supplier Relationship Management (SRM): All processes that focus on the interface between the firm and its suppliers.

The three macro processes manage the flow of information, product, and funds required to generate, receive, and fulfill a customer request. The CRM macro process aims to generate customer demand and facilitate the placement and tracking of orders. It includes processes such as marketing, sales, order management, and call center management. At an industrial distributor like W. W. Grainger, CRM processes would include the preparation of catalogs and other marketing materials, management of the Web site, and management of the call center taking orders and providing service. The ISCM macro process aims to fulfill demand generated by the CRM process in a timely manner and at the lowest possible cost. ISCM processes include the planning of internal production and storage capacity, preparation of demand and supply plans, and internal fulfillment of actual orders. At W. W. Grainger, ISCM processes would include planning for the location and size of warehouses; planning for which products to carry at each warehouse; preparation of inventory management policies; and the picking, packing, and shipping of actual orders. The SRM macro process aims to arrange for and manage supply sources for various goods and services. SRM processes include the evaluation and selection of suppliers, negotiation of supply terms, and communication regarding new products and orders with suppliers. At W. W. Grainger, SRM processes

---

FIGURE 1.11   Supply Chain Macro Processes

Supplier	Firm	Customer
SRM	ISCM	CRM

• Source	• Strategic Planning	• Market
• Negotiate	• Demand Planning	• Sell
• Buy	• Supply Planning	• Call Center
• Design Collaboration	• Fulfillment	• Order Management
• Supply Collaboration	• Field Service	

would include the selection of suppliers for various products, negotiation of pricing and delivery terms with suppliers, sharing of demand and supply plans with suppliers, and the placement of replenishment orders.

All three supply chain macro processes and their component processes are shown in Figure 1.11.

Observe that all three macro processes are aimed at serving the same customer. Thus, for a supply chain to be successful it is crucial that the three macro processes are well integrated. The importance of this integration in the context of supply chain software is discussed in Chapter 17. The organizational structure of the firm has a strong influence on the success or failure of the integration effort. In many firms, marketing is in charge of the CRM macro process, manufacturing handles the ISCM macro process, and purchasing oversees the SRM macro process with very little communication between them. It is not unusual for marketing and manufacturing to have two different forecasts when making their plans. This lack of integration hurts the supply chain's ability to match supply and demand effectively, leading to dissatisfied customers and high costs. Thus, firms should structure a supply chain organization that mirrors the macro processes and ensures good communication and coordination between the owners of processes that interact with each other.

> **Key Point** Within a firm, all supply chain activities belong to one of three macro processes—CRM, ISCM, and SRM. Integration between the three macro processes is crucial for successful supply chain management.

1.4 THE IMPORTANCE OF SUPPLY CHAIN FLOWS

There is a close connection between the design and management of supply chain flows (product, information, and cash) and the success of a supply chain. Dell Computer is an example of a firm that has successfully used good supply chain practices to support its competitive strategy. In contrast, Quaker Oats' acquisition of Snapple is an example in which the inability to design and manage supply chain flows led to failure. Most e-business failures can also be attributed to problems with the design and management of supply chain flows.

Dell has, over a relatively short period of time, become the world's largest PC manufacturer. They have generated margins, profits, and, subsequently, market capitalization beyond any of their competitors' PC businesses. Dell has attributed a significant part of its success to the way it manages flows—product, information, and cash—within its supply chain.

Dell's basic supply chain model is direct sales to customers. As distributors and retailers are bypassed, the Dell supply chain has only three stages—customers, manufacturer, and suppliers—as shown in Figure 1.12.

Because Dell is in direct contact with its customers, it has been able to finely segment them and analyze the needs and profitability of each segment. Close contact with their customers and an understanding of customers' needs also allows Dell to develop better forecasts. To further improve the match between supply and demand, Dell makes an active effort to steer customers in real time, on the phone or via the Internet, toward PC configurations that can be built given the components available.

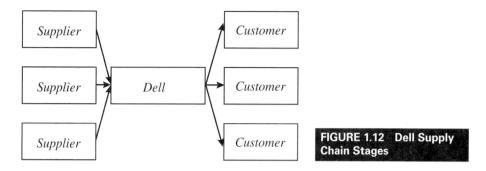

FIGURE 1.12 Dell Supply Chain Stages

On the operational side, inventory turns is a key performance measure that Dell watches very closely. Dell carries less than ten days' worth of inventory; in contrast, the competition, selling through retailers, carries in the vicinity of eighty to one hundred days' worth of inventory. If Intel introduces a new chip, the low level of inventory allows Dell to go to market with a PC containing the chip faster than the competition. If prices suddenly drop, as they often do, Dell has less inventory that loses value relative to its competitors. For some products, such as monitors manufactured by Sony, Dell maintains no inventory. The transportation company simply picks up the appropriate number of computers from Dell's Austin plant and monitors from Sony's factory in Mexico, matches them by customer order, and delivers them to the customers. This procedure allows Dell to save time and money associated with the extra handling of monitors.

The success of the Dell supply chain is facilitated by sophisticated information exchange. Dell provides real time data to suppliers on the current state of demand. Suppliers are able to access their components' inventory levels at the factories along with daily production requirements. Dell has created customized Web pages so that its major suppliers can view demand forecasts and other customer-sensitive information, thus helping suppliers to get a better idea of customer demand and better match their production schedules to that of Dell. The company has production concentrated in five manufacturing centers—Brazil, China, Ireland, Malaysia, and Texas. Because demand at each location is relatively large and stable, suppliers are able to replenish component inventories regularly, allowing for low levels of component inventories to be maintained. In some cases, Dell carries only hours of component inventory at its factory.

Dell's low levels of inventory also help ensure that defects are not introduced into a large quantity of product. When a new product is launched, supplier engineers are stationed right in the plant. If a customer calls in with a problem, production is stopped and flaws are fixed in real time. As there is no finished product in inventory, the amount of defective merchandise produced is minimized.

Dell also manages its cash flows very effectively. By managing receivables and payables very closely, they are able to collect cash from their customers, on average, ten to fifteen days before they have to pay their suppliers.

Clearly, Dell's supply chain design and their management of product, information, and cash flows play a key role in the company's success. This approach has left Dell very well positioned in the PC industry. Given that the PC is to an extent a commodity, the competitive battlefield is more focused on supply chain responsiveness and efficiency. This bodes well for Dell.

Quaker Oats, with its acquisition of Snapple, provides an example in which failure to design and manage supply chain flows led to financial failure. In December 1994, Quaker purchased Snapple, a producer of bottled natural drinks such as teas, at a cost of $1.7 billion. Gatorade, the top-selling brand in the sports drink segment, was Quaker's most successful beverage. Gatorade was very strong in the south and the southwest of the United States while Snapple was strong in the northeast and on the west coast.

Quaker announced that a major motivation of the merger was the potential synergies between the two distribution systems of Snapple and Gatorade. The company, however, was unable to take advantage of these synergies. Problems stemmed from disparate manufacturing facilities to different customer types. Gatorade was manufactured in plants owned by Quaker while Snapple was produced under contract by outside plants. Gatorade sold significant amounts through supermarkets and grocery stores while Snapple sold primarily through restaurants and independent retailers. Over the two years following their acquisition of Snapple, Quaker was unable to gain much synergy between the two distribution systems in their attempts to merge them. Just twenty eight months later, Quaker sold Snapple to Triarc Companies for about $300 million, about 20 percent of the purchase price. The inability to achieve synergies between the two supply chains was a significant reason for the failure of Snapple at Quaker.

The failure of many e-businesses such as Webvan and Kozmo can be attributed to their inability to manage supply chain flows effectively. Webvan was unable to bring the cost of grocery picking and delivery to a competitive level. The recent success of Amazon.com has been primarily driven by the improvements in the management of product inventories and delivery.

> **Key Point** Supply chain decisions play a significant role in the success or failure of a firm.

1.5 EXAMPLES OF SUPPLY CHAINS

In this section, we consider several supply chains and raise questions that would have to be answered during the design, planning, and operations phases of these supply chains. In later chapters, we discuss concepts and present methodologies that can be used to answer these questions.

Gateway: A Direct Sales Manufacturer

Gateway is a manufacturer of PCs that sells directly to customers who place orders at Gateway retail stores, through the telephone, or via the Internet. The company was founded in 1985 and started as a direct sales manufacturer with no retail footprint. In 1996, Gateway was one of the first PC manufacturer's to start selling PCs online. Over the years Gateway expanded its operations worldwide with sales and manufacturing presence in Europe and Asia Pacific. In 1999, the company had three plants in the United States, a plant in Ireland, and one in Malaysia.

In the late 1990s, Gateway introduced an aggressive strategy of opening Gateway retail stores throughout the United States. They invested in many retail stores, increasing their selling, general, and administrative (SG&A) expenses from 12.5 percent of sales in 1997 to 15.1 percent of sales in 1999. As of January 2002, Gateway had about 280 retail stores in the United States. Gateway's strategy has been to not carry any finished-goods inventory at the retail stores but simply use these stores for customers to try the PCs and obtain help in deciding on the right configuration to purchase. Once customers place their order, PCs are manufactured to order and shipped from one of the assembly plants.

Initially, investors rewarded Gateway for this strategy and raised the stock price to over $80 per share in late 1999. By November 2002, however, Gateway shares had dropped to below $4 and Gateway had lost a significant amount of money.

In 2001, Gateway decided to close all overseas operations to focus on its business in the United States. Plants in Ireland and Malaysia were shut. The company has entered into contracts with third parties to provide service and support to customers outside the United States.

Gateway has also shut its production facility in Salt Lake City. The company has closed several of its retail stores in the United States but has not fundamentally changed the way they are used. Gateway has also decided to reduce the number of configurations that will be offered to customers in an effort to lower costs.

The following supply chain decisions have a bearing on the performance of Gateway:

1. Why did Gateway have multiple production facilities in the United States? What advantages or disadvantages does this strategy offer relative to Dell, which has one facility? How does Gateway decide which production facility will produce and ship a customer order?
2. What factors did Gateway consider when deciding which plants to close?
3. Why does Gateway not carry any finished-product inventory at its retail stores?
4. Should a firm with an investment in retail stores carry any finished-goods inventory? What are the characteristics of products that are most suitable to be carried in finished-goods inventory? What characterizes products that are best manufactured to order?
5. Is the Dell model of selling directly without retail stores always less expensive than a supply chain with retail stores?
6. What are the supply chain implications of Gateway's decision to offer fewer configurations?

Answers to these questions determine the appropriateness of Gateway's supply chain decisions. Manufacturers like HP that sell both direct and through resellers will need a different supply chain design to best support their strategy. How should they design and manage their supply chains?

7-Eleven: A Convenience Store

With over 23,000 stores in about 20 countries, 7-Eleven is one of the largest convenience store chains in the world. It has about 9,000 stores in Japan and almost 6,000 in the United States. Its growth in Japan has been phenomenal given that the first 7-Eleven store opened there in 1974. 7-Eleven Japan is one of the most profitable companies listed on the Tokyo stock exchange. It has seen tremendous growth in sales and profitability while simultaneously decreasing its inventory relative to sales. 7-Eleven Japan's success is attributed primarily to its supply chain design and management ability.

7-Eleven Japan aims to provide customers with what they want, when they want it. From a strategic perspective, one of the company's key objectives is to micro-match supply and demand by location, season, and time of day. 7-Eleven designs and manages location, inventory, transportation, and information to support this objective.

7-Eleven Japan follows a dominant location strategy and opens new stores in target areas to establish or enhance a strong presence. They are present in about half of the prefectures (roughly equivalent to a county in the United States). 7-Eleven has a strong presence, however, with several stores in each prefecture where they are located. 7-Eleven's dominant location strategy allows the company the benefits of consolidation in both warehousing and transportation.

In Japan, fresh food constitutes a significant percentage of 7-Eleven's sales. Most of the fresh food is cooked off-site and delivered to the stores. A store placing an order by 10 A.M. has it delivered by dinnertime the same day. There are at least three fresh food deliveries a day per store so that the stock can change for breakfast, lunch, and dinner. All stores are electronically connected to the head office, distribution centers (DCs), and suppliers. All store orders are passed on to the suppliers who package store-specific orders and deliver them to the DC. At the DC, all orders of like products (categorized by temperature) from different suppliers are combined and delivered to the stores. Each delivery truck delivers to more than one store and tries to visit stores during the off-peak hours. 7-Eleven Japan has made an effort to have no direct store delivery from vendors to the stores. Rather, all deliveries pass through and are aggregated at a 7-Eleven DC or warehouse from which they are shipped to the stores. Note that the location strategy helps facilitate this supply strategy.

In the United States, 7-Eleven is taking a similar approach to the one used in Japan. Fresh foods are being introduced into the stores. 7-Eleven has once again decided to avoid on-site cooking by having suppliers cook the fresh food for them. These foods are then delivered to store on a daily basis. In the United States, 7-Eleven has tried to replicate the Japanese model with combined DCs where product is received from suppliers and then shipped to stores. The success of this strategy is reflected by the improved performance of 7-Eleven in the United States. In the United States, however, a large fraction of products are delivered to stores by a distributor and not from the 7-Eleven DC.

In both Japan and the United States, 7-Eleven has invested significant money and effort on a retail information system. Scanner data are collected and analyzed. The resulting information is then made available to headquarters and the stores for use in ordering, product assortment, and merchandising. Information systems play a key role in 7-Eleven's ability to micro-match supply and demand.

7-Eleven has made clear choices in the design of its supply chain. Other convenience store chains have not always made the same choices. We can ask a variety of questions, listed next, concerning 7-Eleven's supply chain choices and its key success factors.

1. What factors influence the decision regarding the opening and closing of stores? Why does 7-Eleven choose to have a preponderance of its stores in a particular location?
2. Why has 7-Eleven chosen off-site preparation of fresh foods and subsequent delivery to stores?
3. Why does 7-Eleven Japan discourage direct store delivery from vendors and make an effort to move all products through combined DCs? How does the presence of the distributor delivering to the stores affect the performance of the delivery system in the United States?
4. Where are DCs located and how many stores does each center serve? How are stores assigned to DCs?
5. Why does 7-Eleven combine fresh food shipments by temperature?
6. What point-of-sales data does 7-Eleven gather and what information is made available to store managers to assist them in their ordering and merchandising decisions? How should the information system be structured?

W. W. Grainger and McMaster Carr: MRO Suppliers

W. W. Grainger and McMaster Carr sell MRO products. Both companies have catalogs that they make available, as well as Web pages through which orders can be placed. W. W. Grainger also has several hundred stores throughout the United States. Customers can walk into a store, call in an order, or place it via the Web. W. W. Grainger orders are either shipped to the customer or picked up by the customer at one of the stores. McMaster Carr, in contrast, ships all orders. W. W. Grainger has several DCs that both replenish stores and fill customer orders. McMaster has DCs from which all orders are filled. Neither McMaster nor W. W. Grainger manufacture any product. They primarily serve the role of a distributor or retailer. Their success is largely linked to their supply chain management ability.

Both firms offer several hundred thousand products to their customers. Each firm stocks about 100,000 products with the rest being obtained from the supplier as needed. Both firms face the following strategic and operational issues:

1. How many DCs should there be and where should they be located?
2. How should product stocking be managed at the DCs? Should all DCs carry all products?
3. What products should be carried in inventory and what products should be left with the supplier?
4. What products should W. W. Grainger carry at a store?
5. How should markets be allocated to DCs in terms of order fulfillment? What should be done if an order cannot be completely filled from a DC? Should there be specified backup locations? How should they be selected?
6. How should replenishment of inventory be managed at the various stocking locations?

7. How should Web orders be handled relative to the existing business? Is it better to integrate the Web business with the existing business or to set up separate distribution?

8. What transportation modes should be used for order fulfillment and stock replenishment?

Toyota: A Global Auto Manufacturer

Toyota Motor Corporation is Japan's top auto manufacturer and has experienced significant growth in global sales over the last two decades. A key issue facing Toyota is the design of its global production and distribution network. Part of Toyota's global strategy is to open factories in every market it serves. Toyota must decide what the production capability of each of the factories will be, as this has a significant impact on the desired distribution system. At one extreme, each plant would be equipped only for local production. At the other extreme, each plant would be capable of supplying every market. Prior to 1996, Toyota used specialized local factories for each market. After the Asian financial crisis in 1996/1997, Toyota focused on redesigning its plants so that they could be shifted quickly to exporting to markets that remain strong. Toyota calls this strategy "global complementation."

Whether to be global or local is also an issue for Toyota's parts plants. Should they be designed for local consumption or should there be few parts plants globally that supply multiple assembly plants?

For any global manufacturer like Toyota, several questions arise regarding the configuration and capability of the supply chain:

1. Where should the plants be located and what degree of flexibility should be built into each? What capacity should each plant have?

2. Should plants be able to produce for all markets or only specific contingency markets?

3. How should markets be allocated to plants and how frequently should this allocation be revised?

4. What kind of flexibility should be built into the distribution system?

5. How should this flexible investment be valued?

6. What actions may be taken during product design to facilitate this flexibility?

Amazon.com: An E-Business

Amazon.com sells books, music, and other items over the Internet and is one of the pioneers of consumer e-business. Amazon is based in Seattle and started by filling all orders using books purchased from a distributor in response to customer orders. This practice differs from that of a traditional bookstore that purchases directly from publishers and stocks books in anticipation of customer orders. Today, Amazon has six warehouses where it holds inventory. Amazon stocks best-selling books, though it still gets other titles from distributors or publishers. It uses the U.S. Postal Service and other package carriers like UPS and FedEx to send books to customers.

Traditional booksellers like Borders and Barnes and Noble have also started selling using the Internet channel. Barnes and Noble has set up BarnesandNoble.com as a separate company, whereas Borders uses Amazon to fulfill its online orders after initially trying to operate an online business. In the case of Barnes and Noble, the retail store and the online supply chains share warehousing and transportation to some extent. This is a departure from their original strategy when BarnesandNoble.com was not visible in any Barnes and Noble Bookstore.

Several questions arise concerning how Amazon is structured and how traditional booksellers have responded:

1. Why is Amazon building more warehouses as it grows? How many warehouses should it have and where should they be located?
2. What advantages does selling books via the Internet provide over a traditional bookstore? Are there any disadvantages of selling via the Internet?
3. Why does Amazon stock best-sellers while buying other titles from distributors?
4. Does the Internet channel provide greater value to a bookseller like Borders with retail outlets or to a company like Amazon?
5. Should traditional booksellers like Barnes and Noble integrate e-commerce into their current supply chain or manage it as a separate supply chain?
6. For what products does the e-commerce channel offer the greatest advantage? What characterizes these products?

1.6 SUMMARY OF LEARNING OBJECTIVES

1. Describe the cycle and push/pull views of a supply chain.

   A cycle view of a supply chain divides processes into cycles, each performed at the interface between two successive stages of a supply chain. Each cycle starts with an order placed by one stage of the supply chain and ends when the order is received from the supplier stage. A push/pull view of a supply chain characterizes processes based on their timing relative to that of a customer order. Pull processes are performed in response to a customer order while push processes are performed in anticipation of customer orders.

2. Classify the supply chain macro processes in a firm.

   All supply chain processes can be classified into three macro processes based on whether they are at the customer or supplier interface or are internal to the firm. The CRM macro process consists of all processes at the interface between the firm and the customer that work to generate, receive, and track cus-

tomer orders. The ISCM macro process consists of all supply chain processes that are internal to the firm and work to plan for and fulfill customer orders. The SRM macro process consists of all supply chain processes at the interface between the firm and its suppliers that work to evaluate and select suppliers and then source goods and services from them.

3. Identify the three key supply chain decision phases and explain the significance of each one.

   Supply chain decisions may be characterized as strategic (design), planning, or operational depending on the duration over which they apply. Strategic decisions relate to supply chain configuration. These decisions have a long-term impact lasting several years. Planning decisions cover a period of a few months to a year and include decisions such as production plans, subcontracting, and promotions over that period. Operational decisions span from minutes to days and include sequencing production and filling specific orders. Strategic decisions define the constraints for planning decisions and planning decisions define the constraints for operational decisions.

4. Discuss the goal of a supply chain and explain the impact of supply chain decisions on the success of a firm.

The goal of a supply chain should be to maximize overall supply chain profitability. Supply chain profitability is the difference between the revenue generated from the customer and the total cost incurred across all stages of the supply chain. Supply chain decisions have a large impact on the success or failure of each firm because they significantly influence both the revenue generated as well as the cost incurred. Successful supply chains manage flows of product, information, and funds to provide a high level of product availability to the customer while keeping costs low.

DISCUSSION QUESTIONS

1. Consider the purchase of a can of soda at a convenience store. Describe the various stages in the supply chain and the different flows involved.
2. Why should a firm like Dell take into account total supply chain profitability when making decisions?
3. What are some strategic, planning, and operational decisions that must be made by an apparel retailer like The Gap?
4. Consider the supply chain involved when a customer purchases a book at a bookstore. Identify the cycles in this supply chain and the location of the push/pull boundary.
5. Consider the supply chain involved when a customer orders a book from Amazon. Identify the push/pull boundary and two processes each in the push and pull phase.
6. In what way do supply chain flows affect the success or failure of a firm like Amazon? List two supply chain decisions that have a significant impact on supply chain profitability.

BIBLIOGRAPHY

Cavinato, Joseph L. 2002. "What's Your Supply Chain Type?" *Supply Chain Management Review* (May–June): 60–66.

Chopra, Sunil. 1995. *Seven Eleven Japan*. Evanston, Ill.: J.L. Kellogg School of Management, Northwestern University.

Fisher, Marshall L. 1997. "What Is the Right Supply Chain for Your Product?" *Harvard Business Review* (March–April): 83–93.

Fuller, J. B., J. O'Conner, and R. Rawlinson. 1993. "Tailored Logistics: The Next Advantage." *Harvard Business Review* (May–June): 87–98.

Lee, Hau L. 2002. "Aligning Supply Chain Strategies with Product Uncertainties." *California Management Review* (Spring): 105–119.

Magretta, Joan. 1998a. "Fast, Global, and Entrepreneurial: Supply Chain Management, Hong Kong Style." *Harvard Business Review* (September–October): 102–114.

———. 1998b. "The Power of Virtual Integration: An Interview with Dell Computer's Michael Dell." *Harvard Business Review* (March–April): 72–84.

Quinn, Francis J. 1999. "Reengineering the Supply Chain: An Interview with Michael Hammer." *Supply Chain Management Review* (Spring): 20–26.

Robeson, James F., and William C. Copacino, eds. 1994. *The Logistics Handbook*. New York: Free Press.

Shapiro, Roy D. 1984. "Get Leverage from Logistics." *Harvard Business Review* (May–June): 199–127.

Supply Chain Performance: Achieving Strategic Fit and Scope

2.1 Competitive and Supply Chain Strategies
2.2 Achieving Strategic Fit
2.3 Expanding Strategic Scope
2.4 Summary of Learning Objectives
Discussion Questions
Bibliography

Learning Objectives

After reading this chapter, you will be able to:

1. Explain why achieving strategic fit is critical to a company's overall success.

2. Describe how a company achieves strategic fit between its supply chain strategy and its competitive strategy.

3. Discuss the importance of expanding the scope of strategic fit across the supply chain.

In Chapter 1, we discuss what a supply chain is and the importance of supply chain design, planning, and operation to a firm's success. In this chapter, we define supply chain strategy and explain how creating a strategic fit between a company's competitive strategy and its supply chain strategy affects performance. We also discuss the importance of expanding the scope of strategic fit from one operation within a company to all stages of the supply chain.

2.1 COMPETITIVE AND SUPPLY CHAIN STRATEGIES

A company's *competitive strategy* defines the set of customer needs that it seeks to satisfy through its products and services. For example, Wal-Mart aims to provide high availability of a variety of reasonable quality products at low prices. Most products sold at Wal-Mart are commonplace (everything from home appliances to clothing) and can be purchased elsewhere. What Wal-Mart provides is a low price and product availability. McMaster Carr sells maintenance, repair, and operations (MRO) products. It offers over 200,000 different products through both a catalog and a Web site. Its competitive strategy is built around providing the customer with convenience, availability, and responsiveness. With this focus on responsiveness, McMaster does not compete based on low price. Clearly, the competitive strategy at Wal-Mart is different from that at McMaster.

We can also contrast Dell, with its build-to-order model, with a firm like HP, selling PCs through retailers. Dell has stressed customization and variety at a reasonable cost, with customers having to wait approximately 1 week to get their product. In contrast, a customer can walk into a computer retailer, be helped by a salesperson, and leave the same day with an HP computer. The amount of variety and customization available at the retailer, however, is limited. In each case, the competitive strategy is defined based on how the customer prioritizes product cost, delivery time, variety, and quality. A McMaster Carr customer places greater emphasis on product variety and response time than on cost. A Wal-Mart customer, in contrast, places greater emphasis on cost. A Dell customer, purchasing online, places great emphasis on product variety and customization. A customer purchasing a PC at a retailer is most concerned with the help in product selection and faster response time. Thus, a firm's competitive strategy will be defined based on the customer's priorities. Competitive strategy targets one or more customer segments and aims to provide products and services that satisfy these customers' needs.

To see the relationship between competitive and supply chain strategies, we start with the value chain for a typical organization, as shown in Figure 2.1.

The value chain begins with new product development, which creates specifications for the product. Marketing and sales generates demand by publicizing the customer priorities that the product and services will satisfy. Marketing also brings customer input back to new product development. Using new product specifications, operations transforms inputs to outputs to create the product. Distribution either takes the product to the customer or brings the customer to the product. Service responds to customer requests during or after the sale. These are core functions that must be performed for a successful sale. Finance, accounting, information technology, and human resources support and facilitate the functioning of the value chain.

FIGURE 2.1 The Value Chain in a Company

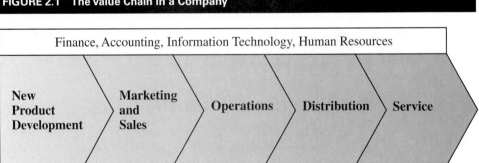

To execute a company's competitive strategy, all these functions play a role and each must develop its own strategy. Here, strategy refers to what each function will try to do particularly well.

A *product development* strategy specifies the portfolio of new products that a company will try to develop. It also dictates whether the development effort will be made internally or outsourced. A *marketing and sales* strategy specifies how the market will be segmented and how the product will be positioned, priced, and promoted. A *supply chain strategy* determines the nature of procurement of raw materials, transportation of materials to and from the company, manufacture of the product or operation to provide the service, and distribution of the product to the customer, along with any follow-up service. From a value chain perspective, supply chain strategy specifies what operations, distribution, and service will try to do particularly well. Additionally, in each company, strategies will also be devised for finance, accounting, information technology, and human resources.

Because our focus here is on supply chain strategy, we define it in a little more detail. Supply chain strategy includes what many traditionally call supplier strategy, operations strategy, and logistics strategy. Decisions regarding inventory, transportation, operating facilities, and information flows in the supply chain are all part of supply chain strategy.

The value chain emphasizes the close relationship between all the functional strategies within a company. Each function is crucial if a company is to profitably satisfy customer needs. Thus, the various functional strategies cannot be formulated in isolation. They are closely intertwined and must fit and support each other if a company is to succeed. We are particularly concerned here with the link between a company's competitive strategy and supply chain strategies. We will seek to answer this question: Given its competitive strategy, what should a company's supply chain try to do particularly well?

2.2   ACHIEVING STRATEGIC FIT

This chapter is built on the idea that for any company to be successful, its supply chain strategy and competitive strategy must fit together. *Strategic fit* means that both the competitive and supply chain strategies have the same goal. It refers to consistency between the customer priorities that the competitive strategy hopes to satisfy and the supply chain capabilities that the supply chain strategy aims to build. The issue of achieving strategic fit is a key consideration during the supply chain strategy or design phase discussed in Chapter 1.

All functions that are part of a company's value chain contribute to its success or failure. These functions do not operate in isolation; no one function can ensure the chain's success. Failure at any one function, however, may lead to failure of the overall chain. A company's success or failure is thus closely linked to the following keys:

1. The competitive strategy and all functional strategies must fit together to form a coordinated overall strategy. Each functional strategy must support other functional strategies and help a firm reach its competitive strategy goal.

2. The different functions in a company must appropriately structure their processes and resources to be able to execute these strategies successfully.

A company may fail either because of a lack of strategic fit or because its processes and resources do not provide the capabilities to support the desired strategic fit. In thinking of the major tasks of a chief executive officer (CEO), there are few greater than the job of aligning all of the core functional strategies with the overall competitive strategy to achieve strategic fit. If this alignment is not achieved, conflicts between different functional goals arise. Such conflicts result in different functions targeting different customer priorities. Because processes and resources are structured to support functional goals, a conflict in functional goals leads to conflicts during execution.

Consider, for example, a situation in which marketing is publicizing the company's ability to provide a large variety of products very quickly; simultaneously, distribution is targeting the lowest cost means of transportation. In this situation, it is very likely that distribution will delay orders so it can get better transportation economies by grouping several orders together. This action conflicts with marketing's stated goal of providing variety quickly.

To elaborate on strategic fit, let us return to the example of Dell Computer from Chapter 1. Dell's competitive strategy is to provide a large variety of customizable products at a reasonable price; customers can select from among thousands of possible PC configurations. In terms of supply chain strategy, a PC manufacturer has a range of options. At one extreme, a company can have an efficient supply chain with a focus on the ability to produce low-cost PCs by limiting variety and exploiting economies of scale. At the other extreme, a company can have a highly flexible and responsive supply chain that is very good at producing a large variety of products. In this second case, costs will be higher than in an efficient supply chain. Both supply chain strategies are viable by themselves. Both do not fit, however, with Dell's competitive strategy. A supply chain strategy that emphasizes flexibility and responsiveness has a better strategic fit with Dell's competitive strategy of providing a large variety of customizable products.

This notion of fit also extends to Dell's other functional strategies. For instance, its new product development strategy should emphasize designing products that are easily customizable, which may include designing common platforms across several products and the use of common components. Dell products use common components and are designed so that they can be assembled quickly. This feature allows Dell to assemble customized PCs quickly in response to a customer order. The design of new products at Dell supports the supply chain's ability to assemble customized PCs in response to customer orders. This capability, in turn, supports Dell's strategic goal of offering customization to its customers. Dell clearly has achieved strong strategic fit between its different functional strategies and its competitive strategy.

How Is Strategic Fit Achieved?

What does a company need to do to achieve that all-important strategic fit between the supply chain and competitive strategies? A competitive strategy will specify, either explicitly or implicitly, one or more customer segments that a company hopes to satisfy.

To achieve strategic fit, a company must ensure that its supply chain capabilities support its ability to satisfy the targeted customer segments.

There are three basic steps to achieving strategic fit:

1. *Understanding the customer and supply chain uncertainty.* First a company must understand the customer needs for each targeted segment and the uncertainty the supply chain faces in satisfying these needs. These needs help the company define the desired cost and service requirements. The supply chain uncertainty helps the company identify the extent of disruption and delay the supply chain must be prepared for.
2. *Understanding the supply chain capabilities.* There are many types of supply chains, each of which is designed to perform different tasks well. A company must understand what its supply chain is designed to do well.
3. *Achieving strategic fit.* If a mismatch exists between what the supply chain does particularly well and the desired customer needs, the company will either need to restructure the supply chain to support the competitive strategy or alter its strategy.

Step 1: Understanding the Customer and Supply Chain Uncertainty

To understand the customer, a company must identify the needs of the customer segment being served. Let us compare 7-Eleven Japan and a discounter such as Sam's Club (a part of Wal-Mart). When customers go to 7-Eleven to purchase detergent, they go there for the convenience of a nearby store and are not necessarily looking for the lowest price. In contrast, a low price is very important to a customer going to Sam's Club. This customer may be willing to tolerate less variety and even purchase very large package sizes as long as the price is low. Even though customers purchase detergent at both places, the demand varies along certain attributes. In the case of 7-Eleven, customers are in a hurry and want convenience. In the case of Sam's Club, they want a low price and are willing to spend time getting it. In general, customer demand from different segments may vary along several attributes as follows:

- **The quantity of the product needed in each lot:** An emergency order for material needed to repair a production line is likely to be small. An order for material to construct a new production line is likely to be large.
- **The response time that customers are willing to tolerate:** The tolerable response time for the emergency order is likely to be short, whereas the allowable response time for the construction order is apt to be long.
- **The variety of products needed:** A customer may place a high premium on the availability of all parts of an emergency repair order from a single supplier. This may not be the case for the construction order.
- **The service level required:** A customer placing an emergency order expects a high level of product availability. This customer may go elsewhere if all parts of the order are not immediately available. This is not apt to happen in the case of the construction order where a long lead time is likely.
- **The price of the product:** The customer placing the emergency order is apt to be much less sensitive to price than the customer placing the construction order.

- **The desired rate of innovation in the product:** Customers at a high-end department store expect a lot of innovation and new designs in the store's apparel. Customers at Wal-Mart may be less sensitive to new product innovation.

Each customer in a particular segment will tend to have similar needs, whereas customers in a different segment can have very different needs.

Although we have described the many attributes along which customer demand varies, our goal is to identify one key measure for combining all of these attributes. This single measure then helps define what the supply chain should do particularly well.

Implied Demand Uncertainty   At first glance, it may appear that each of the customer need categories should be viewed differently, but in a very fundamental sense, each customer need can be translated into the metric of implied demand uncertainty. *Implied demand uncertainty* is the uncertainty that exists due to the portion of demand that the supply chain is required to meet.

We make a distinction between demand uncertainty and implied demand uncertainty. *Demand uncertainty* reflects the uncertainty of customer demand for a product. Implied demand uncertainty, in contrast, is the resulting uncertainty for only the portion of the demand that the supply chain must handle and the attributes the customer desires. For example, a firm supplying only emergency orders for a product will face a higher implied demand uncertainty than a firm that supplies the same product with a long lead time.

Another illustration of the need for this distinction is the impact of service level. As a supply chain raises its level of service, it must be able to meet a higher and higher percentage of actual demand, forcing it to prepare for rare surges in demand. Thus, raising the service level increases the implied demand uncertainty even though the product's underlying demand uncertainty does not change.

Both the product demand uncertainty and various customer needs that the supply chain tries to fill affect implied demand uncertainty. Table 2.1 illustrates how various customer needs affect implied demand uncertainty.

As each individual customer need contributes to the implied demand uncertainty, we can use implied demand uncertainty as a common metric with which to distinguish different types of demand.

Fisher (1997) pointed out that implied demand uncertainty is often correlated with other characteristics of demand, as shown in Table 2.2. An explanation follows:

1. Products with uncertain demand are often less mature and have less direct competition. As a result, margins tend to be high.
2. Forecasting is more accurate when demand is more predictable.
3. Increased implied demand uncertainty leads to increased difficulty matching supply with demand. For a given product, this dynamic can lead to either a stockout or an oversupply situation. Increased implied demand uncertainty thus leads to both higher oversupply and a higher stockout rate.
4. Markdowns are high for products with high implied demand uncertainty because oversupply often results.

TABLE 2.1   Impact of Customer Needs on Implied Demand Uncertainty

Customer Need	Causes Implied Demand Uncertainty to . . .
Range of quantity required increases	Increase because a wider range of the quantity required implies greater variance in demand
Lead time decreases	Increase because there is less time in which to react to orders
Variety of products required increases	Increase because demand per product becomes more disaggregate
Number of channels through which product may be acquired increases	Increase because the total customer demand is now disaggregated over more channels
Rate of innovation increases	Increase because new products tend to have more uncertain demand
Required service level increases	Increase because the firm now has to handle unusual surges in demand

First let us take an example of a product with low implied demand uncertainty—such as table salt. Salt has a very low contribution margin, accurate demand forecasts, low stockout rates, and virtually no markdowns. These characteristics match well with Fisher's chart of characteristics for products with highly certain demand.

On the other end of the spectrum, a new "palmtop" computer has high implied demand uncertainty. It will likely have a high margin, very inaccurate demand forecasts, high stockout rates (if it is successful), and large markdowns (if it is a failure). This too matches well with Table 2.2.

Another example is a circuit board supplier whose customers include two different types of PC manufacturers. One of its customers is a build-to-order PC manufacturer such as Dell that requires same-day lead times. In this case, the supplier might need to build up inventory or have very flexible manufacturing to be prepared for whatever demand Dell had that day. Forecast error would be high and stockouts could be high; because of these factors, margins would likely be higher. The supplier's other customer builds a small variety of PCs and specifies in advance the number and type of PCs to be built. This information gives the supplier a much longer lead time and reduces the forecasting errors and stockout rates. Thus, the supplier would likely get smaller margins from this PC manufacturer. These examples demonstrate that even with the same product, different customer segments can have different implied demand uncertainty given different service requirements.

Lee (2002) pointed out that along with demand uncertainty, it is important to consider uncertainty resulting from the capability of the supply chain. For example,

TABLE 2.2   Correlation Between Implied Demand Uncertainty and Other Attributes

	Low Implied Uncertainty	High Implied Uncertainty
Product margin	Low	High
Average forecast error	10%	40% to 100%
Average stockout rate	1% to 2%	10% to 40%
Average forced season end markdown	0%	10% to 25%

Source: Adapted from "What is the Right Supply Chain for Your Product?" Marshall L. Fisher, *Harvard Business Review* (March–April 1997), 83–93.

TABLE 2.3 Impact of Supply Source Capability on Supply Uncertainty	
Supply Source Capability	*Causes Supply Uncertainty to . . .*
Frequent breakdowns	Increase
Unpredictable and low yields	Increase
Poor quality	Increase
Limited supply capacity	Increase
Inflexible supply capacity	Increase
Evolving production process	Increase

Source: Adapted from "Aligning Supply Chain Strategies with Product Uncertainties." Hau L. Lee, *California Management Review* (Spring 2002), 105–119.

when a new component is introduced in the PC industry, the quality yields of the production process tend to be low and breakdowns are frequent. As a result, companies have difficulty delivering according to a well-defined schedule, resulting in high supply uncertainty for PC manufacturers. As the production technology matures and yields improve, companies are able to follow a fixed delivery schedule, resulting in low supply uncertainty. Table 2.3 illustrates how various characteristics of supply sources affect the supply uncertainty.

Supply uncertainty is also strongly affected by the life cycle position of the product. New products that are being introduced have higher supply uncertainty because designs and production processes are still evolving. In contrast, mature products have less supply uncertainty.

We can create a spectrum of uncertainty by combining the demand and supply uncertainty. This implied uncertainty spectrum is shown in Figure 2.2.

A company introducing a brand-new cell phone based on entirely new components and technology faces high implied demand uncertainty and high supply uncertainty. As a result, the implied uncertainty faced by the supply chain is very high. In contrast, a supermarket selling milk or salt faces low implied demand uncertainty and low levels of supply uncertainty, resulting in a low implied uncertainty. Many agricultural products such as coffee are examples where supply chains face low levels of implied demand uncertainty but significant supply uncertainty based on weather. The supply chain thus has to face an intermediate level of implied uncertainty.

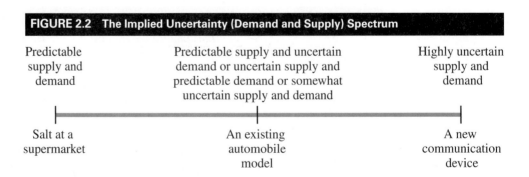

FIGURE 2.2   The Implied Uncertainty (Demand and Supply) Spectrum

Predictable supply and demand	Predictable supply and uncertain demand or uncertain supply and predictable demand or somewhat uncertain supply and demand	Highly uncertain supply and demand
Salt at a supermarket	An existing automobile model	A new communication device

> **Key Point**　The first step in achieving strategic fit between competitive and supply chain strategies is to understand customers and supply chain uncertainty. Uncertainty from the customer and the supply chain can be combined and mapped on the implied uncertainty spectrum.

Step 2: Understanding the Supply Chain

After understanding the uncertainty that the company faces, the next question is: How does the firm best meet demand in that uncertain environment? Creating strategic fit is all about creating a supply chain strategy that best meets demand that a company has targeted given the uncertainty it faces.

We now consider the characteristics of supply chains and categorize them. Similar to the way we placed demand on a one-dimensional spectrum (the implied uncertainty spectrum), we will also place each supply chain on a spectrum. Like customer needs, supply chains have many different characteristics. However, if we search for a single idea to which all characteristics of the supply chain contribute, it is the idea of the trade-off between responsiveness and efficiency.

First we provide some definitions. *Supply chain responsiveness* includes a supply chain's ability to do the following:

- Respond to wide ranges of quantities demanded
- Meet short lead times
- Handle a large variety of products
- Build highly innovative products
- Meet a very high service level
- Handle supply uncertainty

These abilities are similar to many of the characteristics of demand and supply that led to high implied uncertainty. The more of these abilities that a supply chain has, the more responsive it is.

Responsiveness, however, comes at a cost. For instance, to respond to a wider range of quantities demanded, capacity must be increased, which increases costs. This increase in cost leads to the second definition: *Supply chain efficiency* is the cost of making and delivering a product to the customer. Increases in cost lower efficiency. For every strategic choice to increase responsiveness, there are additional costs that lower efficiency.

The *cost-responsiveness efficient frontier* is the curve in Figure 2.3 showing the lowest possible cost for a given level of responsiveness. Lowest is defined based on existing technology; not every firm is able to perform on the efficient frontier. The efficient frontier represents the cost-responsiveness performance of the best supply chains. A firm that is not on the efficient frontier can improve both its responsiveness and its cost performance by moving toward the efficient frontier. In contrast, a firm on the efficient frontier can only improve its responsiveness by increasing cost and becoming less efficient. Such a firm must then make a trade-off between efficiency and responsiveness. Of course, firms on the efficient frontier are also continuously improving their processes and changing technology to shift the efficient frontier itself. Given

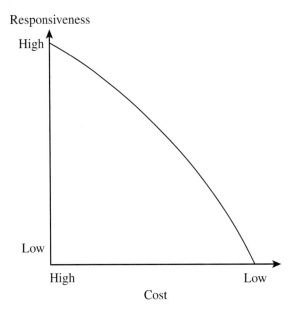

FIGURE 2.3 Cost-Responsiveness Efficient Frontier

the trade-off between cost and responsiveness, a key strategic choice for any supply chain is the level of responsiveness it seeks to provide.

Supply chains range from those that focus solely on being responsive to those that focus on a goal of producing and supplying at the lowest possible cost. Figure 2.4 shows the responsiveness spectrum and where some supply chains fall on this spectrum.

The more capabilities constituting responsiveness that a supply chain has, the more responsive it is. 7-Eleven Japan replenishes its stores with breakfast items in the morning, lunch items in the afternoon, and dinner items at night. As a result, the available product variety changes by time of day. 7-Eleven responds very quickly to orders, with store managers placing replenishment orders less than 12 hours before they are supplied. This practice makes the 7-Eleven supply chain very responsive. The Dell supply chain allows a customer to customize any of several thousand PC configurations.

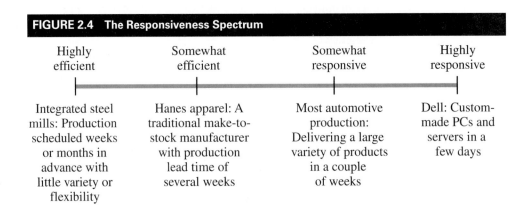

FIGURE 2.4 The Responsiveness Spectrum

Highly efficient	Somewhat efficient	Somewhat responsive	Highly responsive
Integrated steel mills: Production scheduled weeks or months in advance with little variety or flexibility	Hanes apparel: A traditional make-to-stock manufacturer with production lead time of several weeks	Most automotive production: Delivering a large variety of products in a couple of weeks	Dell: Custom-made PCs and servers in a few days

Dell then delivers the appropriate PC to the customer within days. The Dell supply chain would also be considered very responsive. Another example of a responsive supply chain is W. W. Grainger. The company faces both demand and supply uncertainty; therefore, the supply chain has been designed to deal effectively with both. An efficient supply chain, in contrast, lowers cost by eliminating some of its responsive capabilities. For example, Sam's Club sells a limited variety of products in large package sizes. The supply chain is very good at keeping costs down and the focus of this supply chain is clearly on efficiency.

> **Key Point** The second step in achieving strategic fit between competitive and supply chain strategies is to understand the supply chain and map it on the responsiveness spectrum.

Step 3: Achieving Strategic Fit

We have now looked at demand and supply and mapped both to gauge the level of implied uncertainty. We have examined a supply chain to understand where it lies on the responsiveness spectrum. The third and final step in achieving strategic fit is to ensure that what the supply chain does particularly well is consistent with the targeted customer's needs and the uncertainty of the supply chain. The degree of supply chain responsiveness should be consistent with the implied uncertainty.

A useful exercise is to think of the spectrums that we have discussed as two axes on a graph, as shown in Figure 2.5, with implied uncertainty increasing as we move along the horizontal axis (the implied uncertainty spectrum) and responsiveness increasing along the vertical axis (the responsiveness spectrum). This graph is referred to as the uncertainty/responsiveness map. A point in this graph represents a combination of implied uncertainty and supply chain responsiveness. The implied uncertainty represents customer needs or the firm's strategic position and the capability of supply sources. The supply chain's responsiveness represents the supply chain strategy. We can

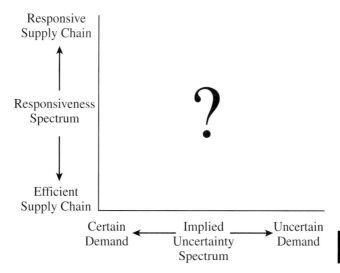

FIGURE 2.5   Uncertainty/ Responsiveness Map

now ask the following question: Which combinations of implied uncertainty and supply chain responsiveness result in strategic fit?

Consider again the example of Dell Computers. For Dell, the competitive strategy targets customers who value having the latest PC models customized to their needs. Further, these customers want the PCs delivered within days. Given the vast variety of PCs, the high level of innovation, and rapid delivery, demand from Dell customers can be characterized as having high demand uncertainty. Some supply uncertainty also exists, especially for newly introduced components. Dell has the option of designing an efficient or responsive supply chain. An efficient supply chain may use slow, inexpensive modes of transportation and economies of scale in production. If Dell made both of these choices, it would have difficulty supporting the customer's desire for rapid delivery and a wide variety of customizable products. Building a responsive supply chain, however, will allow Dell to meet its customers' needs. Therefore, a responsive supply chain strategy is best suited to meet the needs of Dell's targeted customers.

Now, consider a pasta manufacturer like Barilla. Pasta is a product with relatively stable customer demand, giving it a low implied demand uncertainty. Supply is also quite predictable. Barilla could design a highly responsive supply chain in which pasta is custom-made in very small batches in response to customer orders and shipped via a rapid transportation mode such as FedEx. This choice would obviously make the pasta prohibitively expensive, resulting in a loss of customers. Barilla, therefore, is in a much better position if it designs a more efficient supply chain with a focus on cost reduction.

From the preceding discussion, it follows that to achieve strategic fit, the greater the implied uncertainty, the more responsive the supply chain should be. Increasing implied uncertainty from customers and supply sources is best served by increasing responsiveness from the supply chain. This relationship is represented by the "zone of strategic fit" illustrated in Figure 2.6. For a high level of performance, companies should move their competitive strategy (and resulting implied uncertainty) and supply chain strategy (and resulting responsiveness) toward the zone of strategic fit.

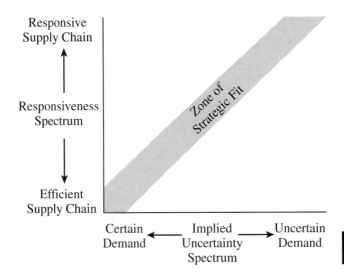

FIGURE 2.6   Finding the Zone of Strategic Fit

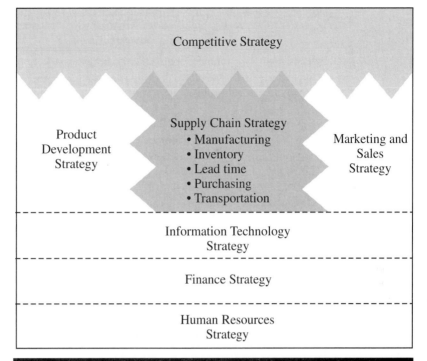

FIGURE 2.7   Fit Between Competitive and Functional Strategies

To achieve complete strategic fit, a firm must consider all functional strategies within the value chain; it must ensure that all functions in the value chain have consistent strategies that support the competitive strategy as shown in Figure 2.7. All functional strategies must support the goals of the competitive strategy and all substrategies within the supply chain such as manufacturing, inventory, and purchasing must also be consistent with the supply chain's level of responsiveness.

Thus, firms with different locations along the responsiveness spectrum must have different functional strategies that support their responsiveness. A highly responsive supply chain must devote all its functional strategies to responsiveness whereas an efficient supply chain must focus all its functional strategies on efficiency. Table 2.4 lists some of the major differences in functional strategy between supply chains that are efficient and those that are responsive.

Key Point   The final step in achieving strategic fit is to match supply chain responsiveness with the implied uncertainty from demand and supply. All functional strategies within the value chain must also support the supply chain's level of responsiveness.

Changing the strategies to achieve strategic fit may sound easy enough to do, but in reality it can be quite difficult. In later chapters, we discuss many of the obstacles to

TABLE 2.4 Comparison of Efficient and Responsive Supply Chains		
	Efficient Supply Chains	*Responsive Supply Chains*
Primary goal	Supply demand at the lowest cost	Respond quickly to demand
Product design strategy	Maximize performance at a minimum product cost	Create *modularity* to allow postponement of product differentiation
Pricing strategy	Lower margins because price is a prime customer driver	Higher margins because price is not a prime customer driver
Manufacturing strategy	Lower costs through high utilization	Maintain capacity flexibility to buffer against demand/supply uncertainty
Inventory strategy	Minimize inventory to lower cost	Maintain *buffer inventory* to deal with demand/supply uncertainty
Lead time strategy	Reduce but not at the expense of costs	Aggressively reduce even if the costs are significant
Supplier strategy	Select based on cost and quality	Select based on speed, flexibility, reliability, and quality

Source: Adapted from "What Is the Right Supply Chain for Your Product?" Marshall L. Fisher, *Harvard Business Review* (March–April 1997), 83–93.

achieving this fit. Right now, the important points to remember from this discussion are the following:

1. There *is no* right supply chain strategy independent of the competitive strategy.
2. There *is* a right supply chain strategy for a given competitive strategy.

The drive for strategic fit should come from the highest levels of the organization. In many companies, different groups devise competitive and functional strategies. Without proper communication between the groups and coordination by high-level management such as the CEO, these strategies are not likely to achieve strategic fit. For many firms, the failure to achieve strategic fit is a key reason for their inability to succeed.

Other Issues Affecting Strategic Fit

Our previous discussion focused on achieving strategic fit when a firm serves a single market segment and the result is a well-defined strategic position. We now consider how multiple products, multiple customer segments, and product life cycle affect strategic fit.

Multiple Products and Customer Segments

Most companies produce and sell multiple products to multiple customer segments, each with different characteristics. A department store may sell seasonal products such as ski jackets with high implied demand uncertainty along with products such as black socks with low implied demand uncertainty. The demand in each case maps to a different part of the uncertainty spectrum. W. W. Grainger sells MRO products to both large firms like Ford and Boeing and small manufacturers and contractors. The customer needs in the two cases are very different. A large firm is much more likely to be concerned with price given the large volumes they generate from W. W. Grainger, whereas a smaller company is apt to go to W. W. Grainger because it is responsive. The two segments served map to different positions along the implied uncertainty spectrum. Another example is Levi Strauss, which sells both customized and standard-sized jeans. Demand for standard-sized jeans has a much lower demand uncertainty than demand for customized jeans.

In each of the aforementioned examples, the firm sells multiple products and serves customer segments with very different needs. As a result, the different products and segments have different implied demand uncertainty. When devising supply chain strategy in these cases, the key issue for a company is to create a supply chain that balances efficiency and responsiveness given its portfolio of products, customer segments, and supply sources.

There are several possible routes a company can take. One is to set up independent supply chains for each different product or customer segment. This strategy is feasible if each segment is large enough to support a dedicated supply chain. It fails, however, to take advantage of any economies of scope that often exist between a company's different products. Therefore, a preferable strategy is to tailor the supply chain to best meet the needs of each product's demand.

Tailoring the supply chain requires sharing some links in the supply chain with some products, while having separate operations for other links. The links are shared to achieve maximum possible efficiency while providing the appropriate level of responsiveness to each segment. For instance, all products may be made on the same line in a plant, but products requiring a high level of responsiveness may be shipped using a fast mode of transportation such as FedEx. Those products that do not have high responsiveness needs may be shipped by slower and less expensive means such as truck, rail, or even ship. In other instances, products requiring high responsiveness may be manufactured using a very flexible process in response to customer orders, whereas products that require less responsiveness may be manufactured using a less responsive but more efficient process. The mode of transportation used in both cases, however, may be the same. In other cases, some products may be held at regional warehouses close to the customer while others may be held in a centralized warehouse far from the customer. W. W. Grainger holds fast-moving items in its decentralized locations close to the customer. It holds slow-moving items with higher implied demand uncertainty in a centralized warehouse. Appropriate tailoring of the supply chain helps a firm achieve varying levels of responsiveness for a low overall cost. The level of responsiveness is tailored to each product or customer segment. We provide various examples of tailored supply chains in subsequent chapters.

Product Life Cycle

As products go through their life cycle, the demand characteristics and the needs of the customer segments being served change. Supply characteristics also change as the product and production technologies mature. High-tech products are particularly prone to these life cycle swings over a very compressed time span. A product goes through life cycle phases from the introductory phase, when only the leading edge of customers is interested in it and supply is uncertain, all the way to the point at which the product becomes a commodity, the market is saturated, and supply is predictable. Thus, if a company is to maintain strategic fit, its supply chain strategy must evolve as its products enter different phases.

Let us consider changes in demand and supply characteristics over the life cycle of a product. Toward the beginning stages of a product's life cycle:

1. Demand is very uncertain and supply may be unpredictable.
2. Margins are often high and time is crucial to gaining sales.
3. Product availability is crucial to capturing the market.
4. Cost is often of secondary consideration.

Consider a pharmaceutical firm introducing a new drug. Initial demand for the drug is highly uncertain, margins are typically very high, and product availability is the key to capturing market share. The introductory phase of a product's life cycle corresponds to high implied uncertainty. In such a situation, responsiveness is the most important characteristic of the supply chain.

As the product becomes a commodity product later in its life cycle, the demand and supply characteristics change. At this stage it is typically the case that:

1. Demand has become more certain and supply is predictable.
2. Margins are lower due to an increase in competitive pressure.
3. Price becomes a significant factor in customer choice.

In the case of the pharmaceutical company, these changes occur when the drug patent expires and generic drugs are introduced. At this stage demand for the drug stabilizes and margins shrink. Customers make their selections from the various choices based on price. Production technologies are well-developed and supply is predictable. This stage corresponds to a low level of implied uncertainty. As a result, the supply chain needs to change. In such a situation, efficiency is the most important characteristic of the supply chain.

This discussion illustrates that as products mature, the corresponding supply chain strategy should, in general, move from being responsive to being efficient, as illustrated in Figure 2.8.

To illustrate these ideas, consider the example of Intel Corporation. Each time Intel introduces a new processor, there is great uncertainty with respect to demand for this new product, as depends on the sales of new high-end PCs. Typically there is high uncertainty regarding how the market will receive these PCs and what the demand will be. Supply is unpredictable because yield is low and variable. At this stage, the Intel supply chain must be very responsive so it can react if demand is very high.

As the Intel processor becomes more mainstream, demand begins to stabilize and yield from the production process is higher and more predictable. At this point demand and supply typically display lower implied uncertainty and price becomes a greater determinant of sales. Now it is important that Intel have an efficient supply chain in place for producing processors.

All PC manufacturers are subject to the cycle described earlier. When a new model is introduced, margins are high, but demand is highly uncertain. In such a

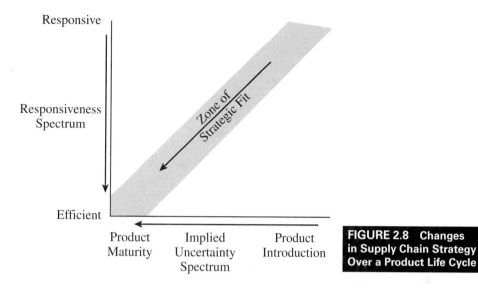

FIGURE 2.8 Changes in Supply Chain Strategy Over a Product Life Cycle

situation, a responsive supply chain best serves the PC manufacturer. As the model matures, demand stabilizes and margins shrink. At this stage it is important that the manufacturer have an efficient supply chain. Apple Computer is an example of a firm that had difficulty during product introduction when it introduced the G4 in 1999. Demand for the machine far exceeded the available supply of processors, resulting in significant lost sales. The supply chain in this case did not display sufficient responsiveness during the product's introductory phase.

The key point here is that demand and supply characteristics change over a product's life cycle. Because demand and supply characteristics change, the supply chain strategy must also change over the product life cycle if a company is to continue achieving strategic fit.

Competitive Changes Over Time

A final dimension to consider when matching supply chain and competitive strategy is changes in competitor behavior. Like product life cycles, competitors can change the landscape, thereby requiring a change in the firm's competitive strategy. An example is the growth of mass customization in various industries over the last decade of the 20th century. As competitors flood the marketplace with product variety, customers are becoming accustomed to having their individual needs satisfied. Thus, the competitive focus today is on producing sufficient variety at a reasonable price. As more firms increase the level of variety offered, supply chains have been forced to develop the ability to supply high variety. As the competitive landscape changes, a firm is forced to alter its competitive strategy. With the change in competitive strategy, a firm must also change its supply chain strategy to maintain strategic fit.

Key Point To achieve strategic fit, a firm must tailor its supply chain to best meet the needs of different customer segments. To retain strategic fit, supply chain strategy must be adjusted over the life cycle of a product and as the competitive landscape changes.

In the next section, we describe how the scope of the supply chain has expanded when achieving strategic fit. We also discuss why expanding the scope of strategic fit is critical to supply chain success.

2.3 EXPANDING STRATEGIC SCOPE

A key issue relating to strategic fit is the scope, in terms of supply chain stages, across which the strategic fit applies. *Scope of strategic fit* refers to the functions and stages that devise an integrated strategy with a shared objective. At one extreme, every operation within each functional area devises its own independent strategy with the objective of optimizing its individual performance. In this case the scope of strategic fit is restricted to an operation in a functional area within a stage of the supply chain. At the opposite extreme, all functional areas within all stages of the supply chain devise strategy jointly with a common objective of maximizing supply chain profit. In this case the scope of strategic fit extends to the entire supply chain.

In this section we discuss how expanding the scope of strategic fit improves supply chain performance. We represent the scope of strategic fit on a two-dimensional grid. Horizontally, the scope of strategic fit is considered across different supply chain stages, starting from suppliers and moving all the way along the chain to the customer. Vertically, the scope is applied to the fit achieved across different functional strategies, competitive, product development, supply chain, and marketing.

Intracompany Intraoperation Scope: The Minimize Local Cost View

The most limited scope over which strategic fit is considered is one operation within a functional area within a company. This is referred to as *intracompany intraoperation scope*. Here each operation within each stage of the supply chain devises strategy independently. In such a setting, the resulting collection of strategies will most likely not come close to maximizing supply chain profit because different functions and operations have conflicting local objectives. This limited scope was the dominant practice during the 1950s and 1960s when each operation within each stage of the supply chain attempted to minimize its own costs. Consider an example of a distribution company where a transportation operation is evaluated based on average shipping cost per unit. Shipping the product individually costs $5/item whereas shipping by truckload costs only $1/item. To minimize cost, the transportation group ships the product in full trucks as this practice results in the lowest shipping cost per unit. This decision, while minimizing transportation cost per unit, increases response time and may undermine a competitive strategy based on responsiveness. The key point here is that the transportation decision was made independent of the rest of the supply chain both within and outside of the company. In this case, the scope of strategic fit is restricted to a portion (transportation) of the distributor stage within the supply chain. The shaded area in Figure 2.9 represents the scope of strategic fit at the distributor in this instance.

Intracompany Intrafunctional Scope: The Minimize Functional Cost View

Given that many operations together form each function within a firm, managers recognized the weakness of the intracompany intraoperation scope. Supply chain

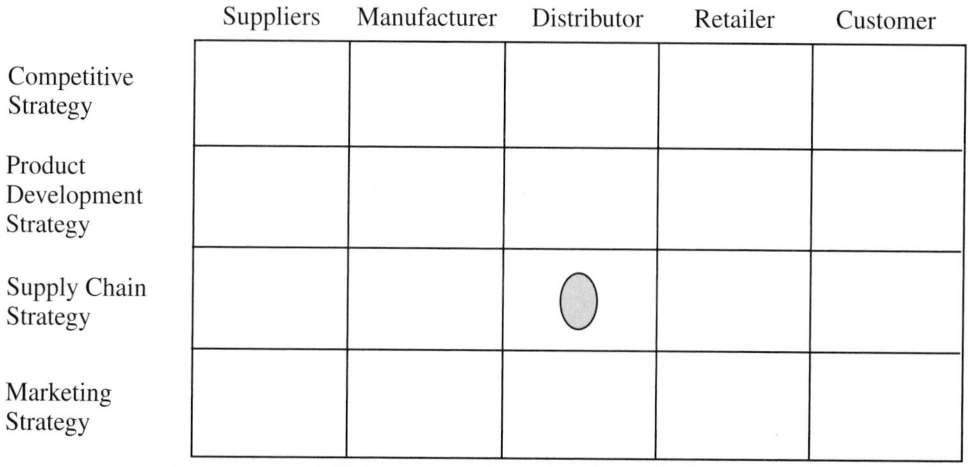

	Suppliers	Manufacturer	Distributor	Retailer	Customer
Competitive Strategy					
Product Development Strategy					
Supply Chain Strategy			◯		
Marketing Strategy					

FIGURE 2.9   An Example of Intracompany Intraoperation Scope of Supply Chain Strategy at a Distributor

operations include manufacturing, warehousing, and transportation, among others. With the intracompany intrafunctional scope, the strategic fit is expanded to include all operations within a function. In this case, the warehousing manager no longer minimizes warehousing costs while the transportation manager independently minimizes transportation costs. By working together and developing a joint strategy, the two minimize the total functional cost.

Applying the intracompany intrafunctional scope and continuing with the distribution example, managers now look at not just transportation costs, but also warehousing and other supply chain related costs. Although truckload transportation saves the company $4/item, it costs an additional $8/item due to increased inventory and warehousing costs. Therefore, it costs less for the company to ship each item individually because the extra $4 transportation charge saves the company $8 in inventory-related costs.

In this case the scope of strategic fit expands to an entire function within a stage of the supply chain. Figure 2.10 shows the intracompany intrafunctional scope as it applies to the supply chain strategy at the distributor.

Intracompany Interfunctional Scope: The Maximize Company Profit View

The key weakness of the intracompany intrafunctional view is that different functions may have conflicting objectives. Over time, companies became aware of this weakness as they saw, for example, marketing and sales focusing on revenue generation and manufacturing and distribution focusing on cost reduction. Actions the two functions took were often in conflict and hurt the firm's overall performance. Companies realized the importance of expanding the scope of strategic fit across all functions within the firm. With the intracompany interfunctional scope, the goal is to maximize company profit. To achieve this goal, all functional strategies are developed to support both each other and the competitive strategy.

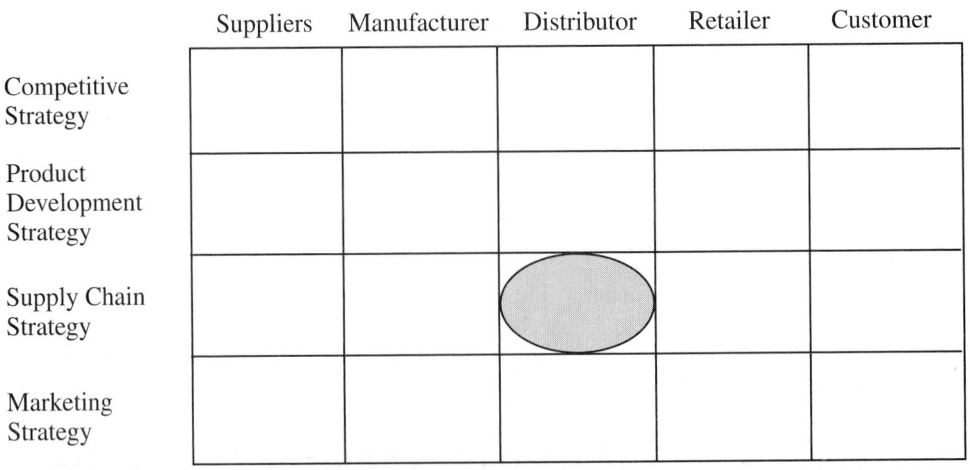

	Suppliers	Manufacturer	Distributor	Retailer	Customer
Competitive Strategy					
Product Development Strategy					
Supply Chain Strategy			⬭		
Marketing Strategy					

FIGURE 2.10 An Example of the Intracompany Intrafunctional Scope of Supply Chain Strategy at a Distributor

How does this change manifest itself? To return to our example, instead of looking only at the supply chain costs, the company will now look at revenue as well. Although the company had already decided to ship individual units to bring down inventory costs, marketing wanted to increase inventory so the company could take advantage of increased sales as a result of higher service levels. If the revenues and margins gained from holding more inventory outweigh the additional costs, the company should go ahead and increase inventory. The basic point is that both operational and marketing decisions have a revenue and a cost impact. They must thus be coordinated. The intracompany interfunctional scope of strategic fit as it applies to the distributor is shown in Figure 2.11.

Intercompany Interfunctional Scope: The Maximize Supply Chain Surplus View

The intracompany interfunctional scope of strategic fit has two major weaknesses. The first derives from the fact that the only positive cash flow for the supply chain occurs when the end customer pays for the product. All other cash flows are simply a resettling of accounts within the supply chain and add to supply chain cost. The difference between what the customer pays and the total cost generated across the supply chain represents the supply chain surplus. The supply chain surplus represents the total profit to be shared across all companies in the supply chain. Increasing supply chain surplus increases the amount to be shared among all members of the supply chain. The intracompany interfunctional scope leads to each stage of the supply chain trying to maximize its own profits, which does not necessarily result in the maximization of supply chain surplus. Supply chain surplus is maximized only when all supply chain stages coordinate strategy together. This occurs with the intercompany interfunctional scope in which all stages of the supply chain coordinate strategy across all functions to ensure that together they best meet the customer's needs and maximize supply chain surplus.

The second major weakness of the intracompany scope was noted in the 1990s when speed became a key driver of supply chain success. Today more and more

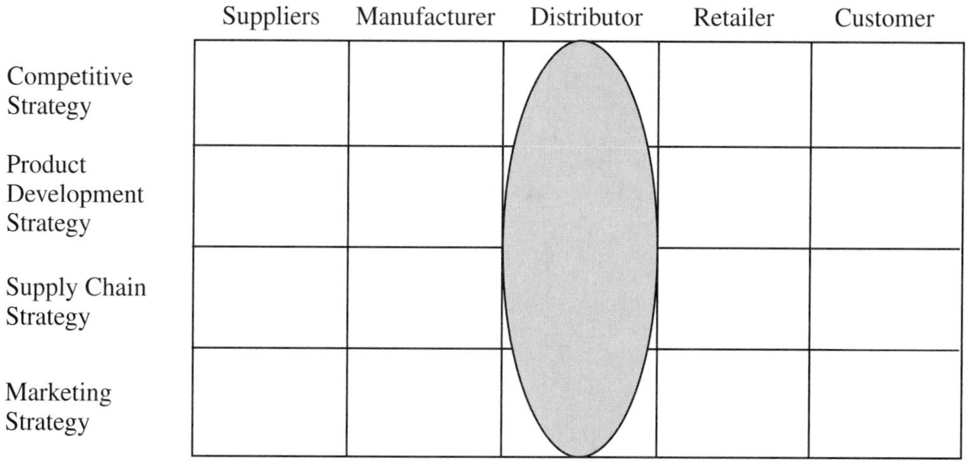

	Suppliers	Manufacturer	Distributor	Retailer	Customer
Competitive Strategy					
Product Development Strategy					
Supply Chain Strategy					
Marketing Strategy					

FIGURE 2.11   An Example of the Intracompany Interfunctional Scope Strategic Fit at a Data Distributor

companies are succeeding not because they have the lowest priced product and not because they have the highest quality or best performing product, but because they are able to respond quickly to market needs and get the right product to the right customer at the right time. Companies like Zara, the Spanish apparel retailer, have used speed as their primary competitive advantage to succeed in the marketplace.

This shift toward speed has forced companies to ask what creates the level of speed that customers are demanding. When this question is examined, the answer for most companies lies to a degree within their own boundaries. The most significant delays, however, are created at the interface between the boundaries of different stages of a supply chain. Thus, managing these interfaces becomes a key to providing speed to customers. The intracompany scope restricts strategic attention within each stage of the supply chain, leading to the interfaces being neglected. The intercompany scope forces every stage of the supply chain to look across the supply chain and evaluate the impact of its actions on other stages as well as on the interfaces.

The intercompany interfunctional scope of strategic fit is shown in Figure 2.12.

> **Key Point**   The intercompany scope of strategic fit is essential today because the competitive playing field has shifted from company versus company to supply chain versus supply chain. A company's partners in the supply chain may well determine the company's success, as the company is intimately tied to its supply chain.

Taking this view requires that each company evaluate its actions in the context of the entire supply chain. This means treating stages in the supply chain that a company does not own as belonging to the company. For example, a major supply chain theme that has received a great deal of press in recent years is the reduction of inventory.

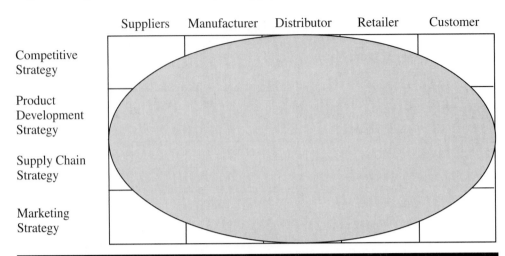

| | Suppliers | Manufacturer | Distributor | Retailer | Customer |

Competitive
Strategy

Product
Development
Strategy

Supply Chain
Strategy

Marketing
Strategy

FIGURE 2.12   The Intercompany Interfunctional Scope of Strategic Fit

Many companies strive to reduce their own inventories because they assume that the less inventory they have, the better. This assumption has led to a rash of changes in ownership of inventory from stage to stage in the supply chain without necessarily achieving any real reduction in overall inventory. Manufacturers feel that if they force their suppliers to own the parts inventory, they will not have to finance this inventory and therefore their costs will go down. But in many cases, the suppliers simply take ownership of the parts inventory without making any changes in the way this inventory is managed. Because holding this inventory increases the suppliers' costs, they are forced to raise their prices to the manufacturer or lower their margins. In the end, there is no real reduction in total cost because the supply chain merely shifts costs back and forth between its links.

The intercompany interfunctional scope proposes a different approach. Instead of just forcing the inventory on the supplier, who then increases price, the manufacturer and the supplier need to work together to actually reduce the amount of inventory that is required. For example, by sharing demand information with the supplier, the manufacturer can lower the amount of inventory needed in the chain, thus reducing overall cost in the supply chain and making the firms in that supply chain better able to compete.

The intercompany scope will result in a supply chain with greater surplus than the intracompany scope. This result will allow the supply chain to either increase profits by sharing the extra surplus or reduce price by passing along some of the surplus to the customer. Overall, the supply chain will be more competitive if it can achieve the intercompany scope of strategic fit.

Key Point   The intercompany scope of strategic fit requires firms to evaluate every action in the context of the entire supply chain. This broad scope increases the size of the surplus to be shared among all stages of the supply chain.

Agile Intercompany Interfunctional Scope

Up to this point, we have discussed strategic fit in a static context; that is, the players in a supply chain and the customer needs do not change over time. The situation in reality is much more dynamic as product life cycles get shorter and companies try to satisfy the changing needs of individual customers. In such a situation, a company may have to partner with many different firms depending on the product being produced and the customer being served. In such a situation it is crucial that strategic fit have agile intercompany scope.

Agile intercompany scope refers to a firm's ability to achieve strategic fit when partnering with supply chain stages that change over time. Firms must think in terms of supply chains consisting of many players at each stage. For example, a manufacturer may interface with a different set of suppliers and distributors depending on the product being produced and the customer being served. The strategy and operations at firms must be agile enough to maintain strategic fit in a changing environment. Further, as customer needs vary over time, firms must have the ability to become part of new supply chains while ensuring strategic fit. This level of agility becomes more important as the competitive environment becomes more dynamic.

2.4 SUMMARY OF LEARNING OBJECTIVES

1. Explain why achieving strategic fit is critical to a company's overall success.

   A lack of strategic fit between the competitive and supply chain strategy can result in the supply chain taking actions that are not consistent with customer needs, leading to a reduction in supply chain surplus and decreasing supply chain profitability. Strategic fit requires that all functions and stages in the supply chain target the same goal, one that is consistent with customer needs.

2. Describe how a company achieves strategic fit between its supply chain strategy and its competitive strategy.

   To achieve strategic fit, a company must first understand the needs of the customers being served, understand the uncertainty of the supply chain, and identify the implied uncertainty. The second step is to understand the supply chain's capabilities in terms of efficiency and responsiveness. The key to strategic fit is ensuring that supply chain responsiveness is consistent with customer needs, supply capabilities, and the resulting implied uncertainty.

3. Discuss the importance of expanding the scope of strategic fit across the supply chain.

   The scope of strategic fit refers to the functions and stages within a supply chain that coordinate strategy and target a common goal. When the scope is narrow, individual functions try to optimize their performance based on their own goals. This practice often results in conflicting actions that reduce the supply chain surplus. As the scope of strategic fit is enlarged to include the entire supply chain, actions are evaluated based on their impact on overall supply chain performance, which helps increase supply chain surplus.

DISCUSSION QUESTIONS

1. How would you characterize the competitive strategy of a high-end department store chain such as Nordstrom? What are the key customer needs that Nordstrom aims to fill?

2. Where would you place the demand faced by Nordstrom on the implied demand uncertainty spectrum? Why?
3. What level of responsiveness would be most appropriate for Nordstrom's supply chain? What should the supply chain be able to do particularly well?
4. How can Nordstrom expand the scope of strategic fit across its supply chain?
5. Reconsider the previous four questions for other companies such as Amazon, a supermarket chain, an auto manufacturer, and a discount retailer such as Wal-Mart.
6. Give arguments to support the statement that Wal-Mart has achieved very good strategic fit between its competitive and supply chain strategies.

BIBLIOGRAPHY

Blackwell, Roger D., and Kristina Blackwell. 1999. "The Century of the Consumer: Converting Supply Chains Into Demand Chains." *Supply Chain Management Review* (Fall): 22–32.

Bovet, David M., and David G. Frentzel. 1999. "The Value Net: Connecting for Profitable Growth." *Supply Chain Management Review* (Fall): 96–104.

Fine, Charles H. 1999. *Clock Speed, Winning Industry Control in the Age of Temporary Advantage.* Reading, Mass.: Perseus Books.

Fisher, Marshall L. 1997. "What Is the Right Supply Chain for Your Product?" *Harvard Business Review* (March–April): 83–93.

Fuller, J. B., J. O'Conner, and R. Rawlinson. 1993. "Tailored Logistics: The Next Advantage." *Harvard Business Review* (May–June): 87–98.

Gilmore, James H., and B. Joseph Pine II. (2000). *Markets of One: Creating Customer Unique Value Through Mass Customization.* Boston: Harvard Business School Press.

Lee, Hau L. 2002. "Aligning Supply Chain Strategies with Product Uncertainties." *California Management Review* (Spring): 105–119.

Magretta, Joan. 1998a. "Fast, Global, and Entrepreneurial: Supply Chain Management, Hong Kong Style." *Harvard Business Review* (September–October): 102–114.

———. 1998b. "The Power of Virtual Integration: An Interview With Dell Computer's Michael Dell." *Harvard Business Review* (March–April): 72–84.

Pine, B. Joseph II. 1999. *Mass Customization.* Boston: Harvard Business School Press.

Shapiro, Roy D. 1984. "Get Leverage from Logistics." *Harvard Business Review* (May–June): 119–127.

Shapiro, Roy D., and James L. Heskett. 1985. *Logistics Strategy: Cases and Concepts.* St. Paul, Minn.: West Publishing Company.

Stalk, George, Jr., and Thomas M. Hout. 1990. *Competing Against Time.* New York: Free Press.

CHAPTER

Supply Chain Drivers and Obstacles

Learning Objectives

After reading this chapter, you will be able to:

1. Identify the major drivers of supply chain performance.

2. Discuss the role each driver plays in creating strategic fit between the supply chain strategy and the competitive strategy.

3. Describe the major obstacles that must be overcome to successfully manage a supply chain.

In this chapter, we introduce the four major drivers—facilities, inventory, transportation, and information—that determine the performance of any supply chain. We discuss how these drivers are used in the design, planning, and operation of the supply chain. We also introduce many of the obstacles supply chain managers face in designing, planning, and operating their supply chains.

3.1 DRIVERS OF SUPPLY CHAIN PERFORMANCE

The strategic fit discussed in Chapter 2 requires that a company achieve the balance between responsiveness and efficiency in its supply chain that best meets the needs of the company's competitive strategy. To understand how a company can improve supply chain performance in terms of responsiveness and efficiency, we must examine the four drivers of supply chain performance: facilities, inventory, transportation, and information. These drivers not only determine the supply chain's performance in terms of responsiveness and efficiency, they also determine whether strategic fit is achieved across the supply chain.

First we define each driver and discuss its impact on the performance of the supply chain.

1. *Facilities* are the places in the supply chain network where product is stored, assembled, or fabricated. The two major types of facilities are production sites and storage sites. Whatever the function of the facility, decisions regarding location, capacity, and flexibility of facilities have a significant impact on the supply chain's performance. For instance, an auto parts distributor striving for responsiveness could have many warehousing facilities located close to customers even though this practice reduces efficiency. Alternatively, a high-efficiency distributor would have fewer warehouses to increase efficiency despite the fact that this practice will reduce responsiveness.

2. *Inventory* is all raw materials, work in process, and finished goods within a supply chain. Inventory is an important supply chain driver because changing inventory policies can dramatically alter the supply chain's efficiency and responsiveness. For example, a clothing retailer can make itself more responsive by stocking large amounts of inventory. With a large inventory, the likelihood is high that the retailer can immediately satisfy customer demand with clothes from its floor. A large inventory, however, will increase the retailer's cost, thereby making it less efficient. Reducing inventory will make the retailer more efficient but will hurt its responsiveness.

3. *Transportation* entails moving inventory from point to point in the supply chain. Transportation can take the form of many combinations of modes and routes, each with its own performance characteristics. Transportation choices have a large impact on supply chain responsiveness and efficiency. For example, a mail order catalog company can use a faster mode of transportation like FedEx to ship products, thus making their supply chain more responsive but also less efficient given the high costs associated with FedEx. Or the company can use slower but cheaper ground transportation to ship the product, making the supply chain efficient but limiting its responsiveness.

4. *Information* consists of data and analysis concerning facilities, inventory, transportation, and customers throughout the supply chain. Information is potentially the biggest driver of performance in the supply chain as it directly affects each of the other drivers. Information presents management with the opportunity to make supply chains more responsive and efficient. For example, with information on customer demand patterns, a pharmaceutical company can produce and stock drugs in anticipation of customer demand, which makes the supply chain very responsive because customers will find the drugs they need when they need them. This demand information can also make the supply chain more efficient because the pharmaceutical firm is better able to forecast demand and produce only the required amount. Information can also make this supply chain more efficient by providing managers with shipping options, for instance, that allow them to choose the lowest cost alternative while still meeting the necessary service requirements.

Before we discuss each of the four drivers in detail, we put these drivers into a framework that helps to clarify the role of each driver in improving supply chain performance.

3.2 A FRAMEWORK FOR STRUCTURING DRIVERS

Recall from Chapter 2 that the goal of a supply chain strategy is to strike the balance between responsiveness and efficiency that results in strategic fit with the competitive strategy. To reach this goal, a company uses the four supply chain drivers discussed earlier. For each of the individual drivers, supply chain managers must make a trade-off between efficiency and responsiveness. The combined impact of these four drivers then determines the responsiveness and efficiency of the entire supply chain.

We provide a visual framework for supply chain decision making in Figure 3.1. Most companies begin with a competitive strategy and then decide what their supply chain strategy ought to be. The supply chain strategy determines how the supply chain should perform with respect to efficiency and responsiveness. The supply chain must then use the supply chain drivers to reach the performance level the supply chain strategy dictates. Although this framework is generally viewed from the top down, in many instances, a study of the four drivers may indicate the need to change both the supply chain and potentially even the competitive strategy.

Consider this framework with Wal-Mart as an example. Wal-Mart's competitive strategy is to be a reliable, low-cost retailer for a very wide variety of mass consumption goods. This strategy dictates that the ideal supply chain will emphasize efficiency but also maintain an adequate level of responsiveness. Wal-Mart uses the four drivers to achieve this type of supply chain performance. With the inventory driver, Wal-Mart maintains an efficient supply chain by keeping relatively low levels of inventory. For

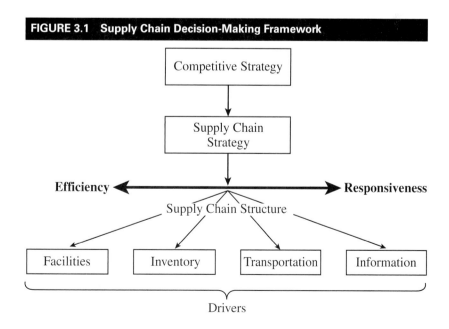

FIGURE 3.1 Supply Chain Decision-Making Framework

instance, Wal-Mart's DCs pioneered cross-docking, a system in which inventory is not stocked in a warehouse but rather is shipped to stores from the manufacturer. These shipments make only brief stops at DCs where they are transferred to trucks making deliveries to stores. This significantly lowers inventory because products are only stocked at stores, not at both stores and warehouses. With respect to inventory, Wal-Mart favors efficiency over responsiveness. On the transportation front, Wal-Mart runs its own fleet to keep responsiveness high. This increases transportation cost and investment, but the benefits in terms of responsiveness justify this cost in Wal-Mart's case because responsive transportation allows Wal-Mart to keep low levels of inventory. In the case of facilities, Wal-Mart uses central DCs within its network of stores to keep the number of facilities low and efficiency high. Wal-Mart only builds facilities where the demand is sufficient to justify having them, thereby increasing efficiency. To utilize information in the supply chain, Wal-Mart has invested significantly more than its competitors on information technology. This has led Wal-Mart to be a leader in its use of the information driver to improve responsiveness and decrease inventory investment. Wal-Mart feeds demand information all the way back up the supply chain to suppliers who manufacture only what is being demanded. The supply chain's ability to share demand information has required large investments, but the result is an improved supply chain in terms of both responsiveness and efficiency. Wal-Mart uses each supply chain driver to achieve the right balance between responsiveness and efficiency so that their competitive strategy and supply chain strategy are in harmony.

We devote the next four sections to a detailed discussion of each of the four drivers and its role in the supply chain.

3.3 FACILITIES

In this section, we discuss the role facilities play in the supply chain as well as critical facility-related decisions that supply chain managers need to make.

Role in the Supply Chain

If we think of inventory as *what* is being passed along the supply chain and transportation as *how* it is passed along, then facilities are the *where* of the supply chain. They are the locations to or from which the inventory is transported. Within a facility, inventory is either processed or transformed into another state (manufacturing) or it is stored before being shipped to the next stage (warehousing).

Role in the Competitive Strategy

Facilities and their corresponding capacities to perform their functions are a key driver of supply chain performance in terms of responsiveness and efficiency. For example, companies can gain economies of scale when a product is manufactured or stored in only one location; this centralization increases efficiency. The cost reduction, however, comes at the expense of responsiveness, as many of a company's customers may be located far from the production facility. The opposite is also true. Locating facilities close to customers increases the number of facilities needed and consequently reduces efficiency. If the customer demands and is willing to pay for the responsiveness that having numerous facilities adds, however, then this facilities decision helps meet the company's competitive strategy goals.

Example 3.1: Toyota and Honda

Both Toyota and Honda use facilities decisions to be more responsive to their customers. These companies have an end goal of opening manufacturing facilities in every major market that they enter. While there are other benefits to opening local facilities, such as protection from currency fluctuation and trade barriers, the increase in responsiveness plays a large role in Toyota and Honda's decision to locate in their local markets.

Components of Facilities Decisions

Decisions regarding facilities are a crucial part of supply chain design. We now identify components of facilities decisions that companies must analyze.

Location

Deciding where a company will locate its facilities constitutes a large part of the design of a supply chain. A basic trade-off here is whether to centralize to gain economies of scale or decentralize to become more responsive by being closer to the customer. Companies must also consider a host of issues related to the various characteristics of the local area in which the facility may be situated. These include macroeconomic factors, quality of workers, cost of workers, cost of facility, availability of infrastructure, proximity to customers and the rest of the network, tax effects, and other strategic factors.

Capacity

Companies must also decide what a facility's capacity to perform its intended function or functions will be. A large amount of excess capacity allows the facility to be very flexible and to respond to wide swings in the demands placed on it. Excess capacity, however, costs money and therefore can decrease efficiency. A facility with little excess capacity will likely be more efficient per unit of product it produces than one with a lot of unused capacity. The high utilization facility will, however, have difficulty responding to demand fluctuations. Therefore, a company must make a trade-off to determine the right amount of capacity to have at each of its facilities.

Operations Methodology

Companies must make a major decision regarding the operations methodology that a facility will use. They must decide whether to design a facility with a product focus or a functional focus. A product-focused facility performs many different functions (e.g., fabrication and assembly) in producing a single type of product. A functional focused facility performs few functions (e.g., only fabrication or only assembly) on many types of products. A product focus tends to result in more expertise about a particular type of product at the expense of the functional expertise that comes from a functional methodology. Firms must decide which type of expertise will best enable them to meet customer needs.

Firms must also make a decision regarding the relative level of flexible versus dedicated capacity in their portfolios. Flexible capacity can be used for many types of products but is often less efficient while dedicated capacity can be used for only a limited number of products but it is more efficient. The trade-off, as in previous instances, is between efficiency and responsiveness.

Warehousing Methodology

As with manufacturing, there are a variety of methodologies from which companies can choose when designing a warehouse facility. Some of these methodologies include:

- Stock keeping unit (SKU) storage: a traditional warehouse that stores all of one type of product together. This is a fairly efficient way to store products.
- Job lot storage: a methodology in which all the different types of products needed to perform a particular job or satisfy a particular type of customer are stored together. This generally requires more storage space but can create a more efficient picking and packing environment.
- Cross-docking: a methodology (pioneered by Wal-Mart) in which goods are not actually warehoused in a facility. Instead, trucks from suppliers, each carrying a different type of product, deliver goods to a facility. There the inventory is broken into smaller lots and quickly loaded onto store-bound trucks that carry a variety of products, some from each of the supplier trucks.

Overall Trade-Off: Responsiveness versus Efficiency

The fundamental trade-off managers face when making facilities decisions is between the cost of the number, location, and type of facilities (efficiency) and the level of responsiveness that these facilities provide the company's customers.

3.4 INVENTORY

In this section we discuss the role inventory plays in the supply chain and how managers use inventory to drive supply chain performance.

Role in the Supply Chain

Inventory exists in the supply chain because of a mismatch between supply and demand. This mismatch is intentional at a steel manufacturer where it is economical to manufacture in large lots that are then stored for future sales. The mismatch is also intentional at a retail store where inventory is held in anticipation of future demand. An important role that inventory plays in the supply chain is to increase the amount of demand that can be satisfied by having product ready and available when the customer wants it. Another significant role inventory plays is to reduce cost by exploiting any economies of scale that may exist during both production and distribution.

Inventory is spread throughout the supply chain from raw materials to work in process to finished goods that suppliers, manufacturers, distributors, and retailers hold. Inventory is a major source of cost in a supply chain and it has a huge impact on responsiveness. If we think of the responsiveness spectrum discussed in Chapter 2, the location and quantity of inventory can move the supply chain from one end of the spectrum to the other. For example, an apparel supply chain with high inventory levels at the retail stage has a high level of responsiveness because a consumer can walk into a store and walk out with the shirt they were looking for. In contrast, an apparel supply chain with little inventory would be very unresponsive. A customer wanting a shirt would have to order it and wait several weeks or even months for it to be manufactured, depending on how little inventory existed in the supply chain.

Inventory also has a significant impact on the material flow time in a supply chain. *Material flow time* is the time that elapses between the point at which material enters the supply chain to the point at which it exits. Another important area where inventory has a significant impact is throughput. For a supply chain, *throughput* is the rate at which sales occur. If inventory is represented by I, flow time by T, and throughput by D, the three can be related using Little's law as follows:

$$I = DT \tag{3.1}$$

For example, if the flow time of an auto assembly process is ten hours and the throughput is 60 units an hour, Little's Law tells us that the inventory is $60 \times 10 = 600$ units. If we were able to reduce inventory to 300 units while holding throughput constant, we would reduce our flow time to five hours (300/60). We note that in this relationship, inventory and throughput must have consistent units.

The logical conclusion here is that inventory and flow time are synonymous in a supply chain. Managers should use actions that lower the amount of inventory needed without increasing cost or reducing responsiveness, because reduced flow time can be a significant advantage in a supply chain.

Role in the Competitive Strategy

Inventory plays a significant role in a supply chain's ability to support a firm's competitive strategy. If a firm's competitive strategy requires a very high level of responsiveness, a company can use inventory to achieve this responsiveness by locating large amounts of inventory close to the customer. Conversely, a company can also use inventory to make itself more efficient by reducing inventory through centralized stocking. The latter strategy would support a competitive strategy of being a low-cost producer. The trade-off implicit in the inventory driver is between the responsiveness that results from more inventory and the efficiency that results from less inventory.

Example 3.2: Nordstrom

Nordstrom's competitive strategy targets upper-end customers with high responsiveness requirements. These customers are willing to pay a premium to have the products they want when they want them. To support this competitive strategy, Nordstrom uses inventory; the company stocks a large variety and quantity of products to ensure a high level of availability. In fact, Nordstrom stocks a significantly larger amount of inventory than other department stores. Nordstrom incurs higher costs because of their large inventory, but they gain extra margin from their customers, who are willing to pay for the level of service that Nordstrom's inventory makes possible.

Components of Inventory Decisions

We now identify major inventory-related decisions that supply chain managers must make to effectively create more responsive and more efficient supply chains.

Cycle Inventory

Cycle inventory is the average amount of inventory used to satisfy demand between receipt of supplier shipments. The size of the cycle inventory is a result of the production or purchase of material in large lots. Companies produce or purchase in large lots to exploit economies of scale in the production, transportation, or purchasing process. With the increase in lot size, however, also comes an increase in carrying costs. As an example of a cycle stock decision, consider an online book retailer. This retailer's sales average around 10 truckloads of books a month. The cycle inventory decisions the retailer must make are how much to order for replenishment and how often to place these orders. The e-retailer could order 10 trucks once each month or it could order one truck every three days. The basic trade-off supply chain managers face is the cost of holding larger lots of inventory (when cycle inventory is high) versus the cost of ordering product frequently (when cycle inventory is low).

Safety Inventory

Safety inventory is inventory held in case demand exceeds expectation; it is held to counter uncertainty. If the world were perfectly predictable, only cycle inventory would be needed. Because demand is uncertain and may exceed expectations, however, companies hold safety inventory to satisfy an unexpectedly high demand. Managers face a key decision when determining how much safety inventory to hold. For example, a toy retailer such as Toys 'R' Us must calculate their safety inventory for the holiday buying season. If they have too much safety inventory, toys go unsold and may have to be discounted after the holidays. If the company has ordered too little safety inventory, however, then Toys 'R' Us will lose sales and the margin those sales would have brought. Therefore, choosing safety inventory involves making a trade-off between the costs of having too much inventory and the costs of losing sales due to not having enough inventory.

Seasonal Inventory

Seasonal inventory is inventory that is built up to counter predictable variability in demand. Companies using seasonal inventory will build up inventory in periods of low demand and store it for periods of high demand when they will not have the capacity to produce all that is demanded. Managers face key decisions in determining whether to build seasonal inventory, and if they do build it, in deciding how much to build. If a company can rapidly change the rate of its production system at very low cost, then it may not need seasonal inventory because the production system can adjust to a period of high demand without incurring large costs. However, if changing the rate of production is expensive (e.g., when workers must be hired or fired), then a company would be wise to have a smooth production rate and build up its inventory during periods of low demand. Therefore, the basic trade-off supply chain managers face in determining how much seasonal inventory to build is the cost of carrying the additional seasonal inventory versus the cost of having a more flexible production rate.

Sourcing

Sourcing is the set of business processes required to purchase goods and services. Managers must first decide the tasks that will be outsourced and those that will be performed within the firm. For each task, the manager must decide whether to source from a single supplier or a portfolio of suppliers. If a portfolio of multiple suppliers is to be carried, the role of each supplier in the portfolio must be clarified. The next step is to identify the set of criterion that will be used to select suppliers and measure their performance. Managers then select suppliers and negotiate contracts with them.

Contracts should be structured to improve supply chain performance and minimize information distortion from one stage to the next. Contracts also clearly define the role of each supply source. Once suppliers and contracts are in place, procurement processes that facilitate the placement and delivery of orders play a major role. Sourcing decisions are crucial for a firm because they affect all other inventory decisions and the level of efficiency and responsiveness the supply chain can achieve.

Overall Trade-Off: Responsiveness versus Efficiency

The fundamental trade-off managers face when making inventory decisions is between responsiveness and efficiency. Increasing inventory will generally make the supply chain more responsive to the customer. This choice, however, comes at a cost as the added inventory decreases efficiency. Therefore, a supply chain manager can use inventory as one of the drivers for reaching the level of responsiveness and efficiency the competitive strategy targets.

3.5   TRANSPORTATION

In this section we discuss the role transportation plays in the supply chain as well as key transportation-related decisions that supply chain managers need to make.

Role in the Supply Chain

Transportation moves product between different stages in a supply chain. Like the other supply chain drivers, transportation has a large impact on both responsiveness and efficiency. Faster transportation, whether in the form of different modes of transportation or different amounts being transported, allows a supply chain to be more responsive but reduces its efficiency. The type of transportation a company uses also affects the inventory and facility locations in the supply chain. Dell, for example, flies some components from Asia because doing so allows the company to lower the level of inventory it holds. Clearly, such a practice increases responsiveness but decreases transportation efficiency because it is more costly than transporting parts by ship.

Role in the Competitive Strategy

The role of transportation in a company's competitive strategy figures prominently when the company is considering the target customer's needs. If a firm's competitive strategy targets a customer that demands a very high level of responsiveness and that customer is willing to pay for this responsiveness, then a firm can use transportation as one driver for making the supply chain more responsive. The opposite is true as well. If a company's competitive strategy targets customers whose main decision criterion is price, then the company can use transportation to lower the cost of the product at the expense of responsiveness. As a company may use both inventory and transportation to increase responsiveness or efficiency, the optimal decision for the company often means finding the right balance between the two.

Example 3.3: Laura Ashley

Laura Ashley sells clothing and other household items through a mail order catalog and uses transportation as part of its competitive strategy. Laura Ashley's customers are willing to pay a premium price for a high level of responsiveness. To meet this level of responsiveness, Laura

Ashley has located their main warehouse near the FedEx hub in Memphis to better utilize the responsive transportation that FedEx offers. When an order is placed, the goods can easily and quickly be sent from the Laura Ashley warehouse to the FedEx hub where they are sent overnight to the customer. This transportation policy enables Laura Ashley's customers to order their goods later than they can at other companies and still receive them next day.

Components of Transportation Decisions

We now identify key components of transportation that companies must analyze when designing and operating a supply chain.

Mode of Transportation

The mode of transportation is the manner in which a product is moved from one location in the supply chain network to another. Companies have six basic modes from which to choose:

- *Air:* The fastest and most expensive mode.
- *Truck:* A relatively quick and inexpensive mode with high levels of flexibility.
- *Rail:* An inexpensive mode used for large quantities.
- *Ship:* The slowest mode but often the only economical choice for large overseas shipments.
- *Pipeline:* Used primarily to transport oil and gas.
- *Electronic transportation:* The newest mode that "transports" goods such as music, previously sent solely by physical modes, electronically via the Internet.

Each mode has different characteristics with respect to the speed, size of shipments (individual parcels to pallets to full trucks to entire ships), cost of shipping, and flexibility that lead companies to choose one particular mode over the others.

Route and Network Selection

Another major decision managers must make is the route and network along which products are shipped. A route is the path along which a product is shipped and a network is the collection of locations and routes along which a product can be shipped. For example, a company needs to decide whether to ship products directly to customers or to use a series of distribution layers. Companies make some routing decisions at the supply chain's design stage while they make others daily or on a short-term basis.

Inhouse or Outsource

Traditionally, much of the transportation function has been performed inhouse. Today, however, much of transportation (and even entire logistics systems) is outsourced. Having to choose between bringing parts of transportation inhouse or outsourcing leads to another dimension of complexity when companies are designing their transportation systems.

Overall Trade-Off: Responsiveness versus Efficiency

The fundamental trade-off for transportation is between the cost of transporting a given product (efficiency) and the speed with which that product is transported (responsiveness). The transportation choice influences other drivers such as inventory and facilities. When supply chain managers think about making transportation decisions, they frame the decision in terms of this trade-off.

3.6   INFORMATION

In this section we discuss the role information plays in the supply chain as well as key information-related decisions that supply chain managers must make.

Role in the Supply Chain

Information could be overlooked as a major supply chain driver because it does not have a physical presence. Information, however, deeply affects every part of the supply chain. Its impact is easy to underestimate as information affects a supply chain in many different ways. Consider the following:

1. Information serves as the connection between the supply chain's various stages, allowing them to coordinate and bring about many of the benefits of maximizing total supply chain profitability.
2. Information is also crucial to the daily operations of each stage in a supply chain. For instance, a production scheduling system uses information on demand to create a schedule that allows a factory to produce the right products in an efficient manner. A warehouse management system uses information to create visibility of the warehouse's inventory. The company can then use this information to determine whether new orders can be filled.

Role in the Competitive Strategy

Information is a driver whose importance has grown as companies have used it to become both more efficient and more responsive. The tremendous growth of the importance of information technology is a testimony to the impact information can have on improving a company. Like all the other drivers, however, even with information, companies reach a point when they must make the trade-off between efficiency and responsiveness.

Another key decision involves what information is most valuable in reducing cost and improving responsiveness within a supply chain. This decision will vary depending on the supply chain structure and the market segments served. Some companies, for example, target customers who require customized products that carry a premium price tag. These companies might find that investments in information allow them to respond more quickly to their customers. The following examples illustrate this kind of investment.

Example 3.4: Andersen Windows

Andersen Windows, a major manufacturer of residential wood windows located in Bayport, Minnesota, has invested in an information system that enables them to rapidly get customized products to the market. This system, called "Window of Knowledge," allows distributors and customers to actually design windows to custom-fit their needs. Users can select from a library of over 50,000 components that can be combined in any number of ways. The system immediately gives the customer price quotes and automatically sends the order to the factory if the customer decides to buy. This information investment not only gives the customer a much wider variety of products, but it allows Andersen to be much more responsive to the customer as they get the customer's order to their factory as soon as the order is placed.

Example 3.5: Dell

Dell operates differently than most PC manufacturers in that it has invested in building up its own channel—a direct channel to the consumer. Most PC manufacturers sell their product through resellers. Dell takes orders directly from consumers over the phone and via the Internet. To build this direct channel required an investment because of the added functions Dell must perform. A large part of that cost can be attributed to information. With the direct channel model, however, Dell is able to view the actual consumer demand much sooner than most PC manufacturers and therefore the company can respond more quickly to changes in consumer needs. Dell can then modify its product offering to meet these new needs. Dell is not the low-cost provider. The company is, however, the most responsive provider and a large part of its responsiveness is due to the information flow between Dell and its customers and Dell and its suppliers that is made possible by its investment in information.

Components of Information Decisions

We now consider key components of information within a supply chain that a company must analyze to increase efficiency and improve responsiveness within its supply chain.

Push Versus Pull

When designing pieces of the supply chain, managers must determine whether these pieces are part of the push or pull phase in the chain. We discussed this distinction in Chapter 1, but we mention it again here because different types of systems require different types of information. Push systems generally require information in the form of elaborate Material Requirements Planning (MRP) systems to take the master production schedule and roll it back, creating schedules for suppliers with part types, quantities, and delivery dates. Pull systems require information on actual demand to be transmitted extremely quickly throughout the entire chain so that production and distribution of parts and products may accurately reflect the real demand.

Coordination and Information Sharing

Supply chain coordination occurs when all the different stages of a supply chain work toward the objective of maximizing total supply chain profitability rather than each stage devoting itself to its own profitability without considering total supply chain profit. Lack of coordination can result in a significant loss of supply chain profit. Managers must decide how to create this coordination in the supply chain and what information must be shared in order to accomplish this goal. Coordination between different stages in a supply chain requires each stage to share appropriate information with other stages. For example, if a supplier is to produce the right parts in a timely manner for a manufacturer in a pull system, the manufacturer must share demand and production information with the supplier. Information sharing is thus crucial to the success of a supply chain.

Forecasting and Aggregate Planning

Forecasting is the art and science of making projections about what future demand and conditions will be. Obtaining forecasting information frequently means using sophisticated techniques to estimate future sales or market conditions. Managers must decide how they will make forecasts and to what extent they will rely on them to make decisions. Companies often use forecasts both on a tactical level to schedule production and on a strategic level to determine whether to build new plants or even whether to enter a new market.

Once a company creates a forecast, the company needs a plan to act on this forecast. *Aggregate planning* transforms forecasts into plans of activity to satisfy the projected demand. A key decision managers face is how to collaborate on aggregate planning throughout the entire supply chain. The aggregate plan becomes a critical piece of information to be shared across the supply chain because it affects both the demand on a firm's suppliers and the supply to its customers.

Pricing and Revenue Management

Pricing is the process by which a firm decides how much to charge customers for its goods and services. Demand and supply information is a fundamental input into the pricing decision. A firm must understand the impact of price and competition on demand and the cost of supply when deciding whether to run a price promotion. Information on the availability of supply chain assets and the demand for these assets is needed for a firm to decide the best pricing strategy.

Revenue management is the use of differential pricing over time or customer segments to maximize profits from a limited set of supply chain assets. For effective revenue management, the supply chain must have good information on asset availability, customer demand, and customer behavior when faced with differential pricing.

Enabling Technologies

Many technologies exist that share and analyze information in the supply chain. Managers must decide which technologies to use and how to integrate these technologies into their companies and their partners' companies. The consequences of these decisions are becoming more and more important as the capabilities of these technologies grow. Some of these technologies include:

1. Electronic Data Interchange (EDI) allows companies to place instantaneous, paperless purchase orders with suppliers. EDI is not only efficient, but it also decreases the time needed to get products to customers as transactions can occur more quickly and accurately than when they are paper based.

2. The Internet has critical advantages over EDI with respect to information sharing. The Internet conveys much more information and therefore offers much more visibility than EDI. Better visibility enables stages in the supply chain to make better decisions. Internet communication between stages in the supply chain is also easier because a standard infrastructure (the World Wide Web) already exists. Thanks to the Internet, e-commerce has become a major force in the supply chain.

3. Enterprise Resource Planning (ERP) systems provide the transactional tracking and global visibility of information from any part of a company and its supply chain that allows intelligent decisions to be made. This real time information helps a supply chain to improve the quality of its operational decisions. ERP systems keep track of the information, whereas the Internet provides one method with which to view this information. A more detailed discussion of ERP systems is in Chapter 17.

4. Supply Chain Management (SCM) software adds a higher layer to ERP systems. This software provides analytical decision support in addition to the visibility of information. ERP systems show a company what is going on while SCM systems help a company decide what it should do. A more detailed discussion of SCM systems is in Chapter 17.

Overall Trade-Off: Responsiveness Versus Efficiency

Good information systems can help a firm improve both its responsiveness and efficiency. The information driver is used to improve the performance of other drivers and the use of information is based on the strategic position the other drivers support. Accurate information can help a firm improve efficiency by decreasing inventory and transportation costs. Accurate information can improve responsiveness by helping a supply chain better match supply and demand.

In the next section, we discuss the main obstacles companies face when striving to achieve strategic fit.

3.7 OBSTACLES TO ACHIEVING STRATEGIC FIT

A company's ability to find a balance between responsiveness and efficiency that best matches the needs of the customer it is targeting is the key to achieving strategic fit. In deciding where this balance should be located on the responsiveness spectrum, companies face many obstacles.

In this section we discuss some of the obstacles and also provide a feel for how the supply chain environment has changed over the years. On one hand, these obstacles have made it much more difficult for companies to create the ideal balance. On the other hand, they have afforded companies increased opportunities for improving supply chain management. Managers need a solid understanding of the impact of these obstacles because they are critical to a company's ability to reap the maximum profitability from its supply chain.

Increasing Variety of Products

Product proliferation is rampant today. With customers demanding ever more customized products, manufacturers have responded with mass customization and even segment-of-one (where companies view each customer as an independent market segment) views of the market. Products that were formerly quite generic are now custom-made for a specific consumer. For example, PCs used to come from the manufacturer in a standard set of configurations. Now one can order a custom PC, built from a variety of configurations that number in the millions. The increase in product variety complicates the supply chain by making forecasting and meeting demand much more difficult. Increased variety tends to raise uncertainty, and uncertainty frequently results in increased cost and decreased responsiveness within the supply chain.

Decreasing Product Lifecycles

In addition to the increasing variety of product types, the life cycle of products has been shrinking. Today there are products whose life cycles can be measured in months compared to the old standard of years. These are not just niche products, either. PCs now have a life cycle of several months, and even some automobile manufacturers have lowered their product life cycles from five plus years to about three years. This decrease in product life cycles makes the job of achieving strategic fit more difficult as the supply chain must constantly adapt to manufacture and deliver new products in addition to coping with these products' demand uncertainty. Shorter life cycles increase uncertainty while reducing the window of opportunity within which the supply chain can achieve fit. Increased uncertainty combined with a smaller window of opportunity has put additional pressure on supply chains to coordinate and create a good match between supply and demand.

Increasingly Demanding Customers

Customers are constantly demanding improvements in delivery lead times, cost, and product performance. If they do not receive these improvements, they move on to new suppliers. Many companies used to have periodic, standard price increases—not due to a rise in demand or any other factor, but simply because raising prices was the way business was done. Now, one repeatedly sees companies that cannot force through *any* price increases without losing market share. Today's customers are demanding faster fulfillment, better quality, and better performing products for the same price they paid years ago. This tremendous growth in customer *demands* (not necessarily *demand*) means that the supply chain must provide more just to maintain its business.

Fragmentation of Supply Chain Ownership

Over the past several decades, most firms have become less vertically integrated. As companies have shed noncore functions, they have been able to take advantage of supplier and customer competencies that they themselves did not have. This new ownership structure, however, has also made managing the supply chain more difficult. With the chain broken into many owners, each with its own policies and interests, the chain is more difficult to coordinate. Potentially, this problem could cause each stage of a supply chain to work only toward its own objectives rather than the whole chain's, resulting in the reduction of overall supply chain profitability.

Globalization

Over the last few decades, governments around the world have loosened trade restrictions, which has resulted in a dramatic trend toward increased global trade. This increase in globalization has had two main impacts on the supply chain. The first is that supply chains are now more likely than ever to be global. Having a global supply chain creates many benefits, such as the ability to source from a global base of suppliers who may offer better or cheaper goods than were available in a company's home nation. Globalization, however, also adds stress to the chain because facilities within the chain are farther apart, making coordination much more difficult.

The second impact of globalization on the supply chain is an increase in competition, as once-protected national players must compete with companies from around the world. In the past, if there were not many companies offering to satisfy customers' needs, then individual companies could take more time responding to these needs. However, in most industries there are now many more firms aggressively pursuing their competitors' business. This competitive situation makes supply chain performance a key to maintaining and growing sales while also putting more strain on supply chains and thus forcing them to make their trade-offs even more precisely.

Difficulty Executing New Strategies

Creating a successful supply chain strategy is not easy. Once a good strategy is formulated, however, actually executing the strategy can be even more difficult. For instance, Toyota's production system, which is a supply chain strategy, has been widely known and understood. Yet this strategy has been a sustained competitive advantage for Toyota for more than two decades. Does Toyota have a brilliant strategy that no one else can figure out? Their strategy *is* brilliant, but many others have figured it out. The difficulty other firms have had is in executing that strategy. Many highly talented employees at all levels of the organization are necessary to make a supply chain strategy successful. Although we deal mostly with the formulation of strategy in this book, one should keep in mind that skillful execution of a strategy can be as important as the strategy itself.

All of the obstacles discussed earlier are making it more difficult for companies to achieve strategic fit by creating the proper balance between responsiveness and efficiency in the supply chain. These obstacles also represent a tremendous opportunity in terms of untapped improvement within the supply chain. The increasing impact of these obstacles has led to supply chain management becoming a major factor in the success or failure of firms.

> **Key Point** Many obstacles, such as growing product variety and shorter life cycles, have made it increasingly difficult for supply chains to achieve strategic fit. Overcoming these obstacles offers a tremendous opportunity for firms to use supply chain management to gain competitive advantage.

3.8 SUMMARY OF LEARNING OBJECTIVES

1. Identify the major drivers of supply chain performance.

   The major drivers of supply chain performance are facilities, inventory, transportation, and information.

2. Discuss the role of each driver in creating strategic fit between the supply chain strategy and the competitive strategy.

   A company achieving strategic fit has found the right balance between responsiveness and efficiency. Each driver affects this balance. Having more facilities generally makes a chain more responsive, whereas having few, central facilities creates higher efficiency.

Holding higher levels of inventory increases the responsiveness of a supply chain, whereas keeping inventory low increases the chain's efficiency. Using faster modes of transportation increases a chain's responsiveness, whereas using slower modes generally increases efficiency. Investing in information can vastly improve the supply chain performance on both dimensions. This investment, however, must be done based on the strategic position supported by the other drivers.

3. Describe the major obstacles that must be overcome to successfully manage a supply chain.

Increasing product variety, decreasing product life cycles, demanding customers, and global competition all make creating supply chain strategies more difficult as these factors can hamper supply chain performance. The increase in globalization of the supply chain and fragmentation of supply chain ownership has also made it more difficult to execute supply chain strategies.

DISCUSSION QUESTIONS

1. How could a grocery retailer use inventory to increase the responsiveness of the company's supply chain?
2. How could an auto manufacturer use transportation to increase the efficiency of its supply chain?
3. How could a bicycle manufacturer increase responsiveness through its facilities?
4. How could an industrial supplies distributor use information to increase its responsiveness?
5. How has globalization made strategic fit even more important to a company's success?
6. What are some industries where products have proliferated and life cycles have shortened? How have the supply chains in these industries adapted?
7. How can the full set of four drivers be used to create strategic fit for a PC manufacturer targeting time-sensitive customers?

BIBLIOGRAPHY

Marien, Edward J. 2000. "The Four Supply Chain Enablers." *Supply Chain Management Review* (March–April): 60–68.

PART

Designing the Supply Chain Network

C H A P T E R   4

Designing the Distribution Network in a Supply Chain

C H A P T E R   5

Network Design in the Supply Chain

C H A P T E R   6

Network Design in an Uncertain Environment

The goal of the chapters in this module is to discuss a set of frameworks and tools used to design supply chain networks. Network design decisions are among the most important supply chain decisions as their implications are significant and long lasting. When designing a supply chain, we need to consider how all four supply chain drivers—facilities, transportation, inventory, and information—should be used together to support the competitive strategy of a firm and maximize supply chain profits.

Chapter 4 explores how to design a distribution network. A variety of distribution network models are presented along with an analysis of the pros and cons of each model. Chapter 5 considers facility related decisions that firms must make when designing their supply chain network. A framework for facility decisions in a supply chain is developed and methodologies for locating facilities and allocating capacity and markets to each facility are described. Chapter 6 highlights how uncertainties in financial factors such as prices, exchange rates, and inflation should be accounted for in supply chain decisions. Methodologies for financial evaluation of supply chain decisions under uncertainty are discussed. These methodologies are then used to evaluate several supply chain decisions.

CHAPTER

4

Designing the Distribution Network in a Supply Chain

4.1 The Role of Distribution in the Supply Chain
4.2 Factors Influencing Distribution Network Design
4.3 Design Options for a Distribution Network
4.4 The Value of Distributors in the Supply Chain
4.5 Distribution Networks in Practice
4.6 Summary of Learning Objectives
Discussion Questions
Bibliography

Learning Objectives

After reading this chapter, you will be able to:

1. Identify the key factors to be considered when designing the distribution network.

2. Discuss the strengths and weaknesses of various distribution options.

3. Understand the role that distributors play in the supply chain.

In this chapter, we provide an understanding of the role of distribution within a supply chain and identify factors that should be considered when designing a distribution network. We identify several potential designs for distribution networks and evaluate the strength and weakness of each option. We also discuss how distributors provide value in a supply chain. Our goal is to provide managers with a logical framework for selecting the appropriate distribution network given product characteristics and the markets being served.

4.1 THE ROLE OF DISTRIBUTION IN THE SUPPLY CHAIN

Distribution refers to the steps taken to move and store a product from the supplier stage to a customer stage in the supply chain. Distribution occurs between every pair of stages in the supply chain. Raw materials and components are moved from suppliers to manufacturers, whereas finished products are moved from the manufacturer to the end consumer. Distribution is a key driver of the overall profitability of a firm because it directly impacts both the supply chain cost and the customer experience. Distribution related costs form about 10.5 percent of the U.S. economy and about 20 percent of the cost of manufacturing. For commodity products, distribution forms an even higher fraction of the product cost. In India, the outbound distribution cost of cement is about 30 percent of the cost of producing and selling cement.

It would be no exaggeration to state that two of the world's most profitable companies, Wal-Mart and 7-Eleven Japan, have built the success of their entire business around outstanding distribution design and operation. In the case of Wal-Mart, distribution allows them to provide good availability of relatively common products at very low cost. In the case of 7-Eleven, distribution allows them to provide a very high level of customer responsiveness at a reasonable cost.

The choice of the distribution network can be used to achieve a variety of supply chain objectives ranging from low cost to high responsiveness. As a result, companies in the same industry often select very different distribution networks. Next, we discuss examples of distribution networks of different companies to highlight the variety of distribution choices and the issues that arise when selecting among these options.

Dell distributes its PCs directly to end consumers, whereas companies like HP distribute through resellers. Dell customers wait several days to get a PC while customers can walk away with an HP PC from a reseller. Gateway opened Gateway Country stores where customers could check out the products and have sales people help them configure a PC that suited their needs. Gateway, however, chose to sell no products at the stores, with all PCs shipped directly from the factory to the customer. In 2001, Gateway closed several of these stores given their poor financial performance. Apple Computer is planning to open retail stores where computers will be sold. These PC companies have chosen three different distribution models. How can we evaluate this wide range of distribution choices? Which ones serve the companies and their customers better?

P&G has chosen to distribute directly to large supermarket chains while making the smaller players buy P&G products from distributors. The product moves faster from P&G to the larger chains while moving through an additional stage when going to the smaller supermarkets. Texas Instruments, which once used only direct sales, now sells about 30 percent of its volume to 98 percent of its customers through distributors, while serving the remaining 2 percent of customers with 70 percent of the volume directly.[1] What value do these distributors provide? When should a distribution network include an additional stage such as a distributor? Proponents of e-business had predicted the death of intermediaries like distributors. Why were they proved wrong in many industries? Distributors play a much more significant role for consumer goods

---

[1] *A Tale of Two Electronic Component Distributors*, Ananth Raman and Bharat P. Rao, Harvard Business School Case, 1997.

distribution in a country such as India compared to the United States. Why may this be the case?

W. W. Grainger stocks about 100,000 SKUs that can be sent to customers within a day of the order being placed. The remaining slower moving products are not stocked but shipped directly from the manufacturer when a customer places an order. It takes several days for the customer to receive the product in this case. Are these distribution choices appropriate? How can they be justified?

As the preceding examples illustrate, firms can make many different choices when designing their distribution network. A poor distribution network can hurt the level of service that customers receive while increasing the cost. An inappropriate network can have a significant negative impact on the profitability of the firm as evident in the failure of many business-to-consumer (B2C) companies such as Webvan. The appropriate choice of the distribution network results in customer needs being satisfied at the lowest possible cost.

In the next section we identify performance measures that need to be considered when designing the distribution network.

4.2   FACTORS INFLUENCING DISTRIBUTION NETWORK DESIGN

At the highest level, performance of a distribution network should be evaluated along two dimensions:

1. Customer needs that are met
2. Cost of meeting customer needs

Thus, a firm must evaluate the impact on customer service and cost as it compares different distribution network options. The customer needs that are met influence the company's revenues, which along with cost decide the profitability of the delivery network.

Although customer service consists of many components, we focus on those measures that are influenced by the structure of the distribution network. These include:

- Response time
- Product variety
- Product availability
- Customer experience
- Order visibility
- Returnability

Response time is the time between when a customer places an order and receives delivery. Product variety is the number of different products/configurations that a customer desires from the distribution network. Availability is the probability of having a product in stock when a customer order arrives. Customer experience includes the ease with which the customer can place and receive their order. It also includes purely experiential aspects such as the possibility of getting a cup of coffee and the value that the sales staff provides. Order visibility is the ability of the customer to track their order from placement to delivery. Returnability is the ease with which a customer can return unsatisfactory merchandise and the ability of the network to handle such returns.

It may seem at first that a customer always wants the highest level of performance along all these dimensions. In practice, however, this is not the case. Customers ordering a book at Amazon.com are willing to wait longer than those that drive to a nearby Borders store to get the same book. In contrast, customers can find a far larger variety of books at Amazon compared to the Borders store.

Firms that target customers who can tolerate a large response time require few locations that may be far from the customer and can focus on increasing the capacity of each location. In contrast, firms that target customers who value short response times need to locate close to them. These firms must have many facilities, with each location having a low capacity. Thus, a decrease in the response time customers desire increases the number of facilities required in the network, as shown in Figure 4.1. For example, Borders provides its customers with books on the same day but requires about 400 stores to achieve this goal for most of the United States. Amazon, in contrast, takes about a week to deliver a book to its customers, but only uses about five locations to store its books.

Changing the distribution network design affects the following supply chain costs (notice that these are the four supply chain drivers we discussed earlier):

- Inventories
- Transportation
- Facilities and handling
- Information

As the number of facilities in a supply chain increases, the inventory and resulting inventory costs also increase (see Chapter 11), as shown in Figure 4.2.

To decrease inventory costs, firms try to consolidate and limit the number of facilities in their supply chain network. For example, with fewer facilities Amazon is able to turn its inventory about 12 times a year, whereas Borders, with about 400 facilities, achieves only about two turns per year.

Inbound transportation costs are the costs incurred in bringing material into a facility. *Outbound transportation costs* are the costs incurred in sending material out of a facility. Outbound transportation costs per unit tend to be higher than inbound costs because inbound lot sizes are typically larger. For example, the Amazon warehouse

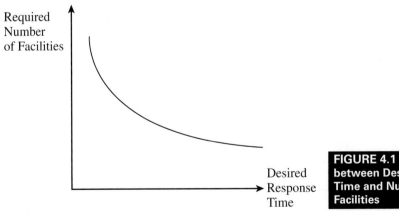

FIGURE 4.1   Relationship between Desired Response Time and Number of Facilities

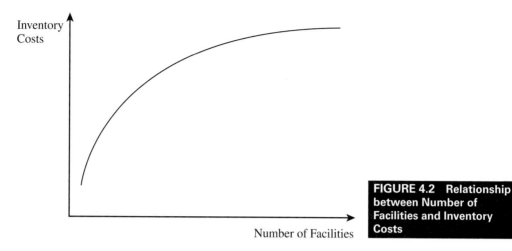

FIGURE 4.2   Relationship between Number of Facilities and Inventory Costs

receives full truckload (TL) shipments of books on the inbound side, but ships out small packages with a few books per customer on the outbound side. Increasing the number of warehouse locations decreases the average outbound distance to a customer and makes outbound transportation distance a smaller fraction of total distance traveled by the product. Thus, as long as inbound transportation economies of scale are maintained, increasing the number of facilities decreases total transportation cost, as shown in Figure 4.3. If the number of facilities is increased to a point where inbound lot sizes are also very small and result in a significant loss of economies of scale in inbound transportation, increasing the number of facilities increases total transportation cost, as shown in Figure 4.3.

A distribution network with more than one warehouse allows Amazon to reduce transportation cost relative to a network with a single warehouse.

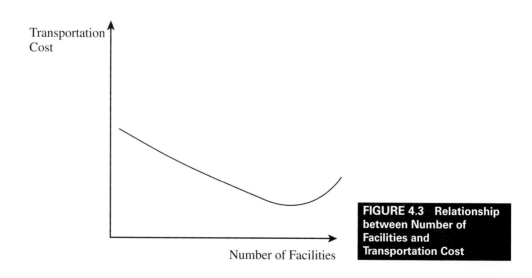

FIGURE 4.3   Relationship between Number of Facilities and Transportation Cost

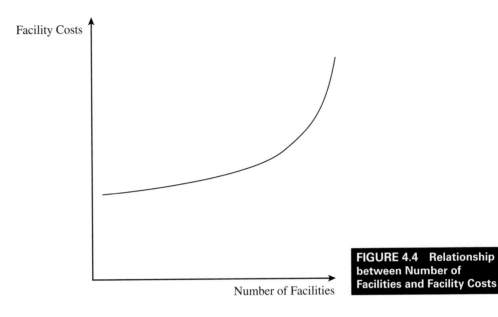

FIGURE 4.4 Relationship between Number of Facilities and Facility Costs

Facility costs decrease as the number of facilities is reduced as shown in Figure 4.4 because a consolidation of facilities allows a firm to exploit economies of scale.

Total logistics costs are the sum of inventory, transportation, and facility costs for a supply chain network. As the number of facilities increases, total logistics costs first decrease and then increase as shown in Figure 4.5. Each firm should have at least the number of facilities that minimize total logistics costs. For example, Amazon has more than one warehouse primarily to reduce its logistics costs (and improve response time). As a firm wants to further reduce the response time to its customers, it may have to increase the number of facilities beyond the point that minimizes logistics costs. A firm

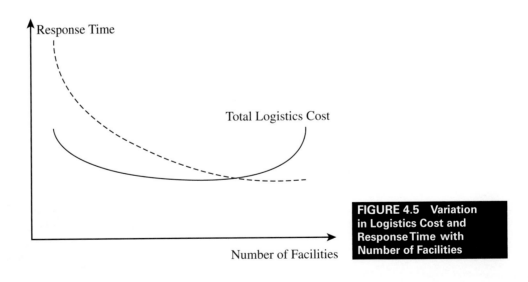

FIGURE 4.5 Variation in Logistics Cost and Response Time with Number of Facilities

should add facilities beyond the cost-minimizing point only if managers are confident that the increase in revenues because of better responsiveness is greater than the increase in costs because of the additional facilities.

The customer service and cost components listed earlier are the primary measures used to evaluate different delivery network designs. In general, no distribution network will outperform others along all dimensions. Thus, it is important to ensure that the strengths of the distribution network fit with the strategic position of the firm.

In the next section, we discuss various distribution networks and their relative strengths and weaknesses.

4.3 DESIGN OPTIONS FOR A DISTRIBUTION NETWORK

We discuss distribution network choices in the context of distribution from the manufacturer to the end consumer. When considering distribution between any other pair of stages, such as supplier to manufacturer, many of the same options still apply. There are two key decisions when designing a distribution network:

1. Will product be delivered to the customer location or picked up from a pre-ordained site?
2. Will product flow through an intermediary (or intermediate location)?

Based on the choices for the two decisions, there are six distinct distribution network designs that may be used to move products from factory to customer. These are classified as follows:

1. Manufacturer storage with direct shipping
2. Manufacturer storage with direct shipping and in-transit merge
3. Distributor storage with package carrier delivery
4. Distributor storage with last mile delivery
5. Manufacturer/distributor storage with costumer pickup
6. Retail storage with customer pickup

Next we describe each distribution option and discuss its strengths and weaknesses.

Manufacturer Storage with Direct Shipping

In this option, product is shipped directly from the manufacturer to the end customer, bypassing the retailer (who takes the order and initiates the delivery request). This option is also referred to as drop-shipping with product delivered directly from the manufacturer to the customer location. The retailer, if they exist independent of the manufacturer, carries no inventories with all inventories stored at the manufacturer. Information flows from the customer, via the retailer, to the manufacturer, whereas product is shipped directly from the manufacturer to customers as shown in Figure 4.6. In some instances like Dell, the manufacturer sells directly to the customer. Online retailers such as eBags and Nordstrom.com use drop-shipping to deliver goods to the end consumer. eBags does not hold any inventory of bags and has them drop-shipped directly from the manufacturer to the customer. Nordstrom carries some products in

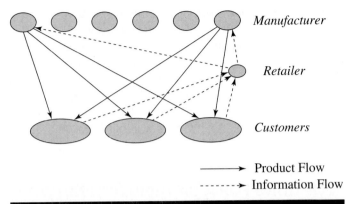

Product Flow
Information Flow

FIGURE 4.6 Manufacturer Storage with Direct Shipping

inventory while using the drop-ship model for slow-moving footwear. W. W. Grainger also uses drop-shipping to deliver slow-moving items that are not carried in inventory.

The biggest advantage of drop-shipping is the ability to centralize inventories at the manufacturer. A manufacturer can aggregate demand across all retailers that they supply. As a result, the supply chain is able to provide a high level of product availability with lower levels of inventory. A key issue with regards to drop-shipping is the ownership structure of the inventory at the manufacturer. If specified portions of inventory at the manufacturer are allocated to individual retailers, there is little benefit of aggregation even though the inventory is physically aggregated. Benefit of aggregation is only achieved if the manufacturer can allocate at least a portion of the available inventory across retailers on an as-needed basis. The benefits from centralization are highest for high-value, low-demand items with unpredictable demand. The decision of Nordstrom to drop-ship low-demand shoes satisfies these criteria. Similarly, bags sold by eBags tend to have high value and relatively low demand per SKU. The inventory benefits of aggregation are small for items with predictable demand and low value. Thus, drop-shipping would not offer a significant inventory advantage to an online grocer selling a staple item like detergent. For slow-moving items, inventory turns can increase by a factor of 6:15 if drop-shipping is used instead of storage at retail stores.

Drop-shipping also offers the manufacturer the opportunity to postpone customization until after the customer order has been placed. Postponement, if implemented, further lowers inventories by aggregating to the component level. Build-to-order companies such as Dell hold inventories as common components and postpone product customization, thus lowering the level of inventories carried.

Transportation costs are high with drop-shipping because the average outbound distance to the end consumer is large and package carriers are used to ship the product. Package carriers have high shipping costs per unit compared to TL or less-than-truckload (LTL) carriers. With drop-shipping, a customer order with items from several manufacturers will involve multiple shipments to the customer. This loss in aggregation in outbound transportation further increases cost.

Supply chains save on the fixed cost of facilities when using drop-shipping because all inventories are centralized at the manufacturer. This eliminates the need for other warehousing space in the supply chain. There can be some savings of handling costs as well because the transfer from manufacturer to retailer no longer occurs. Handling cost savings must be evaluated carefully, however, because the manufacturer is now required to transfer items to the factory warehouse in full cases and then ship out from the warehouse in single units. The inability of a manufacturer to develop single-unit delivery capability can have a significant negative impact on handling cost and response time. Handling costs can be significantly reduced if the manufacturer has the capability to ship orders directly from the production line.

A good information infrastructure is needed between the retailers and the manufacturer so that the retailer can provide product availability information to the customer even though the inventory is located at the manufacturer. The customer should also have visibility into order processing at the manufacturer even though the order is placed with the retailer. Drop-shipping will generally require significant investment in the information infrastructure. The information infrastructure requirement is somewhat simpler for direct sellers like Dell because two stages (retailer and manufacturer) do not need to be integrated.

Response times tend to be large when drop-shipping is used because the order has to be transmitted from the retailer to the manufacturer and shipping distances are on average longer from the manufacturer's centralized site. eBags, for example, states that order processing may take from one to five days and ground transportation after that may take from three to eleven business days. This implies that customer response time at eBags will be four to sixteen days using ground transportation and drop-shipping. Another issue is that the response time need not be identical for every manufacturer that is part of a customer order. Given an order containing products from several sources, the customer will receive multiple partial shipments over time, making receiving more complicated for the customer.

Manufacturer storage allows a high level of product variety to be made available to the customer. With a drop-shipping model, every product at the manufacturer can be made available to the customer without any limits imposed by shelf space. W. W. Grainger is able to offer hundreds of thousands of slow-moving items from thousands of manufacturers using drop-shipping. This would be impossible if each product had to be stored by W. W. Grainger.

Drop-shipping provides a good customer experience in the form of delivery to the customer location. The experience, however, suffers when a single order containing products from several manufacturers is delivered in partial shipments.

Order visibility is very important in the context of manufacturer storage because two stages in the supply chain are involved in every customer order. A failure to provide this capability is likely to have a significant negative impact on customer satisfaction. Order tracking, however, becomes harder to implement in a situation of drop-shipping because it requires complete integration of information systems at both the retailer and the manufacturer. For direct sellers such as Dell, order visibility is simpler to provide.

A manufacturer storage network is likely to have difficulty handling returns, hurting customer satisfaction. The handling of returns is more expensive under drop-shipping because each order may involve shipments from more than one manufacturer. There are two ways that returns can be handled. One is for the customer to return the product directly to the manufacturer. The second approach is for the retailer to set up a separate facility (across all manufacturers) to handle returns. The first approach incurs high transportation and coordination costs whereas the second approach requires investment in a facility to handle returns.

The performance characteristics of drop-shipping along various dimensions are summarized in Table 4.1.

Given its performance characteristics, manufacturer storage with direct shipping is best suited for a large variety of low-demand, high-value items where customers are willing to wait for delivery and accept several partial shipments. Manufacturer storage is also suitable if it allows the manufacturer to postpone customization, thus reducing inventories. For drop-shipping to be effective, there should be few sourcing locations per order. It is thus ideal for direct sellers that are able to build-to-order. Drop-shipping will be hard to implement if there are more than 20 or 30 sourcing locations that have to ship directly to customers on a regular basis. For products with very low demand, however, drop-shipping may be the only option.

TABLE 4.1 Performance Characteristics of Manufacturer Storage with Direct Shipping Network

Cost Factor	Performance
Inventory	Lower costs because of aggregation. Benefits of aggregation are highest for low-demand, high-value items. Benefits are very large if product customization can be postponed at the manufacturer.
Transportation	Higher transportation costs because of increased distance and disaggregate shipping.
Facilities and handling	Lower facility costs because of aggregation. Some saving on handling costs if manufacturer can manage small shipments or ship from production line.
Information	Significant investment in information infrastructure to integrate manufacturer and retailer.

Service Factor	Performance
Response time	High response time of between one to two weeks because of increased distance and two stages for order processing. Response time may vary by product, thus complicating receiving.
Product variety	Easy to provide a very high level of variety.
Product availability	Easy to provide a high level of product availability because of aggregation at manufacturer.
Customer experience	Good in terms of home delivery but can suffer if order from several manufacturers is sent as partial shipments.
Order visibility	More difficult but also more important from a customer service perspective.
Returnability	Expensive and difficult to implement.

Manufacturer Storage with Direct Shipping and In-Transit Merge

Unlike pure drop-shipping where each product in the order is sent directly from its manufacturer to the end customer, in-transit merge combines pieces of the order coming from different locations so that the customer gets a single delivery. Information and product flows for the in-transit merge network are as shown in Figure 4.7. In-transit merge has been used by direct sellers like Dell and Gateway and can be used by companies implementing drop-shipping. When a customer orders a PC from Dell along with a Sony monitor, the package carrier picks up the PC from the Dell factory and the monitor from the Sony factory; it then merges the two together at a hub before making a single delivery to the customer.

As with drop-shipping, the ability to aggregate inventories and postpone product customization is a significant advantage of in-transit merge. In-transit merge allows Dell and Sony to aggregate all their inventories at the factory. This approach will have the greatest benefits for products with high value whose demand is hard to forecast, in particular if product customization can be postponed.

In most cases, transportation costs will be lower than drop-shipping because of the merge that takes place at the carrier hub prior to delivery to the customer. An order with products from three manufacturers thus requires only one delivery to the customer compared to three that would be required with drop-shipping. Fewer deliveries save transportation cost and simplify receiving.

Facility and processing costs for the manufacturer and the retailer are as in drop-shipping. The party performing the in-transit merge has higher facility costs because of the merge capability required. Receiving costs at the customer will be lower because a single delivery is received. Overall supply chain facility and handling costs are somewhat higher than drop-shipping.

A very sophisticated information infrastructure is needed to allow the in-transit merge. Besides information, operations at the retailer, manufacturers, and the carrier must be coordinated. The investment in information infrastructure will be higher than for drop-shipping.

Response times, product variety, and availability will be similar to drop-shipping. Response times may be marginally higher because of the need to perform the merge. Customer experience is likely to be better than drop-shipping because the customer

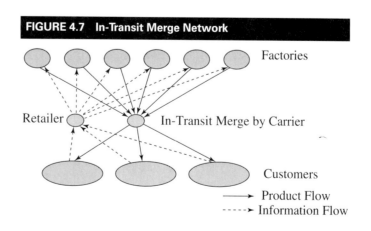

FIGURE 4.7 In-Transit Merge Network

Factories

Retailer

In-Transit Merge by Carrier

Customers

→ Product Flow
----▸ Information Flow

receives only one delivery for their order instead of many partial shipments. Order visibility is a very important requirement. Although the initial setup is difficult because it requires integration of manufacturer, carrier, and retailer, tracking itself becomes easier given the merge that occurs at the carrier hub. Up to the point of merge, the order from each manufacturer is tracked separately. After that the order can be tracked as a single unit. Returnability is similar to drop-shipping. Problems in handling returns are very likely and the reverse supply chain will continue to be expensive and difficult to implement as with drop-shipping.

The performance of factory storage with in-transit merge is compared with drop-shipping in Table 4.2.

The main advantage of in-transit merge over drop-shipping is the somewhat lower transportation cost and improved customer experience. The major disadvantage is the additional effort during the merge itself. Given its performance characteristics, manufacturer storage with in-transit merge is best suited for low- to medium-demand, high-value items where the retailer is sourcing from a limited number of manufacturers. Compared to drop-shipping, in-transit merge requires a higher demand from each manufacturer (not necessarily each product) to be effective. If there are too many sources, in-transit merge can be very difficult to coordinate and implement. In-transit merge is best implemented if there are no more than four or five sourcing locations. The in-transit merge of a Dell PC with a Sony monitor is appropriate because product variety is high but there are few sourcing locations with relatively large total demand from each sourcing location.

Distributor Storage with Carrier Delivery

Under this option, inventory is not held by manufacturers at the factories but is held by distributors/retailers in intermediate warehouses and package carriers are used to transport products from the intermediate location to the final customer. Amazon, as

TABLE 4.2 Performance Characteristics of In-Transit Merge

Cost Factor	Performance
Inventory	Similar to drop-shipping.
Transportation	Somewhat lower transportation costs than drop-shipping.
Facilities and handling	Handling costs higher than drop-shipping at carrier; receiving costs lower at customer.
Information	Investment is somewhat higher than for drop-shipping.

Service Factor	Performance
Response time	Similar to drop-shipping; may be marginally higher.
Product variety	Similar to drop-shipping.
Product availability	Similar to drop-shipping.
Customer experience	Better than drop-shipping because a single delivery has to be received.
Order visibility	Similar to drop-shipping.
Returnability	Similar to drop-shipping.

well as industrial distributors like W. W. Grainger and McMaster Carr, have used this approach combined with drop-shipping from a manufacturer (or distributor). Information and product flows when using distributor storage with delivery by a package carrier are shown in Figure 4.8.

Relative to manufacturer storage, distributor storage will require a higher level of inventory because the distributor/retailer warehouse aggregates demand uncertainty to a lower level than the manufacturer who is able to aggregate demand across all distributors/retailers. From an inventory perspective, distributor storage makes sense for products with somewhat higher demand. This is seen in the operations of both Amazon and W. W. Grainger. They only stock the medium- to fast-moving items at their warehouse with slower moving items stocked further upstream. In some instances, postponement can be implemented with distributor storage but it does require that the warehouse develop some assembly capability. Distributor storage, however, requires much less inventory than a retail network. Amazon achieves about 12 turns of inventory using warehouse storage whereas Borders achieves about two turns using retail stores.

Transportation costs will be somewhat lower for distributor storage compared to manufacturer storage because an economic mode of transportation (e.g., TL) can be employed for inbound shipments to the warehouse, which is closer to the customer. Unlike manufacturer storage where multiple shipments may need to go out for a single customer order with multiple items, distributor storage allows outbound orders to the customer to be bundled into a single shipment, further reducing transportation cost. Transportation savings from distributor storage relative to manufacturer storage increase for faster moving items.

Compared to manufacturer storage, facility costs (of warehousing) will be somewhat higher with distributor storage because of a loss of aggregation. Processing and handling costs will be comparable to manufacturer storage unless the factory is able to ship to the end customer directly from the production line. In that case, distributor storage will have higher processing costs. From a facility cost perspective, distributor storage is not appropriate for extremely slow-moving items.

The information infrastructure needed with distributor storage is significantly less complex than that needed with manufacturer storage. The distributor warehouse

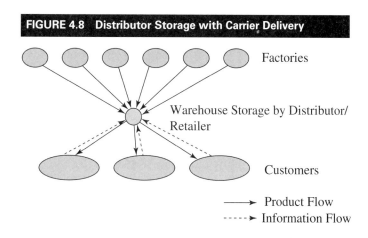

FIGURE 4.8   Distributor Storage with Carrier Delivery

Factories

Warehouse Storage by Distributor/ Retailer

Customers

Product Flow

Information Flow

serves as a buffer between the customer and the manufacturer, decreasing the need to coordinate the two completely. Real time visibility between customers and the warehouse is needed, whereas real time visibility between the customer and the manufacturer is not. Visibility between the distributor warehouse and manufacturer can be achieved at a much lower cost than real time visibility between the customer and manufacturer.

Response time with distributor storage will be better than with manufacturer storage because distributor warehouses are, on average, closer to customers and the entire order is aggregated at the warehouse when shipped. Amazon, for example, processes all warehouse-stored items within a day and then takes three to seven business days using ground transportation for the order to reach the customer. W. W. Grainger processes customer orders on the same day and has enough warehouses to deliver most orders the next day using ground transport. Warehouse storage will limit to some extent the variety of products that can be offered. W. W. Grainger does not store very low-demand items at its warehouse, relying on manufacturers to drop-ship those products to the customer. Customer convenience is high with distributor storage because a single shipment reaches the customer in response to an order. Order visibility becomes easier than with manufacturer storage because there is a single shipment from the warehouse to the customer and only one stage of the supply chain is directly involved in filling the customer order. Returnability is better than with manufacturer storage because all returns can be processed at the warehouse itself. The customer also has to return only one package even if the items are from several manufacturers.

The performance of distributor storage with carrier delivery is summarized in Table 4.3.

Distributor storage with carrier delivery is well suited for medium- to fast-moving items. Distributor storage also makes sense when customers want delivery

TABLE 4.3	**Performance Characteristics of Distributor Storage with Carrier Delivery**
Cost Factor	*Performance*
Inventory	Higher than manufacturer storage. Difference is not large for faster moving items.
Transportation	Lower than manufacturer storage. Reduction is highest for faster moving items.
Facilities and handling	Somewhat higher than manufacturer storage. The difference can be large for slow-moving items.
Information	Simpler infrastructure compared to manufacturer storage.
Service Factor	*Performance*
Response time	Faster than manufacturer storage.
Product variety	Lower than manufacturer storage.
Product availability	Higher cost to provide the same level of availability as manufacturer storage.
Customer experience	Better than manufacturer storage with drop-shipping.
Order visibility	Easier than manufacturer storage.
Returnability	Easier than manufacturer storage.

faster than offered by manufacturer storage but do not need it immediately. Distributor storage can handle somewhat lower variety than manufacturer storage but can handle a much higher level of variety than a chain of retail stores.

Distributor Storage with Last Mile Delivery

Last mile delivery refers to the distributor/retailer delivering the product to the customer's home instead of using a package carrier. Webvan, Peapod, and Alberston's have used last mile delivery in the grocery industry. Companies like Kozmo and Urbanfetch tried to set up home delivery networks for a variety of products but have failed to survive profitably. Unlike package carrier delivery, last mile delivery requires the distributor warehouse to be much closer to the customer. Given the limited radius that can be served with last mile delivery, more warehouses are required compared to the case when package delivery is used. The warehouse storage with last mile delivery network is as shown in Figure 4.9.

Distributor storage with last mile delivery requires higher levels of inventory than the other options (except for retail stores) because it has a lower level of aggregation. From an inventory perspective, warehouse storage with last mile delivery will be suitable for relatively fast-moving items where disaggregation does not lead to a significant increase of inventory. Staple items in the grocery industry fit this description.

Transportation costs will be highest using last mile delivery. This is because package carriers aggregate delivery across many retailers and are able to obtain better economies of scale than available to a distributor/retailer attempting last mile delivery. Delivery costs (including transportation and processing) can be about $30 to $40 per home delivery in the grocery industry. Last mile delivery may be somewhat cheaper in large, dense cities. Transportation costs may also be justifiable for bulky products where the customer is willing to pay for home delivery. Home delivery for water and large bags of rice has proved quite successful in China, where the high population density has helped decrease delivery costs.

Facility and processing costs are very high using this option given the large number of facilities required. Facility costs are somewhat lower than a network with retail stores but much higher than either manufacturer storage or distributor storage with package carrier delivery. Processing costs, however, are much higher than a network of

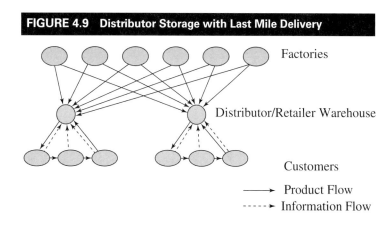

FIGURE 4.9   Distributor Storage with Last Mile Delivery

Factories

Distributor/Retailer Warehouse

Customers

⟶ Product Flow
----▶ Information Flow

retail stores because all customer participation is eliminated. A grocery store doing last mile delivery performs all the processing until the product is delivered to the customer's home, unlike a supermarket where there is much more customer participation.

The information infrastructure with last mile delivery is similar to distributor storage with package carrier delivery. However, it requires the additional capability of scheduling deliveries.

Response times will be faster than the use of package carriers. Kozmo and Urbanfetch tried to provide same day delivery whereas online grocers have typically provided next day delivery. Product variety will generally be lower than distributor storage with package carrier delivery. The cost of providing product availability will be higher than every option other than retail stores. The customer experience can be very good using this option, particularly for bulky, hard-to-carry items. Order visibility is less of an issue given that deliveries are made within twenty four hours. The order-tracking feature does become important to handle exceptions in case of incomplete or undelivered orders. Of all the options discussed, returnability is best with last mile delivery because trucks making deliveries can also pick up returns from customers. Returns will still be more expensive to handle than at a retail store where a customer can bring the product back.

The performance characteristics of distributor storage with last mile delivery are summarized in Table 4.4.

TABLE 4.4   Performance Characteristics of Distributor Storage with Last Mile Delivery

Cost Factor	Performance
Inventory	Higher than distributor storage with package carrier delivery.
Transportation	Very high cost given minimal scale economies. Higher than any other distribution option.
Facilities and handling	Facility costs higher than manufacturer storage or distributor storage with package carrier delivery, but lower than a chain of retail stores.
Information	Similar to distributor storage with package carrier delivery.
Service Factor	*Performance*
Response time	Very quick. Same day to next day delivery.
Product variety	Somewhat less than distributor storage with package carrier delivery but larger than retail stores.
Product availability	More expensive to provide availability than any other option except retail stores.
Customer experience	Very good, particularly for bulky items.
Order traceability	Less of an issue and easier to implement than manufacturer storage or distributor storage with package carrier delivery.
Returnability	Easier to implement than other options. Harder and more expensive than a retail network.

In areas with high labor cost, it is very hard to justify distributor storage with last mile delivery on the basis of efficiency or improved margin. It can only be justified if there is a large enough customer segment willing to pay for this convenience. In that case, an effort should be made to couple last mile delivery with an existing distribution network to exploit economies of scale and improve utilization. An example is Albertson's use of existing grocery store facilities and labor to provide home delivery. A portion of the grocery store serves as a fulfillment center for online orders as well as a replenishment center for the grocery store itself. This helps improve utilization and lower the cost of providing this service. Last mile delivery may be justifiable if customer orders are large enough to provide some economies of scale. Peapod has changed its pricing policies to reflect this idea. Minimum order sizes are for $50 (with a delivery charge of $9.95) and free delivery is no longer provided for orders of any size. One interesting thing that peapod does is to offer discounts for deliveries during times when they aren't busy. These discounts change based on what their schedule looks like. To be profitable, home delivery companies will almost definitely have to eliminate free delivery.

Manufacturer or Distributor Storage with Consumer Pickup

In this approach, inventory is stored at the manufacturer or distributor warehouse but customers place their orders online or on the phone and then come to designated pickup points to collect their orders. Orders are shipped from the storage site to the pickup points as needed. Examples include 7dream.com, operated by 7-Eleven Japan, which allows customers to pick up online orders at a designated store. A business-to-business (B2B) example is W. W. Grainger where customers can pick up their order at one of the W. W. Grainger retail outlets. In the case of 7dream.com, the order is delivered from a manufacturer or distributor warehouse to the pickup location. In the case of W. W. Grainger, some items are stored at the pickup location while others may come from a central location. The information and product flows in the network for 7-Eleven Japan are as shown in Figure 4.10.

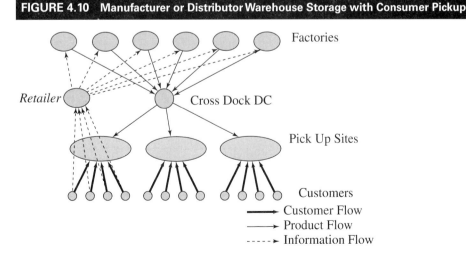

FIGURE 4.10   Manufacturer or Distributor Warehouse Storage with Consumer Pickup

7-Eleven has DCs where product from manufacturers is cross-docked and sent to retail outlets on a daily basis. A retailer delivering an online order can be treated as one of the manufacturers with deliveries cross-docked and sent to the appropriate 7-Eleven outlet. Serving as an outlet for online orders allows 7-Eleven to improve utilization of its existing logistical assets.

Inventory costs using this approach can be kept low with either manufacturer or distributor storage to exploit aggregation. W. W. Grainger keeps its inventory of fast-moving items at pickup locations, whereas slow-moving items are stocked at a central warehouse, or in some cases at the manufacturer.

Transportation cost is lower than any solution using package carriers because significant aggregation is possible when delivering orders to a pickup site. This allows the use of TL or LTL carriers to transport orders to the pickup site. In a case like 7-Eleven Japan, the marginal increase in transportation cost is small because trucks are already making deliveries to the stores and their utilization can be improved by including online orders.

Facility costs will be high if new pickup sites have to be built. A solution using existing sites will lower the additional facility costs. This, for example, is the case with 7dream.com and W. W. Grainger where the stores already exist. Processing costs at the manufacturer or the warehouse will be comparable to other solutions. Processing costs at the pickup site will be high because each order must be matched with a specific customer when they arrive. Creating this capability can increase processing costs significantly if appropriate storage and information systems are not provided. Increased processing cost at the pickup site is the biggest hurdle to the success of this approach.

A significant information infrastructure is needed to provide visibility of the order until the customer picks it up. Very good coordination is needed between the retailer, the storage location, and the pickup location.

A response time comparable to the use of package carriers can be achieved in this case. Variety and availability comparable to any manufacturer or distributor storage option can be provided. There is some loss of customer experience because unlike the other options discussed, customers must come and pick up their orders. On the other hand, customers who do not want to pay online can pay by cash using this option. In countries like Japan where 7-Eleven has over 9,000 outlets, it can be argued that the loss of customer convenience is small because most customers are close to a pickup site and can collect their order at their own convenience. In some cases, this option is considered more convenient because it does not require the customer to be at home at the time of delivery.

Order visibility is extremely important for customer pickups. The customer must be informed when the order has arrived and the order should be easily identified once the customer arrives to pick it up. Such a system will be hard to implement because it requires integration of several stages in the supply chain. Returns can potentially be handled at the pickup site. The problem with some existing sites such as 7-Eleven stores is that they are not equipped to accept and process returns for products not sold at the stores. From a transportation perspective, however, return flows can be handled using the delivery trucks. For customers, returning a product will be easy because they have a physical location to bring it to. Overall, returnability will be fairly good using this option.

TABLE 4.5   Performance Characteristics of Network with Consumer Pickup Sites

Cost Factor	Performance
Inventory	Can match any other option depending on the location of inventory.
Transportation	Lower than the use of package carriers, especially if using an existing delivery network.
Facilities and handling	Facility costs can be very high if new facilities have to be built. Costs are lower if existing facilities are used. The increase in handling cost at the pickup site can be significant.
Information	Significant investment in infrastructure required.

Service Factor	Performance
Response time	Similar to package carrier delivery with manufacturer or distributor storage. Same day delivery possible for items stored locally at pickup site.
Product variety	Similar to other manufacturer or distributor storage options.
Product availability	Similar to other manufacturer or distributor storage options.
Customer experience	Lower than other options because of the lack of home delivery. In areas with high density of population loss of convenience may be small.
Order visibility	Difficult but essential.
Returnability	Somewhat easier given that pickup location can handle returns.

The performance characteristics of manufacturer or distributor storage with consumer pickup sites are summarized in Table 4.5.

The main advantage of a network with consumer pickup sites is that it can lower the delivery cost, thus expanding the set of products sold as well as customers served online. The major hurdle is the increased handling cost at the pickup site. Such a network is likely to be most effective if existing locations such as convenience or grocery stores are used as pickup sites because such a network improves the economies from existing infrastructure. Unfortunately, such sites are typically designed to allow the customer to do the picking and will need to develop the capability of picking a customer specific order.

Retail Storage with Customer Pickup

In this option, inventory is stored locally at retail stores. Customers walk into the retail store or place an order online or on the phone and pick it up at the retail store. Examples of companies that offer multiple options of order placement include Albertson's, which uses part of the facility as a grocery store and part of the facility as an online fulfillment center. Customers can walk into the store or order online. A B2B example is W. W. Grainger, where customers can order online, by phone, or in person and pick up their order at one of the W. W. Grainger retail outlets. Alberston's stores its inventory at the pickup location itself. In the case of W. W. Grainger, some items are stored at the pickup location whereas others may come from a central location.

Local storage increases inventory costs because of lack of aggregation. For very fast-moving items, however, there is marginal increase in inventory even with local storage. Albertson's uses local storage given that most of its products are relatively fast moving and are being stocked at the supermarket in any case. Similarly, W. W. Grainger keeps its inventory of fast-moving items at pickup locations, whereas slow-moving items are stocked at a central warehouse. In general, inventory will increase with local storage.

Transportation cost is much lower than other solutions because inexpensive modes of transport can be used to replenish product at the retail store. Facility costs will be high because many local facilities are required. A minimal information infrastructure is needed if customers walk into the store and place their order. For online orders, however, a significant information infrastructure is needed to provide visibility of the order until the customer picks it up.

Very good response times can be achieved in this case because of local storage. For example, both Alberston's and W. W. Grainger offer same day pickup from their retail locations. Product variety stored locally will be lower than other options. It is more expensive than all other options to provide a high level of product availability. Order visibility is extremely important for customer pickups where orders are placed online or on the phone. Returns can be handled at the pickup site. Overall, returnability will be fairly good using this option.

The performance characteristics of a network with customer pickup sites and local storage (such as retail stores) are summarized in Table 4.6.

The main advantage of a network with local storage is that it can lower the delivery cost and provide a faster response than other networks. The major disadvantage is the increased inventory and facility costs. Such a network is best suited for fast-moving items or items where customers value the rapid response.

TABLE 4.6 Performance Characteristics of Local Storage at Consumer Pickup Sites

Cost Factor	*Performance*
Inventory	Higher than all other options.
Transportation	Lower than all other options.
Facilities and handling	Higher than other options. The increase in handling cost at the pickup site can be significant for online and phone orders.
Information	Some investment in infrastructure required for online and phone orders.

Service Factor	*Performance*
Response time	Same day (immediate) pickup possible for items stored locally at pickup site.
Product variety	Lower than all other options.
Product availability	More expensive to provide than all other options.
Customer experience	Related to whether shopping is viewed as a positive or negative experience by customer.
Order visibility	Trivial for in-store orders. Difficult, but essential, for online and phone orders.
Returnability	Easier than other options given that pickup location can handle returns.

Selecting a Distribution Network Design

A network designer needs to consider product characteristics as well as network requirements when deciding on the appropriate delivery network. The various networks considered earlier have different strengths and weaknesses. In Table 4.7, the various delivery networks are ranked relative to each other along different performance dimensions. A ranking of 1 indicates the best performance along a given dimension; as the relative performance worsens, the ranking gets higher.

Only niche companies will end up using a single distribution network. Most companies are best served by a combination of delivery networks. The combination used will depend on product characteristics as well as the strategic position that the firm is targeting. The suitability of different delivery designs (from a supply chain perspective) in various situations is shown in Table 4.8.

An excellent example of a hybrid network is W. W. Grainger, which combines all the aforementioned options into its distribution network. The network, however, is tailored to match the characteristics of the product or the needs of the customer. Fast-moving and emergency items are stocked locally and customers can either pick them up directly or have them shipped depending on the urgency. Slower moving items are stocked at a national DC from where they are shipped to the customer within a day or two. Very slow-moving items are typically drop-shipped from the manufacturer and involve a longer lead time. Another hybrid network is Amazon, where some items are stocked at their warehouse while other slow-moving items may be drop-shipped from distributors or publishers.

We can revisit the questions raised at the beginning of the chapter. In the computer industry today, customization and high product variety seem to be valued by the customer. PCs are assembled at few sources by a company but with high variety of end product. Demand for any one configuration tends to be low and variable. This is also a purchase for which customers are willing to wait a few days for delivery. Product value is reasonably high. Product postponement can play an important role in reducing inventories. From Table 4.8 it would thus seem to be a product better suited for drop-shipping or

TABLE 4.7 Comparative Performance of Delivery Network Designs

	Retail Storage with Customer Pickup	Manufacturer Storage with Direct Shipping	Manufacturer Storage with In-Transit Merge	Distributor Storage with Package Carrier Delivery	Distributor Storage with Last Mile Delivery	Manufacturer Storage with Pickup
Response time	1	4	4	3	2	4
Product variety	4	1	1	2	3	1
Product availability	4	1	1	2	3	1
Customer experience	5	4	3	2	1	5
Order visibility	1	5	4	3	2	6
Returnability	1	5	5	4	3	2
Inventory	4	1	1	2	3	1
Transportation	1	4	3	2	5	1
Facility and handling	6	1	2	3	4	5
Information	1	4	4	3	2	5

TABLE 4.8 Performance of Delivery Networks for Different Product/Customer Characteristics

	Retail Storage with Customer Pickup	Manufacturer Storage with Direct Shipping	Manufacturer Storage with In-Transit Merge	Distributor Storage with Package Carrier Delivery	Distributor Storage with Last Mile Delivery	Manufacturer Storage with Pickup
High-demand product	+2	−2	−1	0	+1	−1
Medium-demand product	+1	−1	0	+1	0	0
Low-demand product	−1	+1	0	+1	−1	+1
Very low-demand product	−2	+2	+1	0	−2	+1
Many product sources	+1	−1	−1	+2	+1	0
High product value	−1	+2	+1	+1	0	−12
Quick desired response	+2	−2	−2	−1	+1	−2
High product variety	−1	+2	0	+1	0	+2
Low customer effort	−2	+1	+2	+2	+2	−1

+2: Very suitable; +1: Somewhat suitable; 0: Neutral; −1: Somewhat unsuitable; −2: Very unsuitable.

factory storage with pickup from a local site. Thus, at present, IBM's decision to stop selling many slow-moving configurations at retail stores would appear better than that of Gateway to open retail stores. Gateway has created a network of retail stores but is not exploiting any of the supply chain advantages such a network offers because no products are sold there. To fully exploit the benefits of the retail network it would make sense for Gateway to sell their standard configurations (likely to have high demand) at the retail stores with all other configurations drop-shipped from the factory (perhaps with local pickup at the retail stores if it is economical). Apple has decided to open some retail stores (fewer than Gateway) and actually carry product for sale at these stores. If Apple uses these retail stores to sell the fast-moving items and display the configurable items (which can be drop-shipped), it will be a good use of their retail network.

4.4 THE VALUE OF DISTRIBUTORS IN THE SUPPLY CHAIN

As the notion of disintermediation pushed by proponents of online commerce suggests, the value of distributors has always been questioned and it has been assumed that their presence makes the supply chain less efficient. The failure of the Web to eliminate most distributors indicates that they must be providing some value. Although the presence of an intermediary such as a distributor does not always improve supply chain performance, there are many situations where intermediaries add value to the supply chain. We discuss several examples where the presence of distributors improves supply chain performance and then characterize situations where distributors play a positive role.

Distributing Consumer Goods in India

Consider a country like India where consumer goods are sold through tens of millions of small retail outlets. Should manufacturers use distributors when selling fast-moving consumer goods such as soaps and detergent? Soaps and detergents are commodity products with low value. Transportation is an important component of total cost, making it critical for the supply chain to be structured to keep transportation costs low.

The small size of Indian retail outlets limits the amount of inventory they can hold. Thus, each retailer has a small replenishment lot size. A typical replenishment order can be compared with the weekly grocery shopping for a family in the United States. The only way for a manufacturer to keep transportation costs low is to bring full TLs of product close to the market and then distribute locally using milk runs with smaller vehicles. The presence of an intermediary who can receive a full TL shipment, break bulk, and then make smaller deliveries to the retailers is crucial if transportation costs are to be kept low. Most Indian distributors are one-stop shops stocking everything from cooking oil to soaps and detergents made by a variety of manufacturers. Besides the convenience provided by one-stop shopping, distributors are also able to reduce transportation costs for outbound delivery to the retailer by aggregating products across multiple manufacturers during the delivery runs. Distributors are able to replenish retailers with a much shorter response time than a manufacturer would be able to provide.

The presence of distributors thus improves performance of the consumer goods supply chain in India by lowering transportation cost and improving replenishment response time. The major services provided by them are the ability to take in TL shipments, break bulk, store inventory, and provide outbound delivery to retailers.

Distributing MRO Products

MRO products are generally needed in an emergency in small quantities. The typical order is unplanned and has a few items with a small dollar value. The variety of items that may be needed differs from one order to the next and is very large. As a result, products from many manufacturers are typically required to satisfy all MRO needs at a customer. How should the manufacturers move products from their factories to customers? Distributors like W. W. Grainger and McMaster Carr serve as intermediaries in the MRO supply chain. Storing inventory close to the end consumer allows distributors to provide the desired response time of one to two days, which would not be possible for a manufacturer. Inventory at the distributors serves as a buffer given the small, sporadic orders from customers. Replenishment orders placed from distributors to manufacturers are more stable, making it much easier and cheaper for manufacturers to respond. Incoming deliveries from manufacturers to distributors are often TLs, which decreases the overall cost of transportation. By including products from many manufacturers on a single outbound shipment, distributors are also able to lower the transportation cost to the customer. MRO distributors effectively carry the emergency inventory that would otherwise have to be held at each customer. As a result, they aggregate the safety inventory required across all their customers. This aggregation reduces the total safety inventory required in the supply chain. This is particularly important for slow-moving items where the value of this aggregation is high. In the United States, MRO products are entirely sold through distributors given the high value that distributors provide in the supply chain.

Distributing Electronic Components[2]

In the electronics industry, there are a few major component manufacturers like Intel, Texas Instruments, and Motorola, who produce components for a large number of

---

[2]*A Tale of Two Electronic Component Distributors*, Ananth Raman and Bharat P. Rao, Harvard Business School Case, 1997.

original equipment manufacturers (OEMs). The 80:20 rule holds in general with less than 20 percent of the OEMs using over 80 percent of the components. Due to this high demand from the large OEMs, component manufacturers generally sell directly to their large customers. Should they use distributors when serving their small customers?

For distribution to small OEMs, the presence of electronic component distributors improves supply chain performance in several ways. The distributors receive large shipments from component manufacturers at low transportation rates. After breaking bulk, distributors supply the smaller quantities required by the OEMs. This reduces overall transportation cost in the channel. By stocking components from several manufacturers, distributors serve as a one-stop shop for smaller OEMs and are able to improve economies of scale on outbound shipments by combining components from many manufacturers into a single outbound shipment. Distributors hold centralized safety stock for the OEMs, effectively allowing the channel to operate with much lower safety stocks than would be needed if inventories were held separately at each OEM. Thus, distributors add significant value to the supply chain when moving components from manufacturers to smaller OEMs in the electronics industry. This example shows many of the classic areas of value that distributors provide.

In conclusion, distributors add value to a supply chain between a supply stage and a customer stage if there are many small players at the customer stage, each requiring a small amount of the product at a time. The value added increases if distributors carry products from many manufacturers. Improvement in supply chain performance occurs for the following reasons:

- Reduction in inbound transportation cost because of TL shipments from manufacturers to distributor.
- Reduction in outbound transportation cost because the distributor combines products from many manufacturers into a single outbound shipment.
- Reduction in inventory costs because distributor aggregates safety inventory rather than disaggregating at each retailer.
- A more stable order stream from distributor to manufacturer (compared to erratic orders from each retailer) allows manufacturers to lower cost by planning production more effectively.
- By carrying inventory closer to the point of sale, distributors are able to provide a better response time than manufacturers can.
- Distributors are able to offer one-stop shopping with products from several manufacturers.

4.5 DISTRIBUTION NETWORKS IN PRACTICE

The ownership structure of the distribution network can have as big an impact as the type of distribution network. The bulk of this chapter dealt with different types of physical networks and subsequent flows to successfully distribute products. However, equally important is who owns each stage in the distribution network. Distribution networks that have the exact same physical flow but different ownership structures can have vastly different behavior and performance. For example, if a manufacturer owns its distribution network, then the firm can control the network's actions and optimize over the entire network. However, if the manufacturer does not own the distribution network, as is more often the case, a wide variety of issues need to be taken into account to optimize over the network. Obviously, an independent distributor will want to optimize its own enterprise, not necessarily the entire supply chain. Because of this, manufacturers, distributors, and retailers, if independent, develop a complex relationship, with many contractual and legal ramifications, in order to make the distribution network functional. Attempting to optimize over a distribution network with multiple enterprises requires great skill in coordinating the incentives of each of the players and in creating the right relationships. Be sure to consider the impact of both the physical flows and the ownership structure when designing a distribution network.

The choice of a distribution network has very long-term consequences. Many decisions companies make can be changed relatively quickly. However, a distribution network is one of the most difficult decisions to change. The impact often lasts for decades, amplifying the importance of the choice. For example, in the United States, auto manufacturers sell virtually all of their vehicles to consumers through a network of independent dealers set up decades ago. Because dealers are the interface between the consumer and the automotive supply chain, auto manufacturers are very interested in influencing dealers to ensure that this is a positive relationship. However, given that dealers are independent, they have a somewhat different set of goals that is not necessarily consistent with the manufacturers. Further complicating this is the fact that dealers often have relationships with more than one manufacturer and have successfully encouraged legislation that makes it very difficult for manufacturers to use any other distribution channel. Although automakers have tried to implement alternative distribution channels for several years, the dealers have kept the manufacturers captive and remain the only real channel they have. Given the high costs of aggravating their own dealers and limited feasibility of creating other networks, the automakers are essentially stuck with the distribution channel they set up many years ago.

Another example is the PC industry. In the early days, manufacturers sold through independent distributors and retailers. Dell's emergence was a clear example of how the direct model was often superior to the traditional model. Other PC manufacturers, such as HP, made forays into selling PCs directly. However, their existing distribution channels reacted quite negatively to this—as you might expect given it would cannibalize their business. Because distributors often sold other company's PCs, manufacturers were hesitant to aggressively promote their direct efforts for fear of their distributors retaliating by promoting competitors' products. These PC manufacturers therefore ended up with minimal direct business. The manufacturers were essentially shackled by their legacy distribution network. The only way to go direct was a clean break—a move that was just too costly given their distributors owned the relationship with their customers. These examples illustrate the long-term implications of choosing the right distribution network.

Consider whether an exclusive distribution strategy is advantageous. We have discussed how a hybrid distribution network is often the optimal choice. There is an additional variable, however, to be determined even within a particular distribution model. That variable is whether to distribute exclusively or not. For instance, a manufacturer of consumer electronics like Sony could choose to have relationships with many distributors such as Best Buy, Circuit City, and Wal-Mart. In this case, Sony would be interested in increasing the availability of its products to customers and would certainly not mind if its distributors competed with each other to sell Sony products to customers. An alternative, more likely for a manufacturer of very high-end stereo equipment, would be to form an exclusive relationship with a distributor. In this case, customers could only buy this brand's products from a single retailer. The retailer can garner higher margins as they don't have to battle over price with a store next door in the same shopping center. But what's in it for the manufacturer? The manufacturer can often significantly increase their sales because their exclusive distributor will be much more interested in marketing that manufacturer's goods as they have a higher margin and there is less competition.

Product price, commoditization, and criticality have an impact on the type of distribution system preferred by customers. Interactions between a buyer and a seller take time and resources. Many buyers would like to establish a relationship with a single enterprise that can deliver a full line of products. This can be accomplished by a manufacturer with a broad line of products. However, more often than not, this is accomplished by a distributor that has relationships with many manufacturers. The desire for a one-stop-shop depends largely on the type of product itself. A customer's willingness to create a relationship depends not just on the convenience of the relationship, as we consider earlier in the chapter, but also on the type of product they are buying. The more expensive an item is, the more an item has characteristics that make it differentiated; the more important an item is to a customer, the more likely they are to want to have a relationship solely around that particular product.

For example, a consumer may well be content to by a PC direct from a manufacturer. However, very few consumers would be willing to order pens direct from a pen manufacturer, paper directly from a paper manufacturer, and staples directly from a staple manufacturer. Most consumers much prefer a stationary store that carries a very wide range of different manufacturers' products. Even if a pen manufacturer could economically deliver individual pens to customers' homes, the hassle for the consumer of dealing with different entities for each type of office product would be prohibitive. Again, it's crucial to think of the customer's needs when designing a distribution network.

4.6 SUMMARY OF LEARNING OBJECTIVES

1. Identify the key factors to be considered when designing the distribution network.

   A manager must consider the customer needs to be met and the cost of meeting these needs when designing the distribution network. Some key customer needs to be considered include response time, product variety/availability, convenience, order visibility, and returnability. Important costs that managers must consider include inventories, transportation, facilities and handling, and information. Increasing the number of facilities decreases the response time and transportation cost but increases inventory and facility cost.

2. Discuss the strengths and weaknesses of various distribution options.

   Distribution networks that ship directly to the customer are better suited for large variety of high-value products that have low and uncertain demand. These networks will carry low levels of inventory but incur high transportation cost and provide a slow response time. Distribution networks that carry local inventory are suitable for products with high demand, especially if transportation is a large fraction of total cost. These networks incur higher inventory cost but lower transportation cost and provide a faster response time.

3. Understand the role that distributors play in the supply chain.

Distributors add significant value to the supply chain if there are many small retailers to be replenished by the manufacturer. Distributors improve supply chain perfor- mance by decreasing transportation costs through aggregation of inbound and outbound shipments, decreasing inventory costs by aggregating safety inventories, stabilizing the stream of replenishment orders to manufac- turers, providing one-stop shopping, and de- creasing the response time relative to what manufacturers can provide.

DISCUSSION QUESTIONS

1. What differences in the retail environment may justify the fact that the fast- moving consumer goods supply chain in India has far more distributors than in the United States?
2. A specialty chemical company is considering expanding its operations into Brazil where five companies dominate the consumption of specialty chemicals. What sort of distribution network should this company utilize?
3. A distributor has heard that one of the major manufacturers it buys from is con- sidering going direct to the consumer. What can the distributor do about this? What advantages can they offer the manufacturer that the manufacturer is unlikely to be able to reproduce?
4. What types of distribution networks are typically best suited for commodity items?
5. What type of networks are best suited to highly differentiated products?
6. In the future, do you see the value added by distributors decreasing, increasing, or staying about the same?
7. What are some examples of very effective distribution networks?

BIBLIOGRAPHY

Chopra, Sunil. 2003. *Designing the Delivery Network for a Supply Chain.* Transportation Research, Part E (39) 123–140.

Raman, Ananth, and Bharat P. Rao. 1997. *A Tale of Two Electronic Component Distributors.* Harvard Business School Case 9-697-064.

CHAPTER

Network Design in the Supply Chain

Learning Objectives

After reading this chapter, you will be able to:

1. Understand the role of network design in a supply chain.

2. Identify factors influencing supply chain network design decisions.

3. Develop a framework for making network design decisions.

4. Use optimization for facility location and capacity allocation decisions.

In this chapter, we provide an understanding of the role of network design within a supply chain. We focus on the fundamental questions of facility location and capacity allocation when designing a supply chain network. We identify and discuss the role of various factors that influence the facility location and capacity allocation decision. We then establish a framework and discuss various solution methodologies for facility location and capacity allocation decisions in a supply chain.

5.1   THE ROLE OF NETWORK DESIGN IN THE SUPPLY CHAIN

Supply chain *network design decisions* include the location of manufacturing, storage, or transportation-related facilities and the allocation of capacity and roles to each facility. Supply chain network design decisions are classified as follows:

1. *Facility role:* What role should each facility play? What processes are performed at each facility?
2. *Facility location:* Where should facilities be located?
3. *Capacity allocation:* How much capacity should be allocated to each facility?
4. *Market and supply allocation*: What markets should each facility serve? Which supply sources should feed each facility?

All network design decisions affect each other and must be made taking this fact into consideration. Decisions concerning the role of each facility are significant because they determine the amount of flexibility the supply chain has in changing the way it meets demand. For example, Toyota has plants located worldwide in each market that it serves. Prior to 1997, each plant was only capable of serving its local market. This hurt Toyota when the Asian economy went into a recession in the late 1990s. The local plants in Asia had a lot of idle capacity that could not be used to serve other markets that had excess demand. Toyota has now added flexibility to each plant to be able to serve markets other than the local one. This additional flexibility helps Toyota deal more effectively with changing global market conditions.

Facility location decisions have a long-term impact on a supply chain's performance because it is very expensive to shut down a facility or move it to a different location. A good location decision can help a supply chain be responsive while keeping its costs low. Toyota, for example, built its assembly plant in the United States in Lexington, Kentucky, in 1988 and has used the plant since then. The Lexington plant proved very profitable for Toyota when the Yen strengthened and cars produced in Japan were too expensive to be cost competitive with cars produced in the United Sates. The plant allowed Toyota to be responsive to the American market while keeping costs low.

In contrast, a poorly located facility makes it very difficult for a supply chain to perform close to the efficient frontier. For example, Amazon.com found it very difficult to be cost effective in supplying books throughout the United States when it had a single warehouse in Seattle. As a result, the company has added warehouses located in other parts of the country.

Capacity allocation decisions also have a significant impact on supply chain performance. Whereas capacity allocation can be altered more easily than location, capacity decisions do tend to stay in place for several years. Allocating too much capacity to a location results in poor utilization and as a result higher costs. Allocating too little capacity results in poor responsiveness if demand is not satisfied or high cost if demand is filled from a distant facility.

The allocation of supply sources and markets to facilities has a significant impact on performance because it affects total production, inventory, and transportation costs incurred by the supply chain to satisfy customer demand. This decision should be reconsidered on a regular basis so that the allocation can be changed as market conditions or plant capacities change. As we mentioned earlier, Amazon.com has built new warehouses and changed the markets supplied by each warehouse as its customer base has grown. As a result, it has lowered costs and improved responsiveness. Of course, the allocation of markets and supply sources can only be changed if the facilities are flexible enough to serve different markets and receive supply from different sources.

Network design decisions have a significant impact on performance because they determine the supply chain configuration and set constraints within which inventory, transportation, and information can be used to either decrease supply chain cost or increase responsiveness. A company has to focus on network design decisions as its demand grows and its current configuration becomes too expensive or provides poor responsiveness. For example, Dell has decided to build a facility in Brazil to serve its South American market because the factories in Texas, Ireland, and Malaysia could not do so in the most profitable manner.

Network design decisions are also very important when two companies merge. Due to the redundancies and differences in markets served by either of the two separate firms, consolidating some facilities and changing the location and role of others can often help reduce cost and improve responsiveness.

We focus on developing a framework as well as methodologies that can be used for network design in a supply chain. In the next section, we identify various factors that influence network design decisions.

5.2 FACTORS INFLUENCING NETWORK DESIGN DECISIONS

Strategic, technological, macroeconomic, political, infrastructure, competitive, and operational factors influence network design decisions in supply chains.

Strategic Factors

A firm's competitive strategy has a significant impact on network design decisions within the supply chain. Firms focusing on cost leadership tend to find the lowest cost location for their manufacturing facilities, even if that means locating very far from the markets they serve. For example, in the early 1980s, many apparel producers moved all their manufacturing out of the United States to countries with lower labor costs in the hope of lowering their costs.

Firms focusing on responsiveness tend to locate facilities closer to the market and may select a high-cost location if this choice allows the firm to quickly react to changing market needs. Apparel manufacturers in Italy have developed very flexible production facilities that allow them to provide a high level of variety quickly. Companies that value this responsiveness use the Italian manufacturers in spite of their higher cost.

Convenience store chains aim to provide easy access to customers as part of their competitive strategy. Convenience store networks thus contain many stores that cover an area, even though each store is not very large. In contrast, discount stores like Sam's Club have a competitive strategy that focuses on providing low prices. Thus, their networks have very large stores and customers often have to travel several miles to get to one. An area covered by one Sam's Club store may contain many convenience stores.

Global supply chain networks can best support their strategic objectives with facilities in different countries playing different roles. For example, Nike has production facilities located in many countries in Asia. The facilities in China and Indonesia focus on cost and produce the mass-market lower priced shoes for Nike. In contrast, facilities in Korea and Taiwan focus on responsiveness and produce the higher priced new designs. This differentiation allows Nike to satisfy a wide variety of demands in the most profitable manner.

It is important for a firm to identify the mission or strategic role of each facility when designing its global network. Kasra Ferdows (1997) suggests the following classification of possible strategic roles for various facilities in a global supply chain network.[1]

1. *Offshore Facility: Low-cost facility for export production.* An offshore facility serves the role of being a low-cost supply source for markets located outside the country where the facility is located. The location selected for an offshore facility should have low labor and other costs to facilitate low-cost production. Given that many Asian developing countries waive import tariffs if all the output from a factory is exported, they are preferred sites for offshore manufacturing facilities.

2. *Source Facility: Low-cost facility for global production.* A source facility also has low cost as its primary objective, but its strategic role is broader than that of an offshore facility. A source facility is often a primary source of product for the entire global network. Source facilities tend to be located in places where production costs are relatively low, infrastructure is well developed, and a skilled workforce is available. Good offshore facilities migrate over time into source facilities. A good example is Nike's plant network in Korea and Taiwan. Plants in both countries started out as offshore facilities because of low labor costs. Over time, however, these plants have become more involved with new product development and manufacture some products for sale all over the world.

3. *Server Facility: Regional production facility.* A server facility's objective is to supply the market where it is located. A server facility is built because of tax incentives, local content requirement, tariff barriers, or high logistics cost to supply the region from elsewhere. In the late 1970s, Suzuki partnered with the Indian government to set up Maruti Udyog. Initially, Maruti was set up as a server facility and only produced cars for the Indian market. The Maruti facility allowed Suzuki to overcome the high tariffs for imported cars in India.

4. *Contributor Facility: Regional production facility with development skills.* A contributor facility serves the market where it is located but also assumes responsibility for product customization, process improvements, product modifications, or product development. Most well-managed server facilities become contributor facilities over time. The Maruti facility in India today develops many new products for both the Indian and the overseas markets and has moved from being a server to a contributor facility in the Suzuki network.

---

[1]Kasra Ferdows. 1997. "Making the Most of Your Foreign Factories," *Harvard Business Review* (March–April).

5. *Outpost Facility: Regional production facility built to gain local skills.* An outpost facility is located primarily to obtain access to knowledge or skills that may exist within a certain region. Given its location, it also plays the role of a server facility. The primary objective remains one of being a source of knowledge and skills for the entire network. Many global firms have production facilities located in Japan in spite of the high operating costs. Most of these serve as outpost facilities.

6. *Lead Facility: Facility that leads in development and process technologies.* A lead facility creates new products, processes, and technologies for the entire network. Lead facilities are located in areas with good access to a skilled workforce and technological resources.

Technological Factors

Characteristics of available production technologies have a significant impact on network design decisions. If production technology displays significant economies of scale, few high-capacity locations are the most effective. This is the case in the manufacture of computer chips where factories require a very large investment. As a result, most companies build few chip production facilities, and each one they build has a very large capacity.

In contrast, if facilities have lower fixed costs, many local facilities are preferred because this helps lower transportation costs. For example, bottling plants for Coca-Cola do not have a very high fixed cost. To reduce transportation costs, Coca-Cola sets up many bottling plants all over the world, each serving its local market.

Flexibility of the production technology impacts the degree of consolidation that can be achieved in the network. If the production technology is very inflexible and product requirements vary from one country to another, a firm has to set up local facilities to serve the market in each country. Conversely, if the technology is flexible, it becomes easier to consolidate manufacturing in a few large facilities.

Macroeconomic Factors

Macroeconomic factors include taxes, tariffs, exchange rates, and other economic factors that are not internal to an individual firm. As trade has increased and markets have become more global, macroeconomic factors have had a significant influence on the success or failure of supply chain networks. Thus, it is imperative that firms take these factors into account when making network design decisions.

Tariffs and Tax Incentives

Tariffs refer to any duties that must be paid when products and/or equipment are moved across international, state, or city boundaries. Tariffs have a strong influence on location decisions within a supply chain. If a country has very high tariffs, companies either do not serve the local market or set up manufacturing plants within the country to save on duties. High tariffs lead to more production locations within a supply chain network, with each location having a lower allocated capacity. As tariffs have come down with the World Trade Organization, and regional agreements like NAFTA (North America) and MERCOSUR (South America), firms can now supply the market within a country from a plant located outside that country without incurring high duties. As a result, firms have begun to consolidate their global production and distribution facilities. For global firms, a decrease in tariffs has led to a decrease in the number of manufacturing facilities and an increase in the capacity of each facility built.

Tax incentives are a reduction in tariffs or taxes that countries, states, and cities often provide to encourage firms to locate their facilities in specific areas. Many countries vary incentives from city to city to encourage investments in areas with lower economic development. Such incentives are often a key factor in the final location decision for many plants. General Motors built its Saturn facility in Tennessee primarily because of the tax incentives offered by the state. Similarly, BMW built its factory, which assembles the Z3, in Spartanburg, mainly because of the tax incentives offered by South Carolina.

Developing countries often create *free trade zones* where duties and tariffs are relaxed as long as production is used primarily for export. This creates a strong incentive for global firms to set up a plant in these countries to be able to exploit their low labor costs. In China, for example, the establishment of a free trade zone near GuangZhou has led to several global firms locating facilities there.

Many developing countries also provide additional tax incentives based on training, meals, transportation, and other facilities offered to the workforce. Tariffs may also vary based on the product's level of technology. China, for example, waives tariffs entirely for "high-tech" products in an effort to encourage companies to locate there and bring in state-of-the-art technology. Motorola located a large chip manufacturing plant in China to take advantage of the reduced tariffs and other incentives available to high-tech products.

Many countries also place minimum requirements on local content and limits on imports. Such policies lead companies to set up many facilities and source from local suppliers. For example, the United States has limits on the import of apparel from different countries. As a result, companies develop suppliers in many countries to avoid reaching the limit from any one country. Policies that restrict imports from countries lead to an increase in the number of production sites within the supply chain network.

Exchange Rate and Demand Risk

Fluctuation in exchange rates has a significant impact on the profits of any supply chain serving global markets. A firm that sells its product in the United States with production in Japan is exposed to the risk of appreciation of the Yen. The cost of production is incurred in Yen whereas revenues are obtained in dollars. Thus, an increase in the value of the Yen increases the production cost in dollars, decreasing the firm's profits. In the 1980s, many Japanese manufacturers faced this problem when the Yen appreciated in value. At that time most of their production capacity was located in Japan and they served large markets overseas. The appreciation of the Yen decreased their revenues and they saw their profits decline. Most Japanese manufacturers have responded by building production facilities all over the world.

Exchange rate risks may be handled using financial instruments that limit, or hedge against, the loss due to fluctuations. Suitably designed supply chain networks, however, offer the opportunity to take advantage of exchange rate fluctuations and increase profits. An effective way to do this is to build some over-capacity in the network and make the capacity flexible so that it can be used to supply different markets. This flexibility allows the firm to alter production flows within the supply chain to produce more in facilities that have a lower cost based on current exchange rates.

Companies must also take into account fluctuations in demand caused by fluctuations in the economies of different countries. For example, the Asian economies slowed down between 1996 and 1998. Firms that had plants with little flexibility saw a lot of unutilized capacity in their Asian plants. Firms with greater flexibility in their manufacturing facilities were able to use the extra capacity in their Asian plants to meet the needs of other countries where demand was high. As mentioned earlier in the chapter, in 1997 Toyota had assembly plants in Asia that were only capable of producing for the local market. The Asian crisis motivated Toyota to make the plants more flexible to be able to supply demand from other countries.

When designing supply chain networks, companies must build appropriate flexibility to help counter fluctuations in exchange rates and demand across different countries.

Political Factors

The political stability of the country under consideration plays a significant role in the location choice. Companies prefer to locate facilities in politically stable countries where the rules of commerce are well defined. Countries with independent and clear legal systems allow firms to feel that they have recourse in the courts should they need it. This makes it easier for companies to invest in facilities in these countries. Political stability is hard to quantify, so a firm makes an essentially subjective evaluation when designing its supply chain network.

Infrastructure Factors

The availability of good infrastructure is an important prerequisite to locating a facility in a given area. Poor infrastructure adds to the cost of doing business from a given location. Global companies have located their factories in China near Shanghai, Tianjin, or GuangZhou, even though these locations do not have the lowest labor or land cost because of better infrastructure at these locations. Key infrastructure elements to be considered during network design include availability of sites, labor availability, proximity to transportation terminals, rail service, proximity to airports and seaports, highway access, congestion, and local utilities.

Competitive Factors

Companies must consider competitors' strategy, size, and location when designing their supply chain networks. A fundamental decision firms make is whether to locate their facilities close to competitors or far from them. How the firms compete and whether external factors such as raw material or labor availability force them to locate close to each other influence this decision.

Positive Externalities between Firms

Positive externalities are instances where the collocation of multiple firms benefits all of them. Positive externalities lead to competitors locating close to each other. For example, gas stations and retail stores tend to locate close to each other because doing so increases the overall demand, thus benefiting all parties. By locating together in a mall, competing retail stores make it more convenient for customers who need only drive to one location and find everything they are looking for. This increases the total number of customers who visit the mall, increasing demand for all stores located there.

Another example of positive externality is when the presence of a competitor leads to the development of appropriate infrastructure in a developing area. In India, for example, Suzuki was the first foreign auto manufacturer to set up a manufacturing facility. The company went to considerable effort and built a local supplier network. Given the well-established supplier base in India, Suzuki's competitors have also built assembly plants there, because they now find it more effective to build cars in India rather than import them to the country.

Locating to Split the Market

When there are no positive externalities, firms locate to be able to capture the largest possible share of the market. A simple model first proposed by Hotelling explains the issues behind this decision.[2]

When firms do not control price but compete on distance from the customer, they can maximize market share by locating close to each other and splitting the market. Consider a situation where customers are uniformly located along the line segment between 0 and 1 and two firms compete based on their distance from the customer as shown in Figure 5.1. A customer goes to the closest firm and customers that are equidistant from the two firms are evenly split between them.

If total demand is 1 and Firm 1 locates at point a and Firm 2 locates at point $1 - b$, the demand at the two firms, d_1 and d_2, is given by

$$d_1 = a + \frac{1 - b - a}{2} \quad \text{and} \quad d_2 = \frac{1 + b - a}{2} .$$

Clearly, both firms maximize their market share if they move closer to each other and locate at $a = b = 1/2$.

Observe that when both firms locate in the middle of the line segment, the average distance that customers have to travel is 1/4. If one firm locates at 1/4 and the other at 3/4, the average distance customers have to travel drops to 1/8. This set of locations, however, gives both firms an incentive to try and increase market share by moving to the middle. The result of competition is for both firms to locate close together even though doing so increases the average distance to the customer.

In case the firms compete on price and incur the transportation cost to the customer, it may be optimal for the two firms to locate as far apart as possible,[3] with Firm 1 locating at 0 and Firm 2 locating at 1. Locating far from each other minimizes price competition and helps the firms split the market and maximize profits.

Customer Response Time and Local Presence

Firms that target customers who value a short response time must locate close to them. For example, customers are unlikely to come to a convenience store if they have to travel a long distance to get there. It is thus best for a convenience store chain to have

---

[2]Jean Tirole. 1997. *The Theory of Industrial Organization.* Cambridge, Mass.: The MIT Press.
[3]Ibid.

FIGURE 5.1 Two Firms Locating on a Line

many stores distributed in an area so that most people have a convenience store close to them. In contrast, customers shop for larger amounts at supermarkets and are willing to travel longer distances to get to one. Thus, supermarket chains tend to have stores that are much larger than convenience stores and not as densely distributed. Most towns have fewer supermarkets than convenience stores. Discounters like Sam's Club target customers who are even less time sensitive. These stores are even larger than supermarkets and there are fewer of them in an area. W. W. Grainger uses about 350 facilities all over the United States to provide same day delivery of maintenance and repair supplies to many of its customers. McMaster Carr, a competitor, targets customers who are willing to wait for next day delivery. McMaster has only six facilities throughout the United States and is able to provide next day delivery to a large number of customers.

If a firm is delivering its product to customers, use of a rapid means of transportation allows it to build fewer facilities and still provide a short response time. This option, however, increases transportation cost. Moreover, there are many situations where the presence of a facility close to a customer is important. For example, a coffee shop is likely to attract customers who live or work nearby. No faster mode of transport can serve as a substitute and be used to attract customers that are far away.

Logistics and Facility Costs

Logistics and facility costs incurred within a supply chain change as the number of facilities, their location, and capacity allocation is changed. Companies must consider inventory, transportation, and facility costs when designing their supply chain networks.

Inventory and facility costs increase as the number of facilities in a supply chain increase. Transportation costs decrease as the number of facilities is increased. Increasing the number of facilities to a point where inbound economies of scale are lost increases transportation cost. For example, with few facilities Amazon.com has lower inventory and facility costs than Borders, which has about 400 stores. Borders, however, has lower transportation costs.

The supply chain network design is also influenced by the transformation occurring at each facility. When there is a significant reduction in material weight or volume as a result of processing, it may be better to locate facilities closer to the supply source rather than the customer. For example, when iron ore is processed to make steel, the amount of output is a small fraction of the amount of ore used. Locating the steel factory close to the supply source is preferred because it reduces the distance that the large quantity of ore has to travel.

Total logistics costs are a sum of the inventory, transportation, and facility costs. The facilities in a supply chain network must at least equal the number that minimizes total logistics cost. A firm may increase the number of facilities beyond this point to improve the response time to its customers. This decision is justified if the revenue increase from improved response outweighs the increased cost from additional facilities.

In the next section we discuss a framework for making network design decisions.

5.3   A FRAMEWORK FOR NETWORK DESIGN DECISIONS

When faced with a network design decision, the goal of a manager is to design a network that maximizes the firm's profits while satisfying customer needs in terms of demand and responsiveness. To design an effective network a manager must consider all the factors described in Section 5.2. Global network design decisions are made in four phases as shown in Figure 5.2. We describe each phase in greater detail.

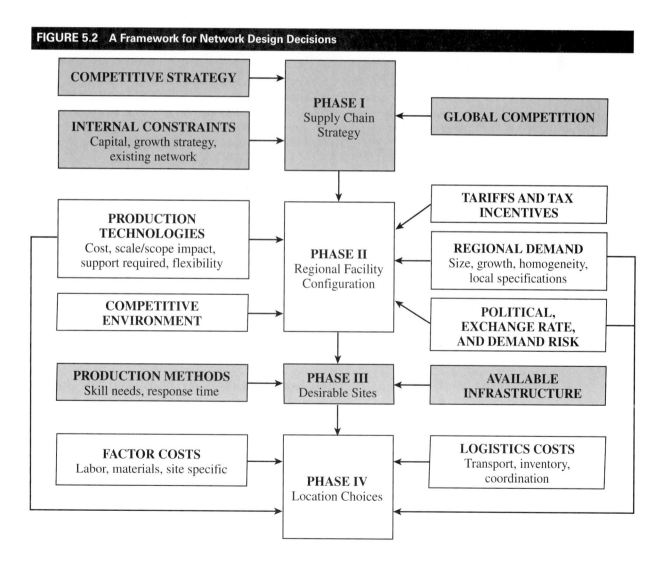

FIGURE 5.2   A Framework for Network Design Decisions

Phase I: Define a Supply Chain Strategy

The objective of the first phase of network design is to define a firm's supply chain strategy. The supply chain strategy specifies what capabilities the supply chain network must have to support a firm's competitive strategy (see Chapter 2).

Phase I starts with a clear definition of the firm's competitive strategy as the set of customer needs that the supply chain aims to satisfy. Next, managers must forecast the likely evolution of global competition and whether competitors in each market will be local or global players. Managers must also identify constraints on available capital and whether growth will be accomplished by acquiring existing facilities, building new facilities, or partnering.

Based on the competitive strategy of the firm, an analysis of the competition, any economies of scale or scope, and any constraints, managers must determine the supply chain strategy for the firm.

Phase II: Define the Regional Facility Configuration

The objective of the second phase of network design is to identify regions where facilities will be located, their potential roles, and their approximate capacity.

An analysis of Phase II is started with a forecast of the demand by country. Such a forecast must include a measure of the size of the demand as well as a determination of whether the customer requirements are homogenous or variable across different countries. Homogenous requirements favor large consolidated facilities whereas requirements that vary across countries favor smaller, localized facilities.

The next step is for managers to identify whether economies of scale or scope can play a significant role in reducing costs given available production technologies. If economies of scale or scope are significant, it may be better to have a few facilities serving many markets. If economies of scale or scope are not significant, it may be better for each market to have its own facility. For example, Coca Cola has bottling plants in every market that it serves because the manufacturing technology does not include large economies of scale. Semiconductor manufacturers like Motorola, in contrast, have very few plants for their global markets given the economies of scale in production.

Next, managers must identify demand risk, exchange rate risk, and political risk associated with different regional markets. They must also identify regional tariffs, any requirements for local production, tax incentives, and any export or import restrictions for each market. The tax and tariff information is used to identify the best location to extract a major share of the profits. In general, it is best to obtain the major share of profits at the location with the lowest tax rate.

Managers must identify competitors in each region and make a case for whether a facility needs to be located close to or far from a competitor's facility. The desired response time for each market must also be identified. Managers must also identify the factor and logistics costs at an aggregate level in each region.

Based on all this information, managers will identify the regional facility configuration for the supply chain network using network design models discussed in the next section. The regional configuration defines the approximate number of facilities in the network, regions where facilities will be set up, and whether a facility will produce all products for a given market or a few products for all markets in the network.

Phase III: Select Desirable Sites

The objective of Phase III is to select a set of desirable sites within each region where facilities are to be located. The set of desirable sites should be larger than the desired number of facilities to be set up so that a precise selection may be made in Phase IV.

Sites should be selected based on an analysis of infrastructure availability to support the desired production methodologies. *Hard infrastructure requirements* include the availability of suppliers, transportation services, communication, utilities, and warehousing infrastructure. *Soft infrastructure requirements* include the availability of skilled workforce, workforce turnover, and the community receptivity to business and industry.

Phase IV: Location Choices

The objective of this phase is to select a precise location and capacity allocation for each facility. Attention is restricted to the desirable sites selected in Phase III. The network is designed to maximize total profits taking into account the expected margin and demand in each market, various logistics and facility costs, and the taxes and tariffs at each location.

In the next section we discuss methodologies for making facility location and capacity allocation decisions during Phase II and Phase IV.

5.4 MODELS FOR FACILITY LOCATION AND CAPACITY ALLOCATION

A manager's goal when locating facilities and allocating capacity should be to maximize the overall profitability of the resulting supply chain network while providing customers with the appropriate responsiveness. Revenues come from the sale of product and costs arise from facilities, labor, transportation, material, and inventories. The profits of the firm are also impacted by taxes and tariffs. Ideally, profits after tariffs and taxes should be maximized when designing a supply chain network.

A manager must consider many tradeoffs during network design. For example, building many facilities to serve local markets reduces transportation cost and provides a fast response time, but it increases the facility and inventory costs incurred by the firm.

Managers use network design models in two different situations. First, these models are used to decide on locations where facilities will be established and the capacity to be assigned to each facility. Managers must make this decision considering a time horizon over which locations and capacities will not be altered (typically in years). Second, these models are used to assign current demand to the available facilities and identify lanes along which product will be transported. Managers must consider this decision at least on an annual basis as demand, prices, and tariffs change. In both cases, the goal is to maximize the profit while satisfying customer needs. The following information must be available before the design decision can be made:

- Location of supply sources and markets
- Location of potential facility sites
- Demand forecast by market
- Facility, labor, and material costs by site

- Transportation costs between each pair of sites
- Inventory costs by site as well as a function of quantity
- Sale price of product in different regions
- Taxes and tariffs as product is moved between locations
- Desired response time and other service factors

Given this information, either gravity or network optimization models may be used to design the network. We organize the models according to the phase of the network design framework where each model is likely to be useful.

Phase II: Network Optimization Models

During Phase II of the network design framework (see Figure 5.2), a manager must consider regional demand, tariffs, economies of scale, and aggregate factor costs to decide the regions in which facilities are to be located. As an example, consider SunOil, a manufacturer of petrochemical products with worldwide sales. The Vice President of Supply Chain can consider several different alternatives to meet demand. One alternative would be to set up a facility in each region. The advantage of such an approach will be that it lowers transportation cost and also helps avoids duties that may be imposed if product is imported from other regions. The disadvantage of this approach is that plants will be sized only to meet local demand and may not fully exploit economies of scale. Another alternative would be to consolidate plants in few regions. This would improve economies of scale but would increase transportation cost and the duties to be paid. During Phase II, the manager must consider these quantifiable tradeoffs along with nonquantifiable factors such as the competitive environment and political risk.

Network optimization models are useful for managers considering regional configuration during Phase II. The first step is to collect the data in a form that can be used for a quantitative model. For SunOil, the Vice President of Supply Chain decides to view the worldwide demand in terms of five regions—North America, South America, Europe, Africa, and Asia. The data collected is shown in Figure 5.3.

Annual demand for each of the five regions is shown in Cells B9:F9. Cells B4:F8 contain the variable production, inventory, and transportation cost (including tariffs and duties) of producing in one region to meet demand in each individual region. For example, as shown in Cell C4, it costs $92,000 (including duties) to produce 1 million

FIGURE 5.3 Cost and Demand Data for SunOil

	A	B	C	D	E	F	G	H	I	J
1	*Inputs - Costs, Capacities, Demands*									
2		*Demand Region*					**Fixed**	**Low**	**Fixed**	**High**
		Production and Transportation Cost per 1,000,000 Units					**Cost ($)**	**Capacity**	**Cost ($)**	**Capacity**
3	*Supply Region*	N. America	S. America	Europe	Asia	Africa				
4	N. America	81	92	101	130	115	6,000	10	9,000	20
5	S. America	117	77	108	98	100	4,500	10	6,750	20
6	Europe	102	105	95	119	111	6,500	10	9,750	20
7	Asia	115	125	90	59	74	4,100	10	6,150	20
8	Africa	142	100	103	105	71	4,000	10	6,000	20
9	*Demand*	12	8	14	16	7				

units in North America and sell them in South America. Observe that the data collected at this stage is at a fairly aggregate level.

There are fixed as well as variable costs associated with facilities, transportation, and inventories at each facility. Fixed costs are those that are incurred no matter how much is produced or shipped from a facility. Variable costs are those that are incurred in proportion to the quantity produced or shipped from a given facility. Variable facility, transportation, and inventory costs generally display economies of scale and the marginal cost decreases as the quantity produced at a facility increases. In the models we consider, however, all variable costs grow linearly with the quantity produced or shipped.

SunOil is considering two different plant sizes in each location. Low-capacity plants can produce 10 million units a year whereas high-capacity plants can produce 20 million units a year as shown in Cells H4:H8 and J4:J8, respectively. High-capacity plants exhibit some economies of scale and have fixed costs that are less than twice the fixed cost of a low-capacity plant as shown in Cells I4:I8. All fixed costs are annualized. The vice president would like to know what the lowest cost network should look like. Next, we discuss the capacitated plant location model, which can be used in this setting.

The Capacitated Plant Location Model

The capacitated plant location network optimization model requires the following inputs:

n = Number of potential plant locations/capacity (each capacity will count as a separate location)
m = Number of markets or demand points
D_j = Annual demand from market j
K_i = Potential capacity of plant i
f_i = Annualized fixed cost of keeping factory i open
c_{ij} = Cost of producing and shipping one unit from factory i to market j (cost includes production, inventory, transportation, and duties)

The supply chain team's goal is to decide on a network design that maximizes profits after taxes. In this model, however, we assume that all demand must be met and taxes on earnings are ignored. The model thus focuses on minimizing the cost of meeting global demand. It can, however, be easily modified to include profits and taxes. Define the following decision variables:

y_i = 1 if plant i is open, 0 otherwise
x_{ij} = Quantity shipped from factory i to market j

The problem is then formulated as the following integer program:

$$Min \sum_{i=1}^{n} f_i y_i + \sum_{i=1}^{n} \sum_{j=1}^{m} c_{ij} x_{ij}$$

Subject to

$$\sum_{i=1}^{n} x_{ij} = D_j \text{ for } j = 1, ..., m \tag{5.1}$$

$$\sum_{j=1}^{m} x_{ij} \leq K_i y_i \text{ for } i = 1,...,n \tag{5.2}$$

$$y_i \in \{0,1\} \quad \text{for } i = 1,...,n \tag{5.3}$$

The objective function minimizes the total cost (fixed + variable) of setting up and operating the network. The constraint in Equation 5.1 requires that the demand at each regional market be satisfied. The constraint in Equation 5.2 states that no plant can supply more than its capacity. (Clearly the capacity is 0 if the plant is closed and K_i if it is open. The product of terms, $K_i y_i$, captures this effect.) The constraint in Equation 5.3 enforces that each plant is either open ($y_i = 1$) or closed ($y_i = 0$). The solution will identify the plants that are to be kept open, their capacity, and the allocation of regional demand to these plants.

The model is solved using the Solver tool in Excel. Given the data, the next step in Excel is to identify cells corresponding to each decision variable as shown in Figure 5.4.

Cells B14:F18 correspond to the decision variables x_{ij} and determine the amount produced in a supply region and shipped to a demand region. Cells G14:G18 contain the decision variables y_i corresponding to the low-capacity plants and Cells H14:H18 contain the decision variables y_i corresponding to the high-capacity plants. Initially, all decision variables are set to be 0.

FIGURE 5.4 Spreadsheet Area for Decision Variables for SunOil

	A	B	C	D	E	F	G	H	I	J
1	*Inputs - Costs, Capacities, Demands*									
2		*Demand Region*					Fixed	Low	Fixed	High
		Production and Transportation Cost per 1,000,000 Units								
3	*Supply Region*	N. America	S. America	Europe	Asia	Africa	Cost ($)	Capacity	Cost ($)	Capacity
4	N. America	81	92	101	130	115	6,000	10	9,000	20
5	S. America	117	77	108	98	100	4,500	10	6,750	20
6	Europe	102	105	95	119	111	6,500	10	9,750	20
7	Asia	115	125	90	59	74	4,100	10	6,150	20
8	Africa	142	100	103	105	71	4,000	10	6,000	20
9	*Demand*	12	8	14	16	7				
10										
11	*Decision Variables*									
12		*Demand Region - Production Allocation (1000 Units)*					Plants	Plants		
13	*Supply Region*	N. America	S. America	Europe	Asia	Africa	(1=open)	(1=open)		
14	N. America	0	0	0	0	0	0	0		
15	S. America	0	0	0	0	0	0	0		
16	Europe	0	0	0	0	0	0	0		
17	Asia	0	0	0	0	0	0	0		
18	Africa	0	0	0	0	0	0	0		

	A	B	C	D	E	F	G	H	I	J
1	*Inputs - Costs, Capacities, Demands*									
2			*Demand Region*				Fixed	Low	Fixed	High
			Production and Transportation Cost per 1,000,000 Units				Cost ($)	Capacity	Cost ($)	Capacity
3	*Supply Region*	N. America	S. America	Europe	Asia	Africa				
4	N. America	81	92	101	130	115	6,000	10	9,000	20
5	S. America	117	77	108	98	100	4,500	10	6,750	20
6	Europe	102	105	95	119	111	6,500	10	9,750	20
7	Asia	115	125	90	59	74	4,100	10	6,150	20
8	Africa	142	100	103	105	71	4,000	10	6,000	20
9	*Demand*	12	8	14	16	7				
10										
11	*Decision Variables*									
12		*Demand Region - Production Allocation (1000 Units)*					Plants	Plants		
13	*Supply Region*	N. America	S. America	Europe	Asia	Africa	(1=open)	(1=open)		
14	N. America	0	0	0	0	0	0	0		
15	S. America	0	0	0	0	0	0	0		
16	Europe	0	0	0	0	0	0	0		
17	Asia	0	0	0	0	0	0	0		
18	Africa	0	0	0	0	0	0	0		
19										
20	*Constraints*									
21	*Supply Region*	*Excess Capacity*								
22	N. America	0								
23	S. America	0								
24	Europe	0								
25	Asia	0								
26	Africa	0								
27		N. America	S. America	Europe	Asia	Africa				
28	*Unmet Demand*	12	8	14	16	7				
29										
30	*Objective Function*									
31	*Cost =*	$ -								

Cell	Cell Formula	Equation	Copied to
B28	=B9 - SUM(B14:B18)	5.1	B28:F28
B22	=G14*H4 + H14*J4 - SUM(B14:F14)	5.2	B22:B26
B31	=SUMPRODUCT(B14:F18,B4:F8) + SUMPRODUCT(G14:G18,G4:G8) + SUMPRODUCT(H14:H18,I4:I8)	Objective Function	—

FIGURE 5.5   Spreadsheet Area for Constraints and Objective Function for SunOil

The next step is to construct cells for the constraints in Equations 5.1 and 5.2 and the objective function. The constraint cells and objective function are shown in Figure 5.5.

Cells B22:B26 contain the capacity constraints in Equation 5.2 and Cells B28:F28 contain the demand constraints in Equation 5.1. The objective function is shown in Cell B31 and measures the total fixed cost plus the variable cost of operating the network.

The next step is to use Tools | Solver to invoke Solver as shown in Figure 5.6.

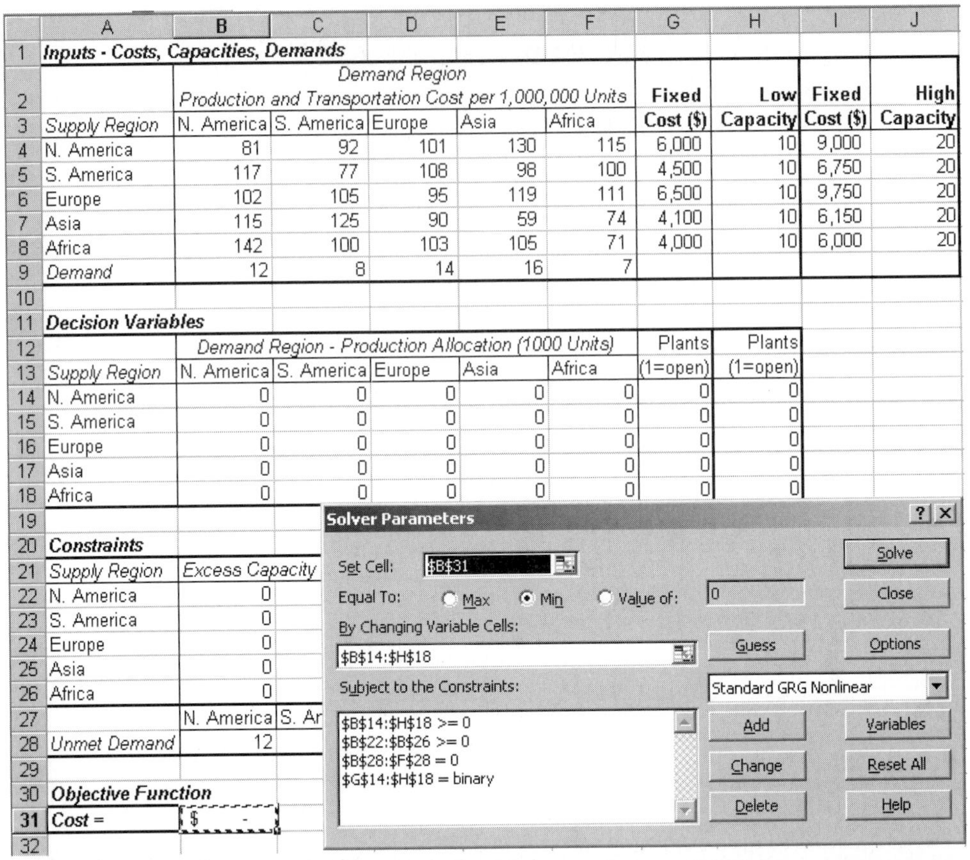

	Demand Region Production and Transportation Cost per 1,000,000 Units					Fixed	Low	Fixed	High
Supply Region	N. America	S. America	Europe	Asia	Africa	Cost ($)	Capacity	Cost ($)	Capacity
N. America	81	92	101	130	115	6,000	10	9,000	20
S. America	117	77	108	98	100	4,500	10	6,750	20
Europe	102	105	95	119	111	6,500	10	9,750	20
Asia	115	125	90	59	74	4,100	10	6,150	20
Africa	142	100	103	105	71	4,000	10	6,000	20
Demand	12	8	14	16	7				

Inputs - Costs, Capacities, Demands

Decision Variables

Demand Region - Production Allocation (1000 Units)						Plants (1=open)	Plants (1=open)
Supply Region	N. America	S. America	Europe	Asia	Africa		
N. America	0	0	0	0	0	0	0
S. America	0	0	0	0	0	0	0
Europe	0	0	0	0	0	0	0
Asia	0	0	0	0	0	0	0
Africa	0	0	0	0	0	0	0

Constraints

Supply Region	Excess Capacity
N. America	0
S. America	0
Europe	0
Asia	0
Africa	0
Unmet Demand	12

Objective Function
Cost = $ -

FIGURE 5.6 Using Solver to Set Regional Configuration for SunOil

Within Solver the goal is to minimize the total cost in Cell B31. The variables are in Cells B14:H18. The constraints are as follows:

B14:H18 ≥ 0 — {All decision variables are nonnegative}

B22:B26 ≥ 0 — $\left\{ K_i y_i - \sum_{j=1}^{m} x_{ij} \geq 0 \text{ for } i = 1,...5 \right\}$

B28:F28 $= 0$ — $\left\{ D_j - \sum_{i=1}^{n} x_{ij} = 0 \text{ for } j = 1,...,5 \right\}$

G14:H18 *binary* — {Location variables y_i are binary; that is, 0 or 1}

	A	B	C	D	E	F	G	H	I	J
1	*Inputs - Costs, Capacities, Demands*									
2			Demand Region				Fixed	Low	Fixed	High
3	*Supply Region*		Production and Transportation Cost per 1,000,000 Units							
3	*Supply Region*	N. America	S. America	Europe	Asia	Africa	Cost ($)	Capacity	Cost ($)	Capacity
4	N. America	81	92	101	130	115	6,000	10	9,000	20
5	S. America	117	77	108	98	100	4,500	10	6,750	20
6	Europe	102	105	95	119	111	6,500	10	9,750	20
7	Asia	115	125	90	59	74	4,100	10	6,150	20
8	Africa	142	100	103	105	71	4,000	10	6,000	20
9	*Demand*	12	8	14	16	7				
10										
11	*Decision Variables*									
12		Demand Region - Production Allocation (1000 Units)					Plants	Plants		
13	*Supply Region*	N. America	S. America	Europe	Asia	Africa	(1=open)	(1=open)		
14	N. America	0	0	0	0	0	0	0		
15	S. America	12	8	0	0	0	0	1		
16	Europe	0	0	0	0	0	0	0		
17	Asia	0	0	4	16	0	0	1		
18	Africa	0	0	10	0	7	0	1		
19										
20	*Constraints*									
21	*Supply Region*	Excess Capacity								
22	N. America	0								
23	S. America	0								
24	Europe	0								
25	Asia	0								
26	Africa	3								
27		N. America	S. America	Europe	Asia	Africa				
28	*Unmet Demand*	0	0	0	0	0				
29										
30	*Objective Function*									
31	Cost =	$ 23,751								

FIGURE 5.7   Optimal Regional Network Configuration for SunOil

Within the *Solver parameters* dialog box, click on *Solve* to obtain the optimal solution as shown in Figure 5.7.

From Figure 5.7, the supply chain team concludes that the lowest cost network will have facilities located in South America, Asia, and Africa. Further, a high-capacity plant should be planned in each region. The plant in South America meets the North American demand whereas the European demand is met from plants in Asia and Africa.

The model discussed earlier can be modified to account for strategic imperatives that require locating a plant in some region. For example, if SunOil decides to locate a plant in Europe for strategic reasons, we can modify the model by adding a constraint that requires one plant to be located in Europe.

Next we consider a model that can be useful during Phase III.

Phase III: Gravity Location Models

During Phase III (see Figure 5.2), a manager must identify potential locations in each region where the company has decided to locate a plant. As a preliminary step, the manager needs to identify the geographical location where potential sites may be considered. Gravity location models can be useful when identifying suitable geographical locations within a region. Gravity models are used to find locations that minimize the cost of transporting raw materials from suppliers and finished goods to the markets served. Next, we discuss a typical scenario where gravity models can be used.

Consider, for example, Steel Appliances (SA), a manufacturer of high-quality refrigerators and cooking ranges. SA has one assembly factory located near Denver from which it has supplied the entire United States. Demand has grown rapidly and the CEO of SA has decided to set up another factory to serve its eastern markets. The supply chain manager is asked to find a suitable location for the new factory. Three parts plants located in Buffalo, Memphis, and St. Louis will supply parts to the new factory, which will serve markets in Atlanta, Boston, Jacksonville, Philadelphia, and New York. The coordinate location, the demand in each market, the required supply from each parts plant, and the shipping cost for each supply source or market are shown in Table 5.1.

Gravity models assume that both the markets and the supply sources can be located as grid points on a plane. All distances are calculated as the geometric distance between two points on the plane. These models also assume that the transportation cost grows linearly with the quantity shipped. We discuss a gravity model for locating a single facility that receives raw material from supply sources and ships finished product to markets. The basic inputs to the model are as follows:

x_n, y_n: Coordinate location of either a market or supply source n

F_n: Cost of shipping one unit for one mile between the facility and either market or supply source n

D_n: Quantity to be shipped between facility and market or supply source n

If (x, y) is the location selected for the facility, the distance d_n between the facility at location (x, y) and the supply source or market n is given by

$$d_n = \sqrt{\left(x - x_n\right)^2 + \left(y - y_n\right)^2}$$

(5.4)

TABLE 5.1 Locations of Supply Sources and Markets for Steel Appliances

Sources/Markets	Transportation Cost $/Ton Mile ($F_n$)	Quantity in Tons (D_n)	Coordinates x_n	y_n
Supply Sources				
Buffalo	0.90	500	700	1200
Memphis	0.95	300	250	600
St. Louis	0.85	700	225	825
Markets				
Atlanta	1.50	225	600	500
Boston	1.50	150	1050	1200
Jacksonville	1.50	250	800	300
Philadelphia	1.50	175	925	975
New York	1.50	300	1000	1080

The total transportation cost (TC) is given by

$$TC = \sum_{n=1}^{k} d_n D_n F_n \qquad (5.5)$$

The optimal location is one that minimizes the total TC in Equation 5.5. The optimal solution for SA is obtained using the Solver tool in Excel as shown in Figure 5.8. The first step is to enter the problem data as shown in Cells B5:G12. Next, we set the decision variables (x, y) corresponding to the location of the new facility in Cells B16 and B17, respectively. In Cells G5:G12, we then calculate the distance d_n from the

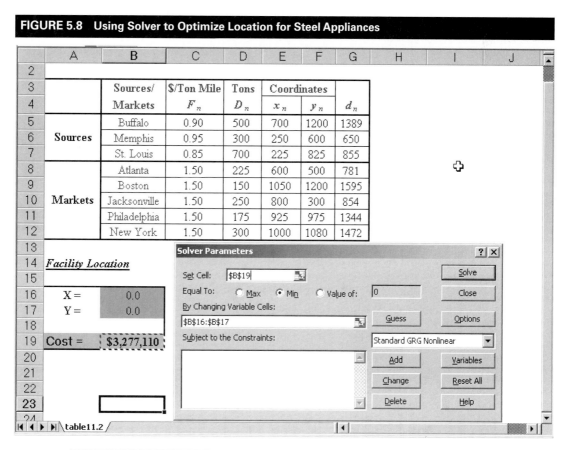

FIGURE 5.8 Using Solver to Optimize Location for Steel Appliances

Cell	Cell Formula	Equation	Copied to
G5	=SQRT(($B$16-E5)^2+($B$17-F5)^2)	5.1	G5:G12
B19	=SUMPRODUCT(G5:G12,D5:D12,C5:C12)	5.2	—

facility location (x, y) to each source or market using Equation 5.4. The total TC is then calculated in Cell B19 using Equation 5.5.

The next step is to use the Tools/Solver to invoke Solver. Within the Solver parameters dialog box (see Figure 5.8), the following information is entered to represent the problem

> Set Target Cell: B19
> Equal to: Select *Min*
> By Changing Cells: B16:B17

Click on the Solve button. The optimal solution is returned in Cells B16 and B17.

The manager thus identifies the coordinates $(x, y) = (681, 882)$ as the location of the factory that minimizes total cost TC. From a map, these coordinates are close to the border of North Carolina and Virginia. The precise coordinates provided by the gravity model may not correspond to a feasible location. The manager should look for desirable sites close to the optimal coordinates that have the required infrastructure as well as the appropriate worker skills available.

Phase IV: Network Optimization Models

During Phase IV (see Figure 5.2), a manager must decide on the location and capacity allocation for each facility. Besides locating the facilities, a manager must also decide how markets will be allocated to facilities. This allocation must account for customer service constraints in terms of response time. The demand allocation decision can be altered on a regular basis as costs change and markets evolve. When designing the network, both location and allocation decisions are made jointly. Network optimization models are critical tools for both the network design and demand allocation decisions.

We illustrate the relevant network optimization models using the example of two manufacturers of fiber optic telecommunication equipment. Both TelecomOne and HighOptic are manufacturers of the latest generation of telecommunication equipment. TelecomOne has focused on the eastern half of the United States. It has manufacturing plants located in Baltimore, Memphis, and Wichita, and serves markets in Atlanta, Boston, and Chicago. HighOptic has targeted the western half of the United States and serves markets in Denver, Omaha, and Portland. HighOptic has plants located in Cheyenne and Salt Lake City.

Plant capacities, market demand, variable production and transportation cost per thousand units shipped, and fixed costs per month at each plant are shown in Table 5.2.

Allocating Demand to Production Facilities

From Table 5.2 observe that TelecomOne has a total production capacity of 71,000 units per month and a total demand of 30,000 units per month whereas HighOptic has a production capacity of 51,000 units per month and a demand of 24,000 units per month. Each year, managers in both companies must decide how to allocate the demand to their production facilities. This decision will be revisited every year as demand and costs change.

TABLE 5.2 Capacity, Demand, and Cost Data for TelecomOne and HighOptic

Supply City	Demand City Production and Transportation Cost per Thousand Units (Thousand $)						Monthly Capacity (Thousand Units) K_i	Monthly Fixed Cost (Thousand $) f_i
	Atlanta	*Boston*	*Chicago*	*Denver*	*Omaha*	*Portland*		
Baltimore	1,675	400	685	1,630	1,160	2,800	18	7,650
Cheyenne	1,460	1,940	970	100	495	1,200	24	3,500
Salt Lake City	1,925	2,400	1,425	500	950	800	27	5,000
Memphis	380	1,355	543	1,045	665	2,321	22	4,100
Wichita	922	1,646	700	508	311	1,797	31	2,200
Monthly demand (thousand units) D_j	10	8	12	6	7	11		

The demand allocation problem can be solved using a demand allocation model. The model requires the following inputs:

n = Number of factory locations
m = Number of markets or demand points
D_j = Annual demand from market j
K_i = Capacity of factory i
c_{ij} = Cost of producing and shipping one unit from factory i to market j (cost includes production, inventory, and transportation)

The goal is to allocate the demand from different markets to the various plants to minimize the total cost of facilities, transportation, and inventory. Define the decision variables

$$x_{ij} = \text{Quantity shipped from factory } i \text{ to market } j$$

The problem is formulated as the following linear program:

$$Min \sum_{i=1}^{n} \sum_{j=1}^{m} c_{ij} x_{ij}$$

Subject to

$$\sum_{i=1}^{n} x_{ij} = D_j \text{ for } j = 1, ..., m \qquad \textbf{(5.6)}$$

$$\sum_{j=1}^{m} x_{ij} \leq K_i \text{ for } i = 1,...,n \qquad \textbf{(5.7)}$$

The constraints in Equation 5.6 ensure that all market demand is satisfied and the constraints in Equation 5.7 ensure that no factory produces more than its capacity.

For both TelecomOne and HighOptic, the demand allocation problem can be solved using the Solver tool within Excel. The optimal demand allocation is presented here in Table 5.3.

Observe that it is optimal for TelecomOne not to produce anything in the Wichita facility even though the facility is operational. With the demand allocation as shown in Table 5.3, TelecomOne incurs a monthly variable cost of $14,886,000 and a monthly fixed cost of $13,950,000 for a total monthly cost of $28,836,000. HighOptic incurs a monthly variable cost of $12,865,000 and a monthly fixed cost of $8,500,000 for a total monthly cost of $21,365,000.

Locating Plants: The Capacitated Plant Location Model

Management at both TelecomOne and HighOptic has decided to merge the two companies into a single entity to be called TelecomOptic. Management feels that significant benefits will result if the two networks are merged appropriately. TelecomOptic will have five factories from which to serve six markets. Management is debating whether all five factories are needed. They have assigned a supply chain team to study the network for the combined company and identify the plants that should be shut down.

The problem of selecting the optimal location and capacity allocation is very similar to the regional configuration problem we have already studied in Phase II. The only difference is that instead of using aggregate costs and duties, we must now use location specific costs and duties. The supply chain team thus decides to use the capacitated plant location model discussed earlier to solve the problem in Phase IV.

Ideally, the problem should be formulated to maximize total profits taking into account costs, taxes, and duties by location. Given that taxes and duties do not vary between the various locations, the supply chain team decides to locate factories and then allocate demand to the open factories to minimize the total cost of facilities, transportation, and inventory. Define the following decision variables:

y_i = 1 if factory i is open, 0 otherwise
x_{ij} = Quantity shipped from factory i to market j

Recall that the problem is then formulated as the following integer program:

$$Min \sum_{i=1}^{n} f_i y_i + \sum_{i=1}^{n} \sum_{j=1}^{m} c_{ij} x_{ij}$$

TABLE 5.3   Optimal Demand Allocation for TelecomOne and HighOptic

		Atlanta	Boston	Chicago	Denver	Omaha	Portland
TelecomOne	Baltimore	0	8	2			
	Memphis	10	0	12			
	Wichita	0	0	0			
HighOptic	Salt Lake				0	0	11
	Cheyenne				6	7	0

Subject to *x* and *y* satisfying the constraints in Equations 5.1, 5.2, and 5.3.

The capacity and demand data along with production, transportation, and inventory costs at different factories for the merged firm TelecomOptic are given in Table 5.2. The supply chain team decides to solve the plant location model using the Solver tool in Excel.

The first step in setting up the Solver model is to enter the cost, demand, and capacity information as shown in Figure 5.9. The fixed costs f_i for the five plants are entered in cells H4 to H8. The capacities K_i of the five plants are entered in cells I4 to I8. The variable costs c_{ij} are entered in cells B4 to G8. The demands D_j of the six markets are entered in cells B9 to G9. Next, corresponding to each decision variable x_{ij} and y_i, a cell is assigned as shown in Figure 5.9. Initially all variables are set to be 0.

Cells H14 to H18 contain the decision variables y_i and cells B14 through G18 contain the decision variables x_{ij}.

The next step is to construct cells for each of the constraints in Equations 5.1 and 5.2. The constraint cells are as shown in Figure 5.10. Cells B22 to B26 contain the capacity constraints in Equation 5.6 whereas cells B29 to G29 contain the demand constraints in Equation 5.5. The constraint in cell B22 corresponds to the capacity constraint for the factory in Baltimore. The cell B29 corresponds to the demand constraint for the market in Atlanta.

The capacity constraints require that the cell value be greater than or equal to ($\geq$) 0 whereas the demand constraints require the cell value be equal to 0.

The next step is to construct the objective function in Cell B32. The objective function measures the total fixed and variable cost of the supply chain network.

FIGURE 5.9   Spreadsheet Area for Decision Variables for TelecomOptic

	A	B	C	D	E	F	G	H	I
1	Inputs - Costs, Capacities, Demands (for TelecomOptic)								
2		Demand City Production and Transportation Cost per 1000 Units						Fixed	
3	Supply City	Atlanta	Boston	Chicago	Denver	Omaha	Portland	Cost ($)	Capacity
4	Baltimore	1,675	400	685	1,630	1,160	2,800	7,650	18
5	Cheyenne	1,460	1,940	970	100	495	1,200	3,500	24
6	Salt Lake	1,925	2,400	1,425	500	950	800	5,000	27
7	Memphis	380	1,355	543	1,045	665	2,321	4,100	22
8	Wichita	922	1,646	700	508	311	1,797	2,200	31
9	Demand	10	8	14	6	7	11		
11	Decision Variables								
12		Demand City - Production Allocation (1000 Units)						Plants	
13	Supply City	Atlanta	Boston	Chicago	Denver	Omaha	Portland	(1=open)	
14	Baltimore	0	0	0	0	0	0	0	
15	Cheyenne	0	0	0	0	0	0	0	
16	Salt Lake	0	0	0	0	0	0	0	
17	Memphis	0	0	0	0	0	0	0	
18	Wichita	0	0	0	0	0	0	0	

Table11.4 HighOptic / Table11.4 TelecomOne / Produ

	A	B	C	D	E	F	G	H	I
1	*Inputs - Costs, Capacities, Demands (for TelecomOptic)*								
2		*Demand City* *Production and Transportation Cost per 1000 Units*						**Fixed**	
3	*Supply City*	Atlanta	Boston	Chicago	Denver	Omaha	Portland	**Cost ($)**	**Capacity**
4	Baltimore	1,675	400	685	1,630	1,160	2,800	7,650	18
5	Cheyenne	1,460	1,940	970	100	495	1,200	3,500	24
6	Salt Lake	1,925	2,400	1,425	500	950	800	5,000	27
7	Memphis	380	1,355	543	1,045	665	2,321	4,100	22
8	Wichita	922	1,646	700	508	311	1,797	2,200	31
9	*Demand*	10	8	14	6	7	11		
11	*Decision Variables*								
12		*Demand City - Production Allocation (1000 Units)*						**Plants**	
13	*Supply City*	Atlanta	Boston	Chicago	Denver	Omaha	Portland	(1=open)	
14	Baltimore	0	0	0	0	0	0	0	
15	Cheyenne	0	0	0	0	0	0	0	
16	Salt Lake	0	0	0	0	0	0	0	
17	Memphis	0	0	0	0	0	0	0	
18	Wichita	0	0	0	0	0	0	0	
20	*Constraints*								
21	*Supply City*	Excess Capacity							
22	Baltimore	0		*Total Available Capacity 0*					
23	Cheyenne	0							
24	Salt Lake	0		Solver					
25	Memphis	0							
26	Wichita	0							
28		Atlanta	Boston	Chicago	Denver	Omaha	Portland		
29	*Unmet Demand*	10	8	14	6	7	11		
31	*Objective Function*								
32	Cost =	$ -							

View Linear Program Formulation

Table11.4 HighOptic / Table11.4 TelecomOne \ Produc

Cell	Formula	Equation	Copied to
B22	= I4*H14 - SUM(B14:G14)	5.6	B22:B26
B29	= B9 - SUM(B14:B18)	5.5	B29:G29
B32	= SUMPRODUCT(B4:G8, B14:G18) + SUMPRODUCT(H4:H8, H14:H18)	Objective function	—

FIGURE 5.10 Spreadsheet Area for Constraints for TelecomOptic

The next step is to use Tools | Solver to invoke Solver as shown in Figure 5.11. Within Solver, the goal is to minimize the total cost in cell B32. The variables are in cells B14:H18. The constraints are as follows:

B14:G18 ≥ 0 {All decision variables are nonnegative}

$$\text{B22:B26} \geq 0 \quad \left\{ K_i y_i - \sum_{j=1}^{m} x_{ij} \geq 0 \text{ for } i = 1,...,5 \right\}$$

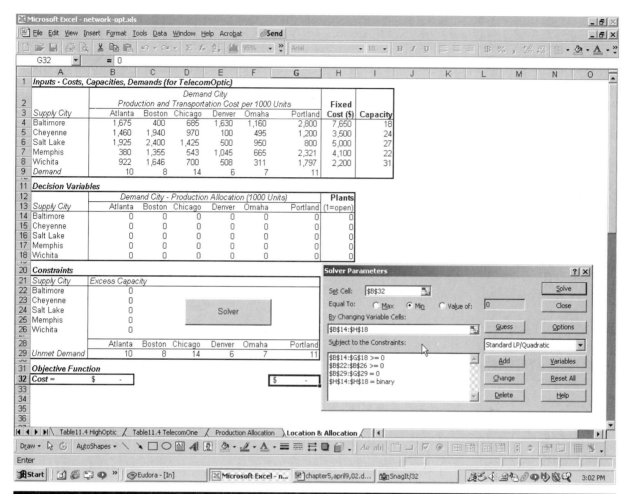

FIGURE 5.11 Solver Dialog Box for TelecomOptic

$$B29{:}G29 = 0 \qquad \left\{ D_j - \sum_{i=1}^{n} x_{ij} = 0 \text{ for } j = 1,...,6 \right\}$$

H14:H18 *binary* {Location variables y_i are binary; that is, 0 or 1}

Within the Solver parameters dialog box, click on Solve to obtain the optimal solution as shown in Figure 5.12.

From Figure 5.12, the supply chain team concludes that it is optimal for TelecomOptic to close the plants in Salt Lake City and Wichita while keeping the plants in Baltimore, Cheyenne, and Memphis open. The total monthly cost of this network and operation is $47,401,000. This cost represents savings of about $3 million per month compared to the situation where TelecomOne and HighOptic operate separate supply chain networks.

	A	B	C	D	E	F	G	H	I
1	*Inputs - Costs, Capacities, Demands (for TelecomOptic)*								
2		*Demand City*						**Fixed**	
3	*Supply City*	Atlanta	Boston	Chicago	Denver	Omaha	Portland	Cost ($)	Capacity
4	Baltimore	1,675	400	685	1,630	1,160	2,800	7,650	18
5	Cheyenne	1,460	1,940	970	100	495	1,200	3,500	24
6	Salt Lake	1,925	2,400	1,425	500	950	800	5,000	27
7	Memphis	380	1,355	543	1,045	665	2,321	4,100	22
8	Wichita	922	1,646	700	508	311	1,797	2,200	31
9	*Demand*	10	8	14	6	7	11		
11	**Decision Variables**								
12		*Demand City - Production Allocation (1000 Units)*						**Plants**	
13	*Supply City*	Atlanta	Boston	Chicago	Denver	Omaha	Portland	(1=open)	
14	Baltimore	0	8	2	0	0	0	1	
15	Cheyenne	0	0	0	6	7	11	1	
16	Salt Lake	0	0	0	0	0	0	0	
17	Memphis	10	0	12	0	0	0	1	
18	Wichita	0	0	0	0	0	0	0	
20	**Constraints**								
21	*Supply City*	*Excess Capacity*							
22	Baltimore	8							
23	Cheyenne	0							
24	Salt Lake	0			Solver			View Linear	
25	Memphis	0						Program	
26	Wichita	0						Formulation	
28		Atlanta	Boston	Chicago	Denver	Omaha	Portland		
29	*Unmet Demand*	0	0	0	0	0	0		
31	**Objective Function**								
32	Cost =	$ 47,401							

Table11.4 HighOptic / Table11.4 TelecomOne / Productio

FIGURE 5.12   Optimal Network Design for TelecomOptic

Locating Plants: The Capacitated Plant Location Model with Single Sourcing

In some cases, companies want to design supply chain networks where a market is supplied from only one factory, referred to as a *single source*. Companies may impose this constraint because it lowers the complexity of coordinating the network and requires less flexibility from each facility. The plant location model discussed earlier needs some modification to accommodate this constraint. The decision variables are redefined as follows:

$y_i = 1$ if factory is located at site i, 0 otherwise
$x_{ij} = 1$ if market j is supplied by factory i, 0 otherwise

The problem is formulated as the following integer program:

$$Min \sum_{i=1}^{n} f_i y_i + \sum_{i=1}^{n} \sum_{j=1}^{m} D_j c_{ij} x_{ij}$$

Subject to

$$\sum_{i=1}^{n} x_{ij} = 1 \text{ for } j = 1, ..., m \qquad (5.8)$$

$$\sum_{j=1}^{m} D_j x_{ij} \le K_i y_i \text{ for } i = 1,...,n \qquad (5.9)$$

$$x_{ij}, y_i \in \{0,1\}. \qquad (5.10)$$

The constraints in Equations 5.8 and 5.10 enforce that each market is supplied by exactly one factory.

Management at the merged company TelecomOptic described earlier would like to identify the optimal supply chain network if each market is to be supplied from a single factory. Using the data in Table 5.2, the plant location model with single sourcing is solved by the supply chain team to obtain the optimal network shown in Table 5.4.

If single sourcing is required, it is optimal for TelecomOptic to close the factories in Baltimore and Cheyenne. This is different from the result in Figure 5.12 where factories in Salt Lake City and Wichita were closed. The monthly cost of operating the network in Table 5.4 is $49,717,000. This cost is about $2.3 million higher than the cost of the network in Figure 5.12, where single sourcing was not required. The supply chain team thus concludes that single sourcing, although making coordination easier and requiring less flexibility from the plants, will add about $2.3 million per month to the cost of the supply chain network.

Locating Plants and Warehouses Simultaneously

A much more general form of the plant location model needs to be considered if the entire supply chain network from the supplier to the customer must be designed. We consider a supply chain in which suppliers send material to factories that supply warehouses that supply markets as shown in Figure 5.13. Location and capacity allocation decisions have to be made for both factories and warehouses. Multiple warehouses may be used to satisfy demand at a market and multiple factories may be used to replenish warehouses. It is also assumed that units have been appropriately adjusted such that one unit of input from a supply source produces one unit of the finished product. The model requires the following inputs:

TABLE 5.4   Optimal Network Configuration for TelecomOptic with Single Sourcing

	Open/Closed	Atlanta	Boston	Chicago	Denver	Omaha	Portland
Baltimore	Closed	0	0	0	0	0	0
Cheyenne	Closed	0	0	0	0	0	0
Salt Lake	Open	0	0	0	6	0	11
Memphis	Open	10	8	0	0	0	0
Wichita	Open	0	0	14	0	7	0

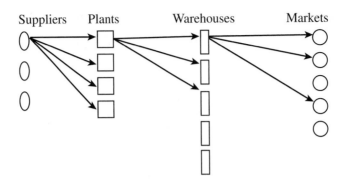

FIGURE 5.13 Stages in a Supply Network

m = Number of markets or demand points
n = Number of potential factory locations
l = Number of suppliers
t = Number of potential warehouse locations
D_j = Annual demand from customer j
K_i = Potential capacity of factory at site i
S_h = Supply capacity at supplier h
W_e = Potential warehouse capacity at site e
F_i = Fixed cost of locating a plant at site i
f_e = Fixed cost of locating a warehouse at site e
c_{hi} = Cost of shipping one unit from supply source h to factory i
c_{ie} = Cost of producing and shipping one unit from factory i to warehouse e
c_{ej} = Cost of shipping one unit from warehouse e to customer j

The goal is to identify plant and warehouse locations as well as quantities shipped between various points that minimize the total fixed and variable costs. Define the following decision variables:

y_i = 1 if factory is located at site i, 0 otherwise
y_e = 1 if warehouse is located at site e, 0 otherwise
x_{ej} = Quantity shipped from warehouse e to market j
x_{ie} = Quantity shipped from factory at site i to warehouse e
x_{hi} = Quantity shipped from supplier h to factory at site i

The problem is formulated as the following integer program:

$$Min \ \sum_{i=1}^{n} f_i y_i + \sum_{e=1}^{t} f_e y_e + \sum_{h=1}^{l}\sum_{i=1}^{n} c_{hi}x_{hi} + \sum_{i=1}^{n}\sum_{e=1}^{t} c_{ie}x_{ie} + \sum_{e=1}^{t}\sum_{j=1}^{m} c_{ej}x_{ej}$$

Subject to

$$\sum_{i=1}^{n} x_{hi} \le S_h \text{ for } h = 1,...,l \qquad (5.11)$$

$$\sum_{h=1}^{l} x_{hi} - \sum_{e=1}^{t} x_{ie} \geq 0 \text{ for } i = 1,\ldots, n \qquad \textbf{(5.12)}$$

$$\sum_{e=1}^{t} x_{ie} \leq K_i y_i \quad \text{ for } i = 1,\ldots, n \qquad \textbf{(5.13)}$$

$$\sum_{i=1}^{n} x_{ie} - \sum_{j=1}^{m} x_{ej} \geq 0 \text{ for } e = 1,\ldots, t \qquad \textbf{(5.14)}$$

$$\sum_{j=1}^{m} x_{ej} \leq W_e y_e \text{ for } e = 1,\ldots, t \qquad \textbf{(5.15)}$$

$$\sum_{e=1}^{t} x_{ej} = D_j \text{ for } j = 1,\ldots, m \qquad \textbf{(5.16)}$$

$$y_i, y_e \in \{0, 1\} \qquad \textbf{(5.17)}$$

The objective function minimizes the total fixed and variable costs of the supply chain network. The constraint in Equation 5.11 specifies that the total amount shipped from a supplier cannot exceed the supplier's capacity. The constraint in Equation 5.12 states that the amount shipped out of a factory cannot exceed the quantity of raw material received. The constraint in Equation 5.13 enforces that the amount produced in the factory cannot exceed its capacity. The constraint in Equation 5.14 specifies that the amount shipped out of a warehouse cannot exceed the quantity received from the factories. The constraint in Equation 5.15 specifies that the amount shipped through a warehouse cannot exceed its capacity. The constraint in Equation 5.16 specifies that the amount shipped to a customer must cover the demand. The constraint in Equation 5.17 enforces that each factory or warehouse is either open or closed.

The model discussed earlier can be modified to allow direct shipments between factories and markets. All the models previously discussed can also be modified to accommodate economies of scale in production, transportation, and inventory costs. However, these requirements make the models more difficult to solve.

Accounting for Taxes, Tariffs, and Customer Requirements

Network design models should be structured such that the resulting supply chain network maximizes profits after tariffs and taxes while meeting customer service requirements. The models discussed earlier can easily be modified to maximize profits accounting for taxes, even when revenues are in different currencies. If r_j is the revenue from selling one unit in market j, the objective function of the capacitated plant location model can be modified to be

$$Max \sum_{j=1}^{m} r_j \sum_{i=1}^{n} x_{ij} - \sum_{i=1}^{n} f_i y_i - \sum_{i=1}^{n} \sum_{j=1}^{m} c_{ij} x_{ij}$$

This objective function maximizes profits for the firm. When using a profit maximization objective function, a manager should modify the constraint in Equation 5.1 to be

$$\sum_{i=1}^{n} x_{ij} \leq D_j \quad \text{for } j = 1, ..., m \tag{5.18}$$

The constraint in Equation 5.18 is more appropriate because it allows the network designer to identify the demand that can be satisfied profitably and the demand that is satisfied at a loss to the firm. The plant location model with Equation 5.18 instead of Equation 5.1 and a profit maximization objective function will only serve that portion of demand that is profitable to serve. This may result in some markets where a portion of the demand is dropped because it cannot be served profitably.

Customer preferences and requirements may be in terms of desired response time and the choice of transportation mode or transportation provider. Consider, for example, two modes of transportation available between plant location i and market j. Mode 1 may be sea and mode 2 may be air. The plant location model is modified by defining two distinct decision variables x_{ij}^1 and x_{ij}^2 corresponding to the quantity shipped from location i to market j using Modes 1 and 2, respectively. The desired response time using each transportation mode is accounted for by only allowing shipments where the time taken is less than the desired response time. For example, if the time from location i to market j using Mode 1 (sea) is longer than would be acceptable to the customer, we simply drop the decision variable x_{ij}^1 from the plant location model. The option among several transportation providers can be modeled similarly.

5.5 MAKING NETWORK DESIGN DECISIONS IN PRACTICE

Managers should keep the following issues in mind when making network design decisions for a supply chain.

Do not underestimate the life span of facilities. Facilities last a long time and have an enduring impact on a firm's performance. Therefore, it is very important that long-term consequences be thought through when making facility decisions. Managers must not only consider future demand and costs but also scenarios where technology may change. Failure to do so may lead to facilities that are useless within a few years and become a financial burden to the firm. For example, an insurance company moved its clerical labor from a metropolitan location to a suburban location to lower costs. With increasing automation, the need for clerical labor decreased significantly and within a few years the facility was no longer needed. The company found it very difficult to sell the facility given its distance from residential areas and airports.[4] Within most supply chains, production facilities are harder to change than storage facilities. Supply chain network designers must consider that any factories that they put in place will stay there for an extended period of a decade or more. Warehouses or storage facilities, particularly those that are not owned by the company, can be changed within a year of making the decision. Managers must consider this difference in the lifetime of a facility when designing supply chain networks.

Do not gloss over the cultural implications. Network design decisions regarding facility location and facility role have a significant impact on the culture of each facility and the firm. The culture at a facility will be influenced by other facilities in its vicinity. Network designers can use this fact to influence the role of the new facility and the focus of people working there. For example, when Ford Motor Company introduced the Lincoln Mark VIII model, management was faced with a dilemma. At that time, the Mark VIII shared a platform with the Mercury Cougar. However, the Mark VIII is part of Ford's luxury Lincoln division. Locating the Mark VIII line with the Cougar would have obvious operational advantages because of shared parts and processes. However, Ford decided to locate the Mark VIII line in the Wixom plant where other Lincoln cars were produced. The primary reason for doing so was to ensure that the focus on quality for the Mark VIII would be consistent with other Ford luxury cars that were produced in Wixom.

The location of a facility has a significant impact on the extent and form of communication that develops in the supply chain network. Locating a facility far from headquarters will likely give it more of a culture of autonomy. This may be beneficial if the firm is starting a new division that needs to function in a manner different from the rest of the company. In contrast, locating two facilities closer together is likely to encourage communication between them. Extensive communication can be very useful if decisions made at either facility have a strong impact on the performance of the other facility.

Do not ignore quality of life issues. The quality of life at selected facility locations has a significant impact on performance because it influences the work force available and their morale. In many instances, a firm may be better off selecting a higher cost location if it provides a much better quality of life. Failure to do so can have dire consequences. For example, an aerospace supplier decided to relocate an entire division to an area with a lower standard of living to reduce costs. Most of the marketing team, however, refused to relocate. As a result, customer relations deteriorated and the company had a very difficult transition. The effort to save costs hurt the company and effectively curtailed the firm's status as a major player in its market.[5]

Focus on tariffs and tax incentives when locating facilities. Managers making facility location decisions should carefully consider tariffs and tax incentives. When considering international locations, it is astounding how often tax incentives drive the choice of location, often overcoming all of the other cost factors combined. For instance,

---

[4]Charles F. Harding. 1988. "Quantifying Abstract Factors in Facility-Location Decisions,. *Industrial Development* (May–June): 24.
[5]Ibid.

Ireland has developed a large high-tech industry by enticing companies with their low taxes to locate their European facilities there. Even within nations, local governments may offer generous packages of low to no taxes and free land when firms decide to locate facilities within their jurisdiction. Toyota, BMW, and Mercedes have all chosen their facility locations in the United States due in large part to tax incentives offered by different states.

5.6   SUMMARY OF LEARNING OBJECTIVES

1. Understand the role of network design decisions in supply chain.

   Network design decisions include identifying facility locations, roles, and capacities as well as allocating markets to be served by different facilities. These decisions are strategic in nature and define the physical constraints within which the network must be operated as market conditions change. Good network design decisions increase supply chain profits whereas poor network design hurts profits.

2. Identify factors influencing supply chain network design decisions.

   Network design decisions are influenced by strategic, technological, macroeconomic, political, infrastructure, competitive, and operational factors.

3. Develop a framework for making network design decisions.

   The goal of network design is to maximize the supply chain's long-term profitability. The process starts by defining the supply chain strategy, which must be aligned with the competitive strategy of the firm. The supply chain strategy, regional demand, costs, infrastructure, and the competitive environment are used to define a regional facility configuration. For regions where facilities are to be located, potentially attractive sites are then selected based on available infrastructure. The optimal configuration is determined from the potential sites using demand, logistics cost, factor costs, and margins in different markets.

4. Use optimization for facility location and capacity allocation decisions.

   Gravity location models identify a location that minimizes inbound and outbound transportation costs. They are simple to implement but do not account for other important costs. Network optimization models can include contribution margins, taxes, tariffs, and production, transportation, and inventory costs and are used to maximize profitability. These models are useful when locating facilities, allocating capacity to facilities, and allocating markets to facilities.

DISCUSSION QUESTIONS

1. How do the location and size of warehouses impact the performance of a firm like Amazon.com? What factors should Amazon.com take into account when making this decision?
2. How do import duties and exchange rates impact the location decision in a supply chain?
3. What are different roles played by production facilities within a global network?
4. Amazon.com has increased the number of warehouses as it has grown. How does this change affect various cost and response times in the Amazon.com supply chain?

5. McMaster Carr sells maintenance, repair, and operations equipment from six warehouses in the United States. W. W. Grainger sells products with over 300 retail locations, supported by several warehouses. In both cases, customers place orders using the Web or on the phone. Discuss the pros and cons of the two strategies.
6. Consider a firm like Dell with very few production facilities worldwide. List the pros and cons of this approach and why it may or may not be suitable for the computer industry.
7. Consider a firm like Ford with over 150 facilities worldwide. List the pros and cons of this approach and why it may or may not be suitable for the automobile industry.

EXERCISES

1. SC Consulting, a supply chain consulting firm, has to decide on the location of its home offices. Their clients are primarily located in the 16 states in Table 5.5. There are four potential sites for home offices: Los Angeles, Tulsa, Denver, and Seattle. The annual fixed cost of locating an office in Los Angeles is $165,428, Tulsa is $131,230, Denver is $140,000, and Seattle is $145,000. The expected number of trips to each state and the travel costs from each potential site are shown in Table 5.5.

TABLE 5.5 Travel Costs and Number of Trips for SC Consulting

State	Travel Costs ($)				Number of Trips
	Los Angeles	*Tulsa*	*Denver*	*Seattle*	
Washington	150	250	200	25	40
Oregon	150	250	200	75	35
California	75	200	150	125	100
Idaho	150	200	125	125	25
Nevada	100	200	125	150	40
Montana	175	175	125	125	25
Wyoming	150	175	100	150	50
Utah	150	150	100	200	30
Arizona	75	200	100	250	50
Colorado	150	125	25	250	65
New Mexico	125	125	75	300	40
North Dakota	300	200	150	200	30
South Dakota	300	175	125	200	20
Nebraska	250	100	125	250	30
Kansas	250	75	75	300	40
Oklahoma	250	25	125	300	55

TABLE 5.6 Production and Transport Costs for DryIce Inc.

	New York	Atlanta	Chicago	San Diego
Annual fixed cost of 200,000 plant	$6 million	$5.5 million	$5.6 million	$6.1 million
Annual fixed cost of 400,000 plant	$10 million	$9.2 million	$9.3 million	$10.2 million
East	$211	$232	$238	$299
South	$232	$212	$230	$280
Midwest	$240	$230	$215	$270
West	$300	$280	$270	$225

Each consultant is expected to take at most 25 trips each year.

  (a) If there are no restrictions on the number of consultants at a site and the goal is to minimize costs, where should the home offices be located and how many consultants should be assigned to each office? What is the annual cost in terms of the facility and travel?

  (b) If at most 10 consultants are to be assigned to a home office, where should the offices be set up? How many consultants should be assigned to each office? What is the annual cost of this network?

  (c) What do you think of a rule where all consulting projects out of a given state are assigned to one home office? How much is this policy likely to add to cost compared to allowing multiple offices to handle a single state?

2. DryIce Inc. is a manufacturer of air conditioners that has seen its demand grow significantly. They anticipate nationwide demand for the year 2001 to be 180,000 units in the South, 120,000 units in the Midwest, 110,000 units in the East, and 100,000 units in the West. Managers at DryIce are designing the manufacturing network and have selected four potential sites—New York, Atlanta, Chicago, and San Diego. Plants could have a capacity of either 200,000 or 400,000 units. The annual fixed costs at the four locations are shown in Table 5.6, along with the cost of producing and shipping an air conditioner to each of the four markets. Where should DryIce build its factories and how large should they be?

3. Sunchem, a manufacturer of printing inks, has five manufacturing plants worldwide. Their locations and capacities are shown in Table 5.7 along with the cost of

TABLE 5.7 Capacity, Demand, Production and Transportation Costs for Sunchem

	North America	South America	Europe	Japan	Asia	Capacity Tons/Year	Production Cost/Ton
United States	600	1,200	1,300	2,000	1,700	185	$10,000
Germany	1,300	1,400	600	1,400	1,300	475	15,000 Marks
Japan	2,000	2,100	1,400	300	900	50	180,000 Yen
Brazil	1,200	800	1,400	2,100	2,100	200	Real
India	2,200	2,300	1,300	1,000	800	80	400,000 Rupees
Demand (tons/year)	270	190	200	120	100		

TABLE 5.8	Anticipated Exchange Rates for 2001				
	US$	*Mark*	*Yen*	*Real*	*Rupee*
US$	1.000	1.993	107.7	1.78	43.55
Mark	0.502	1	54.07	0.89	21.83
Yen	0.0093	0.0185	1	0.016	0.405
Real	0.562	1.124	60.65	1	24.52
Rupee	0.023	0.046	2.47	0.041	1

producing one ton of ink at each facility. The production costs are in the local currency of the country where the plant is located. The major markets for the inks are North America, South America, Europe, Japan, and the rest of Asia. Demand at each market is shown in Table 5.7. Transportation costs from each plant to each market in U.S. dollars are shown in Table 5.7. Management has to come up with a production plan for 2001.

(a) If exchange rates are expected as in Table 5.8, and no plant can run below 50 percent of capacity, how much should each plant produce and which markets should each plant supply?

(b) If there are no limits on the amount produced in a plant, how much should each plant produce?

(c) Can adding 10 tons of capacity in any plant reduce costs?

(d) How should Sunchem account for the fact that exchange rates fluctuate over time?

BIBLIOGRAPHY

Ballou, Ronald H. 1999. *Business Logistics Management.* Upper Saddle River, N.J.: Prentice Hall.

Daskin, Mark S. 1995. *Network and Discrete Location.* New York: John Wiley & Sons.

Ferdows, Kasra. 1997. "Making the Most of Foreign Factories." *Harvard Business Review* (March–April), 73–88.

Harding, Charles F. 1988. "Quantifying Abstract Factors in Facility-Location Decisions." *Industrial Development* (May-June), 24–24.

Korpela, Jukka, Antti Lehmusvaara, and Markku Tuominen. 2001. "Customer Service Based Design of the Supply Chain." *International Journal of Production Economics* 69, 193–204.

MacCormack, Alan D., Lawrence J. Newman III, and Donald B. Rosenfield. 1994. "The New Dynamics of Global Manufacturing Site Location." *Sloan Management Review* (Summer), 69–79.

Note on Facility Location. 1989. Harvard Business School note 9-689-059.

Robeson, James F., and William C. Copacino, eds. 1994. *The Logistics Handbook.* New York: Free Press.

Tayur, Sridhar, Ram Ganeshan, and Michael Magazine, eds. 1999. *Quantitative Models for Supply Chain Management.* Boston: Kluwer Academic Publishers.

Tirole, Jean. 1997. *The Theory of Industrial Organization.* Cambridge, Mass.: The MIT Press.

------------------------------------ C A S E   S T U D Y ------------------------------------

Managing Growth at SportStuff.com

In December 2000, Sanjay Gupta and his management team were busy evaluating the performance at SportStuff.com over the last year. Demand had grown by 80 percent over the year. This growth, however, was a mixed blessing. The venture capitalists supporting the company were very pleased with the growth in sales and the resulting increase in revenue. Sanjay and his team, however, could clearly see that costs would grow faster than revenues if demand continued to grow and the supply chain network was not redesigned. They decided to analyze the performance of the current network to see how it could be redesigned to best cope with the rapid growth anticipated over the next three years.

SPORTSTUFF.COM

Sanjay Gupta founded SportStuff.com in 1996 with a mission of supplying parents with more affordable sports equipment for their children. Parents complained about having to discard expensive skates, skis, jackets, and shoes because children outgrew them rapidly. Sanjay's initial plan was for the company to purchase used equipment and jackets from families and any surplus equipment from manufacturers and retailers and sell these over the Internet. The idea was very well received in the marketplace, demand grew rapidly, and by the end of 1996 the company had sales of $0.8 million. By this time a variety of new and used products were sold and the company received significant venture capital support.

In June 1996, Sanjay leased part of a warehouse in the outskirts of St. Louis to manage the large amount of product being sold. Suppliers sent their product to the warehouse. Customer orders were packed and shipped by UPS from there. As demand grew, SportStuff.com leased more space within the warehouse. By 1999, SportStuff.com leased the entire warehouse and orders were shipped to customers all over the United States. Management divided the United States into six customer zones for planning purposes. Demand from each customer zone in 1999 was as shown in Table 5.9. Sanjay estimated that the next three years would see a growth rate of about 80 percent per year, after which demand would level off.

THE NETWORK OPTIONS

Sanjay and his management team could see that they needed more warehouse space to cope with the anticipated growth. One option was to lease more warehouse space in St. Louis itself. Other options included leasing warehouses all over the country. Leasing a warehouse involved fixed costs based on the size of the warehouse and variable costs that varied with the quantity shipped through the warehouse. Four potential locations for warehouses were identified in Denver, Seattle, Atlanta, and Philadelphia. Warehouses leased could be either small (about 100,000 sq. ft.) or large (200,000 sq. ft.). Small warehouses could handle a flow of up to 2 million units per year whereas large warehouses could handle a flow of up to 4 million units per year. The current warehouse in St. Louis was small. The fixed and variable costs of small and large warehouses in different locations are shown in Table 5.10.

TABLE 5.9 Regional Demand at SportStuff.com for 1999			
Zone	*Demand in 1999*	*Zone*	*Demand in 1999*
Northwest	320,000	Lower Midwest	220,000
Southwest	200,000	Northeast	350,000
Upper Midwest	160,000	Southeast	175,000

TABLE 5.10   Fixed and Variable Costs of Potential Warehouses

| | Small Warehouse | | Large Warehouse | |
Location	Fixed Cost ($/year)	Variable Cost ($/unit flow)	Fixed Cost ($/year)	Variable Cost ($/unit flow)
Seattle	300,000	0.20	500,000	0.2
Denver	250,000	0.20	420,000	0.2
St. Louis	220,000	0.20	375,000	0.2
Atlanta	220,000	0.20	375,000	0.2
Philadelphia	240,000	0.20	400,000	0.2

TABLE 5.11   UPS Charges per Shipment (Four Units)

	Northwest	Southwest	Upper Midwest	Lower Midwest	Northeast	Southeast
Seattle	$2.00	$2.50	$3.50	$4.00	$5.00	$5.50
Denver	$2.50	$2.50	$2.50	$3.00	$4.00	$4.50
St. Louis	$3.50	$3.50	$2.50	$2.50	$3.00	$3.50
Atlanta	$4.00	$4.00	$3.00	$2.50	$3.00	$2.50
Philadelphia	$4.50	$5.00	$3.00	$3.50	$2.50	$4.00

Sanjay estimated that the inventory holding costs at a warehouse (excluding warehouse expense) was about $600 \sqrt{F}$ where F is the number of units flowing through the warehouse per year. Thus, a warehouse handling 1,000,000 units per year incurred an inventory holding cost of $600,000 in the course of the year. If your version of Excel has problems solving the nonlinear objective function, use the following inventory costs:

Range of F	Inventory Cost
0–2 million	$250,000 + 0.310F$
2–4 million	$530,000 + 0.170F$
4–6 million	$678,000 + 0.133F$
Over 6 million	$798,000 + 0.113F$

If students can handle only a single linear inventory cost they should use $475,000 + 0.165F$.

SportStuff.com charged a flat fee of $3 per shipment sent to a customer. An average customer order contained four units. SportStuff.com in turn contracted with UPS to handle all its outbound shipments. UPS charges were based on both the origin and the destination of the shipment and are shown in Table 5.11. Management estimated that inbound transportation costs for shipments from suppliers were likely to remain unchanged, no matter what the warehouse configuration selected.

QUESTIONS

1. What is the cost SportStuff.com incurs if all warehouses leased are in St. Louis?

2. What supply chain network configuration do you recommend for SportStuff.com?

CHAPTER

Network Design in an Uncertain Environment

Learning Objectives

After reading this chapter, you will be able to

1. Identify uncertainties that influence supply chain performance and network design.

2. Understand the methodologies used to evaluate supply chain design decisions under uncertainty.

3. Analyze supply chain network design decisions in an uncertain environment.

In previous chapters, we emphasized that network design decisions have a long-term impact on a supply chain's performance. As a result, managers must account for demand and financial uncertainties over this period when designing a supply chain network. In this chapter, we discuss the methodologies used to evaluate network design decisions under uncertainty and show how they can be used to make better supply chain decisions.

6.1 THE IMPACT OF UNCERTAINTY ON NETWORK DESIGN

During the supply chain design phase, decisions are made regarding significant investments in the supply chain such as the number and size of plants to build, the number of trucks to purchase or lease, and whether to build warehouses or lease warehouse space. These decisions, once made, cannot be altered in the short term. They often remain in place for several years and define the boundaries within which the supply chain must compete. Thus, it is important that these decisions be evaluated as accurately as possible.

Over the life of a supply chain network, the company will experience fluctuations in demand, prices, exchange rates, and the competitive environment. A decision that looks very good under the current environment may be quite poor if the situation were to change. Firms, for example, must decide on the portfolio of long- and short-term contracts for both warehousing and transportation requirements. Long-term contracts will be more effective if the demand and price of warehousing do not change in the future or if the price of warehousing goes up. In contrast, a short-term contract will be more effective if either demand or the price of warehousing drops in the future. The degree of demand and price uncertainty has a significant influence on the appropriate portfolio of long- and short-term warehousing space that a firm should carry.

Uncertainty of demand and price drives the value of building flexible production capacity at a plant. If price and demand do vary over time in a global network, flexible production capacity can be reconfigured to maximize profits in the new environment. Toyota, for example, has made its global assembly plants more flexible so that each plant can supply multiple markets. One of the main benefits of this flexibility is that it allows Toyota to react to fluctuations in demand, exchange rates, and local prices by altering production to maximize profits. A firm may chose to build a flexible global supply chain even in the presence of little demand or supply uncertainty if uncertainty exists in exchange rates or prices. Thus, both supply and demand uncertainty and financial uncertainty must be considered when making network design decisions.

In the next section we discuss a methodology for evaluating any supply chain decision that will be in place for a long period of time.

6.2 DISCOUNTED CASH FLOW ANALYSIS

Because supply chain design decisions remain in place for an extended period of time, they should be evaluated as a sequence of cash flows over that period. The present value of a stream of cash flows is what that stream is worth in today's dollars. *Discounted cash flow* (DCF) analysis evaluates the present value of any stream of future cash flows and allows management to compare two streams of cash flows in terms of their financial value. DCF analysis is based on the fundamental premise that "a dollar today is worth more than a dollar tomorrow" because a dollar today may be invested and earn a return in addition to the dollar invested. This premise provides the basic tool for comparing the relative value of future cash flows that will arrive during different time periods.

The present value of future cash flow is found by using a discount factor. If a dollar today can be invested and earn a rate of return k over the next period, an investment of $1 today will result in $1 + k$ dollars in the next period. An investor would therefore be indifferent between obtaining $1 in the next period or $1/(1 + k)$ in the current period. Thus, $1 in the next period is discounted by the

$$\text{Discount factor} = \frac{1}{1+k}.$$ **(6.1)**

to obtain its present value.

The rate of return k is also referred to as the discount rate, hurdle rate, or opportunity cost of capital. Given a stream of cash flows $C_0, C_1,..., C_T$ over the next T periods, and a rate of return k, the net present value (NPV) of this cash flow stream is given by

$$\text{NPV} = C_0 + \sum_{t=1}^{T} \left(\frac{1}{1+k}\right)^t C_t.$$ **(6.2)**

The NPV of different options should be compared when making supply chain decisions. A negative NPV for an option indicates that the option will lose money for the supply chain. The decision with the highest NPV will provide a supply chain with the highest financial return.

Consider Trips Logistics, a third-party logistics firm that provides warehousing and other logistics services. The general manager at Trips Logistics is facing a decision regarding the amount of space to lease for the upcoming three-year period. He has forecast that Trips Logistics will need to handle a demand of 100,000 units for each of the three years. Historically, Trips Logistics has required 1,000 sq. ft. of warehouse space for every 1,000 units of demand. For the purposes of this discussion, the only cost Trips Logistics faces is the cost for the warehouse.

Trips Logistics receives revenue of $1.22 for each unit of demand. The general manager must decide whether to sign a three-year lease or obtain warehousing space on the spot market each year. The three-year lease will cost $1 per square foot per year and the spot market rate is expected to be $1.20 per square foot per year for each of the three years. Trips Logistics has a discount rate of $k = 0.1$.

The general manager decides to compare the NPV of signing a three-year lease for 100,000 sq. ft. of warehouse space with obtaining the space from the spot market each year.

If the general manager obtains warehousing space from the spot market each year, Trips Logistics will earn $1.22 for each unit and pay $1.20 for one square foot of warehouse space required. The expected annual profit for Trips Logistics in this case is given by the following:

Expected annual profit if warehousing space is obtained from spot market = $100,000 \times \$1.22 - 100,000 \times \$1.20 = \$2,000$.

Obtaining warehouse space from the spot market provides Trips Logistics with an expected positive cash flow of $2,000 in each of the three years. The NPV may be evaluated as follows:

$$NPV\text{(No lease)} = C_0 + \frac{C_1}{1+k} + \frac{C_2}{(1+k)^2} = 2,000 + \frac{2,000}{1.1} + \frac{2,000}{1.1^2} = \$5,471.$$

If the general manager leases 100,000 sq. ft. of warehouse space for the next three years, Trips Logistics pays $1 per square foot of space leased each year. The expected annual profit for Trips Logistics in this case is given by the following:

Expected annual profit with three-year lease =
100,000 × $1.22 – 100,000 × $1.00 = $22,000.

Signing a lease for three years provides Trips Logistics with a positive cash flow of $22,000 in each of the three years. The NPV may be evaluated as

$$NPV(Lease) = C_0 + \frac{C_1}{1+k} + \frac{C_2}{\left(1+k\right)^2} = 22,000 + \frac{22,000}{1.1} + \frac{22,000}{1.1^2} = \$60,182.$$

The NPV of signing the lease is $60,182 – $5,471 = $54,711 higher than obtaining warehousing space on the spot market. The general manager at Trips Logistics thus decides to sign the three-year lease. As we discuss in the next section, however, including uncertainty of future demand and costs may cause the manager to rethink the decision.

6.3   REPRESENTATIONS OF UNCERTAINTY

The manager at Trips Logistics considered both future demand and spot market prices to be predictable. In reality, demand and prices are highly uncertain and are likely to fluctuate during the life of any supply chain decision. For a global supply chain, exchange rates and inflation are also likely to vary over time in different locations. Supply chain managers must incorporate these uncertainties when making network design decisions. Next we discuss some models that can be used to represent uncertainty in factors such as demand, price, and exchange rate.

Binomial Representation of Uncertainty

The binomial representation of uncertainty is based on the assumption that when moving from one period to the next, the value of the underlying factor (such as demand or price) has only two possible outcomes—up or down. In the commonly used multiplicative binomial, it is assumed that the underlying factor either moves up by a factor $u > 1$ with probability p, or down by a factor $d < 1$ with probability $1 - p$. Given a price P in Period 0, the possible outcomes in future periods are as follows:

Period 1: Pu, Pd
Period 2: Pu^2, Pud, Pd^2
Period 3: Pu^3, Pu^2d, Pud^2, Pd^3
Period 4: $Pu^4, Pu^3d, Pu^2d^2, Pud^3, Pd^4$

In general, Period T has all possible outcomes $Pu^t d^{(T-t)}$, for $t = 0, 1, ..., T$. From a state $Pu^a d^{(T-a)}$ in Period t, the price may move to either $Pu^{a+1} d^{(T-a)}$ with probability p or $Pu^a d^{(T-a)+1}$ with probability $(1 - p)$ in Period $t + 1$. This is represented as the binomial tree shown in Figure 6.1.

In the additive binomial, it is assumed that the underlying factor increases by u in a given period with probability p and decreases by d with probability $1 - p$. The additive binomial has the following states in a given period

Period 1: $P + u, P - d$
Period 2: $P + 2u, P + u - d, P - 2d$
Period 3: $P + 3u, P + 2u - d, P + u - 2d, P - 3d$
Period 4: $P + 4u, P + 3u - d, P + 2u - 2d, P + u - 3d, P - 4d$

In general, Period T has all possible outcomes $P + tu - (T - t)d$, for $t = 0, 1, ..., T$.

The multiplicative binomial cannot take on negative values and can be used for factors like demand, price, and exchange rates that cannot become negative. It also has the advantage of the growth or decline in the given factor being proportional to the current value of the factor and not fixed independent of size. For example, a product with a unit price of \$10 is much less likely to see a fluctuation in price of \$5 than a product with a unit price of \$100. This fact is better captured by the multiplicative binomial.

A logical objection to both the multiplicative and additive binomial is the fact that the underlying factor takes on only one of two possible values at the end of each period. Certainly a price can change to more than just two values. But by making the period short enough, this assumption may be justified. The time period selected depends on the factor under consideration and the frequency with which decision

FIGURE 6.1 The Multiplicative Binomial Tree

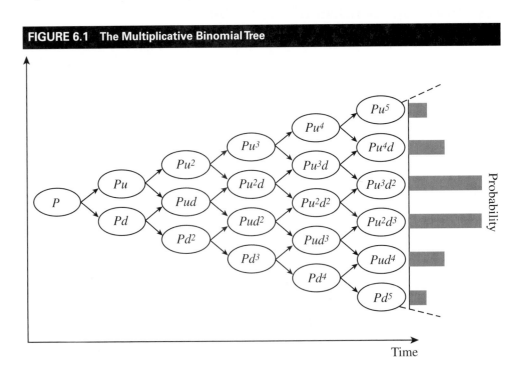

making occurs. For example, if a decision is made monthly, the time period should be no longer than a month. A time period that is shorter than a month may be justified to allow more than two outcomes at the end of each month.

As the number of periods increases, the probability distribution among the end states of the multiplicative binomial becomes smoother and begins to resemble the normal distribution. Observe that as we go further into the future, the range of possibilities of the underlying factor increases. This is a common property of all binomial distributions and is a reasonable assumption for many factors such as demand, price, or exchange rates.

Other Representations of Uncertainty

In the valuation of options, the underlying asset price is often allowed to vary continuously over time. A commonly used process to describe the evolution of the asset price is the log-normal diffusion process. A key feature of this process is that the price never drops below zero. Another feature of the log-normal diffusion process that is similar to the binomial is that the variance of the asset price grows with time. The variance in fact grows proportional to the length of the time horizon.

Another common representation of the evolution of a financial factor is as a mean reverting process. The idea here is that the factor fluctuates about a mean and experiences shocks. When it deviates from the mean it is pulled back toward the mean over time. The further from the mean that the factor deviates, the stronger it is pulled back toward the mean.

6.4 EVALUATING NETWORK DESIGN DECISIONS USING DECISION TREES

A manager makes several different decisions when designing a supply chain network. For instance:

- Should the firm sign a long-term contract for warehousing space or get space from the spot market as needed?
- What should the firm's mix of long-term and spot market be in the portfolio of transportation capacity?
- How much capacity should various facilities have? What fraction of this capacity should be flexible?

If uncertainty is ignored, a manager will always sign long-term contracts because they are typically cheaper and avoid all flexible capacity because it is more expensive. Such a decision, however, can hurt the firm if future demand or prices are not as forecast at the time of the decision.

For example, in the pharmaceutical industry, all production capacity was dedicated until around 1990. Dedicated capacity was cheaper than flexible capacity but could only be used for the drug it was designed for. Pharmaceutical companies, however, have found it very difficult to forecast the demand and price for drugs in the marketplace. Thus, a large fraction of the dedicated capacity can go unused if the forecast demand does not materialize. Today, pharmaceutical companies have a strategy of carrying a portfolio of dedicated and flexible capacity. Most products are introduced in a flexible facility and only moved to a dedicated facility when a reasonably accurate forecast of future demand is available.

During network design, managers thus need a methodology that allows them to estimate the uncertainty in their forecast of demand and price and then incorporate this uncertainty in the decision-making process. Such a methodology is most important for network design decisions because these decisions are hard to change in the short term. In this section we describe such a methodology and show that accounting for uncertainty can have a significant impact on the value of network design decisions.

A *decision tree* is a graphic device used to evaluate decisions under uncertainty. Decision trees with DCFs can be used to evaluate supply chain design decisions given uncertainty in prices, demand, exchange rates, and inflation.

The first step in setting up a decision tree is to identify the number of time periods into the future that will be considered when making the decision. The decision maker should also identify the duration of a period, which could be a day, a month, a quarter, or any other time period. The duration of a period should be the minimum period of time over which factors affecting supply chain decisions may change by a *significant* amount. "Significant" is hard to define, but in most cases it is appropriate to use the duration over which an aggregate plan holds as a period. If planning is done monthly, we set the duration of a period at a month. In the following discussion, T will represent the number of time periods over which the supply chain decision is to be evaluated.

The next step is to identify factors that will affect the value of the decision and are likely to fluctuate over the next T periods. These factors include demand, price, exchange rate, and inflation. Having identified the key factors, the next step is to identify probability distributions that define the fluctuation of each factor from one period to the next. If, for instance, demand and price are identified as the two key factors that impact the decision, the probability of moving from a given value of demand and price in one period to any other value of demand and price in the next period must be defined.

The next step is to identify a periodic discount rate k to be applied to future cash flows. It is not essential that the same discount rate apply to each period or even at every node in a period. The discount rate should take into account the inherent risk associated with the investment. In general, a higher discount rate should apply to investments with higher risk.

The decision is now evaluated using a decision tree, which contains the present and T future periods. Within each period a node must be defined for every possible combination of factor values (say demand and price) that can be achieved. Arrows are drawn from origin nodes in Period i to end nodes in Period $i + 1$. The probability on an arrow is referred to as the transition probability and is the probability of transitioning from the origin node in Period i to the end node in Period $i + 1$.

The decision tree is evaluated starting from nodes in Period T and working back to Period 0. For each node, the decision is optimized taking into account current as well as future values of various factors. The analysis is based on *Bellman's principle,* which states that for any choice of strategy in a given state, the optimal strategy in the next period is the one that is selected if the entire analysis is assumed to begin in the next period. This principle allows the optimal strategy to be solved in a backward fashion starting at the last period. Expected future cash flows are discounted back and included in the decision currently under consideration. The value of the node in Period

0 gives the value of the investment as well as the decisions taken during each time period. Tools like *Treeplan* are available that help solve decision trees on spreadsheets.

The decision tree analysis methodology is summarized as follows:

1. Identify the duration of each period (month, quarter, etc.) and the number of periods T over which the decision is to be evaluated.
2. Identify factors such as demand, price, and exchange rate whose fluctuation will be considered over the next T periods.
3. Identify representations of uncertainty for each factor; that is, determine what distribution to use to model the uncertainty.
4. Identify the periodic discount rate k for each period.
5. Represent the decision tree with defined states in each period as well as the transition probabilities between states in successive periods.
6. Starting at period T, work back to Period 0 identifying the optimal decision and the expected cash flows at each step. Expected cash flows at each state in a given period should be discounted back when included in the previous period.

We illustrate the decision tree analysis methodology by using the lease decision facing the general manager at Trips Logistics. The manager must decide whether to lease warehouse space for the coming three years and the quantity to lease. The long-term lease is currently cheaper than the spot market rate for warehouse space. The manager anticipates uncertainty in demand and spot prices for warehouse space over the coming three years. The long-term lease is cheaper but could go unused if demand is lower than anticipated. The long-term lease may also end up being more expensive if future spot market prices come down. In contrast, spot market rates are high and warehouse space from the spot market will cost a lot if future demand is high. There are three options that the manager is considering:

1. Get all warehousing space from the spot market as needed.
2. Sign a three-year lease for a fixed amount of warehouse space and get additional requirements from the spot market.
3. Sign a flexible lease with a minimum charge that allows variable usage of warehouse space up to a limit with additional requirement from the spot market.

We now discuss how the manager can make the appropriate decision taking uncertainty into account.

One thousand square feet of warehouse space is required for every 1,000 units of demand and the current demand at Trips Logistics is for 100,000 units per year. The manager decides to use a multiplicative binomial representation of uncertainty for both demand and price. From one year to the next, demand may go up by 20 percent with a probability of 0.5 or go down by 20 percent with a probability of 0.5. The probabilities of the two outcomes are unchanged from one year to the next.

The general manager can sign a three-year lease at a price of $1 per square foot per year. Warehouse space is currently available on the spot market for $1.20 per square foot per year. From one year to the next, spot prices for warehouse space may go up by 10 percent with probability 0.5 or go down by 10 percent with probability 0.5

according to a binomial process. The probabilities of the two outcomes are unchanged from one year to the next.

The general manager feels that prices of warehouse space and demand for the product fluctuate independently. Each unit Trips Logistics handles results in revenue of $1.22 and Trips Logistics is committed to handling all demand that arises. Trips Logistics uses a discount rate of $k = 0.1$ for each of the three years.

The general manager assumes that all costs are incurred at the beginning of each year and thus constructs a decision tree with $T = 2$. The decision tree is shown in Figure 6.2, with each node representing demand (D) in thousands of units and price (p) in

FIGURE 6.2 Decision Tree for Trips Logistics Considering Demand and Price Fluctuation

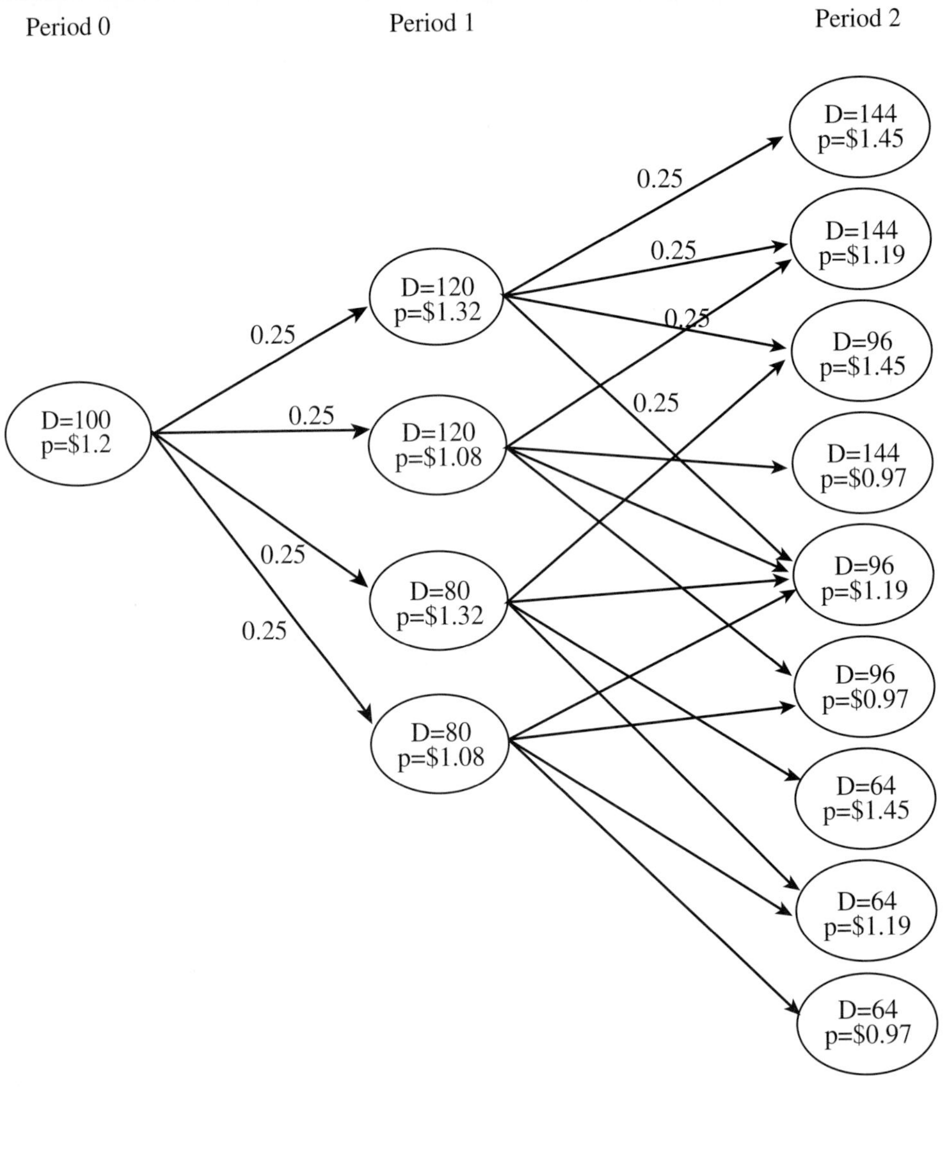

dollars. The probability of each transition is 0.25 because price and demand fluctuate independently.

The manager first analyzes the option of not signing a lease and obtaining all warehouse space from the spot market. He starts with Period 2 and evaluates the profit for Trips Logistics at each node. At the node $D = 144, p = \$1.45$, Trips Logistics must satisfy a demand of 144,000 and faces a spot price of $1.45 per square foot for warehouse space in Period 2. The cost incurred by Trips Logistics in Period 2 at the node $D = 144, p = \$1.45$ is represented by $C(D = 144, p = 1.45, 2)$ and is given by

$$C(D = 144, p = 1.45, 2) = 144,000 \times 1.45 = \$208,800.$$

The profit at Trips Logistics in Period 2 at the node $D = 144, p = \$1.45$ is represented by $P(D = 144, p = 1.45, 2)$ and is given by

$$P(D = 144, p = 1.45, 2) = 144,000 \times 1.22 - C(D = 144, p = 1.45, 2) =$$
$$175,680 - 208,800 = -\$33,120.$$

The profit for Trips Logistics at each of the other nodes in Period 2 is evaluated similarly as shown in Table 6.1.

The manager next evaluates the expected profit at each node in Period 1 to be the profit during Period 1 plus the present value (at the time of Period 1) of the expected profit in Period 2. The expected profit $EP(D =, p =, 1)$ at a node is the expected profit over all four nodes in Period 2 that may result from this node. $PVEP(D =, p =, 1)$ represents the present value of this expected profit and $P(D =, p =, 1)$, the total expected profit, is the sum of the profit in Period 1 and the present value of the expected profit in Period 2. From the node $D = 120, p = \$1.32$ in Period 1, there are four possible states in Period 2. The manager thus evaluates the expected profit in Period 2 over all four states possible from the node $D = 120, p = \$1.32$ in Period 1 to be $EP(D = 120, p = 1.32, 1)$, where

TABLE 6.1   **Period 2 Calculations for Spot Market Option**

	Revenue	Cost $C(D =, p =, 2)$	Profit $P(D =, p =, 2)$
$D = 144, p = 1.45$	$144,000 \times 1.22$	$144,000 \times 1.45$	$-\$33,120$
$D = 144, p = 1.19$	$144,000 \times 1.22$	$144,000 \times 1.19$	$\$4,320$
$D = 144, p = 0.97$	$144,000 \times 1.22$	$144,000 \times 0.97$	$\$36,000$
$D = 96, p = 1.45$	$96,000 \times 1.22$	$96,000 \times 1.45$	$-\$22,080$
$D = 96, p = 1.19$	$96,000 \times 1.22$	$96,000 \times 1.19$	$\$2,880$
$D = 96, p = 0.97$	$96,000 \times 1.22$	$96,000 \times 0.97$	$\$24,000$
$D = 64, p = 1.45$	$64,000 \times 1.22$	$64,000 \times 1.45$	$-\$14,720$
$D = 64, p = 1.19$	$64,000 \times 1.22$	$64,000 \times 1.19$	$\$1,920$
$D = 64, p = 0.97$	$64,000 \times 1.22$	$64,000 \times 0.97$	$\$16,000$

$$EP(D = 120, p = 1.32, 1) = 0.25 \times P(D = 144, p = 1.45, 2) + 0.25 \times$$
$$P(D = 144, p = 1.19, 2) + 0.25 \times P(D = 96, p = 1.45, 2) + 0.25 \times$$
$$P(D = 96, p = 1.19, 2) = -0.25 \times 33,120 + 0.25 \times 4,320 - 0.25 \times$$
$$22,080 + 0.25 \times 2,880 = -\$12,000.$$

The present value of this expected value in Period 1 is given by

$$PVEP(D = 120, p = 1.32, 1) = EP(D = 120, p = 1.32, 1) / (1 + k) =$$
$$-12,000 / 1.1 = -\$10,909.$$

The manager obtains the total expected profit $P(D = 120, p = 1.32, 1)$ at node $D = 120, p = 1.32$ in Period 1 to be the sum of the profit in Period 1 at this node as well as the present value of future expected profits.

$$P(D = 120, p = 1.32, 1) = 120,000 \times 1.22 - 120,000 \times 1.32 +$$
$$PVEP(D = 120, p = 1.32, 1) = -\$12,000 - \$10,909 = -\$22,909.$$

The total expected profit for all other nodes in Period 1 is evaluated as shown in Table 6.2.

For Period 0, the total profit $P(D = 100, p = 1.20, 0)$ is obtained as the sum of the profit at Period 0 and the present value of the expected profit over the four nodes in Period 1.

$$EP(D = 100, p = 1.20, 0) = 0.25 \times P(D = 120, p = 1.32, 1) + 0.25 \times$$
$$P(D = 120, p = 1.08, 1) + 0.25 \times P(D = 96, p = 1.32, 1) + 0.25 \times$$
$$P(D = 96, p = 1.08, 1) = -0.25 \times 22,909 + 025 \times 32,073 - 0.25 \times 15,273 +$$
$$0.25 \times 21,382 = \$3,818$$

$$PVEP(D = 100, p = 1.20, 1) = EP(D = 100, p = 1.20, 0) / (1 + k) = 3,818 / 1.1 = \$3,471$$

$$P(D = 100, p = 1.20, 0) = 100,000 \times 1.22 - 100,000 \times 1.20 + PVEP(D = 100,$$
$$p = 1.20, 0) = \$2,000 + \$3,471 = \$5,471.$$

Thus, the expected NPV of not signing the lease and obtaining all warehousing space from the spot market is given by

$$NPV(\text{Spot Market}) = \$5,471.$$

TABLE 6.2 Period 1 Calculations for Spot Market Option

Node	$EP(D =, p =, 1)$	$P(D =, p =, 1) = D \times 1.22 - D \times p + EP(D =, p =, 1) / (1 + k)$
$D = 120, p = 1.32$	−$12,000	−$22,909
$D = 120, p = 1.08$	$16,800	$32,073
$D = 80, p = 1.32$	−$8,000	−$15,273
$D = 80, p = 1.08$	$11,200	$21,382

The manager next evaluates the alternative where the lease for 100,000 sq. ft. of warehouse space is signed. The evaluation procedure is very similar to the previous case but the outcome in terms of profit changes. For example, at the node $D = 144$, $p = 1.45$, the manager will have to obtain 44,000 sq. ft. of warehouse space from the spot market at \$1.45 per square foot because only 100,000 sq. ft. has been leased at \$1 per square foot. If demand happens to be less than 100,000 units, Trips Logistics still has to pay for the entire 100,000 sq. ft. of leased space. For Period 2 the manager obtains the profit at each of the nine nodes as shown in Table 6.3.

The manager next evaluates the total expected profit for each node in Period 1. Again, the expected profit $EP(D =, p =, 1)$ at a node is the expected profit over all four nodes in Period 2 that may result from this node (see Figure 6.2), and $P(D =, p =, 1)$ is the total expected profit from both Period 1 and 2. The manager thus obtains the results in Table 6.4.

For Period 0, the expected profit $EP(D = 100, p = 1.20, 0)$ over the four nodes in Period 1 is given by

$$EP(D = 100, p = 1.20, 0) = 0.25 \times P(D = 120, p = 1.32, 1) + 0.25 \times$$
$$P(D = 120, p = 1.08, 1) + 0.25 \times P(D = 96, p = 1.32, 1) + 0.25 \times$$
$$P(D = 96, p = 1.08, 1) = 0.25 \times 35,782 + 0.25 \times 45,382 - 0.25 \times$$
$$4,582 - 0.25 \times 4,582 = \$18,000.$$

The present value of the expected profit in Period 0 is given by

$$PVEP(D = 100, p = 1.20, 0) = EP(D = 100, p = 1.20, 0)/(1 + k) = 18,000 / 1.1 = \$16,364.$$

The total expected profit is obtained as the sum of the profit in Period 0 and the present value of the expected profit over all four nodes in Period 1. It is

$$P(D = 100, p = 1.20, 0) = 100,000 \times 1.22 - 100,000 \times 1 + PVEP(D = 100,$$
$$p = 1.20, 0) = \$22,000 + \$16,364 = \$38,364.$$

The NPV of signing a three-year lease for 100,000 sq. ft. of warehouse space is thus

$$\text{NPV(Lease)} = \$38,364.$$

TABLE 6.3   Period 2 Profit Calculations at Trips Logistics for Lease Option

Node	Leased Space	Warehouse Space at Spot Price (S)	Profit $P(D =, p =, 2) =$ $D \times 1.22 - (100,000 \times 1 + S \times p)$
$D = 144, p = 1.45$	100,000 sq. ft.	44,000 sq. ft.	\$11,880
$D = 144, p = 1.19$	100,000 sq. ft.	44,000 sq. ft	\$23,320
$D = 144, p = 0.97$	100,000 sq. ft.	44,000 sq. ft.	\$33,000
$D = 96, p = 1.45$	100,000 sq. ft.	0 sq. ft.	\$17,120
$D = 96, p = 1.19$	100,000 sq. ft.	0 sq. ft.	\$17,120
$D = 96, p = 0.97$	100,000 sq. ft.	0 sq. ft.	\$17,120
$D = 64, p = 1.45$	100,000 sq. ft.	0 sq. ft.	–\$21,920
$D = 64, p = 1.19$	100,000 sq. ft.	0 sq. ft.	–\$21,920
$D = 64, p = 0.97$	100,000 sq. ft.	0 sq. ft.	–\$21,920

TABLE 6.4 Period 1 Profit Calculations at Trips Logistics for Lease Option

Node	$EP(D =, p =, 1)$	Warehouse Space at Spot Price (S)	$P(D =, p =, 1) = D \times 1.22 - (100,000 \times 1 + S \times p) + EP(D =, p =, 1) / (1 + k)$
$D = 120$, $p = 1.32$	$0.25 \times P(D = 144, p = 1.45,2) + 0.25 \times P(D = 144, p = 1.19,2) + 0.25 \times P(D = 96, p = 1.45,2) + 0.25 \times P(D = 96, p = 1.19,2) = 0.25 \times 11,880 + 0.25 \times 23,320 + 0.25 \times 17,120 + 0.25 \times 17,120 = \$17,360$	20,000	\$35,782
$D = 120$, $p = 1.08$	$0.25 \times 23,320 + 0.25 \times 33,000 + 0.25 \times 17,120 + 0.25 \times 17,120 = \$22,640$	20,000	\$45,382
$D = 80$, $p = 1.32$	$0.25 \times 17,120 + 0.25 \times 17,120 - 0.25 \times 21,920 - 0.25 \times 21,920 = -\$2,400$	0	−\$4,582
$D = 80$, $p = 1.08$	$0.25 \times 17,120 + 0.25 \times 17,120 - 0.25 \times 21,920 - 0.25 \times 21,920 = -\$2,400$	0	−\$4,582

Observe that the NPV of the lease option under uncertainty is considerably less than when uncertainty is ignored (\$60,182). This is because the lease is a fixed decision and Trips Logistics is unable to react to market conditions by leasing less space if demand is lower. Rigid contracts are less attractive in the presence of uncertainty.

The presence of uncertainty in demand and price reduces the value of the lease but does not affect the value of the spot market option. The manager, however, still prefers to sign the three-year lease for 100,000 sq. ft. because this option has a higher expected profit.

> **Key Point** Uncertainty in demand and economic factors should be included in the financial evaluation of supply chain design decisions. The inclusion of uncertainty may have a significant impact on this evaluation.

Evaluating Flexibility Using Decision Trees

The decision tree analysis methodology is very useful when evaluating flexibility within a supply chain. We consider the evaluation of flexibility with decision trees in the context of warehousing choices for Trips Logistics.

The general manager at Trips Logistics has been offered a contract in which, for an up-front payment of \$10,000, Trips Logistics will have the flexibility of using between 60,000 sq. ft. and 100,000 sq. ft. of warehouse space at \$1 per square foot per year. Trips Logistics must pay \$60,000 per year for the first 60,000 sq. ft. and can then use up to another 40,000 sq. ft. on demand at \$1 per square foot. The general manager decides to use decision trees to evaluate whether this flexible contract with an up-front payment of \$10,000 is preferable to a fixed contract for 100,000 sq. ft.

The underlying decision tree for evaluating the flexible contract is exactly as in Figure 6.2. The profit at each node, however, will change because of the flexibility. If demand is larger than 100,000 units, Trips Logistics uses all 100,000 sq. ft. of warehouse space even under the flexible contract. If demand is between 60,000 and 100,000 units, Trips Logistics need only pay for the exact amount of warehouse space used rather than

TABLE 6.5 Period 2 Profit Calculations at Trips Logistics for Flexible Lease Option

Node	Warehouse Space at $1 (W)	Warehouse Space at Spot Price (S)	Profit $P(D =, p =, 2) = D \times 1.22 - (W \times 1 + S \times p)$
$D = 144, p = 1.45$	100,000 sq. ft.	44,000 sq. ft.	$11,880
$D = 144, p = 1.19$	100,000 sq. ft.	44,000 sq. ft	$23,320
$D = 144, p = 0.97$	100,000 sq. ft.	44,000 sq. ft.	$34,200
$D = 96, p = 1.45$	96,000 sq. ft.	0 sq. ft.	$21,120
$D = 96, p = 1.19$	96,000 sq. ft.	0 sq. ft.	$21,120
$D = 96, p = 0.97$	96,000 sq. ft.	0 sq. ft.	$22,200
$D = 64, p = 1.45$	64,000 sq. ft.	0 sq. ft.	$14,080
$D = 64, p = 1.19$	64,000 sq. ft.	0 sq. ft.	$14,080
$D = 64, p = 0.97$	64,000 sq. ft.	0 sq. ft.	$14,200

the entire 100,000 sq. ft. under the contract without flexibility. The profit at all nodes where demand is 100,000 or higher remains the same as in Table 6.3. The profit in Period 2 at all nodes where demand is less than 100,000 units increases as shown in Table 6.5.

The general manager evaluates the expected profit $EP(D =, p =, 1)$ from Period 2 and the total expected profit for each node in Period 1 as discussed earlier. The results are shown in Table 6.6.

The total expected profit in Period 0 is the sum of the profit in Period 0 and the present value of the expected profit in Period 1. The manager thus obtains

$$EP(D = 100, p = 1.20, 0) = 0.25 \times P(D = 120, p = 1.32, 1) + 0.25 \times$$
$$P(D = 120, p = 1.08, 1) + 0.25 \times P(D = 96, p = 1.32, 1) + 0.25 \times$$
$$P(D = 96, p = 1.08, 1) = 0.25 \times 37,600 + 0.25 \times 47,718 + 0.25 \times$$
$$33,600 + 0.25 \times 33,873 = \$38,198$$

TABLE 6.6 Period 1 Profit Calculations at Trips Logistics With Flexible Lease Contract

Node	$EP(D =, p =, 1)$	Warehouse Space at $1 (W)	Warehouse Space at Spot Price (S)	$P(D =, p =, 1) = D \times 1.22 - (W \times 1 + S \times p) + EP(D =, p =, 1) / (1 + k)$
$D = 120, p = 1.32$	$0.25 \times 11,880 + 0.25 \times 23,320 + 0.25 \times 21,120 + 0.25 \times 21,120 = \$19,360$	100,000	20,000	$37,600
$D = 120, p = 1.08$	$0.25 \times 23,320 + 0.25 \times 34,200 + 0.25 \times 21,120 + 0.25 \times 22,200 = \$25,210$	100,000	20,000	$47,718
$D = 80, p = 1.32$	$0.25 \times 21,120 + 0.25 \times 21,120 + 0.25 \times 14,080 + 0.25 \times 14,080 = \$17,600$	80,000	0	$33,600
$D = 80, p = 1.08$	$.25 \times 21,120 + 0.25 \times 22,200 + 0.25 \times 14,080 + 0.25 \times 14,200 = \$17,900$	80,000	0	$33,873

TABLE 6.7 Comparison of Different Lease Options for Trips Logistics	
Option	*Value*
All warehouse space from the spot market	$5,471
Lease 100,000 sq. ft. for three years	$38,364
Flexible lease to use between 60,000 and 100,000 sq. ft.	$56,725

$$PVEP(D = 100, p = 1.20, 1) = EP(D = 100, p = 1.20, 0)/(1 + k) = 38{,}198 \, / \, 1.1 = \$34{,}725$$

$$P(D = 100, p = 1.20, 0) = 100{,}000 \times 1.22 - 100{,}000 \times 1 + PVEP(D = 100, p = 1.20, 0) =$$
$$\$22{,}000 + \$34{,}725 = \$56{,}725.$$

The value of flexibility may now be obtained as the difference between the expected present values of the two contracts. Accounting for uncertainty, the manager at Trips Logistics values the three options as shown in Table 6.7.

The flexible contract is thus beneficial for Trips Logistics because it only requires an up-front payment of $10,000. An up-front payment of $10,000 would still result in the flexible contract being $8,361 more valuable than the rigid contract.

> **Key Point** Flexibility should be valued by taking into account uncertainty in demand and economic factors. In general, flexibility will tend to increase in value with an increase in uncertainty.

6.5 AM TIRES: EVALUATION OF SUPPLY CHAIN DESIGN DECISIONS UNDER UNCERTAINTY

In this section we discuss a supply chain design decision at AM Tires, a tire manufacturer, to illustrate the power of the decision tree analysis methodology for making decisions under uncertainty. AM tires is faced with a plant location decision in a global network with fluctuating exchange rates and demand uncertainty.

AM Tires sells its products in both Mexico and the United States. Demand in the United States is currently 100,000 tires per year, and that in Mexico is 50,000 tires per year. From one year to the next, demand in either country is uncertain and may go up by 20 percent with probability 0.5 or go down by 20 percent with probability 0.5. Demand fluctuations in the two countries are independent.

Tires sell for $30/tire in the United States and 240 pesos/tire in Mexico. The current exchange rate is 1US$ = 9 pesos. Exchange rates are expected to fluctuate as per the binomial distribution. From one year to the next, the peso may rise 25 percent or drop 25 percent, each with a probability of 0.5. Exchange rate fluctuations are independent of demand fluctuations.

AM Tires is designing its manufacturing network, which will be in place over the next two years. The company is planning to build a 100,000-unit plant in the United States and a 50,000-unit plant in Mexico. The plants may be dedicated, in which case they can only supply the local market, or flexible, in which case they can supply either market. The fixed and variable costs for each option are shown in Table 6.8.

TABLE 6.8 Fixed and Variable Production Costs for AM Tires				
	Dedicated Plant	*Flexible Plant*		
Plant	*Fixed Cost*	*Variable Cost*	*Fixed Cost*	*Variable Cost*
U.S. 100,000	$1 million/year	$15/tire	$1.1 million/year	$15/tire
Mexico 50,000	4 million pesos/year	110 pesos/tire	4.4 million pesos/year	110 pesos/tire

Observe that the fixed costs have been given per year rather than up front with a future salvage value. Transportation costs between the United States and Mexico are $1 per tire either way. The plant decision has to stay in place over the next two years and the discount rate used by AM Tires is $k = 0.1$. The vice president of operations at AM Tires is working with the CEO to decide on the type of facility to build in each location. The company is bound by agreements with each local government to build a plant in each country.

The vice president constructs a decision tree as shown in Figure 6.3. Each node in a given period leads to eight possible nodes in the next period because demand in each country and the exchange rate may go up or down. The detailed links in Period 2 for one node in Period 1 are shown in Figure 6.3. The transition probability between each pair of linked nodes is $0.5 \times 0.5 \times 0.5 = 0.125$ because demand in the United States as well as Mexico and exchange rate fluctuations are independent and take place with 0.5 probability each. Demand is represented by DU for the United States and DM for Mexico, and is in thousands. The exchange rate is represented by E, where E is the number of pesos to a US$.

There are four possible capacity and flexibility combinations between plants in Mexico and the United States. The vice president at AM Tires first evaluates the case where a dedicated capacity of 100,000 is installed in the United States and a dedicated capacity of 50,000 is installed in Mexico.

Dedicated Capacity of 100,000 in the United States and 50,000 in Mexico

The vice president starts by evaluating profits at each node in Period 2. Each node is represented by the corresponding value of DU, DM, and E. At each node, the vice president must solve a demand allocation problem (see Chapter 5). Given the demand in each market, the existing exchange rate, and the degree of flexibility, demand must be allocated to maximize profits.

Period 2 Evaluation

The detailed analysis for the node $DU = 144$, $DM = 72$, $E = 14.06$ is as follows. All 100,000 of the U.S. capacity and all 50,000 of the Mexican capacity is used for the local markets because capacity is dedicated and demand exceeds capacity in both markets. Revenues and costs are evaluated as follows.

1. *Revenues for $DU = 144$, $DM = 72$, $E = 14.06$.* The revenues in the United States and Mexico are evaluated as follows:

U.S. revenue from manufacture and sale of 100,000 tires = 100,000 × $30 = $3,000,000

Period 0   Period 1   Period 2

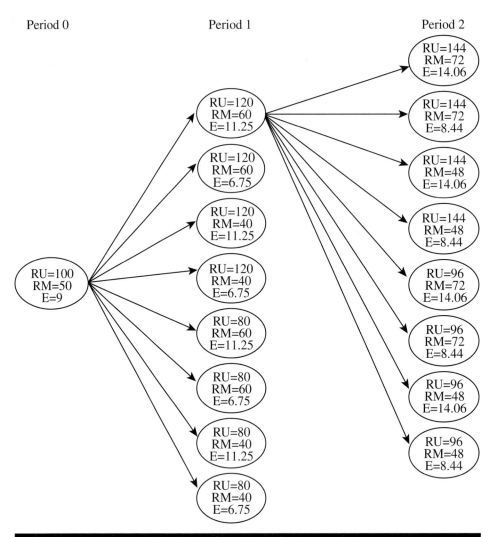

FIGURE 6.3   Partial Decision Tree for AM Tires

Mexico revenue from manufacture and sale of 50,000 tires = 50,000 ×
240 = 12,000,000 pesos = $12,000,000 / E = 12,000,000/14.06 = $853,485

Total revenue = $3,853,485

2. *Costs for DU = 144, DM = 72, E = 14.06.* The costs in the United States and
Mexico are evaluated from the data in Table 6.8. They are:

Fixed cost of U.S. plant = $1,000,000

Variable production cost at U.S. plant = 100,000 × 15 = $1,500,000

Fixed cost of Mexico plant = 4,400,000 pesos = $4,400,000 / E = 4,400,000 /
14.06 = $312,944

Variable production cost at Mexico plant $= 50{,}000 \times 110 = 5{,}500{,}000$ pesos
$$= \$5{,}500{,}000 \,/\, E = 5{,}500{,}000 \,/\, 14.06 = \$391{,}181$$

Total cost $= 1{,}000{,}000 + 1{,}500{,}000 + 312{,}944 + 391{,}181 = \$3{,}204{,}125$

The total profit for AM Tires at the node $DU = 144$, $DM = 72$, $E = 14.06$, is thus given by

$$P(DU = 144, DM = 72, E = 14.06, 2) = 3{,}853{,}485 - 3{,}204{,}125 = \$649{,}360.$$

Using the same approach, the vice president evaluates the profit in each of the 27 states in Period 2 as shown in Table 6.9. Each state in Period 2 is represented by the corresponding value of DU, DM, and E. The amount produced in each plant is the

TABLE 6.9   Period 2 Profits for Dedicated Capacity in Both United States and Mexico

			United States			Mexico			
DU	DM	E	Production	Revenue ($)	Variable Cost ($)	Production	Revenue (Pesos)	Variable Cost (Pesos)	Profit ($)
144	72	14.06	100,000	3,000,000	1,500,000	50,000	12,000,000	5,500,000	649,360
144	72	8.44	100,000	3,000,000	1,500,000	50,000	12,000,000	5,500,000	748,815
144	72	5.06	100,000	3,000,000	1,500,000	50,000	12,000,000	5,500,000	915,020
144	48	14.06	100,000	3,000,000	1,500,000	48,000	11,520,000	5,280,000	630,868
144	48	8.44	100,000	3,000,000	1,500,000	48,000	11,520,000	5,280,000	718,009
144	48	5.06	100,000	3,000,000	1,500,000	48,000	11,520,000	5,280,000	863,636
144	32	14.06	100,000	3,000,000	1,500,000	32,000	7,680,000	3,520,000	482,930
144	32	8.44	100,000	3,000,000	1,500,000	32,000	7,680,000	3,520,000	471,564
144	32	5.06	100,000	3,000,000	1,500,000	32,000	7,680,000	3,520,000	452,569
96	72	14.06	96,000	2,880,000	1,440,000	50,000	12,000,000	5,500,000	589,360
96	72	8.44	96,000	2,880,000	1,440,000	50,000	12,000,000	5,500,000	688,815
96	72	5.06	96,000	2,880,000	1,440,000	50,000	12,000,000	5,500,000	855,020
96	48	14.06	96,000	2,880,000	1,440,000	48,000	11,520,000	5,280,000	570,868
96	48	8.44	96,000	2,880,000	1,440,000	48,000	11,520,000	5,280,000	658,009
96	48	5.06	96,000	2,880,000	1,440,000	48,000	11,520,000	5,280,000	803,636
96	32	14.06	96,000	2,880,000	1,440,000	32,000	7,680,000	3,520,000	422,930
96	32	8.44	96,000	2,880,000	1,440,000	32,000	7,680,000	3,520,000	411,564
96	32	5.06	96,000	2,880,000	1,440,000	32,000	7,680,000	3,520,000	392,569
64	72	14.06	64,000	1,920,000	960,000	50,000	12,000,000	5,500,000	109,360
64	72	8.44	64,000	1,920,000	960,000	50,000	12,000,000	5,500,000	208,815
64	72	5.06	64,000	1,920,000	960,000	50,000	12,000,000	5,500,000	375,020
64	48	14.06	64,000	1,920,000	960,000	48,000	11,520,000	5,280,000	90,868
64	48	8.44	64,000	1,920,000	960,000	48,000	11,520,000	5,280,000	178,009
64	48	5.06	64,000	1,920,000	960,000	48,000	11,520,000	5,280,000	323,636
64	32	14.06	64,000	1,920,000	960,000	32,000	7,680,000	3,520,000	(57,070)
64	32	8.44	64,000	1,920,000	960,000	32,000	7,680,000	3,520,000	(68,436)
64	32	5.06	64,000	1,920,000	960,000	32,000	7,680,000	3,520,000	(87,431)

minimum of plant capacity and local demand because both plants are assumed to be dedicated.

Period 1 Evaluation

In Period 1 there are 8 outcome nodes to be analyzed. A detailed analysis for one of the nodes $DU = 120$, $DM = 60$, $E = 11.25$ is presented here. Besides the revenue and cost at this node, we also need to consider the present value of the expected profit in Period 2 from the eight nodes that may result. The transition probability into each of the eight nodes is 0.125. The expected profit in Period 2 from the node $DU=120$, $DM = 60$, $E = 11.25$ is thus given by

$$EP(DU = 120, DM = 60, E = 11.25, 1) = 0.125 \times [P(DU = 144, DM = 72, E = 14.06, 2) + P(DU = 144, DM = 72, E = 8.44, 2) + P(DU = 144, DM = 48, E = 14.06, 2) + P(DU = 144, DM = 48, E = 8.44, 2) + P(DU = 96, DM = 72, E = 14.06, 2) + P(DU = 96, DM = 72, E = 8.44, 2) + P(DU = 96, DM = 48, E = 14.06, 2) + P(DU = 96, DM = 48, E = 8.44, 2)].$$

From Table 6.9 we thus obtain

$$EP(DU = 120, DM = 60, E = 11.25, 1) = 0.125 \times [649{,}360 + 748{,}815 + 630{,}868 + 718{,}009 + 589{,}360 + 688{,}815 + 570{,}868 + 658{,}009] = \$656{,}763.$$

The present value of the expected profit in Period 2 discounted to Period 1 is given by

$$PVEP(DU = 120, DM = 60, E = 11.25, 1) = EP(DU = 120, DM = 60, E = 11.25, 1) / (1 + k) = 656{,}763/1.1 = \$597{,}057.$$

1. *Revenues for $DU = 120$, $DM = 60$, $E = 11.25$.* Given that both plants are dedicated, the U.S. plant will produce 100,000 tires for the local market and the Mexican plant will produce 50,000 tires for the market there. The revenues in the United States and Mexico are evaluated as follows:

   U.S. revenue from manufacture and sale of 100,000 tires =
   $100{,}000 \times \$30 = \$3{,}000{,}000$

   Mexico revenue from manufacture and sale of 50,000 tires = $50{,}000 \times 240 =$
   12,000,000 pesos = $\$12{,}000{,}000$ / E = 12,000,000 / 11.25 = $\$1{,}066{,}667$

   Total revenue = $\$4{,}066{,}667$

2. *Costs for $DU = 120$, $DM = 60$, $E = 11.25$.* The costs in the United States and Mexico are evaluated from the data in Table 6.8 as follows:

   Fixed cost of U.S. plant = $\$1{,}000{,}000$

   Variable production cost at U.S. plant = $100{,}000 \times 15 = \$1{,}500{,}000$

   Fixed cost of Mexico plant = 4,400,000 pesos = $\$4{,}400{,}000/E =$
   $4{,}400{,}000/11.25 \doteq \$391{,}111$

Variable production cost at Mexico plant = $50,000 \times 110 =$
5,500,000 pesos = \$5,500,000 / E = 5,500,000 / 11.25 = \$488,889

Total cost = 1,000,000 + 1,500,000 + 391,111 + 488,889 = \$3,380,000

The expected profit for AM Tires at the node $DU = 120$, $DM = 60$, $E = 11.25$ is given by

$$P(DU = 120, DM = 60, E = 11.25, 1) = 4,066,667 - 3,380,000 +$$
$$PVEP(DU = 120, DM = 60, E = 11.25, 1) = 686,667 + 597,057 = \$1,283,724.$$

The expected profit for all nodes in Period 1 is given in Table 6.10.

Period 0 Evaluation

In Period 0 the demand and exchange rate are given by $DU = 100$, $DM = 50$, $E = 9$. Besides the revenue and cost at this node, we also need to consider the expected profit from the eight nodes in Period 1. The expected profit is given by

$$EP(DU = 100, DM = 50, E = 9, 0) = 0.125 \times [P(DU = 120, DM = 60, E = 11.25, 1) +$$
$$P(DU = 120, DM = 60, E=6.75, 1) + P(DU = 120, DM = 40, E = 11.25, 1) +$$
$$P(DU = 120, DM = 40, E = 6.75, 1) + P(DU = 80, DM = 60, E = 11.25, 1) +$$
$$P(DU = 80, DM = 60, E = 6.75, 1) + P(DU = 80, DM = 40, E = 11.25, 1) +$$
$$P(DU = 80, DM = 40, E=6.75, 1)].$$

From Table 6.10 we thus obtain

$$EP(DU = 100, DM = 50, E = 9, 0) = 0.125 \times (1,283,724 + 1,521,447 + 1,067,332 +$$
$$1,160,741 + 738,269 + 975,993 + 521,877 + 615,287) = \$985,584.$$

TABLE 6.10 Period 1 Profits for Dedicated Capacity in Both United States and Mexico

DU	DM	E	Expected Profit in Period 2 EP($)	United States Production	Revenue ($)	Variable Cost ($)	Mexico Production	Revenue (Pesos)	Variable Cost (Pesos)	Profit ($)
120	60	11.25	656763	100,000	3,000,000	1,500,000	50,000	12,000,000	5,500,000	1,283,724
120	60	6.75	781370	100,000	3,000,000	1,500,000	50,000	12,000,000	5,500,000	1,521,447
120	40	11.25	545843	100,000	3,000,000	1,500,000	40,000	9,600,000	4,400,000	1,067,332
120	40	6.75	596445	100,000	3,000,000	1,500,000	40,000	9,600,000	4,400,000	1,160,741
80	60	11.25	386763	80,000	2,400,000	1,200,000	50,000	12,000,000	5,500,000	738,269
80	60	6.75	511370	80,000	2,400,000	1,200,000	50,000	12,000,000	5,500,000	975,993
80	40	11.25	275843	80,000	2,400,000	1,200,000	40,000	9,600,000	4,400,000	521,877
80	40	6.75	326445	80,000	2,400,000	1,200,000	40,000	9,600,000	4,400,000	615,287

The present value of the Period 1 profit discounted to Period 0 is given by

$$PVEP(DU = 100, DM = 50, E = 9, 0) = EP(DU = 100, DM = 50, E = 9, 0) / (1 + k) = 985,584/1.1 = \$895,985.$$

1. *Revenues for DU = 100, DM = 50, E = 9.* In this case the U.S. plant produces 100,000 tires for the local market whereas the Mexican plant produces 50,000 tires for the market there. The revenues in Period 0 are given by

   U.S. revenue from manufacture and sale of 100,000 tires = 100,000 × $30 = \$3,000,000.

   Mexico revenue from manufacture and sale of 50,000 tires = 50,000 × 240 = 12,000,000 pesos = \$12,000,000 / E = 12,000,000 / 9 = \$1,333,333

   Total revenue = \$4,333,333

2. *Costs for DU = 100, DM = 50, E = 9.* The costs in Period 0 are given by

   Fixed cost of U.S. plant = \$1,000,000

   Variable production cost at U.S. plant = 100,000 × 15 = \$1,500,000

   Fixed cost of Mexico plant = 4,400,000 pesos = \$4,400,000 / E = 4,400,000 / 9 = \$488,889

   Variable production cost at Mexico plant = 50,000 × 110 = 5,500,000 pesos = \$5,500,000 / E = 5,500,000 / 9 = \$611,111

   Total cost = 1,000,000 + 1,500,000 + 488,889 + 611,111 = \$3,600,000

The expected profit for AM Tires from installing 100,000 units of dedicated capacity in the United States and 50,000 units of dedicated capacity in Mexico is given by

$$P(DU = 100, DM = 50, E = 9, 0) = 4,333,333 - 3,600,000 + 895,985 = \$1,629,318.$$

The vice president of AM Tires thus obtains

NPV(dedicated 100,000 unit capacity in the United States and 50,000 in Mexico) = \$1,629,318.

Flexible Capacity of 100,000 in United States and 50,000 in Mexico

The vice president next evaluates the NPV of installing flexible capacity in both the United States and Mexico. Flexible capacity may be used to produce tires for either country depending on the profit from doing so. The decision tree in this case is as in Figure 6.3 but the profit at each node changes. The vice president first evaluates the profit at each node in Period 2.

Period 2 Evaluation

The detailed analysis for the node $DU = 144, DM = 72, E = 14.06$ for Period 2 is as follows. The vice president first evaluates the margin contribution of producing a tire in one place and selling in each of the two markets as shown in Table 6.11.

From Table 6.11 it is clear that under the given conditions, both U.S. and Mexican production should first be used to satisfy U.S. demand of 144,000. The remaining 6,000 tires are sold in the Mexican market because this action maximizes profits for AM Tires. The example considered here is simple enough for the optimal demand allocation to be obtained by observation. In general, a demand allocation model (see Chapter 5) must be solved at each node of the decision tree.

1. *U.S. production contribution for DU = 144, DM = 72, E = 14.06.* Given a demand in the United States of 144,000 units, all 100,000 units of U.S. production are sent to the local market. Given a margin of $15 per unit the vice president obtains

$$\text{Contribution margin from U.S. production} = 100,000 \times \$15 = \$1,500,000$$

$$\text{Fixed cost of U.S. plant} = \$1,100,000$$

$$\text{Profit from U.S. production} = \$400,000$$

2. *Mexican production contribution for DU = 144, DM = 72, E = 14.06.* Given that there is a higher margin of $21.2 per tire from selling Mexican tires in the United States, 44,000 tires from Mexico are sent to the United States. The remaining 6,000 tires are sold in Mexico with each tire contributing $9.2. Thus

$$\text{Contribution margin from Mexican production} =$$
$$44,000 \times \$21.2 + 6,000 \times \$9.2 = \$988,000$$

$$\text{Fixed cost of Mexican plant} = 4,400,000 \text{ pesos} = \$312,945$$

$$\text{Profit from Mexican production} = \$675,055$$

The total profit for AM Tires is the sum of the profit from U.S. and Mexican production and is given by

$$P(DU = 144, DM = 72, E = 14.06, 2) = \$400,000 + \$675,055 = \$1,075,055.$$

TABLE 6.11 Source/Destination Margins for $DU = 144, DM = 72, E = 14.06$

Source	Destination	Variable Cost	Shipping Cost	E	Sale Price	Margin ($)
U.S.	U.S.	$15	0	14.06	$30	$15
U.S.	Mexico	$15	$1	14.06	240 pesos	$1.1
Mexico	U.S.	110 pesos	$1	14.06	$30	$21.2
Mexico	Mexico	110 pesos	0	14.06	240 pesos	$9.2

Compare the profit at this node with and without flexibility. Flexible capacity gives a profit of $1,075,055, whereas dedicated capacity results in a profit of $649,360. The production flexibility allows AM Tires to exploit exchange rate fluctuations and increase profit by adjusting the markets being served by each plant.

The vice president of operations repeats the aforementioned analysis for each of the 27 nodes in Period 2. The results are shown in Table 6.12.

TABLE 6.12 Period 2 Profits with Flexible Capacity in Both United States and Mexico

			Contribution Margin ($/Unit)				U.S. Production		Profit in U.S. $	Mexico Production		Mexico Profit ($)	Total Profit ($)
DU	DM	E	U.S./U.S.	U.S./Mex	Mex/U.S.	Mex/Mex	For U.S.	For Mexico		For U.S.	For Mexico		
144	72	14.06	15	1.1	21.2	9.2	100,000	—	400,000	44,000	6,000	675,055	1,075,055
144	72	8.44	15	12.4	16.0	15.4	100,000	—	400,000	44,000	6,000	273,630	673,630
144	72	5.06	15	31.4	7.3	25.7	78,000	22,000	761,478	—	50,000	415,020	1,176,498
144	48	14.06	15	1.1	21.2	9.2	100,000	—	400,000	—	48,000	130,868	530,868
144	48	8.44	15	12.4	16.0	15.4	100,000	—	400,000	—	48,000	218,009	618,009
144	48	5.06	15	31.4	7.3	25.7	100,000	—	400,000	2,000	48,000	378,158	778,158
144	32	14.06	15	1.1	21.2	9.2	100,000	—	400,000	44,000	6,000	674,293	1,074,293
144	32	8.44	15	12.4	16.0	15.4	100,000	—	400,000	44,000	6,000	273,630	673,630
144	32	5.06	15	31.4	7.3	25.7	100,000	—	400,000	18,000	32,000	83,265	483,265
96	72	14.06	15	1.1	21.2	9.2	96,000	4,000	344,279	—	50,000	149,360	493,639
96	72	8.44	15	12.4	16.0	15.4	96,000	4,000	389,744	—	50,000	248,815	638,559
96	72	5.06	15	31.4	7.3	25.7	96,000	4,000	465,723	-	50,000	415,020	880,743
96	48	14.06	15	1.1	21.2	9.2	96,000	—	340,000	—	48,000	130,868	470,868
96	48	8.44	15	12.4	16.0	15.4	96,000	—	340,000	—	48,000	218,009	558,009
96	48	5.06	15	31.4	7.3	25.7	96,000	—	340,000	—	48,000	363,636	703,636
96	32	14.06	15	1.1	21.2	9.2	96,000	—	340,000	—	32,000	(17,070)	322,930
96	32	8.44	15	12.4	16.0	15.4	96,000	—	340,000	—	32,000	(28,436)	311,564
96	32	5.06	15	31.4	7.3	25.7	96,000	—	340,000	—	32,000	(47,431)	292,569
64	72	14.06	15	1.1	21.2	9.2	64,000	22,000	(116,467)	—	50,000	149,360	32,893
64	72	8.44	15	12.4	16.0	15.4	64,000	22,000	133,592	—	50,000	248,815	382,408
64	72	5.06	15	31.4	7.3	25.7	64,000	36,000	991,510	—	36,000	55,336	1,046,846
64	48	14.06	15	1.1	21.2	9.2	64,000	—	(140,000)	—	48,000	130,868	(9,132)
64	48	8.44	15	12.4	16.0	15.4	64,000	—	(140,000)	—	48,000	218,009	78,009
64	48	5.06	15	31.4	7.3	25.7	64,000	36,000	991,510	—	12,000	(561,265)	430,245
64	32	14.06	15	1.1	21.2	9.2	64,000	—	(140,000)	—	32,000	(17,070)	(157,070)
64	32	8.44	15	12.4	16.0	15.4	64,000	—	(140,000)	—	32,000	(28,436)	(168,436)
64	32	5.06	15	31.4	7.3	25.7	64,000	32,000	865,787	—	—	(869,565)	(3,779)

Period 1 Evaluation

In Period 1 there are eight outcome nodes to be analyzed. The detailed analysis for the node $DU = 120$, $DM = 60$, $E = 11.25$ is provided. Besides the revenue and cost at this node, we also need to consider the present value of the expected profit from the eight nodes in Period 2 that may result from this node. The transition probability to each of the eight nodes is 0.125. The expected profit is thus given by

$$EP(DU = 120, DM = 60, E = 11.25, 1) = 0.125 \times [P(DU = 144, DM=72, E = 14.06, 2) +$$
$$P(DU = 144, DM = 72, E = 8.44, 2) + P(DU = 144, DM = 48, E = 14.06, 2) +$$
$$P(DU = 144, DM = 48, E = 8.44, 2) + P(DU = 96, DM = 72, E = 14.06, 2) +$$
$$P(DU = 96, DM = 72, E = 8.44, 2) + P(DU = 96, DM = 48, E = 14.06, 2) +$$
$$P(DU = 96, DM = 48, E = 8.44, 2)].$$

From Table 6.12 the vice president thus obtains

$$EP(DU = 120, DM = 60, E = 11.25, 1) = 0.125 \times [1,075,055 + 673,630 + 530,868 +$$
$$618,009 + 493,639 + 638,559 + 470,868 + 558,009] = \$632,330.$$

The present value of the expected profit discounted to Period 1 is given by

$$PVEP(DU = 120, DM = 60, E = 11.25, 1) = EP(DU = 120, DM = 60, E = 11.25, 1) /$$
$$(1 + k) = 632,330/1.1 = \$574,845.$$

The next step is to evaluate the margin contribution of producing a tire in one place and selling in each of the two markets with an exchange rate of $E = 11.25$. The details are contained in Table 6.13.

The next step is to evaluate the profit contribution from each plant by solving a demand allocation problem. Given the simple example, the evaluation is done directly in this case.

1. *U.S. production contribution for DU = 120, DM = 60, E = 11.25.* Given that there is a higher margin from selling U.S. production in the United States, all 100,000 U.S. tires are sent to the local market. Thus

$$\text{Contribution margin from U.S. production} = 100,000 \times \$15 = \$1,500,000$$

$$\text{Fixed cost of U.S. plant} = \$1,100,000$$

$$\text{Profit from U.S. production} = \$400,000$$

TABLE 6.13 Source/Destination Margins for $DU = 120$, $DM = 60$, $E = 11.25$

Source	Destination	Variable Cost	Shipping Cost	E	Sale Price	Margin ($)
U.S.	U.S.	$15	0	11.25	$30	$15
U.S.	Mexico	$15	$1	11.25	240 pesos	$5.3
Mexico	U.S.	110 pesos	$1	11.25	$30	$19.2
Mexico	Mexico	110 pesos	0	11.25	240 pesos	$11.6

2. *Mexican production contribution for DU = 120, DM = 60, E = 11.25.* Given that there is a higher margin from selling Mexican production in the United States, 20,000 tires from Mexico are sent to the United States and 30,000 tires are sold in Mexico. Given the margins in Table 6.13, the vice president thus obtains

$$\text{Contribution margin from Mexican plant} = 20{,}000 \times \$19.2 + 30{,}000 \times \$11.6 = \$732{,}000$$

$$\text{Fixed cost of Mexican plant} = 4{,}400{,}000 \text{ pesos} = \$391{,}111$$

$$\text{Profit from Mexican plant} = \$340{,}889$$

The total expected profit for AM Tires for $DU = 120$, $DM = 60$, $E = 11.25$ in Period 1 is thus given by

$$P(DU = 120, DM = 60, E = 11.25, 1) = \$400{,}000 + \$391{,}111 +$$
$$PVEP(DU = 120, DM = 60, E = 11.25, 1) = \$400{,}000 + \$391{,}111 +$$
$$\$574{,}845 = \$1{,}315{,}734.$$

The expected profit for all other nodes in Period 1 is calculated as earlier and is shown in Table 6.14.

Period 0 Evaluation

In Period 0 the demand and exchange rate are given by $DU = 100$, $DM = 50$, $E = 9$. Besides the revenue and cost at this node, we also need to consider the present value of the expected profit from all nodes in Period 1. Given a transition probability of 0.125 to each node, the expected profit from Period 1 is given by

$$EP(DU = 100, DM = 50, E = 9, 0) = 0.125 \times [P(DU = 120, DM = 60, E = 11.25, 1) +$$
$$P(DU = 120, DM = 60, E = 6.75, 1) + P(DU = 120, DM = 40, E = 11.25, 1) +$$
$$P(DU = 120, DM = 40, E = 6.75, 1) + P(DU = 80, DM = 60, E = 11.25, 1) +$$
$$P(DU = 80, DM = 60, E = 6.75, 1) + P(DU = 80, DM = 40, E = 11.25, 1) +$$
$$P(DU = 80, DM = 40, E = 6.75, 1)].$$

From Table 6.11 the vice president thus obtains

$$EP(DU = 100, DM = 50, E = 9, 0) = 0.125 \times (1{,}315{,}734 + 1{,}444{,}062 + 1{,}185{,}091 +$$
$$1{,}149{,}289 + 741{,}486 + 1{,}295{,}336 + 300{,}746 + 476{,}355) = \$988{,}512.$$

The present value of the expected profit in Period 1 discounted to Period 0 is given by

$$PVEP(DU = 100, DM = 50, E = 9, 0) = EP(DU = 100, DM = 50, E = 9, 0) /$$
$$(1 + k) = 988{,}512/1.1 = \$898{,}647.$$

The next step is to evaluate the margin contribution of producing a tire in one place and selling in each of the two markets in Period 0. The details are contained in Table 6.15.

TABLE 6.14 Period 1 Profits with Flexible Capacity in Both the United States and Mexico

DU	DM	E	Expected Profit in Period 1 EP ($)	Contribution Margin ($/Unit) U.S./U.S.	U.S./Mex	Mex/U.S.	Mex/Mex	U.S. Production For U.S.	For Mexico	Profit in U.S. $	Mexico Production For U.S.	For Mexico	Profit in Mexico ($)	Total Profit ($)
120	60	11.25	632,330	15	5.3	19.2	11.6	100,000	—	400,000	20,000	30,000	340,889	1,315,734
120	60	6.75	753,405	15	19.6	12.7	19.3	90,000	10,000	446,000	—	50,000	313,148	1,444,062
120	40	11.25	570,022	15	5.3	19.2	11.6	90,000	—	250,000	30,000	20,000	416,889	1,185,091
120	40	6.75	552,355	15	19.6	12.7	19.3	100,000	—	400,000	10,000	40,000	247,148	1,149,289
80	60	11.25	330,657	15	5.3	19.2	11.6	80,000	—	100,000	20,000	30,000	340,889	741,486
80	60	6.75	589,807	15	19.6	12.7	19.3	90,000	10,000	446,000	—	50,000	313,148	1,295,336
80	40	11.25	175,843	15	5.3	19.2	11.6	60,000	—	(200,000)	20,000	30,000	340,889	300,746
80	40	6.75	275,227	15	19.6	12.7	19.3	80,000	20,000	492,000	—	20,000	(265,852)	476,355

TABLE 6.15   Source/Destination Margins for *DU* = 100, *DM* = 50, *E* = 9

Source	Destination	Variable Cost	Shipping Cost	E	Sale Price	Margin ($)
U.S.	U.S.	$15	0	9	$30	$15
U.S.	Mexico	$15	$1	9	240 pesos	$10.7
Mexico	U.S.	110 pesos	$1	9	$30	$16.8
Mexico	Mexico	110 pesos	0	9	240 pesos	$14.4

The vice president next evaluates the profit contribution from each plant.

1. *U.S. production contribution for DU = 100, DM = 50, E = 9.* All 100,000 units produced in the United States are sold locally because the U.S. market provides a higher margin. Thus,

Contribution margin from U.S. production = 100,000 × $15 = $1,500,000

Fixed cost of U.S. plant = $1,100,000

Profit from U.S. production = $400,000

2. *Mexican production contribution for DU = 100, DM = 50, E = 9.* All of the Mexican capacity is used to satisfy Mexican demand because there is no unmet demand in the United States. Thus, 50,000 tires are sold in Mexico.

Contribution margin from Mexican production = 50,000 × $14.4 = $720,000

Fixed cost of Mexican plant = 4,400,000 pesos = $4,888,889

Profit from Mexican production = $231,111

The total expected profit for AM Tires in Period 0 is thus given by the following:

$$P(DU = 100, DM = 50, E = 9, 0) = \$400,000 + \$231,111 + PVEP(DU = 100,$$
$$DM = 50, E = 9, 0) = \$400,000 + \$231,111 + \$898,647 = \$1,529,758.$$

The vice president thus obtains the following:

NPV(Flexible 100,000 unit capacity in United States and
50,000 in Mexico) = $1,529,758.

The option of having both plants be flexible yields a lower expected NPV compared to both plants being dedicated. A similar analysis can be used to evaluate the cases where one of the two plants is flexible. The results for the four options are shown in Table 6.16.

TABLE 6.16   NPV of Various Plant Configurations for AM Tires

Plant Configuration		
United States	*Mexico*	*NPV*
Dedicated	Dedicated	$1,629,319
Flexible	Dedicated	$1,514,322
Dedicated	Flexible	$1,722,447
Flexible	Flexible	$1,529,758

The analysis indicates that although flexibility in Mexico is beneficial, flexibility in the U.S. plant ends up costing money. Based on the results in Table 6.16, the CEO of AM Tires decides to build a dedicated plant in the United States and a flexible plant in Mexico.

In summary, the decision tree methodology is quite powerful. As we mentioned earlier, a major factor is in the choice of discount rate. The appropriate discount rate should be risk-adjusted and risk may vary by period and decision node. It is not appropriate to use either the risk-free discount rate or a constant risk adjusted discount in each period. One option is to find the risk adjusted rate for each period and each state and apply that in our decision tree analysis. This would allow for a fair comparison between different investment options.

Other approaches available include contingent claims analysis (CCA) for discrete time analysis and real options for the continuous time case.[1,2] In both cases, transition probabilities are adjusted so that the risk-free discount rate may be applied in each period. This allows for the proper valuation of risk. The solution methodology at that point is exactly the same as with decision tree analysis.

When underlying decision trees are very complex and explicit solutions for the underlying decision tree are difficult to obtain, firms should use simulation for evaluating decisions (see Chapter 12). In a complex decision tree there are thousands of possible paths that may result from the first period to the last. Transition probabilities are used to generate probability weighted random paths within the decision tree. For each path, the stage-by-stage decision as well as the present value of the payoff is evaluated. The paths are generated in such a way that the probability of a path being generated during the simulation is the same as the probability of the path in the decision tree. After generating many paths and evaluating the payoffs in each case, the payoffs obtained during the simulation are used as a representation of the payoffs that would result from the decision tree. The expected payoff is then found by averaging the payoffs obtained in the simulation.

Simulation methods are very good at evaluating a decision where the path itself is not decision dependent. In other words, transition probabilities from one period to the next are not dependent on the decision taken during a period. They can also take into account real world constraints as well as complex decision rules. In addition, they can easily handle different forms of uncertainty even in instances where uncertainty between different factors is correlated.

---

[1]Trigeorgis, Lenos. 1996. *Real Options.* Cambridge, Mass.: The MIT Press.
[2]Amram, Martha, and Nalin Kulatilaka. 1999. *Real Options.* Cambridge, Mass.: Harvard Business School Press.

Simulation models require a higher setup cost to start and operate compared to decision tree tools. However, their main advantage is that they can provide high-quality evaluations of complex situations.

6.6 MAKING SUPPLY CHAIN DESIGN DECISIONS UNDER UNCERTAINTY IN PRACTICE

Managers should consider the following ideas to help them make better network design decisions under uncertainty.

1. *Combine strategic planning and financial planning during network design.* In most organizations, financial planning and strategic planning are performed independently. Strategic planning tries to prepare for future uncertainties but often without rigorous quantitative analysis, whereas financial planning performs quantitative analysis but assumes a predictable or well-defined future. This chapter has presented methodologies that allow integration of financial and strategic planning. Decision makers should design supply chain networks considering a portfolio of strategic options—the option to wait, build excess capacity, build flexible capacity, sign long-term contracts, purchase from the spot market, and so forth. The various options should be evaluated in the context of future uncertainty.

2. *Use multiple metrics to evaluate supply chain networks.* As one metric can only give part of the picture, it is beneficial to examine network design decisions using multiple metrics such as firm profits, supply chain profits, customer service levels, and response times. Often, different metrics will recommend different decisions and by using multiple metrics, the differences between the strategic choices will become clearer. The best decisions can be made when a multitude of metrics are available because each metric enhances the overall view of the alternatives being considered.

3. *Use financial analysis as an input to decision making, not as the decision-making process.* Financial analysis is a great tool in the decision-making process as it often produces an answer and an abundance of quantitative data to back up that answer. However appealing this may be, management should not rely solely on financial analysis to make decisions. Use of this analysis as a large part of the decision-making process is fine, but other inputs into the decision process that are difficult to quantify should be included in the analysis as well. Financial methodologies alone do not provide a complete picture of the alternatives. For instance, there may be strategic benefits to locating a plant in a certain country that are hard to quantify. These impacts should be considered in addition to the raw financial analysis. In the final analysis, management must use other inputs beyond financial analysis in the decision-making process to get the most complete view of the alternatives possible.

4. *Use estimates along with sensitivity analysis.* Many of the inputs into financial analysis can be difficult, if not impossible, to nail down in a very accurate fashion. This can cause financial analysis to be a long and drawn out process. One of the best ways to speed the process along and arrive at a good decision is to use estimates of inputs when it appears that finding a very accurate input would take an inordinate amount of time. As we discuss in some of the other practice-oriented sections, using estimates is fine when the estimates are backed up by sensitivity analysis. It is almost always easier to

come up with a range for an input than it is to come up with a single point. By performing sensitivity analysis on the input's range, managers can often show that no matter where the true input lies within the range, the outcome remains the same. When this is not the case, they have highlighted a key variable to making the decision and it likely deserves more attention to arrive at a more accurate answer. In summary, to effectively make supply chain design decisions, managers need to make estimates of inputs and then test all recommendations with sensitivity analysis.

6.7   SUMMARY OF LEARNING OBJECTIVES

1. Identify uncertainties that influence supply chain performance and network design.

   The main financial measurement for evaluating supply chain alternatives is the present value of the stream of cash flows generated by each alternative. These streams are affected by uncertainty of demand, price, exchange rates, and other economic factors. These uncertainties and any flexibility in the supply chain network must be taken into account when valuing the cash flows.

2. Understand the methodologies used to evaluate supply chain decisions under uncertainty.

   When valuing the streams of cash flows, decision trees are a basic approach to valuing alternatives under uncertainty. Incorporating a binomial representation of uncertainty allows the decision tree to value alternatives given

uncertainty. When decision trees become too complex to reasonably solve, simulation can be used to perform financial evaluations on the decision alternatives.

3. Analyze supply chain network design decisions in an uncertain environment.

   The basic steps in analyzing network design decisions involve gathering financial data on the alternatives, determining what the uncertainties affecting the decision are, quantifying the cash flows for each alternative in each time period, quantifying the uncertainties' impact on the cash flows, and using one of the methodologies to calculate a financial valuation for the different alternatives.

DISCUSSION QUESTIONS

1. Why is it important to consider uncertainty when evaluating supply chain design decisions?
2. What are the major sources of uncertainty that can impact the value of supply chain decisions?
3. Describe the basic principle of DCFs and how it can be used to compare different streams of cash flows.
4. How does the binomial representation of uncertainty relate to the normal distribution?
5. Summarize the basic steps in the decision tree analysis methodology.
6. What are the major financial uncertainties faced by an electronic components manufacturer deciding whether to build a plant in Thailand or the United States?
7. What are some major nonfinancial uncertainties that a company should consider when making decisions on where to source product?

EXERCISES

1. Moon Micro is a small manufacturer of servers that currently builds all of its product in Santa Clara, California. As the market for servers has grown dramatically, the Santa Clara plant has reached capacity of 10,000 servers per year. Moon is considering two options to increase its capacity. The first option is to add 10,000 units of capacity to the Santa Clara plant at an annualized fixed cost of $10,000,000 plus $500 labor per server. The second option is to have Molectron, an independent assembler, manufacture servers for Moon at a cost of $2,000 for each server (excluding raw materials cost). Moon sells each server for $15,000 and raw materials cost $8,000 per server.

   Moon must make this decision for a two-year time horizon. During each year, demand for Moon servers has an 80 percent chance of increasing 50 percent from the year before and a 20 percent chance of remaining the same as the year before. Molectron's prices may change as well. They are fixed for the first year but have a 50 percent chance of increasing 20 percent in the second year and a 50 percent chance of remaining where they are.

   Use a decision tree to determine whether Moon should add capacity to its Santa Clara plant or if it should outsource to Molectron. What are some other factors that would affect this decision that we have not discussed?

2. Unipart, a manufacturer of auto parts, is considering two different B2B marketplaces to purchase their MRO supplies. Both marketplaces offer a full line of supplies at very similar prices for products and shipping. Both provide very similar service levels and lead times.

   However, their fee structures are quite different. The first marketplace, Parts4u.com, sells all of its products with a 5 percent commission tacked on top of the price of the product (not including shipping). AllMRO.com's pricing is based on a subscription fee of $10 million that must be paid up front for a two-year period and a commission of 1 percent on each transaction's product price.

   Unipart spends about $150 million on MRO supplies each year, although this varies with their utilization. Next year will likely be a strong year where high utilization will keep MRO spending at $150 million. However, there is a 25 percent chance that spending will drop by 10 percent. The second year, there is a 50 percent chance the spending level will stay where it was in the first year and a 50 percent chance it will drop by another 10 percent. Unipart uses a discount rate of 20 percent. Assume all costs are incurred at the beginning of each year (so Year 1's costs are incurred now and Year 2 costs are incurred in a year).

   Which B2B marketplace should Unipart buy its parts from?

3. Alphacap, a manufacturer of electronic components, is trying to select a single supplier for the raw materials that go into their main product, the doublecap, a new capacitor that is used by cellular phone manufacturers to protect microprocessors from power spikes. Two companies can provide the necessary materials—MultiChem and Mixemat.

   MultiChem has a very solid reputation for its products and charges a higher price due to their reliability of supply and delivery. MultiChem dedicates plant capacity to each customer and therefore supply is assured. This allows MultiChem to charge $1.20 for the raw materials used in each doublecap.

Mixemat is a small raw materials supplier that has limited capacity. They charge only $.90 for a unit's worth of raw materials but their reliability of supply is in question. They do not have enough capacity to supply all their customers all the time. This means that orders to Mixemat are not guaranteed. In a year of high demand for raw materials, Mixemat will have 90,000 units available for Alphacap. In low demand years, all product will be delivered.

If Alphacap does not get raw materials from their suppliers, they need to buy them on the spot market to supply their customers. Alphacap relies on one major cell phone manufacturer for the majority of its business and failing to deliver could cause them to lose this contract, essentially putting the firm at risk. Therefore, Alphacap will buy raw material on the spot market to make up for any shortfall. Spot prices for single-lot purchases (such as Alphacap would need) are $2.00 when raw materials demand is low and $4.00 when demand is high.

Demand in the raw materials market has a 75 percent chance of being high in the market each of the next two years. Alphacap sold 100,000 doublecaps last year and expects to sell 110,000 this year. However, there is a 25 percent chance they will only sell 100,000. Next year, the demand has a 75 percent chance of rising 20 percent over this year and a 25 percent chance of falling 10 percent. Alphacap uses a discount rate of 20 percent. Assume all costs are incurred at the beginning of each year (Year 1's costs are incurred now and Year 2 costs are incurred in a year) and that Alphacap must make a decision with a two-year horizon. Only one supplier can be chosen as these two suppliers refuse to supply someone who works with their competitor.

Which supplier should Alphacap choose? What other information would you like to have to make this decision?

4. Bell Computer is reaching a crossroads. This PC manufacturer has been growing at a rapid rate. This has been causing problems for their operations as they try to keep up with the surging demand. Bell executives can plainly see that within the next half year, the systems used to coordinate their supply chain are going to fall apart because they will not be able to handle the volume of Bell projects they will have.

To solve this problem, Bell has brought in two supply chain software companies that have made proposals on systems that could cover the volume and the complexity of tasks Bell needs to have handled. These two software companies are offering very different types of products, however.

The first company, SCSoftware, proposes a system that Bell will purchase a license for. This would allow Bell to use the software as long as they want. However, Bell would be responsible for maintaining this software, which would require significant resources.

The second company, SC–ASP, proposes that Bell pay a subscription fee on a monthly basis for SC–ASP to host Bell's supply chain applications on SC–ASP's machines. Bell employees would access information and analysis via a Web browser. Information would automatically be fed from the ASP servers to the Bell servers whenever necessary. Bell would continue to pay this monthly fee for the software but all maintenance would be performed by SC–ASP.

How should Bell go about making a decision regarding which software company to go with? What are the specific pieces of information that Bell needs to know (both about the software and about the future conditions Bell will experience) in order to make a decision? What are some of the qualitative issues Bell must think about in addition to the costs?

BIBLIOGRAPHY

Amram, Martha, and Nalin Kulatilaka. 1999. *Real Options*. Cambridge, Mass.: Harvard Business School Press.

Brealey, Richard A., and Stewart C. Myers. 1996. *Principles of Corporate Finance*, New York: McGraw Hill.

Horngren, Charles T., George Foster, and Srikant M. Datar. 1997. *Cost Accounting*, Upper Saddle River, N.J.: Prentice Hall.

Johnson, Norman L., Samuel Kotz, and N. Balakrishnan. 1994. *Continuous Univariate Distributions*. New York: John Wiley & Sons.

Luehrman, Timothy A. 1995. "Capital Projects as Real Options: An Introduction." *Harvard Business School* case 9-295-074.

Luehrman, Timothy A. 1998. "Investment Opportunities as Real Options: Getting Started on the Numbers." *Harvard Business Review* (July–August): 51–67.

Luehrman, Timothy A. 1998. "Strategy as a Portfolio of Real Options." *Harvard Business Review* (September–October): 89–99.

Ross, Sheldon M. 1983. *Introduction to Stochastic Dynamic Programming*. New York: Academic Press.

Stokey, Nancy L., Robert E. Lucas Jr., and Edward C. Prescott. 1989. *Recursive Methods in Economic Dynamics*. Cambridge, Mass.: Harvard University Press.

Trigeorgis, Lenos. 1996. *Real Options*. Cambridge, Mass.: The MIT Press.

PART

III

Planning Demand and Supply in a Supply Chain

CHAPTER 7

Demand Forecasting in a Supply Chain

CHAPTER 8

Aggregate Planning in the Supply Chain

CHAPTER 9

**Planning Supply and Demand in the Supply Chain:
Managing Predictable Variability**

The goals of the three chapters in Part III are to explain the significance of planning in a supply chain, identify decisions that are part of the planning process, and discuss tools that supply chain managers can use for planning. Planning allows a supply chain manager to be proactive and manage demand and supply to ensure that profits are maximized.

All supply chain decisions are based on an estimate of future demand. Chapter 7 describes methodologies that can be used to forecast future demand based on historical demand data. Given a demand forecast, Chapter 8 describes the aggregate planning methodology that a supply chain manager can use to plan production, distribution, and allocation of resources for the near future (typically a quarter or a year) by making appropriate trade-offs between capacity, inventory, and backlogged orders across the entire supply chain. Chapter 9 then discusses how a supply chain manager can plan pricing and promotions along with supply planning across the supply chain to maximize profits.

CHAPTER

7

Demand Forecasting in a Supply Chain

Learning Objectives

After reading this chapter, you will be able to

1. Understand the role of forecasting for both an enterprise and a supply chain.

2. Identify the components of a demand forecast.

3. Forecast demand in a supply chain given historical demand data using time series methodologies.

4. Analyze demand forecasts to estimate forecast error.

Forecasts of future demand are essential to a supply chain manager's decision-making processes. In this chapter, we explain how historical demand information can be used to forecast future demand and how these forecasts affect the supply chain. We also describe several methods to forecast demand and estimate a forecast's accuracy. We then discuss how these methods can be implemented using Microsoft Excel.

7.1 THE ROLE OF FORECASTING IN A SUPPLY CHAIN

The forecast of demand forms the basis for all strategic and planning decisions in a supply chain. Consider the push/pull view of the supply chain discussed in Chapter 1. Throughout the supply chain, all push processes are performed in anticipation of customer demand whereas all pull processes are performed in response to customer demand. For push processes, a manager must plan the level of production. For pull processes, a manager must plan the level of available capacity and inventory. In both instances, the first step a manager must take is to forecast what customer demand will be.

For example, Dell orders PC components in anticipation of customer orders, whereas it performs assembly in response to a customer orders. To determine the amount of components to have on hand (a push process) and to determine the capacity needed in its plants (for pull production), Dell requires a forecast of future demand. Forecasts are also needed further up the supply chain. For example, Intel faces a similar need in determining their own production and inventory levels to supply Dell. Intel's suppliers also need forecasts for the same reason. When each stage in the supply chain makes its own separate forecast, these forecasts are often very different. The result is a mismatch between supply and demand. When all stages of a supply chain produce a collaborative forecast, it tends to be much more accurate. The resulting forecast accuracy enables supply chains to be both more responsive and more efficient in serving their customers. Leaders in many supply chains, from PC manufacturers to packaged goods retailers, have started moving toward collaborative forecasting to improve their ability to match supply and demand.

We list some decisions that utilize forecasts and can be enhanced through collaborative forecasting among supply chain partners:

- *Production:* Scheduling, inventory control, aggregate planning, purchasing
- *Marketing:* Sales-force allocation, promotions, new product introduction
- *Finance:* Plant/equipment investment, budgetary planning
- *Personnel:* Workforce planning, hiring, layoffs

It is essential that these decisions not be segregated by functional area or even by enterprise, as they influence each other and are best made jointly. For example, Coca-Cola considers the demand forecast over the coming quarter and decides on the timing of various promotions. The promotion information is then used to update the demand forecast. The updated forecast is essential for the bottlers, who are often independent of Coca-Cola, to plan their production as it may require additional investment and hiring decisions. A bottler operating without the updated forecast based on the promotion is unlikely to have sufficient supply available for Coca-Cola. This example illustrates the importance of collaboration—both within the functions of a company as well as among companies in a supply chain.

Mature products with stable demand are usually easiest to forecast. Staple products at a supermarket, such as milk or paper towels, fit this description. Forecasting and the accompanying managerial decisions are extremely difficult when either the supply of raw materials or the demand for the finished product is highly variable. Some examples of items that are difficult to forecast include fashion goods and many high-tech products. Good forecasting is very important in these cases because the time window for sales is narrow and if a firm has over- or underproduced, it has little chance to recover. For a product with a long life cycle, in contrast, the impact of a forecasting error is less significant.

Before we begin an in-depth discussion of the components of forecasts and forecasting methods in the supply chain, we briefly list characteristics of forecasts that a manager must understand to effectively design and manage his or her supply chain.

7.2 CHARACTERISTICS OF FORECASTS

Companies and supply chain managers should be aware of the following characteristics of forecasts:

1. Forecasts are always wrong and should thus include both the expected value of the forecast and a measure of forecast error. To understand the importance of forecast error, consider two car dealers. One of them expects sales to range between 100 and 1,900 whereas the other expects sales to range between 900 and 1,100. Even though both dealers anticipate average sales of 1,000, the sourcing policies for each dealer should be very different given the difference in forecast accuracy. Thus, the forecast error (or demand uncertainty) must be a key input into most supply chain decisions. An estimation of demand uncertainty is unfortunately often missing from forecasts, resulting in estimates that vary widely among different stages of a supply chain that is not forecasting collaboratively.

2. Long-term forecasts are usually less accurate than short-term forecasts; that is, long-term forecasts have a larger standard deviation of error relative to the mean than short-term forecasts. 7-Eleven Japan has exploited this key property to improve its performance. The company has instituted a replenishment process that enables them to respond to an order within hours. For example, if a store manager places an order by 10 A.M., the order is delivered by 7 P.M. the same day. The manager thus has to forecast what will sell that night less than twelve hours before the actual sale. The short lead time allows a manager to take into account current information, such as the weather, which could affect product sales. The forecast in this case is likely to be more accurate than if the store manager had to forecast demand one week in advance.

3. Aggregate forecasts are usually more accurate than disaggregate forecasts as they tend to have a smaller standard deviation of error relative to the mean. For example, it is easy to forecast the Gross Domestic Product (GDP) of the United States for a given year with less than a 2 percent error. However, it is much more difficult to forecast yearly revenue for a company with less than a 2 percent error, and it is even harder to forecast revenue for a given product with the same degree of accuracy. The key difference between the three forecasts is the degree of aggregation. The GDP is an aggregation across many companies and the earnings of a company are an aggregation across several product lines. The greater the degree of aggregation, the more accurate the forecast.

4. In general, the further up the supply chain a company is (or the further they are from the consumer), the greater the distortion of information they receive. One classic

example of this is the bullwhip effect (see Chapter 16) where order variation is amplified as orders move further from the end customer. As a result, the further up the supply chain an enterprise exists, the higher the forecast error. Collaborative forecasting based on sales to the end customer can help enterprises further up the supply chain reduce forecast error.

In the next section, we discuss the basic components of a forecast, explain the four classifications into which forecasting methods fall, and introduce the notion of forecast error.

7.3 COMPONENTS OF A FORECAST AND FORECASTING METHODS

Yogi Berra, the former New York Yankees catcher who is famous for his malapropisms, has been quoted as saying, "Predictions are usually difficult, especially about the future." One may be tempted to treat demand forecasting as magic or art and leave everything to chance. What a firm knows about its customers' past behavior, however, sheds light on their future behavior as well as the responses they are apt to have to actions the firm may take. Demand does not arise in a vacuum. Rather, customer demand is influenced by a variety of factors and can be predicted if a company can determine the relationship between these factors and future demand. To forecast demand, companies must first identify the factors that influence future demand and then ascertain the relationship between these factors and future demand.

Companies must balance objective and subjective factors when forecasting demand. Although we focus on quantitative forecasting methods in this chapter, companies must include human input when they make their final forecast. 7-Eleven Japan illustrates this point.

7-Eleven Japan provides its store managers with a state-of-the-art decision support system to forecast demand. The decision support system makes a forecast and provides a recommended order. The store manager, however, is responsible for making the final forecast and placing the order because he or she may have access to information about market conditions that is not available in historical demand data. This knowledge of market conditions is likely to improve the forecast. For example, if the store manager knows that the weather is likely to be rainy and cold the next day, they can use this information to reduce the size of an ice cream order to be placed with an upstream supplier even if demand was high during the previous few days when the weather was hot. In this instance, a change in market conditions (the weather) would not have been predicted using historical demand data. A supply chain can experience substantial payoffs from improving its demand forecasting through qualitative human inputs.

A company must be knowledgeable about numerous factors that are be related to the demand forecast. Some of these factors are listed next.

- Past demand
- Lead time of product
- Planned advertising or marketing efforts
- State of the economy

- Planned price discounts
- Actions competitors have taken

A company must understand such factors before it can select an appropriate forecasting methodology. For example, historically a firm may have experienced low demand for chicken noodle soup in October and high demand in December and January. If the firm decides to discount the product in October, the situation is likely to change, with some of the future demand shifting to the month of October. The firm should make its forecast taking this factor into consideration.

Forecasting methods are classified according to the following four types:

1. *Qualitative:* Qualitative forecasting methods are primarily subjective and rely on human judgment. They are most appropriate when there is little historical data available or when experts have market intelligence that is critical in making the forecast. Such methods may be necessary to forecast demand several years into the future in a new industry.

2. *Time series:* Time series forecasting methods use historical demand to make a forecast. They are based on the assumption that past demand history is a good indicator of future demand. These methods are most appropriate when the basic demand pattern does not vary significantly from one year to the next. These are the simplest methods to implement and can serve as a good starting point for a demand forecast.

3. *Causal:* Causal forecasting methods assume that the demand forecast is highly correlated with certain factors in the environment (e.g., the state of the economy, interest rates, etc.). Causal forecasting methods find this correlation between demand and environmental factors and use estimates of what environmental factors will be to forecast future demand. For example, product pricing is strongly correlated with demand. Companies can thus use causal methods to determine the impact of price promotions on demand.

4. *Simulation:* Simulation forecasting methods imitate the consumer choices that give rise to demand to arrive at a forecast. Using simulation, a firm can combine time series and causal methods to answer such questions as: What will the impact of a price promotion be? What will the impact be of a competitor opening a store nearby? Airlines simulate customer buying behavior to forecast demand for higher fare seats when there are no seats available at the lower fares.

A company may find it difficult to decide which method is most appropriate for forecasting. In fact, several studies have indicated that using multiple forecasting methods to create a combined forecast is more effective than any individual method.

In this chapter we deal primarily with time series methods, which are most appropriate when future demand is expected to follow historical patterns. When a company attempts to forecast demand based on history, then the historical demand, growth patterns, and any seasonal patterns will influence the forecast. Moreover, with this forecasting method, there is always a random element that cannot be explained by historical demand patterns. Therefore, any observed demand can be broken down into a systematic and a random component:

Observed demand (O) = Systematic component (S) + Random component (R).

The *systematic component* measures the expected value of demand and consists of the *level*, the current deseasonalized demand; *trend*, the rate of growth or decline in demand for the next period; and *seasonality*, the predictable seasonal fluctuations in demand.

A company may forecast demand's level, trend, and seasonality by using historical data to obtain the forecast's systematic component. The *random component* is that part of the forecast that deviates from the systematic part. A company cannot (and should not) forecast the random component. All a company can forecast is its estimated size and variability, which provides a measure of forecast error. Randomness also means that a company cannot forecast this component's direction. On average, a good forecasting method will have an error whose size is comparable to the random component of demand. A manager should be skeptical of a forecasting method that claims to have no forecasting error on historical demand. In this case, the method has merged the historical random component with the systematic component. As a result, the forecasting method will likely perform poorly. The objective of forecasting is to filter out the random component (noise) and estimate the systematic component. The *forecast error* measures the difference between the forecast and actual demand.

7.4 BASIC APPROACH TO DEMAND FORECASTING

The following basic, six-step approach helps an organization perform effective forecasting:

1. Understand the objective of forecasting
2. Integrate demand planning and forecasting throughout the supply chain
3. Understand and identify customer segments
4. Identify the major factors that influence the demand forecast
5. Determine the appropriate forecasting technique
6. Establish performance and error measures for the forecast

Each organization must use all six steps to forecast effectively.

Understand the Objective of Forecasting

The objective of every forecast is to support decisions that are based on the forecast, so an important first step is to clearly identify these decisions. Examples of such decisions include how much of a particular product to make, how much to inventory, and how much to order. All parties affected by a supply chain decision should be aware of the link between the decision and the forecast. For example, if Wal-Mart plans a promotion in which it will discount detergent during the month of July, this information must be shared with the manufacturer, the transporter, and others involved in filling demand, as they all have decisions to make that will be affected by the forecast of demand. All parties should come up with a common forecast for the promotion and a shared plan of action based on the forecast. Failure to make these decisions jointly may result in either too much or too little product in various stages of the supply chain.

Integrate Demand Planning and Forecasting Throughout the Supply Chain

A company should link its forecast to all planning activities throughout the supply chain. These include capacity planning, production planning, promotion planning, and purchasing, among others. This link should exist at both the information system and the human resource management level. As a variety of functions are affected by the outcomes of the planning process, it is important that all of them are integrated into the forecasting process. In one unfortunately common scenario, a retailer develops forecasts based on promotional activities, whereas a manufacturer, unaware of these promotions, develops a different forecast for their production planning. As a result, the manufacturer may not have enough product for the retailer, ultimately leading to poor customer service.

To accomplish this integration, it is a good idea for a firm to have a cross-functional team, with members from each affected function responsible for forecasting demand—and an even better idea to have members of different companies in the supply chain working together to create a forecast.

Understand and Identify Customer Segments

Here a firm must identify the customer segments the supply chain serves. Customers may be grouped by similarities in service requirements, demand volumes, order frequency, demand volatility, seasonality, and so forth. In general, companies may use different forecasting methods for different segments. A clear understanding of the customer segments facilitates an accurate and simplified approach to forecasting.

Identify Major Factors that Influence the Demand Forecast

Next, a firm must identify major factors that influence the demand forecast. A proper analysis of these factors is central to developing an appropriate forecasting technique. The main factors influencing forecasts are demand, supply, and product-related phenomena.

On the demand side, a company must ascertain whether demand is growing, declining, or has a seasonal pattern. These estimates must be based on demand—not sales data. For example, a supermarket may have promoted a certain brand of cereal in July 2002. As a result, the demand for this cereal may have been high while the demand for other, comparable cereal brands was low in July. The supermarket should not use the sales data from 2002 to estimate that demand for this brand will be high in July 2003, because this will only be the case if the same brand is promoted again in July 2003 and other brands respond as they did the previous year. When making the demand forecast, the supermarket must understand what the demand would have been in the absence of promotion activity and how demand is affected by promotions. A combination of these two pieces of information will allow the supermarket to forecast demand for July 2003 given the promotion activity planned for that year.

On the supply side, a company must consider the available supply sources to decide on the accuracy of the forecast desired. If alternate supply sources with short lead times are available, a highly accurate forecast may not be especially important. However, if only a single supplier with a long lead time is available, an accurate forecast will have great value.

On the product side, a firm must know the number of variants of a product being sold and whether these variants substitute for or complement each other. If demand for a product influences or is influenced by demand for another product, the two forecasts are best made jointly. For example, when a firm introduces an improved version of an existing product, it is likely that the demand for the existing product will decline because new customers will buy the improved version. While the decline in demand for the original product would not be indicated by historical data, the historical demand is still useful in that it allows the firm to estimate the combined total demand for the two versions. Clearly, demand for the two products should be forecast jointly.

Determine the Appropriate Forecasting Technique

In selecting an appropriate forecasting technique, a company should first understand the dimensions that will be relevant to the forecast. These dimensions include geographical area, product groups, and customer groups. The company should understand the differences in demand along each dimension. A firm would be wise to have different forecasts and techniques for each dimension. At this stage, a firm selects an appropriate forecasting method from the four methods discussed earlier—qualitative, time series, causal, or simulation. As mentioned earlier, using a combination of these methods is often effective.

Establish Performance and Error Measures for Forecast

Companies should establish clear performance measures to evaluate the accuracy and timeliness of the forecast. These measures should correlate with the objectives of the business decisions based on these forecasts. For example, consider a mail order company that uses a forecast to place orders with its suppliers up the supply chain. Suppliers send in the orders with a two-month lead time and the products are then sold. The objective of the order is to provide the company with a quantity that minimizes both the amount of extra product left over at the end of the sales season and any lost sales that would result if the product were not available. The mail order company must ensure that the forecast is created at least two months before the start of the sales season because suppliers take two months to send the ordered quantities. At the end of the sales season, the company must compare actual demand to forecasted demand to estimate the accuracy of the forecast. The observed accuracy should be compared with the desired accuracy and the resulting gap should be used to identify corrective actions that the mail order company needs to take.

In the next section, we begin by discussing the techniques for static and adaptive time series forecasting.

7.5 TIME SERIES FORECASTING METHODS

The goal of any forecasting method is to predict the systematic component of demand and estimate the random component. The systematic component of demand data, in its most general form, contains a level, a trend, and a seasonal factor. The systematic component may take a variety of forms, as shown following:

- Multiplicative: Systematic component = level × trend × seasonal factor
- Additive: Systematic component = level + trend + seasonal factor
- Mixed: Systematic component = (level + trend) × seasonal factor

The specific form of the systematic component applicable to a given forecast will depend on the nature of demand. Companies may develop both static and adaptive forecasting methods for each form.

Static Methods

A static method assumes that the estimates of level, trend, and seasonality within the systematic component do not vary as new demand is observed. In this case, we estimate each of these parameters based on historical data and then use the same values for all future forecasts. In this section we discuss a static forecasting method for use when demand has a trend as well as a seasonal component. We assume that the systematic component of demand is mixed, that is,

$$\text{systematic component} = (\text{level} + \text{trend}) \times \text{seasonal factor}.$$

A similar approach can be applied for other forms as well. We begin with a few basic definitions:

L = Estimate of level at $t = 0$ (the deseasonalized demand estimate during Period $t = 0$)

T = Estimate of trend (increase or decrease in demand per period)

S_t = Estimate of seasonal factor for Period t

D_t = Actual demand observed in Period t

F_t = Forecast of demand for Period t

In a static forecasting method, the forecast in Period t for demand in Period $t + l$ is given as follows:

$$F_{t+l} = [L + (t + l)\ T]S_{t+l}. \tag{7.1}$$

We now describe one method for estimating the three parameters L, T, and S. As an example, we consider the demand for rock salt used primarily to melt snow and produced by Tahoe Salt. Tahoe Salt's product is sold through a variety of independent retailers around the Lake Tahoe area of the Sierra Nevada Mountains. In the past, Tahoe Salt has relied on estimates of demand from a sample of their retailers but they have noticed that these retailers always overestimated what they would purchase, leaving Tahoe (and even some retailers) stuck with lots of excess inventory. After meeting with their retailers Tahoe has decided to produce a collaborative forecast. Tahoe Salt now has data on the actual retail sales of their salt and they intend to work with the retailers to create a more accurate forecast with this data. This quarterly demand data for the last three years is shown in Table 7.1 and charted in Figure 7.1.

From Figure 7.1 observe that demand for salt is seasonal with demand increasing from the second quarter of a given year to the first quarter of the following year. The second quarter of each year has the lowest demand of all quarters in the year. Each cycle lasts four quarters and the demand pattern repeats itself every year. There is also a growth trend in the demand, with sales growing over the last three years. The

	TABLE 7.1 Quarterly Demand for Tahoe Salt		
Year	Quarter	Period t	Demand D_t
2000	2	1	8,000
2000	3	2	13,000
2000	4	3	23,000
2001	1	4	34,000
2001	2	5	10,000
2001	3	6	18,000
2001	4	7	23,000
2002	1	8	38,000
2002	2	9	12,000
2002	3	10	13,000
2002	4	11	32,000
2003	1	12	41,000

company estimates that growth will continue in the coming year at historical rates. We now describe how each of the three parameters—level, trend, and seasonal factors—may be estimated. The following two steps are necessary to making this estimation:

1. Deseasonalize demand and run linear regression to estimate level and trend
2. Estimate seasonal factors

Estimating Level and Trend

In this step, the objective is to estimate the level at Period 0 and the trend. Before estimating these two parameters, we must *deseasonalize* the demand data. *Deseasonalized demand* represents the demand that would have been observed in the absence of seasonal fluctuations. The *periodicity p* is the number of periods after which the seasonal cycle repeats itself. For the Tahoe Salt's demand, the pattern repeats every

FIGURE 7.1 Quarterly Demand at Tahoe Salt

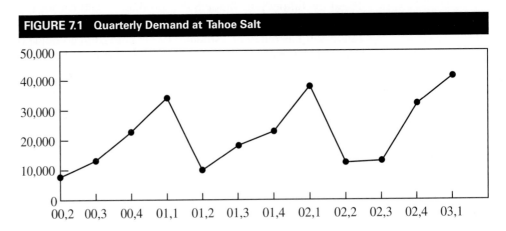

year. Given that we are measuring demand on a quarterly basis, the periodicity for the demand in Table 7.1 is $p = 4$.

To ensure that each season is given equal weight when deseasonalizing demand, we take the average of p consecutive periods of demand. The average of demand from Period $l + 1$ to $l + p$ provides deseasonalized demand for Period $l + (p + 1) / 2$. If p is odd, this method provides deseasonalized demand for an existing period. If p is even, this method provides deseasonalized demand at a point between Period $l + (p / 2)$ and $l + 1 + (p / 2)$. By taking the average of deaseasonalized demand provided by Periods $l + 1$ to $l + p$ and $l + 2$ to $l + p + 1$, we obtain the deseasonalized demand for Period $l + 1 + (p / 2)$. This procedure for obtaining the deseasonalized demand, D_t, for Period t, is formulated as follows:

$$\overline{D_t} = \left[D_{t-(p/2)} + D_{t+(p/2)} + \sum_{i=t+1-(p/2)}^{t-1+(p/2)} 2\, D_i \right] / 2p \text{ for } p \text{ even}$$

$$\sum_{i=t-\lfloor p/2 \rfloor}^{t+\lfloor p/2 \rfloor} D_i / p \text{ for } p \text{ odd} \tag{7.2}$$

In our example, $p = 4$ is even. For $t = 3$, we obtain the deseasonalized demand using Equation (7.2). That demand is as follows:

$$\overline{D_3} = \left\{ D_{t-(p/2)} + D_{t+(p/2)} + \sum_{o=t+1-(p/2)}^{t-1+(p/2)} 2\, D_i \right\} / 2p = \left\{ D_1 + D_5 + \sum_{i=2}^{4} 2\, D_i \right\} / 8$$

With this procedure we can obtain deseasonalized demand between Periods 3 and 10 as shown in Figure 7.2 and Figure 7.3.

FIGURE 7.2 Excel Workbook with Deseasonalized Demand for Tahoe Salt

	A	B	C
1	Period t	Demand D_t	Deseasonalized Demand
2	1	8,000	
3	2	13,000	
4	3	23,000	19,750
5	4	34,000	20,625
6	5	10,000	21,250
7	6	18,000	21,750
8	7	23,000	22,500
9	8	38,000	22,125
10	9	12,000	22,625
11	10	13,000	24,125
12	11	32,000	
13	12	41,000	

Cell	Cell Formula	Equation	Copied to
C4	=(B2+B6+2*SUM(B3:B5))/8	7.2	C5:C11

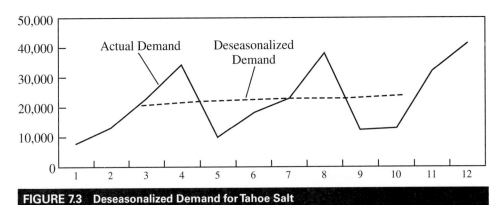

FIGURE 7.3 Deseasonalized Demand for Tahoe Salt

Once demand has been deseasonalized, it is either growing or declining at a steady rate. Thus, there is a linear relationship between the deseasonalized demand, $\overline{D_t}$, and time. This relationship is defined by the following:

$$\overline{D_t} = L + Tt \qquad\qquad (7.3)$$

Note that in Equation 7.3, we use $\overline{D_t}$ to represent deseasonalized demand and not the actual demand in Period t, L represents the *level* or deseasonalized demand at Period 0, and T represents the rate of growth of deseasonalized demand or *trend*. We need to estimate the values of L and T for the deseasonalized demand given in Figure 7.2. We can estimate these two quantities using linear regression with deseasonalized demand in Figure 7.2 as the dependent variable and time as the independent variable. Such a regression can be run using Excel (Tools | Data Analysis | Regression). This sequence of commands opens the Regression dialog box in Excel. For the Tahoe Salt workbook in Table 7.2, in the resulting dialog box we enter

Input Y Range: C4:C11
Input X Range: A4:A11

and click the OK button. A new sheet containing the results of the regression opens up. This new sheet contains estimates for both the initial level L and the trend T. The initial level, L, is obtained as the *intercept coefficient* and the trend, T, is obtained as the *X variable coefficient* (or the slope) from the sheet containing the regression results. For the Tahoe Salt example, we obtain $L = 18{,}439$ and $T = 524$. For this example, deseasonalized demand $\overline{D_t}$ for any Period t is thus given by the following:

$$\overline{D_t} = 18{,}439 + 524t. \qquad\qquad (7.4)$$

Note that it is not appropriate to run a linear regression between the original demand data and time to estimate level and trend because the original demand data are not linear and the resulting linear regression will not be accurate. The demand must be deseasonalized before we run the linear regression.

Estimating Seasonal Factors

We can now obtain deseasonalized demand for each period using Equation 7.4. The seasonal factor $\overline{S_t}$ for Period t is the ratio of actual demand D to deseasonalized demand and is given as follows:

$$\overline{S_t} = D_t / \overline{D_t} \tag{7.5}$$

For the Tahoe Salt example, the deseasonalized demand estimated using Equation 7.4 and the seasonal factors estimated using Equation 7.5 are shown in Figure 7.4.

Given the periodicity, p, we can obtain the seasonal factor for a given period by averaging seasonal factors that correspond to similar periods. For example, if we have a periodicity of $p = 4$, Periods 1, 5, and 9 will have similar seasonal factors. The seasonal factor for these periods is obtained as the average of the three seasonal factors. Given r seasonal cycles in the data, for all periods of the form $pt + i, 1 \leq i \leq p$ we obtain the seasonal factor as follows:

$$S_i = \left(\sum_{j=0}^{r-1} \overline{S}_{jp+i} \right) / r \tag{7.6}$$

FIGURE 7.4   Deseasonalized Demand and Seasonal Factors for Tahoe Salt

	A	B	C	D
1	Period t	Demand D_t	Deseasonalized Demand (Eqn 7.4) $\overline{D_t}$	Seasonal Factor (Eqn 7.5) $\overline{S_t}$
2	1	8,000	18,963	0.42
3	2	13,000	19,487	0.67
4	3	23,000	20,011	1.15
5	4	34,000	20,535	1.66
6	5	10,000	21,059	0.47
7	6	18,000	21,583	0.83
8	7	23,000	22,107	1.04
9	8	38,000	22,631	1.68
10	9	12,000	23,155	0.52
11	10	13,000	23,679	0.55
12	11	32,000	24,203	1.32
13	12	41,000	24,727	1.66

Cell	Cell Formula	Equation	Copied to
C2	=18439+A2*524	7.4	C3:C13
D2	=B2/C2	7.5	D3:D13

For the Tahoe Salt example, a total of 12 periods and a periodicity of $p = 4$ implies that there are $r = 3$ seasonal cycles in the data. We obtain seasonal factors using Equation 7.6 as

$$S_1 = (\bar{S}_1 + \bar{S}_5 + \bar{S}_9) / 3 = (0.42 + 0.47 + 0.52) / 3 = 0.47,$$
$$S_2 = (\bar{S}_2 + \bar{S}_6 + \bar{S}_{10}) / 3 = (0.67 + 0.83 + 0.55) / 3 = 0.68,$$
$$S_3 = (\bar{S}_3 + \bar{S}_7 + \bar{S}_{11}) / 3 = (1.15 + 1.04 + 1.32) / 3 = 1.17,$$
$$S_4 = (\bar{S}_4 + \bar{S}_8 + \bar{S}_{12}) / 3 = (1.66 + 1.68 + 1.66) / 3 = 1.67.$$

At this stage, we have estimated the level, trend, and all seasonal factors. We can now obtain the forecast for the next four quarters using Equation 7.1. In the example, the forecast for the next four periods using the static forecasting method is given by

$$F_{13} = (L + 13T) \, S_{13} = (18{,}439 + 13 \times 524)0.47 = 11{,}868,$$
$$F_{14} = (L + 14T) \, S_{14} = (18{,}439 + 14 \times 524)0.68 = 17{,}527,$$
$$F_{15} = (L + 15T) \, S_{15} = (18{,}439 + 15 \times 524)1.17 = 30{,}770,$$
$$F_{16} = (L + 16T) \, S_{16} = (18{,}439 + 16 \times 524)1.67 = 44{,}794.$$

Tahoe Salt and its retailers now have a more accurate forecast of demand. Without the sharing of sell-through information between the retailers and the manufacturer, this supply chain would have a less accurate forecast and a variety of production and inventory inefficiencies would result.

Adaptive Forecasting

In adaptive forecasting, the estimates of level, trend, and seasonality are updated after each demand observation. We now discuss a basic framework and several methods that can be used for adaptive forecasting. The framework is provided in the most general setting when the systematic component of demand data contains a level, a trend, and a seasonal factor. The framework we present is for the case when the systematic component has the mixed form. It can, however, easily be modified for the other two cases. The framework can also be specialized for the case where the systematic component contains no seasonality or trend. We assume that we have a set of historical data for n periods and that demand is seasonal with periodicity p. Given quarterly data, where the pattern repeats itself every year, we would have a periodicity of $p = 4$.

We begin by defining a few terms:

L_t = Estimate of level at the end of Period t
T_t = Estimate of trend at the end of Period t
S_t = Estimate of seasonal factor for Period t
F_t = Forecast of demand for Period t (made in Period $t - 1$ or earlier)
D_t = Actual demand observed in Period t
E_t = Forecast error in Period t

In adaptive methods, the forecast for Period $t + l$ in Period t is given as follows:

$$F_{t+l} = (L_t + lT_t) \, S_{t+l}. \tag{7.7}$$

The four steps in the adaptive forecasting framework are as follows:

1. *Initialize:* Compute initial estimates of the level (L_0), trend (T_0) and seasonal factors ($S_1, ..., S_p$) from the given data. This is done exactly as in the static forecasting method discussed earlier in the chapter.

2. *Forecast:* Given the estimates in Period *t,* forecast demand for Period *t* + 1 using Equation 7.7. Our first forecast is for Period 1 and is made with the estimates of level, trend, and seasonal factor at Period 0.
3. *Estimate error:* Record the actual demand D_{t+1} for Period *t* + 1 and compute the error E_{t+1} in the forecast for Period *t* + 1 as the difference between the forecast and the actual demand. The error for Period *t* + 1 is stated as follows:

$$E_{t+1} = F_{t+1} - D_{t+1}. \tag{7.8}$$

4. *Modify estimates:* Modify the estimates of level (L_{t+1}), trend (T_{t+1}), and seasonal factor (S_{t+p+1}), given the error E_{t+1} in the forecast. It is desirable that the modification be such that if the demand is lower than forecast, the estimates are revised downward, while if the demand is higher than forecast, the estimates are revised upward.

The revised estimates in Period *t* + 1 are then used to make a forecast for Period *t* + 2 and Steps 2, 3, and 4 are repeated until all historical data up to Period *n* have been covered. The estimates at Period *n* are then used to forecast future demand.

We now discuss various adaptive forecasting methods. The method that is most appropriate depends on the characteristic of demand and the composition of the systematic component of demand. In each case we assume the period under consideration to be *t*.

Moving Average

We use this method when demand has no observable trend or seasonality. In this case

systematic component of demand = level.

In this method, we estimate the level in Period *t* as the average demand over the most recent *N* periods. This represents an *N*-period moving average. Thus, we have the following:

$$L_t = (D_t + D_{t-1} + ... + D_{t-N+1})/N. \tag{7.9}$$

The current forecast for all future periods is the same and is based on the current estimate of level. The forecast is stated as follows:

$$F_{t+1} = L_t \text{ and } F_{t+n} = L_t. \tag{7.10}$$

After observing the demand for Period *t* + 1, we revise the estimates as follows:

$$L_{t+1} = (D_{t+1} + D_t + ... + D_{t-N+2})/N, F_{t+2} = L_{t+1};$$

that is, to compute the new moving average, we simply add the latest observation and drop the oldest one. The revised moving average serves as the next forecast. The moving average corresponds to giving the last *N* periods of data equal weight when forecasting and ignoring all data older than this new moving average. As we increase *N*, the moving average becomes less responsive to the most recently observed demand. We illustrate the use of the moving average in Example 7.1.

Example 7.1: Consider the demand data for Tahoe Salt in Table 7.1. Forecast demand for Period 5 using a four-period moving average.

Analysis: We make the forecast for Period 5 in Period 4. Thus, assume the current period to be $t = 4$. Our first objective is to estimate the level in Period 4. Using Equation (7.9), with $N = 4$, we obtain

$$L_4 = (D_4 + D_3 + D_2 + D_1)/4 = (34{,}000 + 23{,}000 + 13{,}000 + 8{,}000)/4 = 19{,}500.$$

The forecast of demand for Period 5, using Equation (7.10), is expressed as

$$F_5 = L_4 = 19{,}500.$$

As demand in Period 5, D_5 is 10,000, we have a forecast error for Period 5 of

$$E_5 = F_5 - D_5 = 19{,}500 - 10{,}000 = 9{,}500.$$

After observing demand in Period 5, the revised estimate of level for Period 5 is given by

$$L_5 = (D_5 + D_4 + D_3 + D_2)/4 = (10{,}000 + 34{,}000 + 23{,}000 + 13{,}000)/4 = 20{,}000.$$

Simple Exponential Smoothing

This method is appropriate when demand has no observable trend or seasonality. In this case

systematic component of demand = level.

The initial estimate of level, L_0, is taken to be the average of all historical data because demand has been assumed to have no observable trend or seasonality. Given demand data for Periods 1 though n, we have the following:

$$L_0 = \frac{1}{n}\sum_{i=1}^{n} D_i \tag{7.11}$$

The current forecast for all future periods is equal to the current estimate of level and is given as follows:

$$F_{t+1} = L_t \text{ and } F_{t+n} = L_t. \tag{7.12}$$

After observing the demand, D_{t+1}, for Period $t + 1$, we revise the estimate of the level as follows:

$$L_{t+1} = \alpha D_{t+1} + (1 - \alpha)L_t \tag{7.13}$$

where α is a smoothing constant for the level, $0 < \alpha < 1$. The revised value of the level is a weighted average of the observed value of the level (D_{t+1}) in Period $t + 1$ and the old estimate of the level (L_t) in Period t. Using Equation 7.13 we can express the level in a given period as a function of the current demand and the level in the previous period. We can thus rewrite Equation 7.13 as

$$L_{t+1} = \sum_{n=0}^{t+1} \alpha(1-\alpha)^n D_{t+1-n}$$

The current estimate of the level is a weighted average of all of the past observations of demand, with recent observations weighted higher than older observations. A higher value of α corresponds to a forecast that is more responsive to recent observations, whereas a lower value of α represents a more stable forecast that is less responsive to recent observations. We illustrate the use of exponential smoothing in Example 7.2.

Example 7.2: Consider the Tahoe Salt demand data in Table 7.1. Forecast demand for Period 1 using simple exponential smoothing.

Analysis: In this case we have demand data for $n = 12$ periods. Using Equation (7.11), the initial estimate of level is expressed by

$$L_0 = \frac{1}{12}\sum_{i=1}^{12} D_i = 22,083$$

The forecast for Period 1 (using Equation 7.12) is thus given by

$$F_1 = L_0 = 22,083.$$

The observed demand for Period 1 is $D_1 = 8,000$. The forecast error for Period 1 is given by

$$E_1 = F_1 - D_1 = 22,083 - 8,000 = 14,083.$$

Assuming a smoothing constant $\alpha = 0.1$, the revised estimate of level for Period 1 using simple exponential smoothing (Equation 7.13) is given by

$$L_1 = \alpha D_1 + (1 - \alpha)L_0 = 0.1 \times 8,000 + 0.9 \times 22,083 = 20,675.$$

Observe that the estimate of level for Period 1 is lower than for Period 0 because the demand in Period 1 is lower than the forecast for Period 1.

Trend Corrected Exponential Smoothing (Holt's Model)

This method is appropriate when demand is assumed to have a level and a trend in the systematic component but no seasonality. In this case, we have the following:

systematic component of demand = level + trend.

We obtain an initial estimate of level and trend by running a linear regression between demand D_t and time Period t of the form

$$D_t = at + b.$$

In this case, running a linear regression between demand and time periods is appropriate because we have assumed that demand has a trend but no seasonality. The underlying relationship between demand and time is thus linear. The constant b measures the estimate of demand at Period $t = 0$ and is our estimate of the initial level L_0. The slope a measures the rate of change in demand per period and is our initial estimate of the trend T_0.

In Period t, given estimates of level L_t and trend T_t, the forecast for future periods is expressed as follows:

$$F_{t+1} = L_t + T_t, \text{ and } F_{t+n} = L_t + nT_t. \tag{7.14}$$

After observing demand for Period t, we revise the estimates for level and trend as follows:

$$L_{t+1} = \alpha D_{t+1} + (1 - \alpha)(L_t + T_t), \tag{7.15}$$
$$T_{t+1} = \beta(L_{t+1} - L_t) + (1 - \beta)T_t, \tag{7.16}$$

where α is a smoothing constant for the level, $0 < \alpha < 1$, and β is a smoothing constant for the trend, $0 < \beta < 1$. Observe that in each of the two updates, the revised estimate (of level or trend) is a weighted average of the observed value and the old estimate. We illustrate the use of Holt's model in Example 7.3.

Example 7.3: Consider the Tahoe Salt demand data in Table 7.1. Forecast demand for Period 1 using trend corrected exponential smoothing.

Analysis: The first step is to obtain initial estimates of level and trend using linear regression. We first run a linear regression (using the Excel tool Regression Tools|Data Analysis| Regression) between demand and time periods. For the Tahoe Salt workbook in Figure 7.2, in the Regression dialog box we enter

Input Y Range: B2:B11

Input X Range: A2:A11

and click the OK button. A new sheet containing the results of the regression opens up. The estimate of initial level L_0 is obtained as the *intercept coefficient* and the trend T_0 is obtained as the *X variable coefficient* (or the slope). For the Tahoe Salt example, we obtain

$$L_0 = 12,015 \text{ and } T_0 = 1,549.$$

The forecast for Period 1 (using Equation 7.14) is thus given by the following

$$F_1 = L_0 + T_0 = 12,015 + 1,549 = 13,564.$$

The observed demand for Period 1 is $D_1 = 8,000$. The error for Period 1 is thus given by the following

$$E_1 = F_1 - D_1 = 13,564 - 8,000 = 5,564.$$

Assuming smoothing constants $\alpha = 0.1$, $\beta = 0.2$, the revised estimate of level and trend for Period 1 using trend corrected exponential smoothing (Equations 7.15 and 7.16) is given by

$$L_1 = \alpha D_1 + (1 - \alpha)(L_0 + T_0) = 0.1 \times 8,000 + 0.9 \times 13,564 = 13,008,$$

$$T_1 = \beta(L_1 - L_0) + (1 - \beta)T_0 = 0.2 \times (13,008 - 12,015) + 0.8 \times 1,549 = 1,438.$$

Observe that the initial estimates have overforecast demand for Period 1. As a result, our updates have decreased the estimate of level for Period 1 from 13,564 to 13,008 and the estimate of trend from 1,549 to 1,438. Using Equation 7.14, we thus obtain the following forecast for Period 2:

$$F_2 = L_1 + T_1 = 13,008 + 1,438 = 14,446.$$

Trend and Seasonality Corrected Exponential Smoothing (Winter's Model)

This method is appropriate when the systematic component of demand is assumed to have a level, a trend, and a seasonal factor. In this case we have

systematic component of demand = (level + trend) × seasonal factor.

Assume periodicity of demand to be p. To begin, we need initial estimates of level (L_0), trend (T_0), and seasonal factors $(S_1, ..., S_p)$. We obtain these estimates using the procedure for static forecasting described earlier in the chapter.

In Period t, given estimates of level, L_t, trend, T_t, and seasonal factors, S_t, ..., S_{t+p-1}, the forecast for future periods is given by the following:

$$F_{t+1} = (L_t + T_t)S_{t+1} \text{ and } F_{t+l} = (L_t + lT_t)S_{t+l}. \tag{7.17}$$

On observing demand for Period $t + 1$ we revise the estimates for level, trend, and seasonal factors as follows:

$$L_{t+1} = \alpha(D_{t+1}/S_{t+1}) + (1 - \alpha)(L_t+T_t), \tag{7.18}$$
$$T_{t+1} = \beta(L_{t+1} - L_t) + (1 - \beta)T_t, \tag{7.19}$$
$$S_{t+p+1} = \gamma(D_{t+1} / L_{t+1}) + (1 - \gamma)S_{t+1}, \tag{7.20}$$

where α is a smoothing constant for the level, $0 < \alpha < 1$; β is a smoothing constant for the trend, $0 < \beta < 1$; and γ is a smoothing constant for the seasonal factor, $0 < \gamma < 1$. Observe that in each of the updates (level, trend, or seasonal factor), the revised estimate is a weighted average of the observed value and the old estimate. We illustrate the use of Winter's model in Example 7.4.

Example 7.4:   Consider the Tahoe Salt demand data in Table 7.1. Forecast demand for Period 1 using trend and seasonality corrected exponential smoothing.

Analysis: We obtain the initial estimates of level, trend, and seasonal factors exactly as in the static case. They are expressed as follows:

$$L_0 = 18,439, T_0 = 524, S_1 = 0.47, S_2 = 0.68, S_3 = 1.17, S_4 = 1.67.$$

The forecast for Period 1(using Equation 7.17) is thus given by

$$F_1 = (L_0 + T_0)S_1 = (18,439 + 524)0.47 = 8,913.$$

The observed demand for Period 1 is $D_1 = 8,000$. The forecast error for Period 1 is thus given by

$$E_1 = F_1 - D_1 = 8,913 - 8,000 = 913.$$

Assuming smoothing constants $\alpha = 0.1, \beta = 0.2, \gamma = 0.1$, the revised estimate of level and trend for Period 1 and seasonal factor for Period 5, using trend and seasonality corrected exponential smoothing (using Equations 7.18, 7.19, 7.20), is given by the following:

$$L_1 = \alpha(D_1/S_1) + (1 - \alpha)(L_0 + T_0) = 0.1 \times (8,000/0.47) + 0.9 \times (18,439 + 524) = 18,769,$$
$$T_1 = \beta(L_1 - L_0) + (1 - \beta)T_0 = 0.2 \times (18,769 - 18,439) + 0.8 \times 524 = 485,$$
$$S_5 = \gamma(D_1 / L_1) + (1 - \gamma)S_1 = 0.1(8,000 / 18,769) + 0.9 \times 0.47 = 0.47.$$

The forecast of demand for Period 2 (using Equation 7.17) is thus given by

$$F_2 = (L_1 + T_1)S_2 = (18,769 + 485)0.68 = 13,093.$$

The forecasting methods discussed earlier and the situations in which they are generally applicable are shown following.

Forecasting Method	*Applicability*
Moving average	No trend or seasonality
Simple exponential smoothing	No trend or seasonality
Holt's model	Trend but no seasonality
Winter's model	Trend and seasonality

If Tahoe Salt were to use an adaptive forecasting method for the sell-through data obtained from its retailers, Winter's model would be the best choice as their demand undergoes both a trend and seasonality.

If we did not know that Tahoe Salt experienced both a trend and seasonality, how would we find out? Forecast error helps identify instances in which the forecasting method being used is inappropriate. In the next section, we describe the way in which a manager can estimate and use forecast error.

7.6 MEASURES OF FORECAST ERROR

As mentioned earlier, every demand has a random component. A good forecasting method should capture the systematic component of demand but not the random component. The random component manifests itself in the form of a forecast error. Forecast errors contain valuable information and must be analyzed carefully. Managers perform a thorough error analysis on a forecast for the following two key reasons:

1. Managers can use error analysis to determine whether the current forecasting method is accurately predicting the systematic component of demand. For example, if a forecasting method consistently results in a positive error, the manager can assume that the forecasting method is overpredicting the systematic component and take appropriate corrective action.

2. Managers estimate forecast error because any contingency plan must account for such an error. For example, consider a mail order company that has a supplier in the Far East with whom orders are placed two months in advance and another local supplier who supplies with one week's notice. The local supplier is more expensive, whereas the Far East supplier costs less. The mail order company wants to contract a certain amount of contingency capacity with the local supplier to be used if the demand exceeds the quantity the Far East supplier provides. The decision regarding the quantity of local capacity to contract is closely linked to the size of the forecast error.

As long as observed errors are within historical error estimates, firms can continue to use their current forecasting method. If a firm observes an error that is well beyond historical estimates, this finding may indicate that the forecasting method it is using is no longer appropriate. If all of a firm's forecasts tend to consistently over- or underestimate demand, this may be another signal that the firm should change its forecasting method.

As defined earlier, forecast error for Period t is given by E_t, where the following holds:

$$E_t = F_t - D_t.$$

That is, the error in Period t is the difference between the forecast for Period t and the actual demand in Period t. It is important that a manager estimate the error of a forecast made at least as far in advance as the lead time required for the manager to take whatever action the forecast is to be used for. For example, if a forecast will be used to determine an order size and the supplier's lead time is six months, a manager should estimate the error for a forecast made six months before demand arises. In a situation with a six-month lead time, there is no point in estimating errors for a forecast made one month in advance.

One measure of forecast error is the *mean squared error* (MSE), where the following holds:

$$MSE_n = \frac{1}{n} \sum_{t=1}^{n} E_t^2 \qquad (7.21)$$

The MSE can be related to the variance of the forecast error. In effect, we estimate that the random component of demand has a mean of 0 and a variance of MSE.

Define the *absolute deviation* in Period t, A_t to be the absolute value of the error in Period t; that is,

$$A_t = |E_t|.$$

Define the *mean absolute deviation* (MAD) to be the average of the absolute deviation over all periods, as expressed by

$$MAD_n = \frac{1}{n} \sum_{t=1}^{n} A_t \qquad (7.22)$$

The MAD can be used to estimate the standard deviation of the random component assuming that the random component is normally distributed. In this case the standard deviation of the random component is as follows:

$$\sigma = 1.25 \ MAD. \qquad (7.23)$$

We then estimate that the mean of the random component is 0 and the standard deviation of the random component of demand is σ.

The *Mean Absolute Percentage Error* (MAPE) is the average absolute error as a percentage of demand and is given by

$$MAPE_n = \frac{\sum_{t=1}^{n} \left| \frac{E_t}{D_t} \right| 100}{n} \qquad (7.24)$$

To determine whether a forecast method consistently over- or underestimates demand, we can use the sum of forecast errors to evaluate the *bias*, where the following holds:

$$bias_n = \sum_{t=1}^{n} E_t \qquad (7.25)$$

The bias will fluctuate around 0 if the error is truly random and not biased one way or the other. Ideally, if we plot all the errors, the slope of the best straight line passing through should be 0.

The tracking signal (TS) is the ratio of the bias and the MAD and is given as follows:

$$TS_t = \frac{bias_t}{MAD_t} \qquad (7.26)$$

If the TS at any period is outside the range ±6, this is a signal that the forecast is biased and is either underforecasting (TS below –6) or overforecasting (TS above +6). In this case, a firm may decide to choose a new forecasting method. One instance in which a large negative TS will result is when demand has a growth trend and the manager is using a forecasting method such as moving average. Because trend is not included, the average of historical demand will always be lower than future demand. The negative TS will detect that the forecasting method consistently underestimates demand and alert the manager.

7.7 FORECASTING DEMAND AT TAHOE SALT

Recall the Tahoe Salt example earlier in the chapter with the historical sell-through demand from their retailers shown in Table 7.1. The demand data are also shown in column B of Figure 7.5. Tahoe Salt is currently negotiating contracts with suppliers for the four quarters between the second quarter of 2003 and the first quarter of 2004. An important input into this negotiation is the forecast of demand over that period. As we mentioned, Tahoe Salt and their retailers are building collaborative forecasts. To this end, they have put together a team consisting of two sales managers from the retailers and the vice president of operations for Tahoe Salt to come up with this forecast. The forecasting team decides to apply each of the adaptive forecasting methods discussed in this chapter to the given historical data. Their goal is to select the most appropriate forecasting method and then use it to forecast demand for the next four quarters. The team decides to select the forecasting method based on the errors that result when each method is used on the 12 quarters of historical demand data.

Demand in this case clearly has both a trend and seasonality in the systematic component. Thus the team initially expects Winter's model to produce the best forecast. They decide to test this hypothesis by using each of the methods to make the forecast.

Moving Average

The forecasting team initially decides to test a four-period moving average for the forecasting. All calculations are shown in Figure 7.5 and are as discussed in the moving average method section earlier in this chapter. The team uses Equation 7.3 to estimate level and Equation 7.4 to forecast demand.

	Period t	Demand D_t	Level L_t	Forecast F_t	Error E_t	Absolute Error A_t	Squared Error MSE_t	MAD_t	% Error	$MAPE_t$	TS_t
2	1	8,000									
3	2	13,000									
4	3	23,000									
5	4	34,000	19,500								
6	5	10,000	20,000	19,500	9,500	9,500	90,250,000	9,500	95	95	1.00
7	6	18,000	21,250	20,000	2,000	2,000	47,125,000	5,750	11	53	2.00
8	7	23,000	21,250	21,250	-1,750	1,750	32,437,500	4,417	8	38	2.21
9	8	38,000	22,250	21,250	-16,750	16,750	94,468,750	7,500	44	39	-0.93
10	9	12,000	22,750	22,250	10,250	10,250	96,587,500	8,050	85	49	0.40
11	10	13,000	21,500	22,750	9,750	9,750	96,333,333	8,333	75	53	1.56
12	11	32,000	23,750	21,500	-10,500	10,500	98,321,429	8,643	33	50	0.29
13	12	41,000	24,500	23,750	-17,250	17,250	123,226,563	9,719	42	49	-1.52

Cell	Cell Formula	Equation	Copied to
C6	=Average(B3:B6)	7.9	C7:C13
D6	=C5	7.10	D7:D13
E6	=D6-B6	7.8	E7:E13
F6	=Abs(E6)		F7:F13
G6	=Sumsq($E$6:E6)/(A6-4)	7.21	G7:G13
H6	=Sum($F$6:F6)/(A6-4)	7.22	H7:H13
I6	=100*(F6/B6)		I7:I13
J6	=Average($I$6:I6)	7.24	J7:J13
K6	=Sum($E$6:E6)/ H6	7.26	K7:K13

FIGURE 7.5   Tahoe Salt Forecasts Using Four-Period Moving Average

As indicated by column K in Figure 7.5, the TS is well within the ±6 range, which indicates that the forecast using the four-period moving average does not contain any significant bias. It does, however, have a fairly large MAD of 9,719 and MAPE of 49 percent. From Figure 7.5, observe that

$$L_{12} = 24,500.$$

Thus, using a four-period moving average, the forecast for Periods 13 through 16 (using Equation 7.10) is given by the following:

$$F_{13} = F_{14} = F_{15} = F_{16} = L_{12} = 24,500.$$

Given that the MAD is 9,719, the estimate of standard deviation of forecast error, using a four-period moving average, is $1.25 \times 9,719 = 12,148$. In this case, the standard deviation of forecast error is fairly large relative to the size of the forecast.

Simple Exponential Smoothing

The forecasting team next uses a simple exponential smoothing approach with $\alpha = 0.1$ to forecast demand. This method is also tested on the 12 quarters of historical data. Using Equation 7.11, the team estimates the initial level for Period 0 to be the average demand for Periods 1 through 12. The initial level is the average of the demand entries in cells B2 to B14 in Figure 7.6 and results in

$$L_0 = 22{,}083.$$

FIGURE 7.6 Tahoe Salt Forecasts Using Simple Exponential Smoothing

	A	B	C	D	E	F	G	H	I	J	K
1	Period t	Demand D_t	Level L_t	Forecast F_t	Error E_t	Absolute Error A_t	Mean Squared Error MSE_t	MAD_t	% Error	$MAPE_t$	TS_t
2	0		22,083								
3	1	8,000	20,675	22,083	14,083	14,083	198,340,278	14,083	176	176	1
4	2	13,000	19,908	20,675	7,675	7,675	128,622,951	10,879	59	118	2
5	3	23,000	20,217	19,908	-3,093	3,093	88,936,486	8,284	13	83	2
6	4	34,000	21,595	20,217	-13,783	13,783	114,196,860	9,659	41	72	0.51
7	5	10,000	20,436	21,595	11,595	11,595	118,246,641	10,046	116	81	1.64
8	6	18,000	20,192	20,436	2,436	2,436	99,527,532	8,777	14	70	2.15
9	7	23,000	20,473	20,192	-2,808	2,808	86,435,714	7,925	12	62	2.03
10	8	38,000	22,226	20,473	-17,527	17,527	114,031,550	9,125	46	60	-0.16
11	9	12,000	21,203	22,226	10,226	10,226	112,979,315	9,247	85	62	0.95
12	10	13,000	20,383	21,203	8,203	8,203	108,410,265	9,143	63	63	1.86
13	11	32,000	21,544	20,383	-11,617	11,617	110,824,074	9,368	36	60	0.58
14	12	41,000	23,490	21,544	-19,456	19,456	133,132,065	10,208	47	59	-1.38

Cell	Cell Formula	Equation	Copied to
C3	=0.1*B3+(1-0.1)*C2	7.11	C4:C14
D3	=C2	7.12	D4:D14
E3	=D3-B3	7.8	E4:E14
F3	=Abs(E3)		F4:F14
G3	=Sumsq($E$3:E3)/A3	7.21	G4:G14
H3	=Sum($F$3:F3)/A3	7.22	H4:H14
I3	=100*(F3/B3)		I4:I14
J3	=Average($I$3:I3)	7.24	J4:J14
K3	=Sum($E$3:E3)/H3	7.26	K4:K14

The team then uses Equation 7.12 to forecast demand for the succeeding period. The estimate of level is updated each period using Equation 7.13. The results are shown in Figure 7.6.

As indicated by the TS that ranges from −1.38 to 2.25, the forecast using simple exponential smoothing with $\alpha = 0.1$ does not indicate any significant bias. However, it has a fairly large MAD of 10,208 and MAPE of 59 percent. From Figure 7.6 observe that

$$L_{12} = 23,490.$$

Thus, the forecast for the next four quarters (using Equation 7.12) is given by

$$F_{13} = F_{14} = F_{15} = F_{16} = L_{12} = 23,490.$$

In this case, MAD_{12} is 10,208 and $MAPE_{12}$ is 59 percent. Thus, the estimate of standard deviation of forecast error using simple exponential smoothing is $1.25 \times 10,208 = 12,761$. In this case, the standard deviation of forecast error is fairly large relative to the size of the forecast.

Trend Corrected Exponential Smoothing (Holt's Model)

The team next investigates the use of the Holt's model. In this case the systematic component of demand is given by

$$\text{systematic component of demand} = \text{level} + \text{trend}.$$

The team applies the methodology discussed earlier. As a first step, they estimate the level at Period 0 and the initial trend. As described earlier in Example 7.3, this estimate is obtained by running a linear regression between demand, D_t, and time, Period t. From the regression of the available data, the team obtains the following:

$$L_0 = 12,015 \text{ and } T_0 = 1,549.$$

The team now applies Holt's model with $\alpha = 0.1$ and $\beta = 0.2$ to obtain the forecasts for each of the 12 quarters for which demand data are available. They make the forecast using Equation 7.14, they update level using Equation 7.15, and they update the trend using Equation 7.16. The results are shown in Figure 7.7.

As indicated by a TS that ranges from −2.15 to 1.85, trend corrected exponential smoothing with $\alpha = 0.1$ and $\beta = 0.2$ does not seem to significantly over- or underforecast. However, the forecast has a fairly large MAD of 8,836 and MAPE of 52 percent. From Figure 7.7 observe that

$$L_{12} = 30,443 \text{ and } T_{12} = 1,541.$$

	A	B	C	D	E	F	G	H	I	J	K	L
1	Period t	Demand D_t	Level L_t	Trend T_t	Forecast F_t	Error E_t	Absolute Error A_t	Mean Squared Error MSE_t	MAD_t	% Error	$MAPE_t$	TS_t
2	0		12,015	1,549								
3	1	8,000	13,008	1,438	13,564	5,564	5,564	30,958,096	5,564	70	70	1
4	2	13,000	14,301	1,409	14,445	1,445	1,445	16,523,523	3,505	11	40	2
5	3	23,000	16,439	1,555	15,710	-7,290	7,290	28,732,318	4,767	32	37	0
6	4	34,000	19,594	1,875	17,993	-16,007	16,007	85,603,146	7,577	47	39.86	-2.15
7	5	10,000	20,322	1,645	21,469	11,469	11,469	94,788,701	8,355	115	54.83	-0.58
8	6	18,000	21,570	1,566	21,967	3,967	3,967	81,613,705	7,624	22	49.36	-0.11
9	7	23,000	23,123	1,563	23,137	137	137	69,957,267	6,554	1	42.39	-0.11
10	8	38,000	26,018	1,830	24,686	-13,314	13,314	83,369,836	7,399	35	41.48	-1.90
11	9	12,000	26,262	1,513	27,847	15,847	15,847	102,010,079	8,338	132	51.54	0.22
12	10	13,000	26,298	1,217	27,775	14,775	14,775	113,639,348	8,981	114	57.75	1.85
13	11	32,000	27,963	1,307	27,515	-4,485	4,485	105,137,395	8,573	14	53.78	1.41
14	12	41,000	30,443	1,541	29,270	-11,730	11,730	107,841,864	8,836	29	51.68	0.04

Cell	Cell Formula	Equation	Copied to
C3	=0.1*B3+(1-0.1)*(C2+D2)	7.15	C4:C14
D3	=0.2(C3-C2)+(1-0.2)D2	7.16	D4:D14
E3	=C2+D2	7.14	E4:E14
F3	=E3-B3	7.8	F4:F14
G3	=Abs(F3)		G4:G14
H3	=Sumsq($F$3:F3)/A3	7.21	H4:H14
I3	=Sum($F$3:F3)/A3	7.22	I4:I14
J3	=100*(G3/B3)		J4:J14
K3	=Average($J$3:J3)	7.24	K4:K14
L3	=Sum($G$3:G3)/I3	7.26	L4:L14

FIGURE 7.7   Trend Corrected Exponential Smoothing

Thus, using Holt's method (Equation 7.14), the forecast for the next four periods is given by the following:[1]

$$F_{13} = L_{12} + T_{12} = 30{,}443 + 1{,}541 = 31{,}984,$$
$$F_{14} = L_{12} + 2T_{12} = 30{,}443 + 2 \times 1{,}541 = 33{,}525,$$
$$F_{15} = L_{12} + 3T_{12} = 30{,}443 + 3 \times 1{,}541 = 35{,}066,$$
$$F_{16} = L_{12} + 4T_{12} = 30{,}443 + 4 \times 1{,}541 = 36{,}607.$$

---

[1]Due to rounding, calculations done with only significant digits shown in the text may yield a different result. This is the case throughout the book.

In this case, MAD = 8,836. Thus the estimate of standard deviation of forecast error using Holt's model with α = 0.1 and β = 0.2 is 1.25 × 8,836 = 11,045. In this case, the standard deviation of forecast error relative to the size of the forecast is somewhat smaller than it was with the previous two methods. However, it is still fairly large.

Trend and Seasonality Corrected Exponential Smoothing (Winter's Model)

The team next investigates the use of Winter's model to make the forecast. Winter's model assumes that the systematic component of demand is given by

$$\text{systematic component of demand} = (\text{level} + \text{trend}) \times \text{seasonal factor}.$$

The team applies the methodology as we discussed earlier. As a first step they need to estimate the level and trend for Period 0, and seasonal factors for Periods 1 through p = 4. This estimation is done by first deseasonalizing the demand and then estimating initial level and trend by running regression between deseasonalized demand and time. This information is then used to estimate the seasonal factors. For the demand data in Figure 7.2, as discussed in Example 7.4, the team obtains the following:

$$L_0 = 18{,}439, T_0 = 524, S_1 = 0.47, S_2 = 0.68, S_3 = 1.17, S_4 = 1.67.$$

They then apply Winter's model with α = 0.05, β = 0.1, γ = 0.1 to obtain the forecasts. All calculations are shown in Figure 7.8. The team makes forecasts using Equation 7.17, they update level using Equation 7.18, they update the trend using Equation 7.19, and they update seasonal factors using Equation 7.20.

In this case the MAD of 1,469 and MAPE of 8 percent are significantly lower than with any of the other methods. From Figure 7.8 observe the following:

$$L_{12} = 24{,}791, T_{12} = 532, S_{13} = 0.47, S_{14} = 0.68, S_{15} = 1.17, S_{16} = 1.67.$$

Using Winter's model (Equation 7.17), the forecast for the next four periods is given as follows:

$$F_{13} = (L_{12} + T_{12})S_{13} = (24{,}791 + 532) \times 0.47 = 11{,}940,$$
$$F_{14} = (L_{12} + 2T_{12})S_{14} = (24{,}791 + 2 \times 532) \times 0.68 = 17{,}579,$$
$$F_{15} = (L_{12} + 3T_{12})S_{15} = (24{,}791 + 3 \times 532) \times 1.17 = 30{,}930,$$
$$F_{16} = (L_{12} + 4T_{12})S_{16} = (24{,}791 + 4 \times 532) \times 1.67 = 44{,}928.$$

In this case, MAD =1,469. Thus the estimate of standard deviation of forecast error using Winter's model with α = 0.05, β = 0.1, and γ = 0.1 is 1.25 × 1,469 = 1,836. In this case, the standard deviation of forecast error relative to the demand forecast is much smaller than in the other methods.

The team compiles the error estimates for the four forecasting methods as shown in Table 7.2.

	A	B	C	D	E	F	G	H	I	J	K	L	M
1	Period t	Demand D_i	Level L_i	Trend T_i	Seasonal Factor S_i	Forecast F_i	Error E_i	Absolute Error A_i	Mean Squared Error MSE_i	MAD_i	% Error	$MAPE_i$	TS_i
2			18,439	524									
3	1	8,000	18,866	514	0.47	8,913	913	913	832,857	913	11	11.41	1.00
4	2	13,000	19,367	513	0.68	13,179	179	179	432,367	546	1	6.39	2.00
5	3	23,000	19,869	512	1.17	23,260	260	260	310,720	450	1	4.64	3.00
6	4	34,000	20,380	512	1.67	34,036	36	36	233,364	347	0	3.50	4.00
7	5	10,000	20,921	515	0.47	9,723	-277	277	202,036	333	3	3.36	3.34
8	6	18,000	21,689	540	0.68	14,558	-3,442	3,442	2,143,255	851	19	5.98	-2.74
9	7	23,000	22,102	527	1.17	25,981	2,981	2,981	3,106,508	1,155	13	6.98	0.56
10	8	38,000	22,636	528	1.67	37,787	-213	213	2,723,856	1,037	1	6.18	0.42
11	9	12,000	23,291	541	0.47	10,810	-1,190	1,190	2,578,653	1,054	10	6.59	-0.72
12	10	13,000	23,577	515	0.69	16,544	3,544	3,544	3,576,894	1,303	27	8.66	2.14
13	11	32,000	24,271	533	1.16	27,849	-4,151	4,151	4,818,258	1,562	13	9.05	-0.87
14	12	41,000	24,791	532	1.67	41,442	442	442	4,432,987	1,469	1	8.39	-0.63
15	13				0.47	11,940							
16	14				0.68	17,579							
17	15				1.17	30,930							
18	16				1.67	44,928							

Cell	Cell Formula	Equation	Copied to
C3	=0.05*(B3/E3)+(1-0.05)*(C2+D2)	7.18	C4:C14
D3	=0.1*(C3-C2)+(1-0.1)*D2	7.19	D4:D14
E7	=0.1*(B3/C3)+(1-0.1)*E3	7.20	E4:E18
F3	=(C2+D2)*E3	7.17	F4:F18
G3	=F3-B3	7.8	G4:G14
H3	=Abs(G3)		H4:H14
I3	=Sumsq($G$3:G3)/A3	7.21	I4:I14
J3	=Sum($H$3:H3)/A3	7.22	J4:J14
K3	=100*(H3/B3)		K4:K14
L3	=Average($K$3:K3)	7.24	L4:L14
M3	=Sum($G$3:G3)/J3	7.26	M4:M14

FIGURE 7.8 Trend and Seasonality Corrected Exponential Smoothing

Based on the error information in Table 7.2, the forecasting team decides to use Winter's model. It is not surprising that Winter's model results in the most accurate forecast because the demand data has both a growth trend as well as seasonality. Using Winter's model, the team forecasts the following demand for the coming four quarters:

Second Quarter, 2003: 11,940
Third Quarter, 2003: 17,579
Fourth Quarter, 2003: 30,930
First Quarter, 2004: 44,928

The standard deviation of forecast error is 1,836.

TABLE 7.2 Error Estimates for Tahoe Salt Forecasting			
Forecasting Method	*MAD*	*MAPE (%)*	*TS Range*
Four-period moving average	9,719	49	−1.52 to 2.21
Simple exponential smoothing	10,208	59	−1.38 to 2.25
Holt's model	8,836	52	−2.15 to 1.85
Winter's model	1,469	8	−2.74 to 4.00

7.8   FORECASTING IN PRACTICE

Collaborate in building forecasts. As we discussed in the Tahoe Salt example, collaboration with your supply chain partners can often create a much more accurate forecast. However, most forecasts are still made not just within one company, but within one function in a company. It takes an investment of time and effort to build the relationships with your partners to begin sharing information and creating collaborative forecasts. The supply chain benefits of collaboration, however, are often an order of magnitude greater than the cost.

The value of data depends on where you are in the supply chain. Although collaboration is a hot topic, this does not mean that reams and reams of data need to be shared across the supply chain. The value of data depends on where one sits in the supply chain. For instance, a retailer will find point-of-sale data to be quite valuable in measuring the performance of their stores. However, a manufacturer selling to a distributor who in turn sells to retailers does not need all the point-of-sale detail. The manufacturer would find aggregate demand data from the retailer to be quite valuable but there is no value in them having all the detail that is valuable to the retailer. To avoid being overwhelmed with data when collaborating and not being able to sort out what's valuable, think about what data is valuable to each member of the supply chain and share only that data.

Be sure to distinguish between demand and sales. Often, companies make the mistake of looking at historical sales and assuming that this is what the historical demand was. To get true demand, adjustments need to be made for unmet demand due to stockouts, competitor actions, pricing, promotions, and so forth. In many cases, these adjustments are qualitative in nature but are crucial to accurately reflect reality. Although it is not always easy, making an adjustment in a forecast to move toward demand from just sales will increase accuracy and therefore supply chain performance.

7.9   SUMMARY OF LEARNING OBJECTIVES

1. Understand the role of forecasting for an enterprise and a supply chain.

     Forecasting is a key driver of virtually every design and planning decision made in both an enterprise and a supply chain. Enterprises have always forecasted demand and used it to make decisions. A relatively recent phenomenon, however, is to create collaborative forecasts for an entire supply chain and use this as the basis for decisions. Collaborative forecasting greatly increases the accuracy of forecasts and allows the supply chain to maximize its performance. Without collaboration, supply chain stages further from demand will likely have poor forecasts that will lead to supply chain inefficiencies and a lack of responsiveness.

2. Identify the components of a demand forecast.

Demand consists of a systematic and a random component. The systematic component measures the expected value of demand. The random component measures fluctuations in demand from the expected value. The systematic component consists of level, trend, and seasonality. Level measures the current de-seasonalized demand. Trend measures the current rate of growth or decline in demand. Seasonality indicates predictable seasonal fluctuations in demand.

3. Forecast demand in a supply chain given historical data using time series methodologies.

Time series methods for forecasting are categorized as *static* or *adaptive*. In static methods the estimates of parameters and demand patterns are not updated as new demand is

observed. Static methods include regression. In adaptive methods the estimates are updated each time a new demand is observed. Adaptive methods include moving averages, simple exponential smoothing, Holt's model, and Winter's model. Moving averages and simple exponential smoothing are best used when demand displays no trend or seasonality. Holt's model is best when demand displays a trend but no seasonality. Winter's model is appropriate when demand displays both trend and seasonality.

4. Analyze demand forecasts to estimate forecast error.

Forecast error measures the random component of demand. This measure is important because it reveals how inaccurate a forecast is likely to be and what contingencies a firm may have to plan for. The MAD and the MAPE are used to estimate the size of the forecast error. The bias and TS are used to estimate if the forecast consistently over- or underforecasts.

DISCUSSION QUESTIONS

1. What role does forecasting play in the supply chain of a build-to-order manufacturer such as Dell?
2. How could Dell use collaborative forecasting with its suppliers to improve its supply chain?
3. What role does forecasting play in the supply chain of a mail order firm such as L. L. Bean?
4. What are the systematic and random components you would expect in demand for chocolates?
5. Why should a manager be suspicious if a forecaster claims to forecast historical demand without any forecast error?
6. Give examples of products that display seasonality of demand.
7. What is the problem if a manager uses last year's sales data instead of last year's demand to forecast demand for the coming year?
8. How do static and adaptive forecasting methods differ?
9. What information does the MAD and MAPE provide to a manager? How can the manager use this information?
10. What information do the bias and TS provide to a manager? How can the manager use this information?

EXERCISES

1. Consider monthly demand for the ABC Corporation as shown in Table 7.3. Forecast the monthly demand for 2003 using the static method for forecasting. Evaluate the bias, TS, MAD, MAPE, and MSE. Evaluate the quality of the forecast.

2. Weekly sales of pizzas at Hot Pizza are shown following:

Week	Demand ($)	Week	Demand ($)	Week	Demand ($)
1	108	5	96	9	112
2	116	6	119	10	102
3	118	7	96	11	92
4	124	8	102	12	91

Estimate demand for the next four weeks using a four-week moving average as well as simple exponential smoothing with $\alpha = 0.1$. Evaluate the MAD, MAPE, MSE, bias, and TS in each case. Which of the two methods would you prefer? Why?

3. Quarterly sales of flowers at a wholesaler are shown following:

Year	Quarter	Sales ('000 $)	Year	Quarter	Sales ('000 $)
1999	I	98	2001	I	138
	II	106		II	130
	III	109		III	147
	IV	133		IV	141
2000	I	130	2002	I	144
	II	116		II	142
	III	133		III	165
	IV	116		IV	173

TABLE 7.3   Monthly Demand for ABC Corporation

Sales	1998	1999	2000	2001	2002
January	2,000	3,000	2,000	5,000	5,000
February	3,000	4,000	5,000	4,000	2,000
March	3,000	3,000	5,000	4,000	3,000
April	3,000	5,000	3,000	2,000	2,000
May	4,000	5,000	4,000	5,000	7,000
June	6,000	8,000	6,000	7,000	6,000
July	7,000	3,000	7,000	10,000	8,000
August	6,000	8,000	10,000	14,000	10,000
September	10,000	12,000	15,000	16,000	20,000
October	12,000	12,000	15,000	16,000	20,000
November	14,000	16,000	18,000	20,000	22,000
December	8,000	10,000	8,000	12,000	8,000
Total	78,000	89,000	98,000	115,000	113,000

Forecast quarterly sales for 2003 using simple exponential smoothing with $\alpha = 0.1$ as well as Holt's models with $\alpha = 0.1$ and $\beta = 0.1$. Which of the two methods would you prefer? Why?

4. Consider monthly demand for the ABC Corporation as shown in Table 7.3. Forecast the monthly demand for 2003 using moving average, simple exponential smoothing, Holt's model, and Winter's model. In each case evaluate the bias, TS, MAD, MAPE, and MSE. Which forecasting method would you prefer? Why?

BIBLIOGRAPHY

Bernstein, Peter L., and Theodore H. Silbert. 1984. "Are Economic Forecasters Worth Listening To?" *Harvard Business Review* (September–October): 2–8.

Box, G. E. P., and G. M. Jenkins. 1976. *Time Series Analysis: Forecasting and Control.* Oakland, Calif.: Holden-Day.

Bowerman, Bruce L., and Richard T. O'Connell. 1993. *Forecasting and Time Series: An Applied Approach.* 3d ed. Belmont, Calif.: Duxbury Press.

Brown, R. G. 1959. *Statistical Forecasting for Inventory Control.* New York: McGraw-Hill.

Chambers, J. C., K. M. Satinder, and D. D. Smith. 1971. "How to Choose the Right Forecasting Technique." *Harvard Business Review* (July–August): 45–74.

"Forecasting with Regression Analysis." 1994. Cambridge, Mass.: *Harvard Business School* Note #9-894-007.

Georgoff, David M., and Robert G. Murdick. 1986. "Manager's Guide to Forecasting." *Harvard Business Review* (January–February): 2–9.

Gilliland, Michael. "Is Forecasting a Waste of Time?" *Supply Chain Management Review* (July–August): 16–23.

Makridakis, Spyros, and Steven C. Wheelwright. 1989. *Forecasting Methods for Management.* New York: John Wiley & Sons.

Yurkiewicz, Jack. 2000. "Forecasting 2000." *ORMS Today* (February): 58–65.

-------------------------------- C A S E   S T U D Y --------------------------------

Specialty Packaging Corporation, Part A

Julie Williams had a lot on her mind when she left the conference room at Specialty Packaging Corporation (SPC). Her divisional manager had informed her that she would be assigned to a team consisting of SPC's marketing vice president and several staff members from their key customers. The goal of this team was to improve supply chain performance, as SPC had been unable to meet all the demand of their customers over the past several years. This often left SPC's customers scrambling to meet new client demands. Julie had little contact with SPC's customers and wondered how she would add value to this process. She was told by her division manager that the team's first task was to establish a collaborative forecast using data from both SPC and their customers. This forecast would serve as the basis for improving their performance as they could use this more accurate forecast for their production planning. With this in place, SPC would have a key tool to improve delivery performance.

SPC

SPC turns polystyrene resin into recyclable/disposable containers for the food industry. Polystyrene is purchased as a commodity in the form of resin pellets. The resin is unloaded from bulk rail containers or overland trailers into storage silos. Making the food containers is a two-step process. First, resin is conveyed to an extruder, which converts it into polystyrene sheet wound into rolls. The plastic comes in two forms—clear and black. The rolls are either used immediately to make containers or are put into storage. Second, the rolls are loaded onto thermo-forming presses, which form the sheet into containers and trim the containers from the sheet. The two manufacturing steps are shown in Figure 7.9.

Over the past five years, the plastic packaging business has grown steadily. Demand for containers made from clear plastic comes from grocery stores, bakeries, and restaurants. Demand for black plastic trays comes from caterers and grocery stores, who use them as packaging and serving trays. Demand for clear plastic containers peaks in the summer months, whereas demand for black plastic containers peaks in the fall. Capacity on the extruders is not sufficient to cover demand for sheets during the peak seasons. As a result, the plant is forced to build inventory of each type of sheet in anticipation of future demand. Table 7.4 and Figure 7.10 display historical quarterly demand for each of the two types (clear and black) of containers. This demand data was modified from SPC's sales data by the team to take into account the lost sales when SPC was out of stock. Without the customers involved in this team, SPC would never have known this information as they did not keep track of lost orders.

FORECASTING

As a first step in the team's decision making, they want to forecast quarterly demand for each of the two types of containers for the years 2003 to 2005. Based on historical trends, demand is expected to continue to grow until 2005, after which it is expected to plateau. Julie must select the appropriate forecasting method and estimate the likely forecast error. Which method should she choose?

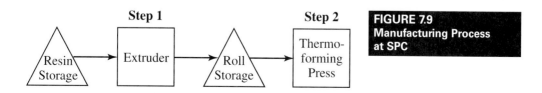

Step 1   **Step 2**

Resin Storage → Extruder → Roll Storage → Thermo-forming Press

FIGURE 7.9
Manufacturing Process at SPC

TABLE 7.4	Quarterly Historical Demand for Clear and Black Plastic Containers		
Year	Quarter	Black Plastic Demand ('000 lbs.)	Clear Plastic Demand ('000 lbs.)
1998	I	2,250	3,200
	II	1,737	7,658
	III	2,412	4,420
	IV	7,269	2,384
1999	I	3,514	3,654
	II	2,143	8,680
	III	3,459	5,695
	IV	7,056	1,953
2000	I	4,120	4,742
	II	2,766	13,673
	III	2,556	6,640
	IV	8,253	2,737
2001	I	5,491	3,486
	II	4,382	13,186
	III	4,315	5,448
	IV	12,035	3,485
2002	I	5,648	7,728
	II	3,696	16,591
	III	4,843	8,236
	IV	13,097	3,316

FIGURE 7.10 Plot of Quarterly Demand for Clear and Black Plastic Containers

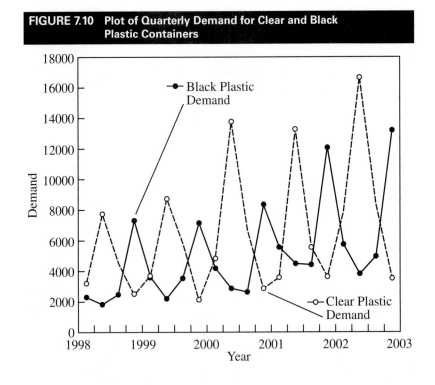

Aggregate Planning in the Supply Chain

Learning Objectives

After reading this chapter, you will be able to

1. Identify the types of decisions that are best solved by aggregate planning.

2. Understand the importance of aggregate planning as a supply chain activity.

3. Describe the kind of information needed to produce an aggregate plan.

4. Explain the basic trade-offs a manager makes when producing an aggregate plan.

5. Formulate and solve aggregate planning problems using Microsoft Excel.

In this chapter, we discuss how the aggregate planning methodology is used to make decisions about production, outsourcing, inventory, and backlogs in a supply chain. We identify the information required to produce an aggregate plan and outline the basic trade-offs that must be considered to create an optimal aggregate plan. We also describe how the aggregate planning problem can be formulated and solved using Microsoft Excel.

8.1 THE ROLE OF AGGREGATE PLANNING IN THE SUPPLY CHAIN

Imagine a world where manufacturing, transportation, storage, and information capacity are all limitless and without cost. Imagine lead times equal to zero, allowing goods to be produced and delivered instantaneously. In this world, there is no need to plan in anticipation of demand as whenever a customer demands a product, the demand can be instantly satisfied. In this world, aggregate planning plays no role.

In our world, however, capacity has a cost and lead times are greater than zero. Therefore, companies must make decisions regarding capacity levels, how to use that capacity, when to outsource, and when to run promotions to spur demand. A company must anticipate demand and determine, in advance of that demand, how it will be met. Should a company invest in a plant with large capacity that is able to produce enough to satisfy demand even in the busiest months? Or should a company build a smaller plant but incur the costs of holding inventory built during slow periods in anticipation of demand in later months? These are the types of questions aggregate planning helps companies answer.

Aggregate planning is a process by which a company determines levels of capacity, production, subcontracting, inventory, stockouts, and even pricing over a specified time horizon. The goal of aggregate planning is to satisfy demand in a way that maximizes profit. Aggregate planning, as the name suggests, solves problems involving aggregate decisions rather than stock keeping unit (SKU) level decisions. For example, aggregate planning will determine the total production level in a plant for a given month, but it will do so without determining the quantity of each individual SKU that will be produced. This level of detail makes aggregate planning a useful tool for thinking about decisions with an intermediate time frame of between roughly three and eighteen months. In this time frame, it is too early to determine SKU by SKU production levels, but it is also generally too late to arrange for additional capacity. Therefore, aggregate planning answers the question, "How should a firm best utilize the facilities that it currently has?"

Traditionally, much of aggregate planning is focused within an enterprise and may not always be seen as a part of supply chain management. Aggregate planning, however, is an important supply chain issue because, to be effective, it requires inputs from throughout the supply chain and its results have a tremendous impact on the supply chain. As we saw in the chapter on forecasting, collaborative forecasts are created by multiple supply chain enterprises and are an important input for aggregate planning. Good forecasts require collaboration with downstream supply chain partners. In addition, many constraints that must be considered in aggregate planning come from supply chain partners outside the enterprise, particularly upstream supply chain partners. Without these inputs from both up and down the supply chain, aggregate planning cannot realize its full potential to create value. The output from aggregate planning is also of value to both up and downstream partners. Production plans for a firm define demand for suppliers and establish supply constraints for customers. This chapter is meant to create a foundation for using aggregate planning both solely within an enterprise as well as across the entire supply chain. The supply chain implications of aggregate planning will become even more clear in Chapter 9 once the foundations of aggregate planning are in place.

For example, consider how a premium paper supply chain uses aggregate planning to maximize profit. Many types of paper mills face seasonal demand as demand ripples up from customers to printers to distributors and finally to the manufacturers. Many types of premium paper have demand peaks in the spring, when annual reports are printed, and in the fall, when new car brochures are released. Building a mill with capacity to meet demand in the spring and fall on an as-needed basis would be too costly because of the high cost of mill capacity. Additionally, premium papers often require special additives and coatings that can be in short supply and need to be ordered far in advance. The paper manufacturer needs to deal with these constraints and maximize profit around them. Therefore, mills use aggregate planning to determine production levels and inventory levels that they should build up in the slower months for sale in the spring and fall when demand is greater than the mill's capacity. By taking into account the inputs from throughout the supply chain, aggregate planning allows the mill and the supply chain to maximize profit.

The aggregate planner's main objective is to identify the following operational parameters over the specified time horizon:

- *Production rate:* the number of units completed per unit time (such as per week or per month).
- *Workforce:* the number of workers/units of capacity needed for production.
- *Overtime:* the amount of overtime production planned.
- *Machine capacity level:* the number of units of machine capacity needed for production.
- *Subcontracting:* the subcontracted capacity required over the planning horizon.
- *Backlog:* demand not satisfied in the period in which it arises but carried over to future periods.
- *Inventory on hand:* the planned inventory carried over the various periods in the planning horizon.

The aggregate plan serves as a broad blueprint for operations and establishes the parameters within which short-term production and distribution decisions are made. The aggregate plan allows the supply chain to alter capacity allocations and change supply contracts. As mentioned in earlier chapters, the entire supply chain should coordinate the planning process. If a manufacturer has planned an increase in production over a given time period, the supplier, transporter, and warehouser must be aware of this plan and incorporate the increase into their own plans. Ideally, all stages of the supply chain should work together on an aggregate plan that will optimize supply chain performance. If each stage develops its own aggregate plan, it is extremely unlikely that all the plans will mesh in a coordinated manner. This lack of coordination will result in shortages or oversupply in the supply chain. Therefore, it is important to perform aggregate plans over as wide a scope of the supply chain as is reasonably possible.

In the next section, we formally define the aggregate planning problem. We specify the information required for aggregate planning and discuss the decision outcomes that aggregate planning can provide.

8.2   THE AGGREGATE PLANNING PROBLEM

The objective of the aggregate plan is to satisfy demand in a way that maximizes profit for the firm. We can formally state the aggregate planning problem as follows:

> Given the demand forecast for each period in the planning horizon, determine the production level, inventory level, and the capacity level (internal and outsourced) for each period that maximizes the firm's profit over the planning horizon.

To create an aggregate plan, a company must specify the planning horizon for the plan. A planning horizon is the time period over which the aggregate plan is to produce a solution—usually between three and eighteen months. A company must also specify the duration of each period within the planning horizon (e.g., weeks, months, or quarters). Next, a company specifies key information required to produce an aggregate plan and the decisions for which an aggregate plan will develop recommendations. This information and the recommendations are specified for a generic aggregate planning problem in this section. The model we propose in the next section is flexible enough to accommodate situation-specific requirements.

An aggregate planner requires the following information:

- Demand forecast F_t for each Period t in the planning horizon that extends over T periods
- Production costs
  - Labor costs, regular time ($/hour), and overtime costs ($/hour)
  - Cost of subcontracting production ($/unit or $/hour)
  - Cost of changing capacity; specifically, cost of hiring/laying off workforce ($/worker) and cost of adding or reducing machine capacity ($/machine)
- Labor/machine hours required per unit
- Inventory holding cost ($/unit/period)
- Stockout or backlog cost ($/unit/period)
- Constraints
  - Limits on overtime
  - Limits on layoffs
  - Limits on capital available
  - Limits on stockouts and backlogs
  - Constraints from suppliers to the enterprise

This information is used to create an aggregate plan that in turn helps a company make the following determinations:

- *Production quantity from regular time, overtime, and subcontracted time:* used to determine number of workers and supplier purchase levels.
- *Inventory held:* used to determine how much warehouse space and working capital is needed.
- *Backlog/stockout quantity:* used to determine what the customer service levels will be.

- *Workforce hired/laid off:* used to determine any labor issues that will be encountered.
- *Machine capacity increase/decrease:* used to determine if new production equipment needs to be purchased or idled.

The quality of an aggregate plan has a significant impact on the profitability of a firm. A poor aggregate plan can result in lost sales and lost profits if the available inventory and capacity are unable to meet demand. A poor aggregate plan may also result in a large amount of excess inventory and capacity, thereby raising costs. Therefore, aggregate planning is a very important tool in helping a supply chain maximize profitability.

8.3 AGGREGATE PLANNING STRATEGIES

The aggregate planner must make a trade-off between capacity, inventory, and backlog costs. An aggregate plan that increases one of these costs typically results in the reduction of the other two. In this sense, the costs represent a trade-off—to lower inventory cost, a planner must increase capacity cost or delay delivery to the customer. Thus the planner has traded inventory cost for capacity or backlog cost. Arriving at the most profitable trade-off is the goal of aggregate planning. Given that demand varies over time, the relative level of the three costs leads to one of them being the key lever the planner uses to maximize profits. If the cost of varying capacity is low, a company may not have to build inventory or carry backlogs. If the cost of varying capacity is high, a company may compensate by building some inventory and carrying some backlogs from peak demand periods to off-peak demand periods.

In general, a company will attempt to use a combination of the three costs to best meet demand. Therefore, the fundamental trade-offs available to a planner are between

- Capacity (regular time, overtime, subcontracted)
- Inventory
- Backlog/lost sales

There are essentially three distinct aggregate planning strategies for achieving balance between these costs. These strategies involve trade-offs between capital investment, workforce size, work hours, inventory, and backlogs/lost sales. Most strategies that a planner actually uses are a combination of these three and are referred to as *mixed strategies.* The three strategies are as follows:

1. *Chase strategy—using capacity as the lever:* With this strategy, the production rate is synchronized with the demand rate by varying machine capacity or hiring and laying off employees as the demand rate varies. In practice, achieving this synchronization can be very problematic because of the difficulty in varying capacity and workforce on short notice. This strategy can be expensive to implement if the cost of varying machine or labor capacity over time is high. It can also have a significant negative impact on the morale of the workforce. The Chase strategy results in low levels of inventory in the supply chain and high levels of change in capacity and workforce. It should be used

when the cost of carrying inventory is very expensive and costs to change levels of machine and labor capacity are low.

2. *Time flexibility strategy—using utilization as the lever:* This strategy may be used if there is excess machine capacity (i.e., if machines are not used twenty four hours a day, seven days a week). In this case the workforce (capacity) is kept stable but the number of hours worked is varied over time in an effort to synchronize production with demand. A planner can use variable amounts of overtime or a flexible schedule to achieve this synchronization. Although this strategy does require that the workforce be flexible, it avoids some of the problems associated with the chase strategy, most notably changing the size of the workforce. This strategy results in low levels of inventory but with lower average utilization. It should be used when inventory carrying costs are relatively high and machine capacity is relatively inexpensive.

3. *Level strategy—using inventory as the lever:* With this strategy, a stable machine capacity and work force are maintained with a constant output rate. Shortages and surpluses result in inventory levels fluctuating over time. Here production is not synchronized with demand. Either inventories are built up in anticipation of future demand or backlogs are carried over from high- to low-demand periods. Employees benefit from stable working conditions. A drawback associated with this strategy is that large inventories may accumulate and customer orders may be delayed. This strategy keeps capacity and costs of changing capacity relatively low. It should be used when inventory carrying and backlog costs are relatively low.

In the next section, we discuss a methodology that is commonly used for aggregate planning.

8.4 AGGREGATE PLANNING USING LINEAR PROGRAMMING

As we discussed earlier, the goal of aggregate planning is to maximize profit while meeting demand. Every company, in its effort to meet customer demand, faces certain constraints, such as the capacity of its facilities or a supplier's ability to deliver a component. A highly effective tool for a company to use when it tries to maximize profits while being subjected to a series of constraints is linear programming. *Linear programming* finds the solution that will create the highest profit while satisfying the constraints that the company faces.

We illustrate linear programming through the discussion of Red Tomato Tools, a small manufacturer of gardening equipment. Red Tomato's operations consist of the assembly of purchased parts into a multipurpose gardening tool. Due to the minimal equipment and space requirements for their assembly operations, Red Tomato's capacity is determined mainly by the size of its workforce.

For this example, we use a six-month time period because this is a large enough time horizon to illustrate the points we make without being unwieldy.

Red Tomato Tools

The demand for Red Tomato's gardening tools from consumers is highly seasonal, peaking in the spring as people plant their gardens. This seasonal demand ripples up the supply chain from the retailer to Red Tomato, the manufacturer. Red Tomato has decided to use aggregate planning to overcome the obstacle of seasonal demand and maximize profits. The options Red Tomato has for handling the seasonality are adding workers during the peak season, subcontracting out some of the work, building up inventory during the slow months, or building up a backlog of orders that will be delivered late to customers. To determine how to best use these options through an aggregate plan, Red Tomato's vice president of supply chain starts with the first task—building a demand forecast. Although Red Tomato could attempt to forecast this demand themselves, a much more accurate forecast would come from a collaborative forecast produced by both Red Tomato and its retailers. The Red Tomato vice president puts together a team with several key retailers to produce a collaborative forecast as shown in Table 8.1.

Red Tomato sells each tool to the retailer for $40. The company has a starting inventory in January of 1,000 tools. At the beginning of January the company has a workforce of 80 employees. The plant has a total of twenty working days in each month and each employee earns $4 per hour regular time. Each employee works eight hours a day of regular time with any remaining hours performed on overtime. As discussed previously, the capacity of the production operation is determined primarily by the total labor hours worked. Therefore, machine capacity does not limit the capacity of the production operation. Due to labor rules, no employee works more than ten hours of overtime per month. The various costs are shown in Table 8.2.

Currently, Red Tomato has no limits on subcontracting, inventories, and stockouts/backlog. All stockouts are backlogged and supplied from the following months' production. Inventory costs are incurred on the ending inventory in the month. The supply chain manager's goal is to obtain the optimal aggregate plan that allows Red Tomato to end June with at least 500 units (i.e., no stockouts at the end of June and at least 500 units in inventory).

The optimal aggregate plan is one that results in the highest profit over the six-month planning horizon. For now, given Red Tomato's desire for a very high level of customer service, assume all demand is to be met although it can be met late with an additional backlog cost. Therefore the revenues earned over the planning horizon can be treated as fixed. In this case, minimizing cost over the planning horizon is the same as maximizing profit. In many instances, a company has the option of not meeting certain demand, or price itself may be a variable that a company will have to determine based on the aggregate plan. In such a scenario, minimizing cost would not be equivalent to maximizing profits.

TABLE 8.1 Demand Forecast at Red Tomato Tools

Month	Demand Forecast
January	1,600
February	3,000
March	3,200
April	3,800
May	2,200
June	2,200

TABLE 8.2 Costs for Red Tomato	
Item	*Cost*
Material cost	$10/unit
Inventory holding cost	$2/unit/month
Marginal cost of stockout/backlog	$5/unit/month
Hiring and training costs	$300/worker
Layoff cost	$500/worker
Labor hours required	4/unit
Regular time cost	$4/hour
Overtime cost	$6/hour
Cost of subcontracting	$30/unit

Decision Variables

The first step in constructing an aggregate planning model is to identify the set of decision variables whose values are to be determined as part of the aggregate plan. For Red Tomato, the following decision variables are defined for the aggregate planning model:

W_t = Workforce size for Month $t, t = 1, \ldots, 6$,
H_t = Number of employees hired at the beginning of Month $t, t = 1, \ldots, 6$,
L_t = Number of employees laid off at the beginning of Month $t, t = 1, \ldots, 6$,
P_t = Number of units produced in Month $t, t = 1, \ldots, 6$,
I_t = Inventory at the end of Month $t, t = 1, \ldots, 6$,
S_t = Number of units stocked out/backlogged at the end of Month $t, t = 1, \ldots, 6$,
C_t = Number of units subcontracted for Month $t, t = 1, \ldots, 6$,
O_t = Number of overtime hours worked in Month $t, t = 1, \ldots, 6$.

The next step in constructing an aggregate planning model is to define the objective function.

Objective Function

Denote the demand in Period t by D_t. The values of D_t are as specified by the demand forecast in Table 8.1. The objective function is to minimize the total cost (equivalent to maximizing total profit as all demand is to be satisfied) incurred during the planning horizon. The cost incurred has the following components:

- Regular time labor cost
- Overtime labor cost
- Cost of hiring and layoffs
- Cost of holding inventory
- Cost of stocking out
- Cost of subcontracting
- Material cost

These costs are evaluated as follows:

1. *Regular time labor cost.* Recall that workers are paid a regular time wage of $640 ($4/hour × eight hours/day × twenty days/month) per month. Because W_t is the number

of workers in Period t, the regular time labor cost over the planning horizon is given by the following:

$$\text{Regular time labor cost} = \sum_{t=1}^{6} 640\, W_t$$

2. *Overtime labor cost.* As overtime labor cost is $6 per hour (see Table 8.2) and O_t represents the number of overtime hours worked in Period t, the overtime cost over the planning horizon is given as follows:

$$\text{Overtime labor cost} = \sum_{t=1}^{6} 6\, O_t$$

3. *Cost of hiring and layoffs.* The cost of hiring a worker is $300 and the cost of laying off a worker is $500 (see Table 8.2). H_t and L_t represent the number hired and the number laid off respectively in Period t. Thus the cost of hiring and layoff is given by the following:

$$\text{Cost of hiring and layoff} = \sum_{t=1}^{6} 300\, H_t + \sum_{t=1}^{6} 500\, L_t$$

4. *Cost of inventory and stockout.* The cost of carrying inventory is $2 per unit per month and the cost of stocking out is $5 per unit per month (see Table 8.2). I_t and S_t represent the units in inventory and the units stocked out, respectively, in Period t. Thus, the cost of holding inventory and stocking out is given as follows:

$$\text{Cost of holding inventory and stocking out} = \sum_{t=1}^{6} 2\, I_t + \sum_{t=1}^{6} 5\, S_t$$

5. *Cost of materials and subcontracting.* The material cost is $10 per unit and the subcontracting cost is $30/unit (see Table 8.2). P_t represents the quantity produced and C_t represents the quantity subcontracted in Period t. Thus, the material and subcontracting cost is given by the following:

$$\text{Cost of materials and subcontracting} = \sum_{t=1}^{6} 10\, P_t + \sum_{t=1}^{6} 30\, C_t$$

The total cost incurred during the planning horizon is a sum of all the aforementioned costs and is given by the following:

$$\sum_{t=1}^{6} 640\, W_t + \sum_{t=1}^{6} 300\, H_t + \sum_{t=1}^{6} 500\, L_t +$$
$$\sum_{t=1}^{6} 6\, O_t + \sum_{t=1}^{6} 2\, I_t + \sum_{t=1}^{6} 5\, S_t + \sum_{t=1}^{6} 10\, P_t + \sum_{t=1}^{6} 30\, C_t \qquad \textbf{(8.1)}$$

Red Tomato's objective is to find an aggregate plan that minimizes the total cost (see Equation 8.1) incurred during the planning horizon.

The values of the decision variables in the objective function cannot be arbitrarily set. They are subject to a variety of constraints. The next step in setting up the aggregate planning model is to clearly define the constraints linking the decision variables.

Constraints

Red Tomato's vice president must now specify the constraints that the decision variables may not violate. They are as follows:

1. *Workforce, hiring, and layoff constraints.* The workforce size W_t in Period t is related to the workforce size W_{t-1} in Period $t-1$, the number hired H_t in Period t, and the number laid off L_t in Period t as follows:

$$W_t = W_{t-1} + H_t - L_t \quad \text{for} \quad t = 1, \ldots, 6 \tag{8.2}$$

The starting workforce size is given by $W_0 = 80$.

2. *Capacity constraints.* In each period, the amount produced cannot exceed the available capacity. This set of constraints limits the total production by the total internally available capacity (which is determined based on the available labor hours, regular or overtime). Subcontracted production is not included in this constraint as the constraint is limited to production within the plant. As each worker can produce 40 units per month on regular time (four hours per unit as specified in Table 8.2) and one unit for every four hours of overtime, we have the following:

$$P_t \leq 40W_t + O_t / 4 \quad \text{for} \quad t = 1, \ldots, 6 \tag{8.3}$$

3. *Inventory balance constraints.* The third set of constraints balances inventory at the end of each period. Net demand for Period t is obtained as the sum of the current demand D_t and the previous backlog S_{t-1}. This demand is either filled from current production (inhouse production P_t or subcontracted production C_t) and previous inventory I_{t-1} (in which case some inventory I_t may be left over) or part of it is backlogged S_t. This relationship is captured by the following equation:

$$I_{t-1} + P_t + C_t = D_t + S_{t-1} + I_t - S_t \quad \text{for} \quad t = 1, \ldots 6 \tag{8.4}$$

The starting inventory is given by $I_0 = 1000$, the ending inventory must be at least 500 units (i.e., $I_6 \geq 500$) and initially there are no backlogs (i.e., $S_0 = 0$).

4. *Overtime limit constraints.* The fourth set of constraints requires that no employee work more than ten hours of overtime each month. This requirement limits the total amount of overtime hours available as follows:

$$O_t \leq 10W_t \quad \text{for} \quad t = 1, \ldots, 6 \tag{8.5}$$

In addition, each variable must be nonnegative and there must be no backlog at the end of Period 6 (i.e., $S_6 = 0$).

When implementing the model in Excel, which we discuss later, it is easiest if all the constraints are written so that the right-hand side for each constraint is 0. The overtime limit constraint (Equation 8.5) in this form would be written as follows:

$$O_t - 10W_t \leq 0 \quad \text{for} \quad t = 1, \ldots, 6$$

Observe that one can easily add constraints that limit the amount purchased from subcontractors each month or the maximum number of employees to be hired or laid off. Any other constraints limiting backlogs or inventories can also be accommodated. Ideally the number of employees should be an integer variable. We can obtain a good approximation, however, by allowing the number of employees to take on fractional values. This change significantly speeds up the time taken to solve the problem. Such a linear program can be solved using the tool Solver in Excel.

If we assume the average inventory in Period t to be the average of the starting and ending inventories, that is, $(I_{t-1} + I_t)/2$, the average inventory over the planning horizon is given by the following:

$$\text{Average inventory} = \left\{ \left[(I_0 + I_T)/2 + \sum_{t=1}^{T-1} I_t \right] / T \right\}$$

The average flow time of the units over the planning horizon is obtained using Little's law (average flow time = average inventory/throughput). The average flow time is given as follows:

$$\text{Average flow time} = \left\{ \left[(I_0 + I_T)/2 + \sum_{t=1}^{T-1} I_t \right] / T \right\} / \left(\sum_{t=1}^{T} D_t / T \right) \qquad \textbf{(8.6)}$$

By optimizing the objective function (minimizing cost in Equation 8.1) subject to the listed constraints (Equations 8.2–8.5), the vice president obtains the aggregate plan shown in Table 8.3. (Later in the chapter we discuss how to perform this optimization using Excel.)

For this aggregate plan we have the following:

Total cost over planning horizon = $422,275.

TABLE 8.3 Aggregate Plan for Red Tomato

Period t	No. Hired H_t	No. Laid Off L_t	Workforce Size W_t	Overtime O_t	Inventory I_t	Stockout S_t	Subcontract C_t	Total Production P_t
0	0	0	80	0	1,000	0	0	
1	0	15	65	0	1,983	0	0	2,583
2	0	0	65	0	1,567	0	0	2,583
3	0	0	65	0	950	0	0	2,583
4	0	0	65	0	0	267	0	2,583
5	0	0	65	0	117	0	0	2,583
6	0	0	65	0	500	0	0	2,583

Red Tomato lays off a total of 15 employees in the beginning of January. After that, the company maintains the workforce and production level. They do not use the subcontractor during the entire planning horizon. They carry a backlog only from April to May. In all other months, they plan no stockouts. In fact, Red Tomato carries inventory in all other periods. We describe this inventory as seasonal inventory because it is carried in anticipation of a future increase in demand. Given the sale price of $40 per unit and total sales of 16,000 units, revenue over the planning horizon is given by

$$\text{Revenue over planning horizon} = 40 \times 16{,}000 = \$640{,}000.$$

The average seasonal inventory during the planning horizon is given by

$$\text{Average seasonal inventory} = \left[(I_0 + I_6)/2 + \sum_{t=1}^{5} I_t \right] / T = 5{,}367/6 = 895$$

The average flow time for this aggregate plan over the planning horizon (using Equation 8.6) is given by

$$\text{Average flow time} = 895 / 2{,}667 = 0.34 \text{ months.}$$

If the seasonal fluctuation of demand grows, synchronization of supply and demand becomes more difficult, resulting in an increase in either inventory or backlogs as well as an increase in the total cost to the supply chain. This is illustrated in Example 8.1, in which the demand forecast is more variable.

Example 8.1

All the data is exactly the same as in our previous discussion of Red Tomato, except for the demand forecast. Assume that the same overall demand (16,000 units) is distributed over the six months in such a way that the seasonal fluctuation of demand is higher, as shown in Table 8.4.

Obtain the optimal aggregate plan in this case.

Analysis: In this case the optimal aggregate plan (using the same costs as those used before) is shown in Table 8.5.

TABLE 8.4 Demand Forecast with Higher Seasonal Fluctuation	
Month	*Demand Forecast*
January	1,000
February	3,000
March	3,800
April	4,800
May	2,000
June	1,400

TABLE 8.5   Optimal Aggregate Plan for Demand in Table 8.4

Period t	No. Hired H_t	No. Laid Off L_t	Workforce Size W_t	Overtime O_t	Inventory I_t	Stockout S_t	Subcontract C_t	Total Production P_t
0	0	0	80	0	1,000	0	0	
1	0	15	65	0	2,583	0	0	2,583
2	0	0	65	0	2,167	0	0	2,583
3	0	0	65	0	950	0	0	2,583
4	0	0	65	0	0	1,267	0	2,583
5	0	0	65	0	0	683	0	2,583
6	0	0	65	0	500	0	0	2,583

Observe that monthly production remains the same but both inventories and stockouts (backlogs) go up compared to the aggregate plan in Table 8.3 for the demand profile in Table 8.1. The cost of meeting the new demand profile in Table 8.4 is higher at $432,858 (compared to $422,275 for the previous demand profile in Table 8.1).

The seasonal inventory during the planning horizon is given by

$$\text{Seasonal inventory} = \left\{ \left[(I_0 + I_T)/2 + \sum_{t=1}^{T-1} I_t \right] / T \right\} = 6{,}450/6 = 1{,}075$$

The average flow time for this aggregate plan over the planning horizon (using Equation 8.6) is given by

$$\text{Average flow time} = 1{,}075 / 2{,}667 = 0.40 \text{ months.}$$

From Example 8.1, we can see that the increase in demand variability at the retailer has an impact up the supply chain in terms of the manufacturer's production schedule as well as the amount of storage space required for inventory.

Using the Red Tomato example, we can also see that the optimal trade-off changes as the costs change. This is illustrated in Example 8.2 where we show that as holding costs increase, it is better to carry less inventory and resort to excess capacity, backlogs, or subcontracting.

Example 8.2

Assume that demand at Red Tomato is as shown in Table 8.1, and all other data is the same except that holding cost per unit is increased from $2 per unit per month to $6 per unit per month. Evaluate the total cost corresponding to the aggregate plan in Table 8.3. Suggest an optimal aggregate plan for the new cost structure.

Analysis: If the holding cost increases from $2 per unit per month to $6 per unit per month, the cost corresponding to the aggregate plan in Table 8.3 would increase from $422,275 to $442,742. Taking this new cost into account and determining a new optimal aggregate plan yields the following plan shown in Table 8.6.

As expected, the inventory carried is reduced (because inventory holding cost has been raised) compared to the aggregate plan in Table 8.3. The aggregate plan has compensated by increasing the amount subcontracted. The total cost of the aggregate plan in Table 8.6 is $441,200 compared to $442,742 (for the aggregate plan in Table 8.3) if the holding cost is $6 per unit per month.

TABLE 8.6   Optimal Aggregate Plan for Holding Cost of $6/Unit/Month

Period t	No. Hired H_t	No. Laid Off O_t	Workforce Size W_t	Overtime O_t	Inventory I_t	Stockout S_t	Subcontract C_t	Total Production P_t
0	0	0	80	0	1,000	0	0	
1	0	23	57	0	1,667	0	0	2,267
2	0	0	57	0	933	0	0	2,267
3	0	0	57	0	0	0	0	2,267
4	0	0	57	0	0	67	1,467	2,267
5	0	0	57	0	0	0	0	2,267
6	0	0	57	0	500	0	433	2,267

The seasonal inventory during the planning horizon is given by

$$\text{Seasonal inventory} = \left\{ \left[(I_0 + I_T)/2 + \sum_{t=1}^{T-1} I_t \right] / T \right\} = 3{,}350 / 6 = 558$$

The average flow time for this aggregate plan over the planning horizon (using Equation 8.6) is given by

$$\text{Average flow time} = 558 / 2{,}667 = 0.21 \text{ months.}$$

From Example 8.2 observe that increasing the cost of one variable not only increases the total cost but also shifts the optimal balance away from that variable. An increase in holding cost at the manufacturer leads to an increase in production outsourced to the subcontractor.

Forecast Error in Aggregate Plans

The aggregate planning methodology we have discussed in this chapter does not take into account any forecast error. However, we know that all forecasts have errors. To improve the quality of these aggregate plans, forecast errors must be taken into account when formulating aggregate plans. Forecasting errors are dealt with using either *safety inventory*, defined as inventory held to satisfy demand that is higher than forecasted (discussed thoroughly in Chapter 11) or *safety capacity*, defined as capacity used to satisfy demand that is higher than forecasted. A company can create a buffer for forecast error using safety inventory and safety capacity in a variety of ways, some of which are listed next.

- Use overtime as a form of safety capacity
- Carry extra workforce permanently as a form of safety capacity
- Use subcontractors as a form of safety capacity
- Build and carry extra inventories as a form of safety inventory
- Purchase capacity or product from an open or spot market as a form of safety capacity

The actions a company might take depend on the relative cost of the choices. Of course, if in practice a company can vary the capacity on short notice by hiring extra people, this is always an option. The problem with this option relates to the cost (monetary as well as morale) of letting them go later.

In the next section, we explain how to implement the linear programming methodology for aggregate planning using Microsoft Excel .

8.5   AGGREGATE PLANNING IN EXCEL

Next we discuss how to generate the aggregate plan for Red Tomato in Table 8.3 using Excel. To access Excel's linear programming capabilities, use Solver (Tools | Solver). To begin, we need to create a table, which we illustrate with Figure 8.1, containing the following decision variables:

W_t = Workforce size for Month t, $t = 1, ..., 6$,
H_t = Number of employees hired at the beginning of Month t, $t = 1, ..., 6$,
L_t = Number of employees laid off at the beginning of Month t, $t = 1, ..., 6$,
P_t = Number of units produced in Month t, $t = 1, ..., 6$,
I_t = Inventory at the end of Month t, $t = 1, ..., 6$,
S_t = Number of units stocked out at the end of Month t, $t = 1, ..., 6$,
C_t = Number of units subcontracted for Month t, $t = 1, ..., 6$,
O_t = Number of overtime hours worked in Month t, $t = 1, ..., 6$.

The first step is to build a table containing each decision variable. Figure 8.1 illustrates what this table should look like. The decision variables are contained in the cells B5 to I10 with each cell corresponding to a decision variable. For example, cell D7 corresponds to the workforce size in Period 3. Begin by setting all the decision variables to 0 as shown in Figure 8.1.

Also note that column J contains the actual demand. The demand information is included because it is required to calculate the aggregate plan.

The second step is to construct a table for the constraints in Equations 8.2 to 8.5. The constraint table may be constructed as shown in Figure 8.2.

FIGURE 8.1   Spreadsheet Area for Decision Variables

	A	B	C	D	E	F	G	H	I	J
1	Aggregate Plan Decision Variables									
2		H_t	L_t	W_t	O_t	I_t	S_t	C_t	P_t	
3	Period	# Hired	# Laid off	# Workforce	Overtime	Inventory	Stockout	Subcontract	Production	Demand
4	0	0	0	80	0	1,000	0	0		
5	1	0	0	0	0	0	0	0	0	1,600
6	2	0	0	0	0	0	0	0	0	3,000
7	3	0	0	0	0	0	0	0	0	3,200
8	4	0	0	0	0	0	0	0	0	3,800
9	5	0	0	0	0	0	0	0	0	2,200
10	6	0	0	0	0	0	0	0	0	2,200

	M	N	O	P
1	**Constraints**			
2				
3	**Workforce**	**Production**	**Inventory**	**Over time**
4				
5	-80	0	-600	0
6	0	0	-3000	0
7	0	0	-3200	0
8	0	0	-3800	0
9	0	0	-2200	0
10	0	0	-2200	0

Cell	Cell Formula	Equation	Copied to
M5	=D5 - D4 - B5 + C5	8.2	M6:M10
N5	=40*D5 + E5/4 - I5	8.3	N6:N10
O5	=F4-G4+I5+H5-J5-F5+G5	8.4	O6:O10
P5	=-E5 + 10*D5	8.5	P6:P10

FIGURE 8.2 Spreadsheet Area for Constraints

Column M contains workforce constraints (Equation 8.2), column N contains capacity constraints (Equation 8.3), column O contains inventory balance constraints (Equation 8.4), and column P contains overtime constraints (Equation 8.5). These constraints are applied to each of the six periods.

Each constraint will eventually be written in solver as

$$\text{Cell value } \{\leq, =, \text{ or } \geq\} \ 0.$$

In our case we have constraints

$$M5 = 0, N5 \geq 0, O5 = 0, P5 \geq 0.$$

The third step is to create a cell containing the objective function, which is how each solution is judged. This cell need not contain the entire formula but can be written as a formula using cells with intermediate cost calculations. For the Red Tomato example, all cost calculations are shown in Figure 8.3. Cell B15, for instance, contains the

FIGURE 8.3 Spreadsheet Area for Cost Calculations

	A	B	C	D	E	F	G	H	I
12	**Aggregate Plan Costs**								
13									
14	**Period**	**Hiring**	**Lay off**	**Regular time**	**Over time**	**Inventory**	**Stockout**	**Subcontract**	**Material**
15	1	0	0	0	0	0	0	0	0
16	2	0	0	0	0	0	0	0	0
17	3	0	0	0	0	0	0	0	0
18	4	0	0	0	0	0	0	0	0
19	5	0	0	0	0	0	0	0	0
20	6	0	0	0	0	0	0	0	0
21									
22	**Total Cost =**	$ -							

hiring costs incurred in Period 1. The formula in cell B15 is the product of cell B5 and the cell containing the hiring cost per worker, which is obtained from Table 8.2. Other cells are similarly filled. Cell C22 contains the sum of cells B15 to I20 and represents the total cost.

The fourth step is to use Tools | Solver to invoke Solver. Within the Solver parameters dialog box, enter the following information to represent the linear programming model:

> Set Target Cell: C22
> Equal to: Select *Min*
> By Changing Cells: B5:I10

Subject to the constraints:

$B5:I10 \geq 0$ {All decision variables are nonnegative},
$F10 \geq 500$ {Inventory at end of Period 6 is at least 500},
$G10 = 0$ {Stockout at end of Period 6 equals 0},
$M5:M10 = 0$ $\{W_t - W_{t-1} - H_t + L_t = 0 \text{ for } t = 1, \ldots, 6\}$,
$N5:N10 \geq 0$ $\{40W_t + O_t/4 - P_t \geq 0 \text{ for } t = 1, \ldots, 6\}$,
$O5:O10 = 0$ $\{I_t - 1 - S_t - 1 + P_t + Ct - D_t - I_t + S_t = 0 \text{ for } t = 1, \ldots, 6\}$,
$P5:P10 \geq 0$ $\{10W_t - Ot \geq 0 \text{ for } t = 1, \ldots, 6\}$.

The Solver parameters dialog box is shown in Figure 8.4.

Within the Solver parameters dialog box, click on Options and then select Assume Linear Model (this will significantly speed up the solution time). Return to the Solver parameters dialog box and click on Solve. The optimal solution should be returned. In case Solver does not return the optimal solution, solve the problem again after saving the solution that Solver has returned. (In some cases multiple repetitions of this step may be required because of some flaws in Solver. Add-Ins are available at relatively low cost that do not have any of the problems associated with Solver.) The optimal solution turns out to be the one shown in Table 8.3.

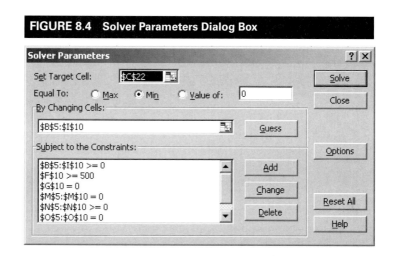

FIGURE 8.4 **Solver Parameters Dialog Box**

8.6 IMPLEMENTING AGGREGATE PLANNING IN PRACTICE

1. *Think beyond the enterprise to the entire supply chain.* Most aggregate planning done today takes only the enterprise as its breadth of scope. However, there are many factors outside the enterprise throughout the supply chain that can dramatically impact the optimal aggregate plan. Therefore, avoid the trap of only thinking about your enterprise when aggregate planning. Work with partners downstream to produce forecasts, with upstream partners to determine constraints, and with any other supply chain entities that can improve the quality of the inputs into the aggregate plan. As the plan is only as good as the quality of the inputs, using the supply chain to increase the quality of the inputs will greatly improve the quality of the aggregate plan. Also make sure to communicate the aggregate plan to all supply chain partners who will be affected by it.

2. *Make plans flexible because forecasts are always wrong.* Aggregate plans are based on forecasts of future demand. Given that these forecasts are always wrong to some degree, the aggregate plan needs to have some flexibility built into it if it is to be useful. By building flexibility into the plan, when future demand changes, or other changes occur such as increases in costs, the plan can appropriately adjust to handle the new situation.

How do we create this flexibility? In addition to the suggestions earlier in the chapter, we recommend that a manager perform sensitivity analysis on the inputs into an aggregate plan. For example, if the plan recommends expanding expensive capacity while facing uncertain demand, examine the outcome of a new aggregate plan when demand is higher and when demand is lower than expected. If this examination reveals a small savings from expanding capacity when demand is high but a large increase in cost when demand is lower than expected, deciding to postpone the capacity investment decision is a potentially attractive option. Using sensitivity analysis on the inputs into the aggregate plan will enable the planner to choose the best solution for the range of possibilities that could occur.

3. *Rerun the aggregate plan as new data emerges.* As we have mentioned, aggregate plans provide a map for the next three to eighteen months. This does not mean that a firm should only run aggregate plans once every three to eighteen months. As inputs into the aggregate plan change, managers should use the latest values of these inputs and rerun the aggregate plan. By using the latest inputs, the plan will avoid suboptimization based on old data and will produce a better solution. For instance, as new demand forecasts become available, aggregate plans should be reevaluated.

4. *Use aggregate planning as capacity utilization increases.* Surprisingly, many companies do not create aggregate plans and instead rely solely on orders from their distributors or warehouses to determine their production schedules. These orders are driven either by actual demand or through inventory management algorithms. If a company has no trouble efficiently meeting demand this way, then one could claim the lack of aggregate planning may not significantly harm the company. However, when utilization becomes high and capacity is an issue, relying on orders to set the production schedule can lead to capacity problems. When utilization is high, the likelihood of producing for all the orders as they arrive is very low. Planning needs to be done to best utilize the capacity to meet the forecasted demand. Therefore, as capacity utilization increases, it becomes more important to perform aggregate planning.

8.7   Summary of Learning Objectives

1. Identify the types of decisions that are best solved by aggregate planning.

   Aggregate planning is best used to determine capacity, production, and inventory decisions for each period of time over a range of three to eighteen months. It is most important to perform aggregate planning under conditions where capacity is limited and lead times are long.

2. Understand the importance of aggregate planning as a supply chain activity.

   Aggregate planning has a significant impact on supply chain performance and must be viewed as an activity that involves all supply chain partners. An aggregate plan prepared by an enterprise in isolation is not very useful because it does not take into account all requirements of the customer stage and constraints from the supplier stage. Localized aggregate planning cannot do a good job of matching supply and demand. Good aggregate planning is done in collaboration with both customers and suppliers because accurate input is required from both stages. The quality of these inputs, both in terms of the demand forecast to be met and the constraints to be dealt with, determines the quality of the aggregate plan. The results of the aggregate plan must also be shared across the supply chain because they influence activities at both customers and suppliers. For suppliers, the aggregate plan determines anticipated orders whereas for customers the aggregate plan determines planned supply.

3. Describe the kind of information needed to produce an aggregate plan.

   To create an aggregate plan, a planner needs a demand forecast, cost and production information, and any supply constraints. The demand forecast consists of an estimate of demand for each period of time in the planning horizon. The production and cost data consist of capacity levels and costs to raise and lower them, costs to produce the product, costs to store the product, costs of stocking out of the product, and any restrictions that limit these factors. Supply constraints determine limits on outsourcing, overtime, or materials.

4. Explain the basic trade-offs a manager makes to produce an aggregate plan.

   The basic trade-offs involve balancing the cost of capacity, the cost of inventory, and the cost of stockouts to maximize profitability. Each of these cost components has many costs within them. How these costs are balanced to maximize profitability is generally expressed by either the chase, flexibility, or level strategies.

5. Formulate and solve aggregate planning problems using Microsoft Excel.

   Aggregate planning problems can be solved in Excel by setting up cells for the objective function and the constraints and using the solver to produce the solution.

Discussion Questions

1. What are some industries in which aggregate planning would be particularly important?
2. What are the characteristics of these industries that make them good candidates for aggregate planning?
3. What are the main differences between the aggregate planning strategies?
4. What types of industries or situations are best suited to the chase strategy? The flexibility strategy? The level strategy?
5. What are the major cost categories needed as inputs for aggregate planning?
6. How does the availability of subcontracting impact the aggregate planning problem?

7. If a company currently employs the chase strategy and the cost of training increases dramatically, how might this change their aggregate planning strategy?
8. How can aggregate planning be used in an environment of high demand uncertainty?

-------------------------------------- C A S E   S T U D Y --------------------------------

Specialty Packaging Corporation, Part B

Julie Williams, facility production planning manager at SPC, left the meeting with the collaborative forecast team with forecasts and error estimates for the next three years. She now needed to determine how to meet this demand. Because SPC sometimes outsourced warehousing, one decision Julie had to make was whether to use public or private warehousing. She also had to decide how much warehouse space to lease or build if she chose to use private warehousing.

SPC

From the discussion of this case in Chapter 7, recall that SPC processes polystyrene resin into recyclable/disposable containers for the food industry. Polystyrene is purchased as a commodity in the form of resin pellets. The resin is unloaded from bulk rail containers or overland trailers into storage silos. Making the food containers is a two-step process. In the first step, resin is conveyed to an extruder, which turns pellets into a polystyrene

sheet that is wound into rolls. The plastic comes in two forms—clear and black. The rolls are then either used immediately to make containers or are put into storage. In the second step, the rolls are loaded onto thermoforming presses, which form the sheet into container cavities and trim the cavities from the sheet. These manufacturing steps are shown in Figure 7.1. SPC currently operates for sixty three working days each quarter. Each work day consists of eight hours of regular time and any overtime that may have been scheduled.

DEMAND FORECAST FOR NEXT THREE YEARS

The collaborative forecasting team used the historical demand data provided in Table 7.4 supplemented with stockout data to develop a forecast for quarterly demand for both clear and black plastic containers. The demand forecast between 2003 and 2005 is shown in Table 8.7.

TABLE 8.7	Demand Forecast for Clear and Black Plastic Containers		
Year	Quarter	Black Plastic Forecast ('000 lbs.)	Clear Plastic Forecast ('000 lbs.)
2003	I	6650	7462
	II	4576	18,250
	III	6293	8894
	IV	13,777	4064
2004	I	7509	8349
	II	5149	20,355
	III	7056	9891
	IV	15,399	4507
2005	I	8367	9235
	II	5721	22,461
	III	7819	10,889
	IV	17,021	4950
		MAD = 608	**MAD = 786**

EXTRUDERS

The extrusion process is capital-intensive, as is the investment in the facilities required to support it. The plant currently has 14 extruders. Each extruder has a rated processing capacity of 3,000 lbs. per hour. A changeover is required whenever the extruder switches between clear and black sheets. SPC estimates that there is a 5 percent capacity loss due to changeovers. The effective processing capacity of an extruder is thus 2,850 lbs. per hour. Each extruder requires 6 workers. SPC pays each worker $15 per hour including benefits. Overtime is paid at 150 percent of regular time salary. Workers are limited to overtime of sixty hours per quarter.

Extruders are fairly expensive and the addition of an extruder requires the hiring of six additional people. Each new extruder incurs a fixed cost of $80,000 per quarter. Any new personnel hired need to be trained. Training cost per person is $3,000. As a result, SPC has decided not to purchase any new extruders over the current planning horizon. During any quarter, available extruders may be idled if they are not to be used. The only savings here is the salary of associated workers. Laying off each worker, however, costs $2,500. If idled extruders are brought online, SPC incurs a training cost of $3,000 per worker.

THERMOFORMING PRESSES

The plant currently has 25 thermoforming presses. Each thermoforming press requires one operator and can produce containers at the rate of 2,000 lbs. per hour. SPC pays each operator $15 per hour including benefits. Overtime is paid at 150 percent of regular time salary. Workers are limited to overtime of sixty hours per quarter. Presses may be idled for the quarter if they are not to be used. Laying off an operator costs $2,500 and training a newly hired operator costs $3,000.

SUBCONTRACTING

SPC has the option of subcontracting the production of plastic sheets to one of its supply chain partners; sufficient capacity is always available on the open market. SPC spends $60 per thousand pounds of plastic sheet produced by a subcontractor.

MATERIALS MANAGEMENT PRACTICES

Resin purchased is stored in silos. As there is no shortage of resin in the market, it can easily be purchased at $10 per 1,000 pounds when needed. As a result, SPC's practice has been to purchase resin on a quarterly basis to match the planned production.

As the extruders produce rolls of plastic sheet, the amount required at the thermoforming presses is passed forward, with the rest driven via shuttle trailer to one of two public warehouses. Transportation is again required to bring the sheets back from the warehouse when they are needed to feed the thermoforming presses. SPC's total transportation cost is $2 per thousand pounds of plastic sheet. Each quarter, SPC follows a policy of first using sheets in storage for thermoforming and only then using the newly produced sheets. Any sheets left over at the end of the quarter are put back into storage. This policy is followed to ensure that sheets do not deteriorate because of time in storage.

PUBLIC WAREHOUSING

Public warehousing charges customers for both material handling and storage. The SPC plant contracts with local warehouses to store material on a per thousand pound basis. Material handling charges are from $4 to $6 per thousand pounds unloaded at the warehouse. Storage charges are from $10 to $12 per thousand pounds in storage at the end of each quarter. The SPC plant negotiates annually with local warehouses to establish rates for each cost element.

PRIVATE WAREHOUSING

Operating a private warehouse requires capitalized investment either to construct a facility or to lease an existing facility. Lease rates in any location are determined by the economics associated with building costs in that location and the option value of a lease versus a long-term capital commitment. Leases are typically in force for three years, but the time span can be shorter depending on a given company's negotiating strengths. Several viable leasing options exist for the SPC plant, all more favorable than the option of building a new facility. Lease rates average $4 per square foot per quarter in each location. On average one square foot is required per thousand pounds in storage.

Private warehousing also results in operating costs, both variable and fixed. Private warehousing is available from a third-party logistics provider who has agreed to charge SPC a variable operating cost of $4 per 1,000 pounds of plastic sheet stored per quarter. To obtain this rate, SPC must sign the lease for a full three years. As a result, SPC will pay for the space each quarter even if it is not used for storage. SPC must take this cost into account when making its decision.

SPC must consider several variables when determining the amount of warehouse space it requires. Usable warehousing space is the fraction of a warehouse that can actually be used to store inventory. Considerations are made for aisle space, shipping and receiving dock space, administrative office space, and ceiling height. Storage density is another consideration. SPC must also take into account velocity and times of materials movement because the staffing level required and storage configurations are dependent on both. For example, if materials must be retrieved readily, the warehouse layout must include a greater ratio of aisle and staging space to actual storage space.

THE ACTIONS AND DECISIONS

Julie and her group must take two actions. The first, given a three-year forecast as shown in Table 8.7, is to come up with an aggregate production plan. The second is to choose from the following three options:

1. Continue with the strategy of storing materials off-site in public warehousing
2. Lease and run a private warehouse to handle off-site inventory
3. Use a combination of both public and private warehousing

In the case of private warehousing, Julie must make a decision regarding the square footage to be leased. This decision will apply over the period 2003 to 2005. Clearly, this decision must be made in conjunction with the preparation of an aggregate plan over the three-year period. Ideally, the two decisions should be made jointly as each will affect the other.

What factors do you think influence the actions and decisions? For example, do you think that the price the subcontractor charges has any relationship to the amount of private warehousing space to be leased?

Julie also has to decide how to handle any potential error in the demand forecast. How do you recommend she handle these errors?

Planning Supply and Demand in the Supply Chain: Managing Predictable Variability

Learning Objectives

After reading this chapter, you will be able to:

1. Manage supply to improve synchronization in the supply chain in the face of predictable variability.

2. Manage demand to improve synchronization in the supply chain in the face of predictable variability.

3. Use aggregate planning to maximize profitability when faced with predictable variability in the supply chain.

In Chapter 8 we discuss how companies manage supply by using aggregate planning to make optimal trade-offs in a way that maximizes profits. In this chapter, we build on the knowledge we gained from Chapter 8 and continue to expand our scope beyond the enterprise to the supply chain as we deal with predictable variability of demand. We also discuss how demand may be managed to counter predictable variability through the use of price and promotion. By managing supply and demand, managers can maximize overall profitability of the supply chain.

9.1   RESPONDING TO PREDICTABLE VARIABILITY IN THE SUPPLY CHAIN

In Chapter 8 we discuss how companies use aggregate planning to plan supply to maximize profits. For products with stable demand, devising an aggregate plan is very simple. In such cases, a firm arranges for sufficient capacity to match the expected demand and then produces an amount to match that demand. Products can be produced close to the time when they will be sold. Therefore, the supply chain carries little inventory.

Demand for many products, however, changes rapidly from period to period, often due to a predictable influence. These influences include seasonal factors that affect products (e.g., lawn mowers and ski jackets), as well as nonseasonal factors (e.g., promotions or product adoption rates) that may cause large, predictable increases and declines in sales.

Predictable variability is change in demand that can be forecasted. Products that undergo this type of change in demand cause numerous problems in the supply chain, ranging from high levels of stockouts during peak demand periods to high levels of excess inventory during periods of low demand. These problems increase the costs and decrease the responsiveness of the supply chain. Supply and demand management will have the greatest impact when it is applied to predictably variable products.

Faced with predictable variability, a company's goal is to respond in a manner that maximizes profitability. A firm must choose how to handle predictable variability by utilizing techniques in two broad categories:

1. Manage supply using capacity, inventory, subcontracting, and backlogs
2. Manage demand using short-term price discounts and trade promotions

The use of these tools enables the supply chain to greatly increase its profitability because it is able to match supply and demand in a much more coordinated fashion.

To illustrate some of the issues involved, let us consider the garden equipment manufacturer discussed in Chapter 8, Red Tomato Tools. Demand for garden tools is seasonal, with sales concentrated in the spring. Red Tomato needs to plan how it will meet the demand to maximize profit. One way to meet demand requires that Red Tomato carry enough manufacturing capacity to meet demand in any period. The advantage of this approach is that Red Tomato incurs very low inventory costs because no inventory needs to be carried from period to period. The disadvantage, however, is that much of the expensive capacity would go unused during most months when demand was lower.

Another approach to meeting demand would be to build up inventory during the off season to keep production stable year round. The advantage of this approach lies in the fact Red Tomato could get by with a smaller, less expensive factory. High inventory carrying costs, however, make this alternative expensive. A third approach would be for Red Tomato to work with their retail partners in the supply chain to offer a price promotion before the spring months during periods of low demand. This promotion shifts some of the spring demand forward into a slow period, thereby spreading demand more evenly throughout the year and reducing the seasonal surge. Such a demand pattern is less expensive to supply. Red Tomato needs to decide which alternative maximizes their profitability.

Often companies divide the task of supply and demand management between different functions. Marketing typically manages demand and Operations typically manages supply. At a higher level, supply chains suffer from this phenomenon as well with retailers independently managing demand and manufacturers independently managing supply. With supply and demand management decisions being made independently, it is increasingly difficult to coordinate the supply chain, thereby decreasing profit. Therefore, maximizing profitability depends on these decisions being made in a coordinated fashion and requires supply chain partners to work together across enterprises. We illustrate how a company can achieve this coordination through further discussion of Red Tomato.

First, we focus on actions that a supply chain can take to improve profitability by managing supply.

9.2 MANAGING SUPPLY

A firm can vary supply of product by controlling a combination of the following two factors:

- Production capacity
- Inventory

The objective is to maximize profit, which, for our discussion, is the difference between revenue generated from sales and the total cost associated with material, capacity, and inventory. In general, companies use a combination of varying capacity and inventory when managing supply. Following we list some specific approaches to managing capacity and inventory with the goal of maximizing profits.

Managing Capacity

When managing capacity to meet predictable variability, firms use a combination of the following approaches.

- *Time flexibility from workforce:* In this approach, a firm uses flexible work hours from the workforce to manage capacity to better meet demand. In many instances, plants do not operate continually and are left idle during portions of the day or week. Therefore, spare plant capacity exists in the form of hours when the plant is not operational. For example, many plants do not run three shifts, so the existing work force could work overtime during peak periods to produce more to meet demand. The overtime used is varied to match the variation in demand. This system would allow production from the plant to more closely match the demand from customers.

If demand fluctuates by day of the week or week of the month and the workforce is willing to be flexible, a firm may schedule the workforce so that the available capacity better matches demand. In such settings, use of a part-time workforce may further increase the capacity flexibility by enabling the firm to have more people at work during peak periods. Telemarketing centers and banks use part-time workers extensively to better match supply and demand.

- *Use of seasonal workforce:* In this approach, a firm uses a temporary workforce during the peak season to increase capacity to match demand. The tourism industry often uses seasonal workers where a base of full-time employees exists and the rest are hired only for the peak season. Toyota regularly uses seasonal workforce in Japan to better match supply and demand. This approach may be hard to sustain if the labor market is tight.

- *Use of subcontracting:* In this approach, a firm subcontracts peak production so that internal production remains level and can be done cheaply. With the subcontractor handling the peaks, the company is able to build a relatively inflexible but low-cost facility where the production rates are kept relatively constant (other than variations that arise from the use of overtime). Peaks are subcontracted out to facilities that are more flexible. A key here is the availability of relatively flexible subcontractor capacity. The subcontractor can often provide flexibility at a lower cost by pooling the fluctuations in demand across different manufacturers. Thus the flexible subcontractor capacity must have both volume (fluctuating demand from a manufacturer) as well as variety flexibility (demand from several manufacturers) to be sustainable. For example, most power companies do not have the capacity to supply their customers with all the electricity demanded on peak days. They instead rely on being able to purchase that power from suppliers and subcontractors who have excess electricity. This allows the power companies to maintain a level supply and, subsequently, a lower cost.

- *Use of dual facilities—dedicated and flexible:* In this approach, a firm builds both dedicated and flexible facilities. Dedicated facilities produce a relatively stable output of products over time in a very efficient manner. Flexible facilities produce a widely varying volume and variety of products but at a higher unit cost. For instance, a PC components manufacturer could have dedicated facilities for specific types of circuit boards as well as a flexible facility that could manufacture all types of circuit boards. Each dedicated facility could produce at a relatively steady rate, with fluctuations being absorbed by the flexible facility.

- *Designing product flexibility into the production processes:* In this approach, a firm has flexible production lines whose production rate can easily be varied. Production is then changed to match demand. Hino Trucks in Japan has several production lines for different product families. The production lines are designed such that changing the number of workers on a line can vary the production rate. As long as variation of demand across different product lines is complementary, (i.e., when one goes up the other tends to go down), the capacity on each line can be varied by moving the workforce from one line to the other. Of course this requires that the work force be multiskilled and easily adapt to being moved from line to line. Production flexibility can also be achieved if the production machinery being used is flexible and can be changed easily from producing one product to another. This approach can only be effective if the overall demand across all the products is relatively constant. Several firms producing products with seasonal demand try and exploit this approach by carrying a portfolio of products that have peak demand seasons distributed over the year. A classic example is that of lawnmower manufacturers also manufacturing snow blowers. In the services field, an example comes from strategy consulting firms that often offer a balanced product portfolio, with growth strategies emphasized when economic times are good and cost cutting projects emphasized when times are bad.

Managing Inventory

When managing inventory to meet predictable variability, firms use a combination of the following approaches:

- *Using common components across multiple products:* In this approach, a firm designs common components used in multiple products, with each product having predictably variable demand that results in relatively constant overall demand. Use of common components across these products will result in the demand for the components being relatively constant. For example, the use of a common engine for both lawn mowers and snow blowers allows for engine demand to be relatively stable even though lawn mower and snow blower demand fluctuates over the year. Therefore, the part of the supply chain producing components can easily synchronize supply with demand and a relatively low inventory of parts will have to be built up. Similarly, in a consulting firm, many of the same consultants produce growth strategies when they are in demand and produce cost reduction strategies when they are in demand.

- *Build inventory of high demand or predictable demand products:* When most of the products a firm produces have the same peak demand season, the previous approach is no longer feasible. A firm must then decide which inventory to build during the off season. The answer is to build products during the off season that have more predictable demand because there is less to be learned about their demand by waiting. As more is known about demand closer to the selling season, production of more uncertain items should take place. As an example, imagine a manufacturer of winter jackets that produces jackets both for retail sale and for the Boston Police and Fire Departments. Demand for the Boston Police and Fire jackets will be much more predictable and these jackets can be made in the off season and stocked up until winter. The retail jacket's demand, however, will likely be better known closer to the time when it is sold because fashion trends can change quickly. Therefore, this jacket manufacturer should manufacture the retail jackets close to the peak season when they are being sold to enable them to gain as much knowledge of demand as they can. This strategy helps the supply chain better synchronize supply and demand.

Next we consider actions a supply chain can take to improve profitability by managing demand.

9.3   MANAGING DEMAND

Supply chains can influence demand by using pricing and other forms of promotion. Marketing and sales often make the promotion and pricing decisions and they typically make them with the objective of maximizing revenue. But as we know from previous chapters, changing the demand pattern can change the cost the company incurs to meet that demand. Thus, pricing decisions based only on revenue considerations often result in a decrease in overall profitability. The same is true when thinking of the supply chain. The retailer sets the price and runs promotions to generate demand. This is regularly done without taking into account the impact on the rest of the supply chain. In this section, our goal is to show how the combination of pricing and aggregate planning (both demand and supply management) may be used to maximize supply chain profitability.

Let us return to Red Tomato Tools, the garden equipment manufacturer. Green Thumb Gardens is a large retail chain that has signed an exclusive contract to sell all products made by Red Tomato Tools. Demand for garden tools peaks in the spring months of March and April as gardeners prepare to begin planting. When planning, the goal of both firms should be to maximize supply chain profits because this outcome leaves them more to divide among each other. For profit maximization to take place, Red Tomato and Green Thumb will need to devise a way to collaborate and, just as important, determine a way to split the supply chain profits. Determining how these profits will be allocated to different members of the supply chain is a key to successful collaboration.

Red Tomato and Green Thumb are exploring how retail promotions can increase their profitability. A key decision they must make is how to time the promotion. Are they in a better position if they offer the price promotion during the peak period of demand or during a low-demand period? Green Thumb's Vice President of Sales favors a promotion during the peak period because this will increase revenue by the largest amount. On the other hand, the Red Tomato's Vice President of Manufacturing is against such a move because it will increase their costs. She favors a promotion during the low-demand season because it will level demand and lower production costs.

Red Tomato and Green Thumb must start by considering the forecasted demand and the resulting optimal aggregate plan (this is the same as we discussed in Chapter 8). Green Thumb and Red Tomato have jointly forecasted demand over the next six months as shown in Table 9.1.

Each tool has a retail price of $40. Red Tomato immediately ships assembled tools to Green Thumb where all inventory is held. Green Thumb has a starting inventory in January of 1,000 tools. At the beginning of January, Red Tomato has a work force of 80 employees. There are a total of twenty working days in each month and Red Tomato workers earn $4 per nonovertime hour. Each employee works eight hours a workday on normal time and the rest on overtime. Because the Red Tomato operation

TABLE 9.1	Demand for Red Tomato Tools
Month	*Demand Forecast*
January	1,600
February	3,000
March	3,200
April	3,800
May	2,200
June	2,200

consists mostly of hand assembly, the capacity of the production operation is determined primarily by the total labor hours worked (i.e., it is not limited by machine capacity). No employee works more than ten hours of over time per month. The various costs are shown in Table 9.2.

There are no limits on subcontracting, inventories, and stockouts. All stockouts are backlogged and supplied from the following month's production. Inventory costs are incurred on the ending inventory of each month. The companies' goal is to obtain the optimal aggregate plan that allows at least 500 units of inventory at the end of June (i.e., no stockouts at the end of June and at least 500 units in inventory).

The optimal aggregate plan for Red Tomato and Green Thumb is shown in Table 9.3.

For this aggregate plan, the supply chain will obtain the following costs and revenues:

$$\text{Total cost over planning horizon} = \$422,275.$$

Given the sale price of $40/unit and total sales of 16,000 units, revenue over the planning horizon is given by the following:

$$\text{Revenue over planning horizon} = 40 \times 16,000 = \$640,000$$
$$\text{Profit over the planning horizon} = \$217,725.$$

TABLE 9.2	Costs for Red Tomato and Green Thumb
Item	*Cost*
Material cost	$10/unit
Inventory holding cost	$2/unit/month
Marginal cost of a stockout	$5/unit/month
Hiring and training costs	$300/worker
Layoff cost	$500/worker
Labor hours required	4/unit
Regular time cost	$4/hour
Over time cost	$6/hour
Cost of subcontracting	$30/unit

TABLE 9.3 Aggregate Plan for Red Tomato and Green Thumb

Period t	No. Hired H_t	No. Laid Off L_t	Workforce Size W_t	Overtime O_t	Inventory I_t	Stockout S_t	Subcontract C_t	Total Production P_t
0	0	0	80	0	1,000	0	0	
1	0	15	65	0	1,983	0	0	2,583
2	0	0	65	0	1,567	0	0	2,583
3	0	0	65	0	950	0	0	2,583
4	0	0	65	0	0	267	0	2,583
5	0	0	65	0	117	0	0	2,583
6	0	0	65	0	500	0	0	2,583

The average seasonal inventory during the planning horizon is given by the following:

$$\text{Average seasonal inventory} = \left[(I_0 + I_6)/2 + \sum_{t=1}^{5} I_t \right] / T = 5{,}367/6 = 895$$

The average flow time for this aggregate plan over the planning horizon is given as follows:

Average flow time = Average inventory / Average sales = 895 / 2,667 = 0.34 months.

These results all pertain to the situation where there is no promotion. Now the companies want to explore if and when to potentially offer a promotion. Four key factors influence the timing of a trade promotion:

- Impact of the promotion on demand
- Product margins
- Cost of holding inventory
- Cost of changing capacity

Management at both companies would like to identify whether each factor favors offering a promotion during the high- or low-demand periods. They start by considering the impact of promotion on demand. When a promotion is offered during a period, that period's demand will go up. This increase in demand results from a combination of the following three factors:

1. *Market growth:* An increase in consumption of the product either from new or existing customers. Toyota provides an example outside the garden tool industry. When Toyota offers a price promotion on the Camry, they may attract buyers who were considering the purchase of a lower end model. Thus, the promotion increases the size of the overall family sedan market as well as increasing Toyota's sales.

2. *Stealing share:* Customers substituting the firm's product for a competitor's product. When Toyota offers a Camry promotion, buyers who might have purchased a Honda

Accord may now purchase a Camry. Thus, the promotion increases Toyota's sales while keeping the overall size of the family sedan market the same.

3. *Forward buying:* Customers move up future purchases (as discussed in Chapter 10) to the present. A promotion may attract buyers who would have purchased a Camry a few months down the road. The promotion does not increase Toyota's sales in the long run and also leaves the family sedan market the same size.

The first two factors increase the overall demand for Toyota, whereas the third simply shifts future demand to the present. It is important to know the relative impact from the three factors as a result of a promotion before making the decision regarding the optimal timing of the promotion. In general, as the fraction of increased demand coming from forward buying grows, offering the promotion during the peak demand period becomes less attractive. Offering a promotion during a peak period that has significant forward buying creates even more variable demand than before the promotion. Product that was once demanded in the slow period is now demanded in the peak period, making this demand pattern even more costly to serve.

Green Thumb has estimated that discounting a Red Tomato tool from $40 to $39 (a $1 discount) results in the period demand increasing by 10 percent because of increased consumption or substitution. Further, 20 percent of each of the two following months' demand is moved forward. Management would like to determine whether it is more effective to offer the discount in January or April.

The team first considers the impact of offering the discount in January. If the discount is offered in January, the demand forecast is as shown in Table 9.4. The optimal aggregate plan is shown in Table 9.5. With a discount in January the supply chain obtains:

$$\text{Total cost over planning horizon} = \$421,915$$
$$\text{Revenue over planning horizon} = \$643,400$$
$$\text{Profit over planning horizon} = \$221,485.$$

Now they consider the impact of offering the discount in April. If Green Thumb offers the discount in April, the demand forecast is as shown in Table 9.6. The optimal aggregate plan is shown in Table 9.7. With a discount in April we have

$$\text{Total cost over planning horizon} = \$438,857$$
$$\text{Revenue over planning horizon} = \$650,140$$
$$\text{Profit over planning horizon} = \$211,283.$$

TABLE 9.4 Demand When Discounting Price in January to $39	
Month	*Demand Forecast*
January	3,000
February	2,400
March	2,560
April	3,800
May	2,200
June	2,200

TABLE 9.5 Optimal Aggregate Plan for Demand in Table 9.4

Period t	No. Hired H_t	No. Laid Off L_t	Workforce Size W_t	Overtime O_t	Inventory I_t	Stockout S_t	Subcontract C_t	Total Production P_t
0	0	0	80	0	1,000	0	0	
1	0	15	65	0	610	0	0	2,610
2	0	0	65	0	820	0	0	2,610
3	0	0	65	0	870	0	0	2,610
4	0	0	65	0	0	320	0	2,610
5	0	0	65	0	90	0	0	2,610
6	0	0	65	0	500	0	0	2,610

TABLE 9.6 Demand Profile on Discounting Price in April to $39

Month	Demand Forecast
January	1,600
February	3,000
March	3,200
April	5,060
May	1,760
June	1,760

TABLE 9.7 Optimal Aggregate Plan for Demand in Table 9.6

Period t	No. Hired H_t	No. Laid Off L_t	Workforce Size W_t	Overtime O_t	Inventory I_t	Stockout S_t	Subcontract C_t	Total Production P_t
0	0	0	80	0	1,000	0	0	
1	0	14	66	0	2,047	0	0	2,647
2	0	0	66	0	1,693	0	0	2,647
3	0	0	66	0	1,140	0	0	2,647
4	0	0	66	0	0	1,273	0	2,647
5	0	0	66	0	0	387	0	2,647
6	0	0	66	0	500	0	0	2,647

TABLE 9.8 Demand Profile from Discounting Price in January to $39 with Large Increase in Demand

Month	Demand Forecast
January	4,440
February	2,400
March	2,560
April	3,800
May	2,200
June	2,200

Observe that the demand fluctuation in Table 9.6 has increased relative to the profile in Table 9.1 because the discount was offered in the highest demand month. The optimal aggregate plan for this demand pattern is shown in Table 9.7.

Observe that a price promotion in January results in a higher supply chain profit than no promotion, whereas a promotion in April results in a lower supply chain profit than no promotion. As a result, Red Tomato and Green Thumb decide to offer the discount in the off-peak month of January. Even though revenues are higher when the discount is offered in April, the increase in operating costs makes it a less profitable option. A promotion in January allows Red Tomato and Green Thumb to increase the profit they can share among themselves. Observe that this analysis is possible only because the retailer and manufacturer have collaborated during the planning phase. This conclusion supports our earlier statement that it is not appropriate for a supply chain to leave pricing decisions solely in the domain of retailers and aggregate planning solely in the domain of manufacturers, with each having their own forecasts. It is crucial that forecasts, pricing, and aggregate planning be coordinated in the supply chain.

The importance of collaboration is further supported by the fact that the optimal action is different if most of the demand increase comes from market growth or stealing market share rather than forward buying. Reconsider the situation where discounting a unit from $40 to $39 results in the period demand increasing by 100 percent because of increased consumption or substitution. Further, 20 percent of each of the

TABLE 9.9 Optimal Aggregate Plan for Demand in Table 9.8

Period t	No. Hired H_t	No. Laid Off L_t	Workforce Size W_t	Overtime O_t	Inventory I_t	Stockout S_t	Subcontract C_t	Total Production P_t
0	0	0	80		1,000	0	0	
1	0	0	80	0	0	240	0	3,200
2	0	11	69	0	140	0	0	2,780
3	0	0	69	0	360	0	0	2,780
4	0	0	69	0	0	660	0	2,780
5	0	0	69	0	0	80	0	2,780
6	0	0	69	0	500	0	0	2,780

TABLE 9.10   Demand Profile on Discounting Price in April to $39 with Large Increase in Demand

Month	Demand Forecast
January	1,600
February	3,000
March	3,200
April	8,480
May	1,760
June	1,760

two following months demand is moved forward. The supply chain team wants to determine whether it is preferable to offer the discount in January or April.

Offering the discount in January results in the demand forecast shown in Table 9.8. The optimal aggregate plan in this case is shown in Table 9.9. With a discount in January the team obtains:

$$\text{Total cost over planning horizon} = \$456,750$$
$$\text{Revenue over planning horizon} = \$699,560$$
$$\text{Profit over planning horizon} = \$242,810.$$

If the discount is offered in April, the demand forecast is as shown in Table 9.10. The optimal aggregate plan in this case is shown in Table 9.11. With a discount in April the team obtains:

$$\text{Total cost over planning horizon} = \$536,200$$
$$\text{Revenue over planning horizon} = \$783,520$$
$$\text{Profit over planning horizon} = \$247,320.$$

When forward buying is a small part of the increase in demand from discounting, the supply chain is better off offering the discount in the peak demand month of April.

Exactly as discussed earlier, the optimal aggregate plan and profitability can also be determined for the case when the unit price is $31 and the discounted price is $30. The results of the various instances are summarized in Table 9.12.

TABLE 9.11   Optimal Aggregate Plan for Demand in Table 9.10

Period t	No. Hired H_t	No. Laid Off L_t	Workforce Size W_t	Overtime O_t	Inventory I_t	Stockout S_t	Subcontract C_t	Total Production P_t
0	0	0	80		1,000	0	0	
1	0	0	80	0	2,600	0	0	3,200
2	0	0	80	0	2,800	0	0	3,200
3	0	0	80	0	2,800	0	0	3,200
4	0	0	80	0	0	2,380	100	3,200
5	0	0	80	0	0	940	0	3,200
6	0	0	80	0	500	0	0	3,200

TABLE 9.12   Supply Chain Performance Under Different Scenarios

Regular Price	Promotion Price	Promotion Period	Percent Increase in Demand	Percent Forward Buy	Profit	Average Inventory
$40	$40	NA	NA	NA	$217,725	895
$40	$39	January	10%	20%	$221,485	523
$40	$39	April	10%	20%	$211,283	938
$40	$39	January	100%	20%	$242,810	208
$40	$39	April	100%	20%	$247,320	1,492
$31	$31	NA	NA	NA	$73,725	895
$31	$30	January	100%	20%	$84,410	208
$31	$30	April	100%	20%	$69,120	1,492

From the results in Table 9.12, we can draw the following conclusions regarding the impact of promotions.

1. As seen in Table 9.12, average inventory increases if a promotion is run during the peak period and decreases if the promotion is run during the off-peak period.

2. Promoting during a peak demand month may decrease overall profitability if a significant fraction of the demand increase results from a forward buy. In Table 9.12, observe that running a promotion in April decreases profitability when forward buying is 20 percent and the demand increase from increased consumption and substitution is 10 percent.

3. As forward buy becomes a smaller fraction of the demand increase from a promotion, it is more profitable to promote during the peak period. From Table 9.12, for a sale price of $40, it is optimal to promote in the off-peak month of January when forward buying is 20 percent and increased consumption is 10 percent. When forward buying is 20 percent and increased consumption is 100 percent, however, it is optimal to promote in the peak month of April.

4. As the product margin declines, promoting during the peak demand period becomes less profitable. In Table 9.12, observe that for a unit price of $40 it is optimal to promote in the peak month of April when forward buying is 20 percent and increased consumption is 100 percent. On the other hand, if the unit price is $31 it is optimal to promote in the off-peak month of January.

Other factors such as holding cost and the cost of changing capacity also affect the optimal timing of promotions. The various factors and their impacts are summarized in Table 9.13.

A key point from the Red Tomato supply chain examples we have considered in this chapter is that faced with seasonal demand, a firm should use a combination of pricing (to manage demand) and production and inventory (to manage supply) to improve profitability. The precise use of each lever varies with the situation. This makes it crucial that enterprises in a supply chain coordinate both their forecasting and planning efforts. Only then are profits maximized.

TABLE 9.13 Summary of Impact on Promotion Timing	
Factor	*Impact on Timing of Promotion*
High forward buying	Favors promotion during low-demand periods
High ability to steal market share	Favors promotion during peak demand periods
High ability to grow overall market	Favors promotion during peak demand periods
High margin	Favors promotion during peak demand periods
Low margin	Favors promotion during low-demand periods
High holding costs	Favors promotion during low-demand periods
High costs of changing capacity	Favors promotion during low-demand periods

9.4   IMPLEMENTING SOLUTIONS TO PREDICTABLE VARIABILITY IN PRACTICE

1. *Coordinate planning across enterprises in the supply chain.* For a supply chain to successfully manage predictable variability, the entire chain must work toward the one goal of maximizing profitability. Everyone in a supply chain may agree with this in principal but in reality, it is very difficult to get an entire supply chain to agree on how to maximize profitability. Firms have even had difficulty getting different functions within an enterprise to plan collaboratively. Incentives play a large role in this. Within a company, marketing often has incentives based on revenue whereas operations has incentives based on cost. Within the supply chain, different enterprises are judged by their own profitability, not necessarily by the overall supply chain's profitability. From the examples considered earlier, it is clear that without working to get companies to work together, the supply chain will return suboptimal profits. Therefore, firms in the supply chain need to collaborate through the formation of joint teams. Incentives of the members of the supply chain must be aligned. High-level support within the organization, including support from the chief executive officer, will also be needed because this coordination often requires groups to act counter to their traditional operating procedures. Although this collaboration is difficult, the payoffs are significant.

2. *Take predictable variability into account when making strategic decisions.* Predictable variability has a tremendous impact on the operations of a company. A firm must always take this impact into account when making strategic decisions. However, predictable variability is not always taken into account when strategic plans are made, such as what type of products to offer, whether or not to build new facilities, and what sort of pricing structure a company should have. As indicated in this chapter, the level of profitability is greatly affected by predictable variability and, therefore, the success or failure of strategic decisions can be determined by it.

3. *Preempt, do not just react to, predictable variability.* Companies often have a tendency to focus on how they can effectively react to predictable variability. This role often falls on operations, which tries to manage supply to best deal with predictable variability. As discussed in this chapter, the management of supply as well as demand provides the best response to predictable variability. Actions like pricing and

promotion that manage demand are preemptive and often in the domain of marketing. It is important for marketing and operations to coordinate their efforts and plan for predictable variability together well before the peak demand is observed. This coordination allows a firm to preempt predictable variability and come up with a response that maximizes profits.

9.5 SUMMARY OF LEARNING OBJECTIVES

1. Manage supply to improve synchronization in the supply chain in the face of predictable variability.

   To manage supply with the goal of maximizing profit, companies must manage their capacity through the use of workforce flexibility, subcontracting, dual facilities, and product flexibility. Companies must also manage supply through the use of inventory by emphasizing common parts and building and holding products with predictable demand ahead of time. These methodologies, combined with aggregate planning, enable a company to effectively manage supply.

2. Manage demand to improve synchronization in the supply chain in the face of predictable variability.

   To manage demand with the goal of maximizing profit, companies must use pricing and promotion decisions. The timing of promotions can often have a tremendous impact on demand. Therefore, using pricing to shape demand can help synchronize the supply chain.

3. Use aggregate planning to maximize profitability when faced with predictable variability in the supply chain.

   To handle predictable variability in a profit-maximizing manner, supply chains must coordinate the management of both supply and demand. This requires coordinated planning across all stages of the supply chain to select aggregate plans that maximize supply chain profit.

DISCUSSION QUESTIONS

1. What are some obstacles to creating a flexible workforce? What are the benefits?
2. Discuss why subcontractors can often offer products and services to a company more cheaply than if the company produced them themselves.
3. In what type of industries would you tend to see dual facility types (some facilities focusing on only one type of product and others able to produce a wide variety)? In what industries would this be relatively rare? Why?
4. Discuss how you would set up a mechanism for multiple enterprises in the supply chain to collaborate.
5. What are some product lines that use common parts across many products? What are the advantages of doing this?
6. Discuss how a company can get marketing and operations to work together with the common goal of coordinating supply and demand to maximize profitability.
7. How can a firm use pricing to change demand patterns?
8. When would a firm want to offer pricing promotions in their peak demand periods?
9. When would a firm want to offer pricing promotions during their low-demand periods?

BIBLIOGRAPHY

Geary, Steve, Paul Childerhouse, and Denis Towill. 2002. "Uncertainty and the Seamless Supply Chain." *Supply Chain Management Review* (July–August): 52–61.

Martin, André J. 2001. "Capacity Planning: The Antidote to Supply Chain Constraints." *Supply Chain Management Review* (November–December): 62–67.

Sodhi, Mohan. 2000. "Getting the Most from Planning Technologies." *Supply Chain Management Review, Special Global Supplement* (Winter).

------------------------------- C A S E   S T U D Y -------------------------------

Mintendo Game Girl

It is late June, and Sandra, head of operations at Mintendo, and Bill, head of sales of We 'R' Toys, are about to get together to discuss production and marketing plans for the next six months. Mintendo is the manufacturer of the popular Game Girl handheld electronic game that is sold exclusively through We 'R' Toys retail stores. The second half of the year is critical to Game Girl's success because a majority of their sales occur during the holiday shopping period.

Sandra is worried about the impact that the upcoming holiday surge in demand will have on her production line. Costs to subcontract assembly of the Game Girls are expected to increase and she has been trying to keep costs down given that her bonus depends on the level of production costs.

Bill is worried about competing toy stores gaining share during the Christmas buying season. He has seen many companies lose their share by failing to keep prices in line with the performance of their products. He would like to maximize the Game Girl market share.

Both Sandra and Bill's teams produce a joint forecast of demand over the next six months, as shown in Table 9.14.

We 'R' Toys sells Game Girls for $50 a piece. At the end of June, the company has an inventory of 50,000 Game Girls. Capacity of the production facility is set purely by the number of workers assem-

TABLE 9.15   Costs for Mintendo/We 'R' Toys

Item	Cost
Material cost	$12/unit
Inventory holding cost	$4/unit/month
Marginal cost of a stockout	$10/unit/month
Hiring and training costs	$3000/worker
Layoff cost	$5000/worker
Labor hours required	.25/unit
Regular time cost	$15/hour
Over time cost	$22.50/hour
Cost of subcontracting	$18/unit

bling the Game Girls. At the end of June, the company has a work force of 300 employees, each of whom work eight hours of nonovertime at $15/hour for twenty days each month. Work rules require that no employee work more than forty hours of overtime a month. The various costs are shown in Table 9.15.

Sandra, concerned about controlling costs during the periods of surging demand over the holidays, proposes to Bill that the price be lowered by $5 for the month of September. This would likely increase September's demand by 50 percent due to new customers attracted to Game Girl. Additionally, 30 percent of each of the following two months of demand would occur in September as forward buys. She strongly believes that this leveling of demand will help the company.

Bill counters with the idea of offering the same promotion in November, during the heart of the buying season. In this case, the promotion increases November's demand by 50 percent due to new customers attracted to Game Girl. Additionally, 30 percent of December's demand would occur in November as forward buying. Bill wants to increase revenue and sees no better way to do this than to offer a promotion during the peak season.

TABLE 9.14   Demand for Game Girls

Month	Demand Forecast
July	100,000
August	110,000
September	130,000
October	180,000
November	250,000
December	300,000

QUESTIONS

1. Which option delivers the maximum profit for the supply chain: Sandra's plan, Bill's plan, or no promotion plan at all?

2. How does the answer change if a discount of $10 must be given to reach the same level of impact that the $5 discount received?

3. Suppose Sandra's fears about increasing outsourcing costs come to fruition and the cost rises to $22/unit for subcontracting. Does this change the decision when the discount is $5?

IV

Planning and Managing Inventories in a Supply Chain

C H A P T E R   1 0

**Managing Economies of Scale in the Supply Chain:
Cycle Inventory**

C H A P T E R   1 1

**Managing Uncertainty in the Supply Chain:
Safety Inventory**

C H A P T E R   1 2

Determining Optimal Level of Product Availability

The goals of the three chapters in Part IV are to describe the role that inventory plays in a supply chain and discuss actions that managers can take to decrease inventories without increasing cost or hurting the level of product availability.

Chapter 10 discusses factors that lead to the increase of cycle inventory within a supply chain. Several managerial actions that allow a supply chain manager to decrease the level of cycle inventory without increasing costs are described. Chapter 11 focuses on the buildup of safety inventory to counter supply or demand uncertainty. Factors influencing the level of safety inventory are discussed. Based on these factors, a variety of managerial levers are explained that can be used to reduce the amount of safety inventory required without hurting the level of product availability. Chapter 12 discusses factors that influence the appropriate level of product availability within a supply chain. Several managerial levers that can be used to increase overall profitability in the supply chain, such as quick response and postponement, are described.

PART IV

Planning and Managing Inventories in a Supply Chain

CHAPTER 11
Managing Economies of Scale in the Supply Chain: Cycle Inventory

CHAPTER 12
Managing Uncertainty in the Supply Chain: Safety Inventory

CHAPTER 13
Determining Optimal Level of Product Availability

C H A P T E R

10

Managing Economies of Scale in the Supply Chain: Cycle Inventory

Learning Objectives

After reading this chapter, you will be able to:

1. Balance the appropriate costs to choose the optimal amount of cycle inventory in the supply chain.

2. Understand the impact of quantity discounts on lot size and cycle inventory.

3. Devise appropriate discounting schemes for the supply chain.

4. Understand the impact of trade promotions on lot size and cycle inventory.

5. Identify managerial levers that reduce lot size and cycle inventory in a supply chain without increasing cost.

Cycle inventory exists because producing or purchasing in large lots allows a stage of the supply chain to exploit economies of scale and lower cost. The presence of fixed costs associated with ordering and transportation, quantity discounts in product pricing, and short-term discounts or trade promotions encourages different stages of a supply chain to exploit economies of scale by ordering in large lots. In this chapter, we study how each of these factors impacts the lot size and cycle inventories within the supply chain. Our goal is to identify managerial levers that reduce cycle inventory in the supply chain without raising cost.

10.1 THE ROLE OF CYCLE INVENTORY IN THE SUPPLY CHAIN

A *lot* or *batch size* is the quantity that a stage of the supply chain either produces or purchases at a given time. Consider, for example, a computer store that sells an average of four printers a day. The store manager, however, orders 80 printers from the manufacturer each time he places an order. The lot or batch size in this case is 80 printers. Given daily sales of four printers, it takes an average of twenty days before the store sells the entire lot and purchases a replenishment lot. The computer store holds an inventory of printers because the manager purchased a lot size larger than the store's daily sales. *Cycle inventory* is the average inventory in the supply chain due to either production or purchases in lot sizes that are larger than those demanded by the customer.

In the rest of this chapter we use the following notation:

Q: Quantity in a lot or batch size
D: Demand per unit time

We ignore the impact of demand variability because it has a marginal impact on lot size and cycle inventory. In this chapter, we assume demand to be stable. In Chapter 11, we introduce demand variability and its impact on safety inventory, where variability has a large effect.

Consider the sale of jeans at Jean-Mart, a department store. Demand for jeans is relatively stable at $D = 100$ jeans per day. First consider the case where the store manager at Jean-Mart purchases in lots of $Q = 1,000$ jeans. We can draw the *inventory profile* of jeans at Jean-Mart, which is a plot depicting the level of inventory over time as shown in Figure 10.1.

Because purchases are in lots of $Q = 1,000$ units, whereas demand is only $D = 100$ units per day, it takes ten days for a lot to be sold. The inventory of jeans at Jean-Mart declines steadily from 1,000 (when the lot arrives) to 0 (when the last pair is sold) over ten days. This sequence of a lot arriving and demand depleting inventory until another lot arrives repeats itself in a cyclical manner every ten days as shown in the inventory profile in Figure 10.1.

When demand is steady, cycle inventory and lot size are related as follows:

$$\text{Cycle Inventory} = \text{Lot Size} / 2 = Q/2. \qquad \textbf{(10.1)}$$

Given a lot size of 1,000 units, Jean-Mart carries a cycle inventory of $Q/2 = 500$ jeans. From the aforementioned relationship (Equation 10.1), we see that cycle inventory is proportional to the lot size. A supply chain where stages produce or purchase in

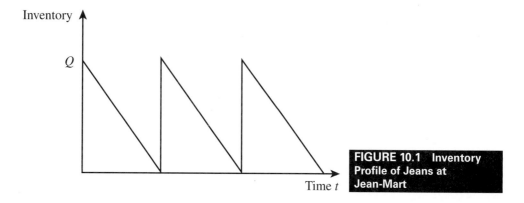

FIGURE 10.1   Inventory Profile of Jeans at Jean-Mart

larger lots will have more cycle inventory than a supply chain where stages purchase in smaller lots. For example, if a competing department store purchases in lot sizes of 200 jeans, it will carry a cycle inventory of only 100 jeans.

Lot sizes and cycle inventory also influence the flow time of material within the supply chain. Recall from Little's Law (Equation 3.1) that

$$\text{Average Flow Time} = \text{Average Inventory/Average Flow Rate.}$$

For any supply chain, average flow rate equals the demand. We thus have

$$\text{Average flow time resulting from cycle inventory} = \text{Cycle Inventory/Demand} = Q/2D.$$

For Jean-Mart, which purchases lot sizes of 1,000 jeans and whose daily demand is 100 jeans, we obtain

$$\text{Average flow time resulting from cycle inventory} = Q/2D = 1{,}000/200 = 5 \text{ days.}$$

Cycle inventory at the Jean-Mart store thus adds five days to the amount of time that jeans spend, on average, in the supply chain. The larger the cycle inventory, the longer the lag time between when a product is produced and when it is sold. All else being equal, a lower level of cycle inventory is always desirable because large time lags leave a firm vulnerable to demand changes in the marketplace. A lower cycle inventory is also desirable because it decreases the working capital requirement for a firm. Toyota, for example, keeps a cycle inventory of only a few hours of production between the factory and most suppliers. As a result, Toyota is never left with parts that it does not need. It also allocates very little space in the factory to inventory.

Before we suggest actions that a manager can take to reduce cycle inventory, it is important to understand why stages of a supply chain produce or purchase in large lots and how lot size reduction impacts supply chain performance.

Cycle inventory is primarily held to take advantage of economies of scale and reduce cost within the supply chain. Increasing the lot size or cycle inventory often decreases the cost incurred by different stages of a supply chain. To understand how the supply chain achieves these economies of scale, we must first identify supply chain costs that are influenced by the lot size.

The *average price paid per unit purchased* is a key cost in the lot sizing decision. A buyer may increase the lot size if this action results in a reduction in the price paid per unit purchased. For example, if the jean manufacturer charges $20 per jean for orders under 500 jeans and $18 per jean for larger orders, the store manager at Jean-Mart may order in lots of at least 500 jeans to get the lower price. The price paid per unit is referred to as the *material cost* and is denoted by C. It is measured in $/unit. In many practical situations, material cost displays economies of scale and increasing the lot size decreases the material cost.

The *fixed ordering cost* includes all costs that do not vary with the size of the order but are incurred each time an order is placed. For example, a fixed administrative cost may be incurred to place an order, a trucking cost may be incurred to transport the order, and a labor cost may be incurred to receive the order. Jean-Mart, for example, incurs a cost of $400 for the truck that brings the shipment of jeans from the manufacturer. Assume that the truck can hold up to 2,000 jeans. The $400 cost is incurred irrespective of the number of jeans shipped on the truck. A lot size of 100 jeans results in a transportation cost of $4 per pair of jeans whereas a lot size of 1,000 jeans results in a transportation cost of $0.40 per pair of jeans. Given the fixed transportation cost per batch, the store manager is inclined to increase lot size to reduce transportation cost per jean. The fixed ordering cost per lot or batch is denoted by S (commonly thought of as a set-up cost) and is measured in $/lot. The ordering cost also displays economies of scale and increasing the lot size decreases the fixed ordering cost per unit purchased.

Holding cost is the cost of carrying one unit in inventory for a specified period of time, usually one year. It is a combination of the cost of capital, the cost of physically storing the inventory, and the cost that results from the product becoming obsolete. The holding cost is denoted by H and is measured in $/unit/year. It may also be obtained as a fraction, h, where h is the cost of holding $1 in inventory for one year. Given a unit cost of C, the holding cost H is given by

$$H = hC. \tag{10.2}$$

The total holding cost increases with an increase in lot size and cycle inventory.

To summarize, the costs that must be considered in any lot sizing decision are:

- Average price per unit purchased, C/unit
- Fixed ordering cost incurred per lot, S/lot
- Holding cost incurred per unit per year, H/unit/year $= hC$

Later in the chapter, we discuss how the various costs may be estimated in practice. However, for the purposes of this discussion, we can assume that they are already known.

The primary role of cycle inventory is to allow different stages in the supply chain to purchase product in lot sizes that minimize the sum of the material, ordering, and holding cost. If a manager were considering the holding cost alone, he or she would reduce the lot size and cycle inventory. Economies of scale in purchasing and ordering, however, motivate a manager to increase the lot size and cycle inventory. A manager must make the trade-off that minimizes the total cost when making the lot sizing decision.

Ideally, cycle inventory decisions should be made considering the total cost across the entire supply chain. In practice, however, each stage often makes its cycle inventory decisions independently. As we discuss later in the chapter, this practice increases the level of cycle inventory as well as the total cost in the supply chain.

> **Key Point**   Cycle inventory exists in a supply chain because different stages exploit economies of scale to lower total cost. The costs considered include material cost, fixed ordering cost, and holding cost.

Any stage of the supply chain exploits economies of scale in its replenishment decisions in the following three typical situations:

1. A fixed cost is incurred each time an order is placed or produced.
2. The supplier offers price discounts based on the quantity purchased per lot.
3. The supplier offers short-term discounts or holds trade promotions.

In the next three sections, we review how managers can take advantage of these situations.

10.2   ECONOMIES OF SCALE TO EXPLOIT FIXED COSTS

To better understand the trade-offs discussed in this section, consider a situation that often arises in our daily life—the purchase of groceries and other household products. These may be purchased at a nearby convenience store or at a Sam's Club (a large warehouse club selling consumer goods), which is generally located much further away. The fixed cost of going shopping is the time it takes to go to either location. This fixed cost is much lower for the convenience store. Prices, however, are higher at the local convenience store. Taking the fixed cost into account, we tend to tailor our lot size decision accordingly. When we only need a small quantity, we go to the nearby convenience store because the fixed costs are low. If we are buying a large quantity, however, we go to Sam's Club where the lower prices over the larger quantity purchased more than make up for the increase in fixed costs.

In this section we focus on the situation in which a supply chain incurs a fixed cost each time an order is placed. As mentioned earlier, this fixed cost may be associated with placing the order, receiving the order, and transporting the order. We identify the appropriate cost trade-offs that need to be considered when making the lot sizing decision. The objective of a lot sizing decision is to minimize the total cost of satisfying demand. We start by considering the lot sizing decision for a single product.

Lot Sizing for a Single Product (Economic Order Quantity)

Consider a computer reseller like Best Buy that sells HP computers. As they sell their current inventory, the Best Buy manager has to place a replenishment order for a new lot of computers. HP ships the order from its distributor using a truck. Best Buy pays for the truck no matter how many computers are on it. The key decision for the manager is how many computers to order from HP in a lot. For this decision, we assume the following inputs:

$$D = \text{Annual demand of the product}$$

$$S = \text{Fixed cost incurred per order}$$

$$C = \text{Cost per unit}$$

$$h = \text{Holding cost per year as a fraction of product cost}$$

Assume that HP does not offer any discounts and each unit costs $C no matter how large an order is. The holding cost is thus given by $H = hC$ (using Equation 10.2).

The Best Buy manager makes the lot sizing decision to minimize the total cost the store incurs. He must consider three costs when deciding on the lot size:

- Annual material cost: Annual cost of material purchased
- Annual order cost: Annual order cost for the lots ordered
- Annual holding cost: Annual cost of holding inventory

Because purchase price is independent of lot size, we have

$$\text{Annual material cost} = CD.$$

Given a lot size of Q, the number of orders must suffice to meet the annual demand. We thus have the following:

$$\text{Number of orders per year} = D/Q. \tag{10.3}$$

Because an order cost of S is incurred for each order placed, we infer the following:

$$\text{Annual order cost} = \left(\frac{D}{Q}\right)S \tag{10.4}$$

Given a lot size of Q, we have an average inventory of $Q/2$. The annual holding cost is thus the cost of holding $Q/2$ units in inventory for one year and is given as follows:

$$\text{Annual holding cost} = \left(\frac{Q}{2}\right)H = \left(\frac{Q}{2}\right)hC$$

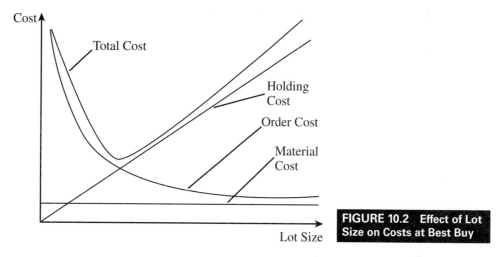

FIGURE 10.2   Effect of Lot Size on Costs at Best Buy

The total annual cost is the sum of all three costs and is given as follows:

$$\text{Total annual cost, } TC = CD + (D/Q)S + (Q/2)hC.$$

Figure 10.2 shows the variation in different costs as the lot size is changed.

Observe that the annual holding cost increases with an increase in lot size. In contrast, the annual order cost declines with an increase in lot size. The material cost is independent of lot size because we have assumed the price to be fixed. The total annual cost thus first declines and then increases with an increase in lot size. The fundamental trade-off the manager must make is between the fixed order cost and the holding cost incurred by Best Buy because material cost in this case is independent of the lot size.

From the perspective of the manager at Best Buy, the optimal lot size is one that minimizes the total cost to Best Buy. It is obtained by taking the first derivative of the total cost with respect to Q and setting it equal to 0 (see Appendix 10A). The optimal lot size is referred to as the *economic order quantity* (EOQ). It is denoted by Q^* and is given by the following equation:

$$\text{Optimal lot size,} Q^* = \sqrt{\frac{2\,DS}{hC}} \qquad \textbf{(10.5)}$$

Note that when using the formula it is important to have the same time units for the holding cost h and the demand D. With each lot or batch of size Q^*, the cycle inventory in the system is given by $Q^*/2$. The flow time spent by each unit in the system is given by $Q^*/(2D)$. Note that as the optimal lot size increases, so does the cycle inventory and the flow time. The optimal ordering frequency is given by n^* where

$$n^* = \frac{D}{Q^*} = \sqrt{\frac{DhC}{2S}} \qquad \textbf{(10.6)}$$

In Example 10.1 we illustrate the *EOQ* formula and the procedure to make lot sizing decisions.

Example 10.1: Economic Order Quantity

Demand for the Deskpro computer at Best Buy is 1,000 units per month. Best Buy incurs a fixed order placement, transportation, and receiving cost of $4,000 each time an order is placed. Each computer costs Best Buy $500 and the retailer has a holding cost of 20 percent. Evaluate the number of computers that the store manager should order in each replenishment lot.

Analysis: In this case, the store manager has the following input

$$\text{Annual demand, } D = 1,000 \times 12 = 12,000 \text{ units,}$$
$$\text{Order cost per lot, } S = \$4,000,$$
$$\text{Unit cost per computer, } C = \$500,$$
$$\text{Holding cost per year as a fraction of inventory value, } h = 0.2.$$

Using the EOQ formula (Equation 10.5), the optimal lot size is as follows

$$\text{Optimal order size} = \sqrt{\frac{2 \times 12,000 \times 4,000}{0.2 \times 500}} = 980$$

To minimize the total cost at Best Buy, the store manager orders a lot size of 980 computers for each replenishment order. For a lot size of $Q^* = 980$, the cycle inventory is the average resulting inventory and (using Equation 10.1) is given by the following:

$$\text{Cycle inventory} = Q^*/2 = 980/2 = 490.$$

For a lot size of $Q^* = 980$, the store manager evaluates

$$\text{Number of orders per year} = D/Q^* = 12,000/980 = 12.24,$$
$$\text{Annual ordering and holding cost} = (D/Q^*)S + (Q^*/2)hC = \$97,980,$$
$$\text{Average flow time} = Q^*/2D = 490/12,000 = 0.041 \text{ year} = 0.49 \text{ month.}$$

Each computer thus spends 0.49 months, on average, at Best Buy before it is sold. This flow time in storage is attributed to lot sizes arising from fixed costs.

A few key insights can be gained from this simple example. First, observe that using a lot size of 1,100 (instead of 980) increases annual costs to $98,636 (from $97,980). Even though the order size is over 10 percent larger than the optimal order size Q^*, total cost increases by only 0.6 percent. This issue can be relevant in practice. For example, Best Buy may find that the economic order quantity for computer diskettes is 6.5 cases. The manufacturer may be reluctant to ship half a case and may want to charge extra for this service. Our discussion illustrates that Best Buy is perhaps better off with lot sizes of six or seven cases because this change has a very small impact on their inventory related costs but can save on any fee that the manufacturer may charge for shipping half a case.

> **Key Point** Total ordering and holding costs are relatively stable around the economic order quantity. A firm is often better served by ordering a convenient lot size close to the economic order quantity rather than the precise EOQ.

If demand at Best Buy increases to 4,000 computers a month (demand has increased by a factor of 4), we can use the EOQ formula to determine that the optimal lot size doubles and the number of orders placed per year also doubles. In contrast, average flow time decreases by a factor of 2. In other words, as demand increases, cycle inventory measured in terms of days (or months) of demand should reduce if the lot sizing decision is made optimally. This observation can be stated as follows:

> **Key Point**   If demand increases by a factor of k, the optimal lot size increases by a factor of $\sqrt{k}$. The number of orders placed per year should also increase by a factor of $\sqrt{k}$. Flow time attributed to cycle inventory should decrease by a factor of $\sqrt{k}$.

Let us return to the instance where monthly demand for the Deskpro model is 1,000 computers. Now assume that the manager would like to reduce the lot size to $Q = 200$ units to reduce flow time. If this lot size is decreased without any other change, we have

$$\text{Annual inventory related costs} = (D/Q)S + (Q/2)hC = \$250{,}000.$$

This is significantly higher than the total cost of $97,980 that Best Buy incurred when ordering in lots of 980 units as in Example 10.1. Thus, there are clear financial reasons why the store manager would be unwilling to reduce the lot size to 200. To make it feasible to reduce the lot size, the Best Buy manager should work to reduce the fixed order cost. For example, if the fixed cost associated with each lot is reduced to $1,000 (from the current value of $4,000), the optimal lot size reduces to 490 (from the current value of 980). We illustrate the relationship between desired lot size and order cost in Example 10.2.

Example 10.2: Relationship between Desired Lot Size and Order Cost

The store manager at Best Buy would like to reduce the optimal lot size from 980 to 200. For this lot size reduction to be optimal, the store manager wants to evaluate how much the order cost per lot should be reduced.

Analysis: In this case we have

$$\text{Desired lot size, } Q^* = 200,$$
$$\text{Annual demand, } D = 1{,}000 \times 12 = 12{,}000 \text{ units,}$$
$$\text{Unit cost per computer, } C = \$500,$$
$$\text{Holding cost per year as a fraction of inventory value, } h = 0.2.$$

Using the EOQ formula (Equation 10.5), the desired order cost is

$$S = \frac{hC(Q^*)^2}{2D} = \frac{0.2 \times 500 \times 200^2}{2 \times 12{,}000} = \$166.7$$

Thus, the store manager at Best Buy would have to reduce the order cost per lot from $4,000 to $166.70 for a lot size of 200 to be optimal.

The observation in Example 10.2 may be stated as follows:

> **Key Point**   To reduce the optimal lot size by a factor of k, the fixed order cost S must be reduced by a factor of k^2.

Aggregating Multiple Products in a Single Order

To effectively reduce the lot size, the store manager needs to understand the source of the fixed cost. As we pointed out earlier, one major source of fixed costs is transportation. In several companies the array of products sold is divided into families or groups with each group managed independently by a separate product manager. For example, Best Buy also purchases the Litepro, Medpro, and Heavypro models from the same manufacturer as the Deskpro. Currently, a separate product manager is responsible for the inventory and sales of each model. As a result, the ordering and delivery for each model is independent. The fixed transportation cost of $4,000 is thus incurred separately for each model. This leads to each product manager ordering a large lot size for their product.

Consider the data from Example 10.1. Assume that the demand for each of the four models is 1,000 units per month. In this case, if each product manager orders separately, he would order a lot size of 980 units. Across the four models, the total cycle inventory would thus be 1960 units.

Now consider the case where the store manager at Best Buy realizes that all four shipments originate from the same source. He asks all the product managers to coordinate their purchasing to ensure that all four products arrive on the same truck. In this case the optimal combined lot size across all four models turns out to be 1,960 units. This is equivalent to 490 units for each model. As a result of aggregating orders and spreading the fixed transportation cost across multiple products originating from the same supplier, it becomes financially optimal for the store manager at Best Buy to reduce the lot size for each individual product. This action significantly reduces the cycle inventory as well as cost to Best Buy.

Another way to achieve this result is to have a single delivery coming from multiple suppliers (allows fixed transportation cost to be spread across multiple suppliers) or have a single truck delivering to multiple retailers (allows fixed transportation cost to be spread across multiple retailers). This observation can be stated as follows:

> **Key Point** Aggregating across products, retailers, or suppliers in a single order allows for a reduction in lot size for individual products because fixed ordering and transportation costs are now spread across multiple products, retailers, or suppliers.

When considering fixed costs, one cannot ignore the receiving or loading costs. As more products are included in a single order, the product variety on a truck increases. The receiving warehouse now has to update inventory records for more items per truck. In addition, the task of putting inventory into storage now becomes more expensive because each distinct item must be stocked in a separate location. Thus, when attempting to reduce lot sizes, it is important to focus on reducing these costs. *Advanced Shipping Notices* (ASN) are files sent electronically by the supplier to the customer that contain precise records of the contents of the truck. These electronic notices facilitate updating of inventory records as well as the decision regarding storage locations, helping to reduce the fixed cost of receiving. The reduced fixed cost of receiving makes it optimal to reduce the lot size ordered, thus reducing cycle inventory. We next analyze how optimal lot sizes may be determined in such a setting.

Lot Sizing with Multiple Products or Customers

Let us return to the example of Best Buy ordering multiple models to be delivered in the same truck. In our earlier discussion, we assumed that the fixed ordering cost is associated with a lot and is not dependent on the variety included in the lot. In practice this is often not the case. In general, a portion of the fixed cost can be related to transportation (this is independent of product variety on the truck). A portion of the fixed cost is related to loading and receiving (this cost increases with variety on the truck). We now discuss how optimal lot sizes may be determined in such a setting.

Our objective is to arrive at lot sizes and an ordering policy that minimize the total cost. We assume the following input:

D_i: Annual demand for product i
S: Order cost incurred each time an order is placed independent of the variety of products included in the order.
s_i: Additional order cost incurred if product i is included in the order

In the case of Best Buy with multiple models, the store manager may consider three approaches to the lot sizing decision:

1. Each product manager orders his model independently.
2. The product managers jointly order every product in each lot.
3. Product managers order jointly but not every order contains every product; that is, each lot contains a selected subset of the products.

The first approach does not use any aggregation and will result in the highest cost. The second approach aggregates all products in each order. The weakness with the second approach is that low-volume products are aggregated with high-volume products in every order, which results in the product-specific order cost for the low-volume product being incurred with each order. In such a situation it may be better to order the low-volume products less frequently than the high-volume products. This practice will result in a reduction of the product-specific order cost associated with the low-volume product. As a result, the third approach is likely to yield the lowest cost.

We consider the example of Best Buy purchasing computers and illustrate the effect of each of the three approaches on supply chain costs.

Lots are Ordered and Delivered Independently for Each Product

This scenario is simple and equivalent to the single product approach using the EOQ formula applied to each product. Example 10.3 illustrates how the lot sizing decision is made in the case where lots are ordered and delivered independently.

Example 10.3: Multiple Products with Lots Ordered and Delivered Independently

Best Buy sells three models of computers, the Litepro, Medpro, and Heavypro. Annual demands for the three products are D_L = 12,000 for the Litepro, D_M = 1,200 units for the Medpro, and D_H = 120 units for the Heavypro. Assume that each model costs Best Buy $500. A fixed transportation cost of $4,000 is incurred each time an order is delivered. For each model ordered and delivered on the same truck, an additional fixed cost of $1,000 is incurred for receiving and storage. Best Buy incurs a holding cost of 20 percent. Evaluate the lot sizes that the Best Buy manager should order if lots for each product are ordered and delivered independently. Also evaluate the annual cost of such a policy.

Analysis: In this example we have the following information:

$$\text{Demand, } D_L = 12{,}000/\text{year}, D_M = 1{,}200/\text{year}, D_H = 120/\text{year};$$
$$\text{Common order cost, } S = \$4{,}000,$$
$$\text{Product-specific order cost, } s_L = \$1{,}000, s_M = \$1{,}000, s_H = \$1{,}000,$$
$$\text{Holding cost, } h = 0.2,$$
$$\text{Unit cost, } C_L = \$500, C_M = \$500, C_H = \$500.$$

Because each model is ordered and delivered independently, a separate truck delivers each model. Thus, a fixed ordering cost of $5,000 (4,000 + 1,000) is incurred for each product delivery. The optimal ordering policies and resulting costs for the three products (when the three products are ordered independently) are evaluated using the EOQ formula (Equation 10.5) and are shown in Table 10.1.

The Litepro model is ordered 11 times a year, the Medpro model is ordered 3.5 times a year, and the Heavypro model is ordered 1.1 times each year. The annual ordering and holding cost Best Buy incurs if the three models are ordered independently turns out to be $155,140.

As mentioned earlier, independent ordering ignores the opportunity of aggregating orders. If the product managers at Best Buy combined orders of the different models in a single truck, the trucking cost of $4,000 would not be incurred separately in each case. We next consider the scenario where all three products are ordered and delivered each time an order is placed.

Lots are Ordered and Delivered Jointly for All Three Models

Here all three models are included each time an order is placed. In this case the combined fixed order cost per order is given by

$$S^* = S + s_L + s_M + s_H.$$

The next step is to identify the optimal ordering frequency. Let n be the number of orders placed per year. We then have,

$$\text{Annual order cost} = S^* n,$$
$$\text{Annual holding cost} = (D_L h C_L/2n) + (D_M h C_M/2n) + (D_H h C_H/2n).$$

TABLE 10.1 Lot Sizes and Costs for Independent Ordering

	Litepro	*Medpro*	*Heavypro*
Demand per year	12,000	1,200	120
Fixed cost/order	$5,000	$5,000	$5,000
Optimal order size	1,095	346	110
Cycle Inventory	548	173	55
Annual holding cost	$54,772	$17,321	$5,477
Order frequency	11.0/year	3.5/year	1.1/year
Annual ordering cost	$54,772	$17,321	$5,477
Average flow time	2.4 weeks	7.5 weeks	23.7 weeks
Annual cost	$109,544	$34,642	$10,954

Note: While these figures are correct, some may differ from calculations due to rounding.

The total annual cost is thus given by

Total annual cost $= (D_L\, h\, C_L/2n) + (D_M\, h\, C_M/2n) + (D_H\, h\, C_H/2n) + S^*\, n.$

The optimal order frequency minimizes the total annual cost and is obtained by taking the first derivative of the total cost with respect to n and setting it equal to 0. This results in the optimal order frequency n^*, where

$$n^* = \sqrt{\frac{D_L\, h\, C_L + D_M h C_M + D_H\, h C_H}{2S^*}} \tag{10.7}$$

In Example 10.4 we consider the case where the product managers at Best Buy order all three models each time they place an order.

Example 10.4: Products Ordered and Delivered Jointly

Consider the Best Buy data in Example 10.3. The three product managers have decided to aggregate and order all three models each time they place an order. Evaluate the optimal lot size for each model.

Analysis: Because all three models are included in each order, the combined order cost is

$$S^* = S + s_A + s_B + s_C = \$7{,}000 \text{ per order.}$$

The optimal order frequency is obtained using Equation 10.7 and is given by

$$n^* = \sqrt{\frac{12{,}000 \times 100 + 1{,}200 \times 100 + 120 \times 100}{2 \times 7{,}000}} = 9.75.$$

Thus, if each model is to be included in every order and delivery, the product managers at Best Buy should place 9.75 orders each year. In this case the ordering policies and costs are as shown in Table 10.2.

Because 9.75 orders are placed each year and each order costs a total of $7,000, we have

Annual order cost $= 9.75 \times 7{,}000 = \$68{,}250.$

The annual ordering and holding cost, across the three sizes, of the aforementioned policy is given by

Annual ordering and holding cost $= \$61{,}512 + \$6{,}151 + \$615 + \$68{,}250 = \$136{,}528.$

Observe that the product managers at Best Buy lower the annual cost from $155,140 to $136,528 by ordering all products jointly. This represents a decrease of about 13 percent.

TABLE 10.2   Lot Sizes and Costs for Joint Ordering at Best Buy

	Litepro	Medpro	Heavypro
Demand per year	12,000	1,200	120
Order frequency	9.75/year	9.75/year	9.75/year
Optimal order size	1,230	123	12.3
Cycle inventory	615	61.5	6.15
Annual holding cost	$61,512	$6,151	$615
Average flow time	2.67 weeks	2.67 weeks	2.67 weeks

The main advantage of this approach is that it is easy to administer and implement. The disadvantage is that it is not selective enough in combining the particular models that should be ordered together. Product-specific order costs of $1,000 are incurred for all three models with each order. Total costs can be reduced if low-demand models are ordered less frequently. Next we consider a policy where the product managers do not necessarily order all models each time an order is placed but still coordinate their orders.

Lots are Ordered and Delivered Jointly for a Selected Subset of the Products

We now discuss a procedure that is more selective in combining products to be jointly ordered. The procedure we discuss here does not necessarily provide the optimal solution. It does, however, yield an ordering policy whose cost is close to optimal.

Of the three products, we first identify the one that is to be ordered most frequently. Once this decision has been made, for each successive product we need to identify those orders in which it is to be included. In general, it is not necessarily optimal for a particular product to be included at regular intervals (i.e., it should be included in every second or third order). In our procedure, however, we make the assumption that each size is included in the order at regular intervals. Once we have identified the most frequently ordered model, for each successive product i we need to identify the frequency m_i, where model i is ordered every m_i deliveries.

We first describe the procedure in general and then apply it to the specific example. Assume that the products are indexed by i where i varies from 1 to n (assuming a total of n products). Each product i has an annual demand D_i, a unit cost C_i, and a product-specific order cost s_i. The common order cost is S.

Step 1: As a first step we identify the most frequently ordered product assuming each product is ordered independently. In this case a fixed cost of $S + s_i$ would be allocated to each product. For each product i (using Equation 10.6), we evaluate the optimal ordering frequency as

$$\overline{n}_i = \sqrt{\frac{h C_i D_i}{2(S + s_i)}}$$

This is the frequency at which product i would be ordered if it were the only product being ordered (in which case a fixed cost of $S + s_i$ would be incurred per order). Let $\overline{n}$ be the frequency of the most frequently ordered product; that is, $\overline{n}$ is the maximum among all $\overline{n}_i$. The most frequently ordered product is included each time an order is placed.

Step 2: Identify the frequency with which other products are included with the most frequently ordered product; that is, calculate the order frequency for each product as a multiple of the order frequency of the most frequently ordered product. We assume that the most frequently ordered product will be ordered each time. All of the fixed cost S is thus allocated to this product. For each of the other products i, we thus only have the product-specific fixed cost component s_i. The order frequency for all other products is thus calculated using only the product-specific fixed cost in Equation 10.6.

For each product i (other than the most frequently ordered product) evaluate the ordering frequency

$$\overline{\overline{n_i}} = \sqrt{\frac{hC_i D_i}{2 s_i}}$$

Evaluate the frequency of product i relative to the most frequently ordered product to be $\overline{m_i}$ where

$$\overline{m_i} = \overline{n} / \overline{\overline{n_i}}$$

In general, $\overline{m_i}$ will contain a fractional component. For each product i (other than the most frequently ordered product), define the frequency m_i with which it is included with the most frequently ordered product, where

$$m_i = \lceil \overline{m_i} \rceil$$

In this case $\lceil \ \rceil$ is the operation that rounds a fraction up to the closest integer.

Step 3: Having decided the ordering frequency of each product, recalculate the ordering frequency of the most frequently ordered product to be n, where

$$n = \sqrt{\frac{\sum hC_i D_i}{2(S + \sum s_i / m_i)}} \tag{10.8}$$

The reason for this step is that in the initial calculation of $\overline{n_i}$, the fixed cost allocated to each order was $S + s_i$, where i is the most frequently ordered product. In reality, the most frequently ordered product is ordered each time, whereas others are ordered once every m_i orders. Thus each product i contributes s_i/m_i to the fixed cost of an order. The effective fixed cost per order thus becomes

$$S + \sum \frac{s_i}{m_i}$$

Using Equation 10.7, we thus obtain the optimal order frequency given in Equation 10.8.

Step 4: For each product, evaluate an order frequency of $n_i = n/m_i$. We can then evaluate the total cost of such an ordering policy.

The procedure described earlier results in *tailored aggregation,* with higher demand products ordered more frequently and lower demand products ordered less frequently when the products are aggregated appropriately. In Example 10.5, we consider tailored aggregation for the Best Buy ordering decision in Example 10.3.

Example 10.5: Lot Sizes Ordered and Delivered Jointly for a Selected Subset that Varies by Order

Consider the Best Buy data in Example 10.3. Product managers have decided to order jointly, but to be selective about which models they include in each order. Evaluate the ordering policy and costs using the procedure previously discussed.

Analysis: Recall that $S = \$4,000$, $s_L = \$1,000$, $s_M = \$1,000$, $s_H = \$1,000$. Applying Step 1, we obtain

$$\overline{n_L} = \sqrt{\frac{h C_L D_L}{2(S + s_L)}} = 11.0, \overline{n_M} = 3.5 \quad \text{and} \quad \overline{n_H} = 1.1$$

Clearly Litepro is the most frequently ordered model. Thus we set $\overline{n} = 11.0$.

We now apply Step 2 to evaluate the frequency with which Medpro and Heavypro are included with Litepro in the order. We first obtain

$$\overline{\overline{n_M}} = \sqrt{\frac{h C_M D_M}{2 s_M}} = 7.7 \quad \text{and} \quad \overline{\overline{n_H}} = 2.4$$

Next we evaluate

$$\overline{m_M} = \overline{n} / \overline{\overline{n_M}} = 11.0 / 7.7 = 1.4 \quad \text{and} \quad \overline{m_H} = 4.5$$

Next we evaluate

$$m_M = \lceil 1.4 \rceil = 2 \quad \text{and} \quad m_L = \lceil 4.5 \rceil = 5$$

Thus, Medpro is included in every other order and Heavypro is included in every fifth order (Litepro, the most frequently ordered model, is included in every order.)

Now that we have decided on the ordering frequency of each model, apply Step 3 (Equation 10.8) to recalculate the ordering frequency of the most frequently ordered model as

$$n = 10.8.$$

Thus the Litepro is ordered 10.8 times per year. Next, we apply Step 4 to obtain an ordering frequency of

$$n_L = 10.8/\text{year}, n_M = 5.4/\text{year and } n_H = 10.8 / 5 = 2.16/\text{year}.$$

The ordering policies and resulting costs for the three products are shown in Table 10.3. The annual holding cost of this policy is $69,444. The annual order cost is given by

$$nS + n_L S_L + n_M S_M + n_H S_H = \$61,560.$$

The total annual cost is thus equal to $131,004. Tailored aggregation results in a cost reduction of $5,554 (about 4 percent) compared to the case when all models are included in each order. The cost reduction results because each model-specific fixed cost of $1,000 is not incurred with every order.

TABLE 10.3   Lot Sizes and Costs for Ordering Policy Using Heuristic

	Litepro	*Medpro*	*Heavypro*
Demand per year	12,000	1,200	120
Order frequency	10.8/year	5.4/year	2.16/year
Order size	1,111	222	56
Cycle inventory	555.5	111	28
Annual holding cost	$55,556	$11,111	$2,778
Average flow time	2.41 weeks	4.81 weeks	12.04 weeks

From the Best Buy examples, it follows that aggregation can provide significant cost savings and reduction in cycle inventory in the supply chain. Simple aggregation of all products into each order will generally do better than the case where each product is ordered independently if product specific order costs are low. Tailored aggregation, however, will provide an even lower cost because it exploits the difference between low- and high-demand products and adjusts their ordering frequency accordingly. In general, complete aggregation should be used when product specific order costs are small and tailored aggregation should be used when product specific order costs are large.

We have looked at fixed ordering costs and their impact on the inventory and costs in the supply chain. What is most significant from this discussion is that the key to reducing lot sizes is to focus on the reduction of fixed costs associated with each lot ordered. These costs and the processes causing them must be well understood so appropriate action may be taken.

> **Key Point** A key to reducing cycle inventory is the reduction of lot size. A key to reducing lot size without increasing costs is to reduce the fixed cost associated with each lot. This may be achieved by reducing the fixed cost itself or by aggregating lots across multiple products, customers, or suppliers. When aggregating across multiple products, customers, or suppliers, tailored aggregation is best, especially if product specific order costs are large.

Next we consider lot sizes when material cost displays economies of scale.

10.3 ECONOMIES OF SCALE TO EXPLOIT QUANTITY DISCOUNTS

In the previous discussion, we assumed that the material cost remains constant regardless of the quantity purchased. There are many instances, however, where the pricing schedule yields economies of scale, with prices decreasing as lot size is increased. This form of pricing is very common in business-to-business transactions. A discount is *lot size based* if the pricing schedule offers discounts based on the quantity ordered in a single lot. A discount is *volume-based* if the discount is based on the total quantity purchased over a given period, regardless of the number of lots purchased over that period. Two commonly used lot size based discount schemes are:

- All unit quantity discounts
- Marginal unit quantity discount or multi-block tariffs

In this section we investigate the impact of such quantity discounts on the supply chain. We must answer the following two basic questions in this context:

1. Given a pricing schedule with quantity discounts, what is the optimal purchasing decision for a buyer seeking to maximize profits? How does this decision impact the supply chain in terms of lot sizes, cycle inventories, and flow times?

2. Under what conditions should a supplier offer quantity discounts? What are appropriate pricing schedules that a supplier, seeking to maximize profits, should offer?

We start by studying the optimal response of a retailer (the buyer) when faced with either of the two lot-size based discount schemes offered by a manufacturer. Because material costs vary with lot size, the retailer needs to consider annual material, order, and holding costs when making the lot sizing decision. The retailer's objective is to select lot sizes to minimize the total annual cost. Next we evaluate the optimal lot size in the case of all unit quantity discounts.

All Unit Quantity Discounts

In all unit quantity discounts, the pricing schedule contains specified break points q_0, $q_1,..., q_r$ where $q_0 = 0$. If an order is placed that is at least as large as q_i but smaller than q_{i+1}, then each unit is obtained at a cost of C_i. In general, the unit cost decreases as the quantity ordered increases; that is, $C_0 \geq C_1 \geq ... C_r$. In the following discussion we focus on a retailer faced with such a pricing schedule. The retailer's objective is to decide on lot sizes to maximize profits or equivalently, to minimize the sum of material, order, and holding costs.

For all unit discounts, the average unit cost varies with the quantity ordered, as shown in Figure 10.3. Observe that under this discount scheme, ordering $q_1 + 1$ units may be less expensive (in terms of material cost) than ordering $q_1 - 1$ units.

The solution procedure evaluates the optimal lot size for each price C_i (this forces a lot size between q_i and q_{i+1}) and then settles on the lot size that minimizes the overall cost. For each value of i, $0 \leq i \leq r$, evaluate the following:

$$Q_i = \sqrt{\frac{2DS}{hC_i}} \tag{10.9}$$

There are three possible cases for Q_i:

1. $q_i \leq Q_i < q_{i+1}$
2. $Q_i < q_i$
3. $Q_i > q_{i+1}$

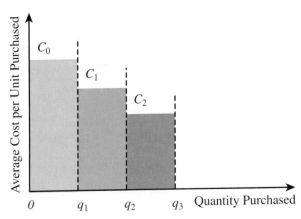

FIGURE 10.3 Average Unit Cost with All Unit Quantity Discounts

Case 1

If $q_i \leq Q_i < q_{i+1}$, then a lot size of Q_i units will result in the discounted price of C_i per unit. In this case the total annual cost of ordering Q_i is given (this includes order cost, holding cost, and material cost) as follows:

$$\text{Total annual cost, } TC_i = \left(\frac{D}{Q_i}\right)S + \left(\frac{Q_i}{2}\right)hC_i + DC_i \qquad \textbf{(10.10)}$$

Case 2

If $Q_i < q_i$, then a lot size of Q_i does not result in a discount. Raising the lot size to q_i units will result in the discounted price of C_i per unit. Ordering more than q_i units will raise the order and holding cost without reducing the material cost. In this case it is thus optimal to order a lot size of q_i units. The annual cost is given by the following:

$$\text{Total annual cost, } TC_i = \left(\frac{D}{q_i}\right)S + \left(\frac{q_i}{2}\right)hC_i + DC_i \qquad \textbf{(10.11)}$$

Case 3

If $Q_i \geq q_{i+1}$, then a lot size of q_{i+1} units will result in the discounted price of C_{i+1} per unit. In this case the total annual cost is based on a lot size of q_{i+1} units and is given by the following:

$$\text{Total annual cost, } TC_i = \left(\frac{D}{q_{i+1}}\right)S + \left(\frac{q_{i+1}}{2}\right)hC_{i+1} + DC_{i+1} \qquad \textbf{(10.12)}$$

For each price C_i we apply the appropriate case and evaluate the total cost TC_i and the corresponding lot size. The solution is to order the lot size that minimizes the total annual cost across all prices in the schedule.

In Example 10.6, we evaluate the optimal lot size given an all unit quantity discount.

Example 10.6: All Unit Quantity Discount

Drugs Online (DO) is an online retailer of prescription drugs and health supplements. Vitamins represent a significant percentage of their sales. Demand for vitamins is 10,000 bottles per month. DO incurs a fixed order placement, transportation, and receiving cost of $100 each time an order for vitamins is placed with the manufacturer. DO incurs a holding cost of 20 percent. The price charged by the manufacturer varies according to the all unit discount pricing schedule shown. Evaluate the number of bottles that the DO manager should order in each lot.

Order Quantity	Unit Price
0–5,000	$3.00
5,000–10,000	$2.96
10,000 or more	$2.92

Analysis: In this case, the manager has the following input

$$q_0 = 0, q_1 = 5{,}000, q_2 = 10{,}000,$$
$$C_0 = \$3.00, C_1 = \$2.96, C_2 = \$2.92,$$
$$D = 120{,}000/\text{year}, S = \$100/\text{lot}, h = 0.2.$$

For $i = 0$, evaluate Q_0 (using Equation 10.9) as $Q_{0=}\sqrt{\dfrac{2\,DS}{h\,C_0}} = 6{,}324 = 6{,}324.$

For $i = 0$, we set the lot size at $q_1 = 5000$ because $6{,}324 > q_1 = 5000$. The total cost incurred in this case is evaluated (using Equation 10.12) as follows:

$$TC_0 = \left(\frac{D}{q_1}\right)S + \left(\frac{q_1}{2}\right)h\,C_1 + DC_1 = \$359{,}080$$

For $i = 1$, using Equation 10.9 we obtain $Q_1 = 6{,}367$ units. Because $5{,}000 < 6{,}367 < 10{,}000$, we set the lot size at $Q_1 = 6{,}367$ units and evaluate the cost of ordering 6,637 units using Equation 10.10 as follows:

$$TC_1 = \left(\frac{D}{Q_1}\right)S + \left(\frac{Q_1}{2}\right)h\,C_1 + DC_1 = \$358{,}969$$

For $i = 2$, using Equation 10.9, we obtain $Q_2 = 6{,}410$ units. Because $6{,}410 < q_2 = 10{,}000$, we set the lot size at $q_2 = 10{,}000$ units and evaluate the cost of ordering 10,000 units using Equation 10.11 as

$$TC_2 = \left(\frac{D}{q_2}\right)S + \left(\frac{q_2}{2}\right)h\,C_2 + DC_2 = \$354{,}520$$

Observe that the lowest total cost is for $i = 2$. Thus, it is optimal for DO to order $q_2 = 10{,}000$ bottles per lot and obtain the discount price of $2.92 per bottle.

If the manufacturer in Example 10.6 sold all bottles for $3, it would be optimal for DO to order in lots of 6,324 bottles. The quantity discount is an incentive for DO to order in larger lots of 10,000 bottles, raising both the cycle inventory and the flow time. The impact of the discount is further magnified if DO works hard to reduce its fixed ordering cost to $S = \$4$. The optimal lot size in the absence of a discount would be 1,265 bottles. In the presence of the all unit quantity discount, the optimal lot size will still be 10,000 bottles. In this case, the presence of quantity discounts leads to an eight-fold increase in average inventory as well as flow time at DO.

Pricing schedules with all unit quantity discounts encourage retailers to increase the size of their lots to take advantage of price discounts, which adds to the average inventory and flow time in a supply chain. This increase in inventory raises a question about the value that all unit quantity discounts offer in the supply chain. Before we consider this question, we discuss marginal unit quantity discounts.

Marginal Unit Quantity Discount

Marginal unit quantity discounts have also been referred to as *multi-block tariffs*. In this case, the pricing schedule contains specified break points $q_0, q_1, \ldots, q_r$. It is not the *average cost* of a unit but the *marginal cost* of a unit that decreases at a breakpoint (in contrast with the all unit discount scheme). If an order of size q is placed, the first $q_1 - q_0$ units are priced at C_0, the next $q_2 - q_1$ are priced at C_1, and so on. The marginal cost per unit varies with the quantity purchased, as shown in Figure 10.4.

Faced with such a pricing schedule, the retailer's objective is to decide on a lot size to maximize profits, which in this scenario is equivalent to minimizing cost.

The solution procedure evaluates the optimal lot size for each marginal price C_i (this forces a lot size between q_i and q_{i+1}) and then settles on the lot size that minimizes the overall cost.

For each value of i, $0 \le i \le r$, let V_i be the cost of ordering q_i units. Define $V_0 = 0$ and V_i for $0 \le i \le r$ as follows:

$$V_i = C_0(q_1 - q_0) + C_1(q_2 - q_1) + \ldots + C_{i-1}(q_i - q_{i-1}) \qquad \textbf{(10.13)}$$

For each value of i, $0 \le i \le r - 1$, consider an order of size Q in the range q_i to q_{i+1} units; that is, $q_{i+1} \ge Q \ge q_i$. The material cost of each order of size Q is given by $V_i + (Q - q_i)C_i$. The various costs associated with such an order are as follows:

$$\text{Annual order cost} = \left(\frac{D}{Q}\right) S$$

$$\text{Annual holding cost} = [V_i + (Q - q_i)C_i]h/2$$

$$\text{Annual material cost} = \frac{D}{Q}[V_i + (Q - q_i)C_i]$$

The total annual cost is the sum of the three costs and is given by the following:

$$\text{Total annual cost} = \left(\frac{D}{Q}\right) S + [V_i + (Q - q_i)C_i]h/2 + \frac{D}{Q}[V_i + (Q - q_i)C_i]$$

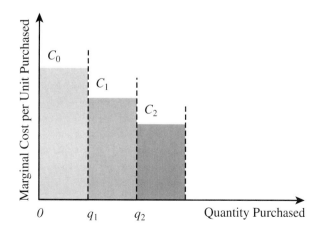

FIGURE 10.4   Marginal Unit Cost with Marginal Unit Quantity Discount

The optimal lot size for this price range is obtained by taking the first derivative of the total cost with respect to the lot size and setting it equal to 0. This results in an optimal lot size for this price range of the following:

$$\text{Optimal lot size for price } C_i = \sqrt{\frac{2D(S + V_i - q_i C_i)}{hC_i}} \qquad \textbf{(10.14)}$$

Observe that the optimal lot size is obtained using a formula very much like the EOQ formula (Equation 10.5) except that the presence of the quantity discount has the effect of raising the fixed cost per order by $V_i - q_i C_i$ (from S to $S + V_i - q_i C_i$). There are three possible cases for Q_i:

1. $q_i \leq Q_i \leq q_{i+1}$
2. $Q_i < q_i$
3. $Q_i > q_{i+1}$

Case 1

If $q_i \leq Q_i \leq q_{i+1}$, then a lot size of Q_i will result in the discounted price in this range. In this case the optimal lot size in this price range is to order Q_i units. The total annual cost of this policy is given by

$$TC_i = \left(\frac{D}{Q_i}\right)S + [V_i + (Q_i - q_i)C_i]h/2 + \frac{D}{Q_i}[V_i + (Q_i - q_i)C_i]$$

Cases 2 and 3

If $Q_i < q_i$ or $Q_i > q_{i+1}$, the lot size in this range is either q_i or q_{i+1} depending on which has the lower total cost. Evaluate the total annual cost

$$TC_i = \text{Min}\left\{\left(\frac{D}{q_i}\right)S + V_i\, h/2 + \frac{D}{q_i}V_i, \left(\frac{D}{q_{i+1}}\right)S + V_{i+1}\, h/2 + \frac{D}{q_{i+1}}V_{i+1}\right\}$$

The lot size for this range then corresponds to the break point giving the minimum total cost. Observe that for each range the optimal lot size is the quantity defined by Equation 10.14 if it is feasible or one of the break points if it is not feasible.

For each i we evaluate the optimal lot size and total cost. The solution is to set the lot size to be the one that minimizes the total annual cost across all ranges i. It can be shown that the overall optimal lot size cannot correspond to Cases 2 and 3 and must correspond to Case 1.

Example 10.7: Marginal Unit Quantity Discount

Let us return to DO from Example 10.6. Assume that the manufacturer uses the following marginal unit discount pricing schedule:

Order Quantity	Marginal Unit Price
0–5,000	$3.00
5,000–10,000	$2.96
Over 10,000	$2.92

This implies that if an order is placed for 7,000 bottles, the first 5,000 are at a unit cost of $3.00, with the remaining 2,000 at a unit cost of $2.96. Evaluate the number of bottles that DO should order in each lot.

Analysis: In this case we have

$q_0 = 0, q_1 = 5,000, q_2 = 10,000,$
$C_0 = \$3.00, C_1 = \$2.96, C_2 = \$2.92,$
$V_0 = 0; V_1 = 3(5,000 - 0) = \$15,000$
$V_2 = 3(5,000 - 0) + 2.96(10,000 - 5,000) = \$29,800$
$D = 120,000/\text{year}, S = \$100/\text{lot}, h = 0.2.$

For $i = 0$, evaluate Q_0 (using Equation 10.14) as follows:

$$Q_0 = \sqrt{\frac{2D(S + V_0 - q_0\, C_0)}{hC_0}} = 6,324$$

Because $6,324 > q_1 = 5,000$, we evaluate the cost of ordering lots of $q_1 = 5,000$ (we do not consider lots of 0). The total annual cost of ordering 5,000 bottles per lot is as follows (set $Q = 5,000$ and $i = 1$):

$$TC_0 = \left(\frac{D}{Q}\right)S + [V_i + (Q - q_i)\,C_i]h/2 + \frac{D}{Q}[V_i + (Q - q_i)\,C_i] = \$363,900$$

For $i = 1$, evaluate Q_1 using Equation 10.14 as follows:

$$Q_1 = \sqrt{\frac{2\,D(S + V_1 - q_1\, C_1)}{hC_1}} = 11,028$$

Because $11,028 > q_2 = 10,000$, we evaluate the cost of ordering lots of $q_2 = 10,000$ (the cost of ordering lots of 5,000 has already been evaluated earlier). The total annual cost of ordering 10,000 bottles per lot is as follows (set $Q = 10,000$ and $i = 2$):

$$TC_1 = \left(\frac{D}{Q}\right)S + [V_i + (Q - q_i)\,C_i]h/2 + \frac{D}{Q}[V_i + (Q - q_i)\,C_i] = \$361,780$$

Because $\$361,780 < \$363,900$, it is less expensive to order in lots of 10,000 than in lots of 5,000. If the lot size is to be 10,000 units or less, we are better off ordering 10,000 units per lot. Now we investigate the cost of ordering in lots larger than 10,000 units; that is, $i = 2$. For $i = 2$, evaluate Q_2 using Equation 10.14 as follows:

$$Q_2 = \sqrt{\frac{2\,D(S + V_2 - q_2\, C_2)}{hC_2}} = 16,961$$

The total annual cost of ordering 16,961 bottles per lot is as follows (set $Q = 16,961$ and $i = 2$):

$$TC_2 = \left(\frac{D}{Q}\right)S + [V_i + (Q - q_i)\,C_i]h/2 + \frac{D}{Q}[V_i + (Q - q_i)\,C_i] = \$360,365$$

DO should order a lot size of 16,961 bottles because that number has the lowest total cost. This is much larger than the optimal lot size of 6,324 in the case where the manufacturer does not offer any discount.

If the fixed cost of ordering is $4, the optimal lot size for DO is 15,755 with the discount compared to a lot size of 1,265 without the discount. This discussion demonstrates that there can be significant order sizes and thus cycle inventory in the absence of any formal fixed ordering costs as long as quantity discounts are offered. Thus, quantity discounts lead to a significant buildup of cycle inventory in the supply chain. In many supply chains, quantity discounts contribute more to cycle inventory than fixed ordering costs. This forces us to once again question the value of quantity discounts in a supply chain.

Why Quantity Discounts?

In this section we develop different arguments supporting the presence of quantity discounts in a supply chain. Quantity discounts can be valuable in a supply chain for the following two reasons:

1. Improved coordination in the supply chain
2. Extraction of surplus through price discrimination

Coordination in the Supply Chain

A supply chain is *coordinated* if the decisions the retailer and supplier make maximize total supply chain profits. This may occur if the supply chain is vertically integrated and the performance at each stage is judged based on total supply chain profits. In reality, each stage has a separate owner and considers its own costs in an effort to maximize its own profits. For example, the retailer makes cycle inventory decisions based on its own profitability considerations. The result of this independent decision making can be a lack of coordination in the supply chain because actions that maximize retailer profits may not maximize supply chain profits.

In this section we discuss how a manufacturer may use appropriate quantity discounts to ensure that coordination results even if the retailer is acting to maximize its own profits given its cost structure.

Quantity Discounts for Commodity Products   Economists have argued that for commodity products like milk, the market sets the price and the firm's objective is to lower costs. Consider, for example, the online retailer DO, discussed earlier. It can be argued that it sells a commodity product. When placing orders with the manufacturer, DO makes its lot sizing decisions based on costs it faces.

Demand for vitamins is 10,000 bottles per month. DO incurs a fixed order placement, transportation, and receiving cost of $100 each time they place an order for vitamins with the manufacturer. DO incurs a holding cost of 20 percent. The manufacturer charges DO $3 for each bottle of vitamins purchased. Using the EOQ formula (Equation 10.5), DO evaluates its optimal lot size to be $Q = 6,324$ bottles. The annual ordering and holding costs incurred by DO as a result of this policy are $3,795.

Each time DO places an order, the manufacturer has to process, pack, and ship the order. The manufacturer has a line packing bottles at a steady rate. The fixed cost of filling each order is $250 for the manufacturer. Each bottle costs them $2 and they incur a holding cost of 20 percent. Given that DO orders in lot sizes of 6,324 bottles, we evaluate the annual ordering and holding cost for the manufacturer as follows:

Annual order cost at manufacturer = (120,000/6,324) × 250 = $4,744,
Annual holding cost at manufacturer = (6,324/2) × 2 × 0.2 = $1,265,
Total order and holding cost at manufacturer = $6,009.

The manufacturer thus incurs an annual cost of $6,009 as a result of DO ordering in lots of 6,324. The total cost, across the supply chain, as a result of DO ordering in lots of 6,324 is thus $6,009 + $3,795 = $9,804.

If DO can be convinced to order in lots of 9,165 units, the total cost in the supply chain decreases to $9,165. There is thus an opportunity for the supply chain to save $638. Observe that ordering in lots of 9,165 bottles raises the cost for DO by $238 per year to $4,059 (even though it reduces overall supply chain costs). The manufacturer's costs, on the other hand, go down by $902 to $5,106 per year. The manufacturer must offer DO a suitable incentive for DO to raise its lot size.

Lot size based quantity discounts are the appropriate incentive in this case. If the manufacturer were to price vitamins so that each bottle cost $3 for all orders with lot sizes under 9,165 and $2.9978 for all orders in lots of 9,165 or more, DO will have an incentive to order in lots of 9,165 bottles. This is because the quantity discount reduces the material cost for DO by just enough to offset the increase in ordering and holding cost. The manufacturer returns $264 to DO as material cost reduction (in the form of a quantity discount) to make it optimal for DO to order in lots of 9,165 bottles. The manufacturer's and the total supply chain's profits increase by $638 in this case. It can be argued that in practice the manufacturer may have to share some of the $638 increase with DO. The precise division of the increase in supply chain profits will depend on the relative bargaining power of the different stages in the supply chain.

Observe that offering a lot size based discount in this case decreases total supply chain cost. It does, however, increase the lot size the retailer purchases and thus increases cycle inventory in the supply chain.

Key Point For commodity products where price is set by the market, manufacturers can use lot size based quantity discounts to achieve coordination in the supply chain and decrease supply chain cost. Lot size based discounts, however, increase cycle inventory in the supply chain.

Our discussion on coordination for commodity products highlights the important link between the lot size based quantity discount offered and the order costs incurred by the manufacturer. As the manufacturer works on lowering his order or setup cost, the discount he offers to retailers should change. This has not always occurred in practice. Often, firms have found that significant efforts to reduce order costs have not reduced cycle inventory in the supply chain because of quantity discounts. In most companies, marketing and sales design quantity discounts while operations works on reducing the setup or order cost. It is very important that the two functions coordinate these activities.

Quantity Discounts for Products where the Firm has Market Power   Now consider the scenario where the manufacturer has invented a new vitamin pill, vitaherb, that is derived from herbal ingredients and has other properties highly valued in the market. Few competitors have a similar product. In this case it can be argued that the price at which DO sells vitaherb will influence demand. Assume that the annual demand faced by DO is given by the demand curve $360,000 - 60,000p$, where p is the price at which DO sells vitaherb. The manufacturer incurs a production cost of $C_S = \$2$ per bottle of vitaherb sold. In this case the manufacturer must decide on the price to charge DO and DO in turn must decide on the price to charge the customer. When the two make their decisions independently, it is optimal for DO to charge a price of $p = \$5$ per bottle and for the manufacturer to charge DO a price of $C_R = \$4$ per bottle. The total market demand in this case is for $360,000 - 60,000p = 60,000$ bottles of vitaherb. The profit at DO as a result of this policy is given by

$$Prof_R = p(360,000 - 60,000p) - (360,000 - 60,000p)C_R = \$60,000.$$

The profit at the manufacturer is given by

$$Prof_M = C_R(180,000 - 30,000C_R) - C_S(180,000 - 30,000C_R) = \$120,000.$$

If the two stages coordinate pricing and DO prices at $p = \$4$, market demand would be 120,000 bottles. The total supply chain profit if the two stages coordinate would be $120,000 \times (\$4 - \$2) = \$240,000$. As a result of each stage settings its price independently, the supply chain thus loses $\$60,000$ in profit. This phenomenon is referred to as double marginalization. Double marginalization leads to a loss in profit because the supply chain margin is divided into two stages but each stage makes its decision considering only its local margin.

> **Key Point** The supply chain profit is lower if each stage of the supply chain independently makes its pricing decisions with the objective of maximizing its own profit. A coordinated solution results in higher profit.

There are two pricing schemes that the manufacturer may use to achieve the coordinated solution and maximize supply chain profits even though DO acts in a way that maximizes its own profit.

1. *Two-part tariff:* In this case the manufacturer charges his entire profit as an up-front franchise fee and then sells to the retailer at cost. It is then optimal for the retailer to price as though the two stages are coordinated. In the case of DO, recall that total supply chain profit when the two stages coordinate is $\$240,000$ with DO charging the customer $\$4$ per bottle of vitaherb. The profit made by DO when the two stages do not coordinate is $\$60,000$. One option available to the manufacturer is to construct a two-part tariff where DO is charged an up-front fee of $\$180,000$ and material cost of $C_R = \$2$ per bottle. DO maximizes its profit if it prices the vitamins at $p = \$4$ per bottle.

It has annual sales of $360,000 - 60,000p = 120,000$ and profits of $60,000. The manufacturer on the other hand makes a profit of $180,000 given his material cost of $2 per bottle.

2. *Volume-based quantity discount:* Observe that the two-part tariff is really a volume-based quantity discount. The average material cost for DO declines as it increases the quantity it purchases per year. This observation can be made explicit by designing a volume-based discount scheme that also achieves coordination. The objective here is to price in a way that the retailer buys the total volume sold when the two stages coordinate pricing. In the case of DO, recall that 120,000 bottles are sold per year when the supply chain is coordinated. The manufacturer must offer DO a volume discount to encourage DO to purchase this quantity. The manufacturer thus offers a price of $C_R = \$4$ per bottle if the quantity DO purchases per year is less than 120,000. If the total volume in the year is 120,000 or higher, DO has to pay only $C_R = \$3.50$. It is then optimal for DO to order 120,000 units and price them at $p = \$4$ per bottle to the customers. The total profit earned by DO is $(360,000 - 60,000 \times p) \times (p - C_R) = \$60,000$. The total profit earned by the manufacturer is $120,000 \times (C_R - \$2) = \$180,000$. The total supply chain profit is $240,000.

> **Key Point**   For products where the firm has market power, two-part tariffs or volume-based quantity discounts can be used to achieve coordination in the supply chain and maximize supply chain profits.

At this stage, we have seen that even in the absence of inventory related costs, quantity discounts play a role in supply chain coordination and improved supply chain profits. The discount schemes that are optimal, however, are volume based and not lot size based. In our analysis, we do not assume any inventory-related costs, so one may argue that in the presence of inventory costs, lot size based discounts may be optimal. It can be shown, however, that even in the presence of inventory costs (order and holding), a two-part tariff or volume-based discount, with the manufacturer passing on some of the fixed cost to the retailer, optimally coordinates the supply chain and maximizes profits given the assumption that customer demand decreases when the retailer increases price.

> **Key Point**   For products where a firm has market power, lot size based discounts are not optimal for the supply chain even in the presence of inventory costs. In such a setting, either a two-part tariff or a volume-based discount, with the supplier passing on some of his fixed cost to the retailer, is needed for the supply chain to be coordinated and maximize profits.

A key distinction between lot size based and volume discounts is that lot size discounts are based on the quantity purchased per lot, not the rate of purchase. Volume discounts, in contrast, are based on the rate of purchase or volume purchased on average per specified time period (say a month, quarter, or year). Lot size based discounts tend to raise the cycle inventory in the supply chain by encouraging retailers to increase the size of each lot. Volume-based discounts, in contrast are compatible with small lots that reduce cycle inventory.

One can make the point that even with volume-based discounts, retailers will tend to increase the size of the lot toward the end of the evaluation period. For example, the manufacturer offers DO a 2 percent discount if the number of bottles of vita-herb purchased over a quarter exceeds 40,000. This policy will not affect the lot sizes DO orders early during the quarter and DO will order in small lots to match the quantity ordered with demand. Consider a situation, however, where DO has sold only 30,000 bottles with a week left before the end of the quarter. To get the quantity discount, DO may order 10,000 bottles over the last week even though it expects to sell only 3,000. In this case, cycle inventory in the supply chain will go up in spite of the fact that there is no lot size based quantity discount. The situation in which orders peak toward the end of a financial horizon is referred to as the *hockey stick phenomenon.* It has been observed in many industries. One possible solution to this phenomenon is to base the volume discounts on a rolling horizon. For example, each week the manufacturer may offer DO the volume discount based on sales over the last twelve weeks. Such a rolling horizon dampens the hockey stick phenomenon by making each week the last week in some twelve-week horizon.

Thus far, we have only discussed the scenario in which the supply chain has a single retailer. One may ask whether our insights are robust and also apply if the supply chain has multiple retailers, each with different demand curves, all supplied by a single manufacturer. As one would expect, the form of the discount scheme to be offered becomes more complicated in these settings (typically, instead of having only one break point at which the volume-based discount is offered there are multiple break-points). The basic form of the optimal pricing scheme, however, does not change. The optimal discount continues to be volume based with the average price charged to the retailers decreasing as the rate of purchase (volume purchased per unit time) increases.

Price Discrimination to Maximize Supplier Profits

Price discrimination is the practice where a firm charges differential prices to maximize profits. A classic user of price discrimination are airlines where passengers traveling on the same plane often pay different prices for their seats. Price discrimination is discussed in detail in Chapter 15. In this section we discuss how price discrimination is a form of quantity discounts.

Let us return to the case where the manufacturer of vitaherb is selling to DO. In such a situation the quantity purchased by DO will depend upon the price charged by the manufacturer, with the quantity purchased decreasing as price increases. Assume that the quantity DO purchases is $200,000 - 50,000C$ where C is the price charged by the manufacturer. The material cost per bottle for the manufacturer is $C_S = \$2$. If the manufacturer is to pick a single price to charge DO, he should charge $3 per bottle. DO purchases 50,000 bottles at this price and the manufacturer makes a profit of $50,000. The demand curve and profits are shown in Figure 10.5.

It is clear that setting a fixed price of $3 does not maximize profits for the manufacturer. In principle, the manufacturer could obtain the entire area under the demand curve above his marginal cost of $2 by pricing each unit differently. The manufacturer could price each unit equal to DO's marginal evaluation at each quantity. The first unit would be priced so DO purchases exactly one unit at that price, the second unit priced

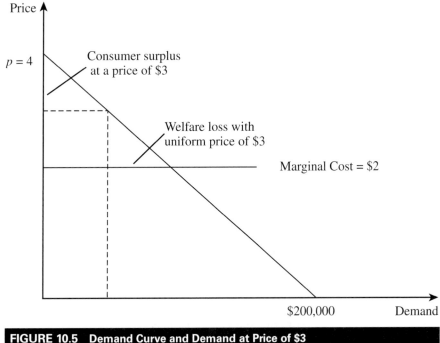

FIGURE 10.5   Demand Curve and Demand at Price of $3

so that DO purchases exactly two units, the third unit priced so that DO purchases exactly three units, and so on. Clearly the price decreases as the quantity increases. The optimal price charged by the manufacturer is thus a form of a quantity discount.

An equivalent approach would be a two-part tariff where the manufacturer asks for the entire area under the demand curve (above the marginal cost of $2) as an up-front franchise fee and then prices each bottle at marginal cost ($2 each). In our example, the manufacturer would ask DO for an up-front payment of $100,000 and then offer a price of $2 per bottle. In this case DO orders 100,000 units (because the up-front payment is sunk) and the manufacturer makes a profit of $100,000. In this situation, the pricing scheme with an up-front fee increases the manufacturer's profits compared to the case when a single fixed price is offered.

Observe that the pricing scheme offered is a quantity discount because the customer pays less per unit as he increases his order. Note that the demand curve represents demand over a specified time period, say a year or a billing period. In other words, the discount offered is a volume discount, not a lot size based discount. Thus the motivation for price discrimination also leads the supplier to offer a volume-based discount, not a lot size based discount.

Key Point   Price discrimination to maximize profits at the manufacturer may also be a reason to offer quantity discounts within a supply chain. Discounts related to price discrimination will also be volume based and not lot size based.

Next we discuss trade promotions and their impact on lot sizes and cycle inventory in the supply chain.

10.4 SHORT-TERM DISCOUNTING: TRADE PROMOTIONS

Manufacturers use *trade promotions* to offer a discounted price and a time period over which the discount is effective. For example, a manufacturer of canned soup may offer a price discount of 10 percent for the shipping period December 15 to January 25. For all purchases within the specified time horizon, retailers get a 10 percent discount. In some cases, the manufacturer may require specific actions from the retailer such as displays, advertising, promotion, and so on to qualify for the trade promotion. Trade promotions are quite common in the consumer packaged goods industry, with manufacturers promoting different products at different times of the year.

The goal of trade promotions is to influence retailers to act in a way that helps the manufacturer achieve its objectives. A few of the key goals (from the manufacturer's perspective) of a trade promotion are as follows[1]:

1. Induce retailers to use price discounts, displays, or advertising to spur sales.
2. Shift inventory from the manufacturer to the retailer and the customer.
3. Defend a brand against competition.

Although these may be the manufacturer's objectives, it is not clear that they are always achieved as the result of a trade promotion. Our goal in this section is to investigate the impact of a trade promotion on the behavior of the retailer and the performance of the entire supply chain. The key to understanding this impact is to focus on how a retailer reacts to a trade promotion that a manufacturer offers. In response to a trade promotion the retailer has the following options:

1. Pass through some or all of the promotion to customers to spur sales.
2. Pass through very little of the promotion to customers but purchase in greater quantity during the promotion period to exploit the temporary reduction in price.

The first action lowers the price of the product for the end customer, leading to increased purchases and thus increased sales for the entire supply chain. The second action does not increase purchases by the customer but increases the amount of inventory held at the retailer. As a result, the cycle inventory and flow time within the supply chain increase.

A *forward buy* is the amount that a retailer purchases in the promotional period for sales in future periods. A forward buy helps reduce the retailer's future cost of goods for product sold after the promotion ends. Although a forward buy is often the retailer's appropriate response and increases their own profits, it usually increases demand variability with a resulting increase in inventory and flow times within the supply chain. As discussed in Chapters 8 and 9, this can decrease supply chain profitability.

Our objective in this section is to understand a retailer's optimal response when faced with a trade promotion. We identify the factors affecting the forward buy and quantify the size of a forward buy by the retailer. We also identify factors that influence

---

[1]See *Sales Promotion: Concepts, Methods, and Strategies.* 1990. Blattberg and Neslin for more details.

the amount of the trade promotion that a retailer passes on to the customer as well as the optimal amount passed on by a retailer.

We first illustrate the impact of a trade promotion on forward buying behavior of the retailer. Consider a Cub Foods supermarket selling chicken noodle soup manufactured by the Campbell Soup Company. Customer demand for chicken noodle soup is D cans per year. The price Campbell charges is $\$C$ per can. Cub Foods incurs a holding cost of h (per dollar of inventory held for a year). Using the EOQ formula (Equation 10.5), Cub Foods normally orders in the following lot sizes:

$$Q^* = \sqrt{\frac{2\,DS}{hC}}$$

Campbell announces that it is offering a discount of $\$d$ per can for the coming four-week period. Cub Foods must decide how much to order at the discounted price compared to the lot size of Q^* that it normally orders. Let Q^d be the lot size ordered at the discounted price.

The costs the retailer must consider when making this decision are material cost, holding cost, and order cost. Increasing the lot size Q^d will lower the material cost for Cub Foods because they purchase more cans (for sale now and in the future) at the discounted price. Increasing the lot size Q^d will raise the holding cost because inventories increase. Increasing the lot size Q^d will lower the order cost for Cub Foods because some orders that would otherwise have been placed are now not necessary. Cub Food's goal is to make the trade-off that minimizes the total cost.

The inventory pattern when a lot size of Q^d is followed by lot sizes of Q^* is shown in Figure 10.6. The objective is to identify Q^d that maximizes the reduction in total cost (material cost + ordering cost + holding cost) over the time interval during which the quantity Q^d (ordered during the promotion period) is consumed.

The precise analysis in this case is complex, so we present a result that holds under some restrictions.[2] The first key assumption is that the discount will only be

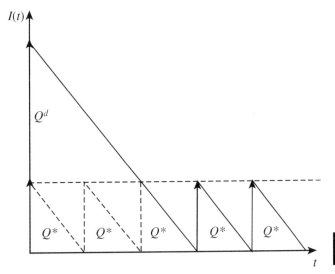

FIGURE 10.6   Inventory Profile for Forward Buying

<hr />

[2]See *Inventory Management and Production Planning and Scheduling.* 1998. Silver, Pyke, and Petersen for a more detailed discussion.

offered once. In all future periods, there will be no discount. The second key assumption is that the order quantity Q^d is a multiple of Q^*. The third key assumption is that the retailer takes no action (such as passing on part of the trade promotion) to influence customer demand. The customer demand thus remains unchanged. With these assumptions, the optimal order quantity at the discounted price is given by

$$Q^d = \frac{dD}{(C-d)h} + \frac{CQ^*}{C-d} \qquad (10.15)$$

In practice, retailers are often aware of the timing of the next promotion. If the demand until the next anticipated trade promotion is Q_1, it is optimal for the retailer to order *min* $\{Q^d, Q_1\}$. Observe that the quantity Q^d ordered as a result of the promotion will be larger than the regular order quantity Q^*. The forward buy in this case is given by

$$\text{Forward buy} = Q^d - Q^*.$$

Even for relatively small discounts, the order size tends to increase by a large quantity, resulting in a large forward buy. We illustrate the impact of trade promotions on lot sizes using Example 10.8.

Example 10.8: Impact of Trade Promotions on Lot Sizes

Recall DO from Example 10.7. DO sells vitaherb, a popular vitamin diet supplement. Demand for vitaherb is 120,000 bottles per year. The manufacturer currently charges $3 for each bottle and DO incurs a holding cost of 20 percent. DO currently orders in lots of $Q^* = 6{,}324$ bottles. The manufacturer has offered a discount of $0.15 for all bottles purchased by retailers over the coming month. Evaluate the number of bottles of vitaherb that DO should order given the promotion.

Analysis: In the absence of any promotion, DO orders in lot sizes of 6,324 bottles. Given a monthly demand of 10,000 bottles, DO normally orders every 0.6324 months. In the absence of the trade promotion we have the following:

$$\text{Cycle inventory at DO} = Q^*/2 = 6{,}324/2 = 3{,}162 \text{ bottles,}$$
$$\text{Average flow time} = Q^*/2D = 6{,}324/(2D) = 0.3162 \text{ months.}$$

The optimal lot size during the promotion is obtained using Equation 10.15 and is given by the following:

$$Q^d = \frac{dD}{(C-d)h} + \frac{CQ^*}{C-d} = \frac{0.15 \times 120{,}000}{(3.00-0.15) \times 0.20} + \frac{3 \times 6{,}324}{3.00-0.15} = 38{,}236$$

During the promotion DO should place an order for a lot size of 38,236. In other words, DO places an order for 3.8236 months worth of demand. In the presence of the trade promotion we have the following:

$$\text{Cycle inventory at DO} = Q^d/2 = 38{,}236/2 = 19{,}118 \text{ bottles,}$$
$$\text{Average flow time} = Q^*/2D = 38{,}236/(2D) = 1.9118 \text{ months.}$$

In the absence of a promotion DO would have ordered 6,324 bottles. In this case, the forward buy is given by

$$\text{Forward buy} = Q^d - Q^* = 38{,}236 - 6{,}324 = 31{,}912 \text{ bottles.}$$

As a result of this forward buy, DO will not place any order for the next 3.8236 months (without a forward buy DO would have placed 31,912 / 6,324 = 5.05 orders for 6,324 bottles each during this period). Observe that a 5 percent discount causes the lot size to increase by more than 500 percent.

As the example illustrates, forward buying as a result of trade promotions leads to a significant increase in inventory (and thus material flow time) at the retailer. The retailer can justify the forward buying because it decreases his total cost. In contrast, the manufacturer can justify this action only if they have either inadvertently built up a lot of excess inventory or the forward buy allows the manufacturer to smooth demand by shifting it from peak to low-demand periods. In practice, manufacturers often build up inventory in anticipation of planned promotions. During the trade promotion this inventory shifts to the retailer, primarily as a forward buy. If the forward buy during trade promotions is a significant fraction of total sales, manufacturers end up reducing the revenues they earn from sales because most of the product is sold at a discount. The increase in inventory and the decrease in revenues often leads to a reduction in manufacturer profits as a result of trade promotions.[3] Total supply chain profits also decrease because of an increase in inventory.

> **Key Point**   Trade promotions lead to a significant increase in lot size and cycle inventory because of forward buying by the retailer. This generally results in reduced supply chain profits unless the trade promotion reduces demand fluctuations.

Now let us consider the extent to which the retailer may find it optimal to pass through some of the discount to the end customer to spur sales. As we shall see in Example 10.9, in general it is not optimal for the retailer to pass through the entire discount to the customer. In other words, it is optimal for the retailer to capture part of the promotion and only pass through part of it to the customer.

Example 10.9

Assume that DO faces a demand curve for vitaherb of $300,000 - 60,000p$. The normal price charged by the manufacturer to the retailer is $C_R = \$3$ per bottle. Ignoring all inventory-related costs, evaluate the optimal response of DO to a discount of $0.15 per unit.

Analysis: The profits for DO, the retailer, are given as follows:

$$Prof_R = (300,000 - 60,000p)p - (300,000 - 60,000p)C_R.$$

The retailer prices to maximize profits and the optimal retail price is obtained by setting the first derivative of retailer profits with respect to p to 0. This implies

$$300,000 - 120,000p + 60,000C_R = 0$$

or

$$p = (300,000 + 60,000C_R)/120,000. \tag{10.16}$$

Substituting $C_R = \$3$ into Equation 10.16, we obtain a retail price of $p = \$4$. As a result the customer demand at the retailer in the absence of the promotion is

$$D_R = 300,000 - 60,000p = 60,000.$$

During the promotion the manufacturer offers a discount of $0.15, resulting in a price to the retailer of $C_R = \$2.85$. Substituting into Equation 10.16, the optimal price set by DO is

---

[3]See Blattberg and Neslin for more details.

$$p = (300,000 + 60,000 \times 2.85)/120,000 = \$3.925.$$

Observe that the retailer's optimal response is to pass through only $0.075 of the $0.15 discount to the customer. The retailer does not pass through the entire discount. At the discounted price, DO experiences a demand of

$$D_R = 300,000 - 60,000p = 64,500.$$

This represents an increase of 7.5 percent in demand. In this case it is optimal for DO to pass on half the trade promotion discount to the customers. This action results in a 7.5 percent increase in customer demand.

From Examples 10.8 and 10.9, observe that the increase in customer demand resulting from a trade promotion (7.5 percent of demand in Example 10.9) is insignificant relative to the increased purchase by the retailer due to forward buying (500 percent from Example 10.8). The impact of the increase in customer demand may be further dampened by customer behavior. For many products like detergent and toothpaste, most of the increase in customer purchases is a forward buy by the customer; customers are unlikely to start brushing their teeth more frequently simply because they have purchased a lot of toothpaste. For such products, a trade promotion does not truly increase demand.

> **Key Point**   Faced with a short-term discount it is optimal for the retailer to pass through only a fraction of the discount to the customer, keeping the rest for themselves. Simultaneously, it is optimal for the retailer to increase the purchase lot size and forward buy for future periods. This leads to an increase of cycle inventory in the supply chain as the result of a trade promotion without a significant increase in customer demand.

Both issues have been commonly observed in industry. Manufacturers have always struggled with the fact that retailers pass along only a small fraction of a trade discount to the customer. Almost a quarter of all distributor inventories in the dry-grocery supply chain in 1990 could be attributed to forward buying.[4]

Our previous discussion supports the claim that trade promotions generally increase cycle inventory in the supply chain and hurt performance. This realization has led many firms including the world's largest retailer, Wal-Mart, and several manufacturers like Procter and Gamble, to adopt Every Day Low Pricing (EDLP). Here the price is fixed over time and no short-term discounts are offered. This eliminates any incentive for forward buying. As a result, all stages of the supply chain purchase in quantities that match demand.

There is one scenario in which trade promotions may make sense—as a competitive response. Consider a situation with competing brands for a product, say cola. In such a category, some customers may be loyal to their brand while others may switch depending on the brand being offered at the lowest price. Consider a situation where one of the competitors, say Pepsi, offers retailers a trade promotion. Retailers increase their purchases of Pepsi and pass through some of the discount to the customer. Price-sensitive customers increase their purchase of Pepsi. If a competitor like Coca-Cola does not respond, they may lose some market share in the form of price sensitive

---

[4]See *Efficient Consumer Response* by Kurt Salmon Associates, Inc. January, 1993.

customers. A case can be made that a trade promotion may be justified in such a setting. Observe that with both competitors offering trade promotions, there is no real increase in demand for either. Inventory in the supply chain, however, does increase for both brands. This is then a situation where trade promotions may be a competitive necessity but they increase supply chain inventory, leading to reduced profits for all competitors.

When trade promotions are offered, they should be designed so that retailers limit their forward buying and pass along more of the discount to end customers. The manufacturer's basic objective is to increase market share and sales without allowing the retailer to forward buy significant amounts. One approach to achieving this outcome is to discount sales to the retailer based on actual sales to customers rather than the amount purchased by the retailer. The discount price thus applies to items sold to customers (*sell-through*) during the promotion, not the quantity purchased by the retailer (*sell-in*). This eliminates all incentive for forward buying.

Given the information technology in place, many manufacturers today offer scanner-based promotions where the retailer receives credit for the promotion discount for every unit sold. It is unlikely, however, that retailers will accept such a scheme for weak brands. Another option is to limit the allocation to a retailer based on past sales. This is also an effort to limit the amount that the retailer can forward buy.

10.5 MANAGING MULTI-ECHELON CYCLE INVENTORY

In our discussions so far we have considered lot sizing decisions to be localized at a single stage of a supply chain. In *multi-echelon* supply chains there are multiple stages, with possibly many players at each stage and one stage supplying another. Each participant in a multi-echelon system must decide on their lot size. One simple approach is for each participant in a multi-echelon system to aggregate its demand and solve for the appropriate EOQ using Equation 10.5 to obtain the lot size. One problem with this approach is that it may result in replenishment orders not being coordinated and the supply chain holding more cycle inventory than required. Another problem with this approach is that it may lead to an unnecessarily large number of orders, resulting in a high order cost in the supply chain. In both cases, the goal is to find ordering policies that coordinate orders across the supply chain.

First consider a simple multi-echelon system with one manufacturer supplying one retailer. Assume that production is instantaneous so the manufacturer can produce a lot when needed. If they have the same optimal lot size Q but are not synchronized, the manufacturer may produce a new lot of size Q right after shipping a lot of size Q to the retailer. Inventory at the two stages is as shown in Figure 10.7. In this case the retailer will carry an average inventory of $Q/2$ and the manufacturer will carry an average inventory of about Q.

In contrast, if the manufacturer synchronizes his production to match shipment to the retailer, he can arrange for his lot to be produced just when the retailer order is to be shipped. In this case, the manufacturer will carry no inventory and the retailer will carry an average inventory of $Q/2$ as before. Synchronization of replenishment orders allows the supply chain to lower total cycle inventory from about $3Q/2$ to $Q/2$ in this case.

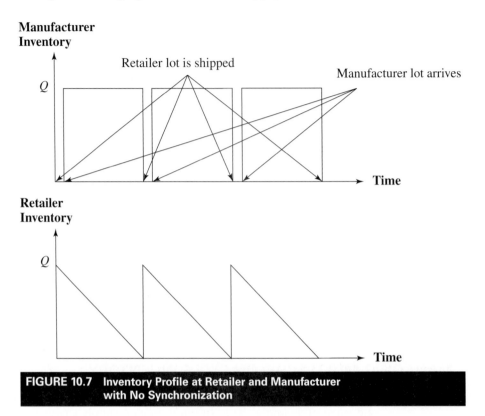

FIGURE 10.7 Inventory Profile at Retailer and Manufacturer with No Synchronization

When a supply chain has a series of stages, the goal is to synchronize lot sizes at different stages in a way that no unnecessary cycle inventory is carried at any stage. One method of achieving synchronization in a supply chain with a single series of stages is to devise inventory policies that are nested and have stationary intervals. An inventory policy is *nested* if a particular stage S and its customers' orders are synchronized such that the replenishment order arrives at stage S just in time for the replenishment order to be shipped to a customer of stage S. Stage S, however, may replenish less frequently than its immediate customer stage. A policy has *stationary intervals* if every stage reorders after a fixed interval of time. Following a nested policy is equivalent to stating that each stage has the opportunity to cross-dock at least a part of its replenishment order because cross-docking can occur when both stages are to be replenished in a coordinated manner. For a supply chain with stages in a single series, ordering policies where the lot size at each stage is an integer multiple of the lot size at its immediate customer (a nested policy) have been shown to be quite close to optimal. Such an ordering policy is equivalent to having lot sizes at each stage be an integer multiple of the amount cross-docked on to the next stage; that is, one out of every k orders from the customer stage is cross-docked where k is an integer. The extent of cross-docking will depend upon the ratio of the fixed cost of ordering S and the holding cost H at each stage. The closer this ratio is between two stages, the higher the optimal percentage of cross-docked product.

A slightly different issue arises when one party in a supply chain supplies multiple parties at the next stage of the supply chain, such as when a distributor supplies many retailers. In this case, a nested policy is not very effective if some retailers have very low demand and others have high demand. Here it may be better for retailers with low demand to order less frequently than the distributor because ordering more frequently will increase the order cost in the supply chain. In this setting, Roundy (1985) has shown that retailers should be grouped such that all retailers in one group order together and for any retailer, either the ordering frequency is an integer multiple of the ordering frequency at the distributor or the ordering frequency at the distributor is an integer multiple of the frequency at the retailer. An example of such a policy is shown in Figure 10.8. Under this policy the distributor places a replenishment order every two weeks. Some retailers place replenishment orders every week and others place replenishment orders every two or four weeks. Observe that for retailers ordering more frequently than the distributor, the retailers' ordering frequency is an integer multiple of the distributor's frequency. For retailers ordering less frequently than the distributor, the distributor's ordering frequency is an integer multiple of the retailers' frequency.

FIGURE 10.8   Illustration of an Integer Replenishment Policy

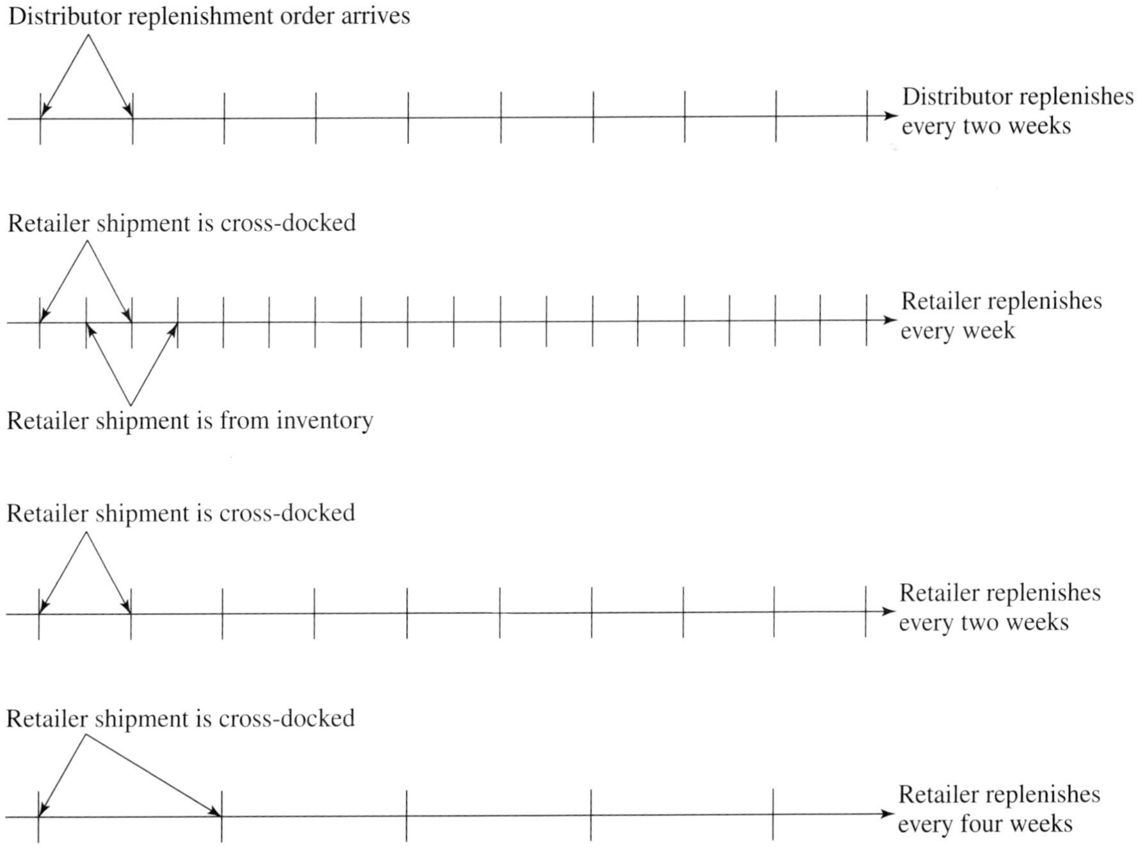

Distributor replenishment order arrives

Distributor replenishes every two weeks

Retailer shipment is cross-docked

Retailer replenishes every week

Retailer shipment is from inventory

Retailer shipment is cross-docked

Retailer replenishes every two weeks

Retailer shipment is cross-docked

Retailer replenishes every four weeks

If the distributor orders more frequently than the retailer, all shipments to the retailer are cross-docked as shown in Figure 10.8. For retailers ordering every four weeks, replenishment at the distributor can be synchronized with shipment to retailers. Thus, every four weeks, the distributor's replenishment order arrives just in time to be cross-docked and shipped to the retailers placing orders once every four weeks as shown in Figure 10.8. If the distributor orders less frequently than the retailer, some of the retailer's replenishment orders are cross-docked, whereas others are shipped from inventory. For retailers ordering every week, every second week the replenishment order at the distributor arrives just in time to be cross-docked and shipped to the retailer as shown in Figure 10.8. Every other week, however, the replenishment order to retailers is shipped from inventory. Thus, half the replenishment orders are cross-docked in this case.

Consider the supply chain shown in Figure 10.9 as a set of stages with all parties at one stage being customers of some party at the previous stage and suppliers to other parties at the next stage. For such a multi-echelon distribution supply chain, a good replenishment policy has the following characteristics:

- All parties within a stage are divided into groups such that all parties within a group order simultaneously from the same supplier.
- When a party receives a replenishment order, the receipt should be synchronized with the shipment of a replenishment order to at least one of its customers. In other words, a portion of any replenishment order at a stage should be cross-docked on to the next stage.

FIGURE 10.9   A Multi-Echelon Distribution Supply Chain

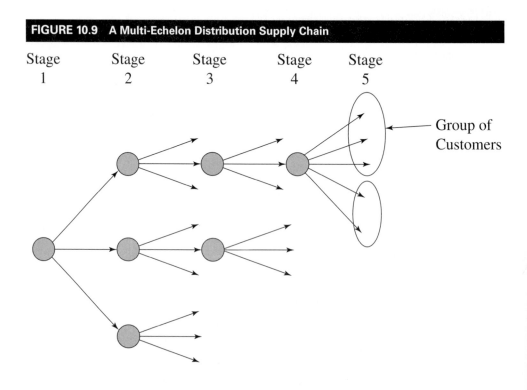

Stage 1   Stage 2   Stage 3   Stage 4   Stage 5

Group of Customers

- If a customer replenishes less frequently than its supplier, the supplier replenishment frequency should be an integer multiple of the customer replenishment frequency and replenishment at both stages should be synchronized to facilitate cross-docking. In other words, a supplier should cross-dock all orders from customers who reorder less frequently than the supplier himself.
- If a customer replenishes more frequently than its supplier, the customer's replenishment frequency should be an integer multiple of the supplier's replenishment frequency and replenishment at both stages should be synchronized to facilitate cross-docking. In other words, a supplier should cross-dock one out of every k shipments to a customer who orders more frequently than himself, where k is an integer.

The relative frequency of reordering will depend upon the setup cost, holding cost, and demand at different parties.

> **Key Point** Replenishment orders in multi-echelon supply chains should be synchronized to keep cycle inventory and order costs low. In general, each stage should attempt to coordinate orders from customers who order less frequently and cross-dock all such orders. Some of the orders from customers that order more frequently should also be cross-docked.

10.6 ESTIMATING CYCLE INVENTORY RELATED COSTS IN PRACTICE

When setting cycle inventory levels in practice, a common hurdle is estimating the various costs that we have included in our discussion so far. The three major costs we have discussed are material cost, order cost, and holding cost. The material cost is typically the easiest to identify in practice. In this section we focus on the components of order and holding cost and discuss how they may be estimated. A key point here is that it is not terribly important to estimate these costs to a high level of precision. It is better to get a good approximation quickly rather than spend a lot of time trying to estimate costs exactly.

In calculating these costs, we need to keep in mind that what we are really concerned with are incremental costs; that is, costs that change as we change our lot sizing decision. Costs that are unchanged with a change in lot size should not be included in the lot sizing decision. For example, if a factory is running at 50 percent of capacity and all labor is full time and not earning overtime, it can be argued that the incremental setup cost for labor is actually zero. Reducing the lot size in this case will not have any impact on setup cost until either labor is fully utilized (and earning overtime) or machines are fully utilized (with a resulting loss in production capacity).

Inventory Holding Cost

Holding cost is estimated as the sum of the following major components, not all of which are applicable to every type of situation. Holding cost is usually estimated as a percentage of the cost of a product.

- *Cost of capital:* This cost is often the most important component of holding cost. The appropriate approach is to evaluate the Weighted Average Cost of Capital (WACC).[5] This cost takes into account the return demanded on the firm's equity and the amount the firm must pay on its debt. These are weighted by the amount of debt and equity financing that the firm has. The formula for the WACC is as follows:

$$WACC = \frac{E}{D+E}(R_f + \beta \times MRP) + \frac{D}{D+E}R_b(1-t)$$

where

E = amount of equity
D = amount of debt
R_f = risk-free rate of return (which is usually in the mid single digits)
β = the firm's beta
MRP = Market risk premium (which is around the high single digits)
R_b = rate at which the firm can borrow money (related to their debt rating)
t = tax rate

We need to keep in mind, however, that the WACC is an after-tax number whereas inventory level calculations are done pre-tax. Therefore, we need to adjust the WACC to use in a pre-tax setting as shown here.

Pre-tax WACC = After-tax WACC/(1 − t).

The pre-tax WACC is the appropriate cost of capital for a firm that could grow its business using the funds released by reducing inventories. Most of these numbers can be found in a company's annual report and in any equity report on the company. The borrowing rate can come from tables listing the rates charged for bonds from firms with the same credit ratings. The risk-free rate is the return on U.S. treasuries, and the market risk premium is the return of the market above the risk-free rate. If a company is private and access to its financial structure is not available, a good approximation can be made by picking companies in the same industry and of somewhat similar size that are public and then using their numbers.

- *Obsolescence (or spoilage) cost:* The obsolescence cost estimates the rate at which the value of the product you are storing drops either because the market value of that product drops or because the product quality deteriorates. This cost can range dramatically from rates of many thousands percent to virtually zero and depend on the type of product we are holding. When setting an inventory level for hamburgers that can only sell for fifteen minutes after they are cooked, the obsolescence rate should be high. It is unlikely that we will be able to sell hamburgers cooked half an hour ago. Even nonperishables that have short life cycles, like microprocessors, can have obsolescence rates topping 100 percent. A product with a life cycle of six months has an effective obsolescence cost of 200 percent. On

---

[5]See *Principles of Corporate Finance* by Brealey and Myers, 2000.

the other end of the spectrum are products like gasoline that take a long time to become obsolete or spoil. For such products a very low obsolescence rate may be applied.

- *Handling cost:* Handling cost should only include receiving and storage costs that vary with the quantity of product received. Quantity-independent handling costs that vary with the number of orders should be included in the order cost. Quantity-dependent handling costs are generally small and often the real cost does not change if quantity varies within a range. If the quantity is within this range (e.g., the range of inventory a crew of four people can unload per period of time), incremental handling cost added to the holding cost is zero. However, if incremental handling cost is incurred, then handling costs associated with this additional inventory should be included in the holding cost.

- *Occupancy cost:* The occupancy cost should reflect the incremental change in space cost due to changing cycle inventory. If the firm is being charged based on the actual number of units held in storage, we have the direct occupancy cost. Firms often lease or purchase a fixed amount of space. As long as a marginal change in cycle inventory does not change the space requirements, the occupancy cost should be considered zero. Occupancy, or space costs, often take the form of a step function with a sudden increase in cost when capacity is fully utilized and new space must be acquired.

- *Miscellaneous costs:* The final component of holding cost deals with a number of other relatively small costs. These costs include theft, security, damage, tax, and additional insurance charges that may be incurred. Once again, it is important to estimate the incremental change in these costs on changing cycle inventory.

Order Cost

The order cost includes all incremental costs associated with placing or receiving an extra order that are incurred regardless of the size of the order. Components of order cost include:

- *Buyer time:* Buyer time is the incremental time of the buyer placing the extra order. This cost should be included only if the buyer is utilized fully. The incremental cost of getting an idle buyer to place an order is zero and does not add to the order cost. Electronic ordering can significantly reduce the buyer time to place an order by making order placement simpler and in some cases automatic.

- *Transportation costs:* A fixed transportation cost is often incurred regardless of the size of the order. For instance, if a truck is sent to deliver every order, it costs the same amount to send a half empty truck as it does a full truck. LTL pricing also includes a fixed component that is independent of the quantity shipped and a variable component that increases with the quantity shipped. The fixed component should be included in the order cost.

- *Receiving costs:* Some receiving costs are incurred regardless of the size of the order. These include any administration work such as purchase order matching and any effort associated with updating inventory records. Receiving costs that are volume dependent should not be included here.

- *Other costs:* Each situation can have costs unique to it that should be considered if they are incurred for each order regardless of the quantity of that order.

The order cost is estimated as the sum of all its component costs. As with carrying cost, it is important to determine that all costs included are the incremental change in real cost for an additional order. The order cost is often a step function; it is zero when the resource is not fully utilized, but takes on a large value when the resource is fully utilized. At that point the order cost is the cost of the additional resource required.

10.7 SUMMARY OF LEARNING OBJECTIVES

1. Balance the appropriate costs in order to choose the optimal amount of cycle inventory in the supply chain.

   Cycle inventory generally equals half the lot size. Therefore, as the lot size grows, so does the cycle inventory. In deciding on the optimal amount of cycle inventory, the supply chain goal is to minimize the total cost—the order cost, holding cost, and material cost. As cycle inventory increases, so does the holding cost. However, the order cost and, in some instances, the material cost go down with an increase in lot size and cycle inventory. The EOQ balances the three costs to obtain the optimal lot size. The higher the order and transportation cost, the higher the lot size and cycle inventory.

2. Understand the impact of quantity discounts on lot size and cycle inventory.

   Lot size based quantity discounts encourage buyers to purchase in larger quantities to take advantage of the decrease in price. Therefore, lot size based quantity discounts increase the lot size and cycle inventory within the supply chain.

3. Devise appropriate discounting schemes for the supply chain.

   Quantity discounts are justified to achieve coordination within the supply chain.

Volume-based discounts are more effective at coordinating the supply chain without increasing lot size and cycle inventory. They are thus more appropriate than lot size based discounts.

4. Understand the impact of trade promotions on lot size and cycle inventory.

   Trade promotions increase forward buying within the supply chain. Forward buying shifts future demand to the present and creates a spike in demand. As a result, trade promotions increase inventory and cost in a supply chain.

5. Identify managerial levers that reduce lot size and cycle inventory in a supply chain without increasing cost.

   The key managerial levers for reducing lot size and thus cycle inventory in the supply chain without increasing cost are the following:

   - Reduce fixed ordering and transportation costs incurred per order.
   - Implement volume-based discounting schemes rather than individual lot size based discounting schemes.
   - Eliminate or reduce trade promotions and encourage EDLP. Base trade promotions on sell-through rather than sell-in to the retailer.

DISCUSSION QUESTIONS

1. Consider a supermarket deciding on the size of its replenishment order from Procter and Gamble. What costs should it take into account when making this decision?
2. Discuss how various costs for the supermarket change as it increases the lot size ordered from Procter & Gamble.
3. As demand at the supermarket chain grows, how would you expect the cycle inventory measured in days of inventory to change? Explain.
4. The manager at the supermarket would like to decrease the lot size without increasing the costs he incurs. What actions can he take to achieve this objective?
5. When are quantity discounts justified in a supply chain?
6. What is the difference between lot size based and volume-based quantity discounts?
7. Why do manufacturers like Kraft and Sara Lee offer trade promotions? What impact do trade promotions have on the supply chain? How should trade promotions be structured to maximize their impact while minimizing the additional cost they impose on the supply chain?
8. Why is it appropriate to include only the incremental cost when estimating the holding and order cost for a firm?

EXERCISES

1. Harley Davidson has its engine assembly plant in Milwaukee and its motorcycle assembly plant in Pennsylvania. Engines are transported between the two plants using trucks. Suppose each truck trip costs $1,000. The motorcycle plant assembles and sells 300 motorcycles each day. Each engine costs $500 and Harley incurs a holding cost of 20 percent per year. How many engines should Harley load onto each truck? What is the cycle inventory of engines at Harley?
2. Harley has decided to implement Just In Time (JIT) manufacturing at the motorcycle assembly plant. As part of this initiative it has reduced the number of engines loaded on each truck to 100. If each truck trip still costs $1,000, how does this decision impact annual costs at Harley? What should the cost of each truck be if a load of 100 engines is to be optimal for Harley?
3. Harley purchases components from three suppliers. Components purchased from Supplier A are priced at $5 each and used at the rate of 20,000 units per month. Components purchased from Supplier B are priced at $4 each and are used at the rate of 2,500 units per month. Components purchased from Supplier C are priced at $5 each and used at the rate of 900 units per month. Currently Harley purchases a separate truckload from each supplier. As part of its JIT drive, Harley has decided to aggregate purchases from the three suppliers. The trucking company charges a fixed cost of $400 for the truck with an additional charge of $100 for each stop. Thus, if Harley asks for a pickup from only one supplier, the trucking company charges $500; from two suppliers it charges $600; and from three suppliers it charges $700. Suggest a replenishment strategy for Harley that minimizes annual cost. Compare the cost of your strategy with Harley's current

strategy of ordering separately from each supplier. What is the cycle inventory of each component at Harley?

4. Prefab, a furniture manufacturer, uses 20,000 square feet of plywood per month. Their trucking company charges Prefab $400 per shipment independent of the quantity purchased. The manufacturer offers an all unit quantity discount with a price of $1 per square foot for orders under 20,000 square feet, $0.98 per square foot for orders between 20,000 square feet and 40,000 square feet, and $0.96 per square foot for orders larger than 40,000 square feet. Prefab incurs a holding cost of 20 percent. What is the optimal lot size for Prefab? What is the annual cost of such a policy? What is the cycle inventory of plywood at Prefab? How does it compare with the cycle inventory if the manufacturer did not offer a quantity discount but sold all plywood at $0.96 per square foot?

5. Reconsider Problem 4 with Prefab. However, the manufacturer now offers a marginal unit quantity discount for the plywood. The first 20,000 square feet of any order is sold at $1 per square foot, the next 20,000 square feet is sold at $0.98 per square foot, and any quantity over 40,000 square feet is sold for $0.96 per square foot. What is the optimal lot size for Prefab given this pricing structure? How much cycle inventory of plywood will Prefab carry given the ordering policy?

6. The Dominick's supermarket chain sells Nut Flakes, a popular cereal manufactured by the Tastee cereal company. Demand for Nut Flakes is 1,000 boxes per week. Dominick's has a holding cost of 25 percent and incurs a fixed trucking cost of $200 for each replenishment order it places with Tastee. Given that Tastee normally charges $2 per box of Nut Flakes, how much should Dominick's order in each replenishment lot? Tastee runs a trade promotion lowering the price of Nut Flakes to $1.80 for a month. How much should Dominick's order given the short-term price reduction?

BIBLIOGRAPHY

Blattberg, Robert C., and Scott A. Neslin. 1990. *Sales Promotion: Concepts, Methods, and Strategies*. Upper Saddle River, N.J.: Prentice Hall.

Brealey, Richard A., and Stewart C. Myers. 2000. *Principles of Corporate Finance*. Boston: Irwin McGraw-Hill.

Buzzell, Robert, John Quelch, and Walter Salmon. 1990. "The Costly Bargain of Trade Promotions." *Harvard Business Review* (March–April): 141–149.

Crowther, J. 1964. "Rationale for Quantity Discounts." *Harvard Business Review* (March–April): 121–127.

Dolan, Robert J. 1987. "Quantity Discounts: Managerial Issues and Research Opportunities." *Marketing Science* 6: 1–24.

Federgruen, A., and Yu-Sheng Zheng. 1993. "Optimal Power-of-Two Replenishment Strategies in Capacitated General Production/Distribution Networks." *Management Science* 39: 710–727.

Kurt Salmon Associates, Inc. 1993. *Efficient Consumer Response*. Washington, D.C.: Food Marketing Institute.

Lee, Hau L., and Corey Billington. 1992. "Managing Supply Chain Inventories: Pitfalls and Opportunities." *Sloan Management Review* (Spring): 65–73.

Maxwell, J. A., and J. A. Muckstadt. 1985. "Establishing Consistent and Realistic Reorder Intervals in Production-Distribution Systems." *Operations Research* 33: 1316–1341.

Roundy, Robin. 1985. "98%-Effective Integer-Ratio Lot-Sizing for One-Warehouse Multi-Retailer Systems." *Management Science* 31: 1416–1429.

Roundy, Robin. 1986. "A 98%-Effective Lot-Sizing Rule for a Multi-Product, Multi-Stage Production Inventory System." *Mathematics of Operations Research* 11: 699–727.

Silver, Edward A., David Pyke, and Rein Petersen. 1998. *Inventory Management and Production Planning and Scheduling*. New York: John Wiley & Sons.

Zipkin, Paul H. 2000. *Foundations of Inventory Management*. Boston: Irwin McGraw-Hill.

------------------------------ C A S E   S T U D Y ------------------------------

Delivery Strategy at MoonChem

John Kresge was very concerned as he left the meeting at MoonChem, a manufacturer of specialty chemicals. The year-end meeting had evaluated financial performance and discussed the fact that the firm was achieving only two inventory turns a year. A more careful look revealed that over half the inventory MoonChem owned was consignment inventory with its customers. This was very surprising given that only 20 percent of its customers carried consignment inventory. John Kresge was Vice President of Supply Chain and thus responsible for inventory as well as transportation. He decided to take a careful look at how consignment inventory was managed and come up with an appropriate plan.

MOONCHEM OPERATIONS

MoonChem is a manufacturer of specialty chemicals used in a variety of industrial applications. MoonChem has eight manufacturing plants and forty distribution centers. The plants manufacture the base chemicals and the distribution centers mix them to produce hundreds of end-products that fit customer specifications. In the specialty chemicals market, MoonChem has decided to differentiate itself in the Midwest region by providing consignment inventory to its customers. MoonChem would like to take this strategy national if it proves effective. MoonChem keeps the chemicals required by each customer in the Midwest region on consignment at the customers' sites. Customers use the chemicals as needed and MoonChem ensures replenishment to ensure that the customers do not run out of inventory. In most instances, consumption of chemicals by customers is very stable. MoonChem is paid for the chemicals as they are used. Thus, all consignment inventories belong to MoonChem.

DISTRIBUTION AT MOONCHEM

MoonChem currently uses Golden trucking, a full truckload carrier for all its shipments. Each truck has a capacity of 40,000 pounds and Golden charges a fixed rate given the origin and destination, irrespective of the quantity shipped on the truck. Currently MoonChem sends full truckloads to each customer to replenish their consignment inventory.

THE ILLINOIS PILOT STUDY

John decided to take a careful look at his distribution operations. He decided to focus on the state of Illinois, which was supplied from the Chicago distribution center. He broke up the state of Illinois into a collection of zip codes that were contiguous, as shown in Figure 10.10. He decided to restrict attention within the Peoria region, which was classified as zip code 615. A careful study of the Peoria region revealed two large customers, six medium-sized customers, and twelve small customers. The annual consumption at each type of customer is as shown in Table 10.4. Golden currently charges $400 for each shipment from Chicago to Peoria and MoonChem's policy is to send a full truckload to each customer when replenishment of consignment inventory is needed.

John checked with Golden to find out what it would take to include shipments for multiple customers on a single load. Golden informed him that they would continue to charge $350 per truck and would then add $50 for each drop-off that Golden was responsible for. Thus, if Golden carried a truck that had to make one delivery, the total charge would be $400. However, if a truck had to make four deliveries, the total charge would be $550.

TABLE 10.4   Customer Profile for MoonChem in Peoria Region

Customer Type	Number of Customers	Consumption (Pounds per Month)
Small	12	1,000
Medium	6	5,000
Large	2	12,000

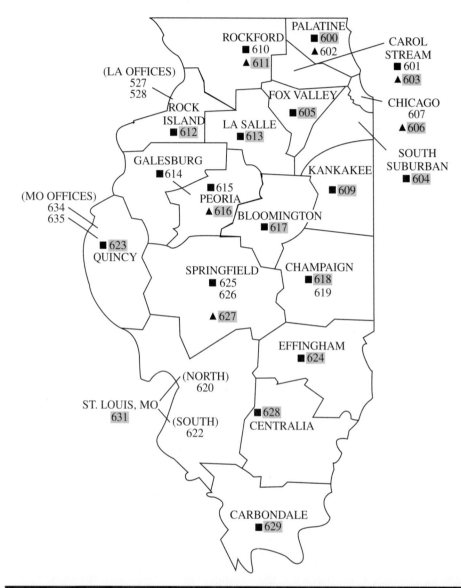

FIGURE 10.10 Illinois Zip Code Map

Each pound of chemical in consignment cost MoonChem $1 and MoonChem had a holding cost of 25 percent. John wanted to analyze different options for distribution available in the Peoria region to decide on the optimal distribution policy. The detailed study of the Peoria region would provide the blueprint for the distribution strategy that MoonChem planned to roll out nationally.

QUESTIONS

1. What is the current annual cost of MoonChem's strategy of sending full truckloads to each customer in the Peoria region to replenish consignment inventory?
2. Consider different delivery options and evaluate the cost of each. What delivery option do you recommend for MoonChem?
3. How does your recommendation impact consignment inventory for MoonChem?

-------------------------------- **A P P E N D I X   1 0 A** --------------------------------

Economic Order Quantity (EOQ)

Objective: Derive the EOQ formula.

Analysis: Given an annual demand D, order cost S, unit cost C, and holding cost h, our goal is to estimate the lot size Q that minimizes the total annual cost. For a lot size of Q, the total annual cost is given by

Total annual cost, $TC = (D/Q)S + (Q/2)hC + CD$.

To minimize the total cost we take the first derivative with respect to the lot size Q and set it to zero. Taking the first derivative with respect to Q, we have

$$\frac{d(TC)}{dQ} = -\frac{DS}{Q^2} + \frac{hC}{2}$$

Setting the first derivative to be zero, the EOQ is given by

$$Q^2 = \frac{2\,DS}{hC}, \quad \text{or} \quad Q = \sqrt{\frac{2\,DS}{hC}}$$

11

Managing Uncertainty in the Supply Chain: Safety Inventory

Learning Objectives

After reading this chapter, you will be able to:

1. Understand the role of safety inventory in a supply chain.

2. Identify factors that influence the required level of safety inventory.

3. Describe different measures of product availability.

4. Utilize managerial levers available to lower safety inventory and improve product availability.

In this chapter, we discuss how safety inventory can help a supply chain improve product availability in the presence of supply and demand variability. We discuss various measures of product availability and how managers can set safety inventory levels to provide the desired product availability. We also explore what managers can do to reduce the amount of safety inventory required while maintaining or even improving product availability.

11.1   THE ROLE OF SAFETY INVENTORY IN THE SUPPLY CHAIN

Safety inventory is inventory carried for the purpose of satisfying demand that exceeds the amount forecasted for a given period. Safety inventory is carried because demand forecasts are uncertain and a product shortage may result if actual demand exceeds the forecast demand. Consider, for example, Bloomingdales, a high-end department store. Bloomingdales sells purses purchased from Gucci, an Italian manufacturer. Given the high transportation cost from Italy, the store manager at Bloomingdales orders in lots of 600 purses. Demand for purses at Bloomingdales averages 100 a week. Gucci takes three weeks to deliver the purses to Bloomingdales in response to an order. If there is no demand uncertainty and exactly 100 purses are sold each week, the store manager at Bloomingdales can place an order when the store has exactly 300 purses remaining. In the absence of demand uncertainty, such a policy ensures that the new lot arrives just as the last purse is being sold at the store.

However, as discussed in Chapter 7, demand forecasts are unlikely to be completely accurate. Given forecast errors, actual demand over the three weeks may be higher or lower than the 300 purses forecasted. If the actual demand at Bloomingdales is higher than 300, some customers will be unable to purchase purses, resulting in a potential loss of margin for Bloomingdales. The store manager thus decides to place an order with Gucci when they still have 400 purses in the store. This policy allows the store manager to improve product availability because the store now runs out of purses only if the demand over the three weeks exceeds 400. Given an average weekly demand of 100 purses, the store will have an average of 100 purses remaining when the replenishment lot arrives. Safety inventory is the average inventory remaining when the replenishment lot arrives. Thus, Bloomingdales carries a safety inventory of 100 purses.

Given a lot size of $Q = 600$ purses, the cycle inventory is $Q/2 = 300$ purses. The inventory profile at Bloomingdales in the presence of safety inventory is shown in Figure 11.1. As Figure 11.1 illustrates, the average inventory at Bloomingdales is the sum of the cycle and safety inventories.

This example illustrates a trade-off that a supply chain manager must consider when planning safety inventory. On one hand, raising the level of safety inventory increases product availability and thus the margin captured from customer purchases. On the other hand, raising the level of safety inventory increases inventory holding costs. This issue is particularly significant in industries where product life cycles are short and demand is very volatile. Carrying excessive inventory can help counter demand volatility but can really hurt if new products come on the market and demand for the product in inventory dries up. The inventory on hand then becomes worthless.

In today's business environment, innovations such as the Internet have made it easier for customers to search across stores for product availability. When shopping for books online, if Amazon.com is out of a title, a customer can easily check to see if BarnesandNoble.com has the title available. The increased ease of searching puts pressure on firms to improve product availability. Simultaneously, product variety has

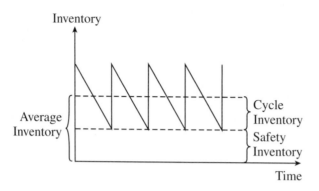

FIGURE 11.1 Inventory Profile with Safety Inventory

grown with increased customization. As a result, markets have become increasingly heterogeneous and demand for individual products is very unstable and difficult to forecast. Both the increased variety and the increased pressure for availability push firms to increase the level of safety inventory they hold. Given the product variety and high demand uncertainty in most high-tech supply chains, a significant fraction of the inventory carried is safety inventory.

As product variety has grown, however, product life cycles have shrunk. Thus, it is more likely that a product that is "hot" today will be obsolete tomorrow, which increases the cost to firms of carrying too much inventory. Thus, a key to the success of any supply chain is to figure out ways to decrease the level of safety inventory carried without hurting the level of product availability.

The importance of reduced safety inventories is emphasized by the experience of Dell and Compaq (now part of HP) in the early part of 1998 when prices dropped. Compaq carried one hundred days of inventory compared to Dell, which only carried ten days of inventory. Declining prices hurt Compaq much worse given the extra inventory that it carried. In fact, this situation resulted in Compaq announcing that it would not be profitable in the first quarter of 1998.

A key to Dell's success has been its ability to provide a high level of product availability to customers while carrying very low levels of safety inventory in its supply chain. This fact has also played a very important role in the success of Wal-Mart and 7-Eleven Japan.

For any supply chain, there are two key questions to consider when planning safety inventory:

1. What is the appropriate level of safety inventory to carry?
2. What actions can be taken to improve product availability while reducing safety inventory?

The remainder of this chapter focuses on answering these questions. Next we consider factors that influence the appropriate level of safety inventory.

11.2 DETERMINING APPROPRIATE LEVEL OF SAFETY INVENTORY

The appropriate level of safety inventory is determined by the following two factors:

- The uncertainty of both demand and supply
- The desired level of product availability

As the uncertainty of supply or demand grows, the required level of safety inventories increases. Consider the sale of Palm personal digital assistants (PDAs) at B&M Office Supplies. When a new Palm model is introduced, demand is highly uncertain. B&M thus carries a much higher level of safety inventory relative to demand. As the market's reaction to the new model becomes more clear, uncertainty is reduced and demand is easier to predict. At that point, B&M can carry a lower level of safety inventory relative to demand.

As the desired level of product availability increases, the required level of safety inventory also increases. If B&M targets a higher level of product availability for the new Palm model, it must carry a higher level of safety inventory for that model.

Next we discuss some measures of demand uncertainty.

Measuring Demand Uncertainty

As discussed in Chapter 7, demand has a systematic as well as a random component. The goal of forecasting is to predict the systematic component and estimate the random component. The estimate of the random component is a measure of demand uncertainty and is usually estimated as the standard deviation of demand. We assume the following inputs for demand:

D: Average demand per period,
σ_D: Standard deviation of demand per period.

For now, we assume that demand is normally distributed. In the case of B&M, weekly demand for the Palm is normally distributed with a mean of D and a standard deviation of σ_D.

Lead time is the gap between when an order is placed and when it is received. In our discussion, we denote the lead time by L. In the B&M example, L is the time between when B&M orders Palms and when they are delivered. In this case, B&M is exposed to the uncertainty of demand during the lead time. Whether B&M is able to satisfy all demand from inventory depends on the demand for Palms experienced during the lead time and the inventory B&M has when a replenishment order is placed. Thus, B&M must estimate the uncertainty of demand during the lead time, not just a single period. We now evaluate the distribution of demand over k periods, given the distribution of demand during each period.

Assume that demand for each period i, $i = 1, \ldots, k$ is normally distributed with a mean D_i and standard deviation σ_i. Let $cov(i, j)$ be the covariance of demand between periods i and j. In this case, the total demand during k periods is normally distributed with a mean of P and a standard deviation of Ω, where the following is true:

$$P = \sum_{i=1}^{k} D_i \quad \text{and} \quad \Omega = \sqrt{\sum_{i=1}^{k} \sigma_i^2 + 2\sum_{i>j} cov(i,j)} \qquad \textbf{(11.1)}$$

The covariance is given by the following:

$$cov(i,j) = \rho\sigma_i\sigma_j,$$

where ρ is the correlation coefficient. Demand in two periods is *perfectly positively correlated* if $\rho = 1$. Demand in two periods is *perfectly negatively correlated* if $\rho = -1$.

Demand in two periods is *independent* if $\rho = 0$. Therefore, if demand during each of the k periods is independent and normally distributed with a mean of D and a standard deviation of σ_D, from Equation 11.1 we find that total demand during the k periods is normally distributed with a mean P and a standard deviation of Ω, where the following is true:

$$P = kD, \Omega = \sqrt{k}\, \sigma_D. \qquad \qquad \textbf{(11.2)}$$

Another important measure of uncertainty is the *coefficient of variation (cv)*, which is the ratio of the standard deviation to the mean. Given demand with a mean of μ and a standard deviation of σ, we have the following:

$$cv = \sigma/\mu.$$

The coefficient of variation measures the size of the uncertainty relative to demand. It captures the fact that a product with mean demand of 100 and a standard deviation of 100 has greater demand uncertainty than a product with mean demand of 1,000 and a standard deviation of 100. Considering the standard deviation alone cannot capture this difference.

Next we discuss some measures of product availability.

Measuring Product Availability

Product availability reflects a firm's ability to fill a customer order out of available inventory. A *stockout* results if a customer order arrives when product is not available. There are several ways to measure product availability. All availability measures are defined on average over a given time frame, which can range from hours to a year. Some of the important measures are as listed next:

1. *Product fill rate* (*fr*) is the fraction of product demand that is satisfied from product in inventory. It is equivalent to the probability that product demand is supplied from available inventory. Assume that B&M receives orders for a total of 100 Palms and has 90 in inventory to satisfy this demand. In this case B&M achieves a fill rate of 90 percent.

2. *Order fill rate* is the fraction of orders that are filled from available inventory. In a multiproduct scenario, an order is filled from inventory only if all products in the order can be supplied from the available inventory. In the case of B&M, a customer may order a Palm along with a calculator. The order is filled from inventory only if both the Palm and the calculator are available through the store. Order fill rates tend to be lower than product fill rates because all products must be in stock for an order to be filled.

3. *Cycle service level* (CSL) is the fraction of *replenishment cycles* that end with all the customer demand being met. A replenishment cycle is the interval between two successive replenishment deliveries. The CSL is equal to the probability of not having a stockout in a replenishment cycle. If B&M orders replenishment lots of 600 Palms, the interval between the arrival of two successive replenishment lots is a replenishment cycle. If the manager at B&M manages inventory such that the store does not run out

of inventory in 6 out of 10 replenishment cycles, the store achieves a CSL of 60 percent. Observe that a CSL of 60 percent will typically result in a much higher fill rate. In the 60 percent of cycles where B&M does not run out of inventory, all customer demand is satisfied from available inventory. In the 40 percent of cycles where a stockout does occur, most of the customer demand is satisfied from inventory. Only the small fraction toward the end of the cycle that arrives after B&M is out of inventory is lost. As a result the fill rate will be much higher than 60 percent.

The distinction between product fill rate and order fill rate is not significant in a single product situation. When a firm is selling multiple products, however, this difference may be significant. For example, if most orders include 10 or more different products that are to be shipped, an out-of-stock situation of one product results in the order not being filled from stock. The firm in this case may have a poor order fill rate even though it has good product fill rates. Tracking order fill rates is important when customers place a high value on the entire order being filled simultaneously.

Next we describe two replenishment policies that are often used in practice.

Replenishment Policies

A replenishment policy consists of decisions regarding when to reorder and how much to reorder. These decisions determine the cycle and safety inventories along with the fr and the CSL. There are several forms that replenishment policies may take. We restrict attention to two instances:

1. *Continuous review:* Inventory is continuously tracked and an order for a lot size Q is placed when the inventory declines to the reorder point (ROP). As an example, consider the store manager at B&M who continuously tracks the inventory of Palms. They order 600 Palms when the inventory drops below 400. In this case, the size of the order does not change from one order to the next. The time between orders may fluctuate given variable demand.

2. *Periodic review:* Inventory status is checked at regular periodic intervals and an order is placed to raise the inventory level to a specified threshold. As an example, consider the purchase of film at B&M. The store manager does not continuously track film inventory. Every Saturday, they check film inventory and the manager orders enough such that the available inventory and the size of the order total 1,000 rolls of films. In this case the time between orders is fixed. The size of each order, however, can fluctuate given variable demand.

These inventory policies are not comprehensive but suffice to illustrate the key managerial issues concerning safety inventories.

Evaluating Cycle Service Level and Fill Rate Given a Replenishment Policy

We now discuss procedures for evaluating the CSL and fr given a replenishment policy. In this section, we restrict our attention to the continuous review policy, which is discussed in detail in section 11.3. The replenishment policy consists of a lot size Q ordered when the inventory on hand declines to the ROP. Assume weekly demand to be normally distributed, with mean D and standard deviation σ_D. Assume replenishment lead time of L weeks.

Evaluating Safety Inventory Given a Replenishment Policy

In the case of B&M, safety inventory corresponds to the average number of Palms on hand when a replenishment order arrives. Given the lead time of L weeks and a mean weekly demand of D, using Equation 11.2, we have the following:

$$\text{Expected demand during lead time} = DL.$$

Given that the store manager places a replenishment order when ROP Palms are on hand, we have the following:

$$\text{Safety inventory, } ss = ROP - DL. \qquad (11.3)$$

This is because, on average, DL Palms will sell over the period between when the order is placed and when the lot arrives. The average inventory when the replenishment lot arrives will thus be $ROP - DL$.

Example 11.1

Assume that weekly demand for Palms at B&M Computer World is normally distributed with a mean of 2,500 and a standard deviation of 500. The manufacturer takes two weeks to fill an order placed by the B&M manager. The store manager currently orders 10,000 Palms when the inventory on hand drops to 6,000. Evaluate the safety inventory carried by B&M and the average inventory carried by B&M. Also evaluate the average time spent by a Palm at B&M.

Analysis: Under this replenishment policy, we have the following:

Average demand per week, $D = 2,500$,
Standard deviation of weekly demand, $\sigma_D = 500$,
Average lead time for replenishment, $L = 2$ weeks,
Reorder point, $ROP = 6,000$,
Average lot size, $Q = 10,000$.

Using Equation 11.3, we thus have the following:

$$\text{Safety inventory, } ss = ROP - DL = 6,000 - 5,000 = 1,000.$$

B&M thus carries a safety inventory of 1,000 Palms. From Chapter 10, recall the following:

$$\text{Cycle inventory} = Q/2 = 10,000/2 = 5,000.$$

We thus have the following:

$$\text{Average inventory} = \text{cycle inventory} + \text{safety inventory} = 5,000 + 1,000 = 6,000.$$

B&M thus carries an average of 6,000 Palms in inventory. Using Little's law (Equation 3.1), we have the following:

$$\text{Average flow time} = \text{Average inventory/Throughput} = 6,000/2,500 = 2.4 \text{ weeks}.$$

Each Palm thus spends an average of 2.4 weeks at B&M.

Next we discuss how to evaluate the CSL given a replenishment policy.

Evaluating Cycle Service Level Given a Replenishment Policy

Given a replenishment policy, our goal is to evaluate CSL, the probability of not stocking out in a replenishment cycle. We return to B&M's continuous review replenishment policy of ordering Q units when the inventory on hand drops to the ROP. The lead time is L weeks and weekly demand is normally distributed with a mean of D and a standard deviation of σ_D. Observe that a stockout occurs in a cycle if demand during the lead time is larger than the ROP. Thus, we have the following:

$$CSL = \text{Prob(Demand during lead time of } L \text{ weeks} \leq ROP).$$

To evaluate this probability, we need to obtain the distribution of demand during the lead time. From Equation 11.2, we know that demand during lead time is normally distributed with a mean of D_L and a standard deviation of σ_L where

$$D_L = DL \quad \text{and} \quad \sigma_L = \sqrt{L}\,\sigma_D$$

Using the notation for the normal distribution from Appendix 11A, the CSL is as follows:

$$CSL = F(ROP, D_L, \sigma_L). \tag{11.4}$$

We now illustrate this evaluation in Example 11.2.

Example 11.2

Weekly demand for Palms at B&M is normally distributed with a mean of 2,500 and a standard deviation of 500. The replenishment lead time is two weeks. Assume that the demand is independent from one week to the next. Evaluate the CSL resulting from a policy of ordering 10,000 Palms when there are 6,000 Palms in inventory.

Analysis: In this case we have the following:

$Q = 10,000, ROP = 6,000, L = 2$ weeks,
$D = 2,500$/week, $\sigma_D = 500$.

Observe that B&M runs the risk of stocking out during the two weeks between when an order is placed and when the replenishment arrives. Thus, whether a stockout occurs or not depends on the demand during the lead time of two weeks.

Because demand across time is independent, we use Equation 11.2 to obtain demand during the lead time to be normally distributed with a mean of D_L and a standard deviation of σ_L where

$$D_L = DL = 2 \times 2,500 = 5,000, \sigma_L = \sqrt{L}\,\sigma_D = \sqrt{2} \times 500 = 707.$$

Using Equation 11.4, The CSL is evaluated as follows:

$$CSL = \text{Probability of not stocking out in a cycle} = F(ROP, D_L, \sigma_L) =$$
$$F(6,000, 5,000, 707).$$

Using Equation 11.19 in Appendix 11B, the CSL is evaluated using the Excel function *NORMDIST* as follows:

$$F(ROP, D_L, \sigma_L) = NORMDIST(ROP, D_L, \sigma_L, 1).$$

We thus obtain a CSL for B&M as follows:

$$CSL = F(6{,}000, 5{,}000, 707) = NORMDIST(6{,}000, 5{,}000, 707, 1) = 0.92.$$

A CSL of 0.92 implies that in 92 percent of the replenishment cycles, B&M is able to supply all demand from available inventory. In the remaining 8 percent of the cycles, stockouts occur and some demand is not satisfied because of the lack of inventory.

Next we discuss the evaluation of the fill rate given a replenishment policy.

Evaluating Fill Rate Given a Replenishment Policy

Recall that fill rate measures the proportion of customer demand that is satisfied from available inventory. From a retailer's perspective, fill rate is a more relevant measure than cycle service level because it allows the retailer to estimate the fraction of demand that is turned into sales. The two measures are very closely related as raising the cycle service level will also raise the fill rate for a firm. Our discussion will focus on evaluating fill rate for a continuous review policy where Q units are ordered when the quantity on hand drops to the ROP.

To evaluate the fill rate it is important to understand the process by which a stockout may occur during a replenishment cycle. A stockout occurs if the demand during the lead time exceeds the ROP. We thus need to evaluate the average amount of demand in excess of the ROP in each replenishment cycle.

The *expected shortage per replenishment cycle* (ESC) is the average units of demand that are not satisfied from inventory in stock per replenishment cycle. Given a lot size of Q (which is also the average demand in a replenishment cycle), the fraction of demand lost is thus ESC/Q. The product fill rate fr is thus given by the following:

$$fr = 1 - ESC/Q = (Q - ESC)/Q. \tag{11.5}$$

A shortage occurs in a replenishment cycle only if the demand during the lead time exceeds the ROP. Let $f(x)$ be the density function of the demand distribution during the lead time. The ESC is given by the following:

$$ESC = \int_{x=ROP}^{\infty} (x - ROP)f(x)dx \tag{11.6}$$

In the case where demand during the lead time is normally distributed with mean D_L and standard deviation σ_L, given a safety inventory ss, Equation 11.6 can be simplified to the following:

$$ESC = -ss\left[1 - F_s\left(\frac{ss}{\sigma_L}\right)\right] + \sigma_L f_s\left(\frac{ss}{\sigma_L}\right) \tag{11.7}$$

where F_S is the standard normal cumulative distribution function and f_S is the standard normal density function. The detailed description of the normal distribution is contained in Appendix 11A. Details of the simplification in Equation 11.7 are described in Appendix 11C. Using Excel functions (Equations 11.22 and 11.23) discussed in Appendix 11B, ESC may be evaluated (using Equation 11.7) as follows:

$$ESC = -ss[1 - NORMDIST(ss/\sigma_L, 0, 1, 1)] + \sigma_L \, NORMDIST(ss/\sigma_L, 0, 1, 0). \quad \textbf{(11.8)}$$

Given the ESC, we can use Equation 11.5 to evaluate the fill rate fr. Next we illustrate this evaluation in Example 11.3.

Example 11.3

From Example 11.2, recall that weekly demand for Palms at B&M is normally distributed with a mean of 2,500 and a standard deviation of 500. The replenishment lead time is two weeks. Assume that the demand is independent from one week to the next. Evaluate the fill rate resulting from the policy of ordering 10,000 Palms when there are 6,000 Palms in inventory.

Analysis: From the analysis of Example 11.2, we have the following:

$$\text{Lot size, } Q = 10{,}000,$$
$$\text{Average demand during lead time, } D_L = 5{,}000,$$
$$\text{Standard deviation of demand during lead time, } \sigma_L = 707.$$

Using Equation 11.3, we obtain the following:

$$\text{Safety inventory, } ss = ROP - DL = 6{,}000 - 5{,}000 = 1{,}000.$$

From Equation 11.8, we thus have the following:

$$ESC = -1{,}000[1 - NORMDIST(1{,}000/707, 0, 1, 1)] + 707 \, NORMDIST(1{,}000/707, 0, 1, 0) = 25.$$

Thus, on average, in each replenishment cycle, 25 Palms are demanded by customers but not available in inventory. Using Equation 11.5, we thus obtain the following fill rate:

$$fr = (Q - ESC)/Q = (10{,}000 - 25)/10{,}000 = 0.9975.$$

In other words, 99.75 percent of the demand is filled from inventory in stock. This is much higher than the CSL of 92 percent that resulted in Example 11.2 for the same replenishment policy.

All the calculations for Example 11.3 may be done easily in Excel, as shown in Figure 11.2.

A few key observations should be made. First, observe that the fill rate (0.9975) in Example 11.3 is significantly higher than the CSL (0.92) in Example 11.2 for the same replenishment policy. Next, by rerunning the examples with a different lot size, we can observe what the impact of lot size changes is on the service level. Increasing the lot size of Palms from 10,000 to 20,000 has no impact on the CSL (which stays at 0.92). The fill rate, however, now increases to 0.9987. This is because an increase in lot size results in fewer replenishment cycles. In the case of B&M, an increase in lot size from 10,000 to 20,000 results in replenishment occurring once every eight weeks instead of once every four. With a 92 percent CSL, a lot size of 10,000 results in, on average, one cycle with a stockout per year. With a lot size of 20,000, we have, on average, one cycle with a stockout every two years. Thus, the fill rate is higher.

> **Key Point**   Both fill rate and cycle service level increase as the safety inventory is increased. For the same safety inventory, an increase in lot size increases the fill rate but not the cycle service level.

We now discuss how the appropriate level of safety inventory may be obtained given a desired CSL or fill rate.

	A	B	C	D	E
1	*Inputs*				
2	Q	R	σ_R	L	ss
3	10,000	2,500	500	2	1,000
4	*Distribution of demand during lead time*				
5	R_L	σ_L			
6	5,000	707			
7	*Cycle Service Level and Fill Rate*				
8	*CSL*	*ESC*	*fr*		
9	0.92	25.13	0.9975		

Cell	Cell Formula	Equation
A6	=B3*D3	11.2
B6	=SQRT(D3)*C3	11.2
A9	=NORMDIST(A6+E3, A6, B6, 1)	11.4
B9	=-E3*(1-NORMDIST(E3/B6, 0, 1, 1)) + B6*NORMDIST(E3/B6, 0, 1, 0)	11.8
C9	=(A3-B9)/A3	11.5

FIGURE 11.2   Excel Solution of Example 11.3

Evaluating Safety Inventory Given Desired Cycle Service Level or Fill Rate

In many practical settings, firms have a desired level of product availability and want to design replenishment polices that achieve this level. For example, Wal-Mart has a desired level of product availability for each product sold in the store. Wal-Mart must design a replenishment policy with the appropriate level of safety inventory to meet this goal. The desired level of product availability may be determined by trading off the cost of holding inventory with the cost of a stockout. This trade-off is discussed in detail in Chapter 12. In other instances, the desired level of product availability (in terms of CSL or fill rate) is explicitly stated in contracts and management must design replenishment policies that achieve the desired target.

Evaluating Required Safety Inventory Given Desired Cycle Service Level

Our goal is to obtain the appropriate level of safety inventory given the desired CSL. We assume that a continuous review replenishment policy is followed. Consider the manager at Wal-Mart responsible for designing replenishment policies for all products in the store. He has targeted a CSL for the basic box of Lego building blocks. Given a lead time of L, the store manager wants to identify a suitable ROP and safety inventory that achieves the desired service level. Assume that demand for Lego at Wal-Mart is normally distributed and independent from one week to the next. We assume the following input:

Desired cycle service level = CSL,
Mean demand during lead time = D_L,
Standard deviation of demand during lead time = σ_L.

From Equation 11.3, recall that $ROP = D_L + ss$. The store manager needs to identify safety inventory ss such that the following is true:

$$\text{Probability(demand during lead time} \leq D_L + ss) = CSL.$$

Given that demand is normally distributed, (using Equation 11.4), the store manager must identify safety inventory ss, such that the following is true:

$$F(D_L + ss, D_L, \sigma_L) = CSL.$$

Given the definition of the inverse normal in Appendix 11A, we obtain the following:

$$D_L + ss = F^{-1}(CSL, D_L, \sigma_L), \text{ or } ss = F^{-1}(CSL, D_L, \sigma_L) - D_L.$$

Using the definition of the standard normal distribution and its inverse from Appendix 11A, it can also be shown that the following is true:

$$ss = F_S^{-1}(CSL) \times \sigma_L. \qquad \textbf{(11.9)}$$

In Example 11.4 we illustrate the evaluation of safety inventory given a desired CSL.

Example 11.4

Weekly demand for Lego at a Wal-Mart store is normally distributed with a mean of 2,500 boxes and a standard deviation of 500. The replenishment lead time is two weeks. Assuming a continuous review replenishment policy, evaluate the safety inventory that the store should carry to achieve a CSL of 90 percent.

Analysis: In this case we have

$Q = 10,000, CSL = 0.9, L = 2$ weeks,
$D = 2,500$/week, $\sigma_D = 500$.

Because demand across time is independent, we use Equation 11.2 to find demand during the lead time to be normally distributed with a mean of D_L and a standard deviation of σ_L where

$$D_L = DL = 2 \times 2,500 = 5,000, \sigma_L = \sqrt{L}\sigma_D = \sqrt{2} \times 500 = 707.$$

Using Equations 11.9 and 11.24 in Appendix 11B, we obtain the following:

$$ss = F_S^{-1}(CSL) \times \sigma_L = NORMSINV(CSL) \times \sigma_L = NORMSINV(.90) \times 707 = 906.$$

Thus, the required safety inventory to achieve a CSL of 90 percent is 906 boxes.

Evaluating Required Safety Inventory Given Desired Fill Rate

We now evaluate the required safety inventory given a desired fill rate fr and the fact that a continuous review replenishment policy is followed. Consider the manager at Wal-Mart targeting a fill rate *fr* for Lego building blocks. The current replenishment lot size is Q. The first step is to obtain the ESC using Equation 11.5. The expected shortage per replenishment cycle is as follows:

$$ESC = (1 - fr)Q.$$

The next step is to obtain a safety inventory *ss* that solves Equation 11.7 (and its Excel equivalent, Equation 11.8) given the ESC evaluated earlier. It is not possible to give a formula that provides the answer. The appropriate safety inventory that solves Equation 11.8 can be obtained easily using Excel and trying different values of *ss*. In Excel the safety inventory may also be obtained directly using the tool GOALSEEK, as illustrated in Example 11.5.

Example 11.5

Weekly demand for Lego at a Wal-Mart store is normally distributed with a mean of 2,500 boxes and a standard deviation of 500. The replenishment lead time is two weeks. The store manager currently orders replenishment lots of 10,000 boxes from Lego. Assuming a continuous review replenishment policy, evaluate the safety inventory the store should carry to achieve a fill rate of 97.5 percent.

Analysis: In this case we have the following:

$$\text{Desired fill rate, } fr = 0.975,$$
$$\text{Lot size, } Q = 10,000 \text{ boxes,}$$
$$\text{Standard deviation of demand during lead time, } \sigma_L = 707.$$

From Equation 11.5, we thus obtain an ESC as follows:

$$ESC = (1 - fr)Q = (1 - 0.975)10,000 = 250.$$

Now we need to solve Equation 11.7 for the safety inventory *ss*, where

$$ESC = 250 = -ss\left[1 - F_s\left(\frac{ss}{\sigma_L}\right)\right] + \sigma_L f_s\left(\frac{ss}{\sigma_L}\right) = -ss\left[1 - F_s\left(\frac{ss}{707}\right)\right] + 707 f_s\left(\frac{ss}{707}\right)$$

Using Equation 11.8, this equation may be restated with Excel functions as follows:

$$250 = -ss[1 - NORMSDIST(ss/707)] + 707 NORMDIST(ss/707). \tag{11.10}$$

Equation 11.10 may be solved in Excel by trying different values of *ss* until the equation is satisfied. A more elegant approach for solving Equation 11.10 is to use the Excel tool *GOALSEEK* as follows.

First set up the spreadsheet as shown in Figure 11.3, where cell D3 can have any value for the safety inventory *ss*.

Invoke *GOALSEEK* using Tools | Goal Seek. In the *GOALSEEK* dialog box enter the data as shown in Figure 11.3 and click the OK button. In this case, Cell D3 is changed until the value of the formula in Cell A6 equals 250.

Using *GOALSEEK*, we obtain a safety inventory of *ss* = 67 boxes as shown in Figure 11.3. Thus, the store manager at Wal-Mart should target a safety inventory of 67 boxes to achieve the desired fill rate of 97.5 percent.

Next we identify the factors that affect the required level of safety inventory.

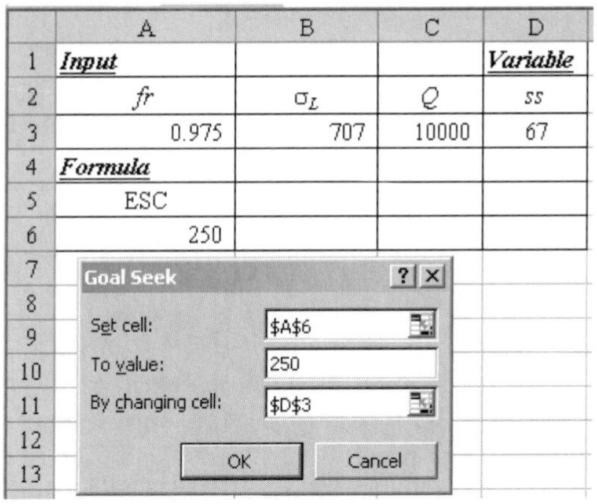

	A	B	C	D
1	*Input*			*Variable*
2	*fr*	σ_L	Q	*ss*
3	0.975	707	10000	67
4	*Formula*			
5	ESC			
6	250			
7				
8				
9				
10				
11				
12				
13				

Goal Seek

Set cell: `$A$6`

To value: `250`

By changing cell: `$D$3`

OK   Cancel

Cell	Cell Formula	Equation
A6	-D3*(1-NORMSDIST(D3/B3)) + B3*NORMDIST(D3/B3, 0, 1, 0)	11.10

FIGURE 11.3 Spreadsheet to Solve for *ss* Using GOALSEEK

Impact of Desired Product Availability and Uncertainty on Safety Inventory

The two key factors that affect the required level of safety inventory are the desired level of product availability and uncertainty. We now discuss the impact that each factor has on the safety inventory.

As the desired product availability goes up, the required safety inventory will also increase because the supply chain must now be able to accommodate uncommonly high demand or uncommonly low supply. For the Wal-Mart situation in Example 11.5, we evaluate the required safety inventory for varying levels of fill rate as shown in Table 11.1.

Observe that raising the fill rate from 97.5 percent to 98.0 percent requires an additional 116 units of safety inventory, whereas raising the fill rate from 99.0 percent to 99.5 percent requires an additional 268 units of safety inventory. Thus, the marginal increase in safety inventory grows as product availability rises. This phenomenon

TABLE 11.1 Required Safety Inventory for Different Values of Fill Rate

Fill Rate	Safety Inventory
97.5%	67
98.0%	183
98.5%	321
99.0%	499
99.5%	767

highlights the importance of selecting suitable product availability levels. It is very important for a supply chain manager to be aware of the products that require a high level of availability and only hold high safety inventories in those instances. It is not appropriate to arbitrarily select a very high level of product availability and require it across all products.

> **Key Point** The required safety inventory grows rapidly with an increase in the desired product availability.

From Equation 11.9, we see that the required safety inventory *ss* is also influenced by the standard deviation of demand during the lead time, σ_L. The standard deviation of demand during the lead time is influenced by the duration of the lead time *L* as well as the standard deviation of periodic demand σ_D, as shown in Equation 11.2. The relationship between safety inventory and σ_D is linear in that a 10 percent increase in σ_D results in a 10 percent increase in safety inventory. Safety inventory also increases with an increase in lead time *L*. The safety inventory, however, is proportional to the square root of the lead time (if demand is independent over time) and thus grows more slowly than the lead time itself.

> **Key Point** The required safety inventory increases with an increase in the lead time and the standard deviation of periodic demand.

A goal of any supply chain manager is to reduce the level of safety inventory required in a way that does not adversely affect product availability. The aforementioned discussion highlights two key managerial levers that may be used to achieve this goal.

1. *Reduce the supplier lead time L:* If lead time decreases by a factor of *k*, the required safety inventory decreases by a factor of $\sqrt{k}$. The only caveat here is that reducing the supplier lead time requires significant effort from the supplier while reduction in safety inventory occurs at the retailer. Thus it is important for the retailer to share some of the resulting benefits as discussed in Chapter 13. Wal-Mart, 7-Eleven Japan, and many other retailers have applied tremendous pressure on their suppliers to reduce the replenishment lead time. Manufacturers like Dell have also required suppliers to reduce their lead times. In each case, the benefit has manifested itself in the form of reduced safety inventory.

2. *Reduce the underlying uncertainty of demand (represented by σ_D):* If σ_D is reduced by a factor of *k*, the required safety inventory also decreases by a factor of *k*. A reduction in σ_D may be achieved by better market intelligence and the use of more sophisticated forecasting methods. 7-Eleven Japan provides its store managers detailed data about prior demand along with weather and other factors that may influence demand. This market intelligence allows the store managers to make better forecasts, reducing uncertainty. In most supply chains, however, the key to reducing the underlying forecast uncertainty is to link all forecasts throughout the supply chain to customer demand data. A lot of the demand uncertainty exists only because each stage of the

supply chain plans and forecasts independently. This distorts demand throughout the supply chain, increasing uncertainty. Improved coordination, as discussed in Chapter 16, can often reduce the demand uncertainty significantly. Both Dell and 7-Eleven Japan share demand information with their suppliers, reducing uncertainty and thus safety inventory within the supply chain.

11.3   IMPACT OF SUPPLY UNCERTAINTY ON SAFETY INVENTORY

In our discussion to this point, we have focused on situations with demand uncertainty in the form of a forecast error. In many practical situations, supply uncertainty also plays a significant role. Consider the case of the Dell assembly plant in Austin. Dell assembles computers to customer order. When planning the level of component inventory, Dell clearly has to take demand uncertainty into account. Suppliers, however, may not be able to deliver the components required on time for a variety of reasons. Dell must also account for this supply uncertainty when planning its safety inventories.

In our previous discussion we considered the replenishment lead time to be fixed. In this section we consider the case where the lead time is uncertain and identify the impact of lead time uncertainty on safety inventories. Assume that the customer demand per period for Dell computers and the replenishment lead time from the component supplier are normally distributed. We are provided the following input:

D: Average demand per period,
σ_D: Standard deviation of demand per period,
L: Average lead time for replenishment,
s_L: Standard deviation of lead time.

We consider the safety inventory requirements given that Dell follows a continuous review policy to manage component inventory. Dell experiences a stockout of components if demand during the lead time exceeds the ROP; that is, the quantity on hand when Dell places a replenishment order. Thus we need to identify the distribution of customer demand during the lead time. Given that both lead time and periodic demand are uncertain, demand during the lead time is normally distributed with a mean of D_L and a standard deviation σ_L, where

$$D_L = DL, \sigma_L = \sqrt{L\,\sigma_D^2 + D^2\,s_L^2} \qquad \textbf{(11.11)}$$

Given the distribution of demand during the lead time in Equation 11.11 and a desired CSL, Dell can obtain the required safety inventory using Equation 11.9. If product availability is specified as a fill rate, Dell can obtain the required safety inventory using the procedure outlined in Example 11.5. In Example 11.6, we illustrate the impact of lead time uncertainty on the required level of safety inventory at Dell.

Example 11.6

Daily demand for PCs at Dell is normally distributed with a mean of 2,500 and a standard deviation of 500. A key component used in the PC assembly is the hard drive. The hard drive supplier takes an average of L = seven days to replenish inventory at Dell. Dell is targeting a CSL of 90 percent (providing a fill rate close to 100 percent) for its hard drive inventory. Evaluate the safety inventory of hard drives that Dell must carry if the standard deviation of the lead time is seven days. Dell is working with the supplier to reduce the standard deviation to zero. Evaluate the reduction in safety inventory that Dell can expect as a result of this initiative.

Analysis: In this case we have the following:

Average demand per period, $D = 2,500$,
Standard deviation of demand per period, $\sigma_D = 500$,
Average lead time for replenishment, $L = 7$ days,
Standard deviation of lead time, $s_L = 7$ days.

We first evaluate the distribution of demand during the lead time. Using Equation 11.11, we have the following:

Mean demand during lead time, $D_L = DL = 2,500 \times 7 = 17,500$,

Standard deviation of demand during lead time $\sigma_L = \sqrt{L\,\sigma_D^2 + D^2\,s_L^2} =$

$$\sqrt{7 \times 500^2 + 2500^2 \times 7^2} = 17,550$$

The required safety inventory is obtained using Equations 11.9 and 11.24 as follows:

$$ss = F_S^{-1}(CSL) \times \sigma_L = NORMSINV(CSL) \times \sigma_L = NORMSINV(0.90) \times 17,550$$
$$= 22,491 \text{ hard drives.}$$

If the standard deviation of lead time is seven days, Dell must carry a safety inventory of 22,491 drives. Observe that this is equivalent to about nine days of demand for hard drives.

In Table 11.2 we provide the required safety inventory as Dell works with the supplier to reduce standard deviation of lead time down to zero.

From Table 11.2, observe that the reduction in lead time uncertainty allows Dell to reduce its safety inventory of hard drives by a significant amount. As the standard deviation of lead time declines from seven days to zero, the amount of safety inventory declines from about nine days of demand to less than a day of demand.

This example emphasizes the impact of lead time variability on safety inventory requirements (and thus material flow time) and the large potential benefits from reducing lead time variability or improving on-time deliveries. Often, safety inventory calculations in practice do not include any measure of supply uncertainty, resulting in levels that may be lower than required. This hurts product availability.

Key Point A reduction in supply uncertainty can help dramatically reduce safety inventory required without hurting product availability.

TABLE 11.2	Required Safety Inventory as a Function of Lead Time Uncertainty		
σ_R	σ_L	ss (units)	ss (days)
6	15,058	19,298	7.72
5	12,570	16,109	6.44
4	10,087	12,927	5.17
3	7,616	9,760	3.90
2	5,172	6,628	2.65
1	2,828	3,625	1.45
0	1,323	1,695	0.68

Variability of supply lead time is caused by practices at both the supplier as well as the party placing the order. Suppliers sometimes have poor planning tools that do not allow them to schedule production in a way that can be executed. Today, most supply chain planning software suites have good production planning tools that allow suppliers to promise lead times that can be met. This should help reduce lead time variability. In other instances, the behavior of the party placing the order often increases lead time variability. In one instance, a distributor placed orders to all suppliers on the same day of the week. As a result, all deliveries arrived on the same day of the week. The surge in deliveries made it impossible for all of them to be recorded into inventory on the day they arrived. This led to a perception that supply lead times were large and variable. By just leveling out the orders over the week, the lead time and the lead time variability were significantly reduced, allowing the distributor to reduce its safety inventory.

Next we discuss how aggregation can help reduce the amount of safety inventory in the supply chain.

11.4   IMPACT OF AGGREGATION ON SAFETY INVENTORY

In practice, supply chains have varying degrees of inventory aggregation. For example, HP sells computers through retail stores like Best Buy with inventory distributed all over the country. Dell, in contrast, has one centralized facility at Austin from which all customer orders are shipped. Borders and Barnes and Noble sell books and music from retail stores with inventory geographically distributed across the country. Amazon.com, in contrast, ships all its books and music from a few facilities. 7-Eleven Japan has small convenience stores densely distributed over areas of Japan where they have a presence. In contrast, supermarkets tend to be much larger with fewer outlets that are not as densely distributed.

A key question to consider is how aggregation in each of the aforementioned cases affects safety inventories. Our goal is to understand how supply chains can exploit inventory aggregation to reduce the level of safety inventory required without hurting product availability.

As discussed in Chapter 7, we show that geographical aggregation of demand improves forecast accuracy. Consider the case where weekly demand for computers in each zip code in the Chicago region is normally distributed with the following characteristics:

D_i: Mean weekly demand in zip code $i, i = 1, ..., k,$
σ_i = Standard deviation of weekly demand in zip code $i, i = 1, ..., k,$
$cov(i, j)$: Covariance of weekly demand for zip codes $i, j, 1 \leq i \neq j \leq k.$

Our objective is to find the distribution of aggregate demand across the entire Chicago region. In this case (similar to Equation 11.1), the aggregate demand is normally distributed with a mean of D^C, standard deviation of σ_D^C, and a variance of $var(D^C)$, where the following is true:

$$D^C = \sum_{j=1}^{k} D_j, \, var(D^C) = \sum_{i=1}^{k} \sigma_1^2 + 2\sum_{i>j} cov(i, j), \sigma_D^C = \sqrt{var(D^C)} \qquad \textbf{(11.12)}$$

Recall that the covariance is given as follows:

$$cov(i,j) = \rho_{ij}\,\sigma_i\,\sigma_j$$

where ρ_{ij} is the correlation coefficient. The stronger the positive correlation of demand in two regions, the closer ρ_{ij} is to one. It can be argued that demand for electricity, natural gas for heating, or oil will be strongly positively correlated across all zip codes in the Chicago area because demand is closely linked to temperature. Conversely, demand for milk across the different zip codes is likely to be independent.

In case demand across all the zip codes is independent, all correlation coefficients and thus covariances are 0. In this case variance and standard deviation of aggregate demand are given by the following equation:

$$var(D^C) = \sum_{i=1}^{k}\sigma_i^2,\ \ \sigma_D^C = \sqrt{var(D^C)} = \sqrt{\sum_{i=1}^{k}\sigma_i^2} \qquad \textbf{(11.13)}$$

From Equation 11.13, observe that $\sigma_D^C \leq \sum_{i=1}^{k}\sigma_i$. This implies that when the demands being aggregated are independent, the standard deviation of aggregate demand is less than the sum of the standard deviations of individual demands.

In contrast, if demand across the different zip codes is perfectly positively correlated, we have all correlation coefficients ρ_{ij} equal to one. In this case, the variance and standard deviation of aggregate demand are given by

$$var(D^C) = \sum_{i=1}^{k}\sigma_i^2 + 2\sum_{i>j} cov(i,j) = \sum_{i=1}^{k}\sigma_i^2 + 2\sum_{i>j}\sigma_i\sigma_j \qquad \textbf{(11.14)}$$

From Equation 11.14, observe that $\sigma_D^C = \sum_{i=1}^{k}\sigma_i$. Thus, if the demands being aggregated are perfectly positively correlated, the standard deviation of aggregate demand is the sum of the standard deviations of individual demands.

From Equations 11.13 and 11.14, it thus follows that aggregation reduces the standard deviation of demand only if demand across the regions being aggregated is not perfectly positively correlated. Because safety inventory is proportional to the standard deviation of demand (see Equation 11.9), aggregating demand is most effective at reducing safety inventory when the correlation amongst the aggregated demand is low. We illustrate the impact of aggregation on safety inventory in Example 11.7.

Example 11.7

A BMW dealership has four retail outlets serving the entire Chicago area (disaggregate option). Weekly demand at each outlet is normally distributed with a mean of $D = 25$ cars and a standard deviation of $\sigma_D = 5$. The lead time for replenishment from the manufacturer is $L = 2$ weeks. Each outlet covers a separate geographical area and the correlation of demand across any pair of areas is ρ. The dealership is considering the possibility of replacing the four outlets with a single large outlet (aggregate option). Assume that the demand in the central outlet would be the sum of the demand across all four areas. The dealership is targeting a CSL of 0.90. Compare the level of safety inventory needed in the two options as the correlation coefficient ρ varies between 0 and 1.

Analysis: We provide a detailed analysis for the case when demand in each area is independent (i.e., $\rho = 0$). For each retail outlet we have the following:

Standard deviation of weekly demand, $\sigma_D = 5$,
Replenishment lead time, $L = 2$ weeks.

Using Equation 11.2, we have the following:

$$\text{Standard deviation of demand during lead time, } \sigma_L = 7.07.$$

Given the desired CSL ($CSL = 0.90$), the required safety inventory at each retail outlet (using Equation 11.9) is given as follows:

$$\text{Required safety inventory, } ss = F_S^{-1}(CSL) \times \sigma_L = F_S^{-1}(0.9) \times 7.07 = 9.06.$$

In the disaggregate option, each retail outlet must carry 9.06 cars as safety inventory. Across all four outlets, in the disaggregate option we have the following:

$$\text{Total safety inventory required for CSL of } 0.90 = 4 \times 9.06 = 36.24 \text{ cars.}$$

Now consider the aggregate option. Because demand in all four areas is independent, using Equation 11.13 we have the following:

Mean demand at central outlet, $D^C = 4 \times 25 = 100$,
Standard deviation of weekly demand at central outlet, $\sigma_D^C = \sqrt{4} \times 5 = 10$.

Given that lead time is two weeks, we have the following:

$$\text{Standard deviation of demand during lead time at central outlet,}$$
$$\sigma_L^C = \sqrt{L}\,\sigma_D^C = \sqrt{2} \times 10 = 14.14$$

For a CSL of 0.90, safety inventory required for the aggregate option (using Equation 11.9) is given as follows:

$$ss = F_S^{-1}(0.90) \times \sigma_L^C = NORMSINV(0.90) \times 14.14 = 18.12.$$

Using the same procedure, the required level of safety inventory for the disaggregate as well as the aggregate option can be obtained for different values of ρ. The results are shown in Table 11.3.

TABLE 11.3	Safety Inventory in the Disaggregate and Aggregate Options	
ρ	*Disaggregate Safety Inventory*	*Aggregate Safety Inventory*
0	36.24	18.12
0.2	36.24	22.92
0.4	36.24	26.88
0.6	36.24	30.32
0.8	36.24	33.41
1.0	36.24	36.24

Observe that the safety inventory for the disaggregate option is higher than for the aggregate option except in the case where all demands are perfectly positively correlated. The benefit of aggregation decreases as demand in different areas is more positively correlated.

Example 11.7 and the previous discussion demonstrate that aggregation reduces demand uncertainty and thus the required safety inventory as long as the demand being aggregated is not perfectly positively correlated. Demand for most products does not show perfect positive correlation across different geographical regions. In case demand in different geographical regions is about the same size and independent, aggregation reduces safety inventory by the square root of the number of areas aggregated. In other words, if the number of independent stocking locations decreases by a factor of n, the average safety inventory is expected to decrease by a factor of $\sqrt{n}$. This principle is referred to as the *square root law*. The square root law is illustrated in Figure 11.4.

There are instances in which companies have physically centralized inventories by having one central warehouse serving the entire United States. In the computer industry, both Dell and Gateway have aggregated their assembly and inventory holding. As for retailers, most e-commerce firms exploit the benefits of aggregation in terms of reduced inventories. The best known example in this regard is Amazon.com, which has aggregated its inventories in a few locations. As a result, it has lower levels of book and music inventories than bookstore chains such as Borders and Barnes and Noble, which must keep inventory in every retail store.

There are, however, situations where physical aggregation of inventories in one location may not be optimal. There are two major disadvantages of aggregating all inventory in one location:

1. Increase in response time to customer order
2. Increase in transportation cost to customer

Both disadvantages result because the average distance between the inventory and the customer increases with aggregation. With this situation, either the customer has to travel more to reach the product or the product has to be shipped over longer

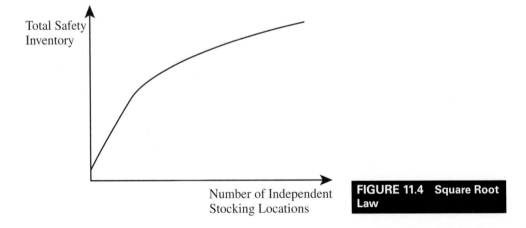

FIGURE 11.4 Square Root Law

distances to reach the customer. For example, a retail chain like The Gap has the option of building many small retail outlets or a few large ones. The Gap tends to have many smaller outlets distributed evenly in a region because this strategy reduces the distance that customers travel to reach a store. If The Gap had one large centralized outlet, the average distance that customers need to travel would increase and thus the response time would increase. A desire to decrease customer response time is thus the impetus for the firm to have multiple outlets. Another example is McMaster Carr, a distributor of MRO supplies. McMaster uses UPS for shipping product to customers. Because shipping charges are based on distance, having one centralized warehouse will increase the average shipping cost as well as the response time to the customer. Thus, McMaster Carr has six warehouses that allow it to provide next day delivery to a large fraction of the United States. Next day delivery with UPS would not be feasible at a reasonable cost if McMaster Carr had only one warehouse. Even Amazon.com, which started with one warehouse in Seattle, has grown to add more warehouses in other parts of the United States in an effort to improve response time and reduce transportation cost to the customer.

These examples highlight instances in which physical aggregation of inventory at one location may not be optimal. However, there are clear benefits to aggregating safety inventory. We now discuss various methods by which a supply chain can extract the benefits of aggregation without having to physically centralize all inventories in one location.

Information Centralization

McMaster Carr uses *information centralization* to virtually aggregate all its inventories despite having six stocking locations. The company has set up an information system that allows access to current inventory records from each warehouse. Consider, for example, a customer from Chicago ordering a motor and a pump. When the customer order arrives, McMaster Carr makes an initial check to see if the Chicago warehouse can fill the entire order. If so, the order is shipped from the Chicago warehouse, minimizing the transportation cost.

In case the Chicago warehouse has motors but is out of pumps, McMaster Carr obtains the pump from the closest warehouse that has the pump in inventory. The pump is shipped from the warehouse to Chicago where it is merged with the motor into a single shipment and sent to the customer. Thus, inventory at all locations is available to all orders, no matter where they originate. Information centralization allows McMaster Carr to reduce the level of inventories required while providing a high level of product availability by virtually aggregating inventories.

The benefit of information centralization derives from the fact that most orders are filled from the warehouse closest to the customer, keeping transportation costs low. In case of a stockout, other warehouses fill the order, improving product availability. As a result, McMaster Carr can reduce its safety inventory without hurting product availability while keeping shipping costs relatively low.

Retailers like The Gap have also used information centralization very effectively. If a store does not have the size or color that a customer wants, store employees can use their information system to inform the customer of the closest store with the product in inventory. The customer can then either go to this store or have the product delivered to their house. The Gap thus uses information centralization to virtually aggregate inventory across all retail stores even though the inventory is physically separated. This allows them to reduce the amount of safety inventory they carry while providing a high level of product availability.

Wal-Mart has an information system that allows store managers to search other stores for an excess of items that may be hot sellers at their stores. Wal-Mart provides transportation that allows store managers to exchange products so they arrive at stores where they are in high demand. In this case, Wal-Mart uses information centralization with a responsive transportation system to reduce the amount of safety inventory carried while providing a high level of product availability.

Specialization

Most supply chains provide a variety of products to customers. When inventory is carried at multiple locations, a key decision for a supply chain manager is whether all products should be stocked at every location. Clearly, a product that does not sell in a geographical region should not be carried in inventory by the warehouse or retail store located there. For example, it does not make sense for a Sears retail store in southern Florida to carry a wide variety of snow boots in inventory.

Another important factor that must be considered when making stocking decisions is the reduction in safety inventory that results from aggregation. If aggregation reduces the required safety inventory for a product by a large amount, it is better to carry the product in one central location. If aggregation reduces the required safety inventory for a product by a small amount, it may be best to carry the product in multiple decentralized locations to reduce response time and transportation cost.

The reduction in safety inventory due to aggregation is strongly influenced by the coefficient of variation of demand. For a product with a very low coefficient of variation, disaggregate demand can be forecast with accuracy. As a result, the benefit from aggregation is minimal. For a product with a high coefficient of variation of demand, disaggregate demand is very difficult to forecast. In this case, aggregation improves forecast accuracy significantly, providing great benefits. We illustrate this idea in Example 11.8.

Example 11.8

Assume that W. W. Grainger, a supplier of MRO products, has 1,600 stores distributed throughout the United States. Consider two products—large electric motors and industrial cleaners. Large electric motors are high value items with low demand, whereas cleaner is a low value item with high demand. Each motor costs $500 while each can of cleaner costs $30. Weekly demand for motors at each store is normally distributed with a mean of 20 and a standard deviation of 40. Weekly demand for cleaner at each store is normally distributed with a mean of 1,000 and a standard deviation of 100. Demand experienced by each store is independent and supply lead time for both motors and cleaner is four weeks. W. W. Grainger has a holding cost of 25 percent. For each of the two products, evaluate the reduction in safety inventories that will result if they are removed from retail stores and only carried in a centralized DC. Assume a desired CSL of 0.95.

Analysis: The evaluation of safety inventories and the value of aggregation for each of the two products is shown in Table 11.4. All calculations use the approach discussed earlier and illustrated in Example 11.5.

As Table 11.4 shows, the benefit from centralizing motors is much larger than the benefit from centralizing cleaner. From this analysis, W. W. Grainger would be advised to stock cleaner

TABLE 11.4 Value of Aggregation at W.W. Grainger		
	Motors	*Cleaner*
Inventory Is Stocked in Each Store		
Mean weekly demand per store	20	1,000
Standard deviation	40	100
Coefficient of variation	2.0	0.1
Safety inventory per store	132	329
Total safety inventory	211,200	526,400
Value of safety inventory	$105,600,000	$15,792,000
Inventory Is Aggregated at the DC		
Mean weekly aggregate demand	32,000	1,600,000
Standard deviation of aggregate demand	1,600	4,000
Coefficient of variation	0.05	0.0025
Aggregate safety inventory	5,264	13,159
Value of safety inventory	$2,632,000	$394,770
Savings		
Total inventory saving on aggregation	$102,968,000	$15,397,230
Total holding cost saving on aggregation	$25,742,000	$3,849,308
Holding cost saving per unit sold	$15.47	$0.046
Savings as a percentage of product cost	3.09%	0.15%

at the stores and motors in the DC. Given that cleaner is a high-demand item, customers will be able to pick it up on the same day at the stores. Given that motors are a low-demand item, customers may be willing to wait the extra day that shipping from the DC will entail.

Key Point   The higher the coefficient of variation of an item, the greater the reduction in safety inventories as a result of centralization.

Items with a very low demand are referred to as *slow-moving items* and typically have a high coefficient of variation, whereas items with high demand are referred to as *fast-moving items* and typically have a low coefficient of variation. For many supply chains, specializing the distribution network with fast-moving items stocked at decentralized locations close to the customer and slow-moving items stocked at a centralized location can significantly reduce the safety inventory carried without hurting customer response time or adding to transportation costs. The centralized location then specializes in handling slow-moving items.

Of course, there are other factors that need to be considered when deciding on the allocation of products to stocking locations. For example, an item that is considered an emergency item because the customer urgently needs it may be stocked at the stores even if it has a high coefficient of variation. One also needs to consider the cost of the item. High-value items will provide a greater benefit from centralization than low-value items.

It is important for firms with brick-and-mortar stores to take the idea of specialization into account when they design their e-commerce strategy. Consider, for example, a bookstore chain like Barnes and Noble. They are able to carry about a hundred thousand titles at each retail store. The titles carried can be divided into two broad categories—best-sellers with high demand and other books with much lower demand. Barnes and Noble can design an e-commerce strategy where the retail stores primarily carry best-sellers in inventory. They would also carry one or at most two copies of each of the other titles to allow customers to browse. Customers could access all titles not in the store via electronic kiosks in the store that provide access to bn.com inventory. This strategy would allow customers to access an increased variety of books from Barnes and Noble stores. Customers could place orders for the low-volume titles with bn.com while purchasing high-volume titles at the store itself. This strategy of specialization would allow Barnes and Noble to aggregate all slow-moving items to be sold by the online channel. All best-sellers would be decentralized and carried close to the customer. The supply chain would thus reduce inventory costs for the slow-moving items at the expense of somewhat higher transportation costs. For the fast-moving items, the supply chain would provide a lower transportation cost and better response time by carrying the items at retail stores close to the customer.

The Gap has followed a similar strategy and integrated its online channel with its retail stores. Terminals are available at the retail stores for placing orders online. The retail stores carry fast-moving items and the customer is able to order slow-moving colors or sizes online. The Gap is thus able to increase the variety of products available to customers while keeping supply chain inventories down.

Product Substitution

Substitution refers to the use of one product to satisfy demand for a different product. There are two instances where substitution may occur:

- *Manufacturer-driven substitution:* In this case the manufacturer or supplier makes the decision to substitute. Typically, the manufacturer will substitute a higher value product for a lower value product not in inventory. For example, Dell may install a 60-gigabyte hard drive into a customer order requiring a 40-gigabyte hard, if the smaller drive is out of stock.
- *Customer-driven substitution:* In this case customers make the decision to substitute. For example, a customer walking into a Wal-Mart store to buy a gallon of detergent may buy the half-gallon size if the gallon size is unavailable. In this case the customer has substituted the half-gallon size for the gallon size.

In both cases, exploiting substitution allows the supply chain to satisfy demand using aggregate inventories, which permits the supply chain to reduce safety inventories without hurting product availability. In general, given two products or components, substitution may be one-way (i.e., only one of the products [components] substitutes for the other) or two-way (i.e., either product [component] substitutes for the other). We briefly discuss one-way substitution in the context of manufacturer-driven substitution and two-way substitution in the context of customer-driven substitution.

Manufacturer-Driven One-Way Substitution

Consider Gateway, a PC manufacturer selling direct to customers. Suppose Gateway offers its customers drives that vary in size from 10 to 100 gigabytes. Customers are charged according to the size of drive that they select, with larger sizes being priced higher. If a customer orders a 40-gigabyte drive and Gateway is out of drives of this size, there are two possible choices: (a) delay or deny the customer order or (b) substitute a larger drive that is in stock (say, a 60-gigabyte drive) and fill the customer order on time. In the first case there is potentially a lost sale or loss of future sales because the customer experiences a delayed delivery. In the second case the manufacturer installs a higher cost component, reducing the company's profit margin. These factors, along with the fact that only larger drives can substitute for smaller drives, must be considered when Gateway makes inventory decisions for individual drive sizes.

Substitution allows Gateway to aggregate demand across the components, reducing safety inventories required. The value of substitution increases as demand uncertainty increases. Thus, Gateway should consider substitution for components displaying very high demand uncertainty.

The desired degree of substitution is influenced by the cost differential between the higher value and lower value component. If the cost differential is very small, Gateway should aggregate most of the demand and carry most of its inventory in the form of the higher value component. As the cost differential increases, the benefit of substitution decreases. In this case, Gateway will find it more profitable to carry inventory of each of the two components and decrease the amount of substitution.

The desired level of substitution is also influenced by the correlation of demand between the products. If demand between two components is strongly positively correlated, there is little value in substitution. As demand for the two components becomes less positively correlated, the benefit of substitution increases.

> **Key Point**   Manufacturer-driven substitution increases overall profitability for the manufacturer by allowing some aggregation of demand, which reduces the inventory requirements for the same level of availability.

Customer-Driven Two-Way Substitution

Consider W. W. Grainger selling two brands of motors, GE and SE, which have very similar performance characteristics. Customers are generally willing to purchase either brand, depending on product availability. If W. W. Grainger managers do not recognize customer substitution, they will not encourage it. For a given level of product availability they will thus have to carry high levels of safety inventory of each brand. If its managers recognize and encourage customer substitution, they can aggregate the safety inventory across the two brands, thereby improving product availability.

W. W. Grainger does a very good job of recognizing customer substitution. When a customer calls or goes online to place an order and the product they request is not available, the customer is immediately told the availability of all equivalent products that they may substitute. Most customers ultimately buy a substitute product in this case. W. W. Grainger exploits this substitution by managing safety inventory of all substitutable products jointly. Recognition and exploitation of customer substitution allows W. W. Grainger to provide a high level of product availability with lower levels of safety inventory.

A good understanding of customer-driven substitution is very important in the retail industry. It must be exploited when merchandising to ensure that substitute products are placed near each other, allowing a customer to buy one if the other is out of stock. In the online channel, substitution requires a retailer to present the availability of substitute products if the one the customer requests is out of stock. The supply chain is thus able to reduce the required level of safety inventory while providing a high level of product availability.

> **Key Point** Recognition of customer-driven substitution and joint management of inventories across substitutable products allows a supply chain to reduce the required safety inventory while ensuring a high level of product availability.

The demand uncertainties as well as the correlation of demand between the substitutable products influence the benefit to a retailer from exploiting substitution. The greater the demand uncertainty, the greater the benefit of substitution. The lower the correlation of demand between substitutable products, the greater the benefit from exploiting substitution.

Component Commonality

In any supply chain, a significant amount of inventory is held in the form of components. A single product like a PC contains hundreds of components. When a supply chain is producing a large variety of products, component inventories can easily become very large. The use of common components in a variety of products has been a very effective supply chain strategy to exploit aggregation and reduce component inventories.

The Dell Corporation sells thousands of different PC configurations to customers. An extreme option for Dell is to design distinct components that are suited to the performance of a particular configuration. In this case Dell would use different memory, hard drive, modem, and other components for each distinct finished product. The other option is to design common components such that different combinations of the components result in different finished products.

Without common components, the uncertainty of demand for any component is the same as the uncertainty of demand for the finished product in which it is used. Given the large number of components in each finished product, demand uncertainty will be very high, resulting in high levels of safety inventory. When common components are designed, each component is used in multiple finished products. The demand for each component is then an aggregation of the demand for all the finished products of which the component is a part. Component demand is thus more predictable than the demand for any one finished product. This fact reduces the component inventories carried in the supply chain. This idea has been a key factor for success in the PC industry and has also started to play a big role in the auto industry. With increasing product variety, component commonality is a key to reducing supply chain inventories without hurting product availability. We illustrate the basic idea behind component commonality in Example 11.9.

Example 11.9

Assume that Dell is to manufacture 27 different PCs with three distinct components: processor, memory, and hard drive. In the disaggregate option, Dell designs specific components for each PC, resulting in $3 \times 27 = 81$ distinct components. In the common component option, Dell designs three distinct processors, three distinct memory units, and three distinct hard drives that can be combined to create 27 different PCs. Each component is thus used in nine different PCs. Monthly demand for each of the 27 different PCs is independent and normally distributed with a mean of 5,000 and a standard deviation of 3,000. The replenishment lead time for each component is one month. Dell is targeting a CSL of 95 percent for component inventory. Evaluate the safety inventory requirements with and without the use of component commonality. Also evaluate the change in safety inventory requirements as the number of finished products of which a component is a part varies from one to nine.

Analysis: We first evaluate the disaggregate option where components are specific to a PC. For each component we have the following:

$$\text{Standard deviation of monthly demand} = 3,000.$$

Given a lead time of one month (using Equation 11.9), required safety inventory per component is given as follows:

$$\text{Safety inventory per component} = NORMSINV(0.95) \times 3,000 = 4,935 \text{ units.}$$

Given a total of 81 components across 27 different PCs, we thus have the following:

$$\text{Total safety inventory required} = 81 \times 4,935 = 399,699 \text{ units.}$$

In the case of component commonality, each component ends up in nine different finished products. Therefore, the demand at the component level is the sum of demand across nine different products. Aggregating across the nine products we get monthly component demand to be normally distributed with the following:

$$\text{Mean demand of common component across 9 products} = 9 \times 5,000 = 45,000,$$
$$\text{Standard deviation of demand of common component across 9 products} = \sqrt{9} \times 3,000 = 9,000.$$

Using Equation 11.9, the safety inventory required for each component is thus as follows:

$$\text{Safety inventory per common component} = NORMSINV(0.95) \times 9,000 = 14,804 \text{ units.}$$

With component commonality there are a total of nine distinct components. The total safety inventory across all nine components is thus as follows:

$$\text{Total safety inventory required} = 9 \times 14,804 = 133,236.$$

Thus, using component commonality, having each component in nine different products results in a reduction in safety inventory for Dell from 399,735 to 133,236 units.

In Table 11.5, we evaluate the marginal benefit in terms of reduction in safety inventory as a result of increasing component commonality. Starting with the required safety inventory when each component is used in only one finished product, we evaluate the safety inventory as the number of products in which a component is used increases to nine.

Observe that component commonality decreases the required safety inventory for Dell. The marginal benefit of commonality, however, declines as a component is used in more and more finished products.

As a component is used in more finished products, it needs to be more flexible. As a result, the cost of producing the component typically increases with increasing commonality. Given that the marginal benefit of component commonality decreases as

TABLE 11.5   Marginal Benefit of Component Commonality

Number of Finished Products per Component	Safety Inventory	Marginal Reduction in Safety Inventory	Total Reduction in Safety Inventory
1	399,699		
2	282,630	117,069	117,069
3	230,766	51,864	168,933
4	199,849	30,917	199,850
5	178,751	21,098	220,948
6	163,176	15,575	236,523
7	151,072	12,104	248,627
8	141,315	9,757	258,384
9	133,233	8,082	266,466

we increase commonality, we need to trade off the increase in component cost and the decrease in safety inventory when deciding on the appropriate level of component commonality.

> **Key Point**   Component commonality decreases the safety inventory required. The marginal benefit, however, decreases with increasing commonality.

Postponement

Postponement is the ability of a supply chain to delay product differentiation or customization until closer to the time the product is sold. The goal is to have common components in the supply chain for most of the push phase and move product differentiation as close to the pull phase of the supply chain as possible. For example, Dell holds all inventory in the form of components that are common across many PC configurations. A PC is assembled in the pull phase of the supply chain after the customer order arrives. Thus, Dell produces product variety only when demand is known with certainty. Postponement coupled with component commonality allows Dell to carry significantly lower safety inventories than a manufacturer like HP that sells through retailers. Given that HP must stock finished inventory at the retailer, they assemble to stock. Thus, HP must forecast demand for each individual configuration when assembling. The assemble-to-order direct sales model of Dell relies on aggregate inventories in the form of components, whereas the assemble to stock, sell-through retailers model relies on disaggregate inventories for each PC configuration.

Another classic example of postponement is the production process at Benetton to make colored knit garments. The original process called for the thread to be dyed and then knitted and assembled into garments. The entire process required up to six months. Because the color of the final garment was fixed the moment the thread was dyed, demand for individual colors had to be forecast far in advance (up to six months). Benetton developed a manufacturing technology that allowed it to dye knitted garments to the appropriate color. Now *greige* thread (the term used for thread that has not yet been dyed) can be purchased, knitted, and assembled into garments

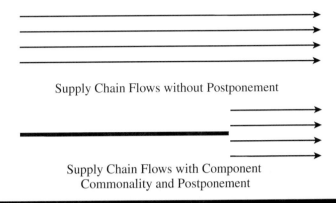

Supply Chain Flows without Postponement

Supply Chain Flows with Component
Commonality and Postponement

FIGURE 11.5   Supply Chain Flows with Postponement

before dyeing. The dyeing of the garments is done much closer to the selling season. In fact, part of the dyeing is done after the start of the selling season when demand is known with great accuracy. In this case Benetton has postponed the color customization of the knit garments. When thread is purchased, only the aggregate demand across all colors needs to be forecast. Given that this decision is made far in advance when forecasts are least likely to be accurate, there is great advantage to this aggregation. However, as Benetton moves closer to the selling season, the forecast uncertainty reduces. At the time Benetton dyes the knit garments, demand is known with a high degree of accuracy. Thus, postponement allows Benetton to exploit aggregation and significantly reduce the level of safety inventory carried. Supply chain flows with and without postponement are illustrated in Figure 11.5.

Without component commonality and postponement, product differentiation occurs early on in the supply chain and most of the supply chain inventories are disaggregate. Postponement allows the supply chain to delay product differentiation. As a result, most of the inventories in the supply chain are aggregate. Postponement thus allows a supply chain to exploit aggregation to reduce safety inventories without hurting product availability.

Postponement can be a powerful concept for the e-commerce channel. When ordering over the Internet, customers are implicitly willing to wait a little for the order to arrive. This delay offers the supply chain an opportunity to reduce inventories by postponing product differentiation until after the customer order arrives. It is important that the manufacturing process be designed in a way that enables assembly to be completed quickly. All PC manufacturers are already postponing assembly for their online orders. Several online furniture manufacturers have also postponed some of the assembly process for their online orders.

11.5   IMPACT OF REPLENISHMENT POLICIES ON SAFETY INVENTORY

In this section we describe the evaluation of safety inventories for both continuous and periodic review replenishment policies. We highlight the fact that periodic review policies require more safety inventory than continuous review policies for the same level of product availability. To simplify the discussion, we focus on the CSL as the measure of product availability. The managerial implications are the same if we use fill rate; the analysis, however, is more cumbersome.

Continuous Review Policies

Given that continuous review policies were discussed in detail in Section 11.2, we only reiterate the main points here. When using a continuous review policy, a manager orders Q units when the inventory drops to the ROP. Clearly, a continuous review policy requires technology that monitors the level of available inventory. This is the case for many firms like Wal-Mart and Dell where inventories are continuously monitored.

Given a desired CSL, our goal is to identify the required safety inventory ss and the ROP. We assume that demand is normally distributed with the following input:

D: Average demand per period,
σ_D: Standard deviation of demand per period,
L: Average lead time for replenishment.

The ROP represents the available inventory to meet demand during the lead time L. A stockout occurs if the demand during the lead time is larger than the ROP. If demand across periods is independent, demand during the lead time is normally distributed with the following:

$$\text{Mean demand during lead time, } D_L = DL,$$
$$\text{Standard deviation of demand during lead time, } \sigma_L = \sqrt{L}\,\sigma_D$$

Given the desired CSL, the required safety inventory (ss) given by Equation 11.9 and the ROP given by Equation 11.3 are as follows:

$$ss = F_S^{-1}(CSL) \times \sigma_L = NORMSINV(CSL) \times \sigma_L, ROP = D_L + ss.$$

When using a continuous review policy, a manager has to account only for the uncertainty of demand during the lead time. This is because the continuous monitoring of inventory allows a manager to adjust the timing of the replenishment order depending on the demand experienced. If demand is very high, the inventory will reach the ROP quickly, leading to a quick replenishment order. If demand is very low, inventory will drop to the ROP slowly, leading to a delayed replenishment order. The manager, however, has no recourse during the lead time once a replenishment order has been placed. The available safety inventory thus must cover for the uncertainty of demand over this period.

Typically in continuous review policies the lot size ordered is kept fixed between replenishment cycles. The optimal lot size may be evaluated using the EOQ formula discussed in Chapter 10.

Periodic Review Policies

In periodic review policies, the inventory levels are reviewed after a fixed period of time T and an order placed such that the level of current inventory plus the replenishment lot size equals a prespecified level called the *order-up-to level* (OUL). The *review interval* is the time T between successive orders. Observe that the size of each order may vary depending on the demand experienced between successive orders and the resulting inventory at the time of ordering. Periodic review policies are simpler to implement for retailers because they do not require that the retailer have the capability of continuously monitoring inventory. Suppliers may also prefer them because they result in replenishment orders placed at regular intervals.

Let us consider the store manager at Wal-Mart responsible for designing a replenishment policy for Lego building blocks. He wants to analyze the impact on safety inventory if he decides to use a periodic review policy. Demand for Lego is normally distributed and independent from one week to the next. We assume the following input:

D: Average demand per period,
σ_D: Standard deviation of demand per period,
L: Average lead time for replenishment,
T: Review interval,
CSL: Desired cycle service level.

To understand the safety inventory requirement, we track the sequence of events over time as the store manager places orders. The store manager places the first order at time 0 such that the lot size ordered and the inventory on hand sum to the order up to level OUL. Once an order is placed, the replenishment lot arrives after the lead time L. The next review period is time T when the store manager places the next order, which then arrives at time $T + L$. The OUL represents the inventory available to meet all demand that arises between periods 0 and $T + L$. The Wal-Mart store will experience a stockout if demand during the time interval between 0 and $T + L$ exceeds the OUL. Thus, the store manager must identify an OUL such that the following is true:

$$\text{Probability(demand during } L + T \leq OUL) = CSL.$$

The next step is to evaluate the distribution of demand during the time interval $T + L$. Using Equation 11.2, demand during the time interval $T + L$ is normally distributed with the following:

Mean demand during $T + L$ periods, $D_{T+L} = (T + L)D$,
Standard deviation of demand during $T + L$ periods, $\sigma_{T+L} = \sqrt{T + L}\sigma_D$.

The safety inventory in this case is the quantity in excess of D_{T+L} carried by Wal-Mart over the time interval $T + L$. The OUL and the safety inventory ss are related as follows:

$$OUL = D_{T+L} + ss. \tag{11.15}$$

Given the desired CSL, the safety inventory (ss) required is given by the following:

$$ss = F_S^{-1}(CSL) \times \sigma_{T+L} = NORMSINV(CSL) \times \sigma_{T+L}. \tag{11.16}$$

The average lot size equals the average demand during the review period T and is given as follows:

$$\text{Average lot size, } Q = D_T = DT. \tag{11.17}$$

We illustrate the periodic review policy for Wal-Mart in Example 11.10.

Example 11.10

Weekly demand for Lego at a Wal-Mart store is normally distributed with a mean of 2,500 boxes and a standard deviation of 500. The replenishment lead time is two weeks and the store manager has decided to review inventory every four weeks. Assuming a periodic review replenishment policy, evaluate the safety inventory that the store should carry to provide a CSL of 90 percent. Evaluate the OUL for such a policy.

Analysis: In this case, we have the following:

$$\text{Average demand per period, } D = 2,500,$$
$$\text{Standard deviation of demand per period, } \sigma_D = 500,$$
$$\text{Average lead time for replenishment, } L = 2 \text{ weeks,}$$
$$\text{Review interval, } T = 4 \text{ weeks.}$$

We first obtain the distribution of demand during the time interval $T + L$. Using Equation 11.2, demand during the time interval $T + L$ is normally distributed with the following:

Mean demand during $T + L$ periods, $D_{T+L} = (T + L)D = (4 + 2)2,500 = 15,000,$

Standard deviation of demand during $T + L$ periods, $\sigma_{T+L} = \sqrt{T + L}\,\sigma_D = (\sqrt{4 + 2})\,500 = 1,225$

From Equation 11.16 (evaluated using Equation 11.24 in Appendix 11B), the required safety inventory for a CSL = 0.90 is given as follows:

$$ss = F_S^{-1}(CSL) \times \sigma_{T+L} = NORMSINV(CSL) \times \sigma_{T+L} =$$
$$NORMSINV(0.90) \times 1,225 = 1,570 \text{ boxes.}$$

Using Equation 11.15, the OUL is given by the following:

$$OUL = D_{T+L} + ss = 15,000 + 1,570 = 16,570.$$

The store manager thus orders the difference between 16,570 and current inventory every four weeks.

We can now compare the safety inventory required when using continuous and periodic review policies. With a continuous review policy, the safety inventory is used to cover for demand uncertainty over the lead time L. With a periodic review policy, the safety inventory is used to cover for demand uncertainty over the lead time and the review interval $L + T$. Given that higher uncertainty must be accounted for, periodic review policies will require a higher level of safety inventory. This argument can be confirmed by comparing the results in Examples 11.4 and 11.10. For a 90 percent CSL, the store manager requires a safety inventory of 906 boxes when using a continuous review and a safety inventory of 1,570 boxes when using a periodic review.

Key Point Periodic review replenishment policies require more safety inventory than continuous review policies for the same lead time and level of product availability.

Of course periodic review policies are somewhat simpler to implement because they do not require continuous tracking of inventory. Given the broad use of bar codes and point-of-sales systems, continuous tracking of all inventories is much more commonplace today than it was a decade ago. In some instances companies partition their products based on their value. High-value products are managed using continuous review policies and low-value products are managed using periodic review policies. This makes sense if the cost of perpetual tracking of inventory is more than the savings in safety inventory that result from switching all products to a continuous review policy.

11.6   MANAGING SAFETY INVENTORY IN A MULTI-ECHELON SUPPLY CHAIN

In our discussion so far, we have assumed that each stage of the supply chain has a well-defined demand and supply distribution that it uses to set its safety inventory levels. In practice this is not true for multi-echelon supply chains. Consider a simple multi-echelon supply chain with a supplier feeding a retailer who sells to the final customer. The retailer needs to know demand as well as supply uncertainty to set safety inventory levels. Supply uncertainty, however, is influenced by the level of safety inventory the supplier chooses to carry. If a retailer order arrives when the supplier has enough inventory, the supply lead time is short. In contrast, if the retailer order arrives when the supplier is out of stock, the replenishment lead time for the retailer increases. Thus, if the supplier were to increase his level of safety inventory, the retailer could reduce the safety inventory he holds. This implies that the level of safety inventory at all stages in a multi-echelon supply chain should be related.

All inventory between a stage and the final customer is called the *echelon inventory*. Echelon inventory at a retailer is just the inventory at the retailer or in the pipeline coming to the retailer. Echelon inventory at a distributor, however, includes inventory at the distributor and all retailers served by the distributor. In a multi-echelon setting, reorder points and order up to levels at any stage should be based on echelon inventory and not local inventory. Thus, a distributor should decide his safety inventory levels based on the level of safety inventory carried by all retailers supplied by him. The more safety inventory retailers carry, the less safety inventory the distributor will need to carry. As retailers decrease the level of safety inventory they carry, the distributor will have to increase his or her safety inventory to insure regular replenishment at the retailers.

If all stages in a supply chain attempt to manage their echelon inventory, the issue of how the inventory is divided among various stages becomes important. Carrying inventory upstream in a supply chain allows for more aggregation and thus reduces the amount of inventory required. Carrying inventory upstream, however, increases the probability that the final customer will have to wait because product is not available at a stage close to him. Thus, in a multi-echelon supply chain a decision must be made with regard to the level of safety inventory carried at different stages. If inventory is very expensive to hold and customers are willing to tolerate a delay, it is better to increase the amount of safety inventory carried upstream, far from the final customer, to exploit the benefits of aggregation. If inventory is inexpensive to hold and customers are very time sensitive, it is better to carry more safety inventory downstream, closer to the final customer.

11.7 ESTIMATING AND MANAGING SAFETY INVENTORY IN PRACTICE

1. *Account for the fact that supply chain demand is lumpy.* In practice, a manufacturer or distributor does not order one unit at a time but instead often orders in a large lot. Thus, demand observed by different stages of the supply chain tends to be lumpy. Lumpiness adds to the variability of demand. Lumpiness of demand is not a significant issue when using periodic review policies. When using a continuous review policy, however, lumpiness may lead to inventory dropping far below the ROP before a replenishment order is placed. On average, inventory will drop below the ROP by about half the average size of an order. The lumpiness can be accounted for in practice by raising the safety inventory suggested by the models discussed earlier by half the average size of an order.

2. *Adjust inventory policies if demand is seasonal.* In practice, demand is often seasonal with the mean and the standard deviation of demand varying by the time of year. Thus, a given reorder point or order up to level may correspond to ten days of demand during the low-demand season and only two days of demand during the peak demand season. If the lead time is one week, stockouts are certain to occur during the peak season. In the presence of seasonality, it is not appropriate to select an average demand and standard deviation over the year to evaluate fixed reorder points and order up to levels. Both the mean and the standard deviation of demand must be adjusted by the time of year to reflect changing demand. Corresponding adjustments in the reorder points, order up to levels, and safety inventories must be made over the year. Adjustments for changes in the mean demand over the year are generally more significant than adjustments for changes in variability.

3. *Use simulation to test inventory policies.* Given that demand may not be perfectly normal and may be seasonal, it is a good idea to test and adjust inventory policies using a computer simulation before they are implemented. The simulation should use a demand pattern that truly reflects actual demand, including any lumpiness as well as seasonality. The inventory policies obtained using the models discussed in the chapter can then be tested and adjusted if needed to obtain the desired service levels. Surprisingly powerful simulations can be built using Excel, as we discuss in Chapter 12. Identifying problems in a simulation can save a lot of time and money compared to facing these problems once the inventory policy is in place.

4. *Start with a pilot.* Even a simulation cannot identify all problems that may arise when using an inventory policy. Once an inventory policy has been selected and tested using simulation, it is often a good idea to start implementation with a pilot program of products representative of the entire set of products in inventory. By starting with a pilot, many of the problems (both in the inventory policies themselves and in the process of applying the policies) can be solved. Getting these problems solved before the policy is rolled out to all the products can save a lot of time and money.

5. *Monitor service levels.* Once an inventory policy has been implemented, it is important that its performance be tracked and monitored. Monitoring is crucial because it allows a supply chain to identify when a policy is not working well and make adjustments before supply chain performance is significantly impacted. Monitoring requires

not just tracking the inventory levels but also tracking any stockouts that may result. Historically, firms have not tracked stockouts very well, partly because they are difficult to track and partly because there is the perception that they impact the customer and not the firm itself. Stockouts can be difficult to measure in a situation like a supermarket where the customer simply does not buy the product when it is not on the shelf. However, there are simple ways to estimate stockouts. At a supermarket, the fraction of time that a shelf does not contain a product may be used to estimate the fill rate. Stockouts are in fact easier to estimate online where the number of clicks on an out-of-stock product can be measured. Given the fraction of clicks that turn into orders and the average size of an order, demand during a stockout can be estimated.

6. *Focus on reducing safety inventories:* Given that safety inventory is often a large fraction of the total inventory in a supply chain, the ability to reduce safety inventory without hurting product availability can significantly increase supply chain profitability. This is particularly important in the high-tech industry where product life cycles are short. In this chapter we discussed a variety of managerial levers that can help reduce safety inventories without hurting availability. Supply chain managers must focus continuously on using these levers to reduce safety inventories.

11.8   SUMMARY OF LEARNING OBJECTIVES

1. Understand the role of safety inventory in a supply chain.

   Safety inventory helps a supply chain provide customers a high level of product availability in spite of supply and demand variability. It is carried just in case demand exceeds the amount forecasted or supply arrives later than expected.

2. Identify factors that influence the required level of safety inventory.

   Safety inventory is influenced by demand uncertainty, replenishment lead times, lead time variability, and desired product availability. As any one of them increases, the required safety inventory also increases. The required safety inventory is also influenced by the inventory policy implemented. Continuous review policies require less safety inventory than periodic review policies.

3. Describe different measures of product availability.

   The three basic measures of product availability are product fill rate, order fill rate, and cycle service level. Product fill rate is the fraction of demand for a product that is successfully filled. Order fill rate is the fraction of orders that are completely filled. Cycle service level is the fraction of replenishment cycles in which no stockouts occur.

4. Utilize managerial levers available to lower safety inventory and improve product availability.

   The required level of safety inventory may be reduced and product availability may be improved if a supply chain can reduce demand variability, replenishment lead times, and the variability of lead times. A switch from periodic monitoring to continuous monitoring can also help reduce inventories. Another key managerial lever to reduce the required safety inventories is to exploit aggregation. This may be achieved by physically aggregating inventories, virtually aggregating inventories using information centralization, specializing inventories based on demand volume, exploiting substitution, using component commonality, and postponing product differentiation.

DISCUSSION QUESTIONS

1. What is the role of safety inventory in the supply chain?
2. Explain how a reduction in lead time can help a supply chain reduce safety inventory without hurting product availability?
3. What are the pros and cons of the various measures of product availability?
4. Describe the two types of ordering policies and the impact that each of them has on safety inventory.
5. What is the impact of supply uncertainty on safety inventory?
6. Why can a Home Depot with a few large stores provide a higher level of product availability with lower inventories than a hardware store chain like Tru-Value with many small stores?
7. Why is Amazon.com able to provide a large variety of books and music with less safety inventory than a bookstore chain selling through retail stores?
8. In the 1980s, paint was sold by color and size in paint stores. Today, paint is mixed at the paint store as per the color required. Discuss what, if any, impact this change has on safety inventories in the supply chain.
9. A new technology allows books to be printed in ten minutes. Borders has decided to purchase these machines for each store. They must decide which books to carry in stock and which books to print on demand using this technology. Do you recommend it for best-sellers or other books? Why?

EXERCISES

1. Weekly demand for Motorola cell phones at a Best Buy store is normally distributed with a mean of 300 and a standard deviation of 200. Motorola takes two weeks to supply a Best Buy order. Best Buy is targeting a CSL of 95 percent and monitors its inventory continuously. How much safety inventory of cell phones should Best Buy carry? What should their ROP be?
2. Reconsider the Best Buy store in Problem 1. The store manager has decided to follow a periodic review policy to manage inventory of cell phones. They plan to order every three weeks. Given a desired CSL of 95 percent, how much safety inventory should the store carry? What should their OUL be?
3. Assume that the Best Buy store has a policy of ordering cell phones from Motorola in lots of 500. Weekly demand for Motorola cell phones at the store is normally distributed with a mean of 300 and a standard deviation of 200. Motorola takes two weeks to supply an order. If the store manager is targeting a fill rate of 99 percent, what safety inventory should they carry? What should their ROP be?
4. Weekly demand for HP printers at a Sam's Club store is normally distributed with a mean of 250 and a standard deviation of 150. The store manager continuously monitors inventory and currently orders 1,000 printers each time the inventory drops to 600 printers. HP currently takes two weeks to fill an order. How much safety inventory does the store carry? What CSL does Sam's Club achieve as a result of this policy? What fill rate does the store achieve?
5. Return to the Sam's Club store in Problem 4. Assume that the supply lead time from HP is normally distributed with a mean of 2 weeks and a standard deviation

of 1.5 weeks. How much safety inventory should Sam's Club carry if they want to provide a CSL of 95 percent? How does the required safety inventory change as the standard deviation of lead time is reduced from 1.5 weeks to zero in intervals of 0.5 weeks?

6. The Gap has started selling through its online channel along with its retail stores. Management has to decide which products to carry at the retail stores and which products to carry at a central warehouse to be sold only via the online channel. The Gap currently has 900 retail stores in the United States. Weekly demand for large Khaki pants at each store is normally distributed with a mean of 800 and a standard deviation of 100. Each pair of pants costs $30. Weekly demand for purple cashmere sweaters at each store is normally distributed with a mean of 50 and a standard deviation of 50. Each sweater costs $100. The Gap has a holding cost of 25 percent. The Gap manages all inventories using a continuous review policy and the supply lead time for both products is four weeks. The targeted CSL is 95 percent. How much reduction in holding cost per unit sold can The Gap expect on moving each of the two products from the stores to the online channel? Which of the two products should The Gap carry at the stores and which should it carry at the central warehouse for the online channel? Why? Assume demand from one week to the next to be independent.

7. Epson produces printers for sale in Europe in its Taiwan factory. Printers sold in different countries differ in terms of the power outlet as well as the language manuals. Currently, Epson assembles and packs printers for sale in individual countries. Weekly demand in different countries is normally distributed with means and standard deviations as shown in Table 11.6.

Assume demand in different countries to be independent. Given that the lead time from the Taiwan factory is eight weeks, how much safety inventory does Epson require in Europe if it targets a CSL of 95 percent?

Epson decides to build a central DC in Europe. It will ship base printers (without power supply) to the DC. When an order is received, the DC will assemble power supplies, add manuals, and ship the printers to the appropriate country. The base printers are still to be manufactured in Taiwan with a lead time of eight weeks. How much saving of safety inventory can Epson expect as a result?

8. Return to the Epson data in Problem 7. Each printer costs Epson $200 and they have a holding cost of 25 percent. What saving in holding cost can they expect as a result of building the European DC? If final assembly in the European DC

TABLE 11.6 Weekly Demand for Epson Printers in Europe

Country	Mean Demand	Standard Deviation
France	3,000	2,000
Germany	4,000	2,200
Spain	2,000	1,400
Italy	2,500	1,600
Portugal	1,000	800
UK	4,000	2,400

adds $5 to the production cost of each printer, would you recommend the move? Suppose that Epson is able to cut the production and delivery lead time from its Taiwan factory to four weeks using good information systems. How much savings in holding cost can they expect without the European DC? How much savings in holding cost can they expect with the European DC?

9. Return to the Epson data in Problem 7. Assume that demand in different countries is not independent. Demand in any pair of countries is correlated with a correlation coefficient of ρ. Evaluate the holding cost savings that Epson gains as a result of building a European DC as ρ increases from 0 (independent demand) to 1 (perfectly positively correlated demand) in intervals of 0.2.

BIBLIOGRAPHY

Feitzinger, Edward, and Hau L. Lee. 1997. "Mass Customization at Hewlett Packard." *Harvard Business Review* (January–February): 116–121.

Geary, Steve, Paul Childerhouse, and Denis Towill. 2002. "Uncertainty and the Seamless Supply Chain." *Supply Chain Management Review* (July–August 2002): 52–61.

Kopczak, Laura, and Hau L. Lee. 1993. "Hewlett-Packard: Deskjet Printer Supply Chain." Stanford University Case.

Lee, Hau L. 1993. "Design for Supply Chain Management: Concepts and Examples." Pp. 45–65 in *Perspectives in Operations Management*, ed. R. Sarin. Norwell, Mass.: Kluwer Academic Publishers.

Lee, Hau L., and Corey Billington. 1992. "Managing Supply Chain Inventory." *Sloan Management Review* (Spring): 65–73.

Lee, Hau L., Corey Billington, and B. Carter. 1993. "Hewlett-Packard Gains Control of Inventory and Service Through Design for Localization." *Interfaces* (July–August): 1–11.

Nahmias, Steven. 1997. *Production and Operations Analysis*. Burr Ridge, Ill.: Richard P. Irwin.

Signorelli, Sergio, and James L. Heskett. 1984. "Benetton (A)." Harvard Business School Case 9-685-014, 1984.

Silver, Edward A., David Pyke, and Rein Petersen. 1998. *Inventory Management and Production Planning and Scheduling*. New York: John Wiley & Sons.

Tayur, Sridhar, Ram Ganeshan, and Michael Magazine, eds. 1999. *Quantitative Models for Supply Chain Management*. Boston: Kluwer Academic Publishers.

Trent, Robert J. 2002. "Managing Inventory Investment Effectively." *Supply Chain Management Review* (March–April): 28–35.

Zipkin, Paul H. 2000. *Foundations of Inventory Management*. Boston: Irwin McGraw-Hill.

--------------------------------C A S E   S T U D Y--------------------------------

Managing Inventories at ALKO Inc.

ALKO started in 1943 in a garage workshop set up by John Williams at his Cleveland home. John had always enjoyed tinkering and in February 1948, he obtained a patent for one of his designs for lighting fixtures. He decided to produce it in his workshop and tried marketing it in the Cleveland area. The product sold well and by 1957 ALKO had grown to a $3 million company. Its lighting fixtures were well known for their outstanding quality. By then, it sold a total of five products.

In 1963 John took the company public. Since then ALKO has been very successful and the company has started distributing its products nationwide. As competition intensified in the 1980s, ALKO started introducing many new lighting fixture designs. The company's profitability, however, started to worsen despite the fact that ALKO had taken great care to ensure that product quality did not suffer. The problem was that margins started to shrink as competition in the market intensified. At this point the board decided that a complete reorganization was needed, starting at the top. Gary Fisher was then hired to reorganize and restructure the company.

When Fisher arrived in 1999, he found a company teetering on the edge. He spent the first few months trying to understand the company business and the way it was structured. Fisher realized that the key was in the operating performance. Although the company had always been outstanding at developing and producing new products, they had historically ignored their distribution system. The feeling within the company was that once you make a good product, the rest takes care of itself. Fisher set up a task force to review the company's current distribution system and come up with recommendations.

THE CURRENT DISTRIBUTION SYSTEM

The task force noted that ALKO had 100 products in its 1999 line. All production occurred at three facilities located in the Cleveland area. For sales purposes, the continental United States was divided into five regions, as shown in Figure 11.6. A DC owned by ALKO operated in each of these regions. Customers placed orders with the DCs, which tried to supply them from product in inventory. As the

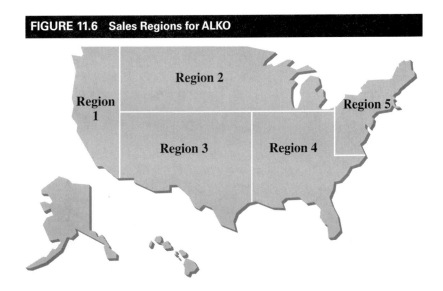

FIGURE 11.6   Sales Regions for ALKO

TABLE 11.7	Distribution of Daily Demand at ALKO				
	Region 1	*Region 2*	*Region 3*	*Region 4*	*Region 5*
Part 1 M	35.48	22.61	17.66	11.81	3.36
Part 1 SD	6.98	6.48	5.26	3.48	4.49
Part 3 M	2.48	4.15	6.15	6.16	7.49
Part 3 SD	3.16	6.20	6.39	6.76	3.56
Part 7 M	0.48	0.73	0.80	1.94	2.54
Part 7 SD	1.98	1.42	2.39	3.76	3.98

inventory for any product diminished, the DC in turn ordered from the plants. The plants scheduled production based on DC orders. Orders were transported from plants to the DCs in TL quantities because order sizes tended to be large. On the other hand, shipments from the DC to the customer were LTL. ALKO used a third-party trucking company for both transportation legs. In 1999 TL costs from the plants to DCs averaged $0.09 per unit. LTL shipping costs from a DC to a customer averaged $0.10 per unit. On average, five days were necessary between the time a DC placed an order with a plant and the time the order was delivered from the plant.

The policy in 1999 was to stock each item in every DC. A detailed study of the product line had shown that there were three basic categories of products in terms of the volume of sales. They were categorized as types High, Medium, and Low. Demand data for a representative product in each category is shown in Table 11.7. Products 1, 3, and 7 are representative of High, Medium, and Low products, respectively. Of the 100 products that ALKO sold, 10 were of type High, 20 of type Medium, and 70 of type Low. Each of their demands was identical to those of the representative products 1, 3, and 7, respectively.

The task force identified that plant capacities allowed any reasonable order to be produced in one day. Thus, a plant shipped out an order one day after receiving it. After another four days in transit, the order reached the DC. The DCs ordered using a periodic review policy with a reorder interval of six days. The holding cost incurred was $0.15 per unit per day whether the unit was in transit or in storage. All DCs carried safety inventories to ensure a CSL of 95 percent.

ALTERNATIVE DISTRIBUTION SYSTEMS

The task force recommended that ALKO build a national distribution center (NDC) outside Chicago. The task force recommended that ALKO close its five DCs and move all inventory to the NDC. Warehouse capacity was measured in terms of the total number of units handled per year (i.e., the warehouse capacity was given in terms of the demand supplied from the warehouse). The cost of constructing a warehouse is shown in Figure 11.7. However, ALKO expected to recover $50,000 for each warehouse that it closed. The CSL out of the NDC would continue to be 95 percent.

Given that Chicago is close to Cleveland, the inbound transportation cost from the plants to the NDC would reduce to $0.05 per unit. Given the increased average distance, however, the outbound transportation cost to customers from the NDC would increase to $0.24 per unit.

Other possibilities the task force considered include building a national distribution center while keeping the regional DCs open. In this case, some products would be stocked at the regional DCs while others would be stocked at the NDC.

FISHER'S DECISION

Gary Fisher pondered the task force report. They had not detailed any of the numbers supporting their decision. He decided to evaluate the numbers before making his decision.

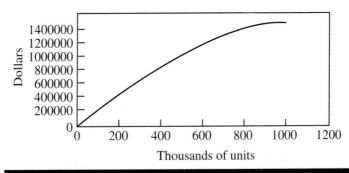

FIGURE 11.7   Construction Costs for NDC

QUESTIONS

1. What is the annual inventory and distribution cost of the current distribution system?

2. What are the savings that would result from following the task force recommendation and setting up an NDC? Evaluate the savings as the correlation coefficient of demand in any pair of regions varies from 0 to 0.5 to 1.0. Do you recommend setting up a NDC?

3. Suggest other options that Fisher should consider. Evaluate each option and recommend a distribution system for ALKO that would be most profitable. How dependent is your recommendation on the correlation coefficient of demand across different regions?

-------------------------------- A P P E N D I X   1 1 A --------------------------------

The Normal Distribution

A continuous random variable X has a *normal distribution* with mean μ and standard deviation $\sigma > 0$ if the probability density function $f(x, \mu, \sigma)$ of the random variable is given by

$$f(x, \mu, \sigma) = \frac{1}{\sigma\sqrt{2\pi}} \exp\left[-\frac{(x-\mu)^2}{2\sigma^2}\right]$$ **(11.18)**

The normal density function is as shown in Figure 11.8.

The *cumulative normal distribution function* is denoted by $F(x, \mu, \sigma)$ and is the probability that a normally distributed random variable with mean μ and standard deviation σ takes on a value less than or equal to x. The cumulative normal distribution function and the density function are related as follows:

$$F(x, \mu, \sigma) = \int_{X=-\infty}^{x} f(X, \mu, \sigma)dX$$

A normal distribution with a mean $\mu = 0$ and standard deviation $\sigma = 1$ is referred to as the *standard normal distribution*. The standard normal density function is denoted by $f_S(x)$ and the cumulative standard normal distribution function is denoted by $F_S(x)$. Thus

$$f_S(x) = f(x, 0, 1) \text{ and } F_S(x) = F(x, 0, 1).$$

Given a probability p, the inverse normal $F^{-1}(p, \mu, \sigma)$ is the value x such that p is the probability that the normal random variable takes on a value x or less. Thus, if $F(x, \mu, \sigma) = p$, then $x = F^{-1}(p, \mu, \sigma)$. The inverse of the standard normal distribution is denoted by $F_S^{-1}(p)$. Thus

$$F_S^{-1}(p) = F^{-1}(p, 0, 1).$$

FIGURE 11.8   Normal Density Function

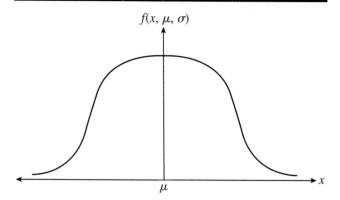

------------------------------- **A P P E N D I X   1 1 B** -------------------------------

The Normal Distribution in Excel

The following Excel functions can be used to evaluate various normal distribution functions:

$$F(x, \mu, \sigma) = NORMDIST(x, \mu, \sigma, 1) \qquad \textbf{(11.19)}$$

$$f(x, \mu, \sigma) = NORMDIST(x, \mu, \sigma, 0) \qquad \textbf{(11.20)}$$

$$F^{-1}(p, \mu, \sigma) = NORMINV(p, \mu, \sigma) \qquad \textbf{(11.21)}$$

The Excel functions to evaluate various standard normal distribution functions are as listed next:

$$F_S(x) = NORMDIST(x, 0, 1, 1) \text{ or } \qquad \textbf{(11.22)}$$
$$NORMSDIST(x)$$

$$f_S(x) = NORMDIST(x, 0, 1, 0) \qquad \textbf{(11.23)}$$

$$F_S^{-1}(p) = NORMSINV(p) \qquad \textbf{(11.24)}$$

------------------------------ A P P E N D I X 1 1 C ------------------------------

Expected Shortage Cost per Cycle

Objective: Establish alternate formula for ESC to be evaluated using Excel.

Analysis: Given a reorder point of $ROP = D_L + ss$, the ESC is given as follows:

$$ESC = \int_{x=ROP}^{\infty} (x - ROP)f(x)dx$$

$$= \int_{x=R_L+ss}^{\infty} (x - D_L - ss)f(x)dx$$

Given that the demand during lead time is normally distributed with a mean D_L and a standard deviation σ_L, we have (using Equation 11.18) the following:

$$ESC = \int_{x=D_L+ss}^{\infty} (x - D_L - ss)\frac{1}{\sqrt{2\pi}\,\sigma_L}\,e^{\frac{-(x-D_L)^2}{2\sigma_L^2}}dx$$

Substitute the following:

$$z = (x - D_L)/\sigma_L$$

This implies the following:

$$dx = \sigma_L\,dz.$$

Thus we have the following:

$$ESC = \int_{z=ss/\sigma_L}^{\infty} (z\sigma_L - ss)\frac{1}{\sqrt{2\pi}}\,e^{-z^2/2}d.$$

$$= -ss\int_{z=ss/\sigma_L}^{\infty} \frac{1}{\sqrt{2\pi}}\,e^{-z^2/2}dz + \sigma_L\int_{z=ss/\sigma_L}^{\infty} z\frac{1}{\sqrt{2\pi}}\,e^{-z^2/2}d$$

Recall that $F_S(\cdot)$ is the cumulative distribution function and $f_S(\cdot)$ is the probability density function for the standard normal distribution with mean 0 and standard deviation 1. Using Equation 11.18 and the definition of the standard normal distribution, we have the following:

$$1 - F_S(y) = \int_{z=y}^{\infty} f_S(z)dz = \int_{z=y}^{\infty} \frac{1}{\sqrt{2\pi}}\,e^{-z^2/2}dz$$

Substitute $w = z^2/2$ into the expression for ESC. This implies the following:

$$ESC = -ss[1 - F_S(ss/\sigma_L)] + \sigma_L\int_{w=ss^2/2\sigma_L^2}^{\infty} \frac{1}{\sqrt{2\pi}}\,e^{-w}dw$$

or,

$$ESC = -ss[1 - F_S(ss/\sigma_L)] + \sigma_L f_S(ss/\sigma_L)$$

Using Equations 11.22 and 11.23, ESC may be evaluated using Excel as follows:

$$ESC = -ss[1 - NORMDIST(ss/\sigma_L, 0, 1, 1)] + \sigma_L NORMDIST(ss/\sigma_L, 0, 1, 0).$$

12

Determining Optimal Level of Product Availability

Learning Objectives

After reading this chapter, you will be able to:

1. Identify the factors affecting the optimal level of product availability and evaluate the optimal cycle service level.

2. Use managerial levers that improve supply chain profitability through optimal service levels.

3. Construct contracts that increase supply chain profitability.

In this chapter, we explore the process of determining the optimal level of availability to be offered to customers. The chapter examines the components that go into the calculation of the optimal service level and the various ways that this calculation can be performed. We discuss and demonstrate how different managerial levers can be used to improve supply chain profitability by increasing the level of product availability while reducing inventories.

12.1   THE IMPORTANCE OF THE LEVEL OF PRODUCT AVAILABILITY

The level of product availability is measured using the cycle service level or the fill rate, which are metrics for the amount of customer demand satisfied from available inventory. The level of product availability is also referred to as the customer service level. The level of product availability is an important component of any supply chain's responsiveness. A supply chain can use a high level of product availability to improve its responsiveness and attract customers. This increases revenues for the supply chain by increasing sales through high product availability when customers come to make a purchase. However, a high level of product availability requires large inventories and large inventories tend to raise costs for the supply chain. Therefore a supply chain needs to achieve a balance between the level of availability and the cost of inventory. This optimal level of product availability is one that maximizes supply chain profitability.

Whether the optimal level of availability is high or low depends on where a particular company believes they can maximize profits. For example, Nordstrom has focused on providing a high level of product availability and has used its reputation for responsiveness to become a very successful department store chain. However, prices at Nordstrom are higher than at a discount store where the level of product availability tends to be lower. Power plants ensure that they (almost) never run out of fuel because a shutdown is extremely expensive and can result in several days of lost production. Some power plants try to maintain several months of fuel supply to avoid any probability of running out. In contrast, most supermarkets carry only a few days' supply of product and out-of-stock situations do occur with some frequency.

With e-commerce, the nature of searching on the Web allows a customer to easily shop at an alternate store if one is out of stock. This competitive environment puts pressure on Web retailers to increase their level of availability. Simultaneously, significant price competition has lowered prices on the Web. Web retailers with excess inventory find it difficult to be profitable. Providing the optimal level of product availability is thus a key to success on the Web.

In the examples described earlier, firms provide different levels of product availability. Every supply chain manager must be aware of the factors that influence the optimal level of product availability. This knowledge can be used to target the optimal level of product availability and identify managerial levers that increase supply chain surplus. Next we identify factors that affect the optimal level of product availability.

12.2   FACTORS AFFECTING OPTIMAL LEVEL OF PRODUCT AVAILABILITY

To understand the factors that influence the optimal level of product availability, consider L. L. Bean, a large mail order company selling apparel. One of the products L. L. Bean sells is ski jackets. The selling season for ski jackets is from November to February. The buyer at L. L. Bean currently purchases the entire season's supply of ski jackets from the manufacturer before the start of the selling season. Providing a high level of product availability requires the purchase of a large number of jackets. Although a high level of product availability is likely to satisfy all demand that arises, it is also likely to result in a large number of unsold jackets at the end of the season, with L. L. Bean losing money on unsold jackets. In contrast, a low level of product availability is likely to result in few unsold jackets. However, it is quite likely that L. L. Bean will have to turn away customers willing to buy jackets because they are sold out. In this scenario, L. L. Bean loses potential profit by losing customers. The buyer at L. L. Bean must balance the loss from having too many unsold jackets (in case the number of jackets ordered is more than demand) and the lost profit from turning away customers (in case the number of jackets ordered is less than demand) when deciding the level of product availability.

The *cost of overstocking* is denoted by C_o and is the loss incurred by a firm for each unsold unit at the end of the selling season. The *cost of understocking* is denoted by C_u and is the margin lost by a firm for each lost sale because there is no inventory on hand. The cost of understocking should include the margin lost from current as well as future sales if the customer does not return. In summary, the two key factors that influence the optimal level of product availability are

- Cost of overstocking the product
- Cost of understocking the product

We illustrate and develop this relationship in the context of a buying decision at L. L. Bean. The first point to observe is that deciding on an optimal level of product availability only makes sense in the context of demand uncertainty. Traditionally, many firms have forecast a consensus estimate of demand without any measure of uncertainty. In this setting, firms do not make a decision regarding the level of availability; they simply order the consensus forecast. Over the last decade, firms have developed a better appreciation for uncertainty and have started developing forecasts that include a measure of uncertainty. Incorporating uncertainty and deciding on the optimal level of product availability can increase profits relative to using a consensus forecast.

L. L. Bean has a buying committee that decides on the quantity of each product to be ordered. Based on demand over the past few years, the buyers have estimated the demand distribution for a red women's ski parka to be as shown in Table 12.1. This is a deviation from their traditional practice of using the average historical demand as the consensus forecast. To simplify the discussion, we assume that all demand is in hundreds of parkas. The manufacturer also requires that L. L. Bean place orders in multiples of 100. In Table 12.1, p_i is the probability that demand equals D_i, and P_i is the probability that demand is less than or equal to D_i.

From Table 12.1, we can evaluate the expected demand of Parkas as follows:

$$\text{Expected demand} = \sum D_i p_i = 1{,}026.$$

Under the old policy of ordering the expected value, the buyers would have ordered 1,000 parkas. However, demand is uncertain and Table 12.1 shows that there is a 51 percent probability that demand will be 1,000 or less. Thus, a policy of ordering a thousand parkas will result in a cycle service level of 51 percent at L. L. Bean. The buying

TABLE 12.1 Demand Distribution for Parkas at L. L. Bean

Demand D_i (in hundreds)	Probability p_i	Cumulative Probability of Demand Being D_i or Less (P_i)	Probability of Demand Being Greater than D_i
4	0.01	0.01	0.99
5	0.02	0.03	0.97
6	0.04	0.07	0.93
7	0.08	0.15	0.85
8	0.09	0.24	0.76
9	0.11	0.35	0.65
10	0.16	0.51	0.49
11	0.20	0.71	0.29
12	0.11	0.82	0.18
13	0.10	0.92	0.08
14	0.04	0.96	0.04
15	0.02	0.98	0.02
16	0.01	0.99	0.01
17	0.01	1.00	0.00

committee must decide on an order size and cycle service level that maximizes the profits from the sale of parkas at L. L. Bean.

The loss that L. L. Bean incurs from an unsold parka as well as the profit that L. L. Bean makes on each parka it sells influence the buying decision. Each parka costs L. L. Bean $c = \$45$ and is priced in the catalog at $p = \$100$. Any unsold parkas at the end of the season are sold at the outlet store for $50. Holding the parka in inventory and transporting it to the outlet store costs L. L. Bean $10. Thus, L. L. Bean recovers a salvage value of $s = \$40$ for each parka that is unsold at the end of the season. L. L. Bean makes a profit of $p - c = \$55$ on each parka it sells and incurs a loss of $c - s = \$5$ on each unsold parka that is sent to the outlet store.

The expected profit from ordering a thousand parkas is given as follows:

$$\text{Expected profit} = \sum_{i=4}^{10} [D_i(p-c) - (1,000 - D_i)(c-s)]p_i$$

$$+ (1 - P_i)1,000(p-c) = \$49,900.$$

To decide whether to order 1,100 parkas, the buying committee needs to determine the potential outcome of buying the extra 100 units. If 1,100 parkas are ordered, the extra 100 are sold (for a profit of $5,500) if demand is 1,100 or higher. Otherwise the extra 100 units are sent to the outlet store at a loss of $500. From Table 12.1, we see that there is a probability of 0.49 that demand is 1,100 or higher and a 0.51 probability that demand is 1,000 or less. Thus, we deduce the following:

Expected profit from the extra 100 parkas = 5,500 × Prob[demand ≥ 1,100] −
500 × Prob[demand < 1,100] = $5,500 × 0.49 − $500 × 0.51 = $2,440.

The total expected profit from ordering 1,100 parkas is thus $52,340, which is almost 5 percent higher than the expected profit from ordering 1,000 parkas. Using the same approach, we can evaluate the marginal contribution of each additional 100 parkas as in Table 12.2.

Note that the expected marginal contribution is positive up to 1,300 parkas, but it is negative from that point on. Thus the optimal order size is 1,300 parkas. From Table 12.2 we have the following:

Expected profit from ordering 1,300 parkas = $49,900 + $2,440 +
$1,240 + $580 = $54,160.

This is over an 8 percent increase in profitability relative to the policy of ordering the expected value of 1,000 parkas.

A plot of total expected profits versus the order quantity is shown in Figure 12.1. The optimal order quantity maximizes the expected profit.

For L. L. Bean, the optimal order quantity is 1,300 parkas, which provides a CSL of 92 percent. Observe that with a CSL of 0.92, L. L. Bean has a fill rate that is much higher. If demand is 1,300 or less, L. L. Bean achieves a fill rate of 100 percent, because all demand is satisfied. If demand is over 1,300 (say D), part of the demand ($D − 1,300$) is not satisfied. In this case a fill rate of $1,300/D$ is achieved. Overall, the fill rate achieved at L. L. Bean if 1,300 parkas are ordered is given by the following:

$$fr = 1 \times \text{Prob(demand} \le 1,300) + \sum_{D_i \ge 1,400} (1,300/D_i)p_i = 0.99.$$

Thus, with a policy of ordering 1,300 parkas, L. L. Bean satisfies on average 99 percent of its demand from parkas in inventory.

In the L. L. Bean example we have a cost of overstocking of $C_o = c − s = \$5$ and a cost of understocking of $C_u = p − c = \$55$. As these costs change, the optimal level of product availability also changes. In the next section we develop the relationship between the desired CSL and the cost of overstocking and understocking for seasonal items.

TABLE 12.2 Expected Marginal Contribution of Each Additional 100 Parkas

Additional Hundreds	Expected Marginal Benefit	Expected Marginal Cost	Expected Marginal Contribution
11th	5,500 × 0.49 = 2,695	500 × 0.51 = 255	2,695 − 255 = 2,440
12th	5,500 × 0.29 = 1,595	500 × 0.71 = 355	1,595 − 355 = 1,240
13th	5,500 × 0.18 = 990	500 × 0.82 = 410	990 − 410 = 580
14th	5,500 × 0.08 = 440	500 × 0.92 = 460	440 − 460 = −20
15th	5,500 × 0.04 = 220	500 × 0.96 = 480	220 − 480 = −260
16th	5,500 × 0.02 = 110	500 × 0.98 = 490	110 − 490 = −380
17th	5,500 × 0.01 = 55	500 × 0.99 = 495	55 − 495 = −440

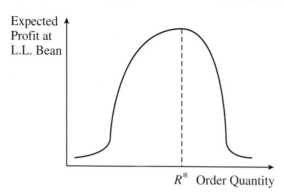

FIGURE 12.1   Expected Profit as a Function of Order Quantity at L. L. Bean

Optimal Cycle Service Level for Seasonal Items with a Single Order in a Season

In this section we focus attention on seasonal products such as ski jackets where all leftover items must be disposed of at the end of the season. The assumption is that the leftover items from the previous season are not used to satisfy demand for the current season. Assume a retail price per unit of p, a cost of c, and a salvage value of s. We consider the following input:

C_o: cost of overstocking by one unit, $C_o = c - s$,
C_u: cost of understocking by one unit, $C_u = p - c$,
CSL^*: optimal cycle service level,
O^*: corresponding optimal order size.

CSL^* is the probability that demand during the season will be at or below O^*. At the optimal cycle service level CSL^*, the marginal contribution of purchasing an additional unit is zero. If the order quantity is raised from O^* to $O^* + 1$, the additional unit sells if demand is larger than O^*. This occurs with probability $1 - CSL^*$ and results in a contribution of $p - c$. We thus have the following:

$$\text{Expected benefit of purchasing extra unit} = (1 - CSL^*)(p - c).$$

The additional unit remains unsold if demand is at or below O^*. This occurs with probability CSL^* and results in a cost of $c - s$. We thus have the following:

$$\text{Expected cost of purchasing extra unit} = CSL^*(c - s).$$

Thus, the expected marginal contribution of raising the order size from O^* to $O^* + 1$ is given by

$$(1 - CSL^*)(p - c) - CSL^*(c - s).$$

Because the expected marginal contribution must be 0 at the optimal cycle service level, we have the following:

$$CSL^* = \text{probability}(\text{demand} \leq O^*) = \frac{p - c}{p - s} = \frac{C_u}{C_u + C_o} = \frac{1}{1 + (C_o / C_u)} \qquad \textbf{(12.1)}$$

A more rigorous derivation of the aforementioned formula is provided in Appendix 12A. The optimal CSL^* has also been referred to as the *critical fractile*. The resulting optimal order quantity maximizes the firm's profit. If demand during the season is normally distributed with a mean of μ and a standard deviation of σ, the optimal order quantity is given by the following:

$$O^* = F^{-1}(CSL^*, \mu, \sigma) = NORMINV(CSL^*, \mu, \sigma) \tag{12.2}$$

When demand is normally distributed with a mean of μ and a standard deviation of σ, the expected profit from ordering O units is given by

$$\text{Expected profit} = (p - s)\mu F_S\left(\frac{O - \mu}{\sigma}\right) - (p - s)\sigma f_S\left(\frac{O - \mu}{\sigma}\right)$$

$$-O(c - s)F(O, \mu, \sigma) + O(p - c)[1 - F(O, \mu, \sigma)].$$

The derivation of this formula is provided in Appendix 12B and Appendix 12C. Here F_S is the standard normal cumulative distribution function and f_S is the standard normal density function discussed in Appendix 11A of Chapter 11. The expected profit from ordering O units is evaluated in Excel using Equations 11.19, 11.22, and 11.23 as follows:

$$\text{Expected profits} = (p - s)\mu\, NORMDIST((O - \mu)/\sigma, 0, 1, 1) -$$
$$(p - s)\sigma NORMDIST((O - \mu)/\sigma, 0, 1, 0) - O(c - s)NORMDIST(O, \mu, \sigma, 1) \tag{12.3}$$
$$+ O(p - c)\,[1 - NORMDIST(O, \mu, \sigma, 1)].$$

Example 12.1 illustrates the use of Equations 12.1 and 12.2 to obtain the optimal cycle service level and order quantity.

Example 12.1

The manager at Sportmart, a sports store, has to decide on the number of skis to purchase for the winter season. Considering past demand data and weather forecasts for the year, management has forecast demand to be normally distributed with a mean of $\mu = 350$ and a standard deviation of $\sigma = 100$. Each pair of skis costs $c = \$100$ and retails for $p = \$250$. Any unsold skis at the end of the season are disposed of for \$85. Assume that it costs \$5 to hold a pair of skis in inventory for the season. Evaluate the number of skis that the manager should order to maximize expected profits.

Analysis: In this case we have the following:

Salvage value $s = \$85 - \$5 = \$80$,
Cost of understocking $= C_u = p - c = \$250 - \$100 = \$150$,
Cost of overstocking $= C_o = c - s = \$100 - \$80 = \$20$.

Using Equation 12.1 we deduce that the optimal CSL is as follows:

$$CSL^* = \text{probability}(\text{demand} \leq R^*) = \frac{C_u}{C_u + C_o} = \frac{150}{150 + 20} = 0.88$$

Using Equation 12.2, the optimal order size is as follows:

$$O^* = NORMINV(CSL^*, \mu, \sigma) = NORMINV(0.88, 350, 100) = 468.$$

Thus it is optimal for the manager at Sportmart to order 468 skis even though the expected number of sales is 350. In this case, because the cost of understocking is much higher than the cost of overstocking, management is better off ordering more than the expected value to cover for the uncertainty of demand.

Using Equation 12.3, the expected profits from ordering O^* units are as follows:

$$\begin{aligned}
\text{Expected profits} &= (p-s)\mu\, NORMDIST((O^*-\mu)/\sigma, 0, 1, 1) - (p-s)\sigma\, NORMDIST((O^* - \\
&\quad \mu)/\sigma, 0, 1, 0) - O^*(c-s)\, NORMDIST(O^*, \mu, \sigma, 1) + O^*(p-c)\,[1 - NORMDIST(O^*, \mu, \sigma, \\
&\quad 1)] = 59{,}500\, NORMDIST(1.18, 0, 1, 1) - 17{,}000\, NORMDIST(1.18, 0, 1, 0) - 9{,}360 \\
&\quad NORMDIST(468, 350, 100, 1) + 70{,}200[1 - NORMDIST(468, 350, 100, 1)] = \$49{,}146.
\end{aligned}$$

The expected profit from ordering 350 skis can be evaluated as \$45,718. Thus ordering 468 skis results in an expected profit that is almost 8 percent higher than the profit obtained from ordering the expected value of 350 skis.

When O units are ordered, a firm is left with either too much or too little inventory, depending on demand. When demand is normally distributed with expected value μ and standard deviation σ, the expected quantity overstocked at the end of the season is given by the following:

$$\text{Expected overstock} = (O - \mu)F_S\left(\frac{O-\mu}{\sigma}\right) + \sigma f_S\left(\frac{O-\mu}{\sigma}\right).$$

The derivation of this formula is provided in Appendix 12D. The formula can be evaluated using Excel as follows:

$$\text{Expected overstock} = (O - \mu)NORMDIST((O - \mu)/\sigma, 0, 1, 1) \qquad \textbf{(12.4)}$$
$$+ \sigma NORMDIST((O - \mu)/\sigma, 0, 1, 0).$$

The expected quantity understocked at the end of the season is given by the following:

$$\text{Expected understock} = (\mu - O)\left[1 - F_S\left(\frac{O-\mu}{\sigma}\right)\right] + \sigma f_S\left(\frac{O-\mu}{\sigma}\right).$$

The derivation of this formula is provided in Appendix 12E. The formula can be evaluated using Excel as follows:

$$\text{Expected understock} = (\mu - O)[1 - NORMDIST((O - \mu)/\sigma, 0, 1, 1)] \qquad \textbf{(12.5)}$$
$$+ \sigma NORMDIST((O - \mu)/\sigma, 0, 1, 0).$$

Example 12.2 illustrates the use of Equations 12.4 and 12.5 to evaluate the quantity expected to be overstocked and understocked as a result of an ordering policy.

Example 12.2

Demand for skis at Sportmart is normally distributed with a mean of $\mu = 350$ and a standard deviation of $\sigma = 100$. The manager has decided to order 450 pairs of skis for the upcoming season. Evaluate expected over- and understock as a result of this policy.

Analysis: In this case we have an order size $O = 450$. An overstock results if demand during the season is below 450. The expected overstock can be obtained using the Equation 12.4 as follows:

$$\begin{aligned}
\text{Expected overstock} &= (O - \mu)NORMDIST((O - \mu)/\sigma, 0, 1, 1) \\
&\quad + \sigma\, NORMDIST((O - \mu)/\sigma, 0, 1, 0) \\
&= (450 - 350)NORMDIST((450 - 350)/100, 0, 1, 1) \\
&\quad + 100 NORMDIST((450 - 350)/100, 0, 1, 0) \\
&= 108.
\end{aligned}$$

Thus, the policy of ordering 450 pairs of skis results in an expected overstock of 108 pairs.

An understock occurs if demand during the season is higher than 450 pairs. The expected understock can be evaluated using Equation 12.5 as follows:

$$
\begin{aligned}
\text{Expected understock} &= (\mu - O)[1 - NORMDIST((O - \mu)/\sigma, 0, 1, 1)] \\
&\quad + \sigma NORMDIST((O - \mu)/\sigma, 0, 1, 0) \\
&= (350 - 450)[1 - NORMDIST((450 - 350)/100, 0, 1, 1)] \\
&\quad + 100 NORMDIST((450 - 350)/100, 0, 1, 0) \\
&= 8.
\end{aligned}
$$

Thus the policy of ordering 450 pairs results in an expected understock of 8 pairs. Note that there is a positive expected understock *and* overstock in virtually every case. This result may initially seem counterintuitive but makes sense as the values used to calculate an expected understock or overstock are always great than or equal to zero. For example if demand is 500 and there are 450 jackets in inventory, there is an understock of 50 and an overstock of 0 (not –50). This guarantees that the expected value will be greater than or equal to zero.

Desired Cycle Service Level for Continuously Stocked Items

In this section we focus on products such as detergent that are ordered repeatedly by a retail store like Wal-Mart. In such a situation, Wal-Mart uses safety inventory to increase the level of availability and decrease the probability of stocking out between successive deliveries. If detergent is left over in a replenishment cycle, it can be sold in the next cycle. It does not have to be disposed of at a lower cost. However, a holding cost is incurred as the product is carried from one cycle to the next. The manager at Wal-Mart is faced with the issue of deciding the CSL to aim for.

Two extreme scenarios should be considered:

1. All demand that arises when the product is out of stock is backlogged and filled later when inventories are replenished.
2. All demand arising when the product is out of stock is lost.

Reality in most instances is somewhere in between, with some of the demand lost and other customers returning when the product is in stock. Here we consider both extreme cases.

We assume that demand per unit time is normally distributed along with the following inputs

   Q: Replenishment lot size,
   S: Fixed cost associated with each order,
ROP: Reorder point,
   D: Average demand per unit time,
   σ: Standard deviation of demand per unit time,
   ss: Safety inventory. Recall that $ss = ROP - D_L,$
CSL: Cycle service level,
   C: Unit cost,
   h: Holding cost as a fraction of product cost per unit time,
   H: Cost of holding one unit for one unit of time. $H = hC.$

Demand During Stockout Is Backlogged

We first consider the case where all demand arising when the product is out of stock is backlogged. Because no demand is lost, minimizing costs becomes equivalent to maximizing profits. As an example, consider a Wal-Mart store selling detergent. The store manager offers a discount of C_u to each customer wanting to buy detergent when it is out of stock. This ensures that all these customers return when inventory is replenished.

If the store manager increases the level of safety inventory, more orders are satisfied from stock, resulting in lower backlogs. This decreases the backlogging cost. However, the cost of holding inventory increases. The store manager must pick a level of safety inventory that minimizes the backlogging and holding costs. In this case, the optimal cycle service level is given by the following:

$$CSL^* = 1 - \frac{HQ}{DC_u} \tag{12.6}$$

Given the optimal cycle service level, the required safety inventory can be evaluated using Equation 11.9 if demand is normally distributed.

From Equation 12.6, observe that increasing the lot size Q allows the store manager at Wal-Mart to reduce the cycle service level and thus the safety inventory carried. This is because increasing the lot size increases the fill rate and thus reduces the quantity backlogged. One should be careful, however, because an increase in lot size raises the cycle inventory. In general, increasing the lot size is not an effective way for a firm to improve product availability.

If the cost of stocking out is known, one can use Equation 12.6 to obtain the appropriate cycle service level (and thus the appropriate level of safety inventory). In many practical settings, it is hard to estimate the cost of stocking out. In such a situation, a manager may want to evaluate the current inventory policy and identify the implied cost of a stockout. Often, when a precise cost of stockout cannot be found, this implied stockout cost will at least give an idea of whether inventory should be increased, decreased, or kept about the same. In Example 12.3 we show how Equation 12.6 can be used to impute a cost of stocking out given an inventory policy.

Example 12.3

Weekly demand for detergent at Wal-Mart is normally distributed with a mean of $\mu = 100$ gallons and a standard deviation of $\sigma = 20$. The replenishment lead time is $L = 2$ weeks. The store manager at Wal-Mart orders 400 gallons when the available inventory drops to 300 gallons. Each gallon of detergent costs $3. The holding cost Wal-Mart incurs is 20 percent. If all unfilled demand is backlogged and carried over to the next cycle, evaluate the cost of stocking out implied by the current replenishment policy.

Analysis: In this case we have the following:

Lot size $Q = 400$ gallons,
Reorder point $ROP = 300$ gallons,
Average demand per week $D = 100$ gallons,
Average demand per year $D_{year} = 100 \times 52 = 5,200$,
Standard deviation of demand per week $\sigma_D = 20$,

Unit cost $C = \$3$,
Holding cost as a fraction of product cost per year $h = 0.2$,
Cost of holding one unit for one year $H = hC = \$0.6$,
Lead time $L = 2$ weeks.

We thus have the following:

$$\text{Mean demand over lead time, } D_L = DL = 200 \text{ gallons,}$$
$$\text{Standard deviation of demand over lead-time, } \sigma_L = \sigma_D\sqrt{L} = 20\sqrt{2} = 28.3$$

Because demand is normally distributed, we can use Equation 11.4 to evaluate the CSL under the current inventory policy as follows:

$$CSL = F(ROP, D_L, \sigma_L) = F(300, 200, 28.3)$$

Using Equation 11.19 from Appendix 11B, we obtain the following:

$$CSL = NORMDIST(300, 200, 28.3, 1) = 0.9998.$$

We can thus deduce that the imputed cost of stocking out (using Equation 12.6) is given by the following:

$$C_u = \frac{HQ}{(1 - CSL)D_{year}} = \frac{0.6 \times 400}{0.0002 \times 5{,}200} = \$230.8 \text{ per gallon}$$

The implication here is that if each shortage of a gallon of detergent costs Wal-Mart $230.8, the current CSL of 0.9998 is optimal. In this particular example, one can claim that the store manager is carrying too much inventory because the cost of stocking out of detergent is unlikely to be $230.8 per gallon.

A manager can use the aforementioned analysis to decide if the imputed cost of stocking out, and thus the inventory policy, is reasonable.

Demand During Stockout Is Lost

For the case where unfilled demand during the stockout period is lost, the optimal cycle service level CSL^* is given as follows:

$$CSL^* = 1 - \frac{HQ}{HQ + DC_u} \qquad \text{(12.7)}$$

In this case we have assumed that C_u is the cost of losing one unit of demand during the stockout period. In Example 12.4, we evaluate the optimal cycle service level if demand is lost during the stockout period.

Example 12.4

Consider the situation in Example 12.3 but make the assumption that all demand during a stockout is lost. Assume that the cost of losing one unit of demand is $2. Evaluate the optimal cycle service level that the store manager at Wal-Mart should target.

Analysis: In this case we have the following:

Lot size $Q = 400$ gallons,
Average demand per year $D_{year} = 100 \times 52 = 5{,}200$,
Cost of holding one unit for one year $H = \$0.6$,
Cost of understocking, $C_u = \$2$.

Using Equation 12.7, the optimal cycle service level is given as follows:

$$CSL^* = 1 - \frac{HQ}{HQ + DC_u} = 1 - \frac{0.6 \times 400}{0.6 \times 400 + 2 \times 5,200} = 0.98.$$

In this case the store manager at Wal-Mart should target a cycle service level of 98 percent.

In general, the optimal cycle service level will be higher if sales are lost than if sales are backlogged.

12.3 MANAGERIAL LEVERS TO IMPROVE SUPPLY CHAIN PROFITABILITY

Having identified the factors that influence the optimal level of product availability, we now focus on actions a manager can take to improve supply chain profitability. We have shown in section 12.2 that the costs of over- and understocking have a direct impact on both the optimal cycle service level and profitability. Two obvious managerial levers to increase profitability are thus as follows:

1. Increasing the salvage value of each unit increases profitability (as well as the optimal cycle service level).
2. Decreasing the margin lost from a stockout increases profitability.

Strategies to increase the salvage value include selling to outlet stores so that left-over units are not merely discarded. Some companies like Sport Obermeyer selling winter wear in the United States sell the surplus in South America, where the winter corresponds to the North American summer. The increased salvage value of the surplus allows Sport Obermeyer to provide a higher level of product availability in the United States and increase its profits.

Strategies to decrease the margin lost in a stockout include arranging for backup sourcing (that may be more expensive) so customers are not lost forever. The practice of purchasing product from a competitor on the open market to satisfy customer demand is observed and justified by the earlier reasoning. In the MRO supply industry, McMaster Carr and W. W. Grainger, two major competitors, are also large customers for each other.

The optimal cycle service level as a function of the ratio of the cost of overstocking and the cost of understocking is shown in Figure 12.2. Observe that as this ratio gets smaller, the optimal level of product availability increases. This fact explains the difference in the level of product availability between a high-end store like Nordstrom and a discount store. Nordstrom has higher margins and thus a higher cost of understocking. It should thus provide a higher level of product availability than a discount store with lower margins and as a result, a lower cost of stocking out.

Another significant managerial lever to improve supply chain profitability is the reduction of demand uncertainty. With reduced demand uncertainty, a supply chain manager can better match supply and demand by reducing both over and understocking. A manager can reduce demand uncertainty via the following means:

1. *Improved forecasting:* Use better market intelligence and collaboration to reduce demand uncertainty.

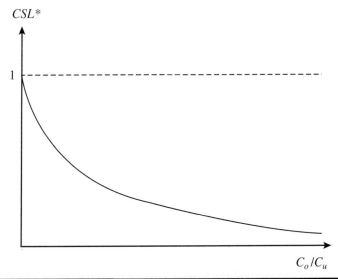

FIGURE 12.2   Impact of Changing C_o/C_u on Optimal Cycle Service Level

2. *Quick response:* Reduce replenishment lead time so that multiple orders may be placed in the selling season.
3. *Postponement:* In a multiproduct setting, postpone product differentiation until closer to the point of sale.
4. *Tailored sourcing:* Use a more expensive short lead time supplier as a backup for a low cost, long lead time supplier.

Next we study the impact of each of these on supply chain performance.

Improving Forecasts: Impact on Profits and Inventories

Companies have tried to better understand their customers and coordinate actions within the supply chain to improve forecast accuracy. The use of demand planning information systems has also helped in this regard. We show that improved forecast accuracy can help a firm significantly increase its profitability while decreasing the excess inventory overstocked as well as the sales lost because of understocking. We illustrate the impact of improving forecast accuracy in Example 12.5.

Example 12.5

Consider a buyer at Bloomingdales responsible for purchasing dinnerware with Christmas patterns. The dinnerware only sells over the Christmas season and the buyer places an order for delivery in early November. Each dinnerware set costs $c = \$100$ and sells for a retail price of $p = \$250$. Any sets unsold by Christmas are heavily discounted in the post-Christmas sales and sold for a salvage value of $s = \$80$. The buyer has estimated that demand is normally distributed with a mean of $\mu = 350$. Historically, forecast errors have had a standard deviation of $\sigma = 150$. The buyer has decided to conduct additional market research to get a better forecast. Evaluate the impact of improved forecast accuracy on profitability and inventories as the buyer reduces σ from 150 to 0 in increments of 30.

Analysis: In this case we have the following:

Cost of understocking $= C_u = p - c = \$250 - \$100 = \$150$
Cost of overstocking $= C_o = c - s = \$100 - \$80 = \$20$

Using Equation 12.1, we have the following:

$$CSL^* = \text{probability (demand} \le O^*) \ge \frac{150}{150 + 20} = 0.88$$

The optimal order size is obtained using Equation 12.2 and the expected profit using Equation 12.3. The order size and expected profit as forecast accuracy (measured by standard deviation of forecast error) varies are shown in Table 12.3.

Example 12.5 illustrates that as a firm improves its forecast accuracy, expected quantity over- and understocked declines and expected profit increases. This relationship is shown in Figure 12.3.

> **Key Point**   An increase in forecast accuracy decreases both the overstocked and understocked quantity and increases a firm's profits.

Quick Response: Impact on Profits and Inventories

Quick response is the set of actions a supply chain takes that lead to a reduction in the replenishment lead time. Supply chain managers are able to increase their forecast accuracy as lead times decrease, which allows them to better match supply with demand and increase supply chain profitability.

To illustrate the issues, consider the example of Saks Fifth Avenue, another high-end department store, purchasing cashmere shawls from India and Nepal. The selling season for cashmere shawls is about fourteen weeks. Historically, replenishment lead times have been on the order of twenty five to thirty weeks. With a thirty-week lead time, the buyer at Saks must order all the store expects to sell well before the start of the sales season. It is difficult for a buyer to make an accurate forecast of demand this far in advance. This results in high demand uncertainty, leading the buyer to order either too many or too few shawls each year. If the Asian manufacturers decrease the replenishment lead time to fifteen weeks, the buyer at Saks must still place the entire

TABLE 12.3   Expected Profit and Order Size at Bloomingdales

Standard Deviation of Forecast Error σ	Optimal Order Size O*	Expected Overstock	Expected Understock	Expected Profit
150	526	186.7	8.6	$47,469
120	491	149.3	6.9	$48,476
90	456	112.0	5.2	$49,482
60	420	74.7	3.5	$50,488
30	385	37.3	1.7	$51,494
0	350	0	0	$52,500

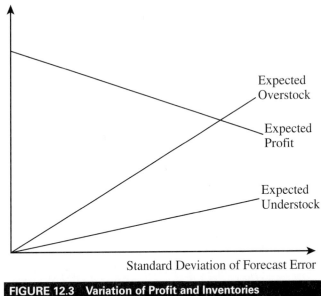

**FIGURE 12.3   Variation of Profit and Inventories
with Forecast Accuracy**

order before the start of the sales season. However, the order can now be placed closer to the sales season, resulting in a more accurate forecast. As was discussed earlier in the chapter, this reduction in uncertainty will increase profits at Saks.

Typically, buyers are able to make very accurate forecasts once they have observed demand for the first week or two in the season. Consider the situation where the manufacturers are able to reduce the replenishment lead time to six weeks. This reduction allows the buyer at Saks to break up the entire season's purchase into two orders. The first order is placed six weeks before the start of the sales season. The buyer orders what the store expects to sell over the first seven weeks of the season. Once sales start, the buyer observes demand for the first week and places a second order after the first week. The second order is to build inventory up to the level that the buyer would like to order for the entire season. The ability to place the second order allows the buyer to match supply and demand much more effectively, resulting in higher profits.

When multiple orders are placed in the season, it is not possible to provide formulas like Equations 12.1–12.5 that specify the optimal order quantity, the expected profit, expected overstock, and expected understock. Rather, we must use simulation (see Appendix 12F) to identify the impact of different ordering policies. We illustrate the impact of being able to place multiple orders using the Saks example discussed earlier.

The buyer at Saks must decide on the quantity of cashmere shawls to order from India and Nepal for the upcoming winter season. The unit cost of each shawl is $40 and the shawl retails for $150. A discount store purchases any leftover shawls at the end of the season for $30. Cost of displaying and holding any unsold shawls is $2 per week in inventory. After the sales season of fourteen weeks, any leftover shawls are sold to the discount store.

Before the start of the sales season, the buyer forecasts weekly demand to be normally distributed with a mean of 20 and a standard deviation of 15. We compare the impact of the following two ordering policies:

1. A single order must arrive at the beginning of the season to cover the entire season's demand.
2. Two orders are placed in the season, one arriving at the beginning of the season and the other arriving at the beginning of the eighth week.

We consider two instances—one where the buyer's forecast accuracy does not improve for the second order and the other where it improves and the buyer is able to reduce the standard deviation of the forecast to 3 instead of 15.

The analysis comparing the two policies is done using a simulation. We compare inventory levels as well as profitability for ordering policies in the single and double order scenario that provide the same level of service.

When placing a single order, the ordering policy consists of a quantity to be ordered at the beginning of the season. When placing two orders, the ordering policy consists of an initial order quantity for the first seven weeks followed by an order-up-to level for the second seven weeks. The idea is that the quantity ordered in the second round should account for sales during the first seven weeks and the inventory remaining. If very little has sold during the first seven weeks, the second order should be small because a lot of inventory remains from the first order. If a lot has sold during the first seven weeks, the second order should be large. The quantity ordered in the second round is the difference between the order-up-to level and the inventory remaining after the first seven weeks.

In the simulation we assume that any unfilled demand is lost. In Table 12.4 we report results for the case when there is no improvement in forecast accuracy for the second order. The results given are an average of 500 different simulations.

TABLE 12.4 Expected Profit and Overstock at Saks Fifth Avenue with No Improvement in Forecast Accuracy for Second Order

| | Single Order for Season | | | Two Orders in the Season | | | | |
CSL	Order Size	Average Overstock	Expected Profit	Initial Order	Order-Up-To Level for Second Order	Average Total Order	Average Overstock	Expected Profit
0.96	378	97	$23,624	209	209	349	69	$26,590
0.94	367	86	$24,034	201	201	342	60	$27,085
0.91	355	73	$24,617	193	193	332	52	$27,154
0.87	343	66	$24,386	184	184	319	43	$26,944
0.81	329	55	$24,609	174	174	313	36	$27,413
0.75	317	41	$25,205	166	166	302	32	$26,915

From the results in Table 12.4, we observe three important consequences of being able to place a second order in the season.

1. The expected total quantity ordered during the season with two orders is less than that with a single order for the same cycle service level. In other words, it is possible to provide the same level of product availability to the customer with less inventory if a second follow-up order is allowed in the sales season.
2. The average overstock to be disposed of at the end of the sales season is less if two orders are allowed.
3. The profits are higher when a second order is allowed during the sales season.

In other words, as the total quantity for the season is broken up into multiple smaller orders, the buyer is better able to match supply and demand and increase profitability for Saks. These relationships are shown in Figures 12.4 and 12.5.

We now consider the case where the buyer improves his or her forecast accuracy for the second order after observing some of the season's demand. As a result, the standard deviation of weekly demand forecast reduces from 15 to 3 for the second ten-week period. To provide the same service level, the second order-up-to level is adjusted appropriately. The results of the simulations are shown in Table 12.5.

From Table 12.5, observe that the reduction in demand uncertainty that occurs after the first seven weeks further enhances the benefits of quick response and the ability to place a second order. Profits at Saks increase and the expected overstock quantity decreases.

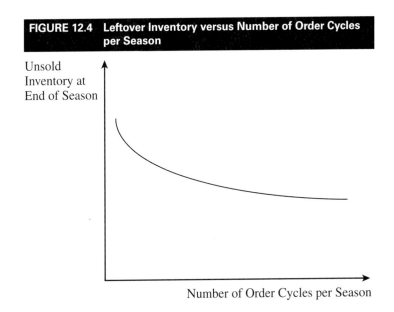

FIGURE 12.4   Leftover Inventory versus Number of Order Cycles per Season

Unsold Inventory at End of Season

Number of Order Cycles per Season

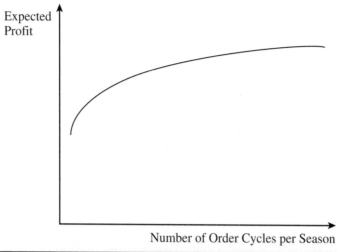

FIGURE 12.5 **Expected Profit versus Number of Order Cycles per Season**

> **Key Point** If quick response allows multiple orders in the season, profits increase and the overstock quantity decreases.

From our previous discussion, quick response is clearly advantageous to a retailer in the supply chain—with one caveat. As the manufacturer reduces replenishment lead times allowing for a second order, we have seen that the retailer's order size drops. In effect, the manufacturer sells less to the retailer. Thus, quick response results in the manufacturer making a lower profit in the short term if all else is unchanged. This is an important point to consider, because decreasing replenishment lead times requires tremendous effort from the manufacturer, yet seems to benefit the retailer at the expense of the manufacturer. The benefits resulting from quick response should be shared appropriately across the supply chain.

TABLE 12.5 **Expected Profit and Overstock at Saks Assuming Forecast Accuracy Improves for Second Order**

	Single Order for Season			Two Orders in the Season				
CSL	Order Size	Average Overstock	Expected Profit	Initial Order	Order-Up-To Level for Second Order	Average Total Order	Average Overstock	Expected Profit
0.96	378	96	$23,707	209	153	292	19	$27,007
0.94	367	84	$24,303	201	152	293	18	$27,371
0.91	355	76	$24,154	193	150	288	17	$26,946
0.87	343	63	$24,807	184	148	288	14	$27,583
0.81	329	52	$24,998	174	146	283	14	$27,162
0.75	317	44	$24,887	166	145	282	14	$27,268

Postponement: Impact on Profits and Inventories

As discussed in Chapter 11, postponement refers to the delay of product differentiation until closer to the sale of the product. With postponement, all activities prior to product differentiation require aggregate forecasts that are more accurate than individual product forecasts. Individual product forecasts are required close to the time of sale when demand is known with greater accuracy. As a result, postponement allows a supply chain to better match supply with demand.

Postponement can be a powerful managerial lever to increase profitability. It can be particularly valuable in e-commerce because of the lag that exists between the time customers place an order and when they expect delivery. If the supply chain can postpone product differentiation until after receiving the customer order, a significant increase in profits and reduction in inventories can be achieved.

The major benefit of postponement arises from the improved matching of supply and demand. There is, however, a cost associated with postponement because the production cost using postponement is typically higher than the production cost without it. For example, the production process at Benetton where assembled knit garments are dyed costs about 10 percent more than if dyed thread is knitted. Similarly, when Hewlett-Packard postpones some assembly steps for its European printers to the European DC, manufacturing costs increase because packing, unpacking, and some other steps have to be duplicated. Given the increased production cost from postponement, a company should quantify the benefits and ensure that they are larger than the additional costs.

Postponement is valuable for a firm that sells a large variety of products with demand that is independent and comparable in size. We illustrate this using the Benetton example. A large fraction of Benetton's sales are from knit garments in solid colors. Starting with thread, there are two steps to completing the garment—dying and knitting. Traditionally, thread was dyed and then the garment was knitted (Option 1). Benetton developed a procedure where dying was postponed until after the garment was knitted (Option 2).

Benetton sells each knit garment at a retail price $p = \$50$. Option 1 results in a manufacturing cost of $20, whereas Option 2 results in a manufacturing cost of $22 per garment. Benetton disposes of any unsold garments at the end of the season in a clearance for $s = \$10$ each. The knitting or manufacturing process takes a total of twenty weeks. For the sake of discussion, we assume that Benetton sells garments in four colors. Twenty weeks in advance, Benetton forecasts demand for each color to be normally distributed with a mean of $\mu = 1,000$ and a standard deviation of $\sigma = 500$. Demand for each color is independent. With Option 1, Benetton makes the buying decision for each color twenty weeks before the sale period and holds separate inventories for each color. With Option 2, Benetton forecasts only the aggregate uncolored thread to purchase twenty weeks in advance. The inventory held is based on the aggregate demand across all four colors. They decide the quantity for individual colors after demand is known. We now quantify the impact of postponement for Benetton.

With Option 1, Benetton must decide on the quantity of colored thread to purchase for each color. For each color we have the following:

Retail price $p = \$50$,
Manufacturing cost $c = \$20$,
Salvage value $s = \$10$.

Using Equation 12.1 we obtain the optimal cycle service level for each color as follows:

$$CSL^* = \frac{p-c}{p-s} = \frac{30}{40} = 0.75$$

Using Equation 12.2, the optimal purchase quantity of thread in each color is as follows:

$$O^* = NORMINV(CSL^*, \mu, \sigma) = NORMINV(0.75, 1000, 500) = 1,337.$$

Thus, it is optimal for Benetton to produce 1,337 units of each color. Using Equation 12.3, the expected profit from each color is as follows:

$$\text{Expected profits} = \$23,644.$$

Using Equations 12.4 and 12.5, the expected over- and understock for each color is as follows:

Expected overstock = 412,
Expected understock = 75.

Using Option 1, across all four colors Benetton thus produces 5,348 sweaters. This results in an expected profit of $94,576, with an average of 1,648 sweaters sold on clearance at the end of the season and 300 customers turned away for lack of sweaters.

Under Option 2, Benetton has to decide on the total number of sweaters across all four colors to be produced because they can be dyed to the appropriate color once demand is known. In this case we have the following:

Retail price $p = \$50$,
Manufacturing cost $c = \$22$,
Salvage value $s = \$10$.

Using Equation 12.1, the optimal cycle service level for each color is as follows:

$$CSL^* = \frac{p-c}{p-s} = \frac{28}{40} = 0.70$$

Given that demand for each color is independent, total demand across all four colors can be evaluated using Equations 11.12 and 11.13 to be normally distributed with a mean of μ_A and a standard deviation of σ_A, where

$$\mu_A = 4 \times 1,000 = 4,000 \qquad \sigma_A = \sqrt{4} \times 500 = 1,000$$

Using Equation 12.2, the optimal aggregate production quantity for Benetton is given by O_A^* where

$$O_A^* = NORMINV(CSL^*, \mu_A, \sigma_A) = NORMINV(0.7, 4000, 1000) = 4{,}524.$$

Under Option 2, it is optimal for Benetton to produce 4,524 undyed sweaters to be dyed as demand by color is available. The expected profit is evaluated using Equation 12.3 as follows:

$$\text{Expected profits} = \$98{,}092.$$

Using Equation 12.4, the expected overstock is 715 and the expected understock is 190. Thus, postponement increases expected profits for Benetton from \$94,576 to \$98,092. Expected overstock declines from 1,648 to 715, and the expected understock declines from 300 to 190. Clearly, the use of postponement and production using Option 2 is a good choice for Benetton in this case.

> **Key Point**   Postponement allows a firm to increase profits and better match supply and demand if the firm produces a large variety of products whose demand is not positively correlated and is of about the same size.

Postponement is not very effective if a large fraction of demand comes from a single product. This is because the benefit from aggregation is small in this case, whereas the increased production cost applies to all items produced. We illustrate this idea once again using Benetton as an example.

Assume that demand for red sweaters at Benetton is forecast to be normally distributed with a mean of $\mu_{red} = 3{,}100$ and a standard deviation of $\sigma_{red} = 800$. Demand for the other three colors is forecast to be normally distributed with a mean of $\mu = 300$ and a standard deviation of $\sigma = 200$. Observe that red sweaters constitute about 80 percent of demand.

Under Option 1, the optimal cycle service level CSL^* is 0.75, as evaluated earlier. Using Equation 12.2, the optimal production of red sweaters is given by the following:

$$O^* = NORMINV(CSL^*, \mu_{red}, \sigma_{red}) = NORMINV(0.75, 3100, 800) = 3{,}640.$$

Using Equation 12.3, the expected profit from red sweaters is \$82,831. Using Equation 12.4, the expected overstock of red sweaters is 659; using Equation 12.5, the expected understock of red sweaters is 119. For each of the other three colors, we can similarly evaluate the optimal production to be 435 sweaters. This results in an expected profit of \$6,458, an expected overstock of 165, and an expected understock of 30. Across all four colors, Option 1 thus results in the following:

Total production = 4,945,
Expected profit = \$102,205,
Expected overstock = 1,154,
Expected understock = 209.

Under Option 2, Benetton has to decide only the total production across all four colors. Given that demand for each color is independent, total demand across all four colors can be evaluated using Equations 11.12 and 11.13 to be normally distributed with a mean of μ_A and a standard deviation of σ_A, where

$$\mu_A = 3{,}100 + 3 \times 300 = 4{,}000, \sigma_A = 872.$$

Under Option 2, we repeat all calculations to obtain the following:

Total production = 4,457,
Expected profit = $99,872,
Expected overstock = 623,
Expected understock = 166.

In this case, Benetton sees its profits decline as a result of postponement. This is because a large fraction of demand is from red sweaters, which can already be forecast with reasonably good accuracy. Postponement and the resulting aggregation thus do little to improve the forecasting accuracy of red sweaters. It does, however, improve the forecasting accuracy for the other three colors, but they represent a small fraction of demand. Meanwhile, the production costs increase for all sweaters. As a result, the increased production costs outweigh the benefits from postponement.

> **Key Point**   Postponement may reduce overall profits for a firm if a single product contributes the majority of the demand because the increased manufacturing expense due to postponement outweighs the small benefit that aggregation provides in this case.

In *tailored postponement,* a firm uses production with postponement to satisfy a part of its demand with the rest being satisfied without postponement. Tailored postponement produces higher profits than when no postponement is used or all products are manufactured using postponement. Under tailored postponement, a firm produces the amount that is very likely to sell using the lower cost production method without postponement. The firm produces the portion of demand that is uncertain using postponement. On the portion of the demand that is certain, postponement provides little value in terms of increased forecast accuracy. The firm thus produces it using the lower cost method to lower manufacturing cost.

On the portion of demand that is uncertain, postponement significantly improves forecast accuracy. The firm is thus willing to incur the increased production cost to achieve the benefit from the improved matching of supply and demand. We illustrate the idea of tailored postponement, returning to the example of Benetton.

Consider the scenario where Benetton is selling four colors and the forecast demand for each color is normally distributed with a mean of $\mu = 1{,}000$ and a standard deviation of $\sigma = 500$. We have observed earlier that the use of postponement increases profits at Benetton. We now consider a situation where Benetton applies tailored postponement and uses both Option 1 (dye thread and then knit garment) and Option 2 (dye knit garment) for production. For each color, Benetton identifies a quantity Q_1 to be manufactured using Option 1 and an aggregate quantity Q_A to be manufactured using Option 2, with colors for the aggregate quantity being assigned when demand is known. We now identify the appropriate tailored postponement policy and its impact on profits and inventories.

TABLE 12.6 Average of 500 Simulations for Tailored Postponement Policies				
Manufacturing Policy		*Average Profit*	*Average Overstock*	*Average Understock*
Q_1	Q_A			
0	4,524	$97,847	510	210
1,337	0	$94,377	1,369	282
700	1,850	$102,730	308	168
800	1,550	$104,603	427	170
900	950	$101,326	607	266
900	1,050	$101,647	664	230
1,000	850	$100,312	815	195
1,000	950	$100,951	803	149
1,100	550	$99,180	1,026	211
1,100	650	$100,510	1,008	185

There is no formula that can be used to evaluate the optimal policy and profits. We thus resort to simulations to study the impact of different policies. The results of various simulations are shown in Table 12.6.

From Table 12.6, we see that Benetton can increase its expected profit to $104,603 by using a tailored postponement policy where 800 units of each color are produced using Option 1 and 1,550 units are produced using Option 2. The resulting profit is higher than if all units are produced entirely using Option 1 or 2. It is quite likely that demand for each color will be 800 or higher. The tailored postponement policy exploits this fact and produces these units using Option 1, which has a low cost. The remaining units are produced using Option 2 so that demand uncertainty can be reduced by aggregation.

> **Key Point** Tailored postponement allows a firm to increase its profitability by only postponing the uncertain part of the demand and producing the predictable part at a lower cost without postponement.

Tailored Sourcing: Impact on Profits and Inventories

In *tailored sourcing,* firms use a combination of two supply sources, one focusing on cost but unable to handle uncertainty well, and the other focusing on flexibility to handle uncertainty, but at a higher cost. For tailored sourcing to be effective, having supply sources where one serves as the backup to the other is not sufficient. The two sources must focus on different capabilities. The low-cost source must focus on being efficient and should only be required to supply the predictable portion of the demand. The flexible source should focus on being responsive and be required to supply the uncertain portion of the demand. As a result, tailored sourcing allows a firm to increase its profits and better match supply and demand. The value of tailored sourcing depends on the reduction in cost that can be achieved as a result of one source facing no variability. If this benefit is small, tailored sourcing may not be ideal because of the added complexity of implementation. Tailored sourcing may be volume based or product based depending on the source of uncertainty.

In volume-based tailored sourcing, the predictable part of a product's demand is produced at an efficient facility, whereas the uncertain portion is produced at a flexible facility. Benetton provides an example of volume-based tailored sourcing.

Benetton requires retailers to commit to about 65 percent of their orders about seven months before the start of the sales season. Benetton subcontracts production of this portion without uncertainty to low-cost sources that have long lead times of several months. For the other 35 percent, Benetton allows retailers to place orders much closer to or even after the start of the selling season. All uncertainty is concentrated in this portion of the order. Benetton produces this portion of the order in a plant they own that is very flexible. Production at the Benetton plant is more expensive than production at the subcontractor's. However, the plant can produce with a lead time of weeks. A combination of the two sources allows Benetton to reduce its inventories while incurring a high cost of production for only a fraction of its demand. This allows it to increase profits.

Volume-based tailored sourcing should be considered by firms that have moved a lot of their production overseas to take advantage of lower costs. The lower costs have also been accompanied by longer lead times. In such a situation, having a flexible local source with short lead times can be very effective even if the local source is more expensive. Long lead times require large safety inventories and the resulting mismatch of supply and demand hurts profits. The presence of the local source allows the firm to carry low safety inventories and supply any excess demand from the local source. The most effective combination is for the overseas source to focus on replenishing cycle inventories ignoring uncertainty. The local source is used as a backup any time demand exceeds the inventory available.

In product-based tailored sourcing, low-volume products with uncertain demand are obtained from a flexible source while high-volume products with less demand uncertainty are obtained from an efficient source. An example of product-based tailored sourcing is Levi Strauss. Levi sells standard-sized jeans as well as jeans that can be customized to fit an individual. Standard jeans have relatively stable demand while demand for custom jeans is unpredictable. Custom jeans are produced at a flexible facility while standard jeans are produced at an efficient facility.

In some instances new products have very uncertain demand while well-established products have more stable demand. Product-based tailored sourcing may be implemented with a flexible facility focusing on new products, and efficient facilities focusing on the well-established products.

12.4 SUPPLY CHAIN CONTRACTS AND THEIR IMPACT ON PROFITABILITY

A *contract* specifies the parameters within which a buyer places orders and a supplier fulfills them. A contract may contain specifications regarding quantity, price, time, and quality. At one extreme, a contract may require the buyer to specify the precise quantity required, with a very long lead time. In this case, the buyer bears the risk of over- and understocking, whereas the supplier has exact order information well in advance of delivery. At the other extreme, buyers may not be required to commit to the precise purchase quantity until they are certain of their demand, with the supply arriving with a short lead time. In this case, the supplier has little advance information, whereas the buyer can wait until demand is known before ordering. As a result, the supplier must build inventory in advance and bear most of the risk of over- or understocking. As contracts change, the risk each stage of the supply chain bears changes, which affects the retailers' and suppliers' decisions and the supply chain's profitability.

Consider, for example, Tech Fiber (TF), a manufacturer of synthetic fibers used in ski jackets and other winter outerwear. TF has patented a new lightweight fiber that is very inexpensive to manufacture but has the warmth and water-repellent properties of very expensive natural fibers. TF has designed a new jacket using this fiber that it wants to bring to the market. The jacket will be sold exclusively through Ski Adventure (SA), a major retailer of winter apparel and sport equipment. Each jacket costs $v = \$10$ to produce and TF plans to charge a wholesale price of $c = \$100$ per jacket from the retailer. The retailer plans to sell the jacket for a price of $p = \$200$. At this price, the manager at SA estimates the demand for the new jacket to be normally distributed with a mean of $\mu = 1,000$ and a standard deviation of $\sigma = 300$. To simplify the discussion, assume that SA is unable to salvage anything for unsold jackets, resulting in a salvage value of $s = \$0$.

Using Equation 12.1, the manager at SA obtains an optimal cycle service level of $CSL^* = 0.5$. Using Equation 12.2, the manager finds it optimal to order 1,000 jackets. Using Equation 12.3, the manager evaluates expected profit at the end of the season as a result of this policy at $76,063. In this case, TF sells 1,000 jackets for a total profit of $90,000. The total expected supply chain profit in this case is $166,063.

Observe that the supply chain makes $190 for each jacket sold. The ordering decision, however, is made by the manager at SA, and SA makes a margin of $100 per jacket, which is lower than the margin for the entire supply chain. Meanwhile, SA loses $100 for each unsold jacket, whereas the supply chain as a whole only loses $10. As a result, the manager at SA orders fewer jackets than is optimal from the perspective of the entire supply chain acting as one. From the perspective of the entire supply chain, the cost of understocking is $190 and the cost of overstocking is $10. It is thus optimal for the supply chain to provide a cycle service level of 0.95 and produce 1,493 jackets. This results in a total supply chain profit of $183,812.

The gap in profit exists because of *double marginalization*. Double marginalization refers to the fact that the total supply chain margin of $190 is divided between $90 for the manufacturer and $100 for the retailer. Thus each party makes decisions considering only a portion of the total supply chain margin. In this case, a decision by the SA manager (the size of the order) affects profits at TF. The manager at SA, however, does not take TF profits into account when making her decision. As a result, her decision does not maximize supply chain profits.

We next consider how TF can offer buy-back contracts to induce the manager at SA to order quantities that increase the total supply chain profit.

Returns Policies: Buy-Back Contracts

A manufacturer can increase the quantity the retailer purchases by offering to buy back any leftover units at the end of the season at a fraction of the purchase price. This action has the effect of increasing the salvage value per unit for the retailer who, as a result, increases its order size. The manufacturer may benefit by taking on some of the cost of overstocking because the supply chain will, on average, end up selling more products.

In a *buy-back contract,* the manufacturer specifies a wholesale price c along with a buy-back price b at which the retailer can return any unsold units at the end of the season. We assume that the manufacturer can salvage $\$s_M$ for any units that the retailer returns.

The optimal order quantity O^* for a retailer in response to a buy-back contract is evaluated using Equations 12.1 and 12.2, where the salvage value for the retailer is $s = b$. The expected retailer profit is evaluated using Equation 12.3. The expected profit at the manufacturer depends on the overstock at the retailer (evaluated using Equation 12.4) that is returned. We obtain

Expected manufacturer profit $= O^*(c - v) - (b - s_M) \times$ Expected overstock at retailer.

Table 12.7 provides the outcome for different buy-back contracts that TF offers SA. The sale price of jackets at SA is $p = \$200$ and demand at this price is normally distributed with a mean of $\mu = 1{,}000$ and a standard deviation of $\sigma = 300$. At this stage we assume that there is no transportation or other cost associated with any returns.

From Table 12.7, observe that a buy-back contract allows both the manufacturer, TF, and the retailer, SA, to increase their profits. In Table 12.7, the use of buy-back contracts increases total supply chain profits by about 10 percent. Also observe that the buy-back price that maximizes supply chain profits is somewhere between zero and the wholesale price. In general, it is optimal for the manufacturer to offer to buy back at a fraction of the wholesale price.

For a fixed wholesale price, increasing the buy-back price always increases retailer profits. In general, there exists a positive buy-back price at which the manufacturer makes a higher profit compared to offering no buyback. Also observe that buybacks increase profits for the manufacturer more as the manufacturer's margin increases. Thus, the greater the manufacturer's margin, the more they stand to benefit through the use of some mechanism like buy-backs.

In 1932, Viking Press was the first book publisher to accept returns. Today, buy-back contracts are very common in the book industry and publishers accept unsold books from retailers. To minimize the cost associated with a return, retailers do not have to return the book but only the cover. This provides publishers with proof that the book did not sell while reducing the cost of the return. Over the years, there has been

TABLE 12.7 Order Sizes and Profits at SA and TF under Different Buy-Back Contracts

Wholesale Price c	Buy-Back Price b	Optimal Order Size for SA	Expected Profit for SA	Expected Returns to TF	Expected Profit for TF	Expected Supply Chain Profit
$100	$0	1,000	$76,063	120	$90,000	$166,063
$100	$30	1,067	$80,154	156	$91,338	$171,492
$100	$60	1,170	$85,724	223	$91,886	$177,610
$110	$0	962	$66,252	102	$96,230	$162,482
$110	$78	1,191	$78,074	239	$100,480	$178,555
$110	$105	1,486	$86,938	493	$96,872	$183,810
$120	$0	924	$56,819	80	$101,640	$158,459
$120	$96	1,221	$70,508	261	$109,225	$179,733
$120	$116	1,501	$77,500	506	$106,310	$183,810

considerable debate about the impact of publishers' returns policy on profits in the industry. Our discussion provides some justification for the approach taken by the publishers.

From Table 12.7, observe that as the wholesale price increases, it is optimal for the manufacturer to increase the buy-back price as well. Also observe that for a fixed wholesale price, as the buy-back price increases, the retailer orders more and also returns more. In our analysis in Table 12.7, we have not considered the cost associated with a return. As the cost associated with a return increases, buy-back contracts become less attractive because the cost of returns reduces supply chain profits. If return costs are very high, buy-back contracts can reduce the total profits of the supply chain far more than is the case without any buy back.

> **Key Point** Manufacturers can use buy-back contracts to increase their own profits as well as total supply chain profits. Buybacks encourage retailers to increase the level of product availability.

In some instances, manufacturers use holding cost subsidies to encourage retailers to order more. With *holding cost subsidies,* manufacturers pay retailers a certain amount for every unit held in inventory over a given period. Holding cost subsidies behave very much like buy-back contracts in their impact on manufacturer and supply chain profits.

Next we discuss how revenue-sharing contracts allow a supply chain to increase total profits.

Revenue-Sharing Contracts

In *revenue-sharing* contracts, the manufacturer charges the retailer a low wholesale price and shares a fraction of the revenue generated by the retailer. Even if no returns are allowed, the lower wholesale price decreases the cost to the retailer in case of an overstock. The retailer thus increases the level of product availability resulting in higher profits for both the manufacturer and the retailer.

Assume that the manufacturer has a production cost v, charges a wholesale price of c, and shares a fraction f of the retailer's revenue. The retailer charges a retail price p and can salvage any leftover units for s_R. The optimal order quantity O^* ordered by the retailer is evaluated using Equations 12.1 and 12.2, where the cost of understocking is $C_u = (1 - f)p - c$ and the cost of overstocking is $C_o = c - s_R$. We thus obtain the following:

$$CSL^* = \text{probability}(\text{demand} \leq O^*) = \frac{C_u}{C_u + C_o} = \frac{(1-f)p - c}{(1-f)p - s_R}.$$

The manufacturer obtains the wholesale price c for each unit purchased by the retailer and a share of the revenue for each unit sold by the retailer. The expected overstock at the retailer is obtained using Equation 12.4. The manufacturer's profits are thus evaluated as follows:

$$\text{Expected manufacturer's profits} = (c - v)\, O^*$$
$$+ fp(O^* - \text{expected overstock at retailer}).$$

The retailer pays a wholesale price c for each unit purchased and obtains a revenue of $(1 - f)p$ for each unit sold and a revenue of s_R for each unit overstocked. The retailer's expected profit is thus evaluated as follows:

$$\text{Expected retailer profit} = (1 - f)p(O^* - \text{expected overstock at retailer})$$
$$+ s_R \times \text{expected overstock at retailer} - cO^*.$$

Consider the example where TF charges only $c = \$10$ for each jacket. SA in turn sells the jacket for $p = \$200$ and shares a fraction f of the revenue with TF. Demand at this price is normally distributed with a mean of $\mu = 1{,}000$ and a standard deviation of $\sigma = 300$. SA is assumed to have no salvage value for any leftover jackets. Table 12.8 provides the outcome for different revenue-sharing fractions.

From Tables 12.7 and 12.8, observe that revenue sharing allows both the manufacturer and retailer to increase their profits in the absence of buybacks. When charging a wholesale price of \$100, TF makes profit of \$90,000 and SA makes a profit of \$76,063 (see Table 12.7). With a revenue-sharing contract that shares 50 percent of the revenue (TF gets revenue of \$100 for each jacket sold), however, TF makes a profit of \$98,580 and SA makes a profit of \$84,735. With a wholesale price of \$10 and 50 percent revenue sharing it is optimal for SA to order 1,384 jackets, whereas with a wholesale price of \$100 and no revenue sharing, SA orders only 1,000 jackets. SA is willing to increase its order size under revenue sharing because the cost of overstocking under revenue sharing is only \$10, whereas the cost of overstocking is \$100 per jacket with a wholesale price of \$100 and no revenue sharing.

Revenue-sharing contracts have been used in the video rental industry. Blockbuster video shares a fraction of the rental revenues with the studios. The studios, in turn, charge Blockbuster a low wholesale price for videos. Revenue sharing increases product availability for the end customer and generates profits for both the manufacturer and retailer.

TABLE 12.8   Order Sizes and Profits at SA and TF under Different Revenue-Sharing Contracts

Wholesale Price c	Revenue-Sharing Fraction f	Optimal Order Size for SA	Expected Overstock at SA	Expected Profit for SA	Expected Profit for TF	Expected Supply Chain Profit
$10	0.3	1,440	449	$124,273	$59,429	$183,702
$10	0.5	1,384	399	$84,735	$98,580	$183,315
$10	0.7	1,290	317	$45,503	$136,278	$181,781
$10	0.9	1,000	120	$7,606	$158,457	$166,063
$20	0.3	1,320	342	$110,523	$71,886	$182,409
$20	0.5	1,252	286	$71,601	$109,176	$180,777
$20	0.7	1,129	195	$33,455	$142,051	$175,506

> **Key Point** Revenue sharing with a lower wholesale price allows both retailers and manufacturers to increase their profit. Revenue sharing encourages retailers to increase the level of product availability.

Next we discuss how quantity flexibility contracts allow a supply chain to increase total profits.

Quantity Flexibility Contracts

In *quantity flexibility contracts*, the manufacturer allows the retailer to change the quantity ordered after observing demand. If a retailer orders O units, the manufacturer commits to providing $Q = (1 + \alpha)O$ units, whereas the retailer is committed to buying at least $q = (1 - \beta)O$ units. Both α and β are between 0 and 1. The retailer can purchase up to Q units depending on the demand they observe. These contracts are similar to buy-back contracts in that the manufacturer now bears some of the risk of having excess inventory. Because no returns are required, these contracts can be more effective than buy-back contracts when the cost of returns is high. Quantity flexibility contracts increase the average amount the retailer purchases and may increase total supply chain profits.

Assume that the manufacturer incurs a production cost of $v per unit and charges a wholesale price of $c from the retailer. The retailer in turn sells to customers for a price of $p. The retailer salvages any leftover units for s_R. The manufacturer salvages any leftover units for s_M. If retailer demand is normally distributed with a mean of μ and a standard deviation of σ, we can evaluate the impact of a quantity flexibility contract. If the retailer orders O units, the manufacturer is committed to supplying Q units. As a result, we assume that the manufacturer produces Q units. The retailer purchases q units if demand D is less than q, D units if demand D is between q and Q, and Q units if demand is higher than Q. We thus obtain

Expected quantity purchased by retailer, $Q_R = qF(q) + Q[1 - F(Q)] +$

$$\mu\left[F_S\left(\frac{Q-\mu}{\sigma}\right) - F_S\left(\frac{q-\mu}{\sigma}\right)\right] - \sigma\left[f_S\left(\frac{Q-\mu}{\sigma}\right) - f_S\left(\frac{q-\mu}{\sigma}\right)\right],$$

Expected quantity sold by retailer $D_R = Q[1 - F(Q)] + \mu F_S\left(\frac{Q-\mu}{\sigma}\right) - \sigma f_S\left(\frac{Q-\mu}{\sigma}\right)$,
Expected overstock at retailer = $Q_R - D_R$,
Expected retailer profit = $D_R \times p + (Q_R - D_R)s_R - Q_R \times c$,
Expected manufacturer profit = $Q_R \times c + (Q - Q_R)s_M - Q \times v$.

We return to the example of TF selling jackets to SA at a wholesale price of $c = \$100$. TF incurs a cost of $v = \$10$ to produce each jacket. SA sells jackets to consumers at a retail price of $p = \$200$. At this price, demand is normally distributed with a mean of $\mu = 1,000$ and a standard deviation of $\sigma = 300$. We assume a salvage value of $0 at both the retailer SA and manufacturer TF. In Table 12.9, we show the impact of

TABLE 12.9 Profits at TF and SA under Different Quantity Flexibility Contracts

α	β	Wholesale Price c	Order Size O	Expected Purchase by SA	Expected Sale by SA	Expected Profits for SA	Expected Profits for TF	Expected Supply Chain Profit
0.00	0.00	$100	1,000	1,000	880	$76,063	$90,000	$166,063
0.20	0.20	$100	1,050	1,024	968	$91,167	$89,830	$180,997
0.40	0.40	$100	1,070	1,011	994	$97,689	$86,122	$183,811
0.00	0.00	$110	962	962	860	$66,252	$96,200	$162,452
0.15	0.15	$110	1,014	1,009	945	$78,153	$99,282	$177,435
0.42	0.42	$110	1,048	1,007	993	$87,932	$95,879	$183,811
0.00	0.00	$120	924	924	838	$56,819	$101,640	$158,459
0.20	0.20	$120	1,000	1,000	955	$70,933	$108,000	$178,933
0.50	0.50	$120	1,040	1,005	994	$78,171	$105,640	$183,811

different quantity flexibility contracts on supply chain profitability. All contracts considered are such that $\alpha = \beta$.

From Table 12.9, observe that quantity flexibility contracts allow both the manufacturer, TF, and the retailer, SA, to increase their profits. It is often in the manufacturer's best interest to offer a quantity flexibility contract to the retailer. In Table 12.9, observe that for wholesale prices of $110 and $120, the manufacturer, TF, increases its profits by offering a quantity flexibility contract. Total supply chain profits also increase with quantity flexibility. Observe that as the manufacturer increases the wholesale price, it is optimal for them to offer greater quantity flexibility to the retailer.

Quantity flexibility contracts are common for components in the electronic and computer industry. In the aforementioned discussion, we considered fairly simple quantity flexibility contracts. Benetton has successfully used sophisticated quantity flexibility contracts with its retailers to increase supply chain profits. We describe such a contract in the context of colored knit garments.[1]

Seven months before delivery, Benetton retailers are required to place their orders. Consider a retailer placing an order for 100 sweaters each in red, blue, and yellow. One to three months before delivery, retailers may alter up to 30 percent of the quantity ordered in any color and assign it to another color. The aggregate order, however, cannot be adjusted at this stage. Potentially the retailer may change the order to 70 red, 70 blue, and 160 yellow sweaters. After the start of the sales season, retailers are allowed to order up to 10 percent of their previous order in any color. Potentially the retailer can order another 30 yellow sweaters. In this quantity flexibility contract, Benetton retailers have a flexibility of up to 10 percent on the aggregate order across all colors and of about 40 percent for individual colors. Retailers can increase the aggregate quantity ordered by up to 10 percent and the quantity for any individual color can be adjusted by up to 40 percent. This flexibility is consistent with the fact that aggregate forecasts are more accurate than forecasts for individual colors. As a result, retailers can better match product availability with demand. The quantity flexibility

[1]See *Benetton (A)*, 1984, by Sergio Signorelli and James L. Heskett.

contract Benetton offers allows both the retailers and Benetton to increase their profits.

> **Key Point**   Manufacturers can use contracts with quantity flexibility to increase their own profits as well as total supply chain profits.

Vendor-Managed Inventory

With *vendor-managed inventory* (VMI), the manufacturer or supplier is responsible for all decisions regarding product inventories at the retailer. As a result, the control of the replenishment decision moves to the manufacturer instead of the retailer. VMI requires the retailer to share demand information with the manufacturer to allow them to make inventory replenishment decisions. VMI can allow a manufacturer to increase their profits as well as profits for the entire supply chain by mitigating some of the effects of double marginalization. Profits increase only if both retailer and manufacturer margins are considered when making inventory decisions. Several firms, including Campbell Soup and Proctor & Gamble, have had successful VMI relationships with retailers.

VMI also helps by conveying customer demand data to the manufacturer, who can then plan production accordingly. This helps improve manufacturer forecasts and better match manufacturer production with customer demand.

One drawback to VMI arises because retailers often sell products from competing manufacturers that are substitutes in the customer's mind. For example, a customer may substitute detergent manufactured by Procter & Gamble with detergent manufactured by Lever Brothers. If the retailer has a VMI agreement with both manufacturers, each manufacturer will ignore the impact of substitution when making their inventory decisions. As a result, inventories at the retailer will be higher than optimal. In such a setting, the retailer may be better positioned to decide on the replenishment policy. Demand data can still be shared with the manufacturer responsible for implementing the replenishment policy.

12.5   SETTING OPTIMAL LEVELS OF PRODUCT AVAILABILITY IN PRACTICE

1. *Use the analytic frameworks in this chapter to increase profits.* Many firms set inventory levels without any supporting analysis. Managers can provide significant value to a firm by introducing the concepts discussed in this chapter. The concepts not only provide an approach for a firm to target the optimal level of product availability, they also help identify key managerial levers that may be used to increase profitability.

2. *Beware of preset levels of availability.* Often companies have a preset target of product availability without any justification. In such a situation, managers should probe the rationale for the targeted level of product availability. A manager can provide significant value by adjusting the targeted level of product availability to one that maximizes profits.

3. *Use approximate costs because profit maximizing solutions are quite robust.* Companies should avoid spending an inordinate amount of effort to get exact estimates of various costs used to evaluate optimal levels of product availability. Levels of

product availability close to optimal will often produce a profit that is very close to the optimal profit. Thus, it is not crucial that all costs be estimated precisely. A reasonable approximation of the costs will generally produce targeted levels of product availability that are close to optimal.

4. *Estimate a range for the cost of stocking out.* Firms' efforts to set levels of product availability often get bogged down in debate over the cost of stocking out. The sometimes controversial nature of this cost and its hard-to-quantify components (such as loss of customer good will) make it a difficult number for people from different functions to agree upon. However, it is often not necessary to estimate a precise cost of stocking out. Using a range of the cost of stocking out, a manager can identify appropriate levels of availability and the associated profits. Often, profits do not change significantly in the range, thus eliminating the need for a more precise estimation of the cost of stocking out.

5. *Ensure levels of product availability fit with strategy.* A manager should use the level of product availability suggested by the analysis along with the firm's strategic objectives when setting the targeted level of product availability. In some instances, a firm may find it appropriate to provide a high level of product availability for a low-demand item that is not very profitable but is required by important customers. A firm trying to project a reputation for product availability may find it appropriate to provide a high level of availability for all products, even if the margins of each individual product do not justify it.

12.6 SUMMARY OF LEARNING OBJECTIVES

1. Identify the factors affecting the optimal level of product availability and evaluate the optimal cycle service level.

   The cost of overstocking by one unit and the lost current and future margin from understocking by one unit are the two major factors that affect the optimal level of product availability. The optimal level of availability is obtained by balancing the costs of over- and understocking. As the cost of overstocking increases, it is optimal to lower the targeted level of product availability. As the lost margin from being out of stock increases, it is optimal to raise the targeted level of product availability.

2. Use managerial levers that improve supply chain profitability through optimal service levels.

   A manager may increase supply chain profitability by (a) increasing the salvage value of each unit overstocked, (b) decreasing the margin lost from a stockout, (c) using improved forecasting to reduce demand uncertainty, (d) using quick response to reduce lead times and allow multiple orders in a season, (e) using postponement to delay product differentiation, and (f) using tailored sourcing with a flexible, short lead time supply source serving as a backup for a low-cost, long supply source with long lead times.

3. Construct contracts that increase supply chain profitability.

   Using contracts that counteract double marginalization increases supply chain profitability. In many instances, a manager can increase supply chain profitability by structuring contracts that allow (a) return of surplus inventory, (b) subsidies for holding inventory, (c) revenue sharing, (d) quantity flexibility when ordering, and (e) VMI.

DISCUSSION QUESTIONS

1. Consider two products with the same cost but different margins. Which product should have a higher level of product availability? Why?
2. Consider two products with the same margin carried by a retail store. Any left-over units of one product are worthless. Leftover units of the other product can be sold to outlet stores. Which product should have a higher level of availability? Why?
3. A firm improves its forecast accuracy using better market intelligence? What impact will this have on supply chain inventories and profitability? Why?
4. How can postponement of product differentiation be used to improve supply chain profitability?
5. Mattel has historically allowed toy retailers to place two orders for the holiday shopping season. Mattel is considering allowing retailers to place only one order. What impact will this have on retailer orders? What impact will this have on supply chain profits?
6. Discuss how an expensive supplier with short lead times who is used as a backup for a low-cost supplier with long lead times can result in higher profits than using only the low-cost supplier.
7. How does a contract with buy backs allow a manufacturer to increase their profits as well as supply chain profits?
8. How does a contract with revenue sharing and a low wholesale price allow both the manufacturer and retailer to increase their profits?
9. How does a contract with quantity flexibility allow a manufacturer to increase their profits as well as supply chain profits?

EXERCISES

1. Green Thumb, a manufacturer of lawn care equipment, has introduced a new product. The anticipated demand is normally distributed with a mean of $\mu = 100$ and a standard deviation of $\sigma = 40$. Each unit costs $150 to manufacture and the introductory price is to be $200 to achieve this level of sales. Any unsold units at the end of the season are unlikely to be very valuable and will be disposed of in a fire sale for $50 each. It costs $20 to hold a unit in inventory for the entire season. How many units should Green Thumb manufacture for sale? What is the expected profit from this policy? On average, how many customers does Green Thumb expect to turn away because of stocking out?
2. The general manager at Green Thumb decides to conduct extensive market research for its new product. At the end of the market research, the manager estimates demand to be normally distributed with a mean of $\mu = 100$ and a standard deviation of $\sigma = 15$. How should Green Thumb alter its production plans in Problem 1 as a result of the market research? How much increase in profit are they likely to observe? How does the improved forecast impact the demand lost by Green Thumb because of understocking? Use cost and price information from Problem 1.
3. The manager at Goodstone Tires, a distributor of tires in Illinois, uses a continuous review policy to manage their inventory. The manager currently orders

10,000 tires when the inventory of tires drops to 6,000. Weekly demand for tires is normally distributed with a mean of 2,000 and a standard deviation of 500. The replenishment lead time for tires is two weeks. Each tire costs Goodstone $40 and the company sells each tire for $80. Goodstone incurs a holding cost of 25 percent. How much safety inventory does Goodstone currently carry? At what cost of understocking is the manager's current inventory policy justified? How much safety inventory should Goodstone carry if the cost of understocking is $80 per tire in lost current and future margin?

4. Champion manufactures winter fleece jackets for sale in the United States. Demand for jackets during the season is normally distributed with a mean of 20,000 and a standard deviation of 10,000. Each jacket sells for $60 and costs $30 to produce. Any leftover jackets at the end of the season are currently sold for $25 at the year-end clearance sale. Holding jackets until the year-end sale adds another $5 to their cost. A recent recruit has suggested shipping leftover jackets to South America for sale in the winter there rather than running a clearance. Each jacket will fetch a price of $35 in South America and all jackets sent there are likely to sell. Shipping costs add $5 to the cost of any jacket sold in South America. Would you recommend the South American option? How will this decision impact production decisions at Champion? How will it impact profitability at Champion? On average, how many jackets will Champion ship to South America each season?

5. Snoblo, a manufacturer of snow blowers, currently sells four models. The base model, Reguplo, has demand that is normally distributed with a mean of 10,000 and a standard deviation of 1,000. The three other models have additional features and each has demand that is normally distributed with a mean of 1,000 and a standard deviation of 700. Currently all four models are manufactured on the same line at a cost of $100 for Reguplo and $110 for each of the other three models. Reguplo sells for $200 while each of the other three models sells for $220. Any unsold blowers are sold at the end of the season for $80. Snoblo is considering the use of tailored sourcing by setting up two separate lines, one for Reguplo and one for the other three. Given that no changeovers will be required on the Reguplo line, the production cost of Reguplo is expected to decline to $90. The production cost of the other three products, however, will now increase to $120. Do you recommend tailored sourcing for Snoblo? How will tailored sourcing impact production and profits? Ignore holding costs for snow blowers.

6. AnyLogo supplies firms with apparel containing their logo to be used for promotional purposes. Currently AnyLogo has four major customers—IBM, AT&T, HP, and Cisco. During the holiday season, the logos are adorned with a Christmas motif. Demand from each firm for apparel with the Christmas motif is normally distributed as shown in Table 12.10.

TABLE 12.10 Demand Distribution for AnyLogo				
	IBM	*AT&T*	*HP*	*Cisco*
Mean	5,000	7,000	4,000	4,000
SD	2,000	2,500	2,000	2,200

AnyLogo currently produces all the apparel including the logo embroidery in Sri Lanka in advance of the holiday season. Each unit costs $15 and is sold by AnyLogo for $50. Any leftover inventory at the end of the holiday season is essentially worthless and is donated by AnyLogo to charity. Holding the apparel in inventory adds another $3 to the cost per unit donated to inventory. However, the donation allows AnyLogo to recover $6 per unit in tax savings. What production quantities do you recommend for AnyLogo? What is the expected profit from the policy? On average, how much does AnyLogo expect to donate to charity each year?

7. The manager at AnyLogo is considering the purchase of high-speed embroidery machines that will allow them to embroider on demand. In this case the apparel will be made in Sri Lanka without any logo; the logo embroidery is postponed and will be done in the United States on demand. This will raise the cost per unit to $18. However, AnyLogo will not have any holiday or company-specific apparel to be disposed of at the end of the season. The apparel without logos can be sold for $18 a unit to retailers. The cost of holding inventory and shipping adds $4 to the cost of any apparel left over after the holiday season. With all other information as in Problem 6, do you recommend that the manager at AnyLogo implement postponement? What will the impact of postponement be on profits and inventories?

BIBLIOGRAPHY

Cachon, G., and M. L. Fisher. 1997. "Campbell Soup's Continuous Product Replenishment Program: Evaluation and Enhanced Decision Rules." *Production and Operations Management* 6: 266–276.

Cachon, G. P., and M. A. Lariviere. 2001. "Turning the Supply Chain into a Revenue Chain." *Harvard Business Review* (March): 20–21.

Clark, T., and J. Hammond. 1997. "Reengineering Channel Reordering Processes to Improve Total Supply Chain Performance." *Production and Operations Management* 6: 248–265.

Fisher, M. L., J. H. Hammond, W. R. Obermeyer, and A. Raman. 1994. "Making Supply Meet Demand in an Uncertain World." *Harvard Business Review* (May–June): 83–93.

Nahmias, Steven. 1997. *Production and Operations Analysis*. Burr Ridge, Ill.: Richard P. Irwin.

Padmanabhan, V., and I. P. L. Png. 1995. "Returns Policies: Making Money by Making Good." *Sloan Management Review* (Fall): 65–72.

Pasternack, B. A. (1985). "Optimal Pricing and Return Policies for Perishable Commodities." *Marketing Science* 4: 166–176.

Signorelli, Sergio, and James L. Heskett. 1984. "Benetton (A)." Harvard Business School Case 9-685-014.

Silver, Edward A., David Pyke, and Rein Petersen. 1998. *Inventory Management and Production Planning and Scheduling*. New York: John Wiley & Sons.

Tayur, Sridhar, Ram Ganeshan, and Michael Magazine, eds. 1999. *Quantitative Models for Supply Chain Management*. Boston: Kluwer Academic Publishers.

"The Critical-Fractile Method for Inventory Planning." 1991. Harvard Business School Note 9-191-132.

---------------------------------- A P P E N D I X   1 2 A ----------------------------------

Optimal Level of Product Availability

Objective: Evaluate level of product availability that maximizes profit.

Analysis: In this analysis we assume that the demand is a continuous nonnegative random variable with density function $f(x)$ and cumulative distribution function $F(x)$. C_u is the margin per unit and as a result the cost of understocking per unit. C_o is the cost of overstocking per unit.

Assume that Q units are purchased and a demand of x units arises. If $Q < x$, all Q units are sold and a profit of QC_u results. On the other hand, if $Q \geq x$, only x units are sold and a profit of $xC_u - (Q - x)C_o$ results. The expected profit $P(Q)$ is thus given by

$$P(Q) = \int_0^Q [xC_u - (Q-x)C_o]f(x)dx + \int_Q^\infty QC_u f(x)dx$$

To determine the value of Q that maximizes the expected profit $P(Q)$, we have

$$\frac{dP(Q)}{d(Q)} = -C_o\int_0^Q f(x)dx + C_u\int_Q^\infty f(x)dx = C_u[1 - F(Q)] - C_o F(Q) = 0$$

This implies an optimal order size of Q^* where

$$F(Q^*) = \frac{C_u}{C_u + C_o}$$

It is easy to verify that the second derivative is negative, implying that the total expected profit is maximized at Q^*.

-------------------------------**A P P E N D I X   1 2 B**---------------------------

An Intermediate Evaluation

Objective: Given that x is normally distributed with a mean μ and standard deviation σ, show that

$$A = \int_{x=-\infty}^{a} xf(x)dx = \mu F_S((a-\mu)/\sigma) - \sigma f_S((a-\mu)/\sigma) \tag{12.8}$$

Here $f(x)$ is the normal density function, $f_S(\ )$ the standard normal density function, and $F_S(\ )$ is the standard normal cumulative distribution function.

Analysis: Using Equation 8.18 we have

$$A = \int_{x=-\infty}^{a} xf(x)dx = \int_{x=-\infty}^{a} x \frac{1}{\sqrt{2\pi}\sigma} e^{\frac{-(x-\mu)^2}{2\sigma^2}} dx$$

Substitute $z = (x - \mu)/\sigma$. This implies $dx = \sigma dz$. Thus, we have

$$A = \int_{z=-\infty}^{(a-\mu)/\sigma} (z\sigma + \mu) \frac{1}{\sqrt{2\pi}} e^{-z^2/2} dz$$

$$= \mu \int_{z=-\infty}^{(a-\mu)/\sigma} \frac{1}{\sqrt{2\pi}} e^{-z^2/2} dz + \sigma \int_{z=-\infty}^{(a-\mu)/\sigma} z \frac{1}{\sqrt{2\pi}} e^{-z^2/2} dz$$

Given the relationship between the cumulative distribution function and the probability density function, we use the definition of the standard normal distribution and Equation 11.18 to obtain

$$F_S(t) = \int_{z=-\infty}^{t} f_S(z)dz = \int_{z=-\infty}^{t} \frac{1}{\sqrt{2\pi}} e^{-z^2/2} dz$$

Substitute $w = z^2/2$ into the expression for A. This implies that $dw = zdz$. Thus,

$$A = \mu F_S((a-\mu)/\sigma) + \sigma \int_{w=\infty}^{(a-\mu)^2/2\sigma^2} \frac{1}{\sqrt{2\pi}} e^{-w} dw$$

$$A = \mu F_S((a-\mu)/\sigma) - \sigma f_S((a-\mu)/\sigma)$$

Expected Profit from an Order

Objective: Assume demand to be normally distributed with a mean μ and standard deviation σ. Each unit sells for a price $\$p$ and costs $\$c$. Any unsold units fetch a salvage value of $\$s$. Obtain an expression for the expected profit if O units are ordered.

Analysis: If O units are ordered and demand turns out to be $x < O$, each of the x units sold contribute $p - c$ while each of the $(O - x)$ units unsold result in a loss of $c - s$. If demand is larger than O, each of the O units sold contribute $p - c$. We thus obtain

$$\text{Expected profits} = \int_{x=-\infty}^{O} [(p-c)x - (c-s)(O-x)]f(x)dx + \int_{x=O}^{\infty} O(p-c)f(x)dx$$

$$= \int_{x=-\infty}^{O} [(p-s)x - O(c-s)]f(x)dx + \int_{x=O}^{\infty} O(p-c)f(x)dx$$

Using Equation 12.8 we obtain,

$$\int_{x=-\infty}^{O} xf(x)dx = \mu F_S\left(\frac{O-\mu}{\sigma}\right) - \sigma f_S\left(\frac{O-\mu}{\sigma}\right)$$

We can thus evaluate the expected profits as

$$\text{Expected profits} = (p-s)\mu F_S\left(\frac{O-\mu}{\sigma}\right) - (p-s)\sigma f_S\left(\frac{O-\mu}{\sigma}\right)$$

$$-O(c-s)F(O,\mu,\sigma) + O(p-c)[1 - F(O,\mu,\sigma)]$$

Expected Overstock from an Order

Objective: Assume demand to be normally distributed with a mean μ and standard deviation σ. Obtain an expression for the expected overstock if O units are ordered.

Analysis: If O units are ordered, an overstock results only if demand is $x < O$. We thus have

$$\text{Expected overstock} = \int_{x=-\infty}^{O} (O-x)f(x)dx = \int_{x=-\infty}^{O} Of(x)dx - \int_{x=-\infty}^{O} xf(x)dx$$

$$= OF_S\left(\frac{O-\mu}{\sigma}\right) - \int_{x=-\infty}^{O} xf(x)dx$$

Using Equation 12.8, we thus obtain

$$\text{Expected overstock} = OF_S\left(\frac{O-\mu}{\sigma}\right) - \mu F_S\left(\frac{O-\mu}{\sigma}\right) + \sigma f_S\left(\frac{O-\mu}{\sigma}\right)$$

$$= (O-\mu)F_S\left(\frac{O-\mu}{\sigma}\right) + \sigma f_S\left(\frac{O-\mu}{\sigma}\right)$$

-------------------------------- A P P E N D I X   1 2 E --------------------------------

Expected Understock from an Order

Objective: Assume demand to be normally distributed with a mean μ and standard deviation σ. Obtain an expression for the expected understock if O units are ordered.

Analysis: If O units are ordered, an understock results only if demand is $x > O$. We thus have

$$\text{Expected understock} = \int_{x=O}^{\infty} (x - O)f(x)dx = \int_{x=O}^{\infty} xf(x)dx - \int_{x=O}^{\infty} Of(x)dx$$

$$= \int_{x=-\infty}^{\infty} xf(x)dx - \int_{x=-\infty}^{O} xf(x)dx - O\left[1 - F_S\left(\frac{O-\mu}{\sigma}\right)\right]$$

$$= (\mu - O) + OF_S\left(\frac{O-\mu}{\sigma}\right) - \int_{x=-\infty}^{O} xf(x)dx$$

Using Equation 12.8, we thus obtain

$$\text{Expected understock} = (\mu - O) + OF_S\left(\frac{O-\mu}{\sigma}\right) - \mu F_S\left(\frac{O-\mu}{\sigma}\right) + \sigma f_S\left(\frac{O-\mu}{\sigma}\right)$$

$$= (\mu - O)\left[1 - F_S\left(\frac{O-\mu}{\sigma}\right)\right] + \sigma f_S\left(\frac{O-\mu}{\sigma}\right)$$

-------------------------------- A P P E N D I X 1 2 F --------------------------------

Simulation Using Spreadsheets

A simulation is a computer model that replicates a real life situation allowing the user to estimate what the potential outcome would be from each of a set of actions. Simulation is a very powerful tool that helps evaluate the impact of business decisions on performance in an uncertain environment. In some instances, future scenarios can be modeled mathematically without simulation and formulas can be obtained for the impact of different policies on performance. In other cases, formulas are difficult or impossible to obtain and one must use simulation. Simulations are powerful because they can accommodate any number of complications. Problems that are impossible to solve analytically can often be solved fairly easily with simulation. A good simulation is an inexpensive way to test different actions and identify the most effective decision given an uncertain future.

Consider Land's End, a mail order firm selling apparel. Land's End faces uncertain demand and has to make decisions regarding the number of catalogs to print and mail, the number of units of each product to order, and the contracts to enter into with its suppliers. The general manager at Land's End would like to evaluate different policies before implementing them. A simulation requires the manager to create a computer model that mimics the orders placed, inventory held, customer demand, and other processes that are part of the Land's End supply chain.

An *instance* of demand refers to random demand obtained from a demand distribution. Each time demand is generated from a distribution, a new instance results. Based on estimates of the future demand distribution, instances of demand for different products are generated randomly. The impact of an ordering policy is evaluated for each instance of demand generated. Based on a large number of demand instances, the manager can evaluate the mean and variability of the performance of a policy. Different policies can then be compared.

GENERATING RANDOM NUMBERS USING EXCEL

A fundamental step in any simulation is the generation of random numbers that correspond to the distribution that has been estimated for future demand or some other parameter. For example, if Land's End has estimated demand for cashmere sweaters from the winter catalog to be normally distributed with a mean of 3,000 and a standard deviation of 1,000, the manager needs to generate several instances of demand from this distribution. There are several functions available in Excel that generate random numbers.

The *RAND()* function generates a random number that is uniformly distributed between 0 and 1. There is thus a 10 percent probability that *RAND()* will generate a number between 0 and 0.1, a 50 percent probability that it will generate a random number between 0 and 0.5, and a 90 percent probability that it will generate a random number between 0 and 0.9. The *RAND()* function can be used to generate random numbers from a variety of distributions.

The Excel function $NORMINV(RAND(), \mu, \sigma)$, generates a random number that is normally distributed with mean μ and standard deviation σ. The Excel function $NORMSINV(RAND())$ generates a random number that is normally distributed with a mean of 0 and standard deviation of 1. The fact that both *NORMINV* and *NORMSINV* can generate negative numbers often poses problems when they are used to generate demand. One option is to use the maximum of 0 and $NORMINV(RAND(), \mu, \sigma)$ to generate demand. This is appropriate if the coefficient of variation *cv* is less than 0.4. For larger coefficients of variation it is better to use the lognormal distribution because it only generates nonnegative numbers. The Excel function $LOGINV(RAND(), \mu, \sigma)$ generates a random number X that follows the lognormal distribution where $ln(X)$ is normally distributed with mean μ and standard deviation σ.

There are several other demand distributions that may be generated using other Excel functions.

SETTING UP A SIMULATION MODEL

Land's End plans to sell cashmere sweaters in its winter catalog for $150 each. The manager expects demand to be normally distributed with a mean of $\mu = 3,000$ and a standard deviation of $\sigma = 1,000$. Toward the end of the winter season, Land's End sends out a sales catalog with discounted prices on unsold items. The discounted price determines the demand in response to the sales catalog. The manager anticipates that the sales catalog will generate demand for cashmere sweaters with a mean of $1,000 - 5p$ and a standard deviation of $(1,000 - 5p)/3$, where p is the discounted price charged. Any leftover sweaters after the sales catalog are donated to charity. Each sweater costs Land's End $50. Thus, the donation to charity fetches $25 in tax benefits. Land's End incurs a cost of $5 per unsold sweater to store and transport them to charity, resulting in a salvage value of $s = \$20$ per sweaters sent to charity. The manager has decided to charge a discount price of $\max(\$25, \$150 - n/20)$, where n is the number of sweaters left over after the winter catalog. The manager would like to identify the number of sweaters that should be purchased at the start of the winter season.

The first step is to set up a simulation model that evaluates the net profit for an instance of demand during the winter season. The model constructed is shown in Figure 12.6.

FIGURE 12.6 Excel Simulation Model for Land's End

	A	B	C	D	E	F	G	H	I
1	*Ordering and Pricing at Land's End*								
2									
3	Cost of sweaters =			$50					
4	Sale Price in winter catalog =			$150					
5	Mean demand from winter catalog =			3,000					
6	SD of demand from winter catalog =			1,000					
7	Mean discounted demand =			341					
8	SD of discounted demand =			113.58					
9									
10	Initial Quantity ordered =			3000		Cost of sweaters ordered =			$150,000
11	Winter catalog demand =			2637		Revenue from winter sales =			$395,550
12	Sweaters to be discounted =			363		Revenue from discounted sales =			$30,194
13	Discounted price, p =			$131.90		Net benefit from donation =			$2,680
14	Demand at discounted price =			229		Net profit =			**$278,424**
15	Number sold at discount =			229					
16	Number donated to charity =			134					
17									
18	Average profit =		$266,702			Average number of sweaters discounted =			376
19	SD of profit =		$64,959			Average number donated to charity =			180

Cell Number	Cell Formula	Cell Number	Cell Formula
D7	=1000-5*D13	D16	=D12-D15
D8	=D7/3	I10	=D3*D10
D11	=int(max(0,norminv(rand(),D5,D6)))	I11	=min(D10,D11)*D4
D12	=max(0,D10-D11)	I12	=D15*D13
D13	=max(25,150-D12/20)	I13	=D16*20
D14	=int(max(0,norminv(rand(),D7,D8)))	I14	=sum(I11:I13)-I10
D15	=min(D12,D14)		

USING DATA TABLE TO CREATE MANY INSTANCES

Having set up the simulation model, the next step is to create many instances of random demand and evaluate the average profits from ordering 3,000 units. In Excel, *Data Tables* can be used to achieve multiple replications of the simulation. The goal is to evaluate the mean and standard deviation of profits, average number of sweaters discounted, and average number of sweaters donated to charity over the multiple replications. A data table is constructed in the range A23:D522 to replicate the results of the simulation for 500 instances of demand as follows:

1. Enter formula =I14 in cell B23, =D12 in cell C23, and =D16 in cell D23. As a result, the profit is copied into cell B23, the quantity discounted is copied into cell C23, and the quantity given to charity is copied into cell D23.

2. Select the range A23:D522. From the toolbar select *Data|Table*. In the *Table* dialog box point to cell A23 as the *Column input cell*. Click on OK.

The data table is created in the range A23:D522. Each row of the data table gives the profit, quantity discounted, and quantity given to charity for an instance of random demand. Excel recalculates the simulation using new random numbers for each row in the data table. We can now obtain the average profit, average number of sweaters discounted, and average number of sweaters donated to charity from the data table. These are calculated in cells C18, I18, and I19, respectively, in Figure 12.6.

Each time the F9 key is pressed, new random numbers are generated and all entries are recalculated. The manager at Land's End can use the simulation to evaluate the impact of different initial ordering policies on performance.

Sourcing, Transporting, and Pricing Products

C H A P T E R   1 3

Sourcing Decisions in a Supply Chain

C H A P T E R   1 4

Transportation in the Supply Chain

C H A P T E R   1 5

Pricing and Revenue Management in the Supply Chain

Part V deals with three topics all related to actions generally taken between a company and its supply chain partners. Chapter 13 deals with decisions focused on sourcing from upstream suppliers, Chapter 14 deals with transporting goods from upstream stages and to downstream stages, and Chapter 15 focuses on pricing to downstream customers.

Chapter 13 focuses on sourcing strategies for interacting with suppliers. A full lifecycle of actions is discussed, from product design to steady state procurement procedures. A framework is presented to grade and select, contract with, and procure from suppliers.

Chapter 14 describes the strengths and weaknesses of various modes of transportation and different options for designing transportation networks. Trade-offs between transportation cost, inventory cost, and responsiveness that must be considered when designing a supply chain are also discussed. Methodologies that firms can use to design delivery routes are described.

Chapter 15 discusses the role of pricing and revenue management in maximizing profitability from supply chain assets. Conditions under which revenue management is applicable are discussed and in each case the basic trade-offs are identified.

CHAPTER

13

Sourcing Decisions in a Supply Chain

Learning Objectives

After reading this chapter, you will be able to

1. Understand the role of sourcing in a supply chain.

2. Identify dimensions of supplier performance that impact total cost.

3. Describe the impact of different contracts on supplier performance and information distortion.

4. Categorize purchased products and services and discuss the desired focus of procurement in each case.

13.1 THE ROLE OF SOURCING IN A SUPPLY CHAIN

Purchasing, also known as procurement, is the process by which companies acquire raw materials, components, products, services, and other resources from suppliers to execute their operations. Sourcing is the entire set of business processes required to purchase goods and services. Sourcing processes include the selection of suppliers, design of supplier contracts, product design collaboration, procurement of material, and evaluation of supplier performance, as shown in Figure 13.1.

Supplier scoring and assessment is the process used to rate supplier performance. For many firms, price has traditionally been the only dimension that suppliers have been compared on. There are many other supplier characteristics such as lead time, reliability, quality, and design capability that impact the total cost of doing business with a supplier. A good supplier scoring and assessment process must identify and track performance along all dimensions that affect the total cost of a using a supplier. *Supplier selection* uses the output from supplier scoring and assessment to identify the appropriate supplier(s). A supply contract is then negotiated with the supplier. A good contract should account for all factors that impact supply chain performance and should be designed to increase supply chain profits in a way that benefits both the supplier and the buyer.

Given that about 80 percent of the cost of a product is determined during design, it is crucial that suppliers be actively involved at this stage. *Design collaboration* allows the supplier and the manufacturer to work together when designing components for the final product. Design collaboration also ensures that any design changes are communicated effectively to all parties involved with designing and manufacturing the product. Once the product has been designed, *procurement* is the process in which the supplier sends product in response to orders placed by the buyer. The goal of procurement is to enable orders to be placed and delivered on schedule at the lowest possible overall cost. Finally, the role of *sourcing planning and analysis* is to analyze spending across various suppliers and component categories to identify opportunities for decreasing the total cost.

Cost of Goods Sold (COGS) represents well over 50 percent of sales for most major manufacturers. Purchased parts are a much higher fraction than they were several decades ago. This change has occurred because companies have reduced vertical integration and outsourced manufacture of many components. Companies such as Cisco have gone further and also outsourced a significant fraction of the assembly capacity. As there is greater pressure on firms to achieve lower costs and the suppliers' share of the COGS grows, good sourcing decisions will have greater impact on the cost leadership and competitive advantage enjoyed by a firm.

Effective sourcing processes within a firm can improve profits for the firm and total supply chain surplus in a variety of ways. It is important that the drivers of

FIGURE 13.1   Key Sourcing-Related Processes

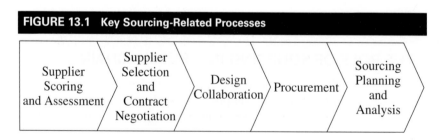

improved profits be clearly identified when making sourcing decisions. Some of the benefits from effective sourcing decisions are the following:

- Better economies of scale can be achieved if orders within a firm are aggregated.
- More efficient procurement transactions can significantly reduce the overall cost of purchasing. This is most important for items where a large number of low-value transactions occur.
- Design collaboration can result in products that are easier to manufacture and distribute resulting in lower overall costs. This factor is most important for supplier products that contribute a significant amount to product cost and value.
- Good procurement processes can facilitate coordination with the supplier and improve forecasting and planning. Better coordination lowers inventories and improves the matching of supply and demand.
- Appropriate supplier contracts can allow for the sharing of risk, resulting in higher profits for both the supplier and the buyer.
- Firms can achieve a lower purchase price by increasing competition through the use of auctions.

When designing a sourcing strategy it is important for a firm to be clear on the factors that have the greatest influence on performance and target improvement on those areas. For example, if most of the spending for a firm is on materials with only a few high-value transactions, improving the efficiency of procurement transactions will provide little value whereas improving design collaboration and coordination with the supplier will provide significant value. In contrast, when sourcing items with many low-value transactions, increasing the efficiency of procurement transactions will be very valuable.

In the following sections we study the various sourcing processes in greater detail and identify strategies that improve supply chain performance.

13.2 SUPPLIER SCORING AND ASSESSMENT

When comparing suppliers, many firms make the fundamental mistake of focusing only on the quoted price, ignoring the fact that suppliers may differ on other important dimensions that impact the total cost of using a supplier. For instance, suppliers have different replenishment lead times. Does it pay to select a more expensive supplier with a shorter lead time? Or consider suppliers that have different on-time performance. Is the more reliable supplier worth the few extra pennies he charges per piece?

In each of the aforementioned instances, the price charged by the supplier is only one of many factors that affect the total cost of the product. When scoring and assessing suppliers, the following factors other than quoted price must be considered:

- Replenishment lead time
- On-time performance
- Supply flexibility
- Delivery frequency/minimum lot size
- Supply quality

- Inbound transportation cost
- Pricing terms
- Information coordination capability
- Design collaboration capability
- Exchange rates, taxes, and duties
- Supplier viability

Supplier performance must be rated on each of these factors because they impact the total supply chain cost. Next we discuss how each factor affects total supply chain cost and how a supplier's rating on the factor can be used to infer a total cost of using the supplier.

1. *Replenishment lead time:* As the replenishment lead time from a supplier grows, the amount of safety inventory that needs to be held by the buyer also grows proportional to the square root of the replenishment lead time (see Chapter 11). Lead time performance by a supplier can directly be translated into the required safety inventory using Equation 11.9. Scoring the performance of suppliers in terms of replenishment lead time thus allows the firm to evaluate the impact each supplier has on the cost of holding safety inventory.

2. *On-time performance:* On-time performance affects the variability of the lead time. A reliable supplier has low variability of lead time whereas an unreliable supplier has high variability. As the variability of lead time grows, the required safety inventory at the firm grows very rapidly (see Chapter 11). On-time performance can be translated into lead time variability, which is converted to required safety inventory using Equation 11.11. A firm can use the discussion in Chapter 11 to evaluate the impact of poor on-time performance by a supplier on the cost of holding safety inventory.

3. *Supply flexibility:* Supply flexibility is the amount of variation in order quantity that a supplier can tolerate without letting other performance factors deteriorate. The less flexible a supplier is, the more lead time variability he will display as order quantities change. Supply flexibility thus impacts the level of safety inventory that the firm will have to carry.

4. *Delivery frequency/minimum lot size:* The delivery frequency and the minimum lot size offered by a supplier affect the size of each replenishment lot ordered by a firm. As the replenishment lot size grows, the cycle inventory at the firm grows, thus increasing the cost of holding inventory (see Chapter 10). Delivery frequency is converted to cycle inventory using Equation 10.1. For a firm using a periodic review policy, delivery frequency also impacts the required safety inventory (see Equation 11.16). Thus, delivery frequency of a supplier can be converted into the cost of holding cycle and safety inventory.

5. *Supply quality:* A worsening of supply quality increases the variability of the supply of components available to a firm. Quality affects the lead time taken by the supplier to complete the replenishment order and also the variability of this lead time because follow-up orders often need to be fulfilled to replace defective products. As a result, the firm will have to carry more safety inventory (see Chapter 11) from a low-quality supplier compared to a high-quality supplier. Once a relationship between supply

quality, lead time, and lead time variability is established, each supplier's quality level can be converted to the required safety inventory and the associated holding cost. The component quality also impacts customer satisfaction and product cost because of rework, lost material, and the cost of inspection.

6. *Inbound transportation cost:* The total cost of using a supplier includes the inbound transportation cost of bringing material in from the supplier. Sourcing a product overseas may have lower product cost but will generally incur a higher inbound transportation cost, which must be accounted for when comparing suppliers. The distance, mode of transportation, and the delivery frequency affect the inbound transportation cost associated with each supplier.

7. *Pricing terms:* Pricing terms include the allowable time delay before payment has to be made and any quantity discounts offered by the supplier. Allowable time delays in payment to suppliers save the buyer working capital. The cost of working capital savings for each supplier can be quantified. Price terms also include discounts for purchases above certain quantities. Quantity discounts lower the unit cost but tend to increase the required batch size and as a result the cycle inventory (see Chapter 10). As discussed in Chapter 10, the impact of quantity discounts on material cost and inventory cost can be quantified for each supplier.

8. *Information coordination capability:* The information coordination capability of a supplier impacts the ability of a firm to match supply and demand. Good coordination will result in better replenishment planning, thus decreasing both the inventory carried as well as the sales lost because of lack of availability. Good information coordination also decreases the bullwhip effect (see Chapter 16) and results in lower production, inventory, and transportation costs while improving responsiveness to the customer. The value of better coordination will be linked to the amount of variability introduced into the supply chain as a result of the bullwhip effect.

9. *Design collaboration capability:* Given that a large part of product cost is fixed at design, collaboration capability of a supplier is significant. Good design collaboration for manufacturability and supply chain can also decrease required inventories and transportation cost. As manufacturers are increasingly outsourcing both the design and manufacture of components, their ability to coordinate design across many suppliers is critical to the ultimate success of the product and the speed of introduction. As a result, design collaboration capability of suppliers is becoming increasingly important.

10. *Exchange rates, taxes, and duties:* Exchange rates, taxes, and duties can be significant for a firm with a global manufacturing and supply base. In many instances, currency fluctuations impact component price more than all other factors put together. Financial hedges can be put into place to counter exchange rate fluctuations. It is important, however, to analyze various supply options in a global supply chain to account for demand and macroeconomic variability as discussed in Chapter 6. Similarly, the level of taxes and duties can make a significant difference on total cost depending upon the location of the supplier.

11. *Supplier viability:* Given the impact suppliers have on a company's performance, an important factor in picking a supplier is the likelihood that they will be around to fulfill the promises they make. This consideration can be especially important if the

supplier is providing mission-critical products and they would be difficult to find a replacement for. Note that this is not necessarily a bias for larger companies—many small companies, and even some startups, can provide an acceptable level of viability.

Each supplier should be rated on all the aforementioned dimensions besides the price charged per unit. The impact of each factor on total cost is summarized in Table 13.1.

The factors in Table 13.1 allow a firm to rate and compare various suppliers with different performance on each dimension. We have discussed how performance along most of the factors can be quantified in terms of impact on cost. The overall performance of each supplier can thus be characterized in terms of total cost and a rating on the nonquantifiable factors.

> **Key Point**   Supplier performance should be compared based on their impact on total cost. Besides purchase price, the total cost is influenced by replenishment lead time, on-time performance, supply flexibility, delivery frequency, supply quality, inbound transportation cost, pricing terms, the ability of the supplier to coordinate forecasting and planning, the design collaboration capability of the supplier, exchange rates and taxes, and supplier viability.

In Example 13.1, we illustrate the comparison of two suppliers with different prices and other performance characteristics.

Example 13.1

Green Thumb, a manufacturer of lawn mowers and snow blowers, has historically purchased a thousand bearings per week from a local supplier who charges $1.00 per bearing. The purchasing manager has identified another potential source willing to supply the bearings at $0.97 per bearing. Before making his decision, the purchasing manager evaluates the performance of the

TABLE 13.1 **Supplier Performance Factors and Their Impact on Total Cost**					
	Purchase Price of Component	*Inventory*		*Transportation Cost*	*Product Introduction Time*
		Cycle	*Safety*		
Replenishment lead time			X		
On-time performance			X		
Supply flexibility			X		
Delivery frequency		X	X	X	
Supply quality	X		X		
Inbound transport cost				X	
Pricing terms	X	X			
Information coordination			X	X	
Design collaboration	X	X	X	X	X
Exchange rates and taxes	X				
Supplier viability			X		X

two suppliers. The local supplier has an average lead time of two weeks and has agreed to deliver the bearings in batches of 2,000. Based on past on-time performance, the purchasing manager estimates that the lead time has a standard deviation of one week. The new source has an average lead time of six weeks with a standard deviation of four weeks. The new source requires a minimum batch size of 8,000 bearings. Which supplier should the purchasing manager go with? Green thumb has a holding cost of 25 percent. They currently use a continuous review policy for managing inventory and aim for a cycle service level of 95 percent.

Analysis: The suppliers' performance along lead time and lead time variability affects the safety inventory that Green Thumb must hold, and the minimum batch size requirement affects the cycle inventory held. Thus, the purchasing manager should evaluate the total cost of using each supplier. First consider the cost of using the current local supplier:

Annual material cost = $1,000 \times 52 \times 1 = \$52,000$,
Average cycle inventory (using Equation 10.1) = $2,000/2 = 1,000$,
Annual cost of holding cycle inventory = $1,000 \times 1 \times 0.25 = \$250$,
Standard deviation of demand during lead time (using Equation 11.11) =

$$\sqrt{2 \times 300^2 + 1000^2 \times 1^2} = 1,086.28,$$

Safety inventory required with new supplier (using Equation 11.9) = $NORMSINV(.95) \times 1086.28 = 3,787$,
Annual cost of holding safety inventory = $3,787 \times 1 \times 0.25 = \$946.75$,
Annual cost of using current supplier = $52,000 + 250 + 946.75 = \$53,196.75$.

Next consider the cost of using the new supplier:

Annual material cost = $1,000 \times 52 \times 0.97 = \$50,440$,
Average cycle inventory (using Equation 10.1) = $8,000/2 = 4,000$,
Annual cost of holding cycle inventory = $4,000 \times 0.97 \times 0.25 = \$970$,
Standard deviation of demand during lead time (using Equation 11.11) =

$$\sqrt{6 \times 300^2 + 1000^2 \times 4^2} = 4,066.94,$$

Safety inventory required with current supplier (using Equation 11.9) = $NORMSINV(.95) \times 4,066.94 = 12,690$,
Annual cost of holding safety inventory = $12,690 \times 0.97 \times 0.25 = \$3,077.21$,
Annual cost of using the new supplier = $50,440 + 970 + 3,077.21 = \$54,487.21$.

Observe that the new supplier has a lower annual material cost but a higher annual total cost. Taking all performance characteristics into account, the purchasing manager should continue to use the current supplier.

13.3   SUPPLIER SELECTION AND CONTRACTS

Once the aforementioned scorecard analysis has been completed, a list of promising suppliers will emerge. The firm can then select desired suppliers using a variety of mechanisms including off-line competitive bids, reverse auctions, or direct negotiations. No matter what mechanism is used, supplier selection should be based on total cost of using a supplier and not just the purchase price.

Before selecting suppliers, a firm must decide whether it will use single sourcing or will have multiple suppliers from which to source the product. Single sourcing is used to guarantee the supplier sufficient business when the supplier has to make a significant buyer-specific investment. The buyer-specific investment can take the form of plant and equipment designed to produce a part that is specific to the buyer or could take the form of expertise that needs to be developed. Single sourcing is also used in the automotive industry for parts such as seats that must arrive in the sequence of production. Coordinating such sequencing would be impossible with multiple sources. As a result, auto companies have a single-seat source for each plant but multiple-seat sources across their manufacturing network. Having multiple sources ensures a degree of competition and also the possibility of a backup should a source fail to deliver.

A good test of whether a firm has the right number of suppliers is to analyze what impact deleting or adding a supplier will have. Unless each supplier has a somewhat different role, it is very likely that the supply base is too large. In contrast, unless adding a supplier with a unique and valuable capability clearly adds to total cost, the supply base may be too small.

Once suppliers have been selected, contracts have to be structured between the buyer and each supplier. A supply contract specifies parameters governing the buyer–supplier relationship. Besides making the terms of the buyer–supplier relationship explicit, contracts have significant impact on the behavior and performance of all stages in a supply chain. Contracts should be designed to facilitate desirable supply chain outcomes and minimize actions that hurt performance. A manager should ask the following three questions when designing a supply chain contract:

1. How will the contract impact the firm's profits and total supply chain profits?
2. Will the incentives in the contract introduce any information distortion?
3. How will the contract influence supplier performance along key performance measures?

Ideally, a contract should be structured to increase the firm's profits and supply chain profits, discourage information distortion, and offer incentives to the supplier to improve performance along key dimensions.

Contracts for Product Availability and Supply Chain Profits

Many shortcomings in supply chain performance occur because the buyer and supplier are two different entities, each trying to optimize their own profits. Actions taken by the two parties in the supply chain thus result in profits that are lower than what could be achieved if the supply chain were to coordinate its actions with a common objective of maximizing supply chain profits.

Consider a product whose demand is significantly impacted by retail price. The retailer decides his price (and thus sales quantity) based on his margin. The retailer's margin is only a fraction of the supply chain margin leading to a retail price that is higher than optimal and a sales quantity that is lower than optimal for the supply chain. This phenomenon is referred to as double marginalization (see Chapters 10 and 12). As discussed in Chapter 10, the supplier can increase supply chain profits by offering a volume discount where the retailer pays a lower price if the total quantity purchased exceeds a threshold.

Another example of double marginalization arises in the presence of demand uncertainty. A manufacturer will want the retailer to carry a large inventory of his product to ensure that any surge in demand can be satisfied. The retailer, on the other hand, loses money on any unsold inventory. As a result he prefers to carry a lower level of inventory. This tension leads to a supply chain outcome that is suboptimal.

In a contract where the supplier specifies a fixed price and the buyer decides on the quantity to be purchased, the most common cause for suboptimal supply chain performance is double marginalization (again see Chapter 12). The retailer makes his buying decision before demand is realized and thus bears all the demand uncertainty. If demand is less than his inventory, the retailer has to liquidate unsold product at a discount. Given uncertain demand, the retailer decides on the purchase quantity based on his margin and the cost of overstocking. The retailer's margin, however, is lower than the contribution margin for the entire supply chain, whereas his cost of overstocking is higher than that for the entire supply chain. As a result, the retailer is conservative and aims for a lower level of product availability than would be optimal for the supply chain.

Consider a music store that sells compact discs. The supplier buys (or manufactures) compact discs at $1 per unit and sells them to the music store at $5 per unit. The retailer sells each disc to the end consumer at $10. The retailer has a margin of $5 per disc and can potentially lose $5 for each unsold disc. Using Equation 12.1, it is optimal for the retailer to aim for a service level of 0.5. The supplier and the retailer together have a margin of $9 and can lose a maximum of only $1 per unsold disc. For the entire supply chain it is thus optimal to aim for a service level of 0.9. The music store is thus conservative and carries fewer discs than are optimal for the supply chain.

To improve overall profits, the supplier must design a contract that encourages the buyer to purchase more and increase the level of product availability. This requires the supplier to share in some of the buyer's demand uncertainty. Three contracts that increase overall profits by making the supplier share some of the buyer's demand uncertainty are as follows (see Chapter 12 for more details):

1. Buyback or returns contracts
2. Revenue-sharing contracts
3. Quantity flexibility contracts

We illustrate each of the three contracts using the example of the music store and discuss their performance in terms of the three questions raised earlier.

Buyback Contracts

A buyback or returns clause in a contract (see Chapter 12) allows a retailer to return unsold inventory up to a specified amount, at an agreed upon price. For example, the supplier to the music store may agree to buy back discs that have not sold at $3 per disc. This lowers the loss to the retailer for each unsold disc from $5 to $2. The supplier absorbs the $3 per unsold disc as a reduction in margin. The presence of the buyback clause makes it optimal for the retailer to order more discs, resulting in higher product availability and higher profits for both the retailer and the supplier. Buyback contracts are most effective for products with a low variable cost. Examples include music, software, books, magazines, and newspapers.

A downside to the buyback clause is that it leads to surplus inventory that must be salvaged or disposed. The task of returning unsold product increases supply chain costs. The cost of returns can be eliminated if the manufacturer gives the retailer a markdown allowance and allows him to sell the product at a significant discount. Publishers today generally do not ask retailers to return unsold books. Instead, they give a markdown allowance for unsold books. Retailers mark them down and sell them for a considerable discount.

For a given level of product availability at the retailer, the presence of a buyback clause can also hurt sales because it leads the retailer to exert less effort to sell than he would if there were no buybacks. The reduction in retailer effort in the presence of buyback occurs because his loss from unsold inventory is higher when there is no buyback, leading to a higher sales effort. The supplier can counter the reduction in sales effort by limiting the amount of buyback permitted.

In the high-tech industry, where products lose value rapidly as new generations are introduced, a retailer will tend to be conservative and provide a lower level of product availability than is optimal from the perspective of the manufacturer and the supply chain. Manufacturers can share risk by providing *price support* to retailers. Many manufacturers guarantee that in the event they drop prices, they will also lower prices for all inventories that the retailer is currently carrying. As a result, the cost of overstocking at the retailer is limited to the cost of capital and physical storage and does not include obsolescence, which can be over 100 percent a year. The retailer thus increases the level of product availability in the presence of price support. Providing price support is equivalent to a buyback clause.

The structure of a buyback clause leads to the entire supply chain reacting to the order placed by the retailer and not actual customer demand. If a supplier is selling to multiple retailers, he will produce based on the orders placed by each retailer. Each retailer will base their order on their cost of over- and understocking (see Chapter 12). After actual sales materialize, unsold inventory is returned to the supplier separately from each retailer. The structure of the buyback clause increases information distortion when a supplier is selling to multiple retailers. At the end of the sales season, however, the supplier does obtain information on actual sales. Information distortion is driven primarily by the fact that inventory is disaggregated at the retailers. If inventory is centralized at the supplier and only sent out as needed to the retailers, information distortion can be reduced. With centralized inventory, the supplier can exploit independence of demand across retailers to carry a lower level of inventory. In practice, most buyback contracts, however, have decentralized inventory at retailers. As a result, there is a high level of information distortion.

> **Key Point** Buyback contracts counter double marginalization by lowering the cost of overstocking for the retailer. These contracts, however, lead to a lower retailer effort in case of overstocking and increased information distortion.

Revenue-Sharing Contracts

In a revenue-sharing contract, the buyer pays a minimal amount for each unit purchased from the supplier but shares a fraction of the revenue for each unit sold. For example, the supplier agrees to sell each disc to the music store at $1 but the music store agrees to share 50 percent of the revenue from each disc sold. If each disc is priced at $10, the supplier gets $5 for each disc sold and the music store keeps $5. The music store makes the same margin of $5 per disc as before and the supplier also makes the same margin of $4 per disc. The music store, however, will increase the number of discs they carry because they lose only $1 per unsold disc (instead of $5 per disc without revenue sharing), while making a margin of $5 for each disc that sells. When sharing 50 percent of the revenue with the manufacturer, they will target a service level of 83.3 percent (see Equation 12.1). As a result, profits for both the retailer and the manufacturer will increase.

Revenue-sharing contracts have a similar effect as buyback contracts in that they increase the level of product availability while increasing profits for the entire supply chain. Revenue sharing contracts also result in lower retailer effort compared to the case when the retailer pays an up front wholesale price and keeps the entire revenue from a sale. The drop in effort results because the retailer gets only a fraction of the revenue from each sale. One advantage of revenue sharing contracts over buyback contracts is that no product needs to be returned, thus eliminating the cost of returns. Revenue-sharing contracts are best suited for products with low variable cost and a high cost of return. A good example of revenue-sharing contracts is between Blockbuster video rentals and movie studios. The studios sell each cassette to Blockbuster at a low price and then share in the revenue generated from each rental. Given the low price, Blockbuster purchases many copies resulting in more rentals and higher profits for both Blockbuster and the studios.

The revenue-sharing contract does require an information infrastructure that allows the supplier to monitor sales at the retailer. Such an infrastructure can be expensive to build. As a result, revenue-sharing contracts may be difficult to manage for a supplier selling to many small buyers.

As in buyback contracts, revenue-sharing contracts also result in the supply chain producing to retailer orders rather than actual consumer demand. This information distortion results in excess inventory in the supply chain and a greater mismatch of supply and demand. The information distortion increases as the number of retailers that the supplier sells to grows. As with buyback contracts, information distortion from revenue-sharing contracts can be reduced if retailers reserve production capacity or inventory at the supplier rather than buying product and holding it in inventory themselves. This allows aggregation of the variability across multiple retailers and the supplier has to hold a lower level of capacity or inventory. In practice, however, most revenue-sharing contracts are implemented with the retailer buying and holding inventory.

Key Point Revenue-sharing contracts counter double marginalization by decreasing the cost per unit charged to the retailer, thus effectively decreasing the cost of overstocking. Revenue-sharing contracts increase information distortion and lead to a lower retailer effort in case of overstocking just as buyback contracts.

Quantity Flexibility Contracts

A quantity flexibility clause allows the buyer to modify the order (within limits agreed to by the supplier) as demand visibility increases closer to the point of sale. In our example, the music store would place an initial order for, say, 1,000 discs. Closer to the release date, as the store got a better idea of actual demand, they would be allowed to modify their order to any number between (say) 950 and 1,050. In this contract, the retailer modifies his order as he gains better market intelligence over time. The supplier in turn only sends the modified order quantity. The amount ordered by the retailer will be more in line with actual demand resulting in higher profits for the supply chain. For a supplier, the quantity flexibility contract makes sense if he has flexible capacity that can be used to produce at least the uncertain part of the order after the retailer has decided on the modification. A quantity flexibility contract is also very effective if a supplier is selling to multiple retailers with independent demand. A classic example of a quantity flexibility contract is Benetton. They allow retailers to modify about 30 percent of their order close to the actual sales season. The guaranteed portion of the order is manufactured using an inexpensive but long lead time production process. The flexible part of the order (about 30 percent) is manufactured using postponement. The result is a better matching of supply and demand at lower cost than in the absence of such a contract.

If the supplier has flexible capacity, a quantity flexibility contract will increase profits for the entire supply chain and also each party. The quantity flexibility contract requires either inventory or excess flexible capacity to be available at the supplier. If the supplier is selling to multiple retailers with independent demand, the aggregation of inventory leads to a smaller surplus inventory (see Chapter 11) with a quantity flexibility contract compared to either a buyback or revenue-sharing contract. Inventories can be further reduced if the supplier has excess flexible capacity. Quantity flexibility contracts are thus preferred for products with high marginal cost or in instances where surplus capacity is available. To be effective, quantity flexibility contracts require the retailer to be good at gathering market intelligence and improving their forecasts closer to the point of sale.

Relative to buyback and revenue-sharing contracts, quantity flexibility contracts have less information distortion. Consider the case with multiple retailers. With a buyback contract, the supply chain must produce based on the retailer orders that are placed well before actual demand arises. This leads to surplus inventory being disaggregated at each retailer. With a quantity flexibility contract, retailers only specify the range in which they will purchase well before actual demand arises. If demand at various retailers is independent, the supplier does not need to plan production to the high end of the order range for each retailer. He can aggregate uncertainty across all retailers and build a lower level of surplus inventory than would be needed if inventory were to be disaggregated at each retailer. Retailers then order closer to the point of sale when demand is more visible and less uncertain. The aggregation of uncertainty results in less information distortion with a quantity flexibility contract.

Like the other contracts discussed, quantity flexibility contracts result in lower retailer effort. In fact, any contract that gets the retailer to provide a higher level of product availability by not making them fully responsible for overstocking will result in a lowering of retailer effort for a given level of inventory.

> **Key Point**   Quantity flexibility contracts counter double marginalization by giving the retailer the ability to modify the order based on improved forecasts closer to the point of sale. These contracts result in lower information distortion than buyback or revenue-sharing contracts in case of a supplier selling to multiple buyers or if the supplier has excess, flexible capacity.

Contracts to Coordinate Supply Chain Costs

Differences in costs at the buyer and supplier also lead to decisions that increase total supply chain costs. An example is the replenishment lot size decision typically made by the buyer. The buyer decides on his optimal lot size based on his fixed cost per lot and the cost of holding inventory. He does not account for the supplier's costs. If the supplier has a high fixed cost per lot, the optimal lot size for the buyer increases total cost for the supplier and the supply chain. In such a situation, the supplier can use a quantity discount contract to encourage the buyer to order in lot sizes that minimize total costs (see Chapter 10). The objective of such a contract is to encourage the retailer to buy in larger lot sizes that lower cost for the supplier and the entire supply chain.

A quantity discount contract decreases overall costs but leads to higher lot sizes and thus higher levels of inventory in the supply chain. It is typically justified only for commodity products where the supplier has high fixed costs per lot. It is important to modify the terms of the contract as operational improvements are made at the supplier, resulting in lower fixed costs per batch.

Quantity discounts increase information distortion in the supply chain because such contracts increase order batching. Retailers order less frequently and any demand variations are exaggerated when orders are placed. The supplier receives information less frequently and all variations are increased because of this batching. This information distortion is discussed in greater detail in Chapter 16.

> **Key Point**   Quantity discounts can coordinate supply chain costs if the supplier has large fixed costs per lot. Quantity discounts, however, increase information distortion due to order batching.

Contracts to Increase Agent Effort

Supply chains have many instances where agents act on behalf of a principal and the agents' effort affects the reward for the principal. As an example, consider a car dealer (the agent) selling cars for DaimlerChrysler (the principal). The dealer also sells other brands and used cars. Every month the dealer allocates his sales effort (advertising, promotions, etc.) across all brands he sells and the used cars. Earnings for DaimlerChrysler are based on sales of their brands, which in turn are affected by the effort exerted by the dealer. Sales can be observed directly, whereas effort is hard to observe and measure. Given double marginalization, the dealer will always exert less effort than is optimal from the perspective of DaimlerChrysler and the supply chain. Thus, DaimlerChrysler must offer an incentive contract that encourages the dealer to increase effort.

In theory, a two-part tariff offers the right incentives for the dealer to exert the appropriate amount of effort. In a two-part tariff, DaimlerChrysler extracts their profits up front as a franchise fee and then sells cars to the dealer at cost. The dealer's margin is then the same as the supply chain margin, and the dealer exerts the right amount of effort.

Another contract, observed more frequently in practice, increases the margin for the dealer as sales cross certain thresholds. DaimlerChrysler offered such a contract to dealers in the first quarter of 2001, roughly structured as follows. Dealers would keep the margin made from customers if sales for the month were under 75 percent of an agreed upon target. However, if sales exceeded 75 percent but were below 100 percent, the dealer would get an additional $150 per car sold. If sales exceeded 100 percent but were under 110 percent, the dealer would get an additional $250 per car sold. If sales exceeded 110 percent, the dealer would get an additional $500 per car sold. DaimlerChrysler's hope was that by increasing the margin for higher thresholds, the dealer would have an incentive to increase effort on sales of DaimlerChrysler cars.

Although threshold contracts clearly encourage the dealer to try and reach higher thresholds, they can significantly increase information distortion by encouraging the agent to exacerbate demand variability. The first month after the new contract was announced, the U.S. car industry saw sales drop. DaimlerChrysler, however, saw sales drop by twice the industry average. There are two potential causes for this behavior. First, under the contract, the dealer makes more money selling 900 cars one month and 1,100 the next month compared to selling a thousand cars each month. The dealer has an incentive to shift demand over time to achieve such an outcome, thus increasing information distortion and observed demand variation. The second cause is that within the first week of the month the dealer has an idea of the threshold range he is likely to reach. For example, if the dealer feels that he can easily cross the 75 percent threshold but has little chance of crossing the 100 percent threshold, he will decrease his effort for the month and save it for later, because the marginal benefit of selling an additional car is only $150. In contrast, if demand for the month is high and the dealer feels he can easily cross the 100 percent threshold, he is likely to exert additional effort to reach the 110 percent threshold because the marginal benefit from reaching that threshold is very high. Thus, DaimlerChrysler's incentive contract increases variation in dealer effort, further exaggerating any existing demand variation.

Information distortion is also observed in threshold contracts often offered by companies to their sales staff. Under these contracts, staff is offered rewards for crossing sales thresholds during a specified period of time (e.g., a quarter). The problem observed is that sales effort and orders peak during the last week or two of the quarter, as salespeople try to cross the threshold. Observed sales are thus highly uneven during the quarter. This information distortion arises because the incentive is offered over a fixed time period making the last week or two of each quarter a period of intense activity for all sales staff.

Given the information distortion arising from threshold contracts, a key question is how a firm can decrease information distortion while maintaining the incentive for the agent to exert extra effort. One approach is to offer threshold incentives over a rolling horizon. For example, if a firm offers its sales staff weekly incentives based on sales over the last thirteen weeks, each week becomes the last week of a thirteen-week period. Sales effort thus becomes more even compared to the case when the entire sales staff has the same last week for their bonus evaluation. Given the presence of ERP systems, implementing a rolling horizon contract is much easier today than it once was.

> **Key Point** Two-part tariffs and threshold contracts can be used to counter double marginalization and increase agent effort in a supply chain. Threshold contracts, however, increase information distortion and are best implemented on a rolling horizon.

Contracts to Induce Performance Improvement

There are many instances where a buyer wants performance improvement from a supplier who has little incentive to do so. A buyer with sufficient power in the supply chain may be able to force the supplier to comply. A buyer without sufficient power will require an appropriate contract to induce the supplier to improve performance. Even for a powerful buyer, however, an appropriate contract designed to encourage supplier cooperation will result in a better outcome.

As an example, consider a buyer who wants the supplier to improve performance by reducing lead time for a seasonal item. This is an important component of all quick response (QR) initiatives in a supply chain. With a lower lead time, the buyer hopes to have better forecasts and be able to better match supply and demand. Most of the work for lead time reduction has to be done by the supplier, whereas most of the benefit will accrue to the buyer. In fact, the supplier will lose sales because the buyer will now carry less safety inventory because of shorter lead times and better forecasts. To induce the supplier to reduce lead time, the buyer can use a *shared savings contract*, with the supplier getting a fraction of the savings that result from lead time reduction. As long as the supplier's share of the savings compensates for any effort he has to put in, his incentive will be aligned with that of the buyer, resulting in an outcome that benefits both parties.

A similar issue arises when a buyer wants to encourage the supplier to improve quality. Improving supply quality will improve the buyer's costs but is likely to require additional effort from the supplier. Once again, a shared savings contract is a good way to align incentives between the buyer and supplier. The buyer can share savings from improved quality with the supplier. This will encourage the supplier to improve quality to a higher level than what the supplier would pick in the absence of the shared savings.

Another example arises in the context of toxic chemicals that may be used by a manufacturer. The manufacturer would like to decrease the use of these toxic chemicals. Generally, the supplier is better equipped to identify ways of reducing use of these chemicals because this is his core business. He has no incentive to work with the buyer on reducing use of these chemicals because that will reduce the supplier's sales. A shared savings contract can be used to align incentives between the supplier and the manufacturer. If the manufacturer shares the savings that result from a reduction in the use of toxic chemicals with the supplier, the supplier will make the effort to reduce use of the chemicals as long as his share of the savings compensates for the loss in margin from reduced sales.

In general, shared savings contracts are effective in aligning supplier and buyer incentives when the supplier is required to improve performance along a particular dimension and most of the benefits of improvement accrue to the buyer. A powerful buyer may couple shared savings with penalties for a lack of improvement to further encourage the supplier to improve performance. Such contracts will increase profits for both the buyer and the supplier while achieving outcomes that are beneficial to the supply chain.

> **Key Point** Shared savings contracts can be used to induce performance improvement from a supplier along dimensions, such as lead time, where the benefit of improvement accrues primarily to the buyer, whereas the effort for improvement comes primarily from the supplier.

13.4 DESIGN COLLABORATION

Two important statistics highlight the importance of design collaboration between a manufacturer and suppliers. Today, between 50 and 70 percent of the spending at a manufacturer is through procurement, compared to only about 20 percent several decades ago. It is generally accepted that about 80 percent of the cost of a purchased part is fixed during the design stage. Thus, it is crucial for a manufacturer to collaborate with suppliers during the design stage if product costs are to be kept low. Design collaboration can lower the cost of purchased material and also lower logistics and manufacturing costs. Design collaboration is also important for a company trying to provide a lot of variety and customization because failure to do so can significantly raise the cost of variety.

Working with suppliers can significantly speed up product development time. This is crucial in an era where product life cycles are shrinking and bringing a product to market before the competition offers a significant competitive advantage. Finally, integrating the supplier into the design phase allows the manufacturer to focus on system integration, resulting in a higher quality product at lower cost. For example, auto manufacturers are increasingly playing the role of system integrators rather than component designers. This is an approach that has been used even more extensively in the high-tech industry.

As suppliers take on a bigger design role, it is important for manufacturers to also become design coordinators for the supply chain. Common part descriptions should be available to all parties involved in the design and any design changes by one party should be communicated to all suppliers affected. A good database of existing parts and designs can save significant amount of money and time. For example, when Johnson Controls finds a seat frame from its database that fulfills all customer requirements, they save the customer about twenty million dollars on the design, development, tooling, and prototyping expense.

A survey by the Procurement and Supply Chain Benchmarking Consortium at Michigan State University dramatically demonstrates the impact of successfully integrating suppliers in product design. The most successful integration efforts have seen costs decrease by 20 percent, quality improve by 30 percent, and time-to-market decrease by 50 percent.

Key themes that must be communicated to suppliers as they take greater responsibility for design are design for logistics and design for manufacturability. Design for logistics attempts to reduce transportation, handling, and inventory costs during distribution by taking appropriate actions during design. To reduce transportation and handling costs, the manufacturer must convey expected order sizes from retailers and the end consumer to the designer. Packages can then be designed such that transportation cost is lowered and handling is minimized. To reduce transportation cost, packaging is kept as compact as possible and also designed to ensure easy stacking. To reduce handling costs, package sizes are designed to minimize the need to break open a pack to fulfill an order.

To reduce inventory costs, the primary approach is to design the product for postponement and mass customization (see Chapter 11). Postponement strategies aim to design a product and production process such that features that differentiate end products are introduced late in the manufacturing phase. As discussed in Chapter 11, Dell designs its PCs such that all components where customers have a choice are assembled after the customer order arrives. This allows Dell to lower inventories by aggregating them as components. Mass customization strategies use a similar approach by designing the product such that inventory can be carried in a form that aggregates across multiple end products. The goal is to design a product such that customization occurs along a combination of the following three categories: modular, adjustable, and dimensional. To provide modular customization, the product is designed as an assembly of modules that fit together. All inventory is then maintained as modules that are assembled to order. A good example of modular customization is PC assembly at Dell. An example of adjustable customization is a washing machine designed by Matsushita that can automatically select from among 600 different cycles. All inventory is thus maintained as a single product while each customer uses the machine to match their specific needs. An example of dimensional customization given by Joseph Pine is a machine that makes custom house gutters on site that can then be cut to fit the dimensions of the house. Another example is National Bicycle, which cuts the frame tubing to fit the body size of the customer.

Design for manufacturability attempts to design products for ease of manufacture. Some of the key principles used include part commonality, eliminating right-hand and left-hand parts, designing symmetrical parts, combining parts, using catalog parts rather than designing a new part, and designing parts to provide access for other parts and tools.

> **Key Point**   Design collaboration with suppliers can help a firm reduce cost, improve quality, and decrease time to market. As design responsibility moves to suppliers it is important to ensure design for logistics and design for manufacturability principles are followed. To be successful, manufacturers will have to become effective design coordinators in the supply chain.

A good area to view design collaboration efforts is in the automotive industry. OEMs all over the world are asking suppliers to participate in every aspect of product development, from conceptual design to manufacturing. Ford, for example, asked suppliers for the Thunderbird to not only manufacture the components and subsystems, but also to be responsible for their design. Solid integration throughout the supply chain allowed Ford to bring the new model to market within thirty six months of program approval. To ensure effective communication, Ford required all its vendors to be on the same software platform for design. Ford also opened all its internal databases to its suppliers and collocated many of the suppliers at its offices. Ford engineers were in constant communication with the suppliers and helped coordinate the overall design. The result was a significant improvement in cost, time, and quality.

13.5 THE PROCUREMENT PROCESS

Once suppliers have been selected, contracts are in place, and the product has been designed, the buyer and suppliers engage in procurement transactions that begin with the buyer placing the order and end with the buyer receiving and paying for the order. When designing the procurement process, it is important to consider goods that the process will be used to purchase. There are two main categories of purchased goods: Direct and indirect materials. *Direct materials* are components used to make finished goods. For example, memory, hard drives, and CD drives are direct materials for a PC manufacturer. *Indirect materials* are goods used to support the operations of a firm. PCs are examples of indirect materials for an automotive manufacturer. All procurement processes within a company relate to the purchase of direct and indirect materials. Important differences between direct and indirect materials that affect procurement are shown in Table 13.2.

Given the direct link to production, the procurement process for direct materials should be designed to ensure that components are available in the right place, in the right quantity, and at the right time. The primary goal of the procurement process for direct materials is to coordinate the entire supply chain and ensure matching of supply and demand. The procurement process should thus be designed to make production plans and current levels of component inventory at the manufacturer visible to the supplier. This visibility allows suppliers to schedule component production to match the needs of the manufacturer. The available capacity at the suppliers should be made visible to the manufacturer so orders for components may be allocated to the appropriate supplier to ensure on-time delivery. The procurement process should also have built in alerts that warn both the buyer and the supplier of potential mismatches between supply and demand.

A good example of a procurement process that focuses on these objectives is the eHub initiative at Cisco. eHub is designed to provide synchronized planning and end-to-end supply chain visibility. Ultimately, Cisco plans to include more than 2,000 of

TABLE 13.2 Differences between Direct and Indirect Materials		
	Direct Materials	*Indirect Materials*
Use	Production	Maintenance, repair, and support operations
Accounting	Cost of goods sold	SG&A
Impact on production	Any delay will delay production	Less direct impact
Processing cost relative to value of transaction	Low	High
Number of transactions	Low	High

its suppliers, distributors, and contract electronic manufacturers in its private trading network. Another example is the relationship between Johnson Controls and DaimlerChrysler for the 2002 Jeep Liberty. Johnson Controls integrates components from 35 suppliers and delivers the assembly to Chrysler as a cockpit module. As soon as Chrysler notifies them of an order for a Jeep, Johnson Controls has two hundred four minutes in which to build and deliver the module. This is done 900 times every day from about 200 different color and interior combinations. The focus of the procurement process is to completely synchronize production at DaimlerChrysler and Johnson Controls. The result is a significant reduction in inventory and a better matching of product supply with end customer demand.

Given the focus on numerous, low-value transactions, the procurement process for indirect materials should focus on reducing the transaction cost of each order. Transaction costs for indirect materials are high because of the difficulty in selecting goods (many catalogs that are often out of date), getting approval, and creating and sending a purchase order. The problem is often exaggerated because companies do not have one system for indirect materials. Instead, they use several processes that are not streamlined or integrated. A good e-procurement process that makes search easy and automates approval and transmission of the purchase order can help reduce transaction costs. The e-procurement process should also update other interested parties such as accounts payable and receiving. Clearly this is only possible with suppliers that implement online catalogs and automate all transactions with the buyer. Successful examples of e-procurement implementations for indirect materials include Johnson Controls and Pfizer. In both cases the firms built their e-procurement solution by integrating existing software. Johnson Controls integrated a Commerce One solution with existing Oracle accounting software while Pfizer integrated an Ariba system with an American Express corporate purchasing card program. Both have extracted significant savings as a result.

Another important requirement for the procurement process for both direct and indirect materials is to be able to aggregate orders by product and supplier. For direct materials, the consolidation of orders improves economies of scale at the supplier and during transport and allows the firm to take advantage of any quantity discounts that may be offered by the supplier. For indirect materials, the consolidation of spending with a supplier often allows the firm to negotiate better purchasing discounts.

Key Point The procurement process for direct materials should focus on improving coordination and visibility with the supplier. The procurement process for indirect materials should focus on decreasing the transaction cost for each order. The procurement process in both cases should consolidate orders to take advantage of economies of scale and quantity discounts.

In addition to the categorization of materials into direct and indirect, all products purchased may also be categorized as shown in Figure 13.2, based on their value/cost and how critical they are.

Most indirect materials are included in general items. The goal of procurement in this case should be to lower the cost of acquisition or the transaction cost. Direct materials can be further classified into bulk purchase, critical, and strategic items. For most

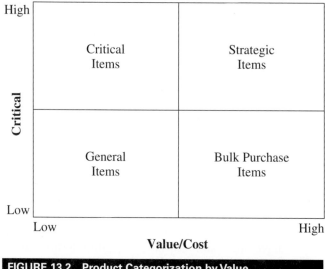

FIGURE 13.2 Product Categorization by Value and Criticality

bulk purchase items, such as packaging materials and bulk chemicals, suppliers will tend to have the same selling price. It is thus important for purchasing to make a distinction between suppliers based on the services they provide and their performance along all dimensions that impact the total cost of ownership. The use of well-designed auctions is likely to be most effective for bulk purchase items. Critical items include components with long lead times and specialty chemicals. The key sourcing objective for critical items is not low price but to ensure availability. In this case, purchasing should work to improve coordination of production plans at both the buyer and supplier. The presence of a responsive, even if high cost, supply source as an alternate can be very valuable for critical items. The last category, strategic items, would include examples such as electronics for an auto manufacturer. For strategic items, the buyer and supplier relationship will be long term. Thus suppliers should be evaluated based on the lifetime cost/value of the relationship. Purchasing should look for suppliers who can collaborate in the design phase and coordinate design and production activities with other players in the supply chain.

13.6 SOURCING PLANNING AND ANALYSIS

Periodically, each firm must analyze its procurement spending and supplier performance and use this as input for future sourcing decisions. One important analysis is the aggregation of spending across and within categories and suppliers. Aggregation provides visibility into what a company is purchasing and from whom the product is being purchased. Managers can use this information to determine economic order quantities, volume discounts, and projected quantity discounts on future volumes. A simple step is to consolidate spending and ensure that the firm's economic order quantity matches with the supplier's economic production quantity. Managers can thus realize better economies of scale and utilize resources more effectively.

The second piece of analysis relates to supplier performance. Supplier performance should be measured against plan on all dimensions that impact total cost such as responsiveness, lead times, on-time delivery, quality, and delivery accuracy.

Spending and supplier performance analysis should be used to decide on the portfolio of suppliers to be used and the allocation of demand among the chosen suppliers. As discussed in Chapter 12, the portfolio should generally not consist of similar suppliers. The portfolio should be constructed such that one supply source performs very well on one dimension, whereas the other source performs very well on a complementary dimension. For example, a company can source more effectively using a low-cost supplier with longer lead times along with a high-cost supplier with short lead times compared to using only one type of supplier. Similarly, one should not ignore a somewhat lower quality source if it is much cheaper than other sources. It would also not be effective to use only the cheaper but lower quality source. In this instance it may be very effective to use the cheaper but lower quality source along with a higher quality but more expensive source.

Once a supplier portfolio has been determined, the next question is the allocation of demand among the suppliers. The allocation should be related to the economic manufacturing quantity for each source and their cost of supply. The low-cost supplier is given large, steady orders independent of demand, whereas the flexible source is given small orders that fluctuate with demand. The flexible source has smaller economic order quantities and is better able to adjust to the fluctuations. The combination of suppliers results in a better matching of supply and demand at lower cost than using one type of supplier.

> **Key Point** Procurement spending should be analyzed by part and supplier to ensure appropriate economies of scale. Supplier performance analysis should be used to build a portfolio of suppliers with complementary strengths. Cheaper, but lower performing, suppliers should be used to supply the base demand, whereas higher performing, but more expensive, suppliers should be used to buffer against variation in demand and supply from the other source.

13.7 MAKING SOURCING DECISIONS IN PRACTICE

1. *Use multifunctional teams.* Effective strategies for sourcing result from multifunctional collaboration within the firm. A sourcing strategy from the purchasing group is likely to be narrow and focus on purchase price. A strategy developed with the collaboration of purchasing, manufacturing, engineering, and planning is much more likely to identify the correct drivers of total cost. The collaboration must be continued beyond strategy formulation to the procurement phase because that is where manufacturing and engineering are most likely to realize the full benefits of good sourcing strategy.

2. *Ensure appropriate coordination across regions and business units.* Coordination of purchasing across all regions and business units allows a firm to maximize economies of scale in purchasing and also to reduce transaction costs. Other opportunities from improved sourcing, such as better supply chain coordination and design collaboration, however, may require strong involvement at the business unit level to be really

effective. Mandating global coordination across all business units may complicate these efforts. Items such as MRO supplies, where transaction costs and total purchase volume have a significant impact on total cost, benefit the most from coordinated purchasing across geography and business unit. On the other hand, items where most of the value is extracted from better design collaboration and coordinated supply chain forecasting and fulfillment are better served with somewhat more decentralized sourcing.

3. *Always evaluate the total cost of ownership.* An effective sourcing strategy should not make price reduction its sole objective. All factors that influence the total cost of ownership should be identified and used for supplier selection. Supplier performance along all relevant dimensions should be measured and its impact on total cost should be quantified. Focusing on the total cost of ownership also allows a buyer to better identify opportunities for better collaboration in design, planning, and fulfillment.

4. *Build long-term relationships with key suppliers.* A basic principle of good sourcing is that a buyer and supplier working together will generate more opportunities for savings than the two parties working independently. Solid cooperation is likely to result only when the two parties have a long-term relationship and a degree of trust. A long-term relationship encourages the supplier to expend greater effort on issues that are important to a particular buyer. This includes investment in buyer-specific technology and design collaboration. A long-term relationship also improves communication and coordination between the two parties. These capabilities are very important when sourcing direct materials. Thus, long-term relationships should be nurtured with suppliers of critical and strategic direct materials.

13.8 SUMMARY OF LEARNING OBJECTIVES

1. Understand the role of sourcing in a supply chain.

   Sourcing encompasses all processes required for a firm to purchase goods from suppliers. Over the last decade, manufacturing firms have increased the fraction of purchased parts. Effective sourcing decisions thus have a significant impact on financial performance. Good sourcing decisions can improve supply chain performance by aggregating orders, making procurement transactions more efficient, achieving design collaboration with suppliers, facilitating coordinated forecasting and planning with suppliers, designing supply chain contracts that increase profitability while minimizing information distortion, and decreasing the purchase price through increased competition among suppliers.

2. Identify dimensions of supplier performance that impact total cost.

   Besides the quoted price, the total cost of using a supplier is affected by the replenishment lead time, on-time performance, supply flexibility, delivery frequency/minimum lot size, supply quality, inbound transportation cost, pricing terms, the information coordination capability, the design collaboration capability of the supplier, and the supplier's viability. These factors must be evaluated when comparing different suppliers to get a real measure of their effectiveness.

3. Describe the role of supply contracts and their impact on supplier performance and information distortion.

   Supply contracts must take into account the desired objective of the buyer and supplier and the resulting impact on supply chain performance. Contracts can be designed to increase product availability, coordinate supply chain costs, increase agent effort, and induce performance improvement from the supplier. Contracts to increase product availability include buyback, revenue sharing, and quantity flexibility contracts. They are designed to counter the problem of double marginalization. Buyback and revenue-sharing contracts increase information distortion relative to quantity flexibility contracts. Quantity discounts coordinate supply chain costs when both the supplier and the buyer have significant fixed costs per lot. Quantity discounts increase information distortion because of order batching. Two-part tariffs and threshold contracts are designed to increase agent effort. Threshold contracts can significantly increase information distortion and are best implemented over a rolling horizon. Shared savings contracts are most effective when a buyer wants the supplier to improve performance along dimensions such as lead time and quality.

4. Categorize purchased products and services and discuss the desired focus of procurement in each case.

Direct materials are components that are used to make the finished product. Indirect materials and services are used to support the main production process. Direct materials can be further categorized into bulk purchase, critical, and strategic items based on the value of the item and how critical it is for the buyer. Procurement should focus on aggregating the spending and reducing transaction costs when purchasing indirect materials. For bulk purchase items, procurement should focus on the value-added service provided and performance along other dimensions that impact total cost. For critical items, procurement should focus on improving coordination of forecasting and fulfillment with the supplier. For strategic items, procurement should focus on improving design and manufacturing collaboration with the supplier.

DISCUSSION QUESTIONS

1. What are some ways that a firm like Wal-Mart benefits from good sourcing decisions?
2. How can a supplier with a lower price end up costing the buyer more than a supplier with a higher price?
3. Explain why for the same inventory level, a revenue-sharing contract will result in a lower sales effort from the retailer than if the retailer has paid for the product and is responsible for all remaining inventory?
4. For a manufacturer selling to many retailers, why does a quantity flexibility contract result in less information distortion than a buyback contract?
5. Most firms offer their sales force monetary incentives based on crossing a specified target. What are some pros and cons of this approach? How would you modify these contracts to rectify some of the problems?
6. An auto manufacturer sources both office supplies and subsystems such as seats. What, if any, difference in sourcing strategy would you recommend for the two types of products?
7. How can design collaboration with suppliers help a PC manufacturer improve performance?

BIBLIOGRAPHY

Banfield, Emiko. 1999. *Harnessing Value in the Supply Chain: Strategic Sourcing in Action.* New York: John Wiley & Sons.

Cavinato, Joseph L., and Ralph Kauffman. 2000. *The Purchasing Handbook: A Guide for the Purchasing and Supply Professional.* New York: McGraw Hill.

Chopra, Sunil, Darren Dougan, and Gareth Taylor. 2001. "B2B E-Commerce Opportunities." *Supply Chain Management Review* (May–June): 50–58.

Grosvenor, Franklin, and Terrence A. Austin. 2001. "Cisco's eHub Initiative." *Supply Chain Management Review* (July–August): 18–26.

Laseter, Timothy M. 1998. *Balanced Sourcing: Cooperation and Competition in Supplier Relationships.* San Francisco: Jossey-Bass Publishers.

Martin, Lisa. 2002. "Charting Pfizer's Path to E-Procurement." *Supply Chain Management Review* (May–June): 20–26.

Monczka, R., G. Ragatz, R. Handfield, R. Trent, and D. Frayer. 1997. "Executive Summary: Supplier Integration into New Product Development: A Strategy for Competitive Advantage." The Global Procurement and Supply Chain Benchmarking Initiative, Michigan State University, The Eli Broad Graduate School of Management.

Monczka, Robert, Robert Trent, and Robert Handfield. 2002. *Purchasing and Supply Chain Management.* Cincinnati, Ohio: South-Western.

Neef, Dale. 2001. *E-Procurement: From Strategy to Implementation.* Upper Saddle River, N.J.: Prentice Hall.

Pierson, John C. 2002. "Johnson Controls' Journey to E-Procurement." *Supply Chain Management Review* (January–February): 56–62.

Smeltzer, Larry R., and Joseph R. Carter. 2001. "How to Build an E-Procurement Strategy." *Supply Chain Management Review* (March–April): 76–83.

Toupin, Laurie. 2002. "Needed: Suppliers Who Can Collaborate throughout the Supply Chain." Special Advertising Section: Automotive. *Supply Chain Management Review* (July–August): 5–8.

CHAPTER

14

Transportation in the Supply Chain

Learning Objectives

After reading this chapter, you will be able to

1. Understand the role of transportation in a supply chain.

2. Evaluate the strengths and weaknesses of different modes of transportation.

3. Identify various transportation network design options and their relative strengths and weaknesses.

4. Identify trade-offs that shippers must consider when designing their transportation network.

5. Use methodologies for routing and scheduling deliveries in transportation networks.

In this chapter, we discuss the role of transportation within a supply chain and identify trade-offs that need to be considered when making transportation decisions. Our goal is to enable managers responsible for transportation decisions to make transportation strategy and design, planning, and operational decisions with an understanding of all the pros and cons of their choices.

14.1 THE ROLE OF TRANSPORTATION IN THE SUPPLY CHAIN

Transportation refers to the movement of product from one location to another as it makes its way from the beginning of a supply chain to the customer's hands. Transportation plays a key role in every supply chain because products are rarely produced and consumed in the same location. Transportation is a significant component of the cost most supply chains incur. Freight transportation costs in the United States amount to about 6 percent of the GDP.[1] With the growth in e-commerce and the associated home delivery of products, transportation costs have become even more significant in retailing. From the book industry to the grocery industry, online firms are delivering products in small packages to the customer's home instead of in full trucks to a retail outlet. As a result, transportation cost is a larger fraction of the delivered cost of products sold online. For example, shipping a truck of books to a Borders retail store costs a few cents per book. In contrast, when Borders.com sends a package to a customer's home, the transportation cost is over a dollar per book.

Any supply chain's success is closely linked to the appropriate use of transportation. Wal-Mart has effectively used a responsive transportation system to lower its overall costs. To achieve a high level of product availability at a reasonable price, Wal-Mart carries a low level of inventory (relative to demand) at its stores and replenishes frequently as product is sold. To lower the transportation cost of frequent replenishment, Wal-Mart aggregates products destined for different retail stores on trucks leaving a supplier. At DCs, Wal-Mart uses *cross-docking,* a process in which product is exchanged between trucks so that each truck going to a retail store has products from different suppliers. Wal-Mart also uses its transportation system to allow stores to exchange products based on where shortages and surpluses occur. The use of a responsive transportation system and cross-docking allows the company to lower inventories and costs and therefore increase profits. Transportation is thus a key to Wal-Mart's ability to improve the matching of supply and demand while keeping costs low.

7-Eleven Japan has a goal of carrying products in its stores to match the needs of customers as they vary by geographical location or time of day. To help achieve this goal, 7-Eleven uses a very responsive transportation system that replenishes its stores several times a day so that the products available match customers' needs. Products from different suppliers are aggregated on trucks according to the required temperature to help achieve very frequent deliveries at a reasonable cost. 7-Eleven uses a responsive transportation system along with aggregation to decrease its transportation and receiving costs while ensuring that product availability closely matches customer demand.

Supply chains also use responsive transportation to centralize inventories and operate with fewer facilities. For example, Amazon.com relies on package carriers and the postal system to deliver customer orders from centralized warehouses. Dell manufactures out of one location in the United States and uses responsive transportation provided by package carriers like Airborne to provide customers with highly customized products at a reasonable price.

---

[1]*Distribution*, July 1997.

Transportation is a significant link between different stages in a global supply chain. Dell currently has suppliers worldwide and sells to customers all over the world from just a few plants. Transportation allows products to move from suppliers to the assembly plants to customers. Similarly, global transportation allows Wal-Mart to sell products manufactured all over the world in the United States.

In the next section, we discuss factors that affect transportation decisions for different members of a supply chain.

14.2   FACTORS AFFECTING TRANSPORTATION DECISIONS

There are two key players in any transportation that takes place within a supply chain. The *shipper* is the party that requires the movement of the product between two points in the supply chain. The *carrier* is the party that moves or transports the product. For example, when Dell uses UPS to ship its computers from the factory to the customer, Dell is the shipper and UPS is the carrier.

When making transportation-related decisions, factors to be considered vary depending on whether one takes the perspective of a carrier or shipper. A carrier makes investment decisions regarding the transportation infrastructure (rails, locomotives, trucks, airplanes, etc.) and then makes operating decisions to try to maximize the return from these assets. A shipper, in contrast, uses transportation to minimize the total cost (transportation, inventory, information, and facility) while providing an appropriate level of responsiveness to the customer.

Factors Affecting Carrier Decisions

A carrier's goal is to make investment decisions and set operating policies that maximize the return on its assets. A carrier such as an airline, railroad, or trucking company must account for the following costs when investing in assets or setting pricing and operating policies.

1. *Vehicle-related cost:* This is the cost a carrier incurs for the purchase or lease of the vehicle used to transport goods. The vehicle-related cost is incurred whether the vehicle is operating or not and is considered fixed for short-term operational decisions by the carrier. When making long-term strategic decisions or medium-term planning decisions, these costs are variable and the number of vehicles purchased or leased is one of the choices that a carrier makes. The vehicle-related cost is proportional to the number of vehicles leased or purchased.

2. *Fixed operating cost:* This includes any cost associated with terminals, airport gates, and labor that are incurred whether vehicles are in operation or not. Examples include the fixed cost of a trucking terminal facility or airport hub that is incurred independent of the number of trucks visiting the terminal or flights landing at the hub. If drivers were paid independent of their travel schedule, their salary would also be included in this category. For operational decisions, these costs are fixed. For planning and strategic decisions concerning the location and size of facilities, these costs are variable. The fixed operating cost is generally proportional to the size of operating facilities.

3. *Trip-related cost:* This cost includes the price of labor and fuel incurred for each trip independent of the quantity transported. The trip-related cost depends on the length and duration of the trip but is independent of the quantity shipped. This cost is considered variable when making strategic or planning decisions. The cost is also considered variable when making operational decisions that impact the length and duration of a trip.

4. *Quantity-related cost:* This category includes loading/unloading costs and a portion of the fuel cost that varies with the quantity being transported. These costs are generally variable in all transportation decisions unless labor used for loading and unloading is fixed.

5. *Overhead cost:* This category includes the cost of planning and scheduling a transportation network as well as any investment in information technology. When a trucking company invests in routing software that allows a manager to devise good delivery routes, the investment in the software and its operation is included in overhead. Airlines include the cost of groups that schedule and route planes and crew in overhead.

For strategic and planning decisions a carrier should consider all of the costs previously discussed to be variable. For operational decisions, most of the aforementioned costs become fixed.

A carrier's decisions are also affected by the responsiveness it seeks to provide its target segment and the prices that the market will bear. For example, FedEx designed a hub-and-spoke airline network for transporting packages to provide fast, reliable delivery times. UPS, in contrast, uses a combination of aircraft and trucks to provide cheaper transportation with somewhat longer delivery times. The difference between the two transportation networks is reflected in the pricing schedule. FedEx charges for packages based primarily on the size. UPS, in contrast, charges based on both size and destination. From a supply chain perspective, a hub-and-spoke air network is more appropriate when prices are independent of destination and rapid delivery is important, whereas a trucking network is more appropriate when prices vary with destination and a somewhat slower delivery is acceptable.

Factors Affecting Shippers Decisions

Shipper's decisions include the design of the transportation network, choice of means of transport, and the assignment of each customer shipment to a particular means of transport. A shipper's goal is to minimize the total cost of fulfilling a customer order while achieving the responsiveness promised. A shipper must account for the following costs when making transportation decisions.

1. *Transportation cost:* This is the total amount paid to various carriers for transporting products to customers. It depends on the prices offered by different carriers and the extent to which the shipper uses inexpensive and slow, or expensive and fast, means of transportation. Transportation costs are considered variable for all shipper decisions as long as the shipper does not own the carrier.

2. *Inventory cost:* This is the cost of holding inventory incurred by the shipper's supply chain network. Inventory costs are considered fixed for short-term transportation decisions that assign each customer shipment to a carrier. Inventory costs are considered

variable when a shipper is designing the transportation network or planning operating policies.

3. *Facility cost:* This is the cost of various facilities in the shipper's supply chain network. Facility costs are considered variable when supply chain managers make strategic design decisions but are considered fixed for all other transportation decisions.

4. *Processing cost:* This is the cost of loading/unloading orders as well as other processing costs associated with transportation. These are considered variable for all transportation decisions.

5. *Service level cost:* This is the cost of not being able to meet delivery commitments. In some cases it may clearly be specified as part of a contract while in other cases it may be reflected in customer satisfaction. This cost should be considered in strategic, planning, and operational decisions.

A shipper must make a trade-off between all these costs when making transportation decisions. A shipper's decisions are also impacted by the responsiveness it seeks to provide its customers and the margins generated from different products and customers. For example, a firm promising delivery within a time window specified by the customer will require more trucks than a firm whose customers are willing to accept delivery at any time.

In the next section we discuss different modes of transportation and their cost and performance characteristics.

14.3 MODES OF TRANSPORTATION AND THEIR PERFORMANCE CHARACTERISTICS

Supply chains use a combination of the following modes of transportation:

- Air
- Package carriers
- Truck
- Rail
- Water
- Pipeline
- Intermodal

We discuss the costs, pricing structure, and performance characteristics of the various modes summarized in Table 14.1.

Air

Major airlines in the United States that carry both passenger and cargo include American and Delta Airlines. Airlines have a high fixed cost in infrastructure and equipment. Labor and fuel costs are largely trip-related and independent of the number of passengers or amount of cargo carried on a flight. An airline's goal is to maximize the daily flying time of a plane and the revenue generated per trip. Given the large fixed costs and relatively low variable costs, revenue management (see Chapter 15), in which airlines vary seat prices and allocate seats to different price classes, is

TABLE 14.1	**Transportation Facts**				
Mode	*Freight Expense ($ Billions)*	*Intercity Ton-Miles (Billions)*	*Intercity Tonnage (Millions)*	*Revenue/ Ton-Mile (cents)*	*Average Length of Haul (miles)*
Air	22.67	13.87	16.3	56.25	1,260
Truck/TL	401.68	1,051	3,745	9.13	289
Truck/LTL				26.12	629
Rail	35.35	1,421	1,972	2.40	722
Water	25.35	473	1,005	0.73	Rivers/canals 481 Great Lakes 509 Coastwise 1,653
Pipeline	8.74	628 (Oil)	1,142	1.37	Crude 761 Products 394

Adapted from *Transportation in America,* 1998.

a significant factor in the success of passenger airlines. At present, airlines practice revenue management for passengers but not for cargo.

Air carriers offer a very fast and fairly expensive mode of transportation. Small, high-value items or time-sensitive emergency shipments that have to travel a long distance are best suited for air transport. Normally air carriers move shipments under 500 pounds, including high-value but lightweight high-tech products. For example, Dell uses airfreight to ship many of its components from Asia. Given the growth in high technology, the weight of freight carried by air has diminished over the last two decades even as the value of the freight has increased somewhat.

Key issues air carriers face include identifying the location and number of hubs, assigning planes to routes, setting up maintenance schedules for planes, scheduling crews, and managing prices and availability at different prices.

Package Carriers

Package carriers are transportation companies like FedEx, UPS, and the U.S. postal system that carry small packages ranging from letters to shipments weighing about 150 pounds. Package carriers use air, truck, and rail to transport time-critical smaller packages. Package carriers are expensive and cannot compete with LTL carriers on price for large shipments. The major service they offer the shipper is rapid and reliable delivery. Thus, shippers use package carriers for small and time-sensitive shipments. Package carriers also provide other value-added services that allow shippers to speed inventory flow and track order status. By tracking order status, shippers can proactively inform customers about their packages. Package carriers also pick up the package from the source and deliver it to the destination site. With an increase in JIT deliveries and focus on inventory reduction, demand for package carriers has grown.

Package carriers are the preferred mode of transport for e-businesses like Amazon.com and Dell as well as companies like W. W. Grainger and McMaster Carr that send small packages to customers. With the growth in e-business, the use of package carriers has increased significantly over the last few years. Package carriers like

FedEx that primarily use airplanes are similar to air cargo carriers except that they seek out smaller and more time-sensitive shipments where tracking and other value-added services are more important. FedEx uses trucks to pick up packages at the source and deliver them to the final destination. Air cargo carriers do not provide this combined service. Companies use air cargo carriers for larger shipments and package carriers for smaller, more time-sensitive ones. For example, Dell uses air cargo to bring components from Asia but uses package carriers to deliver PCs to customers.

Given the small size of packages and several delivery points, consolidation of shipments is a key factor in increasing utilization and decreasing costs for package carriers. Package carriers have trucks that make local deliveries and pick up packages. Packages are then taken to large sort centers from which they are sent by full TL or air to the sort center closest to the delivery point. From the delivery point sort center, the package is sent to customers on small trucks making milk runs (discussed later in the chapter). Key issues in this industry include the location and capacity of transfer points as well as information capability to facilitate and track package flow. For the final delivery to a customer, an important consideration is the scheduling and routing of the delivery trucks.

Truck

Truck is the dominant mode of freight transportation in the United States and accounts for over 75 percent of the nation's freight bill.[2] The trucking industry consists of two major segments—TL or LTL. TL operations charge for the full truck independent of the quantity shipped. Rates vary with the distance traveled. LTL operations charge based on the quantity loaded and the distance traveled. The LTL rates exhibit economies of scale. Trucking is more expensive than rail but offers the advantage of door-to-door shipment and a shorter delivery time. It also has the advantage of requiring no transfer between pickup and delivery. Major TL carriers include Schneider National, JB Hunt, Ryder Integrated, Werner, and Swift Transportation.

TL operations have relatively low fixed costs and owning a few trucks is often sufficient to enter the business. As a result there are many TL carriers in the industry. Schneider National, the largest TL carrier, had only 17 percent of the market share among the top 40 firms in the United States in 1996. The idle time and travel distance between successive loads adds to cost in the TL industry. Carriers thus try to schedule shipments to meet service requirements while minimizing both their trucks' idle and empty travel time.

TL pricing displays economies of scale with respect to the distance traveled. Given trailers of different size, pricing also displays economies of scale with respect to the size of the trailer used. TL shipping is suited for transportation between manufacturing facilities and warehouses or between suppliers and manufacturers. For example, Proctor & Gamble offers TL shipping to customer warehouses.

LTL operations are priced to encourage shipments in small lots, usually less than half a TL as TL tends to be cheaper for larger shipments. Prices display some economies of scale with the quantity shipped as well as the distance traveled. LTL shipments take longer than TL shipments because of other loads that need to be picked up

---

[2]*Transportation in America,* 1998.

and dropped off. LTL shipping is suited for shipments that are too large to be mailed as small packages but constitute less than half a TL.

A key to reducing LTL costs is the degree of consolidation that carriers can achieve for the loads carried. LTL carriers use consolidation centers where trucks bring in many small loads originating from a geographical area and leave with many small loads destined for the same geographical area. This allows LTL carriers to improve their truck use although it increases delivery time somewhat. Larger firms enjoy an advantage in the LTL industry given the importance of consolidation and the fixed cost of setting up consolidation centers. Strong regional players have developed in the LTL industry because of the advantage offered by a high density of pickup and delivery points in a geographical area.

Key issues for the LTL industry include location of consolidation centers, assigning of loads to trucks, and scheduling and routing of pickup and delivery. The goal is to minimize costs through consolidation without hurting delivery time and reliability.

Rail

Major rail carriers in North America include Burlington Northern Santa Fe, Canadian National, CSX Transportation, and Norfolk Southern. Rail carriers incur a high fixed cost in terms of rails, locomotives, cars, and yards. There is also a significant trip-related labor and fuel cost that is independent of the number of cars (fuel costs do vary somewhat with the number of cars) but does vary with the distance traveled and the time taken. Any idle time, once a train is powered, is very expensive because labor and fuel costs are incurred even though trains are not moving. Idle time occurs when trains exchange cars for different destinations. It also occurs because of track congestion. Labor and fuel together account for over 60 percent of railroad expense. From an operational perspective, it is thus important for railroads to keep locomotives and crew well utilized.

Rail is priced to encourage large shipments over a long distance. Prices display economies of scale in the quantity shipped as well as the distance traveled. The price structure and the heavy load capability makes rail an ideal mode for carrying large, heavy, or high-density products over long distances. Transportation time by rail, however, can be large. Rail is thus ideal for very heavy, low-value shipments that are not very time sensitive. The resulting transportation cost tends to be low. Coal, for example, is a major part of each railroad's shipments. Small, time-sensitive, short distance, or short lead time shipments rarely use rail.

Railroad revenues have not grown significantly over the past two decades and hover in the mid $30 billion range. Most of the improvement in financial performance over that period has come from abandoning unprofitable lines and making better use of existing assets. The growth in the intermodal sector (discussed later in the chapter) has also helped railroad performance during this period.

A major goal in railroads is to keep locomotives and crew well utilized. Major operational issues at railroads include vehicle and staff scheduling, track and terminal delays, and poor on-time performance. Railroad performance is hurt by the large amount of time taken at each transition. The travel time is usually a small fraction of the total time for a rail shipment. Delays get exaggerated because trains today are typically not scheduled but "built." In other words, a train leaves once there are enough cars to constitute the train. Cars wait for the train to build, adding to the uncertainty of the delivery time for a shipper. A railroad can improve on-time performance by scheduling some of the trains instead of building all of them. In such a setting, a more sophisticated pricing strategy that includes revenue management (see Chapter 15) will need to be instituted for scheduled trains.

Water

Major ocean carriers include Maersk Sealand, Evergreen Group, American President Lines, and Hanjin Shipping Co. Water transport, by its nature, is limited to certain areas. Within the United States, water transport takes place via the inland waterway system (Great Lakes and rivers) or coastal waters. Water transport is ideally suited for carrying very large loads at low cost. Within the United States, water transport is used primarily for the movement of large bulk commodity shipments and is the cheapest mode for carrying such loads. It is, however, the slowest of all the modes and significant delays occur at ports and terminals. This makes water transport difficult to operate for short-haul trips though it is used effectively in Japan and parts of Europe for daily short-haul trips of a few miles.

Within the United States, the passage of the Ocean Shipping Reform Act of 1998 has been a significant event for water transport. This bill allows carriers and shippers to enter into confidential contracts, effectively deregulating the industry. The bill is similar to the deregulation that occurred in the trucking and airline industries over two decades ago and is likely to have a similar impact on the shipping industry.

In global trade, water transport is the dominant mode for shipping all kinds of products. Cars, grain, apparel, and other products are shipped by sea. For the quantities shipped and the distances involved, water transport is by far the cheapest mode of transport for global shipping. Delays at ports, customs, and the management of containers used are major issues in global shipping.

Pipeline

Pipeline is used primarily for the transport of crude petroleum, refined petroleum products, and natural gas. A significant initial fixed cost is incurred in setting up the pipeline and related infrastructure that does not vary significantly with the diameter of the pipeline. Pipeline operations are typically optimized at about 80 to 90 percent of pipeline capacity. Given the nature of the costs, pipelines are best suited when relatively stable and large flows are required. Pipeline may be an effective way of getting crude oil to a port or a refinery. Sending gasoline to a gas station does not justify investment in a pipeline and is done better with a truck. Pipeline pricing usually consists of two components—a fixed component related to the shipper's peak usage and a second charge relating to the actual quantity transported. This pricing structure encourages the shipper to use the pipeline for the predictable component of demand with other modes often being used to cover fluctuations.

Intermodal

Intermodal transportation is the use of more than one mode of transport to move a shipment to its destination. A variety of intermodal combinations are possible, with the most common being truck/rail. Major intermodal providers with rail include CSX

Intermodal, Pacer Stacktrain, and Triple Crown. Intermodal traffic has grown considerably with the increased use of containers for shipping and the rise of global trade. Containers are easy to transfer from one mode to another and their use facilitates intermodal transportation. Containerized freight often uses truck/water/rail combinations, particularly for global freight. For global trade, intermodal is often the only option because factories and markets may not be next to ports. As the quantity shipped using containers has grown, the truck/water/rail intermodal combination has also grown. In 1996, intermodal activity contributed 16 percent of rail revenues.[3] On land, the rail/truck intermodal system offers the benefit of lower cost than TL and delivery times that are better than rail, thereby bringing together different modes of transport to create a price/service offering that cannot be matched by any single mode. It also creates convenience for shippers who now deal with only one entity representing all carriers who together provide the intermodal service.

Key issues in the intermodal industry involve the exchange of information to facilitate shipment transfers between different modes because these transfers often involve considerable delays, hurting delivery time performance.

14.4 DESIGN OPTIONS FOR A TRANSPORTATION NETWORK

The design of a transportation network impacts the performance of a supply chain by establishing the infrastructure within which operational transportation decisions regarding scheduling and routing are made. A well-designed transportation network allows a supply chain to achieve the desired degree of responsiveness at a low cost. We discuss a variety of design options for transportation networks and the strengths and weaknesses for each option in the context of a retail chain with many stores and several suppliers.

Direct Shipping Network

With this option, the retail chain structures its transportation network to have all shipments come directly from suppliers to retail stores as shown in Figure 14.1. With a direct shipment network, the routing of each shipment is specified and the supply chain manager only needs to decide on the quantity to ship and the mode of transportation to use. This decision involves a trade-off between transportation and inventory costs as discussed later in the chapter.

The major advantage of a direct shipment transportation network is the elimination of intermediate warehouses and its simplicity of operation and coordination. The shipment decision is completely local and the decision made for one shipment does not influence others. The transportation time from supplier to retail store will be short because each shipment goes direct.

A direct shipment network is justified if retail stores are large enough such that optimal replenishment lot sizes are close to a TL from each supplier to each retailer. With small retail stores, however, a direct shipment network tends to have high costs. If a TL carrier is used for transportation, the high fixed cost of each truck results in large

[3]*Distribution*, July 1997.

Suppliers   Retail Stores

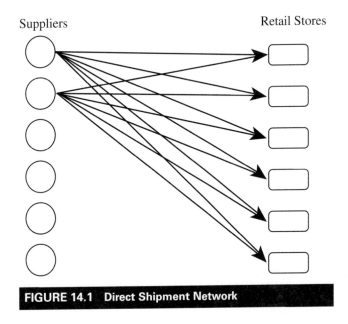

FIGURE 14.1   Direct Shipment Network

lots moving from suppliers to each retail store, resulting in high supply chain inventories. If an LTL carrier is used, the transportation cost and the delivery time increase though inventories are lower. If package carriers are used, transportation cost will be very high. With direct deliveries from each supplier, receiving costs will be high because each supplier must make a separate delivery.

Direct Shipping with Milk Runs

A *milk run* is a route in which a truck either delivers product from a single supplier to multiple retailers or goes from multiple suppliers to a single retailer as shown in Figure 14.2. In direct shipping with milk runs, a supplier delivers directly to multiple retail stores on a truck or a truck picks up deliveries from many suppliers destined for the same retail store. When using this option, a supply chain manager has to decide on the routing of each milk run.

Direct shipping provides the benefit of eliminating intermediate warehouses, whereas milk runs lower transportation cost by consolidating shipments to multiple stores on a single truck. For example, the replenishment lot size for each retail store may be small and require LTL shipping if sent directly. The use of milk runs allows deliveries to multiple stores to be consolidated on a single truck, resulting in a better utilization of the truck and somewhat lower costs. Companies like Frito-Lay that make direct store deliveries use milk runs to lower their transportation cost. If very frequent, small deliveries are needed on a regular basis and either a set of suppliers or a set of retailers is in geographical proximity, the use of milk runs can significantly reduce transportation costs. For example, Toyota uses milk runs from suppliers to support its JIT manufacturing system in both Japan and the United States. In Japan, Toyota has many assembly plants located close together and thus uses milk runs from a single

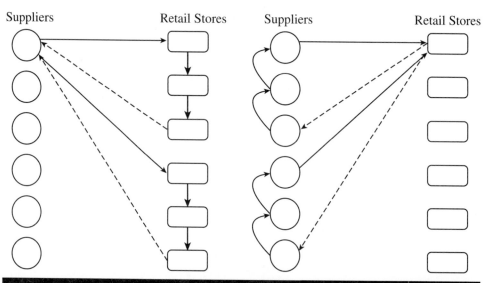

FIGURE 14.2 Milk Runs from Multiple Suppliers or to Multiple Retailers

supplier to many plants. In the United States, however, Toyota uses milk runs from many suppliers to its assembly plants.

All Shipments via Central DC

With this option, suppliers do not send shipments directly to retail stores. The retail chain divides stores by geographical region and a DC is built for each region. Suppliers send their shipments to the DC and the DC then forwards appropriate shipments to each retail store as shown in Figure 14.3.

The DC is an extra layer between suppliers and retailers and can play two different roles. One is to store inventory and the other is to serve as a transfer location. In either case, the presence of DCs can help reduce supply chain costs when suppliers are located far from the retail stores and transportation costs are high. The presence of a DC allows a supply chain to achieve economies of scale for inbound transportation to a point close to the final destination because each supplier sends a large shipment to the DC containing product for all stores the DC serves. Because DCs serve stores located nearby, the outbound transportation cost is not very large.

If transportation economies require very large shipments on the inbound side, DCs hold inventory and send product to retail stores in smaller replenishment lots. For example, when Wal-Mart sources from an overseas supplier, the product is held in inventory at the DC because the lot size on the inbound side is much larger than the sum of the lot sizes for the stores served by the DC. If replenishment lots for the stores served by the DC are large enough to achieve economies of scale on inbound transportation, the DC does not need to hold inventory. In this case the DC can cross-dock product arriving from many suppliers on inbound trucks by breaking each inbound shipment into smaller shipments that are then loaded onto trucks going to each retail store. When a DC cross-docks product, each inbound truck contains product from a

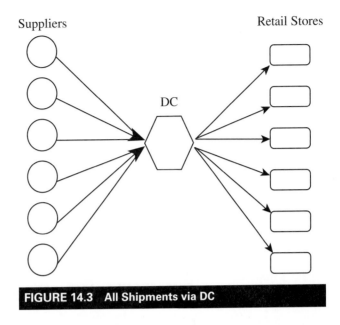

Suppliers

Retail Stores

DC

FIGURE 14.3   All Shipments via DC

supplier for several retail stores while each outbound truck contains product for a retail store from several suppliers. A major benefit of cross-docking is that little inventory needs to be held and product flows faster in the supply chain. Cross-docking also saves on handling cost because product does not have to be moved into and out of storage. Successful cross-docking, however, does require a significant degree of coordination and synchronization between the incoming and outgoing shipments.

Cross-docking is appropriate for products with large, predictable demands and requires that DCs be set up such that economies of scale in transportation can be achieved on both the inbound and outbound side. Wal-Mart has successfully used cross-docking to decrease inventories in the supply chain without incurring excessive transportation costs. Wal-Mart builds many large stores in a geographical area supported by a DC. As a result, the total lot size to all stores from each supplier fills trucks on the inbound side to achieve economies of scale. On the outbound side, the sum of the lot sizes from all suppliers to each retail store fills up the truck to achieve economies of scale.

Shipping via DC Using Milk Runs

As shown in Figure 14.4, milk runs can be used from a DC if lot sizes to be delivered to each retail store are small. Milk runs reduce outbound transportation costs by consolidating small shipments. For example, 7-Eleven Japan cross-docks deliveries from its fresh food suppliers at its DCs and sends out milk runs to the retail outlets because the total shipment to a store from all suppliers does not fill a truck. The use of cross-docking and milk runs allows 7-Eleven to lower its transportation cost while sending small replenishment lots to each store. The use of cross-docking with milk runs requires a significant degree of coordination and suitable routing and scheduling of milk runs.

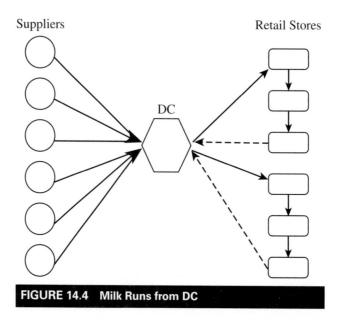

FIGURE 14.4   Milk Runs from DC

The online grocer Peapod uses milk runs from DCs when making customer deliveries to help reduce transportation costs for small shipments to be delivered to homes. OshKosh B'Gosh, a manufacturer of children's wear, has used this idea to virtually eliminate LTL shipments from its DC in Tennessee to retail stores.

Tailored Network

This option is a suitable combination of previous options that reduces the cost and improves responsiveness of the supply chain. Here transportation uses a combination of cross-docking, milk runs, and TL and LTL carriers, along with package carriers in

TABLE 14.2   Pros and Cons of Different Transportation Networks

Network Structure	Pros	Cons
Direct shipping	No intermediate warehouse Simple to coordinate	High inventories (due to large lot size) Significant receiving expense
Direct shipping with milk runs	Lower transportation costs for small lots Lower inventories	Increased coordination complexity
All shipments via central DC with inventory storage	Lower inbound transportation cost through consolidation	Increased inventory cost Increased handling at DC
All shipments via central DC with cross-dock	Very low inventory requirement Lower transportation cost through consolidation	Increased coordination complexity
Shipping via DC using milk runs	Lower outbound transportation cost for small lots	Further increase in coordination complexity
Tailored network	Transportation choice best matches needs of individual product and store	Highest coordination complexity

some cases. The goal is to use the appropriate option in each situation. High-demand products to high-demand retail outlets may be shipped directly while low-demand products or shipments to low-demand retail outlets are consolidated to and from the DC. The complexity of managing this transportation network is high because different shipping procedures are used for each product and retail outlet. Operating a tailored network requires significant investment in information infrastructure to facilitate the coordination. Such a network, however, allows for the selective use of the shipment method to minimize the transportation as well as inventory costs.

Table 14.2 summarizes the pros and cons of the various transportation network options discussed.

In the next section we discuss a variety of trade-offs that supply chain managers need to consider when designing and operating a transportation network.

14.5   TRADE-OFFS IN TRANSPORTATION DESIGN

All transportation decisions in a supply chain network must be made taking into account their impact on inventory costs, facility and processing costs, the cost of coordinating operations, as well as the level of responsiveness provided to customers. For example, Dell's use of package carriers for delivering PCs to customers increases transportation cost but allows Dell to centralize its facilities and reduce inventory costs. If Dell wants to reduce its transportation costs, the company must either sacrifice responsiveness to customers or increase the number of facilities and resulting inventories to move closer to customers.

The cost of coordinating operations is generally hard to quantify. Companies should evaluate different transportation options in terms of various costs as well as revenues and then rank them according to coordination complexity. A manager can then make the appropriate transportation decision. Managers must consider the following trade-offs when making transportation decisions:

- Transportation and inventory cost trade-off
- Transportation cost and customer responsiveness trade-off

Transportation and Inventory Cost Trade-off

The trade-off between transportation and inventory costs is significant when designing a supply chain network. Two fundamental supply chain decisions involving this trade-off are

- Choice of transportation mode
- Inventory aggregation

Choice of Transportation Mode

Selecting a transportation mode is both a planning and an operational decision in a supply chain. The decision regarding carriers with which a company contracts is a planning decision, whereas the choice of transportation mode for a particular shipment is an operational decision. For both decisions, a shipper must balance transportation and inventory costs. The mode of transportation that results in the lowest transportation cost does not necessarily lower total costs for a supply chain. Cheaper modes of transport typically have longer lead times and larger minimum shipment quantities, both of which result in higher levels of inventory in the supply chain. Modes that allow for shipping in small quantities lower inventory levels but tend to be more expensive. Dell, for example, airfreights several of its components from Asia. This choice cannot be justified on the basis of transportation cost alone. It can only be justified because the use of a faster mode of transportation for shipping valuable components allows Dell to carry low levels of inventory.

The impact of using different modes of transportation on inventories, response time, and costs in the supply chain is shown in Table 14.3. Each transportation mode is ranked along various dimensions with 1 being the lowest and 6 being the highest.

Faster modes of transportation are preferred for products with a high value to weight ratio where reducing inventories is important, whereas slower modes are preferred for products with a small value to weight ratio where reducing transportation costs is important.

Ignoring inventory costs when making transportation decisions can result in choices that worsen the performance of a supply chain. To illustrate the importance of evaluating the trade-off between transportation and inventory costs, consider the example of Eastern Electric (EE), a major appliance manufacturer with a large plant in the Chicago area.[4] EE purchases all the motors for its appliances from Westview Motors located near Dallas. EE currently purchases 120,000 motors each year from Westview at a price of $120 per motor. Demand has been relatively constant for several years and is expected to stay that way. Each motor averages about 10 lbs. in weight and EE has traditionally purchased in lots of 3,000 motors. Westview ships each EE order within a day of receiving it. At its assembly plant, EE carries a safety inventory equal to 50 percent of the average demand for motors during the delivery lead time.

The plant manager at EE has received several proposals for transportation and must decide on the one to accept. The details of various proposals are provided in Table 14.4, where one cwt. is equal to a hundred pounds.

Golden's pricing represents a marginal unit quantity discount (see Chapter 10). Golden's representative has proposed lowering the marginal rate for the quantity over 2500 cwt. in a shipment from $4/cwt. to $3/cwt. Golden's new proposal will result in very low transportation costs for EE if the plant manager orders in lots of 400 motors.

The plant manager, however, decides to include inventory costs in the transportation decision. Eastern Electric's annual cost of holding inventory is 25 percent, which

TABLE 14.3 Impact of Transportation Modes on Supply Chain Performance

	Rail	*TL*	*LTL*	*Package*	*Air*	*Water*
Lot size	5	4	3	1	2	6
Safety inventory	5	4	3	1	2	6
In-transit inventory	5	4	3	1	2	6
Transportation cost	2	3	4	6	5	1
Transportation time	5	3	4	1	2	6

---

[4]This example is inspired by the Honfleur Corporation case in *Logistics Strategy: Cases and Concepts* by R. D. Shapiro and J. L. Heskett, 1985.

TABLE 14.4 Transportation Proposals for EE Electric		
Carrier	*Range of Quantity Shipped (cwt.)*	*Shipping Cost ($/cwt.)*
AM Railroad	200 +	6.50
Northeast Trucking	100 +	7.50
Golden Freightways	50–150	8.00
Golden Freightways	150–250	6.00
Golden Freightways	250–400	4.00

implies an annual holding cost of $H = \$120 \times 0.25 = \$30$ per motor. Shipments by rail require a five-day transit time, whereas shipments by truck have a transit time of three days. The transportation decision affects the cycle inventory, safety inventory, and in-transit inventory for EE. Therefore, the plant manager decides to evaluate the total transportation and inventory cost for each transportation option.

The AM Rail proposal requires a minimum shipment of 20,000 lb. or 2,000 motors. The replenishment lead time in this case is $L = 5 + 1 = 6$ days. For a lot size of $Q = 2,000$ motors, the plant manager obtains the following:

$$\text{Cycle inventory} = Q/2 = 2,000/2 = 1,000 \text{ motors,}$$
$$\text{Safety inventory} = L/2 \text{ days of demand} = (6/2)(120,000/365)$$
$$= 986 \text{ motors,}$$
$$\text{In-transit inventory} = 120,000(5/365) = 1,644 \text{ motors,}$$
$$\text{Total average inventory} = 1,000 + 986 + 1,644 = 3,630 \text{ motors,}$$
Annual holding cost using AM Rail $= 3,630 \times 30 = \$108,900$.

AM Rail charges \$6.50 per cwt. resulting in a transportation cost of \$0.65 per motor because each motor weighs 10 lbs. Thus,

$$\text{Annual transportation cost using AM Rail} = 120,000 \times .65 = \$78,000.$$

The total annual cost for inventory and transportation using AM Rail is thus \$186,900.

The plant manager then evaluates the cost associated with each transportation option as shown in Table 14.5.

Based on the analysis in Table 14.5, the plant manager decides to sign a contract with Golden Freightways and order motors in lots of 500. This option has the highest transportation cost but the lowest overall cost. If the selection of the transportation option was made using only the transportation cost incurred, Golden's new proposal lowering the price for large shipments would look attractive. In reality, Eastern pays a high overall cost for this proposal. Thus, considering the trade-off between inventory and transportation costs allows the plant manager to make a transportation decision that minimizes Eastern's total cost.

> **Key Point** When selecting a mode of transportation, managers must account for inventory costs. Modes with high transportation cost can be justified if they result in significantly lower inventories.

TABLE 14.5   Analysis of Transportation Options for Eastern Electric

Alternative	Lot Size (Motors)	Transportation Cost	Cycle Inventory	Safety Inventory	In-Transit Inventory	Inventory Cost	Total Cost
AM Rail	2,000	$78,000	1,000	986	1,644	$108,900	$186,900
Northeast Trucking	1,000	$90,000	500	658	986	$64,320	$154,320
Golden	500	$96,000	250	658	986	$56,820	$152,820
Golden	1,500	$96,000	750	658	986	$71,820	$167,820
Golden	2,500	$86,400	1,250	658	986	$86,820	$173,220
Golden	3,000	$78,000	1,500	658	986	$94,320	$172,320
Golden (old proposal)	4,000	$72,000	2,000	658	986	$109,320	$181,320
Golden (new proposal)	4,000	$67,500	2,000	658	986	$109,320	$176,820

Inventory Aggregation

Firms can significantly reduce the safety inventory they require by physically aggregating inventories in one location (see Chapter 11). Most e-businesses have used this technique to gain advantage over firms with facilities in many locations. For example, Amazon.com has focused on decreasing its facility and inventory costs by holding inventory in a few warehouses, whereas booksellers like Borders and Barnes and Noble have to hold inventory in many retail stores.

Transportation cost, however, increases when inventory is aggregated. Consider a bookstore chain such as Borders. The inbound transportation cost to Borders is due to the replenishment of bookstores with new books. There is no outbound cost because customers transport their own books home. If Borders decides to close all its bookstores and only sell online, it will have to incur both inbound and outbound transportation costs. The inbound transportation cost to warehouses will be lower than to all bookstores. On the outbound side, however, transportation cost will increase significantly because the outbound shipment to each customer will be small and will require an expensive mode such as a package carrier. The total transportation cost will increase on aggregation because each book will travel the same distance as when it was sold through a bookstore, except that a large fraction of the distance will be on the outbound side using an expensive mode of transportation. As the degree of inventory aggregation increases, total transportation cost goes up. Thus, all firms planning inventory aggregation must consider the trade-off between transportation, inventory, and facility costs when making this decision.

Inventory aggregation is a good idea when inventory and facility costs form a large fraction of a supply chain's total costs. Inventory aggregation is useful for products with a large value to weight ratio and for products with high demand uncertainty. For example, inventory aggregation is very valuable in the PC industry for new products because PCs have a large value to weight ratio and demand is uncertain. Inventory aggregation is also a good idea if customer orders are large enough to ensure sufficient economies of scale on outbound transportation. When products have a low value to weight ratio and customer orders are small, however, inventory aggregation may hurt a supply chain's performance because of high transportation costs. Compared to PCs, the value of inventory aggregation is smaller for best-selling books that have a lower value to weight ratio and more predictable demand.

We illustrate the trade-off involved in making aggregation decisions in the context of HighMed Inc., a manufacturer of medical equipment used in heart procedures. HighMed is located in Wisconsin and cardiologists all over North America use its equipment. The medical equipment is not sold through purchasing agents but directly to doctors. HighMed has currently divided the United States into 24 territories, each with its own sales force. All product inventories are maintained locally and replenished from Madison every four weeks using UPS. The average replenishment lead time using UPS is one week. UPS charges at a rate of $0.66 + 0.26x$, where x is the quantity shipped in pounds. The products sold fall into two categories—Highval and Lowval. Highval products weigh 0.1 lbs. and cost $200 each. Lowval products weigh 0.04 lbs. and cost $30 each.

Weekly demand for Highval products in each territory is normally distributed with a mean of $\mu_H = 2$ and a standard deviation of $\sigma_H = 5$. Weekly demand for Lowval products in each territory is normally distributed with a mean of $\mu_L = 20$ and a standard deviation of $\sigma_L = 5$. HighMed maintains sufficient safety inventories in each territory to provide a CSL of 0.997 for each product. Holding cost at HighMed is 25 percent.

The management team at HighMed wants to evaluate the operating cost of the current operating procedure and compare it with two other options they have been considering.

1. *Option A:* Keep the current structure but start replenishing inventory once a week rather than once every four weeks.
2. *Option B:* Eliminate inventories in the territories, aggregate all inventories in a finished goods warehouse at Madison, and replenish the warehouse once a week.

If inventories are aggregated at Madison, orders will be shipped using FedEx, which charges $5.53 + 0.53x$ per shipment, where x is the quantity shipped in pounds. The factory requires a one-week lead time to replenish finished goods inventories at the Madison warehouse. An average customer order is for 1 unit of HighVal and 10 units of LowVal.

HighMed can reduce transportation cost by aggregating the quantity shipped at a time because prices for both UPS and FedEx display economies of scale. When comparing Option A with the current system, the management team must trade off the savings in transportation cost through less frequent replenishment with the savings in inventory cost with more frequent replenishment. When considering Option B, the management team must trade off the increase in transportation cost upon aggregation of inventories and the use of a faster but more expensive carrier (FedEx) with the decrease in inventory cost.

The management team first analyzes the current situation. For each territory,

Replenishment lead time $L = 1$ week,
Reorder interval $T = 4$ weeks,
$CSL = 0.997$.

1. *HighMed inventory costs (current scenario):* For HighVal in each territory, the management team obtains the following:

Average lot size Q_H = Expected demand during T weeks = $T\mu_H = 4 \times 2 = 8$ units,

Safety inventory $ss_H = F^{-1}(CSL) \times \sigma_{T+L} = F^{-1}(CSL) \times \sqrt{T+L} \times \sigma_H =$

$$F^{-1}(0.997) \times \sqrt{4+1} \times 5 = 30.7 \text{ units (see Equation 11.16)},$$

Total HighVal inventory = $Q_H/2 + ss_H = (8/2) + 30.7 = 34.7$ units.

Across all 24 territories, HighMed thus carries HighVal inventory of $24 \times 34.7 = 832.8$ units. For LowVal in each territory, the management team obtains the following:

Average lot size Q_L = Expected demand during T weeks = $T\mu_L = 4 \times 20 = 80$ units,

Safety inventory $ss_H = F^{-1}(CSL) \times \sigma_{T+L} = F^{-1}(CSL) \times \sqrt{T+L} \times \sigma_L$

$$= F^{-1}(0.997) \times \sqrt{4+1} \times 5 = 30.7 \text{ units},$$

Total LowVal inventory = $Q_H/2 + ss_H = (80/2) + 30.7 = 70.7$ units.

Across all 24 territories HighMed thus carries LowVal inventory = $24 \times 70.7 = 1696.8$ units.

The management team thus obtains the following:

Annual inventory holding cost for HighMed = (Average HighVal inventory
$\times$ \$200 + Average LowVal inventory $\times$ \$30) $\times$ 0.25
= (832.8 $\times$ \$200 + 1696.8 $\times$ \$30) $\times$ 0.25 = \$54,366.

2. *HighMed transportation cost (current scenario):* The average replenishment order from each territory consists of Q_H units of HighVal and Q_L units of LowVal. Thus

Average weight of each replenishment order = $0.1Q_H + 0.04Q_L = 0.1 \times 8 + 0.04$
$\times 80 = 4$ lbs,
Shipping cost per replenishment order = \$0.66 + 0.26 $\times$ 4 = \$1.7.

Each territory has 13 replenishment orders per year and there are 24 territories. Thus

Annual transportation cost = \$1.7 $\times$ 13 $\times$ 24 = \$530.

3. *HighMed total cost (current scenario):* Annual inventory and transportation cost at HighMed = Inventory cost + Transportation cost = \$54,366 + \$530.4 = \$54,896. The HighMed management team evaluates the costs for Option A and Option B similarly and the results are summarized in Table 14.6.

From Table 14.6 observe that increasing the replenishment frequency under Option A decreases total cost at HighMed. The increase in transportation costs is much smaller than the decrease in inventory costs resulting from smaller lots. HighMed is able to reduce total cost the most by aggregating all inventories and using FedEx for transportation because the decrease in inventories on aggregation is larger than the increase in transportation costs.

If customer order sizes are small, the increase in transportation cost on aggregation can be significant and inventory aggregation may increase total costs. Consider the case of HighMed where each customer order averages 0.5 *HighVal* and 5 *LowVal* (half the size considered earlier). The costs for the current option as well as option A remain unchanged because HighMed does not pay for outbound transportation and only

TABLE 14.6   HighMed Costs Under Different Network Options

	Current Scenario	*Option A*	*Option B*
Number of stocking locations	24	24	1
Reorder interval	4 weeks	1 week	1 week
HighVal cycle inventory	96 units	24 units	24 units
HighVal safety inventory	736.8 units	466 units	95.2 units
HighVal inventory	832.8 units	490 units	119.2 units
LowVal cycle inventory	960 units	240 units	240 units
LowVal safety inventory	736.8 units	466 units	95.2 units
LowVal inventory	1,696.8 units	706 units	335.2 units
Annual inventory cost	$54,366	$29,795	$8,474
Shipment type	Replenishment	Replenishment	Customer order
Shipment size	8 HighVal + 80 LowVal	2 HighVal + 20 LowVal	1 HighVal + 10 LowVal
Shipment weight	4 lbs.	1 lb.	0.5 lb.
Annual transport cost	$530	$1,148	$14,464
Total annual cost	$54,896	$30,943	$22,938

incurs the cost of transporting replenishment orders under both options. Option B, however, becomes more expensive because outbound transportation costs increase with a decrease in customer order size. The costs under Option B are as follows:

$$\text{Average weight of each customer order} = 0.1 \times 0.5 + 0.04 \times 5 = 0.25 \text{ lbs,}$$
$$\text{Shipping cost per customer order} = \$5.53 + 0.53 \times 0.25 = \$5.66$$
$$\text{Number of customer orders per territory per week} = 4,$$
$$\text{Total customer orders per year} = 4 \times 24 \times 52 = 4,992,$$
$$\text{Annual transportation cost} = 4,992 \times 5.66 = \$28,255,$$
$$\text{Total annual cost} = \text{inventory cost}$$
$$+ \text{transportation cost} = \$8,474 + \$28,255 = \$36,729.$$

Thus, with small customer orders, inventory aggregation is no longer the lowest cost option for HighMed because of the large increase in transportation costs. The company is better off maintaining inventory in each territory and using Option A, which gives a lower total cost.

Key Point   Inventory aggregation decisions must account for inventory and transportation costs. Inventory aggregation decreases supply chain costs if the product has a high value to weight ratio, high demand uncertainty, and customer orders are large. If a product has a low value to weight ratio, low demand uncertainty, or customer orders are small, inventory aggregation may increase supply chain costs.

Trade-Off between Transportation Cost and Customer Responsiveness

The transportation cost a supply chain incurs is closely linked to the degree of responsiveness the supply chain aims to provide. If a firm has high responsiveness and ships all orders within a day of their receipt from the customer, it will have small outbound shipments resulting in a high transportation cost. If it decreases its responsiveness and aggregates orders over a longer time horizon before shipping them out, it will be able to exploit economies of scale and incur a lower transportation cost because of larger shipments. *Temporal aggregation* is the process of combining orders across time. Temporal aggregation decreases a firm's responsiveness because of shipping delay but also decreases transportation costs because of economies of scale that result from larger shipments. Thus, a firm must consider the trade-off between responsiveness and transportation cost when designing its transportation network.

Consider Alloy Steel, a steel service center in the Cleveland area. Alloy ships all orders to customers using an LTL carrier that charges $100 + 0.01x$, where x is the number of pounds of steel shipped on the truck. The LTL carrier also charges $10 for each customer delivery. Currently, Alloy Steel ships orders on the day they are received. Allowing for two days in transit, this policy allows Alloy to achieve a response time of two days. Daily demand at Alloy Steel over a two-week period is shown in Table 14.7.

The general manager at Alloy Steel feels that customers do not really value the 2-day response time and would be satisfied with a four-day response. As the response time increases, Alloy Steel has the opportunity to aggregate demand over multiple days for shipping. For a response time of three days, Alloy Steel can aggregate demand over two successive days before shipping. For a response time of four days, Alloy Steel can aggregate demand over three days before shipping. The manager evaluates the quantity shipped and transportation costs for different response times over the two-week period as shown in Table 14.8.

From Table 14.8 observe that the transportation cost for Alloy Steel decreases as the response time increases. The benefit of temporal consolidation, however, diminishes rapidly on increasing the response time. As the response time increases from two to three days, transportation cost over the two-week window decreases by $700. Increasing the response time from three to four days reduces the transportation cost by only $200. Thus a limited amount of temporal aggregation can be very effective at reducing transportation cost in a supply chain. Firms, however, must trade off the decrease in transportation cost on temporal aggregation with the loss of revenue because of poorer responsiveness when choosing the appropriate response time.

Temporal consolidation also improves transportation performance because it results in more stable shipments. For example, in Table 14.7, when Alloy Steel sends daily shipments, the coefficient of variation is 0.44, whereas temporal aggregation across three days (achieved with a four-day response time) has a coefficient of

TABLE 14.7 Daily Demand at Alloy Steel Over Two-Week Period						
Week 1	19,970	17,470	11,316	26,192	20,263	8,381	25,377
Week 2	39,171	2,158	20,633	23,370	24,100	19,603	18,442

		2-Day Response		3-Day Response		4-Day Response	
Day	Demand	Quantity Shipped	Cost	Quantity Shipped	Cost	Quantity Shipped	Cost
1	19,970	19,970	$ 299.7	0	$ —	0	$ —
2	17,470	17,470	$ 274.70	37,440	$ 474.40	0	$ —
3	11,316	11,316	$ 213.16	0	$ —	48,756	$ 587.56
4	26,192	26,192	$ 361.92	37,508	$ 475.08	0	$ —
5	20,263	20,263	$ 302.63	0	$ —	0	$ —
6	8,381	8,381	$ 183.81	28,644	$ 386.44	54,836	$ 648.36
7	25,377	25,377	$ 353.77	0	$ —	0	$ —
8	39,171	39,171	$ 491.71	64,548	$ 745.48	0	$ —
9	2,158	2,158	$ 121.58	0	$ —	66,706	$ 767.06
10	20,633	20,633	$ 306.33	22,791	$ 327.91	0	$ —
11	23,370	23,370	$ 333.70	0	$ —	0	$ —
12	24,100	24,100	$ 341.00	47,470	$ 574.70	68,103	$ 781.03
13	19,603	19,603	$ 296.03	0	$ —	0	$ —
14	18,442	18,442	$ 284.42	38,045	$ 480.45	38,045	$ 480.45
			$4,164.46		$3,464.46		$3,264.46

TABLE 14.8   Quantity Shipped and Transportation Cost as a Function of Response Time

variation of only 0.16. More stable shipments allow both Alloy Steel and the carrier to better plan operations and improve utilization of their assets.

> **Key Point**   Temporal aggregation of demand results in a reduction of transportation costs because it entails larger shipments and also reduces the variation in shipment sizes from one shipment to the next. It does, however, hurt customer response time. The marginal benefit of temporal aggregation declines as the time window over which aggregation takes place increases.

In the next section we discuss how transportation networks can be appropriately structured to supply customers with differing needs.

14.6   TAILORED TRANSPORTATION

Tailored transportation is the use of different transportation networks and modes based on customer and product characteristics. Most firms sell a variety of products and serve many different customer segments. For example, W. W. Grainger sells over 200,000 MRO supply products to both small contractors and very large firms. Products vary in size and value and customers vary in the quantity purchased, responsiveness required, uncertainty of the orders, and distance from W. W. Grainger branches and DCs. Given these differences, a firm like W. W. Grainger should not design a common transportation network to meet all needs. A firm can meet customer needs at a lower cost by using tailored transportation to provide the appropriate transportation choice based on customer and product characteristics. In the following sections we describe various forms of tailored transportation in supply chains.

Tailored Transportation by Customer Density and Distance

Firms must consider customer density and distance from warehouse when designing transportation networks. The ideal transportation options based on density and distance are shown in Table 14.9.

When a firm serves a very high density of customers close to the DC, it is often best for the firm to own a fleet of trucks that are used with milk runs originating at the DC to supply customers because this scenario makes very good use of the vehicles. If customer density is high but distance from the warehouse is large, it does not pay to send milk runs from the warehouse because trucks will travel a long distance empty on the return trip. In such a situation it is better to use a public carrier with large trucks to haul the shipments to a cross-dock center close to the customer area, where the shipments are loaded onto smaller trucks that deliver product to customers using milk runs. In this situation, it may not be ideal for a firm to own its own fleet. As customer density decreases, use of an LTL carrier or a third party doing milk runs is more economical because the third-party carrier can aggregate shipments across many firms. If a firm wants to serve an area with a very low density of customers far from the warehouse, even LTL carriers may not be feasible and the use of package carriers may be the best option. Boise Cascade Office Products, an industrial distributor of office supplies, has designed a transportation network consistent with the suggestion in Table 14.9.

Customer density and distance should also be considered when firms decide on the degree of temporal aggregation to use when supplying customers. Firms should serve areas with high customer density more frequently because these areas are likely to provide sufficient economies of scale in transportation, making temporal aggregation less valuable. To lower transportation costs, firms should use a higher degree of temporal aggregation when serving areas with a low customer density.

Tailored Transportation by Size of Customer

Firms must consider customer size and location when designing transportation networks. Very large customers can be supplied using a TL carrier, whereas smaller customers will require an LTL carrier or milk runs. When using milk runs, a shipper incurs two types of costs:

- Transportation cost based on total route distance
- Delivery cost based on number of deliveries

TABLE 14.9 Transportation Options Based on Customer Density and Distance

	Short Distance	*Medium Distance*	*Long Distance*
High density	Private Fleet with milk runs	Cross-dock with milk runs	Cross-dock with milk runs
Medium density	Third-party milk runs	LTL carrier	LTL or package carrier
Low density	Third-party milk runs or LTL carrier	LTL or package carrier	Package carrier

The transportation cost is the same whether going to a large or small customer. If a delivery is to be made to a large customer, including other small customers on the same truck can save on transportation cost. For each small customer, however, the delivery cost per unit is higher than for large customers. Thus, it is not optimal to deliver to small and large customers with the same frequency at the same price. One option firms have is to charge a higher delivery cost for smaller customers. Another option is to tailor milk runs so that they visit larger customers with a higher frequency than smaller customers. Firms can partition customers into large (L), medium (M), and small (S) based on the demand at each. The optimal frequency of visits can be evaluated based on the transportation and delivery costs (see Section 10.2). If large customers are to be visited every milk run, medium customers every other milk run, and low-demand customers every three milk runs, suitable milk runs can be designed by combining large, medium, and small customers on each run. Medium customers would be partitioned into two subsets (M_1, M_2) and small customers would be partitioned into three subsets (S_1, S_2, S_3). The firm can sequence the following six milk runs to ensure that each customer is visited with the appropriate frequency: (L, M_1, S_1), (L, M_2, S_2), (L, M_1, S_3), (L, M_2, S_1), (L, M_1, S_2), (L, M_2, S_3). This tailored sequence has the advantage that each truck carries about the same load and larger customers are provided more frequent delivery than smaller customers, consistent with their relative costs of delivery.

Tailored Transportation by Product Demand and Value

The degree of inventory aggregation and the modes of transportation used in a supply chain network should vary with the demand and value of a product as shown in Table 14.10.

The cycle inventory for high-value products with high demand is disaggregated to save on transportation costs because this allows replenishment orders to be transported less expensively. Safety inventory for such products can be aggregated to reduce inventories (see Chapter 11) and a fast mode of transportation can be used if the safety inventory is required to meet customer demand. For high-demand products with low value, all inventories should be disaggregated and held close to the customer to reduce transportation costs. For low-demand, high-value products, all inventories should be aggregated to save on inventory costs. For low-demand, low-value products, cycle inventories can be held close to the customer and safety inventories aggregated

TABLE 14.10   Impact of Value and Demand of Product on Aggregation

Product Type	High Value	Low Value
High Demand	Disaggregate cycle inventory. Aggregate safety inventory. Inexpensive mode of transportation for replenishing cycle inventory and fast mode when using safety inventory.	Disaggregate all inventories and use inexpensive mode of transportation for replenishment
Low Demand	Aggregate all inventories. If needed, use fast mode of transportation for filling customer orders.	Aggregate only safety inventory. Use inexpensive mode of transportation for replenishing cycle inventory.

to reduce transportation costs while taking some advantage of aggregation. Cycle inventories are replenished using an inexpensive mode of transportation to save costs.

> **Key Point**   Tailoring transportation based on customer density and distance, customer size, or product demand and value allows a supply chain to achieve appropriate responsiveness and cost.

14.7   ROUTING AND SCHEDULING IN TRANSPORTATION

The most important operational decision related to transportation in a supply chain is the routing and scheduling of deliveries. Managers must decide on the customers to be visited by a particular vehicle and the sequence in which they will be visited. For example, an online grocer like Peapod is built on delivering customer orders to their homes. The success of its operations turns on its ability to decrease transportation and delivery costs while providing the promised level of responsiveness to the customer. Given a set of customer orders, the goal is to route and schedule delivery vehicles such that the costs incurred to meet delivery promises are as low as possible. Typical objectives when routing and scheduling vehicles are a combination of minimizing cost by decreasing the number of vehicles needed, the total distance traveled by vehicles, and the total travel time of vehicles, as well as eliminating service failures such as a delay in shipments.

We discuss routing and scheduling problems in the context of the manager of a Peapod DC. After customers place orders for groceries online, staff at the DC has to pick the items needed and load them on trucks for delivery. The manager must decide which trucks will deliver to which customers and the route that each truck will take when making deliveries. The manager must also ensure that no truck is overloaded and that promised delivery times are met.

One morning, the DC manager at Peapod has orders from 13 different customers that are to be delivered. The location of the DC, each customer on a grid, and the order size from each customer are shown in Table 14.11. The manager has four trucks, each capable of carrying up to 200 units. The manager feels that the delivery costs are strongly linked to the total distance the trucks travel and that the distance between two points on the grid is correlated with the actual distance that a vehicle will travel between those two points. The manager thus decides to assign customers to trucks and identify a route for each truck with a goal of minimizing the total distance traveled.

The DC manager must first assign customers to be served by each vehicle and then decide on each vehicle's route. After the initial assignment, route sequencing and route improvement procedures are used to decide on the route for each vehicle. The DC manager decides to use the following computational procedures to support his decision:

- The savings matrix method
- The generalized assignment method

We discuss how each method can be used to solve the routing and scheduling decision at Peapod.

TABLE 14.11 Customer Location and Demand for Peapod			
	X-Coordinate	*Y-Coordinate*	*Order Size a_i*
Warehouse	0	0	
Customer 1	0	12	48
Customer 2	6	5	36
Customer 3	7	15	43
Customer 4	9	12	92
Customer 5	15	3	57
Customer 6	20	0	16
Customer 7	17	-2	56
Customer 8	7	-4	30
Customer 9	1	-6	57
Customer 10	15	-6	47
Customer 11	20	-7	91
Customer 12	7	-9	55
Customer 13	2	-15	38

Savings Matrix Method

This method is simple to implement and can be used to assign customers to vehicles even when delivery time windows or other constraints exist. The major steps in the savings matrix method are

1. Identify the distance matrix
2. Identify the savings matrix
3. Assign customers to vehicles or routes
4. Sequence customers within routes

The first three steps are used to assign customers to vehicles and the fourth step is used to route each vehicle to minimize the distance traveled.

Identify the Distance Matrix

The *distance matrix* identifies the distance between every pair of locations to be visited. The distance is used as a surrogate for the cost of traveling between the pair of locations. If the transportation costs between every pair of locations are known, the costs can be used in place of distances. The distance $Dist(A, B)$ on a grid between a point A with coordinates (x_A, y_A) and a point B with coordinates (x_B, y_B) is evaluated as

$$Dist(A, B) = \sqrt{(x_A - x_B)^2 + (y_A - y_B)^2} \tag{14.1}$$

The distance between every pair of locations for Peapod is shown in Table 14.12.

The distances between every pair of locations are next used to evaluate the savings matrix.

TABLE 14.12 Distance Matrix for Peapod Deliveries

	DC	Cust 1	Cust 2	Cust 3	Cust 4	Cust 5	Cust 6	Cust 7	Cust 8	Cust 9	Cust 10	Cust 11	Cust 12	Cust 13
DC	0													
Cust 1	12	0												
Cust 2	8	9	0											
Cust 3	17	8	10	0										
Cust 4	15	9	8	4	0									
Cust 5	15	17	9	14	11	0								
Cust 6	20	23	15	20	16	6	0							
Cust 7	17	22	13	20	16	5	4	0						
Cust 8	8	17	9	19	16	11	14	10	0					
Cust 9	6	18	12	22	20	17	20	16	6	0				
Cust 10	16	23	14	22	19	9	8	4	8	14	0			
Cust 11	21	28	18	26	22	11	7	6	13	19	5	0		
Cust 12	11	22	14	24	21	14	16	12	5	7	9	13	0	
Cust 13	15	27	20	30	28	22	23	20	12	9	16	20	8	0

Identify the Savings Matrix

The *savings matrix* represents the savings that accrue on consolidating two customers on a single truck. Savings may be evaluated in terms of distance, time, or money. The manager at Peapod constructs the savings matrix in terms of distance. A *trip* is identified as the sequence of locations a vehicle visits. The trip DC → Cust x → DC

TABLE 14.13 Savings Matrix for Peapod Deliveries

	Cust 1	Cust 2	Cust 3	Cust 4	Cust 5	Cust 6	Cust 7	Cust 8	Cust 9	Cust 10	Cust 11	Cust 12	Cust 13
Cust 1	0												
Cust 2	11	0											
Cust 3	21	15	0										
Cust 4	18	15	28	0									
Cust 5	10	14	18	19	0								
Cust 6	9	13	17	19	29	0							
Cust 7	7	12	14	16	27	33	0						
Cust 8	3	7	6	7	12	14	15	0					
Cust 9	0	2	1	1	4	6	7	8	0				
Cust 10	5	10	11	12	22	28	29	16	8	0			
Cust 11	5	11	12	14	25	34	32	16	8	32	0		
Cust 12	1	5	4	5	12	15	16	14	10	18	19	0	
Cust 13	0	3	2	2	8	12	12	11	12	15	16	18	0

starts at the DC, visits customer x, and returns to the DC. The savings $S(x,y)$ is the distance saved if the trips DC → Cust x → DC and DC → Cust y → DC are combined to a single trip DC → Cust x → Cust y → DC. This saving can be calculated by the following formula:

$$S(x,y) = Dist(DC, x) + Dist(DC, y) - Dist(x, y). \qquad \textbf{(14.2)}$$

For example, using Table 14.12 the manager evaluates $S(1,2) = 12 + 8 - 9 = 11$. The savings matrix for the Peapod deliveries is shown in Table 14.13. The savings matrix is then used to assign customers to vehicles or routes.

Assign Customers to Vehicles or Routes

When assigning customers to vehicles, the manager attempts to maximize savings. An iterative procedure is used to make this assignment. Initially each customer is assigned to a separate route. Two routes can be combined into a *feasible* route if the total deliveries across both routes do not exceed the vehicle's capacity. At each iterative step, the Peapod manager attempts to combine routes with the highest savings into

FIGURE 14.5   Delivery Route by Assigning 6 and 11 to a Common Route

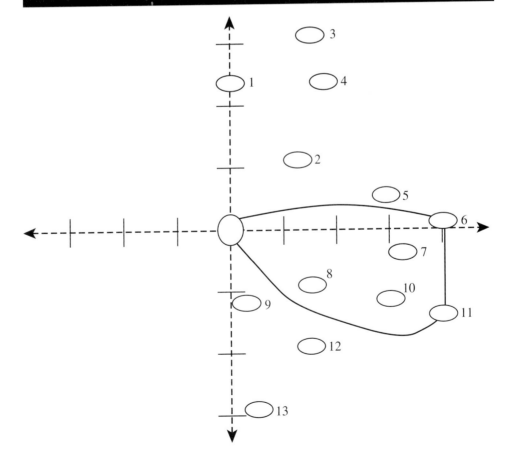

a new feasible route. The procedure is continued until no more combinations are feasible.

At the first step, the highest savings of 34 results on combining truck Routes 6 and 11. The combined route is feasible because the total load is 16 + 91 = 107, which is below 200. The two customers are thus combined on a single route as shown in Figure 14.5 and the saving 34 is eliminated from further consideration.

The next highest saving is 33 on adding Customer 7 to the route for Customer 6. This is feasible because the resulting load is 107 + 56 = 163, which is under 200. Thus, Customer 7 is also added to Route 6 as shown in Figure 14.6.

The next highest saving now is 32 on adding Customer 10 to Route 6 (we need not consider the saving of 32 on combining Customer 7 with Customer 11 because both are already in Route 6). This, however, cannot be done because the addition of Customer 10 results in a delivery of 47 units and adding this amount to the deliveries already on Route 6 would exceed the vehicle capacity of 200. The next highest saving is 29 on adding either Customer 5 or 10 to Route 6. Each of these is also infeasible

FIGURE 14.6 Delivery Route by Assigning 6, 7, and 11 to a Common Route

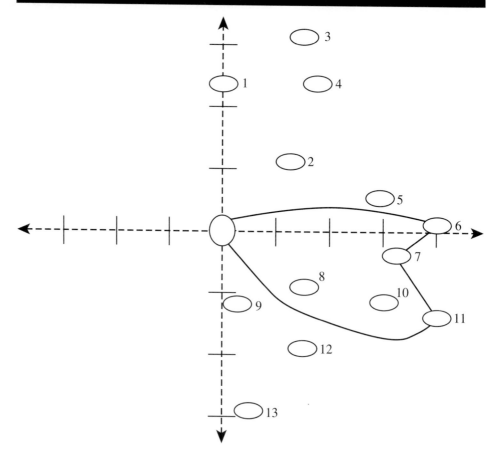

because of the capacity constraint. The next highest saving is 28 on combining Routes 3 and 4, which is feasible. The two routes are combined into a single route as shown in Figure 14.7.

Continuing the iterative procedure, the manager partitions customers into four groups $\{1, 3, 4\}, \{2, 9\}, \{6, 7, 8, 11\}, \{5, 10, 12, 13\}$ with each group assigned to a single vehicle. The next step is to identify the sequence in which each vehicle will visit customers.

Sequence Customers within Routes

At this stage the manager's goal is to sequence customer visits so as to minimize the distance each vehicle must travel. Changing the sequence in which deliveries are made can have a significant impact on the distance traveled by vehicles. Consider the truck that has been assigned deliveries to Customers 5, 10, 12, and 13. If the deliveries are in the sequence 5, 10, 12, 13, the total distance traveled by the truck is $15 + 9 + 9 + 8 + 15 = 56$ (distances are obtained from Table 14.12). In contrast, if deliveries are in the sequence 12, 5, 13, 10, the truck covers a larger distance of $11 + 14 + 22 + 16 + 16 = 79$. Delivery sequences are determined by obtaining a initial route sequence and then

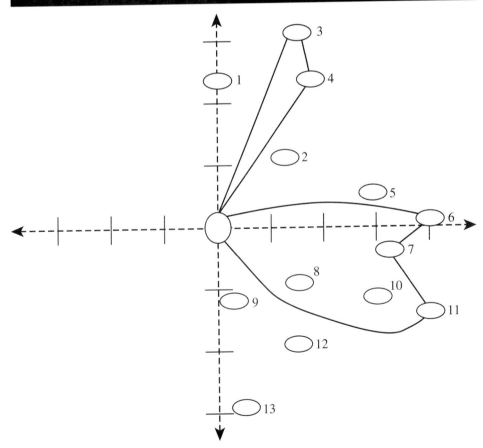

FIGURE 14.7   Delivery Route by Assigning 3 and 4 to a Common Route

using route improvement procedures to obtain delivery sequences with a lower transportation distance or cost.

Route Sequencing Procedures   The manager at Peapod can use route sequencing procedures to obtain an initial trip for each vehicle. The initial trip is then improved using the route improvement procedure discussed later in the chapter. All route sequencing procedures are illustrated for the vehicle assigned to Customers 5, 10, 12, and 13.

1. *Farthest insert.* Given a vehicle trip (including a trip consisting of only the DC) for each remaining customer, find the minimum increase in length for this customer to be inserted from all the potential points in the trip that they could be inserted. Then choose to actually insert the customer with the largest minimum increase to obtain a new trip. This step is referred to as a farthest insert because the customer farthest from the current trip is inserted. The process is continued until all remaining customers to be visited by the vehicle are included in a trip.

   For the Peapod example, the manager is seeking a trip starting at the DC and visiting Customers 5, 10, 12, 13. The initial trip consists of just the DC with a length of 0. Including Customer 5 in the trip adds 30 to its length, including Customer 10 adds 32, including Customer 12 adds 22, and including Customer 13 adds 30 (see Table 14.12). Using farthest insert, the manager adds Customer 10 to obtain a new trip (DC, 10, DC) of length 32.

   At the next step, inserting Customer 5 in the trip raises the length of the trip to a minimum of 40, inserting Customer 12 raises it to 36, inserting Customer 13 raises it to 46. The manager thus inserts the farthest Customer 13 to obtain the new trip (DC, 10, 13, DC) of length 46. This still leaves Customers 5 and 12 to be inserted. The minimum cost insertion for Customer 5 is (DC, 5, 10, 13, DC) for a length of 55 and the minimum cost insertion for Customer 12 is (DC, 10, 12, 13, DC) for a length of 48. The manager thus inserts Customer 5 to obtain the trip (DC, 5, 10, 13, DC) of length 55. Customer 12 is then inserted between Customers 10 and 13 to obtain the trip (DC, 5, 10, 12 13, DC) of length 56.

2. *Nearest insert.* Given a vehicle trip (including a trip consisting of only the DC), for each remaining customer, find the minimum increase in length for this customer to be inserted from all the potential points in the trip that they could be inserted. Insert the customer with the smallest minimum increase to obtain a new trip. This step is referred to as a nearest insert because the customer closest to the current trip is inserted. The process is continued until all remaining customers the vehicle will visit are included in a trip.

   For the Peapod example, the manager applies the nearest insert to the vehicle serving Customers 5, 10, 12, and 13. Starting at the DC, the nearest customer is 12. Inserting Customer 12 results in the trip (DC, 12, DC) of length 22. At the next step, inserting Customer 5 results in a trip of length 40, inserting Customer 10 in a trip of length 36, and inserting Customer 13 in a trip of length 34. Customer 13 results in the smallest increase and is inserted to obtain the trip (DC, 12, 13, DC) of length 34. The next nearest insertion is Customer 10 resulting in the trip (DC, 10, 12, 13, DC) of length 48 and the final insertion of Customer 5 results in the trip (DC, 5, 10, 12, 13, DC) of length 56.

3. *Nearest neighbor.* Starting at the DC, this procedure adds the closest customer to extend the trip. At each step, the trip is built by adding the customer closest to the point last visited by the vehicle until all customers have been visited.

For the Peapod example, the customer closest to the DC is 12 (see Table 14.12). This results in the path (DC, 12). The customer closest to Customer 12 is 10, extending the path to (DC, 12, 10). The nearest neighbor of Customer 10 is 5 and the nearest neighbor of Customer 5 is 13. The Peapod manager thus obtains the trip (DC, 12, 10, 5, 13, DC) of length 66.

4. *Sweep.* In the sweep procedure, any point on the grid is selected (generally the DC itself) and a line is swept either clockwise or counterclockwise from that point. The trip is constructed by sequencing customers in the order they are encountered during the sweep.

The Peapod manager uses the sweep procedure with the line centered at the DC. Customers are encountered in the sequence 5, 10, 12, 13 to obtain the trip (DC, 5, 10, 12 13, DC) for a length of 56.

The initial trips resulting from each route sequencing procedure and their lengths are summarized in Table 14.14.

Route Improvement Procedures Route improvement procedures start with a trip obtained using a route sequencing procedure and improve the trip to shorten its length. The Peapod manager next applies route improvement procedures to alter the sequence of customers visited by a vehicle and shorten the distance a vehicle must travel. The two route improvement procedures discussed are illustrated on the trip obtained as a result of the nearest neighbor procedure.

1. *2-OPT.* The 2-OPT procedure starts with a trip and breaks it at two places. This results in the trip breaking into two paths, which can be reconnected in two possible ways. The length for each reconnection is evaluated and the smaller of the two is used to define a new trip. The procedure is continued on the new trip until no further improvement results.

For example, the trip (DC, 12, 10, 5, 13, DC) resulting from the nearest neighbor procedure can be broken into two paths (13, DC) and (12, 10, 5) and reconnected into the trip (DC, 5, 10, 12, 13, DC) as shown in Figure 14.8. The new trip has length 56, which is an improvement over the existing trip.

2. *3-OPT.* The 3-OPT procedure breaks a trip at three points to obtain three paths that can be reconnected to form up to eight different trips. The length of each of the eight

TABLE 14.14	Initial Trips Using Different Route Sequencing Procedures at Peapod	
Route Sequencing Procedure	*Resulting Trip*	*Trip Length*
Farthest insert	DC, 5, 10, 12, 13, DC	56
Nearest insert	DC, 5, 10, 12, 13, DC	56
Nearest neighbor	DC, 12, 10, 5, 13, DC	66
Sweep	DC, 5, 10, 12, 13, DC	56

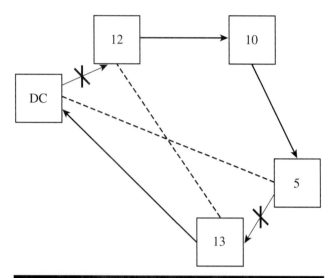

FIGURE 14.8 Improving Route Sequencing Using 2-OPT

possible trips is evaluated and the shortest trip is retained. The procedure is continued on the new trip until no further improvement results.

The trip (DC, 5, 10, 12, 13, DC) resulting from the 2-OPT procedure is broken up into three paths (DC), (5, 10), (12, 13). The various resulting trips on reconnecting the three paths are (DC, 12, 13, 5, 10, DC) of length 65, (DC, 12, 13, 10, 5, DC) of length 81, and (DC, 13, 12, 5, 10, DC) of length 61. All other trips correspond to one of these four trips reversed. This application of the 3-OPT procedure does not improve the trip because the current trip is the shortest. At this stage the Peapod manager can form three new paths from the trip and repeat the procedure.

The Peapod manager uses route sequencing and improvement procedures to obtain delivery trips for each of the four trucks as shown in Table 14.15 and Figure 14.9. The total travel distance for the delivery schedule is 185.

Generalized Assignment Method

The generalized assignment method is more sophisticated than the savings matrix method and usually results in better solutions when there are few delivery constraints to be satisfied. The procedure for routing and sequencing of vehicles consists of the following steps:

TABLE 14.15 Peapod Delivery Schedule Using Saving Matrix Method

Truck	Trip	Length of Trip	Load on Truck
1	DC, 2, 9, DC	32	93
2	DC, 1, 3, 4, DC	39	183
3	DC, 8, 11, 6, 7, DC	58	193
4	DC, 5, 10, 12, 13, DC	56	197

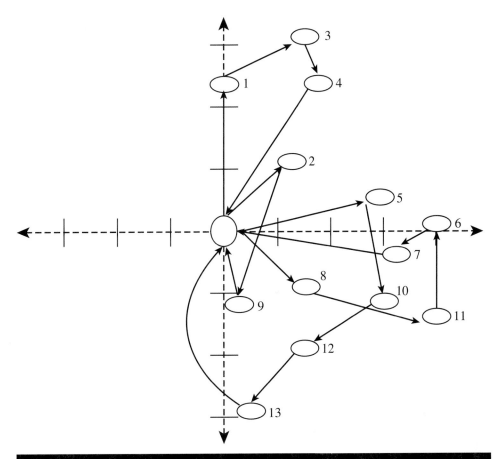

FIGURE 14.9 Delivery Routes at Peapod Using Savings Matrix Method

1. Assign seed points for each route
2. Evaluate insertion cost for each customer
3. Assign customers to routes
4. Sequence customers within routes

The first three steps assign customers to vehicles and the fourth step identifies a route for each vehicle to minimize the distance traveled. We discuss each step in greater detail in the context of the delivery decision at Peapod.

Assign Seed Points for Each Route

The goal of this step is to determine a seed point corresponding to the center of the trip taken by each vehicle using the following procedure:

1. Divide the total load to be shipped to all customers by the number of trucks to obtain L_{seed}, the average load allocated to each seed point.
2. Starting at any customer, use a ray starting at the DC to sweep clockwise to obtain cones assigned to each seed point. Each cone is assigned a load of L_{seed}.

3. Within each cone, the seed point is located in the middle (in terms of angle) at a distance equal to that of the customer (with a partial or complete load allocated to the cone) farthest from the DC.

The manager at Peapod uses the procedure described earlier to obtain seed points for the deliveries described in Table 14.11. Given four vehicles and a total delivery load across all customers of 666 units, the manager obtains an average load per vehicle of $L_{seed} = 666/4 = 166.5$ units.

The next step is to sweep clockwise with a ray emanating from the DC to obtain four cones, one for each vehicle, including all customers. The first step in defining the cones is to obtain the angular position of each customer. The angular position (θ_i) of customer i with coordinates (x_i, y_i) is the angle made relative to the x axis by the line joining the customer i to the origin (DC) as shown in Figure 14.10.

The angular position of each customer is obtained as the inverse tangent of the ratio of its y coordinate to the x coordinate.

$$\theta_i = \tan^{-1}(y_i/x_i) \tag{14.3}$$

The inverse tangent can be evaluated using the Excel function *ATAN()* as

$$\theta_i = ATAN(y_i/x_i). \tag{14.4}$$

The angular position of each customer is obtained using Equation 14.4 as shown in Table 14.16.

The next step is to sweep clockwise and order the customers as encountered. For Peapod, a clockwise sweep encounters customers in the order 1, 3, 4, 2, 5, 6, 7, 11, 10, 8, 12, 9, and 13. Starting with Customer 1, four cones, each representing a load of $L_{seed} = 166.5$ units, are to be formed. Customers 1 and 3 combine to load 91 units on the truck. Customer 4 is encountered next in the sweep. Adding the entire load for Customer 4

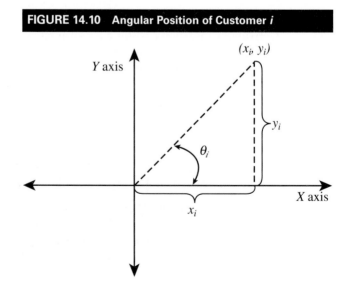

FIGURE 14.10 Angular Position of Customer *i*

TABLE 14.16   Angular Positions of Peapod Customers

	X Coordinate	Y Coordinate	Angular Position (Radians)	Demand
DC	0	0		
Customer 1	0	12	1.57	48
Customer 2	6	5	0.69	36
Customer 3	7	15	1.13	43
Customer 4	9	12	0.93	92
Customer 5	15	3	0.20	57
Customer 6	20	0	0.00	16
Customer 7	17	−2	−0.12	56
Customer 8	7	−4	−0.52	30
Customer 9	1	−6	−1.41	57
Customer 10	15	−6	−0.38	47
Customer 11	20	−7	−0.34	91
Customer 12	7	−9	−0.91	55
Customer 13	2	−15	−1.44	38

would result in a load of 183, which is larger than L_{seed} = 166.5. To get a load of 166.5, only 166.5 − 91 = 75.5 units of the load should be included. Thus, the first cone extends to a point that is 75.5 / 92 of the angle between Customers 3 and 4. Customer 3 has an angular position of 1.13 and Customer 4 has an angular position of 0.93, resulting in an angle between them of 1.13 − 0.93 = 0.20. The first cone thus extends to an angle (75.5/92) × 0.20 beyond Customer 3 with a resulting angle of 1.13 − (75.5/92) × 0.20 = 0.97. The first cone thus has one end at Customer 1 (angle of 1.57) and the other at an angle of 0.97 as shown in Figure 14.11.

The seed point is then located at an angle α_1 = (0.97 + 1.57)/2 = 1.27 in the middle of the cone at a distance equal to that of the farthest customer included. Customer 3, at a distance $d_1 = \sqrt{(7-0)^2 + (15-0)^2}$ = 17, is the farthest customer in the first cone. Given the distance d_1, the coordinates (X_1, Y_1) of the Seed Point 1 are thus given by

$$X_1 = d_1\cos(\alpha) = 17\cos(1.27) = 5, \text{and } Y_1 = d_1\sin(\alpha) = 17\sin(1.27) = 16$$

The second cone starts at the angle 0.97 and includes 92 − 75.5 = 16.5 units of the Customer 4 load. On sweeping clockwise, Customers 2, 5, 6, and 7 are encountered before a load of 166.5 is exceeded. To get a load of exactly 166.5, only 41/56 of Customer 7 load is needed. The angular position of the end of the cone is thus 41/56 between Customers 6 and 7. Customer 6 is at angle of 0.00 and Customer 7 is at the angle of −0.12. The second cone thus ends at an angle of 0.00 − 0.12 × (41/56) = −0.09. The second cone has one end at an angle of 0.33 and the other at an angle of −0.09. The seed point is thus located at an angle α_2 in the middle of the cone; that is, α_2 = (0.33 − 0.09)/2 = 0.12. The distance d_2 of the seed point for the second cone is the same as Customer 6, the farthest customer in the cone. This corresponds to a distance of d_2 = 20 (see Table 14.12). The coordinates (X_2, Y_2) of the Seed Point 2 are thus given by

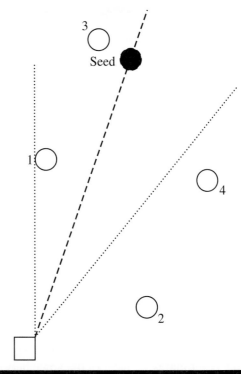

FIGURE 14.11 Sweep Method to Locate Seed 1

$$X_2 = d_2 \cos(\alpha_2) = 20 \cos(0.12) = 20, \text{ and } Y_2 = d_2 \sin(\alpha_2) = 20 \sin(0.12) = 2.$$

Proceeding in the same manner, the manager at the Peapod DC forms four cones to determine the four seed points as shown in Table 14.17.

Evaluate Insertion Cost for Each Customer

For each Seed Point S_k and Customer i, the *insertion cost* c_{ik} is the extra distance that would be traveled if the customer is inserted into a trip from the DC to the seed point and back and is given by

$$c_{ik} = Dist(\text{DC}, i) + Dist(i, S_k) - Dist(\text{DC}, S_k),$$

TABLE 14.17 Seed Point Coordinates for Peapod Deliveries		
Seed Point	*X Coordinate*	*Y Coordinate*
S_1	5	16
S_2	20	2
S_3	19	−5
S_4	5	−5

where the *Dist()* function is evaluated as in Equation 14.1. For Customer 1 and Seed Point 1, the insertion cost is given by

$$c_{11} = Dist(DC, 1) + Dist(1, S_1) - Dist(DC, S_1) = 12 + 10 - 17 = 5.$$

The manager at the Peapod DC evaluates all insertion costs c_{ik} as shown in Table 14.18.

Assign Customers to Routes

The manager next assigns customers to each of the four vehicles to minimize total insertion cost while respecting vehicle capacity constraints. The assignment problem is formulated as an integer program and requires the following input:

$$c_{ik} = \text{insertion cost of Customer } i \text{ and Seed Point } k,$$
$$a_i = \text{order size from Customer } i,$$
$$b_k = \text{capacity of Vehicle } k.$$

Define the following decision variables

$$y_{ik} = 1 \text{ if Customer } i \text{ is assigned to Vehicle } k, 0 \text{ otherwise.}$$

The integer program for assigning customers to vehicles is given by

$$Min \sum_{k=1}^{K} \sum_{i=1}^{n} c_{ik} y_{ik}$$

TABLE 14.18	Insertion Costs for Peapod Deliveries for Each Customer and Seed Point			
Customer	*Seed Point 1*	*Seed Point 2*	*Seed Point 3*	*Seed Point 4*
1	2	14	18	23
2	2	2	5	11
3	2	15	21	30
4	4	10	15	25
5	15	0	4	21
6	25	2	5	29
7	22	2	1	22
8	11	2	0	3
9	12	7	4	3
10	24	5	0	19
11	32	10	4	29
12	20	8	4	8
13	30	20	15	18

subject to

$$\sum_{k=1}^{K} y_{ik} = 1, i = 1, \ldots ,n,$$

$$\sum_{i=1}^{n} a_i\, y_{ik} \leq b_k, k = 1, \ldots , k,$$

$$y_{ik} = 0 \text{ or } 1 \quad \text{for all } i \text{ and } k$$

For Peapod, the order size for each customer is given in Table 14.11, the insertion cost c_{ik} is obtained from Table 14.20, and the capacity of each vehicle is 200 units. The manager at Peapod solves the integer program using the tool Solver in Excel to obtain the assignment of customers to vehicles as shown in Table 14.19 and Figure 14.12. The sequencing of customers within each trip is obtained using the route sequencing and route improvement procedures discussed earlier. The total distance traveled for the delivery schedule is 159.

Applicability of Routing and Scheduling Methods

The delivery schedule for Peapod resulting from the generalized assignment method in Table 14.18 is superior to the solution obtained from the savings matrix method in Table 14.14. The generalized assignment method is more sophisticated and generally gives a better solution than the savings matrix method when the delivery schedule has no constraints other than vehicle capacity. The main disadvantage of the generalized assignment method is that it has difficulty generating good delivery schedules as more constraints are included. For example, if Peapod has fixed time windows within which deliveries must be made to customers, it is difficult to use the generalized assignment method to generate a delivery schedule. The generalized assignment method is recommended if the constraints are limited to vehicle capacity or total travel time.

The main strength of the savings matrix method is its simplicity and robustness. The method is simple enough to be easily modified to include delivery time windows and other constraints and robust enough to give a reasonably good solution that can be implemented in practice. Its main weakness is the quality of the solution. It is often possible to find better delivery schedules using more sophisticated methods. The savings matrix method is recommended in case there are many constraints that need to be satisfied by the delivery schedule. Software packages for transportation planning and

TABLE 14.19 Peapod Delivery Schedule Using Generalized Assignment Method

Truck	Trip	Length of Trip	Load on Truck
1	DC, 1, 3, 4, DC	39	183
2	DC, 2, 5, 6, 7, 8, DC	45	195
3	DC, 10, 11, 12, DC	45	193
4	DC, 9, 13, DC	30	95

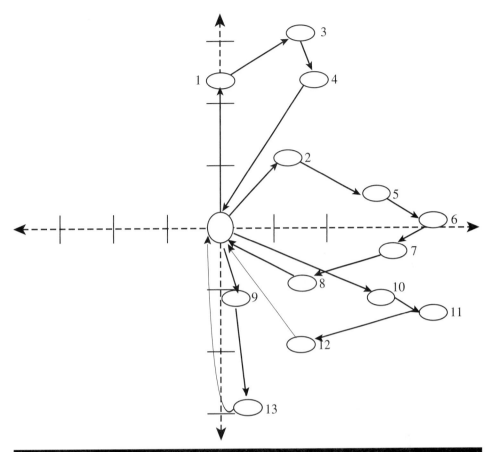

FIGURE 14.12   Delivery Routes at Peapod Using Generalized Assignment

routing and scheduling of deliveries are available from many supply chain software companies (see Chapter 17).

14.8   MAKING TRANSPORTATION DECISIONS IN PRACTICE

1. *Align transportation strategy with competitive strategy:* Managers should ensure that a firm's transportation strategy supports its competitive strategy. They should design functional incentives that help achieve this goal. Historically, the transportation function within firms has been evaluated based on the extent to which it can lower transportation costs. Such a focus leads to decisions that lower transportation costs but hurt the level of responsiveness provided to customers and may raise the firm's total cost. If the dispatcher at a DC is evaluated solely based on the extent to which trucks are loaded, he or she is likely to delay shipments and hurt customer responsiveness to achieve a larger load. Firms should evaluate the transportation function based on a

combination of transportation cost, other costs such as inventory affected by transportation decisions, and the level of responsiveness achieved with customers.

2. *Consider both in-house and outsourced transportation:* Managers should consider an appropriate combination of company-owned and outsourced transportation to meet their needs. This decision should be based on a firm's ability to handle transportation profitably as well as the strategic importance of transportation to the success of the firm. In general, outsourcing is a better option when shipment sizes are small, whereas owning the transportation fleet is better when shipment sizes are large and responsiveness is important. For example, Wal-Mart has used responsive transportation to reduce inventories in its supply chain. Given the importance of transportation to the success of their strategy, they own their transportation fleet and manage it themselves. This is made easier by the fact that they achieve good utilization from their transportation assets because most of their shipments are large. In contrast, firms like W.W. Grainger and McMaster Carr send small shipments to customers; inventory management rather than transportation is the key to their success. A third-party carrier can lower costs for them by aggregating their shipments with those of other companies. As a result, both companies use third-party carriers for their transportation.

3. *Design a transportation network that can handle e-commerce:* The growth in e-commerce for most B2C firms has resulted in a decrease in shipment sizes and a growth in home delivery. Transportation systems for the new economy need to be very responsive but must also be able to exploit every opportunity for aggregation, in some cases even with competitors, to help decrease the transportation cost of small shipments. Whereas replenishment orders are large and can use rail or TL carriers, most e-commerce shipments require more expensive package carriers or LTL carriers given their smaller size. The growth in JIT manufacturing and the focus on reduced inventories and frequent replenishment has further increased the need to handle small shipments. If managers do not take these trends into account when designing their transportation networks, firms are likely to see a significant increase in transportation cost along with a drop in responsiveness to the customer.

4. *Use technology to improve transportation performance:* Managers must use the information technology available to help decrease costs and improve responsiveness in their transportation networks. Software is crucial to helping managers do transportation planning, modal selection, and build delivery routes and schedules. Available technology allows carriers to identify the precise location of each vehicle as well as the shipments the vehicle carries. Satellite-based communication systems allow carriers to communicate with each vehicle in their fleet. These technologies can help a carrier become much more responsive and also help lower costs by better matching shipments from customers with vehicles that are best suited to carry them. These technologies also help a firm react better to unforeseen changes caused by the weather or other unpredictable factors.

5. *Design flexibility into the transportation network:* When designing transportation networks, managers should take into account uncertainty in demand as well as availability of transportation. Ignoring uncertainty encourages a greater use of inexpensive and inflexible transportation modes that perform well when everything goes as planned. Such networks, however, perform very poorly when plans change. When managers

account for uncertainty, they are more likely to include flexible, though more expensive, modes of transportation within their network. Although these modes may be more expensive for a particular shipment, including them in the transportation options allows a firm to reduce the overall cost of providing a high level of responsiveness.

14.9   SUMMARY OF LEARNING OBJECTIVES

1. Understand the role of transportation within a supply chain.

   Transportation refers to the movement of product from one location to another within a supply chain. The importance of transportation has grown with the increasing globalization in supply chains as well as the growth in e-commerce because both trends increase the distance products travel. Transportation decisions impact supply chain profitability and influence both inventory and facility decisions within a supply chain.

2. Evaluate the strengths and weaknesses of different modes of transportation.

   The various modes of transportation include water, rail, intermodal, truck, air, pipeline, and package carriers. Water is typically the least expensive mode but is also the slowest whereas air and package carriers are the most expensive and the fastest. Rail and water are best suited for low-value, large shipments that do not need to be moved in a hurry. Air and package carriers are best suited for small, high-value, emergency shipments. Intermodal and TL carriers are faster than rail and water but somewhat more expensive. LTL carriers are best suited for small shipments that are too large for package carriers but much less than a TL.

3. Identify various transportation network design options and their relative strengths and weaknesses.

   Networks are designed to either ship directly from origin to destination or move the product through a consolidation point. Direct shipments are most effective when large quantities are to be moved. When shipments are small, use of an intermediate warehouse or DC takes longer and is more complex but lowers transportation cost by aggregating the smaller shipments. Shipments may also be consolidated with a single vehicle either picking up from multiple locations or dropping off in multiple locations.

4. Identify trade-offs that shippers need to consider when designing their transportation network.

   When designing transportation networks, shippers must consider the trade-off between transportation cost, inventory cost, operating cost, and customer responsiveness. The supply chain goal is to minimize the total cost while providing the desired level of responsiveness to customers.

5. Use methodologies for routing and scheduling deliveries in transportation networks.

   The savings matrix and the generalized assignment methodology can be used to route vehicles and sequence deliveries. The methods can be used to minimize the transportation cost while meeting delivery commitments to customers. Several companies provide software that allows a manager to set delivery schedules.

DISCUSSION QUESTIONS

1. What modes of transportation are best suited for large, low-value shipments? Why?
2. Wal-Mart designs its networks to have a DC support several large retail stores. Explain how the company can use such a network to reduce transportation costs while replenishing inventories frequently.

3. Compare the transportation costs for an e-business like Amazon.com and a retailer like Home Depot when selling home improvement materials.
4. What transportation challenges does Peapod face? Compare transportation costs at online grocers and supermarket chains.
5. Do you expect aggregation of inventory at one location to be more effective when a company like Dell sells computers or when a company like Amazon.com sells books? Explain by considering transportation and inventory costs.
6. Discuss key drivers that may be used to tailor transportation. How does tailoring help?
7. What are the strengths and weaknesses of using the savings matrix method or the generalized assignment method for routing and scheduling of vehicles?

EXERCISES

1. A power plant in California uses coal at the rate of 100,000 lbs. each day. It also uses MRO material at the rate of 1,000 lbs. each day. The coal comes from Wyoming and the MRO material comes from Chicago. Coal costs $0.01 per lb. whereas MRO material costs $10 per lb., on average. Holding costs at the power plant are 25 percent. Transportation choices available are as follows:

TRAIN
Lead time = 15 days
Carload (100,000 lbs.) at $400 per carload
Full train (70 cars) at $15,000 per train

TRUCK
Lead time = 4 days
Minimum cost = $100
Up to 10,000 lbs. at $0.08 per lb.
Between 10,000 and 20,000 lbs. at $0.07 per lb. for entire load
Between 25,000 and 40,000 lbs. at $0.06 per lb. for entire load
Small TL (40,000 lbs.) for $2,000
Large TL (60,000 lbs.) for $2,600

Safety inventory of coal and MRO materials is kept at twice the consumption during the lead time of supply. What mode of transport do you recommend for each of the two products? Why?

2. Books-On-Line, an online bookseller, charges its customers a shipping charge of $4 for the first book and $1 for each additional book. The average customer order contains 4 books. Books-On-Line currently has one warehouse in Seattle and ships all orders from there. For shipping purposes, Books-On-Line divides the US into three zones—western, central, and eastern. Shipping cost incurred by Books-On-Line per customer order (average 4 books) is $2 within the same zone, $3 between adjacent zones, and $4 between nonadjacent zones.

Weekly demand from each zone is independent and normally distributed with a mean of 50,000 and a standard deviation of 25,000. Each book costs on average $10 and the holding cost incurred by Books-On-Line is 25 percent. Books-On-Line replenishes inventory every week and aims for a 99.7 percent CSL. Assume a replenishment lead time of one week.

A warehouse is designed to carry 50 percent more than the replenishment order + safety stock. The fixed cost of a warehouse is $200,000 + x$, where x is its capacity in books. The weekly operating cost of a warehouse is $0.01y$, where y is the number of books shipped. Books-On-Line is planning its network strategy. Which zones should have warehouses? Detail all costs involved.

3. A European manufacturer of industrial furniture has a factory located in Munich and four warehouses in Western Europe. The warehouses collect customer orders, which are then shipped from the factory. Upon receipt, the warehouse distributes customer orders using small trucks. Daily demand at each of the four warehouses along with distance from Munich is as shown following:

Warehouse	Daily Demand (Kg)	Distance (km)
Milan	25,000	800
Paris	35,000	1,000
Copenhagen	20,000	600
Madrid	20,000	1,300

All shipments are by truck. There are three truck sizes available with capacity— 40,000 (small), 60,000 (medium), and 80,000 kg (large). Transportation costs for the three types of trucks are:

Small: $100 + 0.1x$ Euro,
Medium: $125 + 0.1x$ Euro,
Large: $150 + 0.1x$ Euro.

x is the distance to be traveled in km. For replenishment frequency varying between one and four days for each warehouse, identify the optimal transportation option and the associated cost. What other factors should be considered before deciding on the replenishment frequency?

4. The manager at Albertson's, a grocery chain also selling online, has 12 orders that are to be delivered to customers. The location and order size for each customer is shown in Table 14.20.

TABLE 14.20   Customer Locations and Order Sizes for Albertson's

	X Coordinate	Y Coordinate	Order Size
DC	0	0	
Customer 1	–12	0	74
Customer 2	–5	6	55
Customer 3	–15	7	68
Customer 4	–12	9	109
Customer 5	–3	15	81
Customer 6	0	20	41
Customer 7	2	17	74
Customer 8	4	7	52
Customer 9	6	1	80
Customer 10	6	15	69
Customer 11	7	20	103
Customer 12	9	7	75

The Alberston's fulfillment store has five trucks, each capable of carrying up to 225 units. Use the savings matrix and generalized assignment methods to devise suitable delivery schedules. What is the total distance traveled under each schedule?

BIBLIOGRAPHY

Ampuja, Jack, and Ray Pucci. 2002. "Inbound Freight: Often a Missed Opportunity." *Supply Chain Management Review* (March–April): 50–57.

Ballou, Ronald H. 1999. *Business Logistics Management.* Upper Saddle River, N.J.: Prentice Hall.

Bowersox, D. J., D. J. Closs, and O. K. Helferich. 1986. *Logistical Management.* New York: Macmillan Publishing Company.

Coyle, John J., Edward J. Bardi, and Robert A. Novack. 2000. *Transportation.* Cincinnati, Ohio: South-Western College Publishing.

Christofides, N., and S. Eilon. 1969. "An Algorithm for the Vehicle Dispatching Problem." *Operations Research Quarterly* 20: 309–318.

Fisher, M. L., A. J. Greenfield, R. Jaikumar, and J. T. Lester III. 1982. "A Computerized Vehicle Routing Application." *Interfaces* (August): 42–52.

Fisher, M. L., and R. Jaikumar. 1981. "A Generalized Assignment Heuristic for Vehicle Routing." *Networks* 11: 109–124.

Hammond, J. H., and J. E. P. Morrison. 1988. *Note on the U.S. Transportation Industry.* Harvard Business School Note 688080.

Lin, S., and B. Kernighan. 1973. "An Effective Heuristic Algorithm for the Traveling Salesman Problem." *Operations Research* 21: 498–516.

Robeson, J. F., and W. C. Copacino. 1994. *The Logistics Handbook.* New York: The Free Press.

Shapiro, R. D., and J. L. Heskett. 1985. *Logistics Strategy: Cases and Concepts.* St. Paul, Minn.: West Publishing Co.

Eno Transportation Foundation Inc. 1998. *Transportation in America 1998,* Washington DC.

Tyworth, J. E., J. L. Cavinato, and C. J. Langley, Jr. 1991. *Traffic Management: Planning, Operations, and Control.* Prospect Heights, Ill.: Waveland Press.

CHAPTER

15

Pricing and Revenue Management in the Supply Chain

Learning Objectives

After reading this chapter, you will be able to

1. Understand the role of revenue management in a supply chain.

2. Identify conditions under which revenue management tactics can be effective.

3. Describe trade-offs that must be considered when making revenue management decisions.

15.1 THE ROLE OF REVENUE MANAGEMENT IN THE SUPPLY CHAIN

So far in this book we have focused on managing demand and supply to grow supply chain profits. Altering inventories and capacity can change available supply. Advertising and marketing can be used to spur demand. Besides these levers, pricing is an important lever to increase supply chain profits by better matching supply and demand. Pricing may influence demand if customers are price sensitive. In any event, pricing will influence the total revenue generated. *Revenue Management* is the use of pricing to increase the profit generated from a limited supply of supply chain assets.

Supply chain assets exist in two forms—capacity and inventory. Capacity assets in the supply chain exist for production, transportation, and storage. Inventory assets exist throughout the supply chain and are carried to improve product availability.

Management decisions should try to maximize the total margin earned from these assets. To increase the total margin, managers must use all available levers, including price. This is the primary role of revenue management. Traditionally, firms have often invested in or eliminated assets to reduce the imbalance between supply and demand. Firms build additional capacity during the growth part of a business cycle and shut some of the capacity down during a downturn. Ideas from revenue management suggest that a firm should first use pricing to achieve some balance between supply and demand and only then invest in or eliminate assets.

Consider a trucking company that owns 10 trucks. One approach that the firm can take is to set a fixed price for their services and use advertising to spur demand in case surplus capacity is available. Using revenue management, however, the firm would seek to do much more. One approach would be to charge a lower price for customers willing to commit their orders far in advance and a higher price for customers looking for transportation capacity at the last minute. Another approach would be to charge a lower price for customers with long-term contracts and a higher price for customers looking to purchase capacity at the last minute. A third approach would be to charge a higher price during periods of high demand and lower prices during periods of low demand. Another example is a retailer who purchases seasonal apparel for sale. A strategy that adjusts prices based on product availability, customer demand, and remaining duration of the sales season will result in higher supply chain profits than a strategy that fixes price for the duration of the sales season.

All of these are revenue management strategies that use variable pricing as a critical lever to maximize earnings from available assets. Revenue management may also be defined as the use of differential pricing based on customer segment, time of use, and product or capacity availability to increase supply chain surplus. The impact of revenue management on supply chain performance can be significant. One of the most often cited examples is the successful use of revenue management by American Airlines to counter and finally defeat PeopleExpress in the mid 1980s. PeopleExpress started in Newark, New Jersey, and offered fares that were 50 to 80 percent lower than other carriers. At first the other airlines ignored PeopleExpress because they were not interested in the low-fare market segment. By 1983, however, PeopleExpress was flying 40 aircraft and achieved load factors over 74 percent. PeopleExpress and other new entrants were making significant inroads into the turf of existing airlines. The existing airlines could not compete by cutting prices to the level of PeopleExpress because they had higher operating costs. American Airlines was the first to come up with an effective countermeasure using revenue management. Rather than lower the price of all their seats, they lowered prices of a portion of the seats to prices at or below PeopleExpress. Soon other airlines such as United followed suit, attracting many of PeopleExpress's passengers. This was sufficient to drive down load factors for PeopleExpress to below 50 percent, a level at which the airline could not survive. Before the end of 1986 PeopleExpress collapsed.

The success of American Airlines was primarily because they used differential pricing to lower prices for a fraction of the seats and attract passengers who would otherwise have flown PeopleExpress. They did not lower prices for the fraction of seats used by business travelers who were not flying with PeopleExpress. Targeted differential pricing is at the heart of successful revenue management.

Revenue management adjusts the pricing and available supply of assets to maximize profits. Revenue management has a significant impact on supply chain profitability when one or more of the following four conditions exist:

1. The value of the product varies in different market segments
2. The product is highly perishable or product wastage occurs
3. Demand has seasonal and other peaks
4. The product is sold both in bulk and the spot market

Airline seats are a good example of a product whose value varies by market segment. A business traveler is willing to pay a higher fare for a flight that matches his or her schedule. In contrast, a leisure traveler will often alter his or her schedule to get a lower fare. An airline that can extract a higher price from the business traveler compared to the leisure traveler will always do better than an airline that charges the same price for all travelers.

Fashion and seasonal apparel are examples of highly perishable products. Production, storage, or transportation capacity is an example of a product that is wasted if not utilized. The goal of revenue management in such a setting is to adjust the price over time to maximize the profit obtained from the available inventory or capacity.

Orders at Amazon.com follow a seasonal pattern with a peak in December prior to Christmas. Serving this peak would require Amazon.com to deploy a significant amount of temporary processing capacity at high cost. Amazon.com uses revenue management ideas to offer free shipping prior to the December peak. This shifts some of the demand from the peak to the off-peak period and increases total profit for Amazon.com. Some commuter railroads use a similar strategy to deal with the distinct peaks in passenger travel. They charge higher fares during the peak periods and lower fares for off-peak travel. Differential pricing over peak and off-peak periods results in significantly higher profits.

Every product and every unit of capacity can be sold both in bulk and in the spot market. An example is the owner of a warehouse who must decide whether to lease the entire warehouse to customers willing to sign long-term contracts or save a portion of the warehouse for use in the spot market. The long-term contract is more secure but typically fetches a lower average price than the spot market. Revenue management increases profits by finding the right portfolio of long-term and spot market customers.

Revenue management can be a powerful tool for every owner of assets in a supply chain. Owners of any form of capacity (production, transportation, or storage) can use revenue management if there is seasonal demand or if there are segments that are willing to pay different prices for different lead times to use the capacity. Revenue management can be effective if there is a segment that wants to use capacity at the last minute and is willing to pay for it, and there is another segment that wants a lower price and is willing to commit far in advance. Revenue management is essential for owners of any perishable inventory. Most successful examples of the use of revenue management are from the travel and hospitality industry and include airlines, car rentals, and hotels although these analytic pricing ideas are now beginning to be used in many other industries as well. American Airlines has stated that revenue management techniques increase their revenues by over one billion dollars each year. Revenue management techniques at Marriott raise annual revenues by over one hundred million dollars. Revenue management can have a similar impact on all stages of a supply chain that satisfy one or more of the four conditions identified earlier.

In the following sections we discuss various situations in which revenue management is effective and the techniques used in each case.

15.2 REVENUE MANAGEMENT FOR MULTIPLE CUSTOMER SEGMENTS

A classic example of a market with multiple customer segments is the airline industry, where business travelers are willing to pay a higher fare to travel a specific schedule, and leisure travelers are willing to shift their schedule to take advantage of lower fares. Many similar instances arise in a supply chain. Consider ToFrom, a trucking firm that has purchased six trucks to use for transport between Chicago and St. Louis with a total capacity of six thousand cubic feet. The monthly lease charge, driver, and maintenance expense is $1,500 per truck. Market research has indicated that the demand curve for trucking capacity is

$$d = 10{,}000 - 2{,}000p,$$

where d is the demand from each segment and p is the transport cost per cubic foot. A price of $2 per cubic foot results in a demand of 6,000 cubic feet, a revenue of $12,000, and a profit of $3,000, whereas a price of $3.50 per cubic foot results in a demand of 3,000, a revenue of $10,500 and a profit of $1,500. The real question is whether the

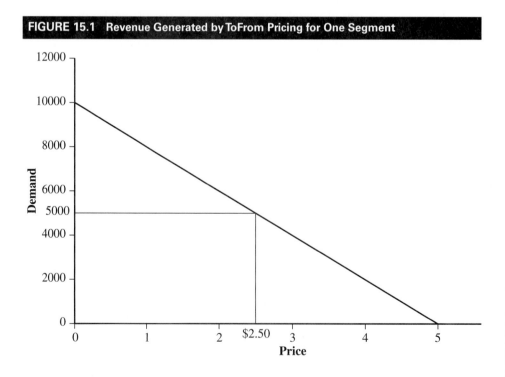

FIGURE 15.1 Revenue Generated by ToFrom Pricing for One Segment

3,000 cubic feet of demand at a price of $3.50 is from a different segment than the 3,000 additional cubic feet of demand generated at a price of $2 per cubic foot. If ToFrom assumes that all demand comes from a single segment, the optimal price is $2.50 per cubic foot, resulting in a demand of 5,000 cubic feet and revenue of $12,500, as shown in Figure 15.1.

However, if ToFrom can differentiate the segment that buys 3,000 cubic feet at $3.50 from the segment that buys 3,000 cubic feet only at $2.00, the firm can use revenue management to improve revenues and profits. They should charge $3.50 for the segment willing to pay that price and $2.00 for the 3,000 cubic feet that only sells at that price. They thus extract a revenue of $10,500 from the segment willing to pay $3.50 and a revenue of $6,000 from the segment willing to pay only $2.00 per cubic foot as shown in Figure 15.2. In the presence of different segments that have different values for trucking capacity, revenue management increases the revenue from $12,500 to $16,500 and results in a significant improvement in profits.

In theory, the concept of differential pricing increases total profits for a firm. There are two fundamental issues, however, that must be handled in practice. First, how can the firm differentiate between the two segments and structure its pricing to make one segment pay more than the other? Second, how can the firm control demand such that the lower paying segment does not utilize the entire availability of the asset?

To differentiate between the various segments, the firm must create barriers by identifying product or service attributes that the segments value differently. For example, business travelers on an airline want to book at the last minute and only stay just as long as they must. Leisure travelers, on the other hand, are willing to book far in advance and adjust the duration of stay. Plans for business travelers are also subject to

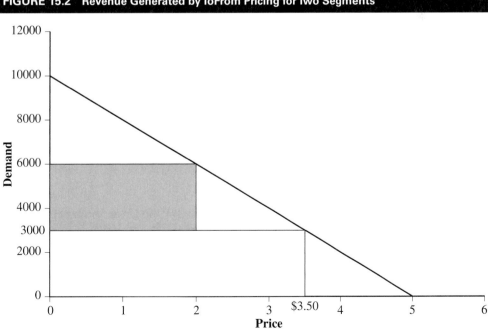

FIGURE 15.2 Revenue Generated by ToFrom Pricing for Two Segments

change. Thus, advance booking, a required Saturday night stay, and a penalty for changes on the lower fare separate the leisure traveler from the business traveler. For a transportation provider like ToFrom, the segments can be differentiated based on how far in advance a customer is willing to commit and pay for the transportation capacity. Similar separation can also occur for production and storage-related assets in a supply chain.

In most instances of differential pricing, demand from the segment paying the lower price arises earlier in time than demand from the segment paying the higher price. A supplier may charge a lower price for a buyer willing to commit far in advance and a higher price for buyers wanting to place their order at the last minute. To take advantage of revenue management, the supplier must limit the amount of capacity committed to lower price buyers even if sufficient demand exists from the lower price segment to use the entire available capacity. This raises the question of how much capacity to save for the higher price segment. The answer would be simple if demand were predictable. In practice, demand is uncertain and firms must make this decision taking uncertainty into account.

The basic trade-off to be considered by the supplier with production capacity is between committing to an order from a lower price buyer or waiting for a high-price buyer to arrive later on. The two risks in such a situation are *spoilage* and *spill*. Spoilage occurs when the capacity reserved for higher price buyers is wasted because demand from the higher price segment does not materialize. Spill occurs if higher price buyers have to be turned away because the capacity has already been committed to lower price buyers. The supplier should decide on the capacity to commit for the higher price buyers so as to minimize the expected cost of spoilage and spill. A current order from a lower price buyer should be compared with the expected revenue from waiting for a higher price buyer. The order from the lower price buyer should be accepted if the expected revenue from the higher price buyer is lower than the current revenue from the lower price buyer.

We now develop the aforementioned trade-off in terms of a formula that can be used when the supplier is working with two customer segments. Let p_L be the price charged to the lower price segment and p_H be the price charged to the higher price segment. Assume that the anticipated demand for the higher price segment is normally distributed with a mean of D_H and a standard deviation of σ_H. If we reserve a capacity C_H for the higher price segment, the expected marginal revenue $R_H(C_H)$ from reserving more capacity is given by

$$R_H(C_H) = \text{Probability(demand from higher price segment} > C_H) \times p_H.$$

The reserved quantity for the higher price segment should be chosen such that the expected marginal revenue from the higher price segment equals the current marginal revenue from the lower priced segment; that is, $R_H(C_H) = p_L$. In other words, the quantity C_H reserved for the higher price segment should be such that

$$\text{Probability(demand from higher price segment} > C_H) = p_L/p_H. \qquad \textbf{(15.1)}$$

If demand for the high-price segment is normally distributed with mean of D_H and a standard deviation of σ_H, we can obtain the reservation quantity to be

$$C_H = F^{-1}(1 - p_L/p_H, D_H, \sigma_H) = \text{NORMINV}(1 - p_L/p_H, D_H, \sigma_H). \qquad \textbf{(15.2)}$$

If there are more than two customer segments, the same philosophy can be used to obtain a set of nested reservations. The quantity C_1 reserved for the highest price segment should be such that the expected marginal revenue from the highest priced segment equals the price of the next highest priced segment. The quantity C_2 reserved for the two highest priced segments should be such that the expected marginal revenue from the two highest priced segments equals the price of the third highest priced segment. This sequential approach can be used to obtain a set of nested reservations of capacity for all but the lowest priced segment.

An important point to observe is that the use of differential pricing increases the level of asset availability for the high-price segment. Capacity is being saved for them because of their willingness to pay more for the asset. Thus, effective use of revenue management increases firm profits and also improves service for the more valuable customer segment.

Example 15.1

ToFrom Trucking serves two segments of customers. One segment (A) is willing to pay $3.50 per cubic foot but wants to commit to a shipment with only twenty four hours notice. The other segment (B) is willing to pay only $2.00 per cubic foot and is willing to commit to a shipment with up to one weeks notice. With two weeks to go, demand for segment A is forecast to be normally distributed with a mean 3,000 cubic feet and a standard deviation of 1,000. How much of the available capacity should be reserved for segment A? How should ToFrom change their decision if segment A is willing to pay $5 per cubic foot?

Analysis: In this case we have

$$\text{Revenue from segment A}, p_A = \$3.50 \text{ per cubic foot,}$$
$$\text{Revenue from segment B}, p_B = \$2.00 \text{ per cubic foot,}$$
$$\text{Mean demand for segment A}, D_A = 3{,}000 \text{ cubic feet,}$$
$$\text{Standard deviation of demand for segment A}, \sigma_A = 1{,}000 \text{ cubic feet.}$$

Using Equation 15.2, the capacity to be reserved for segment A is given by

$$C_A = \text{NORMINV}(1 - p_B/p_A, D_A, \sigma_A)$$
$$= \text{NORMINV}(1 - 2.00/3.50, 3000, 1000) = 2{,}820 \text{ cubic feet.}$$

Thus, ToFrom should reserve 2,820 cubic feet of production capacity for segment A when customers from this segment are willing to pay $3.50 per cubic foot. If the amount customers are willing to pay increases from $3.50 to $5.00, the reserved capacity should be increased to

$$C_A = \text{NORMINV}(1 - p_B/p_A, D_A, \sigma_A)$$
$$= \text{NORMINV}(1 - 2.00/5.00, 3000, 1000) = 3{,}253 \text{ cubic feet.}$$

Ideally, the demand forecast for all customer segments should be revised each time a customer order is processed and a new reservation quantity calculated. In practice, such a procedure would be very difficult to implement. It is more practical to revise the forecast and the reservation quantity after a period of time over which either the forecast demand or the forecast accuracy has changed by a significant amount.

Another approach to differential pricing is to create different versions of a product targeted at different segments. Publishers introduce new books from best-selling authors as hardcover editions and charge a higher price. The same books are introduced later as paperback editions at a lower price. The two versions are used to charge a higher price from the segment that wants to read the book as soon as it is introduced. Different versions can also be created by bundling different options and services with the same basic product. Automobile manufacturers create a high-end, a mid-level, and a low-end version of the most popular models based on the options provided. This policy allows them to charge differential prices from different segments for the same core product. Many contact lens manufacturers sell the same lens with a one-week, one-month, and six-month warranty. In this instance, the same product with different services in the form of warranty is used to charge differential prices.

To successfully use revenue management when serving multiple customer segments, a firm must use the following tactics effectively:

- Price based on the value assigned by each segment
- Use different prices for each segment
- Forecast at the segment level

Freight railroads and trucking firms have not used revenue management with multiple segments effectively. Airlines, in contrast, have been much more effective with this approach. A major hindrance for the railroads is the lack of scheduled trains. Without scheduled trains it is hard to separate between the higher price and the lower price segment. To take advantage of revenue management opportunities, owners of transportation assets in the supply chain will have to offer some scheduled services as a mechanism for separating the higher and lower price segments. Without scheduled services it is difficult to separate customers that are willing to commit early and those that want to use the service at the last minute.

> **Key Point**   If a supplier serves multiple customer segments with a fixed asset, he or she can improve revenues by setting different prices for each segment. Prices must be set with barriers such that the segment willing to pay more is not able to pay the lower price. The amount of the asset reserved for the higher price segment is such that the expected marginal revenue from the higher priced segment equals the price to the lower price segment.

15.3   REVENUE MANAGEMENT FOR PERISHABLE ASSETS

Any asset that loses value over time is perishable. Clearly fruits, vegetables, and pharmaceuticals are perishable. This list also includes products such as computers and cell phones that lose value as new models are introduced. High fashion apparel is perishable because it is hard to sell at full price once the season is past. Perishable assets also include all forms of production, transportation, and storage capacity that is wasted if not fully utilized. Unused capacity from the past has no value. Thus all unutilized capacity is equivalent to perished capacity.

Dell uses revenue management when selling PCs. The year is divided into short sales cycles of about two weeks. Once the sales organization makes a forecast for the next sales cycle, operations ensures the availability of components and production capacity. At this point the investment in inventory and capacity assets for the next sales cycle is fixed. Sales then attempts to maximize the revenue that can be obtained from the available assets by adjusting price and availability.

A well-known example of revenue management in retailing of apparel is Filene's Basement in Boston. Merchandise is first sold at the main store at full price. Leftover merchandise is moved to the basement and its price is reduced incrementally over a thirty five-day period until it sells. Any unsold merchandise is then given away to charity.

Another example of revenue management for a perishable asset is the use of overbooking by the airline industry. An airplane seat loses all value once the plane takes off. Given that people often do not show up for a plane even with a reservation, airlines sell more reservations than the capacity of the plane to maximize expected revenue.

The two revenue management tactics used for perishable assets are

1. Vary price over time to maximize expected revenue
2. Overbook sales of the asset to account for cancellations

The tactic of varying price over time is suitable for assets such as fashion apparel that have a clear date beyond which they lose a lot of their value. Apparel designed for the winter does not have much value by the time it is April. A retailer who has purchased 100 ski jackets in October has many options with regard to his pricing strategy. He can charge a high price initially. This strategy will result in fewer sales early in the season (though at a higher price), leaving more jackets to be sold later during the season when they have lower value to the customer. Another option is to charge a lower price initially, selling more jackets early in the season (though at a lower price) and leaving fewer jackets to be sold at a discount. This trade-off determines the profits for the retailer. To effectively vary price over time for a perishable asset, the asset owner must be able to estimate the value of the asset over time and effectively forecast the impact of price on customer demand. Effective differential pricing over time will generally increase the level of product availability for the consumer willing to pay full price and also increase total profits for the retailer.

The tactic of overbooking or overselling of the available asset is suitable in any situation where customers are able to cancel orders and the value of the asset drops significantly after a deadline. Examples include airline seats, items designed specially for Christmas, and production capacity at a supplier. In each case, there is a limited amount of the asset available, customers are allowed to cancel orders, and the asset loses value beyond a certain date. If the cancellation or the return rate can be predicted accurately, the overbooking level is easy to determine. In practice, however, the cancellation or return rate is uncertain.

The basic trade-off to consider during overbooking is between having wasted capacity (or inventory) because of excessive cancellations or having a shortage of capacity (or inventory) because of few cancellations, in which case an expensive backup needs to be arranged. The cost of wasted capacity is the margin that would have been generated if the capacity had been used for production. The cost of a capacity shortage is the reduction in margin that results from having to go to a backup source. The goal when making the overbooking decision is to maximize supply chain profits by minimizing the cost of wasted capacity and the cost of capacity shortage.

We now develop this trade-off in terms of a formula that can be used to set overbooking levels for an asset. Let p be the price at which each unit of the asset is sold and let c be the cost of using or producing each unit of the asset. In case of asset shortage, let b be the cost per unit at which a backup can be used. Thus, the marginal cost of having wasted capacity is $C_w = p - c$ and the marginal cost of having a capacity shortage is $C_s = b - c$. The trade-off to obtain the optimal overbooking level is very similar to the trade-off in Chapter 12 to obtain the optimal cycle service level for seasonal items given by Equation 12.1. Let O^* be the optimal overbooking level and let s^* be the probability that cancellations will be less than or equal to O^*. Similar to the derivation of Equation 12.1, the optimal overbooking level is obtained as follows

$$s^* = \text{Probability (Cancellations} \leq O^*) = \frac{C_w}{C_w + C_s}. \tag{15.3}$$

If the distribution of cancellations is known in absolute terms to be normally distributed with a mean of μ_c and a standard deviation of σ_c, the optimal overbooking level is evaluated as follows

$$O^* = F^{-1}(s^*, \mu_c, \sigma_c) = \text{NORMINV}(s^*, \mu_c, \sigma_c). \tag{15.4}$$

If the cancellation distribution is only known as a function of the booking level (capacity L + overbooking O) to have a mean of $\mu(L + O)$ and a standard deviation of $\sigma(L + O)$, the optimal overbooking level is obtained as a solution to the following equation

$$O = F^{-1}(s^*, \mu(L + O), \sigma(L + O)) = \text{NORMINV}(s^*, \mu(L + O), \sigma(L + O)). \tag{15.5}$$

Observe that the optimal level of overbooking should increase as the margin per unit increases and the level of overbooking should decrease as the cost of replacement capacity goes up. Also observe that the use of overbooking will increase asset utilization by the customers. The use of overbooking decreases the number of customers that are turned away and thus improves asset availability to the customer, while improving profits for the asset owner.

Example 15.2

Consider an apparel supplier who is taking orders for dresses with a Christmas motif. The production capacity available with the supplier is 5,000 dresses and he makes $10 for each dress sold. The supplier is currently taking orders from retailers and must decide on how many orders to commit to at this time. If he has orders that exceed capacity, he has to arrange for backup capacity that costs him $5 per dress more than his own capacity.

Retailers have been known to cancel their orders near the winter season as they have better visibility into expected demand. How many orders should the supplier accept if cancellations are normally distributed with a mean of 800 and a standard deviation of 400? How many orders should the supplier accept if cancellations are normally distributed with a mean of 15 percent of the orders accepted and a coefficient of variation of 0.5?

Analysis: The supplier has the following parameters

Cost of wasted capacity, $C_w = \$10$ per dress,
Cost of capacity shortage, $C_s = \$5$ per dress.

Using Equation 15.3 we thus obtain

$$s^* = \frac{C_w}{C_w + C_s} = \frac{10}{10 + 5} = 0.667.$$

If cancellations are normally distributed with a mean of 800 and a standard deviation of 400, the optimal overbooking level is obtained using Equation 15.4 to be

$$O^* = \text{NORMINV}(s^*, \mu_c, \sigma_c) = \text{NORMINV}(0.667, 800, 400) = 973.$$

In this case, the supplier should overbook by 973 dresses and take orders for a total of 5,973 dresses.

If cancellations are normally distributed with a mean of 15 percent of the booking level and a coefficient of variation of 0.5, the optimal overbooking level is obtained using Equation 15.5 to be the solution of the following equation

$$O = \text{NORMINV}(0.667, 0.15(5000 + O), 0.075(5000 + O)).$$

This equation can be solved using the Excel tool Solver to obtain the optimal overbooking level of $O^* = 1{,}115$.

In this case, the supplier should overbook by 1,115 dresses and take an order for up to 6,115 dresses.

Overbooking as a tactic has been used in the airline, passenger rail, and hotel industries. It has, however, not been used to the extent it should be in many supply chain scenarios including production, warehousing, and transportation capacity. There is no reason that a third-party warehouse that rents to multiple customers should not sell total space that exceeds the available space. A backup will clearly be needed if all customers use warehouse space to capacity. In all other cases, the available warehouse capacity will cover the need for space. Overbooking in this case will improve revenues for the warehouse while allowing more customers to use the available warehouse space.

> **Key Point** Overbooking or overselling of a supply chain asset is a valuable tactic if order cancellations occur and the asset is perishable. The level of overbooking is based on the trade-off between the cost of wasting the asset if too many cancellations lead to unused assets and the cost of arranging a backup if too few cancellations lead to committed orders being larger than the available capacity.

15.4 REVENUE MANAGEMENT FOR SEASONAL DEMAND

Seasonal peaks of demand are a common occurrence in many supply chains. Most retailers in the United States achieve a significant fraction of their annual sales during the month of December. One such example is Amazon.com. As a result of the seasonal peak, there is a significant increase in the requirement of picking and packing as well as transportation capacity for Amazon.com. Bringing in short-term capacity is expensive and decreases Amazon's margins. As discussed in Chapter 9, off-peak discounting is an effective method of shifting demand from the peak to the off-peak period. Amazon.com typically offers free shipping for orders that are placed in November. The price discount encourages some customers to shift their demand from December to November, thereby reducing the December peak for Amazon.com and allowing them to extract a higher profit. Simultaneously, this strategy offers a price break to customers willing to order early.

Faced with seasonal peaks, an effective revenue management tactic is to charge a higher price during the peak period and a lower price during off-peak periods. The result is a demand shift from peak to off-peak periods. Such an outcome is beneficial if the discount given during the off-peak period is more than offset by the decrease in cost because of a smaller peak and the increase in revenue during the off-peak period. See Chapter 9 for a detailed discussion of the trade-offs involved when a firm uses pricing to deal with seasonal peaks.

The hotel industry has used differential pricing by day of week and time of the year. The Marriott Corporation has been quite successful in this effort. Demand for hotel rooms is known to vary by day of the week. For Marriott, which targets business customers, peak demand days occur in the middle of the week. Marriott has offered lower rates during the weekend to encourage families to use the hotel during that time. Another revenue management tactic that Marriott has used is to charge customers a lower rate if they stay over a longer period that also covers low-demand days.

Off-peak discounting can be an effective revenue management tactic for owners of production or transportation capacity in any supply chain facing seasonal peak demand. This tactic increases profits for the owner of assets, decreases the price paid by a fraction of customers, and also brings in potentially new customers during the off-peak discount.

15.5 REVENUE MANAGEMENT FOR BULK AND SPOT CUSTOMERS

Most firms face a market where some customers purchase in bulk at a discount and others buy single units or small lots at a higher price. Consider an owner of warehousing capacity in a supply chain. Warehousing capacity may be leased in bulk to a large company or in small amounts to large companies for their emergency needs or to small companies. The large company leasing space in bulk typically gets a discount compared to the others. The owner of warehousing space thus faces the following trade-off. He could lease the space to the bulk buyer at a discount or save some of the space for higher priced demand for small amounts of warehouse space that may or may not arise.

In most instances, owners of supply chain assets prefer to fulfill all demand that arises from bulk sales and only try to serve small customers if any assets are left over. In contrast, a firm like McMaster Carr only targets customers with emergency demand for MRO goods. They will turn down any bulk buyer seeking a discount. Using this strategy, McMaster Carr has been a very profitable firm. For a firm wanting to be a niche player, targeting one of the two extremes is a sensible strategy. It allows the firm to focus its operations on either serving only the bulk segment or only the spot market. For other firms, however, a hybrid strategy of serving both segments is appropriate. In this case, firms must decide what fraction of the asset to sell in bulk and what fraction of the asset to save for the spot market. The fundamental trade-off is similar to the case when a firm serves two market segments (see Section 15.2). The firm needs to decide on the amount of the asset to reserve for the spot market. The amount reserved for the spot market should be such that the expected marginal revenue from the spot market equals the current revenue from a bulk sale. The reserved quantity will be affected by the difference in margin between the spot market and the bulk sale and also the distribution of demand from the spot market. If we consider the spot market to be the higher price segment and the bulk purchasers to be the lower price segment, the amount of asset to be saved for the spot market can be obtained using Equations 15.1 and 15.2.

A similar decision needs to be made by each purchaser of production, warehousing, and transportation assets in a supply chain. Consider a company looking for shipping capacity for their global operations. One option is for them to sign a long-term bulk contract with a shipping firm. Another option is to go and purchase shipping capacity on the spot market. The long-term bulk contract has the advantage of a fixed, low price but has the disadvantage of being wasted if it is not utilized. The spot market has the disadvantage of a higher average price but has the advantage of never being wasted. The purchaser must consider this trade-off when deciding the amount of long-term bulk shipping contracts to sign.

Given that both the spot market price and the purchaser's need for the asset are uncertain, a decision tree approach as discussed in Chapter 6 should be used to evaluate the amount of long-term bulk contract to sign. For the simple case where the spot market price is known but demand is uncertain, the extent of the bulk contract can be evaluated using a formula. Let c_B be the bulk rate and let c_S be the spot market price for the asset. Let Q^* be the optimal amount of the asset to be purchased in bulk and let p^* be the probability that demand for the asset does not exceed Q^*. The marginal cost of purchasing another unit in bulk is c_B. The expected marginal cost of not purchasing another unit in bulk and then purchasing it in the spot market is $(1 - p^*)c_S$. If the optimal amount of the asset is purchased in bulk, the marginal cost of the bulk purchase should equal the expected marginal cost of the spot market purchase; that is, $c_B = (1 - p^*)c_S$. Thus, the optimal value p^* is obtained as follows

$$p^* = \frac{c_S - c_B}{c_S}. \tag{15.6}$$

If demand is normally distributed with a mean of μ and a standard deviation of σ, the optimal amount, Q^*, of the asset purchased in bulk is obtained as follows

$$Q^* = F^{-1}(p^*, \mu, \sigma) = \text{NORMINV}(p^*, \mu, \sigma). \tag{15.7}$$

Observe that the amount of bulk purchase increases if either the spot market price increases or the bulk price decreases.

Example 15.3

A manufacturer sources several components from China and has monthly transportation needs that are normally distributed with a mean of $\mu = 10$ million units and a standard deviation of $\sigma = 4$ million. The manufacturer must decide on the portfolio of transportation contracts to carry. A long-term bulk contract costs \$10,000 per month for a million units. Transportation capacity is also available in the spot market at an average price of $12,500 per million units. How much transportation capacity should the manufacturer sign a long-term bulk contract for?

Analysis: In this case we have

Bulk contract cost, c_B = $10,000 per million units,
  Spot market cost, c_S = $12,500 per million units.

Using Equation 15.6, we thus obtain

$$p^* = \frac{c_S - c_B}{c_S} = \frac{12,500 - 10,000}{12,500} = 0.2.$$

The optimal amount to be purchased using the long-term bulk contract is thus obtained using Equation 15.7 to be

$$Q^* = \text{NORMINV}(p^*, \mu, \sigma) = \text{NORMINV}(0.2, 10, 4) = 6.63.$$

Thus, the manufacturer should sign a long-term bulk contract for 6.63 million units per month and purchase any transportation capacity beyond that on the spot market.

Key Point Most consumers of production, warehousing, and transportation assets in a supply chain face the problem of constructing a portfolio of long-term bulk contracts and spot market contracts. The basic decision is the size of the bulk contract. The fundamental trade-off is between wasting a portion of a low-cost bulk contract and paying more for the asset on the spot market.

15.6 USING REVENUE MANAGEMENT IN PRACTICE

1. *Evaluate your market carefully.* The first step in revenue management is to identify the customer segments being served and their needs. The goal is to understand what the customer is buying as opposed to what you are selling. If an airline thinks of itself as only selling seats, it cannot use revenue management. It has to think of itself as selling seats, the ability to book at the last minute, the ability to alter flight plans, and the ability to pick a convenient flight schedule. Only then do revenue management opportunities present themselves.

Having identified the market needs, it is crucial to gather accurate and complete data relating to products offered, prices, competition, and most important, customer behavior. Information about customer behavior is a valuable asset that helps identify consumer preferences. Ultimately, a proper understanding of customer preferences and a quantification of the impact of various tactics on consumer behavior are at the core of successful revenue management.

2. *Quantify the benefits of revenue management.* It is critical to quantify the expected benefits from revenue management before starting the project. Ideally, historical data and a good model of customer preferences should be used to estimate the benefits through a simulation. The outcome of this step should be explicit revenue targets that are to be achieved as a result of revenue management. The revenue targets should be such that all people involved believe in them. The revenue management effort should then be compared to the expected benefit.

3. *Implement a forecasting process.* The foundation of any revenue management system is the forecasting function. To use overbooking with any degree of success, an airline must be able to forecast cancellation patterns. By forecasting we do not mean obtaining an estimate that is always accurate. Forecasting involves estimating demand and also attributing an expected error to the forecast itself. Both the estimated value and the expected error are important inputs into any revenue management model.

It is generally very difficult to forecast at a micro level where all behavior is essentially idiosyncratic. For example, an airline with 100 fare classes will find it very difficult to forecast demand for each class and also forecast the behavior of customers when they find a fare class full. It is thus important to ensure that revenue management tactics are planned over an aggregate enough level that effective forecasting is possible.

Finally, as new information becomes available, reforecast to see if the revenue management tactics currently in place are still appropriate. The frequency of forecasting will depend on the amount of market activity. Ideally, the forecast and the revenue management decision should be evaluated after every transaction.

4. *Apply optimization to obtain the revenue management decision.* The goal of optimization is to use forecasts of customer behavior to identify a revenue management tactic that will be most effective. The decision to use overbooking by a hotel is only the beginning of the revenue management process. The ultimate success of this effort will depend on the level of overbooking used by the hotel. Too high a level of overbooking will lead to upset customers and a high cost of providing them space. Too low a level of overbooking will lead to empty rooms and lost revenue. Optimization allows the hotel to identify the level of overbooking that maximizes profits.

5. *Involve both sales and operations.* Salespeople must understand the revenue management tactic in place so they can align their sales pitch accordingly. It makes no sense for a firm to offer an off-peak discount if the sales force continues to push people toward the period with highest prices. The sales force must differentiate between those customers who truly need the supply chain asset during the peak period and those that will benefit from moving their order to the off-peak period. Such an approach will increase profits for the firm while also satisfying customers. Operations must understand the potential outcomes of the revenue management tactics in place and be informed of actual outcomes taking place. For example, operations in an airline using overbooking must be ready to book passengers unable to depart on the full flight onto other feasible flights.

6. *Understand and inform the customer.* Customers will have a negative perception of revenue management tactics if they are simply presented as a mechanism for extracting maximum revenue. Such a perception is likely to diminish customer loyalty in the long term. Thus, it is important for the firm to structure its revenue management program in a way that revenue increases while improving service along some dimension that is important to customers that pay the highest price. As discussed earlier in the chapter, a proper implementation of revenue management tactics should achieve both outcomes. It is important for the firm to convey this information to their most valuable customers. Remember, a change in behavior by this set of customers can destroy any potential benefit of a revenue management program!

7. *Integrate supply planning with revenue management.* Although the supply planning and revenue management ideas we discuss in this book are valuable in their own right, combining them can create significantly more value. The point here is to not just use revenue management in isolation—but rather combine it with decisions on the supply side. For instance, if, after applying revenue management, a manufacturer finds that the production of a short lead time facility provides the majority of their profit, they should look into adding more short lead time capacity. Understanding and acting on the interaction between supply, demand, and pricing can bring about powerful results.

15.7 SUMMARY OF LEARNING OBJECTIVES

1. Understand the role of revenue management in a supply chain.

Revenue management uses differential pricing to better match supply and demand and increase supply chain profits. Traditionally, firms have changed the availability of assets to match supply and demand. Revenue management aims to reduce any supply/demand imbalance by using pricing as a lever. A big advantage of using revenue management is that a change in pricing is much easier to reverse compared to an investment in supply chain assets. When used properly, revenue management increases firm profits while leaving valuable customers more satisfied through greater asset availability.

2. Identify conditions under which revenue management tactics can be effective.

Revenue management tactics can be very effective if the firm serves multiple segments, each placing a different value on the supply chain asset, or the asset is perishable and loses value over time, or demand for the asset has distinct seasonal peaks, or the asset can be bought and sold both using long-term bulk contracts and on the spot market.

3. Describe trade-offs that must be considered when making revenue management decisions.

When serving multiple customer segments, the basic revenue management decision is the amount of the asset to save for the higher price segment. The trade-off is between saving too much and spoiling the asset if the higher price demand does not materialize and turning away higher price customers because too little of the asset was saved. When the asset is perishable, the revenue management decisions are about how to change the asset price over time and the degree to which the asset should be over-booked or oversold. When changing the asset price over time, the trade-off is between charging a higher price initially and having too much inventory left over to discount later on, and charging a low initial price and having little inventory left over. When overbooking, the trade-off is between not overbooking enough and wasting the available asset and overbooking too much and having to arrange for backup capacity at high cost. When demand has distinct seasonal peaks, the revenue management decision is the timing and extent of the off-peak discount. The trade-off is between the additional cost of serving the seasonal peak, and the impact on demand and thus revenue from offering an off-peak discount. For a seller using both long-term bulk contracts and the spot market, the revenue management decision is the fraction of the asset to save for the spot market. The trade-off is between getting a committed demand at a lower price with the bulk contract and potentially getting a high price on the spot market. For a buyer, the decision is the fraction of anticipated demand to purchase from a long-term bulk contract. The trade-off is between getting a long-term bulk contract at a low price that may not be fully used, and purchasing only the amount required from the spot market but at a higher price.

DISCUSSION QUESTIONS

1. In what ways can a retailer like Nordstrom take advantage of revenue management opportunities?
2. What revenue management opportunities are available to a manufacturer? How can they take advantage of these opportunities?
3. What revenue management opportunities are available to a trucking firm? How can they take advantage of these opportunities?
4. What revenue management opportunities are available to the owner of a warehouse and how can they take advantage of them?
5. Explain the use of outlet stores by retailers like Saks Fifth Avenue in the context of revenue management. How does the presence of outlet stores help Saks? How does it help their more valuable customer who is willing to pay full price?
6. Demand for hairdressers is much higher over the weekend when people are not at work. What revenue management techniques can be used by such a business?
7. How can a golf course use revenue management to improve financial performance?

EXERCISES

1. Felgas, a manufacturer of felt gaskets, has production capacity of 1,000 units per day. Currently, the firm sells production capacity for $5 per unit. At this price, all production capacity gets booked about one week in advance. A group of customers have said that they would be willing to pay twice as much ($10 per unit) if only Felgas had capacity available on the last day. About ten days in advance, demand for the high-price segment is normally distributed with a mean of 250 and a standard deviation of 100. How much production capacity should Felgas reserve for the last day?
2. The GoGo Bunny is a very hot toy this Christmas, and the manufacturer has decided to ration supply to all retailers. A large retail chain owns two channels—a discount channel and a high-service channel. The retailer plans to sell the toy at a margin of $4 in the discount channel and a margin of $8 in the high-service channel. The manufacturer sends 500,000 GoGo Bunnies to the retailer. The retailer has forecast that the demand for the toy at the high-service channel is normally distributed with a mean of 400,000 and a standard deviation of 150,000. How many toys should the retailer send to the high-service channel?
3. A small warehouse has 100,000 square feet of capacity. The manager at the warehouse is in the process of signing contracts for storage space with customers. The contract has an upfront monthly fee of $200 per customer and then a fee of $3 per square foot based on actual usage. The warehouse guarantees the contracted amount even if they have to arrange for extra space at a price of $6 per square foot. The manager feels that customers are unlikely to use the full contracted amount at all times. Thus, he is thinking of signing contracts that exceed 100,000 square feet. He forecasts that unused space will be normally distributed with a mean of 20,000 square feet and a standard deviation of 10,000 square feet. What is the total size of the contracts he should sign? If he forecasts that unused space

will be normally distributed with a mean of 15 percent of the contracted amount and a coefficient of variation of 0.6, what is the total space that he should sign contracts for?

4. A trucking firm has current capacity of 200,000 cubic feet. A large manufacturer is willing to purchase the entire capacity at $0.10 per cubic foot per day. The manager at the trucking firm has observed that on the spot market, trucking capacity sells for an average of $0.13 per cubic foot per day. Demand, however, is not guaranteed at this price. The manager forecasts daily demand on the spot market to be normally distributed with a mean of 60,000 cubic feet and a standard deviation of 20,000. How much trucking capacity should the manager save for the spot market?

5. The manager at a large manufacturer is planning warehousing needs for the coming year. She predicts that warehousing needs will be normally distributed with a mean of 500,000 square feet and a standard deviation of 150,000. The manager can obtain a full-year lease at $0.50 per square foot per month or purchase storage space on the spot market. Spot market rates have averaged $0.70 per square foot per month. How large an annual contract should the manager sign?

BIBLIOGRAPHY

Cross, Robert G. 1997. *Revenue Management.* New York: Bantam Doubleday Dell Publishing.

Daudel, Sylvain, and Georges Vialle. 1994. *Yield Management: Applications to Air Transport and Other Service Industries.* Paris: Institut du Transport Aerien.

Tayur, Sridhar, Ram Ganeshan, and Michael Magazine, eds. 1999. *Quantitative Models for Supply Chain Management.* Boston: Kluwer Academic Publishers.

Coordination and Technology in the Supply Chain

C H A P T E R   1 6

Coordination in the Supply Chain

C H A P T E R   1 7

Information Technology and the Supply Chain

C H A P T E R   1 8

E-Business and the Supply Chain

The goals of the chapters in Part VI are to highlight the importance of coordination in a supply chain and discuss how information technology and e-business can help a supply chain improve performance.

Coordination helps ensure that each part of the supply chain takes actions that increase total supply chain profits and avoids actions that improve its local profits but hurt total profits. Chapter 16 discusses how the lack of coordination across different members of a supply chain can result in poor performance, even when each stage is doing the best it can given its own objectives. The bullwhip effect is described and the primary causes of this phenomenon are identified. Ideas discussed in all previous chapters are brought together to identify managerial actions that can help a supply chain dampen the bullwhip effect and achieve coordination.

Chapter 17 discusses the impact of information technology on the success of a supply chain. A framework is presented to describe the landscape of enterprise software and the role played by each type of software system when designing, planning, and operating a supply chain.

Chapter 18 uses the concepts developed in earlier chapters relating to the design, planning, and operation of a supply chain to analyze the development of e-business and discuss how firms can best integrate e-business when formulating strategy and designing their supply chains. A framework is presented to help determine whether or not e-business is a good fit for a particular company. Different industry examples are analyzed from a supply chain perspective to illustrate the value that e-business provides in each case.

16

Coordination
in the Supply Chain

Learning Objectives

After reading this chapter, you will be able to

1. Describe supply chain coordination and the bullwhip effect and their impact on performance.

2. Identify causes of the bullwhip effect and obstacles to coordination in the supply chain.

3. Discuss managerial levers that help achieve coordination in the supply chain.

4. Describe actions that facilitate the building of strategic partnerships and trust within the supply chain.

In this chapter, we discuss how lack of coordination leads to a degradation of responsiveness and an increase in cost within a supply chain. We describe various obstacles that lead to this lack of coordination and exacerbate variability through the supply chain. We then identify appropriate managerial levers that can help overcome the obstacles and achieve coordination. In this context, we also discuss actions that facilitate strategic partnerships and the building of trust within the supply chain.

16.1 LACK OF SUPPLY CHAIN COORDINATION AND THE BULLWHIP EFFECT

Supply chain coordination improves if all stages of the chain take actions that together increase total supply chain profits. Supply chain coordination requires each stage of the supply chain to take into account the impact its actions have on other stages.

A lack of coordination occurs either because different stages of the supply chain have objectives that conflict or because information moving between stages gets delayed and distorted. Different stages of a supply chain may have objectives that conflict if each stage has a different owner. As a result, each stage tries to maximize its own profits, resulting in actions that often diminish total supply chain profits (see Chapters 10 and 12). Today, supply chains consist of potentially hundreds, or even thousands, of independently owned enterprises. For example, Ford Motor Company has thousands of suppliers from Goodyear to Motorola, and each of these suppliers has many suppliers in turn. Information is distorted as it moves within the supply chain because complete information is not shared between stages. This distortion is exaggerated by the fact that supply chains today produce a large amount of product variety. For example, Ford produces many different models with many options for each model. The increased variety makes it difficult for Ford to coordinate information exchange with thousands of suppliers and dealers. The fundamental challenge today is for supply chains to achieve coordination in spite of multiple ownership and increased product variety.

Many firms have observed the *bullwhip effect* in which fluctuations in orders increase as they move up the supply chain from retailers to wholesalers to manufacturers to suppliers, as shown in Figure 16.1. The bullwhip effect distorts demand information within the supply chain, with different stages having a very different estimate of what demand looks like. The result is a loss of supply chain coordination.

Procter & Gamble (P&G) has observed the bullwhip effect in the supply chain for Pampers diapers.[1] The company found that raw material orders from P&G to its suppliers fluctuated significantly over time. Further down the chain, when sales at retail stores were studied, it was found that the fluctuations, while present, were small. It is reasonable to assume that the consumers of diapers (babies) at the last stage of the supply chain used them at a steady rate. Although consumption of the end product was stable, orders for raw material were highly variable, increasing costs and making it difficult for supply to match demand.

HP also found that the fluctuation in orders increased significantly as they moved from the resellers up the supply chain to the printer division to the integrated circuit division.[2] Once again, while product demand showed some variability, orders placed with the integrated circuit division were much more variable. This made it difficult for HP to fill orders on time and increased the cost of doing so.

Studies of the apparel and grocery industry have shown a similar phenomenon; the fluctuation in orders increases as we move upstream in the supply chain from retail to manufacturing. Barilla, an Italian manufacturer of pasta, observed that weekly orders placed by a local distribution center fluctuated by up to a factor of 70 in the

---

[1]Lee, Hau L., V. Padmanabhan, and S. Whang. 1997. "The Bullwhip Effect in Supply Chains," *Sloan Management Review*, Spring.
[2]Ibid.

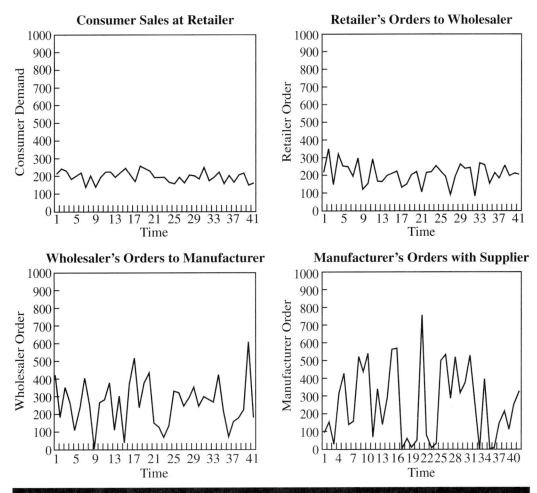

FIGURE 16.1   Demand Fluctuations at Different Stages of a Supply Chain

course of the year, whereas weekly sales at the distribution center (representing orders placed by supermarkets) fluctuated by a factor of less than three.[3] Barilla was thus facing demand that was much more variable than customer demand. This led to increased inventories, poorer product availability, and a drop in profits.

A similar phenomenon, over a longer time frame, has been observed in several industries that are quite prone to "boom and bust" cycles. A good example is the production of memory chips for personal computers. Between 1985 and 1998 there were at least two cycles where prices of memory chips fluctuated by a factor of over three. These large fluctuations in price were driven by either large shortages or surpluses in capacity. The shortages were exacerbated by panic buying and over ordering that was followed by a sudden drop in demand.

---

[3]Hammond, J. H., 1994, "Barilla Spa (A-D)." Harvard Business School Case.

In the next section we consider how the lack of coordination impacts supply chain performance.

16.2   EFFECT OF LACK OF COORDINATION ON PERFORMANCE

Lack of coordination results if each stage of the supply chain only optimizes its local objective without considering the impact on the complete chain. Total supply chain profits are thus less than what could be achieved through coordination (see Chapters 10 and 12). Each stage of the supply chain, in trying to optimize its local objective, takes actions that end up hurting the performance of the entire supply chain.

Lack of coordination also results if information distortion occurs within the supply chain. As an example, consider the bullwhip effect P&G observed within the diaper supply chain. As a result of the bullwhip effect, orders P&G receives from its distributors are much more variable than demand for diapers at retailers. We discuss the impact of this increase in variability on various measures of performance in the diaper supply chain.

Manufacturing Cost

The bullwhip effect increases manufacturing cost in the supply chain. As a result of the bullwhip effect, P&G and its suppliers try to satisfy a stream of orders that is much more variable than customer demand. P&G can respond to the increased variability by either building excess capacity or holding excess inventory (see Chapter 11), both of which increase the manufacturing cost per unit produced.

Inventory Cost

The bullwhip effect increases inventory cost in the supply chain. To handle the increased variability in demand, P&G has to carry a higher level of inventory than would be required in the absence of the bullwhip effect. As a result, inventory costs in the supply chain increase. The high levels of inventory also increase the warehousing space required and thus the warehousing cost incurred.

Replenishment Lead Time

The bullwhip effect increases replenishment lead times in the supply chain. The increased variability as a result of the bullwhip effect makes scheduling at P&G and supplier plants much more difficult compared to a situation with level demand. There are times when the available capacity and inventory cannot supply the orders coming in. This results in higher replenishment lead times within the supply chain from both P&G and its suppliers.

Transportation Cost

The bullwhip effect increases transportation cost within the supply chain. The transportation requirements over time at P&G and its suppliers are correlated with the orders being filled. As a result of the bullwhip effect, transportation requirements fluctuate significantly over time. This raises transportation cost because surplus transportation capacity needs to be maintained to cover high-demand periods.

Labor Cost for Shipping and Receiving

The bullwhip effect increases labor costs associated with shipping and receiving in the supply chain. Labor requirements for shipping at P&G and its suppliers fluctuate with orders. A similar fluctuation will occur for the labor requirements for receiving at distributors and retailers. The various stages have the option of carrying excess labor capacity or varying labor capacity in response to the fluctuation in orders. Either option increases total labor cost.

Level of Product Availability

The bullwhip effect hurts the level of product availability and results in more stockouts within the supply chain. The large fluctuations in orders make it harder for P&G to supply all distributor and retailer orders on time. This increases the likelihood that retailers will run out of stock, resulting in lost sales for the supply chain.

Relationships across the Supply Chain

The bullwhip effect negatively impacts performance at every stage and thus hurts the relationships between different stages of the supply chain. There is the tendency to assign blame to other stages of the supply chain because each stage feels it is doing the best it can. The bullwhip effect thus leads to a loss of trust between different stages of the supply chain and makes any potential coordination efforts more difficult.

From the earlier discussion, it follows that the bullwhip effect and the resulting lack of coordination have a significant negative impact on the supply chain's performance. The bullwhip effect moves a supply chain away from the efficient frontier by increasing cost and decreasing responsiveness. The impact of the bullwhip effect on different performance measures is summarized in Table 16.1.

> **Key Point**   The bullwhip effect reduces the profitability of a supply chain by making it more expensive to provide a given level of product availability.

In the next section we discuss various obstacles to achieving coordination in the supply chain.

TABLE 16.1   Impact of Bullwhip Effect on Supply Chain Performance

Performance Measure	Impact of Bullwhip Effect
Manufacturing cost	Increases
Inventory cost	Increases
Replenishment lead time	Increases
Transportation cost	Increases
Shipping and receiving cost	Increases
Level of product availability	Decreases
Profitability	Decreases

16.3 OBSTACLES TO COORDINATION IN THE SUPPLY CHAIN

Any factor that leads to either local optimization by different stages of the supply chain, or an increase in information delay, distortion, and variability within the supply chain, is an obstacle to coordination. If managers in a supply chain are able to identify the key obstacles, they can then take suitable actions that help achieve coordination. We divide the major obstacles into five categories.

- Incentive obstacles
- Information processing obstacles
- Operational obstacles
- Pricing obstacles
- Behavioral obstacles

Incentive Obstacles

Incentive obstacles refer to situations where incentives offered to different stages or participants in a supply chain lead to actions that increase variability and reduce total supply chain profits.

Local Optimization within Functions or Stages of a Supply Chain

Incentives that focus only on the local impact of an action result in decisions that do not maximize total supply chain profits. For example, if a transportation manager at a firm has her compensation linked to the average transportation cost per unit, she is likely to take actions that lower transportation costs even if they increase inventory costs or hurt customer service. It is natural for any participant in the supply chain to take actions that optimize performance measures along which they are evaluated. For example, managers at a retailer such as K-Mart make all their purchasing and inventory decisions to maximize K-Mart profits, not total supply chain profits. Buying decisions based on maximizing profits at a single stage of the supply chain lead to ordering policies that do not maximize supply chain profits (see Chapters 10 and 12).

Sales Force Incentives

Improperly structured sales force incentives are a significant obstacle to coordination in the supply chain. In many firms, sales force incentives are based on the amount the sales force sells during an evaluation period of a month or quarter. The sales typically measured by a manufacturer are the quantity sold to distributors or retailers (sell-in), not the quantity sold to final customers (sell-through). Measuring performance based on sell-in is often justified on the grounds that the manufacturer's sales force does not control sell-through. For example, Barilla offered its sales force incentives based on the quantity sold to distributors during a four- to six-week promotion period. To maximize their bonuses, the Barilla sales force urged distributors to buy more pasta toward the end of the evaluation period, even if distributors were not selling as much to retailers. The sales force offered discounts they controlled to spur end-of-period sales. This increased variability in the order pattern, with a jump in orders towards the end of the evaluation period followed by very few orders at the beginning of the next evaluation period. Order sizes from distributors to Barilla fluctuated by a factor of up to 70 from one week to the next. A sales force incentive based on sell-in thus results in order variability being larger than customer demand variability.

Information Processing Obstacles

Information processing obstacles refer to situations where demand information is distorted as it moves between different stages of the supply chain, leading to increased variability in orders within the supply chain.

Forecasting Based on Orders and Not Customer Demand

When stages within a supply chain make forecasts that are based on orders they receive, any variability in customer demand is magnified as orders move up the supply chain to manufacturers and suppliers. In supply chains that exhibit the bullwhip effect, the fundamental means of communication between different stages are the orders that are placed. Each stage views its primary role within the supply chain as one of filling orders placed by its downstream partner. Thus, each stage views its demand to be the stream of orders received and produces a forecast based on this information.

In such a scenario, a small change in customer demand becomes magnified as it moves up the supply chain in the form of customer orders. Consider the impact of a random increase in customer demand at the retailer. The retailer may interpret part of this random increase to be a growth trend. This interpretation will lead the retailer to order more than the observed increase in demand because the retailer expects growth to continue into the future and thus orders to cover for future anticipated growth. The increase in the order placed with the wholesaler is thus larger than the observed increase in demand at the retailer. Part of the increase is a one-time increase. The wholesaler, however, has no way to interpret the order increase correctly. The wholesaler simply observes a jump in the order size and infers a growth trend. The growth trend inferred by the wholesaler will be larger than that inferred by the retailer (recall that the retailer had increased the order size to account for future growth). The wholesaler will thus place an even larger order with the manufacturer. As we go further up the supply chain, the order size will be magnified.

Now assume that periods of random increase are followed by periods of random decrease in demand. Using the same forecasting logic as earlier, the retailer will now anticipate a declining trend and reduce order size. This reduction will also become magnified as we move up the supply chain.

> **Key Point**   The fact that each stage in a supply chain forecasts demand based on the stream of orders received from the downstream stage results in a magnification of fluctuations in demand as we move up the supply chain from the retailer to the manufacturer.

Lack of Information Sharing

The lack of information sharing between stages of the supply chain magnifies the bullwhip effect. For example, a retailer such as Wal-Mart may increase the size of a particular order because of a planned promotion. If the manufacturer is not aware of the planned promotion, they may interpret the larger order as a permanent increase in demand and place orders with suppliers accordingly. The manufacturer and suppliers thus have a lot of inventory right after Wal-Mart has finished their promotion. Given the excess inventory, as future Wal-Mart orders return to normal, manufacturer orders will be smaller than before. The lack of information sharing between the retailer and manufacturer thus leads to a large fluctuation in manufacturer orders.

Operational Obstacles

Operational obstacles refer to actions taken in the course of placing and filling orders that lead to an increase in variability.

Ordering in Large Lots

When a firm places orders in lot sizes that are much larger than the lot sizes in which demand arises, variability of orders is magnified up the supply chain. Firms may order in large lots because there is a significant fixed cost associated with placing, receiving, or transporting an order (see Chapter 10). Large lots may also occur if the supplier offers quantity discounts based on lot size (see Chapter 10). Figure 16.2 shows both the demand and the order stream for a firm placing an order every five weeks. Observe that the order stream is far more erratic than the demand stream.

Because orders are batched and placed every five weeks, the order stream has four weeks without orders followed by a large order that equals five weeks of demand.

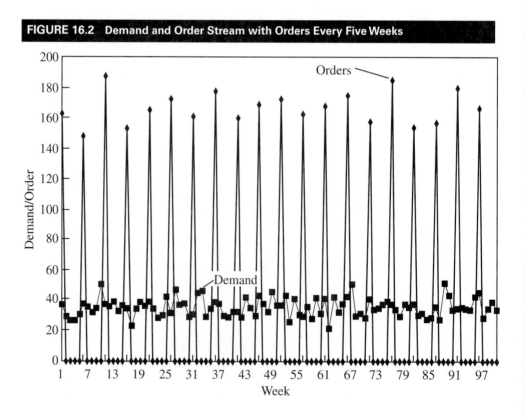

FIGURE 16.2 Demand and Order Stream with Orders Every Five Weeks

A manufacturer supplying several retailers who batch their orders will face an order stream that is much more variable than the demand the retailers experience. If the manufacturer further batches their orders to suppliers, the effect is further magnified. In many instances there are certain focal point periods like the first or the last week of a month when a majority of the orders arrive. This concentration of orders further exacerbates the impact of batching.

Large Replenishment Lead Times

The bullwhip effect is magnified if replenishment lead times between stages are long. Consider a situation where a retailer has misinterpreted a random increase in demand as a growth trend. If the retailer faces a lead time of two weeks, they will incorporate the anticipated growth over two weeks when placing the order. In contrast, if the retailer faces a lead time of two months, they will incorporate into their order the anticipated growth over two months (which will be much larger). The same applies when a random decrease in demand is interpreted as a declining trend.

Rationing and Shortage Gaming

Rationing schemes that allocate limited production in proportion to the orders placed by retailers lead to a magnification of the bullwhip effect. A situation where a high-demand product is in short supply often arises within the supply chain. HP, for example, has faced many situations where a new product has demand that far exceeds supply. In such a situation, manufacturers come up with a variety of mechanisms to ration the scarce supply of product among various distributors or retailers. One commonly used rationing scheme is to allocate the available supply of product based on orders placed. Under this rationing scheme, if the supply available is 75 percent of the total orders received, each retailer receives 75 percent of their order.

This rationing scheme results in a game in which retailers try to increase the size of their orders to increase the amount supplied to them. A retailer needing 75 units will order 100 units in the hope that 75 will then be made available. The net impact of this rationing scheme is to artificially inflate orders for the product. In addition, a retailer ordering based on what they expect to sell will get less and as a result lose sales, whereas a retailer inflating its order is rewarded.

If the manufacturer is using orders to forecast future demand, they will interpret the increase in orders as an increase in demand even though customer demand is unchanged. The manufacturer may respond by building enough capacity to be able to fill all orders received. Once sufficient capacity becomes available, orders return to their normal level because they were inflated in response to the rationing scheme. The manufacturer is now left with a surplus of product and capacity. These boom and bust cycles then tend to alternate.

This phenomenon is fairly common in the computer industry where alternating periods of component shortages followed by a component surplus are often observed. In particular, memory chip manufacturing has experienced a couple of such cycles over the last decade.

Pricing Obstacles

Pricing obstacles refer to situations in which the pricing policies for a product lead to an increase in variability of orders placed.

Lots Size Based Quantity Discounts

Lot size based quantity discounts increase the lot size of orders placed within the supply chain (see Chapter 10). As discussed earlier, the resulting large lots magnify the bullwhip effect within the supply chain.

Price Fluctuations

Trade promotions and other short-term discounts offered by a manufacturer result in forward buying where a wholesaler or retailer purchases large lots during the discounting period to cover demand during future periods. Forward buying results in large orders during the promotion period followed by very small orders after that (see Chapter 10), as shown in Figure 16.3 for chicken noodle soup.

Observe that the shipments during the peak period are higher than the sales during the peak period because of a promotion offered during this period. The peak shipment period is followed by a period of very low shipments from the manufacturer, indicating significant forward buying by distributors. The promotion thus results in a variability in manufacturer shipments that is significantly higher than the variability in retailer sales.

Behavioral Obstacles

Behavioral obstacles refer to problems in learning within organizations that contribute to the bullwhip effect. These problems are often related to the way the supply chain is structured and the communication between different stages. Some of the behavioral obstacles are as follows:

FIGURE 16.3 Retailer Sales and Manufacturer Shipments of Soup

Source: Adapted from "What is the Right Supply Chain for Your Product?" by Marshall L. Fisher. *Harvard Business Review* (March-April 1997), 83-93.

1. Each stage of the supply chain views its actions locally and is unable to see the impact of its actions on other stages.
2. Different stages of the supply chain react to the current local situation rather than trying to identify the root causes.
3. Based on local analysis, different stages of the supply chain blame each other for the fluctuations, with successive stages in the supply chain becoming enemies rather than partners.
4. No stage of the supply chain learns from its actions over time because the most significant consequences of the actions any one stage takes occur elsewhere. The result is a vicious cycle where actions taken by a stage create the very problems that the stage blames on others.
5. A lack of trust between supply chain partners causes them to be opportunistic at the expense of overall supply chain performance. The lack of trust also results in significant duplication of effort. More important, information available at different stages is either not shared or is ignored because it is not trusted.

16.4   MANAGERIAL LEVERS TO ACHIEVE COORDINATION

Having identified obstacles to coordination, we now focus on actions a manager may take to help overcome the obstacles and achieve coordination in the supply chain. The following managerial actions in the supply chain increase total supply chain profits and moderate the bullwhip effect.

- Aligning of goals and incentives
- Improving information accuracy
- Improving operational performance
- Designing pricing strategies to stabilize orders
- Building partnerships and trust

Aligning of Goals and Incentives

Managers can improve coordination within the supply chain by aligning goals and incentives such that every participant in supply chain activities works to maximize total supply chain profits.

Aligning Incentives across Functions

One key to coordinated decisions within a firm is to ensure that the objective any function uses to evaluate a decision is aligned with the firm's overall objective. All facility, transportation, and inventory decisions should be evaluated based on their impact on profitability, not total costs, or even worse, just local costs. This helps avoid situations such as a transportation manager making decisions that lower transportation cost but increase overall supply chain costs (see Chapter 14).

Pricing for Coordination

A manufacturer can use lot size based quantity discounts to achieve coordination for commodity products if the manufacturer has large fixed costs associated with each lot (see Chapter 10). For products where a firm has market power, a manager can use two-part tariffs and volume discounts to help achieve coordination (see Chapter 10).

Given demand uncertainty, manufacturers can use buy-back, revenue sharing, and quantity flexibility contracts to spur retailers to provide levels of product availability that maximize supply chain profits. Buy-back contracts have been used in the publishing industry to increase total supply chain profits. Quantity flexibility contracts have helped Benetton increase supply chain profits.

Altering Sales Force Incentives from Sell-In to Sell-Through

Any change that reduces the incentive for a salesperson to push product to the retailer will reduce the bullwhip effect. If sales force incentives are based on sales over a rolling horizon, the incentive to push product is reduced. This helps reduce forward buying and the resulting fluctuation in orders. Another action that managers can take is to link incentives for the sales staff to sell-through by the retailer rather than sell-in to the retailer. This action eliminates any motivation that sales staff may have to encourage forward buying. The elimination of forward buying helps reduce fluctuations in the order stream.

Improving Information Accuracy

Managers can achieve coordination by improving the accuracy of information available to different stages in the supply chain.

Sharing Point of Sales Data

Sharing point of sales (POS) data across the supply chain can help reduce the bullwhip effect. A primary cause for the bullwhip effect is the fact that each stage of the supply chain uses orders to forecast future demand. Given that orders received by different stages vary, forecasts at different stages also vary. In reality, the only demand that the supply chain needs to satisfy is from the final customer. If retailers share POS data with other supply chain stages, all supply chain stages can forecast future demand based on customer demand. Sharing of POS data helps reduce the bullwhip effect because all stages now respond to the same change in customer demand. Observe that sharing aggregate POS data is sufficient to dampen the bullwhip effect. We do not necessarily need to share detailed POS data. Use of appropriate information systems facilitates the sharing of such data (see Chapter 17). Companies have also used the Internet to share data with suppliers. For direct sales companies like Dell, and companies involved in e-commerce, POS data is available in a form that can easily be shared. Dell shares demand data as well as current inventory positions of components with many of its suppliers on the Internet, thereby helping to avoid unnecessary fluctuations in supply and orders placed. P&G has convinced many retailers to share demand data. P&G in turn shares the data with its suppliers, improving coordination in the supply chain.

Implementing Collaborative Forecasting and Planning

Once point of sales data is shared, different stages of the supply chain must forecast and plan jointly if complete coordination is to be achieved. Without collaborative planning, sharing of POS data does not guarantee coordination. A retailer may have observed large demand in the month of January because it ran a promotion. If no promotion is planned in the upcoming January, the retailer's forecast will differ from the manufacturer's forecast even if both have past POS data. The manufacturer must be aware of the retailer's promotion plans to achieve coordination. The key is to ensure that the entire supply chain is operating to a common forecast. Wal-Mart has observed that a lack of collaborative planning has a significant impact on its supply chain performance. Wal-Mart has a joint initiative with P&G called collaborative forecasting and replenishment (CFAR) that has had significant success in this regard. Teams consisting of managers from both Wal-Mart and P&G jointly forecast sales of P&G products at Wal-Mart stores and then jointly plan replenishment strategies. This ensures that there is no gap between what Wal-Mart plans to sell and what P&G plans to produce. To facilitate this type of coordination in the supply chain environment, the Voluntary Interindustry Commerce Standards (VICS) Association has set up a Collaborative Planning, Forecasting, and Replenishment (CPFR) committee to identify best practices and design guidelines for collaborative planning and forecasting. The use of IT systems helps facilitate collaborative forecasting and planning within the supply chain (see Chapter 17).

Designing Single Stage Control of Replenishment

Designing a supply chain in which a single stage controls replenishment decisions for the entire supply chain can help diminish the bullwhip effect. As we mentioned earlier, a key cause for the bullwhip effect is the fact that each stage of the supply chain uses orders from the previous stage as its historical demand. As a result, each stage views its role as one of replenishing orders placed by the next stage. In reality, the key replenishment is at the retailer, because that is where the final customer purchases. When a single stage controls replenishment decisions for the entire chain, the problem of multiple forecasts is eliminated and coordination within the supply chain follows.

For a manufacturer like Dell that sells directly to customers, single control of replenishment is automatic because there is no intermediary between the manufacturer and the customer. The manufacturer automatically becomes the single point of control for replenishment decisions.

When sales occur through retailers, there are several industry practices that result in single point control of replenishment. In *continuous replenishment programs* (CRP), the wholesaler or manufacturer replenishes a retailer regularly based on POS data. CRP could be supplier, distributor, or third-party managed. In most instances CRP systems are driven by actual withdrawals of inventory from retailer warehouses rather than POS data at the retailer level. Tying CRP systems to warehouse withdrawals is easier to implement and retailers are often more comfortable sharing data at this level. IT systems that are linked across the supply chain provide a good information infrastructure on which a continuous replenishment program may be based.

In VMI, the distributor or manufacturer monitors and manages inventories at the wholesaler or retailer. This centralizes the replenishment decision for all retailers at the upstream distributor or manufacturer. This practice existed in retailing before the growth of enabling technologies. Frito-Lay truck drivers restock retailer shelves and make restocking decisions rather than having the retailer manage the inventory. The existence of suitable information systems facilitates the implementation of VMI. VMI has been implemented with significant success by, among others, K-Mart (with about 50 suppliers) and Fred Meyer. K-Mart has seen inventory turns on seasonal items increase from 3 to between 9 and 11, and for nonseasonal items from 12–15 to 17–20. Fred Meyer has seen inventories reduce by 30 to 40 percent while fill rates have increased to 98 percent.

In each of the instances cited earlier, the single forecast and control of replenishment by a single stage are what help eliminate the increased fluctuations because of the bullwhip effect.

Improving Operational Performance

Managers can help dampen the bullwhip effect by improving operational performance and designing appropriate product rationing schemes in case of shortages.

Reducing Replenishment Lead Time

By reducing the replenishment lead time, managers can decrease the uncertainty of demand during the lead time (see Chapter 11). A reduction in lead time is especially beneficial for seasonal items because it allows for multiple orders to be placed in the season with a significant increase in the accuracy of the forecast (see Chapter 12). Thus, a reduction in replenishment lead time helps dampen the bullwhip effect by reducing the underlying uncertainty of demand.

Managers can take a variety of actions at different stages of the supply chain to help reduce replenishment lead times. Electronic Data Interchange (EDI) and other electronic forms of communication can be used to significantly cut the lead time associated with order placement and information transfer. At manufacturing plants, increased flexibility and cellular manufacturing can be used to achieve a significant reduction in lead times. A dampening of the bullwhip effect further reduces lead times because of stabilized demand and, as a result, improved scheduling. This is particularly true when manufacturing is producing a large variety of products. ASNs can be used to reduce the lead time as well as effort associated with receiving. Cross-docking can be used to reduce the lead time associated with moving the product between stages in the supply chain. Wal-Mart has successfully used many of the aforementioned approaches to significantly reduce lead time within its supply chain.

Reducing Lot Sizes

Managers can dampen the bullwhip effect by implementing operational improvements that reduce lot sizes. A reduction of lot sizes decreases the amount of fluctuation that can accumulate between any pair of stages of a supply chain, thus decreasing the bullwhip effect. To reduce lot sizes, managers must take actions that help reduce the fixed costs associated with ordering, transporting, and receiving each lot (see Chapter 10). Wal-Mart and 7-Eleven Japan have been very successful at reducing replenishment lot sizes by aggregating deliveries across many products and suppliers.

Computer-assisted ordering (CAO) refers to the substitution through technology of the functions of a retail order clerk in preparing an order through the use of computers that integrate information about product sales, market factors affecting demand, inventory levels, product receipts, and desired service levels. CAO and EDI help reduce the fixed costs associated with placing each order. Today, the growing use of Web-based ordering by companies such as W. W. Grainger and McMaster Carr has facilitated ordering in small lots because of reduced ordering costs for customers and reduced fulfillment costs for companies themselves. The growth of B2B e-commerce is also reducing ordering costs. For example, General Motors and Ford require many of their suppliers to be equipped to receive orders on the Web in an attempt to make ordering more efficient. More discussion of this idea is included in Chapter 17.

In some cases, managers can simplify ordering by eliminating the use of purchase orders. In the auto industry, some suppliers are paid based on the number of cars produced, eliminating the need for individual purchase orders. This eliminates the order processing cost associated with each replenishment order. Information systems also facilitate the settlement of financial transactions, eliminating the cost associated with individual purchase orders.

The large gap in the prices of TL and LTL shipping encourages shipment in TL quantities. In fact, with the efforts to reduce order processing costs, transportation costs are now the major barrier to smaller lots in most supply chains. Managers can reduce lot sizes without increasing transportation costs by filling a truck using smaller lots from a variety of products (see Chapter 10). P&G, for example, requires all orders from retailers to be a full TL. The TL, however, may be built from any combination of products. A retailer can thus order small lots of each product as long as a sufficiently large variety of products is included on each truck. 7-Eleven Japan has effectively used this strategy with *combined trucks* where the separation is by the temperature at which the truck is maintained. All products to be shipped at a particular temperature are on the same truck. This has allowed 7-Eleven to reduce the number of trucks sent to retail outlets while keeping product variety high. Some firms in the grocery industry use trucks with different compartments, each at a different temperature and carrying a variety of products, to help reduce lot sizes.

Managers can also reduce lot sizes by having milk runs that combine shipments for several retailers on a single truck (see Chapter 14). In many cases third-party transporters combine shipments to competing retail outlets on a single truck. This reduces the fixed transportation cost per retailer and allows each retailer to order in smaller lots. In Japan, Toyota uses a single truck from a supplier to supply multiple assembly plants, which enables managers to reduce the lot size received by any one plant. Managers can also reduce lot sizes by combining shipments from multiple suppliers on a single truck. In the United States, Toyota uses this approach to reduce the lot size it receives from any one supplier.

As smaller lots are ordered and delivered, both the pressure on and the cost of receiving can grow significantly. Thus, managers must implement technologies that simplify the receiving process and reduce the cost associated with receiving. For example, ASNs electronically identify shipment content, count, and time of delivery and help reduce unloading time and increase cross-dock efficiency. ASNs can be used to update inventory records electronically, thus reducing the cost of receiving. Bar coding of pallets also facilitates receiving and delivery. DEX and NEX are two receiving technologies that allow the direct updating of inventory records once the item count has been verified.

Each of these technologies works to simplify the task of shipping, transporting, and receiving complex orders with small lots of many products. This facilitates the reduction of lot size, counteracting the bullwhip effect.

Another simple way to minimize the impact of batching is to encourage different customers to order in a way that demand is evenly distributed over time. Frequently, customers that order once a week tend to do so on either a Monday or Friday. Customers ordering once a month tend to do so either at the beginning or end of the month. In such situations it is better to evenly distribute customers ordering once a week across all days of the week, and customers ordering once a month across all days of the month. In fact, regular ordering days may be scheduled in advance for each customer. This generally does not affect retailers but it does level out the order stream arriving at the manufacturer, thus dampening the bullwhip effect.

Rationing Based on Past Sales and Share Information to Limit Gaming

To diminish the bullwhip effect, managers can design rationing schemes that discourage retailers from artificially inflating their orders in the case of a shortage. One approach, referred to as *turn-and-earn*, is to allocate the available supply based on past retailer sales rather than current retailer orders. Tying allocation to past sales removes any incentive a retailer may have to inflate orders, as a result dampening the bullwhip effect. In fact, during low-demand periods, the turn-and-earn approach pushes retailers to try and sell more to increase the allocation they receive during periods of shortage. Several firms, including General Motors, have historically used the turn-and-earn mechanism to ration available product in case of a shortage. Others like HP have historically allocated based on retailer orders but are now switching to past sales.

Other firms have tried to share information across the supply chain to minimize shortage situations. Firms like Sport Obermeyer offer incentives to their large customers to preorder at least a part of their annual order. This information allows Sport Obermeyer to improve the accuracy of its own forecast and allocate production capacity accordingly. Once capacity has been allocated appropriately across different products, it is less likely that shortage situations will arise, thus dampening the bullwhip effect. The availability of flexible capacity can also help in this regard, because flexible capacity can easily be shifted from a product whose demand is lower than expected to one whose demand is higher than expected.

Designing Pricing Strategies to Stabilize Orders

Managers can diminish the bullwhip effect by devising pricing strategies that encourage retailers to order in smaller lots and reduce forward buying.

Moving from Lot Size-Based to Volume-Based Quantity Discounts

As a result of lot size-based quantity discounts, retailers increase their lot size to take full advantage of the discount. Offering volume-based quantity discounts eliminates the incentive to increase the size of a single lot because volume-based discounts consider the total purchases during a specified period (say a year) rather than purchases in a single lot (see Chapter 10). Volume-based quantity discounts result in smaller lot sizes, thus reducing order variability in the supply chain. Volume-based discounts with a fixed end date at which discounts will be evaluated may lead to large lots close to the end date. Offering the discounts over a rolling time horizon helps dampen this effect. HP is experimenting with a move away from lot size based discounts to volume-based discounts.

Stabilizing Pricing

Managers can dampen the bullwhip effect by eliminating promotions and charging an EDLP. The elimination of promotions removes forward buying by retailers and results in orders that match customer demand. P&G, Campbell Soup, and several other manufacturers have implemented EDLP to dampen the bullwhip effect.

Managers can place limits on the quantity that may be purchased during a promotion to decrease forward buying. This limit should be retailer specific and linked to historical sales by the retailer. Another approach is to tie the promotion dollars paid to the retailer to the amount of sell-through rather than the amount purchased by the retailer. As a result, retailers obtain no benefit from forward buying and purchase more only if they can sell more. Promotions based on sell-through significantly dampen the bullwhip effect. The presence of specific information systems facilitates the tying of promotions directly to customer sales.

Building Strategic Partnerships and Trust

Managers find it easier to use the levers discussed earlier to diminish the bullwhip effect and achieve coordination if trust and strategic partnerships are built within the supply chain. Sharing of accurate information that is trusted by every stage results in a better matching of supply and demand throughout the supply chain and a lower cost. A better relationship also tends to lower the transaction cost between supply chain stages. For example, a supplier can eliminate its forecasting effort if it trusts orders and forecast information received from the retailer. Similarly, the retailer can lessen the receiving effort by decreasing counting and inspections if it trusts the supplier's quality and delivery. In general, stages in a supply chain can eliminate duplicated effort on the basis of improved trust and a better relationship. This lowering of transaction cost along with accurate shared information helps mitigate the bullwhip effect. Wal-Mart and P&G have been trying to build a strategic partnership that will be mutually beneficial and help reduce the bullwhip effect.

Managerial levers that help a supply chain achieve better coordination fall into two broad categories. *Action-oriented levers* include information sharing, changing of incentives, operational improvements, and stabilization of pricing. *Relationship oriented levers* involve the building of cooperation and trust within the supply chain. In the next section we discuss relationship oriented levers in greater detail.

16.5 BUILDING STRATEGIC PARTNERSHIPS AND TRUST WITHIN A SUPPLY CHAIN

A *trust-based relationship* between two stages of a supply chain includes *dependability* of the two stages, and the ability of each stage to make a *leap of faith*.[4] Trust involves a belief that each stage is interested in the other's welfare and would not take actions without considering their impact on the other stage. Cooperation and trust within the supply chain help improve performance for the following reasons:

---

[4]Kumar, N. 1996. "The Power of Trust in Manufacturer-Retailer Relationships," *Harvard Business Review*.

1. A more natural aligning of incentives and objectives is achieved. When stages trust each other, they are more likely to take the other party's objective into consideration when making decisions.
2. Action-oriented managerial levers to achieve coordination become easier to implement. Sharing of information is natural between parties that trust each other. Similarly, operational improvements are easier to implement and appropriate pricing schemes are easier to design if both parties are aiming for the common good.
3. An increase in supply chain productivity results, either by elimination of duplicated effort or by allocating effort to the appropriate stage. For example, a manufacturer receives material from a supplier without inspecting it as long as the supplier shares process control charts. Another example may be the situation in which a distributor aids the postponement strategy of a manufacturer by performing customization just before the point of sale.
4. A greater sharing of detailed sales and production information results. This sharing allows the supply chain to coordinate production and distribution decisions. As a result, the supply chain is better able to match supply and demand, resulting in better coordination.

The benefits of trust are highlighted in Table 16.2, in the context of a replacement automotive parts supply chain. The table contains average ratings of over 400 retailers classified into low or high categories (and scaled relative to the level of low trust respondents) based on their trust in the manufacturer. For example, the average retailer with high trust toward their manufacturers developed fewer alternative supply sources, were more committed to the manufacturer, sold more of the manufacturer's products, and were rated higher by the manufacturer. It also highlights that the retailers themselves were likely happier when they had greater trust in the manufacturer—exhibited by the fact that they were less likely to search for alternative supply sources.

Historically, supply chain relationships have been based either on power or trust. In a power-based relationship, the stronger party dictates its view. Although exploiting power may be advantageous in the short term, its negative consequences are felt in the long term for three main reasons:

1. Exploiting power results in one stage of the supply chain maximizing its profits, often at the expense of other stages. This decreases total supply chain profits.

TABLE 16.2 Comparison of Retailers by Level of Trust

Measure of Comparison	Low Trust	High Trust
Retailers' development of alternative supply sources	100	78
Retailers' commitment to the manufacturer	100	112
Retailers' sales of manufacturer product line	100	178
Retailers' performance as rated by manufacturer	100	111

Source: Adapted from N. Kumar. 1996. "The Power of Trust in Manufacturer-Retailer Relationships," *Harvard Business Review* (November–December): 92–106.

2. Exploiting power to extract unfair concessions can hurt a company once the balance of power changes. This reversal of power has occurred over the last two decades with retailers in Europe and the United States becoming more powerful than manufacturers in many supply chains.
3. When a stage of a supply chain systematically exploits its power advantage, the other stages seek ways to resist. In many instances where retailers have tried to exploit their power, manufacturers have sought ways to directly access the consumer. These include selling over the Internet and setting up company stores. The result can be a decrease in supply chain profits because different stages are competing rather than cooperating.

Although everybody agrees that cooperation and trust in a supply chain is valuable, these qualities are very hard to initiate and sustain. There are two views regarding how cooperation and trust can be built into any supply chain relationship:

- *Deterrence-based view:* In this view the parties involved use a variety of formal contracts to ensure cooperation. With the contracts in place, parties are assumed to behave in a trusting manner purely for reasons of self-interest.
- *Process-based view:* With this view, trust and cooperation are built over time as a result of a series of interactions between the parties involved. Positive interactions strengthen the belief in the cooperation of the other party.

In most practical situations, neither view holds exclusively. It is impossible to design a contract that will take into account every contingency that may arise in the future. Thus, parties that may not yet trust each other have to rely on the building of trust to resolve issues that are not included in the contract. Conversely, parties that trust each other and have a long relationship still rely on contracts. In most effective partnerships, a combination of the two approaches is used. An example is the situation in which suppliers sign an initial contract containing contingencies with manufacturers and then they never want to refer to the contract again. Their hope is that all contingencies can be resolved through negotiation in a way that is best for the supply chain.

In most strong supply chain relationships, the initial period often relies more on the deterrence-based view. Over time, the relationship evolves toward a greater reliance on the process-based view. From the supply chain perspective, the ideal goal is *co-identification,* where each party considers the other party's objective as its own. Co-identification ensures that each stage accounts for total supply chain profits when making decisions.

There are two phases to any long-term supply chain relationship. In the *design phase,* ground rules are established and the relationship is initiated. In the *management phase,* interactions based on the ground rules occur and the relationship as well as the ground rules evolve. A manager seeking to build a supply chain relationship must consider how cooperation and trust can be encouraged during both phases of the relationship. Careful consideration is very important because in most supply chains, power tends to be concentrated in relatively few hands. The concentration of power often leads managers to ignore the effort required to build trust and cooperation, hurting supply chain performance in the long term.

Next we discuss how a manager can design a supply chain relationship to encourage cooperation and trust.

Designing a Relationship with Cooperation and Trust

The key steps in designing effective supply chain partnerships are as follows:

1. Assessing the value of the relationship
2. Identifying operational roles and decision rights for each party
3. Creating effective contracts
4. Designing effective conflict resolution mechanisms

Assessing the Value of the Relationship and Contributions

The first step in designing a supply chain relationship is to clearly identify the mutual benefit that the relationship provides. In most supply chains, each member of the partnership brings distinct skills, all of which are needed to supply a customer order. For example, a manufacturer produces the product, a carrier transports it between stages, and a retailer makes the product available to the final customer. The next step is to identify the criteria used for evaluating the relationship as well as the contribution of each party. A common criterion is the increase in total profits as a result of the relationship. *Equity,* defined as fair dealing, should be another important criterion when evaluating and designing a relationship.[5] Equity measures the fairness of the division of the total profits between the parties involved.

Stages of the supply chain are unlikely to work at utilizing the various managerial levers that achieve coordination unless they are confident that the resulting increase in profits will be shared equitably. For example, when suppliers work hard to reduce replenishment lead times, the supply chain benefits because of reduced safety inventories at manufacturers and retailers. Suppliers are unlikely to put in the effort if the manufacturers and retailers are not willing to share the increase in profits with them. Thus, a supply chain relationship is likely to be sustainable only if it increases total profits and this increase is shared equitably between the parties involved.

The next step is to clarify the contribution of each party as well as the benefits that will accrue to each. For example, if a manufacturer and distributor are to implement postponement together, it is important to clarify the role of each party in implementing postponement, the value of this strategy to the supply chain, and how the increased profits are to be shared between the parties. Flexible mechanisms should be designed that allow the partners to periodically monitor the relationship and adjust both contributions and the allocation of resulting benefits. For example, DiamlerChrysler negotiates a certain level of improvement per year with each supplier. It does not, however, specify areas within which the improvement must be achieved. This flexibility allows suppliers to identify areas where the largest improvement can result with the minimum effort and creates a win-win situation for both sides.

[5]Ring, P. S., and A. H. Van de Ven, 1994, "Developmental Processes of Cooperative Inter-Organizational Relationships," *Academy of Management Review*.

Identifying Operational Roles and Decision Rights for each Party

When identifying operational roles and decision rights for different parties in a supply chain relationship, managers must consider the resulting interdependence between the parties. A source of conflict may arise if the tasks are divided in a way that makes one party more dependent on the other. In many partnerships, an inefficient allocation of tasks results simply because neither party is willing to give the other a perceived upper hand based on the tasks assigned.

The allocation of tasks results in a *sequential interdependence* if the activities of one partner precede the other. Traditionally, supply chain relationships have been sequential, with one stage completing all its tasks and then handing off to the next stage. In *reciprocal interdependence,* parties come together and exchange information and inputs in both directions. P&G and Wal-Mart are attempting to create reciprocal interdependence through collaborative forecasting and replenishment teams. The teams contain people from both Wal-Mart and P&G. Wal-Mart brings in demand information and P&G brings in information on available capacity. The teams then decide on the production and replenishment policy that is best for the supply chain.

Reciprocal interdependence requires a significant effort to manage and can increase the transaction costs if not managed properly. However, reciprocal interdependence is more likely to result in decisions that maximize supply chain profitability because all decisions must take the objectives of both parties into account. Reciprocal interdependence increases the interactions between the two parties, increasing the chances of trust and cooperation if positive interactions occur. Reciprocal interdependence also makes it harder for one party to be opportunistic and take self-serving actions that hurt the other party. Thus, greater reciprocal interdependence in the allocation of operational roles and decision rights increases the chances of an effective relationship, as shown in Figure 16.4.

Managers must ensure that tasks that are required from each party for a successful handoff of the product from one to the other be well defined. Consider the relationship between Dell, Sony, and Airborne. Dell takes orders for computers it assembles and monitors that Sony manufactures. Airborne picks up the computer from the Dell warehouse in Texas and the monitor from the Sony warehouse in Mexico. It then merges the two and sends a combined order to the customer. For an order to be filled on time, all three parties must coordinate and complete their tasks. To achieve cooperation, managers must also put in place some mechanism, such as appropriate information systems, that helps accurately track all failures to their source.

Creating Effective Contracts

Managers can help promote trust by creating contracts that encourage negotiation as unplanned contingencies arise. Contracts are most effective for governance when *complete information* is available and all future contingencies can be accounted for. In practice, uncertainty with respect to the future value of the relationship and the future business environment makes it impossible to design a contract with all contingencies included. For example, when considering VMI or CRP, it is very difficult to design a contract for all possible future scenarios. Thus, it is essential that the supplier and the retailer develop a relationship that allows trust to compensate for gaps in the contract. The relationship often develops between appropriate individuals that have

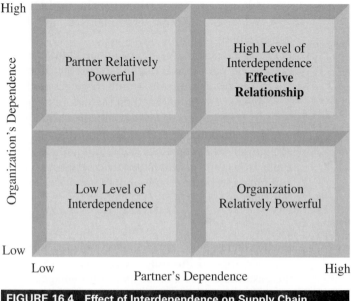

FIGURE 16.4   Effect of Interdependence on Supply Chain Relationships

Source: Adapted from N. Kumar. 1996. "The Power of Trust in Manufacturer-Retailer Relationships," *Harvard Business Review* (November–December): 92–106.

been assigned from each side. Over time, the informal understandings and commitments between the individuals tend to be formalized when new contracts are drawn up. When designing the partnership and initial contract, it should be understood that informal understandings will operate side by side and these will contribute to the development of the formal contract over time. Thus, contracts that evolve over time are likely to be much more effective than contracts that are completely defined at the beginning of the partnership.

Over the long term, contracts can only play a partial role in maintaining effective partnerships in a supply chain. A good example is the relationship between Caterpillar and their dealerships in which either the dealer or Caterpillar can terminate agreements without cause with ninety days notice. Clearly it is not the contract alone that keeps the relationship effective. A combination of a contract, the mutual benefit of the relationship, along with trust that compensates for gaps in the contract, results in effective supply chain partnerships.

Designing Effective Conflict Resolution Mechanisms

Effective conflict resolution mechanisms can significantly strengthen any supply chain relationship. Conflicts are bound to arise in any relationship. Unsatisfactory resolutions cause the partnership to worsen, whereas satisfactory resolutions strengthen the partnership. A good conflict resolution mechanism should give the parties an opportunity to communicate and work through their differences, in the process building greater trust.

An initial formal specification of rules and guidelines for financial procedures and technological transactions can help build trust between partners. The specification of rules and guidelines facilitates the sharing of information among the partners in the supply chain. The sharing of information over time helps move the relationship from deterrence-based trust to process-based trust. Once process-based trust is built between the parties, it facilitates conflict resolution.

To facilitate communication, regular and frequent meetings should be held between managers and staff assigned to the partnership. These meetings allow issues to be raised and discussed before they turn into major conflicts. They also provide a basis for resolution at a higher level, should resolution at a lower level not take place. An important goal of meetings and other formal conflict resolution mechanisms is to ensure that disputes about financial or technological issues do not turn into interpersonal squabbles.

When designing conflict resolution mechanisms, it is important to be sensitive to the context of the partnership. In the United States, parties are sometimes comfortable returning to the detailed contract to resolve a dispute. The help of a court or an intermediary can also be sought to interpret the contract. Thus, detailed contracts can be quite effective in the United States. In Asia, in contrast, conflict resolution mechanisms involving courts are unlikely to be very effective. Parties are much more comfortable directly negotiating resolutions to every conflict. Flexible contracts that allow for such negotiation are effective in building trust in that context.

Managing Supply Chain Relationships for Cooperation and Trust

Effectively managed supply chain relationships foster cooperation and trust, thus increasing supply chain coordination. In contrast, poorly managed relationships lead to each party being opportunistic, resulting in a loss of total supply chain profits. The management of a relationship is often seen as a tedious and routine task. Top management, in particular, is often very involved in the design of a new partnership but rarely involved in its management. This has led to a mixed record in running successful supply chain alliances and partnerships.

Figure 16.5 shows the basic process by which any supply chain partnership or alliance evolves. Once the partnership has been designed and established, both partners learn about the environment in which the partnership will operate, the tasks and processes to be performed by each partner, the skills required and available on each side, and the emerging goals of each side. The performance of each side is evaluated based on the improvement in profitability and on equity or fairness. At this stage, a better evaluation of the value of the partnership becomes available, which provides both parties in the supply chain partnership an opportunity to revise the conditions of the partnership to improve profitability and fairness. It is important that the initial contracts be designed with sufficient flexibility to facilitate such alterations. Formal contracts may be restructured to reflect the changes. As the business environment and company goals change, the cycle repeats itself and the relationship evolves. Any successful supply chain partnership will go through many such cycles.

A supply chain partnership falters if the perceived benefit from the relationship diminishes or one party is seen as being opportunistic. Problems arise when communication between the two parties is weak and the mutual benefit of the relationship is not

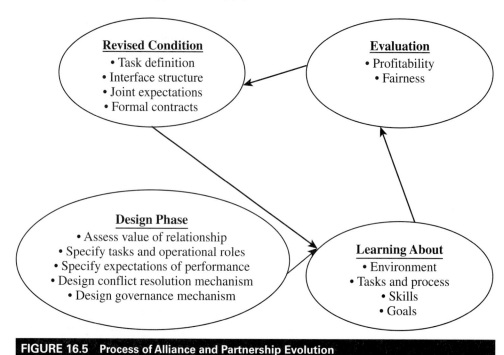

FIGURE 16.5 Process of Alliance and Partnership Evolution

Source: Adapted from *Alliance Advantage* by Y. L. Doz and G. Hamel

reiterated regularly. When managing a supply chain relationship, managers should focus on the following factors to improve the chances of success of a supply chain partnership:

1. The presence of flexibility, trust, and commitment in both parties helps a supply chain relationship succeed. In particular, commitment of top management on both sides is crucial for success. The manager directly responsible for the partnership can also facilitate the development of the relationship by clearly identifying the value of the partnership for each party in terms of his own expectations.
2. Good organizational arrangements, especially for information sharing and conflict resolution, improve chances of success. Lack of information sharing and the inability to resolve conflicts are the two major factors that lead to the breakdown of supply chain partnerships.
3. Mechanisms that make the actions of each party and resulting outcomes visible help avoid conflicts and resolve disputes. Such mechanisms make it harder for either party to be opportunistic and help identify defective processes, increasing the value of the relationship for both parties.
4. The more fairly the stronger partner treats the weaker, vulnerable partner, the stronger the supply chain relationship tends to be.

The issue of fairness is extremely important in the supply chain context because most relationships will involve parties with unequal power. Unanticipated situations that hurt one party more than the other often arise. The more powerful party often has greater control over how the resolution occurs. The fairness of the resolution influences the strength of the relationship in the future.

Fairness requires that the benefits and costs of the relationship be shared between the two parties in a way that makes both winners. A relationship based on power would maximize all benefits on one side. A long-term supply chain relationship cannot be maintained if this is the case. For a strong supply chain relationship to develop, the stronger party must realize its responsibility for its partner's profitability. The relationship between Mark's & Spencer and a manufacturer of a kitchen product provides an excellent example of a fair sharing of benefits.[6] A few months after the product's introduction, the manufacturer realized that costs had been miscalculated and exceeded the price at which the product was being sold to Mark's & Spencer. Meanwhile, given its low retail price, customers found the product an outstanding value and made it a big hit. When the manufacturer brought the problem to the attention of Mark's & Spencer, their managers helped the manufacturer reengineer both the product and the process to lower cost. Mark's & Spencer also lowered its margin to provide a sufficient profit for the manufacturer. The outcome is one where the relationship is strengthened between the two partners because Mark's & Spencer's fairness allowed a resolution that recognized the manufacturer's needs. In the long run, both partners benefit and a higher level of trust develops.

Procedures and policies govern the interaction between parties in a supply chain relationship. It is thus important that the weaker party perceive the fairness of the stronger party's procedures and policies for dealing with its partners. The stronger party is in control of its policies and procedures and should not bias the policies in a way that is opportunistic and does not benefit the entire supply chain. Fair procedures should encourage two-way communication between the partners. The procedures should be impartial and should allow the weaker party an opportunity to appeal the stronger party's decisions. Finally, the stronger party should be willing to explain all its decisions.

16.6 ACHIEVING COORDINATION IN PRACTICE

1. *Quantify the bullwhip effect:* Companies often have no idea that the bullwhip effect plays a significant role in their supply chain. Managers should start by comparing the variability in the orders they receive from their customers with the variability in orders they place with their suppliers. This helps a firm quantify its own contribution to the bullwhip effect. Once its contribution is visible, it becomes easier for a firm to accept the fact that all stages in the supply chain contribute to the bullwhip effect, leading to a significant loss in profits. In the absence of this concrete information, companies try to react better to the variability rather than eliminate the variability itself. This leads companies to invest significant amounts in inventory management and scheduling systems, only to see little improvement in performance or profits. Evidence of the size of the bullwhip effect is very effective in getting different stages of the supply chain to focus

---

[6]Kumar, N. 1996. "The Power of Trust in Manufacturer-Retailer Relationships," *Harvard Business Review.*

on efforts to achieve coordination and eliminate the variability created within the supply chain.

2. *Get top management commitment for coordination:* More than any other aspect of supply chain management, coordination can only succeed with top management's commitment. Coordination requires managers at all stages of the supply chain to subordinate their local interests to the greater interest of the firm and even the supply chain. Coordination often requires the resolution of tradeoffs in a way that requires many functions in the supply chain to change their traditional practices. These changes often run counter to approaches that were put in place when each function only focused on its local objective. Such changes within a supply chain cannot be implemented without strong top management commitment. Top management commitment was a key factor in helping Wal-Mart and P&G set up collaborative forecasting and replenishment teams.

3. *Devote resources to coordination:* Coordination cannot be achieved without all parties involved devoting significant managerial resources to this effort. Companies often do not devote resources to coordination because they either assume that lack of coordination is something they have to live with or hope that coordination will occur on its own. The problem with this approach is that it leaves all managers involved with only the separate areas that they control, while no one is responsible for highlighting the impact one manager's actions have on other parts of the supply chain. One of the best ways to solve coordination problems is through teams made up of members from different companies throughout the supply chain. These teams should be made responsible for coordination and given the power to implement the changes required. Setting up a coordination team is fruitless unless the team has the power to act because the team will run into conflict with functional managers who are currently maximizing local objectives. Coordination teams can only be effective once a sufficient level of trust builds between members from different firms. If used properly, coordination teams can provide significant benefit as is the case with the collaborative forecasting and replenishment teams set up by Wal-Mart and P&G.

4. *Focus on communication with other stages:* Good communication with other stages of a supply chain often creates situations that highlight the value of coordination for both sides. Companies often do not communicate with other stages of the supply chain and are unwilling to share information. However, often all companies in the supply chain are frustrated with the lack of coordination and would be happy to share information if it helped the supply chain operate in a more effective manner. Regular communication between the parties involved facilitates change in such a setting. For instance, a major PC company had been ordering their microprocessors in batches of several weeks of production. They were trying to move to a build-to-order environment where they would place microprocessor orders on a daily basis. They assumed that the microprocessor supplier would be reluctant to go along with this approach. However, once communication was opened up with the supplier, the opposite turned out to be true. The supplier also wanted to reduce lot sizes and increase the frequency of orders. They had just assumed that the PC manufacturer wanted large lots and thus never requested a change. Regular communication helps different stages of the supply chain share their goals and identify common goals and mutually beneficial actions that improve coordination.

5. *Try to achieve coordination in the entire supply chain network:* The complete benefit of coordination is only achieved when the entire supply chain network is coordinated. It is not enough for two stages in a supply chain to coordinate. The most powerful party in a supply chain should make an effort to achieve coordination in the entire network. Toyota has been very effective in achieving knowledge sharing and coordination in its entire network.

6. *Use technology to improve connectivity in the supply chain:* The Internet and a variety of different types of software systems can be used to increase the visibility of information throughout the supply chain. Until now, most IT implementations have achieved only visibility of information within a firm. Visibility across the supply chain still requires additional effort in most cases. From the discussion in this chapter, it should be clear that the major benefits of IT systems can only be realized if the systems help increase visibility across the supply chain and facilitate coordination. If firms are to realize the full benefit of the huge investments they make in their current IT systems, particularly ERP systems, it is crucial that they make the extra effort required to use these systems to facilitate collaborative forecasting and planning across the supply chain. The Internet should be used to share information and increase connectivity in the supply chain.

7. *Share the benefits of coordination equitably:* The greatest hurdle to coordination in the supply chain is the feeling on the part of any stage that the benefits of coordination are not being shared equitably. Managers from the stronger party in the supply chain relationship must be sensitive to this fact and ensure that all parties perceive that the way benefits are shared is fair.

16.7 SUMMARY OF LEARNING OBJECTIVES

1. Describe supply chain coordination and the bullwhip effect and their impact on supply chain performance.

   Supply chain coordination requires all stages to take actions that maximize total supply chain profits. A lack of coordination results if different stages focus on optimizing their local objectives or if information is distorted as it moves across the supply chain. The phenomenon where the fluctuation in orders increases as one moves up the supply chain from retailers to wholesalers to manufacturers to suppliers is referred to as the bullwhip effect. The bullwhip effect results in an increase in all costs in the supply chain and a decrease in customer service levels. The bullwhip effect moves all parties in the supply chain away from the efficient frontier and results in a decrease of both customer satisfaction and profitability within the supply chain.

2. Identify causes of the bullwhip effect and obstacles to coordination in the supply chain.

   A key obstacle to coordination in the supply chain is misaligned incentives that result in different stages optimizing local objectives instead of total supply chain profits. Other obstacles include lack of information sharing, operational inefficiencies leading to large replenishment lead times and large lots, sales force incentives that encourage forward buying, rationing schemes that encourage inflation of orders, promotions that encourage forward buying, and a lack of trust that makes any effort toward coordination difficult.

3. Discuss managerial levers that help achieve coordination in the supply chain.

   Managers can help achieve coordination in the supply chain by aligning goals and incentives across different functions and stages of the supply chain. Other actions that managers can take to achieve coordination include sharing of sales information and collaborative forecasting and planning, implementation of single point control of replenishment, improving operations to reduce lead times and lot sizes, EDLP and other strategies that limit forward buying, and the building of trust and strategic partnerships within the supply chain.

4. Describe actions that facilitate the building of strategic partnerships and trust within the supply chain.

A manager can help build trust and strategic partnerships by designing a relationship where the mutual benefit to both sides is clear, both parties are mutually interdependent, contracts are allowed to evolve over time, and conflicts are effectively resolved. When managing the relationship, flexibility, information sharing, visibility of effort and performance of each party, and fairness from the stronger party when distributing costs and benefits help foster trust and facilitate coordination in the supply chain.

DISCUSSION QUESTIONS

1. What is the bullwhip effect and how does it relate to lack of coordination in the supply chain?
2. What is the impact of lack of coordination on the performance of the supply chain?
3. In what way can improper incentives lead to a lack of coordination in the supply chain? What countermeasures can be used to offset this effect?
4. What problems result if each stage of the supply chain views its demand as the orders placed by the downstream stage? How should firms within the supply chain communicate to facilitate coordination?
5. What factors lead to a batching of orders within a supply chain? How does this impact coordination? What actions can minimize large batches and improve coordination?
6. How do trade promotions and price fluctuations impact coordination in the supply chain? What pricing and promotion policies can facilitate coordination?
7. How is the building of strategic partnerships and trust valuable within a supply chain?
8. What issues must be considered when designing a supply chain relationship to improve the chances of developing cooperation and trust?
9. What issues must be considered when managing a supply chain relationship to improve the chances of developing cooperation and trust?

BIBLIOGRAPHY

Bowersox, Donald J., David J. Closs, and Theodore P. Stank. 1999. "21st Century Logistics: Making Supply Chain Integration a Reality." *Supply Chain Management Review* (Fall): 44–49.

Brunell, Tom. 1999. "Managing a Multicompany Supply Chain." *Supply Chain Management Review* (Spring): 45–52.

Child, John, and David Faulkner. 1998. *Strategies of Cooperation.* Oxford, England: Oxford University Press.

Doz, Yves L. 1996. "The Evolution of Cooperation in Strategic Alliances: Initial Conditions or Learning Process?" *Strategic Management Journal* 17: 55–83.

Doz, Yves L., and Gary Hamel. 1998. *Alliance Advantage.* Boston: Harvard Business School Press.

Dyer, J. H., and K. Nobeoka. 2000. "Creating and Managing a High-Performance Knowledge-Sharing Network: The Toyota Case." *Strategic Management Journal* 21 (March): 345–367.

Gulati, R., and Harbir Singh. 1998. "The Architecture of Cooperation: Managing Coordination Costs and Appropriation Concerns in Strategic Alliances." *Administrative Science Quarterly* 43: 781–814.

Hammond, J. H. 1994. *Barilla Spa (A–D)*. Harvard Business School Case 9-694-046.

Joint Industry Project on Efficient Consumer Response. 1994. *Continuous Replenishment: An ECR Best Practices Report*. Kurt Salmon and Associates.

Joint Industry Project on Efficient Consumer Response. 1994. *Computer Assisted Ordering: An ECR Best Practices Report*. Kurt Salmon and Associates.

Kumar, N. 1996. "The Power of Trust in Manufacturer–Retailer Relationships." *Harvard Business Review* (November–December): 92–106.

Lee, Hau L., V. Padmanabhan, S. Whang. 1997. "The Bullwhip Effect in Supply Chains," *Sloan Management Review* (Spring): 93–102.

Mariotti, John L. 1999. "The Trust Factor in Supply Chain Management." *Supply Chain Management Review* (Spring): 70–77.

Ring, P. S., and A. H. Van de Ven. 1994. "Developmental Processes of Cooperative Interorganizational Relationships." *Academy of Management Review* 19: 90–118.

Sabath, Robert E., and John Fontanella. 2002. "The Unfulfilled Promise of Supply Chain Collaboration." *Supply Chain Management Review* (July–August): 24–29.

Senge, Peter M. 1990. *The Fifth Discipline*. New York: Currency and Doubleday.

Smeltzer, Larry R. 2001. "Integration Means Everybody— Big and Small." *Supply Chain Management Review* (September–October): 36–44.

------------------------------ A P P E N D I X   1 6 A ------------------------------

The Beer Game

The Beer Game originated at MIT and has been used to simulate the performance of a simple supply chain with one player at each stage. The game is often used to illustrate the bullwhip effect in a simple supply chain. The supply chain consists of a manufacturer, a distributor, a wholesaler, and a retailer as shown in Figure 16.6.

Customers come to the retailer to purchase beer. The retailer tries to fill customer orders from beer in inventory. Any unfilled demand is carried over to the future as backlogged demand. The retailer places replenishment orders with the wholesaler, who tries to fill the orders from beer in inventory. The wholesaler in turn orders from the distributor and the distributor from the manufacturer. The manufacturer receives raw materials from a supplier. It takes two periods for orders and product to move between stages. In the game, the delay is accomplished by introducing an in-transit stage between every pair of stages in the supply chain, as shown in Figure 16.6. The game is played by assigning two people to each of the four stages (retailer to manufacturer) of the supply chain. Several supply chains can operate simultaneously.

Each supply chain requires a customer board, a supplier board, four identical boards corresponding to each of the four stages, and three identical in-transit boards. The four different types of boards are shown in Figure 16.7.

The boards are ordered as in Figure 16.6 with the retailer, wholesaler, distributor, and manufacturer getting a stage board each. An in-transit board is placed between every pair of stages, resulting in three in-transit boards. The customer board is placed before the retailer, and the supplier board is placed after the manufacturer.

Each of the four stages gets a recording sheet, as shown in Table 16.3.

Current period demand is the size of the order received in this period. *Gross demand* during a period is the sum of the *current period demand* and *backlog* from the previous period. Gross demand represents the amount that a stage has to try to supply this period. *Amount shipped* is the quantity shipped during the period. Amount shipped should equal gross demand if there is sufficient inventory available. If gross demand exceeds inventory available, then the entire inventory will be shipped and

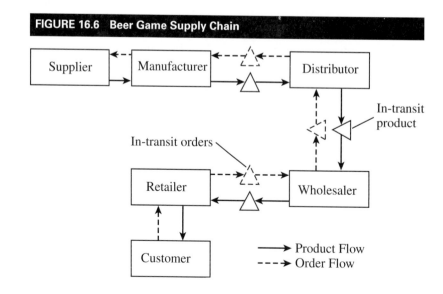

FIGURE 16.6 Beer Game Supply Chain

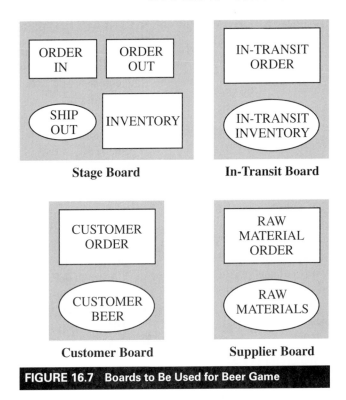

FIGURE 16.7   Boards to Be Used for Beer Game

the unfilled demand added to the backlog. *Ending inventory* measures the cases of beer in inventory right after a shipment has been sent. *Backlog* is the amount of demand that has not yet been supplied. For any period

Backlog = previous period backlog + max {0, gross demand – amount shipped}.

Order placed is the amount ordered by a stage with its supplier.

A cost of $1 is incurred for each case of beer in *ending inventory* per period. A cost of $2 is incurred for each case of demand in *backlog* per period. The

goal of each stage is to minimize the total cost incurred over the period when the game is played. The performance of a stage will be compared with the performance of the same stage in other supply chains.

During the game, orders are written on pieces of paper and pennies are used to represent cases of beer. The game starts with a sequence of orders placed in the customer order box. The game is played through multiple periods. At the start of each period, the following layout exists.

1. The ORDER-IN box at each of the four stages contains an order.

TABLE 16.3   Recording Sheet for Beer Game

Period	Current Period Demand	Gross Demand	Amount Shipped	Ending Inventory	Backlog	Order Placed
1						
2						

2. Each IN-TRANSIT ORDER box contains an order and each IN-TRANSIT INVENTORY box contains some pennies representing beer in transit.
3. The RAW-MATERIAL ORDER box contains an order.

During each period, the activities performed by each stage are divided into two phases. The game works best if one person at each stage takes responsibility for the first phase and the other person takes responsibility for the second phase. The completion of both phases completes all activities to be performed during a period. All four stages must have finished Phase I before any of them can start Phase II in a period. At the end of each period, the layout looks the way it did at the start of the period. The supply chain then moves on to the next period. We now describe the activities performed in each phase of the period at all four stages.

PHASE I ACTIVITIES (COMMON TO ALL FOUR STAGES)

The goal during this phase is to fill the incoming order and place a replenishment order. Phase I activities are identical for all four stages of the supply chain.

1. Pick order from ORDER-IN box and record on recording sheet as *Current Period Demand*.
2. Compute *Gross Demand* by adding *Current Period Demand* (from this period) and *Backlog* (from previous period).
3. Transfer the minimum of the amount in the INVENTORY box and *Gross Demand* from the INVENTORY box to the SHIP OUT box. Record the amount transferred as the *Amount Shipped*.
4. Record *Ending Inventory* as the amount remaining in the INVENTORY box.
5. Compute *Backlog* = max{*Gross Demand* − *Amount Shipped*, 0} and record on recording sheet.
6. Place a replenishment order with the supplier on an order slip and place the order slip in the ORDER-OUT box. Record *Order Placed* on the recording sheet.

PHASE II ACTIVITIES FOR RETAILER

In this phase the retailer receives orders from the customer, beer from the wholesaler, and moves beer to the customer and orders to the wholesaler.

1. Move order from IN-TRANSIT ORDER box between retailer and wholesaler to the ORDER-IN box of the wholesaler.
2. Move order from ORDER-OUT box of retailer to IN-TRANSIT ORDER box between retailer and wholesaler.
3. Move beer from IN-TRANSIT INVENTORY box between retailer and wholesaler to INVENTORY box at retailer.
4. Move beer from SHIP-OUT box of wholesaler to IN-TRANSIT INVENTORY box between retailer and wholesaler.
5. Mover order at top of pile in CUSTOMER ORDER box to ORDER-IN box of retailer.
6. Move beer from SHIP-OUT box of retailer to CUSTOMER BEER box.

PHASE II ACTIVITIES FOR WHOLESALER

In this phase, the wholesaler moves orders to the distributor and receives beer from the distributor.

1. Move order from IN-TRANSIT ORDER box between wholesaler and distributor to ORDER-IN box at distributor.
2. Move order from ORDER-OUT box at wholesaler to IN-TRANSIT ORDER box between wholesaler and distributor.
3. Move beer from IN-TRANSIT ORDER box between wholesaler and distributor to INVENTORY box at wholesaler.
4. Move beer from SHIP-OUT box at wholesaler to IN-TRANSIT ORDER box between retailer and wholesaler.

PHASE II ACTIVITIES FOR DISTRIBUTOR

In this phase, the distributor moves orders to the manufacturer and receives beer from the manufacturer.

1. Move order from IN-TRANSIT ORDER box between distributor and manufacturer to ORDER-IN box at manufacturer.
2. Move order from ORDER-OUT box at distributor to IN-TRANSIT ORDER box between distributor and manufacturer.
3. Move beer from IN-TRANSIT ORDER box between distributor and manufacturer to INVENTORY box at distributor.
4. Move beer from SHIP-OUT box at distributor to IN-TRANSIT ORDER box between distributor and manufacturer.

PHASE II ACTIVITIES FOR MANUFACTURER

In this phase the manufacturer receives raw materials from the supplier and moves the next order to the supplier.

1. Take order from RAW-MATERIAL ORDER box at SUPPLIER and move equivalent amount of beer from RAW MATERIALS box at supplier to INVENTORY box at manufacturer.
2. Move order from ORDER-OUT box at manufacturer to RAW-MATERIAL ORDER box at supplier.

The game is stopped after a suitable number of periods have expired. Each stage then evaluates the total cost it has incurred and plots the orders it received. With this information, each stage should come up with a guess at what the customer demand pattern looked like for the periods that the game is played.

17

Information Technology and the Supply Chain

Learning Objectives

After reading this chapter, you will be able to

1. Understand the importance of information and information technology in a supply chain.

2. Know at a high level how each supply chain driver uses information.

3. Understand the major applications of supply chain information technology and the processes that they enable.

Information is crucial to the performance of a supply chain because it provides the basis upon which supply chain managers make decisions. Information technology (IT) consists of the tools used to gain awareness of information, analyze this information, and act on it to improve the performance of the supply chain. In this chapter we explore the importance of information, its uses, and the technologies that enable supply chain managers to use information to make better decisions.

17.1   THE ROLE OF IT IN THE SUPPLY CHAIN

All supply chain drivers discussed up until this point have dealt directly with some physical aspect of the supply chain. Chapters 10, 11, and 12 discussed how to manage inventories, Chapter 14 discussed transporting the product through the supply chain network and Chapters 4, 5, and 6 discussed issues regarding facility location and capacity that managers face when designing a supply chain network. This chapter, instead, focuses on information about both the product and the supply chain that produces the product. Information is the supply chain driver that serves as the glue allowing the other three drivers to work together to create an integrated, coordinated supply chain.

Information is crucial to supply chain performance because it provides the foundation on which supply chain processes execute transactions and managers make decisions. Without information, a manager will not know what customers want, how much inventory is in stock, and when more product should be produced and shipped. In short, without information a manager can only make decisions blindly. Therefore, information makes the supply chain visible to a manager. With this visibility, a manager can make decisions to improve the supply chain's performance. In many ways, information is the most important of the four supply chain drivers because without it, none of the other drivers can be used to deliver a high level of performance.

Given the role of information in a supply chain's success, managers must understand how information is gathered and analyzed. This is where IT comes into play. IT consists of the hardware and software throughout a supply chain that gather, analyze, and act on information. IT serves as the eyes and ears (and sometimes a portion of the brain) of management in a supply chain, capturing and analyzing the information necessary to make a good decision. For instance, an IT system at a PC manufacturer may tell a manager how many Pentium chips are currently in stock. IT is also used to analyze the information and recommend an action. In this role, an IT system at a PC manufacturer could take the number of chips in inventory, look at demand forecasts, and determine whether to order more chips from Intel.

Using IT systems to capture and analyze information can have a significant impact on a firm's performance. For example, a major manufacturer of computer workstations and servers found that much of the information on customer demand was not being used to set production schedules and inventory levels. The manufacturing group lacked this demand information, which forced them to make inventory and production decisions blindly. By installing a supply chain software system, the company was able to gather and analyze data to produce recommended stocking levels. Using the IT system enabled the company to cut its inventory in half because managers could now make decisions based on information rather than educated guesses. Large impacts like this underscore the importance of IT as a driver of supply chain performance.

Information is the key to the success of a supply chain because it enables management to make decisions over a broad scope that crosses both functions and companies. As discussed in Chapter 2, successful supply chain strategy results from viewing the supply chain as a whole rather than looking only at the individual stages. By taking a global scope across the entire supply chain, a manager is able to craft strategies that take into account all factors that affect the supply chain rather than just those factors affecting a particular stage or function within the supply chain. Taking the entire chain into account maximizes the profit of the total supply chain, which then leads to higher profits for each individual company within the supply chain.

How does a manager take this broad scope? The supply chain scope is made up entirely of information and the breadth of this information determines whether the scope is global or local. To obtain a global scope of the supply chain, a manager needs accurate and timely information on all company functions and organizations in the supply chain. For example, it is not enough for the workstation manufacturer mentioned earlier to know how much inventory is on hand within the company when trying to determine production schedules. The company also needs to know the downstream demand and even the upstream supplier lead times and variability. With this broader scope, the company is able to set production schedules and inventory levels that maximize profitability.

Information must have the following characteristics to be useful when making supply chain decisions:

1. *Information must be accurate.* Without information that gives the true picture of the state of the supply chain, it is very difficult to make good decisions. That is not to say all information must be 100 percent correct but rather that the data available paint a picture of reality that is at least directionally correct.

2. *Information must be accessible in a timely manner.* Often accurate information exists, but by the time it is available, it is either out of date or if it is current, it is not in an accessible form. To make good decisions, a manager needs to have up-to-date information that is easily accessible.

3. *Information must be of the right kind.* Decision makers need information that they can use. Often companies will have large amounts of data that is not helpful with decision making. Companies must think about what information should be recorded so that valuable resources are not wasted collecting meaningless data while important data goes unrecorded.

When managers have good information, they have supply chain visibility, enabling them to take a global scope. With this global scope, they are able to make the best decisions for the supply chain. Therefore, information is a key to supply chain success.

Information is a key ingredient not just at each stage of the supply chain, but also within each phase of supply chain decision making—from the strategic phase to the planning phase to the operational phase (see Chapter 1). For instance, information and its analysis plays a significant role during the formulation of supply chain strategy by providing the basis for decisions such as the location of the push/pull boundary of the supply chain. Information also plays a key role at the other end of the spectrum in operational decisions such as what products will be produced during today's production run. Managers need to be able to understand how to analyze information to make good decisions. Much of this book deals with just that idea—how to identify a supply chain problem that needs to be solved, obtain information, analyze it, and then make a good decision to act on that information.

For example, Wal-Mart has been a pioneer not only in capturing information, but also in understanding how to analyze that information to make good supply chain decisions. Wal-Mart collects data in real time on what products are being purchased at each of their stores and sends this data back to the manufacturers. Wal-Mart analyzes this demand information to determine how much inventory to hold at each store and to decide when to ship new loads of product from the manufacturer. The manufacturer uses this information to set its production schedules so that it produces products in time to meet Wal-Mart's demand. Both Wal-Mart and its key suppliers do not just capture the information they have; they analyze it and base their actions on this analysis.

Information is used when making a wide variety of decisions about inventories, transportation, and facilities within a supply chain, as discussed here.

1. *Inventory:* Setting optimal inventory policies requires information that includes demand patterns, cost of carrying inventory, costs of stocking out, and costs of ordering (see Chapters 10, 11, and 12). For example, Wal-Mart collects detailed demand, cost, margin, and supplier information to make these inventory policy decisions.

2. *Transportation:* Deciding on transportation networks, routings, modes, shipments, and vendors requires information including costs, customer locations, and shipment sizes to make good decisions (see Chapter 14). Wal-Mart uses information to tightly integrate its operations with those of its suppliers. This integration allows Wal-Mart to implement cross-docking in its transportation network, saving on both inventory and transportation costs.

3. *Facility:* Determining the location, capacity, and schedules of a facility requires information on the trade-offs between efficiency and flexibility, demand, exchange rates, taxes, and so on (see Chapters 4, 5, and 6). Wal-Mart's suppliers use the demand information from Wal-Mart's stores to set their production schedules. Wal-Mart uses information on demand to determine where to place its new stores and cross-docking facilities.

In summary, information is crucial to making good supply chain decisions at all three levels of decision making (strategy, planning, and operations) and in each of the other supply chain drivers (inventory, transportation, and facilities). IT enables not only the gathering of this data to create supply chain visibility, but also the analysis of this data so that the supply chain decisions made will maximize profitability.

17.2 THE SUPPLY CHAIN IT FRAMEWORK

Given the wide realm of information discussed earlier, it is important to develop a framework that helps a manager understand how this information is utilized by the various segments of IT within the supply chain. Our vision of this framework is presented in the next several sections of this chapter. It is valuable to note that the driver of IT in the supply chain has increasingly been the enterprise software developed to enable processes both within and across companies. Enterprise software collects transaction data, analyzes this data to make decisions, and executes on these decisions both within an enterprise and across its supply chain. Certainly other parts of IT beyond enterprise software such as hardware, implementation services, and support are all crucial to making IT effective. Within a supply chain, however, the different capabilities provided by IT have as their most basic building block the capabilities of the supply chain's enterprise software. In many ways, software shapes the entire industry of IT as the other components follow the software lead. It is for this reason that we use enterprise software and its evolution as the primary guide in analyzing IT and its impact on the supply chain. The evolution of enterprise software provides insights not only into the future of IT, but also into what the key supply chain processes are. We now discuss this evolution and its impact on companies' supply chain processes.

The enterprise software landscape became increasingly overpopulated during the late 1990s. The unprecedented flow of venture capital into new software companies led not just to an increase in the number of software companies, but also to the proliferation of entire categories of software. The growth of the number of software companies, the emergence of new categories, and the expansion of software product lines combined to create an enterprise software landscape that was not only much more crowded than in the past, but also much more dynamic. It was an environment ripe for significant evolutionary change to take place.

The downturn in technology spending since the second half of 2000 has brought about this evolutionary pressure, thereby causing many software companies to cease operations or merge with existing software firms. Some entire software categories are well on their way to extinction, with many of the recently created categories landing on this endangered species list.

What drives this evolution of the enterprise software landscape? Why are some categories of software companies headed for a profitable long-term future, whereas others have failed? Certainly there are a wide variety of factors affecting the natural selection of software companies. We propose, however, that three of the main drivers of the evolution taking place in enterprise software are the three major groups of supply chain processes, which we call supply chain *macro processes*. The successful categories of software will be those focused on the macro processes. The failures, on the other hand, will not have such a focus.

The Supply Chain Macro Processes

The emergence of supply chain management has broadened the scope across which companies make decisions. This scope has expanded from trying to optimize performance across the division, to the enterprise, and now to the entire supply chain. This broadening of scope emphasizes the importance of including processes all along the supply chain when making decisions. From an enterprise's perspective, all processes within its supply chain can be categorized into three main areas: processes focused downstream, processes focused internally, and processes focused upstream. We use this classification to define the three macro supply chain processes (see Chapter 1) as follows:

- Customer Relationship Management (CRM): Processes that focus on downstream interactions between the enterprise and its customers.
- Internal Supply Chain Management (ISCM): Processes that focus on internal operations within the enterprise. Note that the software industry commonly calls this "supply chain management" (without the word "internal") even though the focus is entirely within the enterprise. In our definition,

supply chain management includes all three macro processes CRM, ISCM, and SRM.

- Supplier Relationship Management (SRM): Processes that focus on upstream interactions between the enterprise and its suppliers.

We must also note that there is a fourth important software building block that provides the foundation upon which the macro processes rest. We call this category the transaction management foundation (TMF), which includes basic ERP systems (and its components such as financials and human resources), infrastructure software, and integration software. TMF software is necessary for the three macro processes to function and to communicate with each other. The relationship between the three macro processes and the transaction management foundation can be seen in Figure 17.1.

Why Focus on the Macro Processes?

As the performance of an enterprise becomes more closely linked to the performance of its supply chain, it is crucial that firms focus on these macro processes. After decades of focusing on internal processes, a firm must expand the scope beyond internal processes and look at the entire supply chain to achieve breakthrough performance. As we have discussed, the goal should be to increase the total profitability of the supply chain (also referred to as the supply chain surplus). Good supply chain management is not a zero sum game where one stage of the supply chain increases profits at the expense of another. As discussed in Chapter 2, good supply chain management is instead a positive sum game where supply chain partners can increase their overall level of profitability by working together. Therefore, to increase the supply chain surplus (and therefore their firm's own profitability) most effectively, firms must expand their scope beyond their enterprise and think in terms of all three macro processes.

Macro Processes Applied to the Evolution of Software

As the downturn in technology spending has applied evolutionary pressure on the enterprise software landscape, we see a distinct pattern emerging. The majority of survivors have chosen to focus their products on improving their customers' macro

---

FIGURE 17.1   The Macro Processes in a Supply Chain

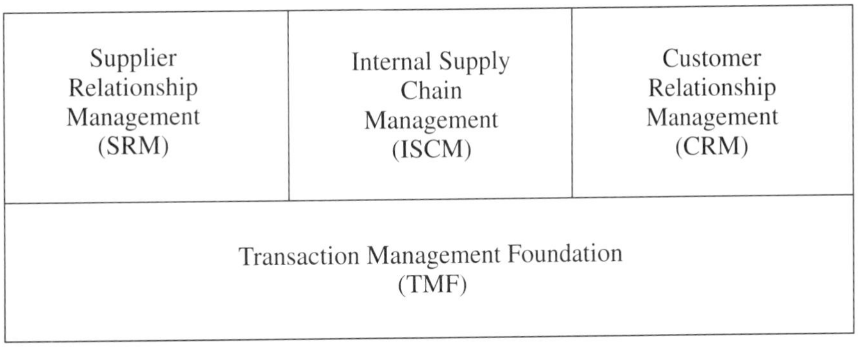

Supplier Relationship Management (SRM)	Internal Supply Chain Management (ISCM)	Customer Relationship Management (CRM)
Transaction Management Foundation (TMF)		

processes. Some software firms cross over into more than one macro process, whereas others only address a small portion of a macro process. But the common theme we see is that to survive, and particularly to thrive, enterprise software firms must focus on one or more of these macro processes. Almost all areas of enterprise software growth exist within CRM, ISCM, or SRM. Both new companies and large firms within enterprise software are now targeting these three macro processes much more sharply. In the future, we see the ability to improve the three macro processes driving the winners and losers in enterprise software.

Examples of failures that did not focus on these macro processes are B2B marketplaces and the software companies providing marketplace software that proliferated during 1999 and 2000. Marketplaces focused more on creating whole new information intermediaries within the supply chain rather than on improving the performance of the macro processes within supply chains. This lack of focus on the macro processes was a key contributor to the downfall of marketplaces.

The software firms behind the marketplaces have also had a difficult time, with the major players Ariba and Commerce One losing well over 95 percent of their peak market capitalization. To survive, these companies have evolved away from being marketplace providers and toward being software firms focused on a macro process. Both Ariba and Commerce One now focus almost exclusively on the SRM macro process. Surviving marketplaces have also started focusing on improving the performance of a macro process within the supply chain, rather than trying to be independent intermediaries as marketplace operators.

A third example of a software category that is being transformed by a focus on macro processes is the ERP category. ERP software has been successful in improving data integrity within the supply chain, but by itself, data integrity provides little value. The real improvement from more accurate data results only when the data can be used to improve decision making. This is where the three macro processes enter the picture. The real value from having ERP systems in place can only be obtained if these systems can be used to improve decision making in the three macro processes. Every major ERP player has realized this and is remaking themselves into a company emphasizing products focused on the macro processes.

The drivers of the software landscape are not just important to software providers. Companies that are users of software must understand these macro processes as well. By understanding whether or not software companies are addressing the macro processes and actually enabling improvements in performance in these areas, a company can better gauge whether or not a particular type of software is valuable for them.

The Software Winners within a Macro Process
Among software firms focused on a macro process, the following three factors determine their success:

1. Functional performance
2. Integration with other macro processes
3. Strength of the software firm's ecosystem

Functional performance is important to customers because it provides them with capabilities to create a competitive advantage. In addition to raw functional performance (qualities such as the ability to optimize both price and supply in an integrated fashion), we believe that the ease of use is crucial to success in this category. Some software has very advanced functionality but is very difficult to use. As a result, the advanced functionality is rarely utilized. Software firms with lower levels of functionality but with high ease of use can, in essence, provide more "usable" functionality to their customers and therefore gain an edge.

The ability to integrate is important to a customer for a variety of reasons. Applications that are easy to integrate are generally easier to get implemented and producing value. Integration is also crucial across different macro processes. Applications that integrate across macro processes will be able to provide the benefits of making decisions for the extended supply chain. This gives an edge to firms that offer a full line of integrated solutions in all three macro processes.

Finally, a firm's ecosystem—the network of software partners and, more importantly, systems integrators and installed base—provides assistance in selling and implementing software. Firms that work well with implementation partners and build up large groups of customers trained on their solutions have built a highly defensible position. For another firm to capture this business requires that they be so far superior that it is worth the retraining and reintegration effort, which is often quite significant. For a customer, a strong ecosystem means a strong network to provide support both during implementation and down the road.

As we stressed earlier, these criteria are also important for customers of supply chain software. These criteria are the key to success for software companies precisely because they improve supply chain performance for firms. Thus, companies should evaluate software providers along these lines to determine their choice of software vendor.

We now discuss each of the macro processes, what segments they consist of, who the players are, and what the future will look like.

17.3 CUSTOMER RELATIONSHIP MANAGEMENT

The CRM macro process consists of processes that take place between an enterprise and its customers downstream in the supply chain. The goal of the CRM macro process is to generate customer demand and facilitate transmission and tracking of orders. Weakness in this process results in demand being lost and a poor customer experience because orders are not processed and executed effectively. The key processes under CRM are as follows:

- *Marketing:* Marketing processes involve decisions regarding which customers to target, how to target customers, what products to offer, how to price products, and how to manage the actual campaigns targeting customers. Successful software vendors in the marketing area within CRM provide analytics that improve the marketing decisions on pricing, product profitability, and customer profitability, among other functions.
- *Sell:* The Sell process focuses on making an actual sale to a customer (compared to marketing where processes are more focused on planning who to sell to and what to sell). The sell process includes providing the sales force the information they need to make a sale and then executing the actual sale. Executing the sale may require the sales person (or the customer) to

build and configure orders by choosing among a variety of options and features. The sell process also requires such functionality as the ability to quote due dates and access information related to a customer order. Successful software providers have targeted sales force automation, configuration, and personalization to improve the sell process.

- *Order Management:* The process of managing customer orders as they flow through an enterprise is important for the customer to track his order and for the enterprise to plan and execute order fulfillment. This process ties together demand from the customer with supply from the enterprise. Order management software has traditionally been handled by legacy systems or been a part of an ERP system. Recently, new order management systems have emerged with additional functionality that enables visibility of orders across the often numerous order management systems that exist within a company.

- *Call/Service center:* A call/service center is often the primary point of contact between a company and its customers. A call/service center helps customers place orders, suggests products, solves problems, and provides information on order status. Successful software providers have helped improve call/service center operations by facilitating and reducing work done by customer service representatives, often by allowing customers to do the work themselves.

The aforementioned CRM processes are crucial to the supply chain as they cover a vast amount of interaction between an enterprise and its customers. The customer must be the starting point when trying to increase the supply chain surplus because all demand, and therefore revenue, ultimately arises from them. Thus, the CRM macro process is the starting point when improving supply chain performance. It is also important to note that CRM processes (and also CRM software) must be integrated with internal operations to optimize performance. Too often companies operate with their customer-focused units working independently from their internal operations. The need for integration between CRM and internal operations emphasizes the importance of CRM to an effective supply chain.

CRM software has been the fastest growing, and is now the largest, category of the three macro processes. Software providers in the CRM space have focused on improving CRM processes themselves, but have more work to do to improve integration between CRM and internal operational processes. Future success will be partially driven by the ability to integrate CRM applications into internal operations.

The CRM software landscape consists of three categories of companies: the best-of-breed winner, the best-of-breed startups, and the ERP players. CRM is currently dominated by Siebel Systems, the sole company in the best-of-breed winner category. However, Siebel does face serious competition from both best-of-breed startups who emphasize functional expertise as well as from the ERP players, such as SAP, Oracle, and Peoplesoft, who provide a powerful integration story and strong ecosystems.

Looking forward, Seibel, the best-of-breed winner, provides a combination of superior functionality and a strong ecosystem within CRM. It does lack, however, the ability to integrate across all three macro processes. The ERP players lag somewhat on functionality but can successfully compete with their strengths in integration and ecosystems. Small best-of-breed players will face a very difficult future within CRM given the strength of the best-of-breed winner and the focus ERP players are putting on CRM. Their only chance is to focus on an area of functionality currently lacking in the other players and gain a large lead there—a difficult, though not impossible, task.

17.4 INTERNAL SUPPLY CHAIN MANAGEMENT

ISCM, as we discussed earlier, is focused on operations *internal* to the enterprise. ISCM includes all processes involved in planning for and fulfilling a customer order. The various processes included in ISCM are as follows:

- *Strategic planning:* The goal of this process is to plan resource availability in the supply chain network. The decisions made include where to locate plants and warehouses, what type of facilities to build, and what markets to serve from each facility. Although a few people make these decisions infrequently, the impact on supply chain performance can be quite large and is felt potentially for years. Successful software providers with this functionality are including the capability of analyzing strategic plans under uncertain future environments.
- *Demand planning:* This set of processes involves forecasting future customer demand. In addition to forecasts, demand planning also includes decisions to manage demand, such as promotions planning. Successful software providers in this area allow the firm to come up with a demand plan accounting for marketing and promotional efforts.
- *Supply planning:* The supply planning process takes as an input the demand forecasts produced by demand planning and the resources made available by strategic planning, and then produces an optimal plan to meet this demand. Factory planning and inventory planning capabilities are typically provided by supply planning software.
- *Fulfillment:* Once a plan is in place to supply the demand, it must be executed. The fulfillment process links each order to a specific supply source and means of transportation. The software applications that typically fall into the fulfillment segment are transportation and warehousing applications.
- *Field service:* Finally, after the product has been delivered to the customer, it eventually must be serviced. Service processes focus on setting inventory levels for spare parts as well as scheduling service calls.

Given that the ISCM macro process aims to fulfill demand that is generated by CRM processes, there needs to be strong integration between the ISCM and CRM macro processes. When forecasting demand, interaction with CRM is essential as the CRM applications are touching the customer and have the most data and insight on customer behavior. Similarly, the ISCM processes should have strong integration with the SRM macro process. Supply planning, fulfillment, and field service are all dependent on suppliers and therefore the SRM processes. It is of little use for your factory to have the production capacity to meet demand if your supplier cannot supply the parts to make your product. Order management, which we discussed in CRM, must integrate closely with fulfillment and be an input for effective demand planning. Again, good supply chain management requires that we integrate across the macro processes.

Successful ISCM software providers have helped improve decision making within ISCM processes. Good integration with CRM and SRM, however, is still largely inadequate at both the organizational and software levels. Future opportunities are likely to arise partly in improving each ISCM process, but primarily in improving integration with CRM and SRM.

Like CRM, today's ISCM landscape consists of three categories—the best-of-breed winners, the best-of-breed startups, and the ERP players. Unlike CRM, however, there is not a clear leader. There are two best-of-breed winners, i2 Technologies and Manugistics, which were ISCM pioneers and are currently the functional leaders. Startups with superior functionality and ERP players are making inroads into their leadership, however. In fact, one ERP player, SAP, has claimed to have taken the top spot in ISCM revenue away from i2.

The best-of-breed ISCM players have the leading functionality, but lack strong integration and ecosystems. These companies have been working to offer more products in the SRM and CRM space to improve their integrated offering. The ERP players' advantages are their integrated product and their ecosystems, although some ERP players' functionality is becoming more and more competitive. Relative to the CRM space where Seibel has a large lead over the ERP providers in terms of functionality, the functionality gap in the ISCM space between the best-of-breed players and some of the ERP providers (in particular, SAP) is smaller and shrinking. As a result, an ERP provider such as SAP has the potential to dominate the ISCM space. To stay competitive, best-of-breed leaders will have to relentlessly improve functionality while providing acceptable integration and ecosystems. There are some smaller players in ISCM taking advantage of new functionality that will remain viable, especially those targeting customers in specific industries that are very dependent on advanced functionality.

17.5 SUPPLIER RELATIONSHIP MANAGEMENT

SRM includes those processes focused on the interaction between the enterprise and suppliers that are upstream in the supply chain. There is a very natural fit between SRM processes and the ISCM processes as integrating supplier constraints is crucial when creating internal plans. The major SRM processes are as follows:

- *Design collaboration:* The goal of this process is to improve the design of products through such ideas as the joint selection (with suppliers) of components that have positive supply chain characteristics such as ease of manufacturability or commonality across several end products. Other design collaboration activities include the sharing of engineering change orders between a manufacturer and its suppliers. This eliminates the costly delays that occur when several suppliers are concurrently designing components for the manufacturer's product. Good collaboration at this stage can create huge value because about 80 percent of product cost is determined at the design stage. Successful software in this area facilitates such collaboration.

- *Source:* The source process qualifies suppliers and helps in supplier selection, contract management, and supplier evaluation. A key goal is to analyze the amount that an enterprise spends with each supplier, often revealing valuable trends or areas for improvement. Suppliers are evaluated along several key criteria including lead time, reliability, quality, and price. This evaluation helps improve supplier performance and aids in supplier selection. Contract management is also an important part of sourcing, as many supplier contracts have complex details that must be tracked (such as price reductions for reaching certain volume targets). Successful software in this area helps analyze supplier performance and manage contracts.
- *Negotiate:* Negotiations with suppliers involve many steps starting with a request for quote (RFQ). The negotiation process may also include the design and execution of auctions. The goal of this process is to negotiate an effective contract that specifies price and delivery parameters for a supplier in a way that best matches the enterprises needs. Successful software automates the RFQ process and the execution of auctions.
- *Buy:* The buy process executes the actual procurement of material from suppliers. This includes the creation, management, and approval of purchase orders. Successful software in this area automates the procurement process and helps decrease processing cost and time.
- *Supply collaboration:* Once an agreement for supply is established between the enterprise and a supplier, supply chain performance can be improved by collaborating on forecasts, production plans, and inventory levels. The goal of collaboration is to ensure a common plan across the supply chain. Good software in this area should be able to facilitate collaborative forecasting and planning in a supply chain.

Significant improvement in supply chain performance can be achieved if SRM processes are well integrated with appropriate CRM and ISCM processes. For instance, when designing a product, incorporating input from customers is a natural way to improve the design. This would require inputs from processes within CRM. Sourcing, negotiating, buying, and collaborating primarily tie into ISCM as the supplier inputs are needed to produce and execute an optimal plan. But even these segments have the need to interface with CRM processes such as order management. Again, the theme of integrating the three macro processes is crucial for improved supply chain performance.

The SRM space has four groupings of competitors. There are two best-of-breed groups that focus exclusively on SRM, one focused on design collaboration and another focused on procurement. Leading design collaboration firms include Agile and Matrix One while leading procurement firms are Ariba and Commerce One. The third type of player in SRM is the best-of-breed ISCM vendor that has made the natural extension of ISCM into SRM—companies such as i2 and Manugistics. Finally, the fourth category consists of the ERP players moving up into the macro processes again. SAP is the largest SRM player among the ERP vendors and has shown the most commitment to entering this space.

Given the youth of the SRM space, the solely SRM focused players have not had a chance to develop large functional leads and their ecosystems are virtually

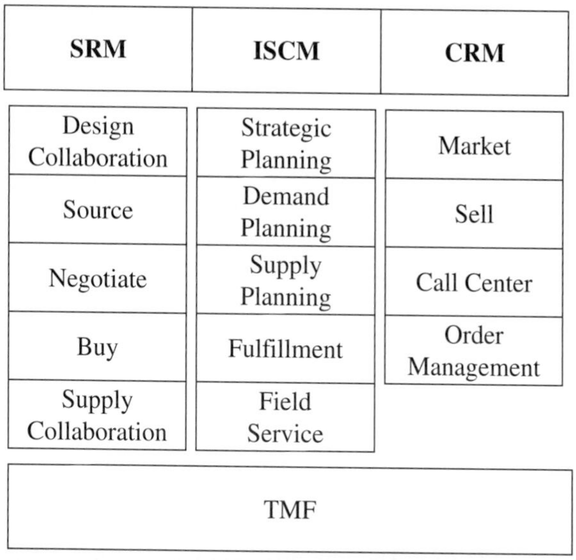

SRM	ISCM	CRM
Design Collaboration	Strategic Planning	Market
Source	Demand Planning	Sell
Negotiate	Supply Planning	Call Center
Buy	Fulfillment	Order Management
Supply Collaboration	Field Service	

TMF

FIGURE 17.2 The Macro Processes and Their Processes

nonexistent. SRM has already attracted all the big players from both ISCM and ERP. Therefore, the solely SRM focused players mentioned earlier will have to battle the much larger ISCM and ERP players who have superior integration capability and far superior ecosystems. Without a tremendous functional advantage, it will be difficult for SRM best-of-breed players to survive on their own. Therefore, the future SRM landscape is likely to be dominated by one or two ISCM players and one or two ERP players.

All three macro processes and their processes can be seen in Figure 17.2.

17.6 THE TRANSACTION MANAGEMENT FOUNDATION

The transaction management foundation is the historical home for the largest enterprise software players. In the early 1990s, when much of the thinking in supply chain management was just getting off the ground and ERP systems were rapidly gaining popularity, there was little focus on the three macro processes we discussed earlier. In fact, there was little emphasis on software applications focused on improving decisions. Instead, the focus at that time was on building transaction management and process automation systems that proved to be the foundation for future decision support applications. These systems excelled at the automation of simple transactions and processes as well as the creation of an integrated way to store and view data across the division (and sometimes the enterprise).

The huge demand for these systems during the 1990s drove the ERP players to become the largest enterprise software companies. SAP has continued as the market leader but other powerful ERP players included Oracle, Peoplesoft, JD Edwards, and Baan. Eventually, however, ERP sales slowed and one of the big five, Baan, even ceased to exist independently.

The real value of the transaction management foundation can only be extracted if decision making within the supply chain is improved. Thus, most recent growth in enterprise software has come from companies focused on improving decision making in the three macro processes. This has set the stage for what we are seeing today and will continue to see in the future—the realignment of the ERP companies into CRM, ISCM, and SRM companies. We expect this shift will continue in the next few years with the majority of the ERP players' revenue coming from applications in the three macro processes. A major advantage that ERP players have relative to best-of-breed providers is the inherent ability to integrate across the three macro process, often through the transaction management foundation. In our opinion, ERP players that focus on integrating across the macro processes along with developing good functionality in one or more macro process will occupy a position of strength.

17.7 THE FUTURE OF IT IN THE SUPPLY CHAIN

At the highest level, we believe that the three SCM macro processes will continue to drive the evolution of enterprise software. To this end, we expect to see software focused on the macro processes become a larger share of the total enterprise software landscape and software firms that focus on the macro processes to be much more successful than those that focus elsewhere. For firms targeting a macro process, we see functionality, the ability to integrate across macro processes, and the strength of their ecosystems as the keys to success.

This conclusion has important implications for companies that are users of software. As we mentioned earlier, the criteria for successful software companies were chosen precisely because they are the characteristics of software that improve performance of its users. Thus, a user of supply chain software should first identify areas within the three macro processes where improvement will provide the maximum leverage. Software and IT decisions should then support the goal of improving performance along these processes.

There is one final note worth mentioning with regard to the future of new software players in this area. One might conclude from our analysis that it will be very difficult for a new company to break into the ranks of successful enterprise software companies given the lead in functionality, integration, and ecosystems that existing firms already have. We believe, however, that there are two potential paths for a company to enter the market. The first is through superior functionality, whether it be specific functionality needed by a particular industry or an application that improves the ease of use of existing functionality, allowing users to take full advantage of the functionality. In this area we see startups adding a significant amount of value to enterprise software.

The other path consists of providing an integrated product that increases the linkage between the macro processes. Certainly, it will be difficult for a startup to garner the resources to build an integrated product across CRM, ISCM, and SRM. However, a large software company with tremendous resources and a history of pulling disparate products into an integrated package could take this path. The one company that comes to mind here is Microsoft. Microsoft has certainly noticed the growth and size of the enterprise software market and has begun to make a significant effort to enter this space. They have made two acquisitions over $1B and are showing more signs that this will be a focus of theirs in the future. Even with these acquisitions,

Microsoft is not yet a significant player in supply chain software and has targeted only small companies as their customers, leaving the large customers and the large revenues to the existing players. Given Microsoft's tried-and-true strategy of going in on the low end and expanding upward, however, they are certainly a company to watch for on the enterprise software landscape.

17.8 SUPPLY CHAIN IT IN PRACTICE

Although there are different sets of practical suggestions for each supply chain macro process, there are several general ideas that managers need to keep in mind when making a decision regarding supply chain IT.

1. *Select an IT system that addresses the company's key success factors.* Every industry and even companies within an industry can have very different key success factors. By key success factors, we mean the two or three elements that really determine whether or not a company is going to be successful. It is important to select supply chain IT systems that are able to give a company an advantage in the areas most crucial to the success of the business. For instance, the ability to optimally set inventory levels is crucial in the PC business where product life cycles are short and inventory becomes obsolete very quickly. However, inventory levels are not nearly as crucial for an oil company where demand is fairly stable and the product has a very long life cycle. For the oil company, the key to success would depend more on utilization of the refinery. Given these success factors, a PC company might pick a package that is strong in setting inventory levels even if it is weak in maximizing utilization of production capacity. However, the oil company should choose a different product, one that excels at maximizing utilization even if its inventory components are not especially strong.

2. *Take incremental steps and measure value.* Some of the worst IT disasters are due to the fact that companies try to implement IT systems in a wide variety of processes at the same time and end up with their projects being failures (often called the big bang approach). The impact of these failures is amplified by the fact that many of a company's processes are tied up in the same debugging cycle all at once, causing productivity to come to a standstill. One way to help ensure success of IT projects is to design them so that they have incremental steps. For instance, instead of installing a complete supply chain system across your company all at once, start first by getting your demand planning up and running and then move on to supply planning. Along the way, make sure each step is adding value through improvement in the performance of the three macro processes. This incremental approach does not mean that one should not take a big picture perspective (in fact, one *must* take a big picture perspective) but rather that the big picture perspective should be implemented in digestible pieces.

3. *Align the level of sophistication with the need for sophistication.* Management must consider the depth to which an IT system deals with the firm's key success factors. There is a trade-off between the ease of implementing a system and the system's level of complexity. Therefore, it is important to consider just how much sophistication a company needs to achieve its goals and then ensure that the system chosen matches that level. This is important because erring on the less sophisticated side leaves the firm

with a competitive weakness, whereas trying to be too sophisticated leads to a higher possibility of the entire system failing.

4. *Use IT systems to support decision making, not to make decisions.* Although the software available today can make many supply chain decisions for management, this does not mean that IT applications should make all of the decisions. A mistake companies can make is installing a supply chain system and then reducing the amount of managerial effort they spend on supply chain issues. Management must keep its focus on the supply chain because as the competitive and customer landscape changes, there needs to be a corresponding change in the supply chain.

5. *Think about the future.* Although it is more difficult to make a decision about an IT system with the future in mind than the present, it is very important that managers include the future state of the business in the decision process. If there are trends in a company's industry indicating that insignificant characteristics will become crucial in the future, managers need to make sure their IT choices take these trends into account. As IT systems often last for many more years than was originally planned, managers need to spend time exploring how flexible the systems will be if, or rather when, changes are required in the future. This exploration can go so far as to include the viability of the supply chain software developer itself. If it is unclear whether a company will be able to get support from a software company in the future, management needs to be sure that the other advantages of this product outweigh this disadvantage. The key here is to ensure that the software not only fits a company's current needs but also, and even more important, that it will meet the company's future needs.

17.9 SUMMARY OF LEARNING OBJECTIVES

1. Understand the importance of information and IT in a supply chain.

   Information is essential to making good supply chain decisions because it provides the global scope needed to make optimal decisions. IT provides the tools to gather this information and analyze it to make the best supply chain decisions.

2. Know at a high level how each supply chain driver uses information.

   Each of the supply chain drivers that we have discussed in previous chapters (inventory, transportation, and facilities) require the fourth driver, information, for decisions to be made. Information is the factual component on which decisions about each of the other drivers are based. In essence, information is the glue that holds the entire supply chain together and

allows it to function, making information the most important supply chain driver.

3. Understand the major applications of supply chain IT and the processes that they enable.

   A company's supply chain processes can be grouped into three main macro processes. CRM includes processes that enable interaction between an enterprise and its customers. ISCM includes processes focused on the internal operations of an enterprise. SRM includes processes that enable interaction between an enterprise and its suppliers. IT is a large enabler of these processes as well as enabling integration across these processes. Good IT systems not only allow the collection of data across the supply chain, but also the analysis of decisions that maximize supply chain profitability.

DISCUSSION QUESTIONS

1. What processes within each macro process are best suited to being enabled by IT? What processes are least suited?
2. What are the key advantages that best-of-breed software companies provide?
3. What are the key advantages that large software companies, such as the ERP players, provide?
4. What types of industries would be most likely to choose a best-of-breed approach to their IT systems? What types would be more likely to choose a large single integrated solution?
5. Discuss why the high-tech industry has been the leader in adopting supply chain IT systems.
6. Are manufacturers better candidates for IT?
7. Will the future enterprise software landscape be dominated by one or two vendors with products spanning CRM, ISCM, and SRM or will best-of-breed winners dominate? What are other possible outcomes?

BIBLIOGRAPHY

Drayer, Ralph, and Robert Wright. 2002. "Getting the Most from Your ERP System." *Supply Chain Management Review* (May–June): 44–52.

Escalle, Cedric X., Mark Cotteleer, and Robert D. Austin. 1999. *Enterprise Resource Planning, Technology Note.* Harvard Business School note 9-699-020.

Meyer, Michelle M. 2001. "Why IBM is Linking Logistics and Information." *Supply Chain Management Review* (September–October): 56–62.

Rutner, Stephen M., Brian J. Gibson, Kate L. Vitasek, and Craig M. Gustin. 2001. "Is Technology Filling the Information Gap?" *Supply Chain Management Review* (March–April): 58–64.

Shankar, Venkatesh, and Tony O'Driscoll. 2002. "How Wireless Networks are Reshaping the Supply Chain." *Supply Chain Management Review* (July–August): 44–51.

Soni, Ashok, M. A. Venkataramanan, and Vincent A. Mabert. 2001. "Enterprise Resource Planning: Common Myths vs. Evolving Reality." *Business Horizons* 44 (3): 69–76.

FOR MORE INFORMATION

For more information on IT in the supply chain, see the following periodicals: *Red Herring, InformationWeek,* and *Manufacturing Systems.* In addition, a number of investment banks periodically publish overviews of the enterprise software industry that provide a large amount of useful information on how IT is being used in the supply chain.

CHAPTER

18

E-Business
and the Supply Chain

Learning Objectives

After reading this chapter, you will be able to

1. Identify the role of e-business in a supply chain.

2. Understand the impact e-business can have on supply chain performance.

3. Utilize the e-business frameworks to evaluate whether a company is a good candidate for e-business and where they should target their e-business efforts.

In this chapter we discuss how e-business can be used to improve supply chain performance. We discuss why the value of e-business varies based on both a company's industry and their stage in the supply chain. Our goal is to enable managers to analyze their supply chains to identify if and how they can use e-business most beneficially.

18.1 THE ROLE OF E-BUSINESS IN SUPPLY CHAINS

E-business is the execution of business transactions via the Internet. Supply chain transactions that involve e-business include the flow of information, product, and funds. For instance, the following are all transactions that can be executed with e-business:

- Providing product information to participants across the supply chain
- Placing orders with suppliers

- Allowing customers to place orders
- Allowing customers to track orders
- Filling and delivering orders to customers
- Receiving payment from customers

These transactions are obviously not new tasks that have come into existence through the creation of e-business. Rather, they are traditional tasks performed by businesses for decades. E-business, however, can enhance these transactions by allowing them to take place over the Internet where they can often be executed more efficiently and with a higher level of responsiveness. For example, mail order companies like Lands End have used catalogs to convey product information to customers for decades. E-business allows Lands End to publish their catalog online, allowing customers instant access to the latest products (improved responsiveness vs. waiting for a new catalog in the mail) at virtually no cost to Lands End (improved efficiency vs. printing and mailing out millions of catalogs).

Today, the Internet plays a significant role in many supply chains and companies are using the Internet to conduct a wide variety of supply chain transactions. Examples of e-business are abundant. Dell displays all its product information over the Internet so customers are able to identify all options available for a PC they want to purchase along with the price of the configuration they select. Dell also shares demand and inventory information online with its suppliers. Using Web-based systems, Solectron, a contract manufacturer, collaborates with PC companies on product design. Companies use the Internet for negotiations and auctions to set prices of products and services. Companies like eBay allow people to auction products over the Internet. Exchanges like Freemarkets allow companies to auction their products and services over the Internet and seek bids from potential suppliers. UPS and FedEx allow customers to track their packages over the Internet. Many software and online music companies deliver orders over the Internet through downloads of electronic products. Customers can pay for their purchases over the Internet using their credit cards and businesses can pay their invoices electronically.

E-business can be divided into two main categories. B2C e-business involves transactions between a company and a consumer. Examples include Amazon.com, Dell, and Wal-Mart selling products to customers over the Internet. A B2B e-business involves transactions between two companies. Examples include Dell selling computers to corporations and Intel selling microprocessors to Dell.

The initial growth of e-business was in B2C supply chains. The most famous example is Amazon.com, which started by selling books over the Internet and has now expanded to include music, toys, electronics, software, and more. The bulk of e-business, however, is conducted between businesses themselves. Companies like Dell, W. W. Grainger, Cisco Systems Inc., and Intel Corp. were the first to move many supply chain processes online. At Intel, automated online ordering systems have replaced several hundred order clerks. Cisco handles over 75 percent of its sales online. At General Electric, employees order office supplies from pre-qualified vendors over the Internet. Ford Motor Co. is using the Internet to bring together engineers from its operations all over the world to collaborate on projects with a goal of designing basic components that can be used everywhere.

After its hype reached a pinnacle in 2000, e-business has endured a significant amount of criticism. Unbridled optimism regarding the value of e-business has been replaced by deep skepticism toward anything characterized as e-business. A key question facing executives is whether they should continue their e-business efforts. In this chapter we emphasize the point that the failure was not in e-business itself. The failure resulted from how companies chose to implement e-business. Why did Webvan fail in trying to sell groceries over the Internet? Why has Dell been able to utilize e-business to create one of the most successful companies anywhere? Our goal is to identify factors that led to failure in one case and significant success in another.

We believe e-business will allow businesses to create significant value in the future. The value of e-business, however, will vary depending upon the industry and the stage in the supply chain a firm occupies. Successful firms will be those that are able to tailor their e-business implementation to support areas where the maximum value can be extracted. Our goal is to provide a framework that can be used by executives to identify where the value lies, the magnitude of the value, and how value can best be extracted after considering the effort involved.

18.2   THE E-BUSINESS FRAMEWORK

In this section we present a framework for determining the impact of e-business on a company conducting transactions with consumers. We then apply the framework to several examples.

Our e-business framework consists of a scorecard that can be evaluated by a firm to gauge the impact of e-business and gain insight into whether or not e-business makes sense for them. At its most basic level, the scorecard can be broken up into two categories:

- Impact on responsiveness (which primarily affects a company's ability to grow and protect revenue)
- Impact on efficiency (which primarily affects a company's costs)

We now detail the contents of each category.

Impact of E-Business on Responsiveness

Improved responsiveness primarily enables a company to gain new revenue or to protect existing revenue. An e-business allows a firm or supply chain to exploit the following responsiveness, and therefore revenue-enhancing, opportunities:

- Direct sales to customers
- Twenty-four-hour access from any location
- Wider product portfolio and information aggregation
- Personalization/customization
- Faster time to market
- Flexible pricing, product portfolio, and promotions
- Price and service discrimination
- Efficient funds transfer
- Lower stockout levels
- Convenience/automated processes

Direct Sales to Customers

An e-business allows manufacturers and other members of the supply chain that do not have direct contact with customers in traditional channels to enhance revenues by bypassing intermediaries and selling directly to customers, thereby collecting the intermediary's incremental revenue. For example, Dell Computers sells PCs online direct to customers. As a result Dell is able to grow revenue and enhance margins because it shares no part of the revenue with a distributor or retailer. In contrast, a PC manufacturer like HP that sells through retailers must share some of the product revenue with the distributor and retailer, resulting in lower revenue and margins for HP.

Twenty-Four-Hour Access from Any Location

Unlike most retail stores, an e-business can attract customers who may not be able to place orders during regular business hours because an e-business is always open. At a retail store, customers place an order and receive the product at the same time. At an e-business, however, a customer can place an order even if the fulfillment process is shut down. For example, a customer can place an order at Grainger.com even though the W. W. Grainger store where he will pick up his order is closed. In fact, W. W. Grainger has observed a surge in online orders after their brick-and-mortar stores close.

E-business also allows a firm to access customers who may be geographically distant. For example, a small specialty retail store located near Chicago can reach customers all over the United States, or even the world, by setting up an e-business. Without an e-business, only the customers located near the store are likely to shop there. Access to an e-business is limited only by the customers' access to the Internet.

Wider Product Portfolio and Information Aggregation

An e-business allows a firm to increase sales by offering a very large selection of products that would be unrealistic in a brick-and-mortar store. For example, Dell offers customers a very large selection of computers and peripherals. Amazon.com offers a tremendously large selection of books. Offering the same selection at a retail store would require a huge site with a correspondingly large amount of inventory.

Making a large variety available does not necessarily mean that a customer will be able to access all the variety offered. Firms have often gone overboard by offering seemingly limitless variety without giving customers the tools to navigate the site and quickly identify what they want. The ability to offer a large selection is only effective if appropriate search tools are provided.

Personalization/Customization

The Internet offers an e-business the ability to use personal information to intelligently guide each customer's buying experience and increase sales. Some e-businesses use information on birthdays and other events provided by customers to send reminders and purchase recommendations. Firms can set up customer-specific sites to display information on products that the customer buys most frequently. Available technologies allow an e-business to use individual preferences and a customer's historical purchases to rank currently available choices. The Internet thus offers the potential of creating an individualized buying experience for each customer, which can increase the look-to-buy ratios significantly compared to a physical store.

Firms that focus on mass customization can use the Internet to help customers select a product that suits their needs. For example, Dell allows customers to customize their computers by using the options available on the Dell Web site. Lands' End will allow shoppers to use a body measurement system to virtually try on clothing before they buy it.

Faster Time to Market

A firm can use e-business to introduce new products much faster than a firm that uses physical channels. A firm selling PCs through physical channels must produce enough units to stock the shelves at their distributors and retailers before they start to see revenue from the new product. This requires considerable time and effort. An e-business, in contrast, introduces a new product by making it available on the Web site—the distribution lag to fill the physical channels is not present. A new product can be made available as soon as the first unit is ready to be produced. This is evident in the computer industry where Dell often introduces new products earlier than its competitors using traditional channels.

Flexible Pricing, Product Portfolio, and Promotions

An e-business can easily alter prices by changing one entry in the database linked to its Web site. This ability allows an e-business to maximize revenues by setting prices based on current inventories and demand. The airlines provide a good example of this ability—they make last-minute, low-cost fares available on the Web on routes with unsold seats. Dell also changes prices for different PC configurations regularly based on demand and component availability. Firms can change prices at an e-business much more easily than most traditional channels. If Dell or L. L. Bean were to use paper catalogs to convey a discount in prices, they would have to print new catalogs and mail them to potential customers. With an e-business, however, they only have to update the price on their Web site. Similarly, an e-business can easily alter the product portfolio that they offer as well as the promotions they are running.

Price and Service Discrimination

An e-business can price discriminate, meaning they can alter prices based on the characteristics of individual customers to enhance their own revenues. The ability to ask different customer segments to pay different prices allows a firm to increase revenues compared to a situation where a firm charges a single price to all customers. The airlines have used various forms of price discrimination for years but with e-business, many other industries are implementing similar types of price discrimination processes. In addition to prices, the services offered can also be customized to particular types of customers. For instance, in an attempt to keep one's best customers satisfied, highly profitable customers may be offered certain services that are unavailable to regular customers. Again, this is possible without e-business for some industries but for others, e-business is the chief enabler of this capability.

Efficient Funds Transfer

An e-business can enhance revenues by speeding up collection. An excellent example shows how e-business impacts areas even outside the business world. Within forty eight hours of John McCain's 2000 presidential primary victory in New Hampshire, Senator McCain's campaign collected $1 million through his Web site. In contrast, it would have taken a campaign receiving checks worth $1 million much more time and effort to process all the payments.

Lower Stockout Levels

E-business can greatly increase the speed with which information on customer demand is disseminated throughout the supply chain, giving rise to more accurate forecasts and significantly decreasing the negative aspects of the bullwhip effect (see Chapter 16). These improved forecasts and the more accurate view of customer demand leads to a better match between supply and demand. On the inventory front, this translates into having more of the inventory that customers demand and less of the inventory they do not. Therefore, stockouts are lower and sales that might have once been lost can now be captured.

Convenience/Automated Processes

For both consumers and businesses, e-business can increase the ease with which one does business. For instance, there is the convenience of not having to leave home or work to make a purchase. E-business can also help automate the purchasing process, increasing the speed of conducting business as well as decreasing the costs of placing orders. Examples include the ability of an online grocer like Peapod to pull up past orders to serve as a starting point for a new order as well as procurement systems used by businesses that automate the creation of purchase orders and the approval process.

Potential Revenue Disadvantage of E-Business

For the sale of physical products that cannot be downloaded, an e-business has one major disadvantage relative to physical channels. Whereas a retail store selling clothing can provide a customer her desired shirt immediately, an e-business without a physical retail outlet will take longer because of the shipping time. Thus, customers that require a short response time may not use the Internet to order a product.

There is no such delay, however, for products that can be downloaded. Going online may offer a time advantage in many cases. For example, the prospectus for a mutual fund or music can be downloaded from the Web. A physical mailing of these products or even making a trip to a music store takes much longer.

Impact of E-Business on Cost

On the cost side, e-business impacts all four supply chain drivers introduced in Chapter 3, namely inventory, facilities, transportation, and information. It is important to observe that the impact in each case is not necessarily positive.

Inventory

E-business can lower inventory levels and inventory cost by improving supply chain coordination and creating a better match between supply and demand. Additionally, an e-business can aggregate inventories far from customers because most customers are willing to wait for delivery of online orders. Due to geographical aggregation, an e-business requires less inventory (see Chapter 11). For example, Amazon.com is able to aggregate all its inventory of books and music at a few warehouses. In contrast, Borders and Barnes and Noble need more inventory because they must carry a significant fraction of their inventory at retail stores. A key point to note is that the relative benefit of aggregation is small for high-demand items with a small coefficient of variation but large for low-demand items with a high coefficient of variation.

An e-business can significantly lower its inventories if it can postpone the introduction of variety until after the customer order is received. The time lag between when a customer places the order and when he expects delivery offers an e-business a window of opportunity to implement postponement. For example, Dell keeps its inventory as components and assembles its PCs after receiving the customer order. The amount of component inventory required is much lower than it would be if Dell kept its inventories in the form of assembled PCs (see Chapter 11). E-business thus allows Dell to decrease its inventory holding costs relative to a firm carrying its inventory at retail stores in finished goods form.

Facilities

There are two basic types of facilities costs that must be included in the analysis—costs related to the number and location of facilities in a network, and costs associated with the operations that take place in these facilities. An e-business can reduce network facility costs by centralizing operations, thereby decreasing the number of facilities required. For example, Amazon.com is able to satisfy demand from a few warehouses, whereas Borders and Barnes and Noble must incur facility costs for all the retail outlets they operate.

With regards to ongoing operating costs, customer participation in selection and order placement allows an e-business to lower its resource costs. For example, when a customer goes to the Lands' End Web site, she makes the effort to check on product availability and then place the order. When the same customer phones in an order, the firm incurs the additional cost of its employees checking product availability and placing the order. An e-business can lower its order fulfillment costs because it does not have to fill an order as soon as it arrives. A retail store or supermarket must staff its sales counters so that more cashiers are available when more customers are shopping. As a result, they require greater staffing during weekends and at times when people are not at work. At an e-business, if a reasonable buffer of unfilled orders is maintained, the rate of order fulfillment can be made significantly smoother than the rate at which orders arrive, which reduces the peak load for order fulfillment and thus reduces resource requirements and cost.

Additionally, operating costs can be decreased for a manufacturer using e-business to sell direct to customers because fewer supply chain stages touch the product as it makes its way to a customer, thereby reducing handling costs.

On the downside, however, for some products, like groceries, an e-business has to perform tasks currently performed by the customer at retail stores, affecting both handling costs and transportation costs. In such situations, an e-business will incur higher handling and delivery costs than a retail store. For example, whereas a customer picks out the required items at a grocery store, an e-business like Peapod incurs higher handling costs because they must pick a customer's order from the warehouse shelves.

Transportation

If a firm can put its product in a form that can be downloaded, the Internet will save on the cost and time for delivery. For example, the MP3 format for music offers an opportunity to eliminate all costs associated with transporting compact discs. Similarly, the ability to download software eliminates the cost and time associated with producing CDs, packaging them, and transporting them to retail stores.

For nondigital products, two components of transportation cost must be considered—inbound and outbound. A firm incurs inbound transportation costs to bring the replenishment order in from the supplier. A firm incurs outbound transportation cost to take the product to the customer. Typically, replenishment orders tend to be larger than customer orders and thus the unit transportation cost is lower for inbound transportation than for outbound transportation. Aggregating inventories increases the distance a customer order travels while decreasing the distance a replenishment order travels. Compared to a business with many retail outlets, an e-business with aggregated inventories will tend to have higher transportation costs (across the entire supply chain) per unit due to the increase in outbound costs.

Information

An e-business can share demand information throughout the supply chain to dampen the bullwhip effect and improve coordination. The Internet may also be used to share planning and forecasting information within the supply chain, further improving coordination. This helps reduce overall supply chain costs and better match supply and demand, as we discussed earlier. Here we see that information is an enabler of many of the benefits discussed in both the earlier revenue and cost sections.

There are additional information costs, however, that are incurred by an e-business. The cost of software and hardware to set up an e-business can often be significant. These costs need to be weighed against the benefits that will be derived. Keep in mind that much of the IT infrastructure for e-business may already be in place to operate the regular brick-and-mortar business. This can greatly reduce the incremental amount that needs to be spent on e-business.

The B2C e-business scorecard shown in Table 18.1 aims to summarize the impact of e-business on each of the areas identified earlier.

To evaluate the potential impact of e-business and to determine whether e-business is appropriate for the firm, a manager should walk through each item on the scorecard and rate the impact it would have. Once the scorecard is completed, this understanding of the impact of e-business can give insight to managers making decisions on whether e-business is a good fit for their business.

TABLE 18.1   The E-Business Scorecard

Area	Impact	Area	Impact
Direct sales		Efficient funds transfer	
24-hour access		Lower stockouts	
Wider product portfolio		Convenience/automated processes	
Personalization/ customization		Inventory	
Faster time to market		Facilities	
Flexible pricing, portfolio, promotions		Transportation	
Price discrimination		Information	

++ Very Positive; + Positive; = Neutral; – Negative; — Very Negative

In the next section we go through several examples applying this e-business scorecard.

Applying the E-Business Framework

The value of setting up an e-business is not the same in every industry. Whereas Dell has seen its profits increase after going online, Webvan and many other online grocers have gone out of business. At its core, the value of e-business for an industry depends on the extent to which firms are able to exploit opportunities offered by the Internet to increase revenues and decrease costs.

Using E-Business to Sell PCs: Dell

The PC industry is well suited to exploit the opportunities the Internet offers to increase profits. Dell has already used e-business extensively and virtually all PC manufacturers are working to expand their sales over the Internet.

As shown in Figure 18.1 Dell sells PCs directly to customers, both companies and consumers, and starts assembly after receiving a customer order (shown by the fact that Dell is above the push/pull boundary). Traditional PC manufacturers, in contrast, assemble the PC in the push phase of the supply chain because they must have an assembled PC available for purchase at a retail store.

Revenue Impact of E-Business on the PC Industry

The main revenue disadvantage for Dell of selling PCs over the Internet is that customers who are unwilling to wait five to ten days to receive their PC cannot be attracted. The PC, however, is usually a planned purchase and most people are willing to wait for its delivery. Dell also does not attract customers who need a lot of help when selecting a PC. However, the segment of people that are comfortable selecting their own PC and willing to wait for its delivery is quite large and growing. Dell and other PC manufacturers selling over the Internet target this group of customers.

Dell is able to exploit most of the revenue enhancing opportunities offered by an e-business. The company uses the Internet to increase revenues by offering a very large number of different PC configurations. Customers are allowed to select recommended PC configurations or customize them to have the desired processor, memory, hard

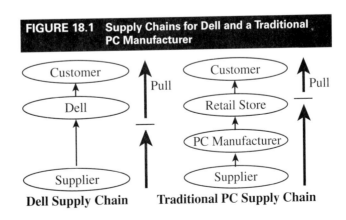

FIGURE 18.1   Supply Chains for Dell and a Traditional PC Manufacturer

drive, and other components. Customization allows Dell to satisfy customers by giving them a product that is close to their specific requirements. The customization options are very easy to display over the Internet and allow Dell to attract customers that value this choice. Dell also uses customized Web pages to enable large business customers to place orders.

Dell has fully exploited the Internet to increase revenues by bringing new products to market faster, allowing the company to attract customers who are willing to pay higher prices to get the latest technology. This is particularly important as products in the PC industry have short life cycles of a few months. Thus a firm like Dell that brings products to market faster than the competition enjoys huge revenue advantages until competing products come to market. Competing firms that sell through distributors and retailers have to fill shelves at their distributors and retailers before a product reaches the customer. Dell, in contrast, introduces a new product to customers on the Internet as soon as the first PC of that model is ready to be assembled. As a result, Dell can offer new components in its products as soon as they are available. It takes PC manufacturers selling through distributors and retailers much longer to bring new components to market.

Although the company cannot compete with a retailer in terms of response time for a PC the retailer has in stock, Dell is one of the fastest at providing customers with customized PCs. The company has designed products and processes in order to assemble the customized PC after a customer order arrives. Without the direct interaction between the consumer and Dell that e-business affords, Dell's reaction would be slower and they could not be as responsive with customized products. Decreasing the response time by a few days allows Dell to attract more time-sensitive customers.

Dell also uses the price flexibility the Internet offers to increase revenues. The sales people at Dell change prices and delivery time daily based on demand and supply of components to maximize the revenue that can be extracted from available resources. The company lowers prices on configurations that contain components with excess inventory to spur sales.

By using the Internet to sell PCs directly to customers, Dell is able to eliminate distributor and retailer margins and increase its own margin. The Internet allows Dell customers to place orders at any time of the day. Relative to other channels, the Internet makes it much cheaper to provide access by decreasing the workforce required. Computer stores, for example, would likely find the cost to stay open all night unjustifiable.

E-business allows Dell to collect payment for its PCs in a matter of days after they are sold. Dell, however, pays its suppliers according to the more traditional schedules in which payment is due in weeks (e.g., thirty days). Given its low levels of inventory, Dell is able to operate the business with negative working capital because it receives payment for its PCs about fifteen days before it pays its suppliers for their components. A PC supply chain including distributors and retailers finds it impossible to achieve these results.

Cost Impact of E-Business on the PC Industry

Inventory Costs E-business offers Dell the opportunity to reduce its inventories by geographically aggregating them in a few locations. Whereas a chain of retail stores selling computers must carry inventory in each store, Dell aggregates all inventories in a few locations (in Dell's case, they have five manufacturing facilities worldwide serving North America, Asia, Europe, Brazil, and China). The benefit of geographical aggregation for a product like a PC, however, will be marginal because a model that is selling well on the East Coast is also likely to sell well in the West Coast. Thus PC demand across different geographical regions is likely to be strongly correlated, reducing the benefit of aggregation (see Chapter 11).

The real benefit comes because e-business enables Dell to reduce inventories by exploiting the time that elapses from the point at which an online order arrives to the point at which it must be shipped. Dell products and assembly lines are designed such that all components on which customers are offered customization can be assembled in a very short period of time. This allows Dell to postpone assembly until after the customer order has been placed. As a result, Dell holds all inventory in the form of components that are common across multiple finished products. Postponement, coupled with component commonality, allows Dell to significantly reduce inventories (see Chapters 11 and 12). Dell maximizes the benefit of postponement by focusing on new PC models where demand is hard to forecast.

A PC manufacturer that sells through distributors and retailers finds it difficult to implement postponement. As a result, traditional PC manufacturers often find that they are stuck with PC configurations that are not selling while simultaneously being out of the configurations that are selling. Dell, in contrast, is better able to match supply and demand.

E-business also allows Dell to reduce inventories by enabling the company to share information across the supply chain, thereby dampening the bullwhip effect (see Chapter 16). This fact reduces costs and improves performance in the Dell supply chain by a significant amount.

Facility Costs E-business allows the Dell supply chain to lower facility costs because the company has no physical distribution or retail outlets. Dell only incurs the cost of the manufacturing facility and warehousing space for components. A PC supply chain selling through retail stores must pay for the distribution warehouses and retail stores as well.

E-business also allows Dell to take advantage of customer participation in order placement and decrease processing costs at its facility. Dell saves on the cost of call center representatives because customers do all the work when placing an order online.

Transportation Costs As a result of e-business, total transportation costs in the Dell supply chain are higher than in a supply chain selling PCs through distributors and retailers. Dell sends individual PCs to customers from its factories, whereas a manufacturer selling through distributors and retailers sends large shipments on trucks to warehouses and to the retailer. The Dell supply chain thus has higher outbound transportation costs. Relative to the price of a PC, however, the outbound transportation cost is low (typically 2 to 3 percent) and thus it does not have a major impact on the overall cost.

Information Costs Although Dell has made a significant investment in information technology to implement their build-to-order model, these costs are more than made up for by the benefits discussed earlier. Additionally, the majority of these IT costs need to be incurred regardless of whether Dell is an e-business or not. Therefore, e-business does add incrementally to Dell's information costs but this is not a significant factor.

E-business Impact on Performance at Dell

As summarized in the e-business scorecard in Table 18.2, e-business allows Dell to significantly improve its performance.

From Table 18.2 it is clear that Dell is very well suited for e-business. Observe that e-business improves both responsiveness and efficiency at Dell. As a result, customers are happier while Dell is able to reduce costs. Dell, to the delight of its shareholders, has exploited every advantage that the Internet offers to improve performance.

Value of E-business for a Traditional PC Manufacturer

It may seem at first glance that Dell, with its build-to-order business model, is best equipped to exploit the benefits of e-business. A careful study, however, indicates that a traditional PC manufacturer, selling through distributors and retailers, has a lot to gain as well. The PC manufacturer should use an e-business to sell new products or customized PC configurations whose demand is hard to forecast and let the regular channel sell standard configurations whose demand is easier to forecast. Manufacturers should introduce new models on the Internet and as demand for some of them grows, these models should be added to the retail channel. Another option is to introduce recommended configurations of new models at retail stores, while selling all customized configurations on the Internet. The manufacturer is thus able to lower inventories by aggregating all high-variability production and satisfying that demand online. These models should be built to order using as many common components as is feasible. The standard models can be produced using a longer lead time but low-cost approach. Selling standardized models through distributors and retail stores allows the supply chain to save on transportation costs, which are likely to be more significant for

TABLE 18.2 Impact of E-Business on Dell Performance

Area	Impact	Area	Impact
Direct sales	++	Efficient funds transfer	++
24-hour access	+	Lower stockouts	+
Wider product portfolio	++	Convenience/automated processes	=
Personalization/customization	++	Inventory	++
Faster time to market	++	Facilities	++
Flexible pricing, portfolio, promotions	++	Transportation	–
Price discrimination	=	Information	=

++ Very Positive; + Positive; = Neutral; – Negative; — Very Negative

these low-cost configurations. Retailers can be allowed to participate in the e-business by having kiosks where customers can configure models of their choice or order standardized models that are out of stock. It is important that traditional PC manufacturers give retailers a chance to participate in any e-business to avoid damaging existing channel relationships.

A traditional manufacturer can use the two-pronged approach outlined earlier to utilize both the strengths of e-business and those of traditional retail and distribution channels. Gateway has largely failed in their effort with retail stores because they did not use any of the supply chain strengths of the brick-and-mortar channel. Instead of only helping people with configuration at their retail stores (as Gateway has chosen to do), they would have been better served by also carrying recommended configurations of their PCs in the stores. This would immediately satisfy customers who wanted the recommended configuration while allowing Gateway to produce the more customized configurations efficiently.

Using E-Business to Sell Books: Amazon

The book industry was one of the first to feel the impact of e-business with the launching of Amazon.com in July 1995. Since 1995, Amazon.com has added music, toys, electronics, software, and home improvement equipment to its list of products offerings. Unlike Dell, however, Amazon.com has generally lost money though it has recently moved closer to profitability.

Amazon.com purchases some of its books direct from the publisher and buys the remaining titles from distributors as shown in Figure 18.2. A traditional bookstore chain, in contrast, purchases all books directly from publishers.

Revenue Impact of E-Business on the Book Industry

There are several reasons why e-business has not helped profits in the book industry. As shown in Figure 18.2, the Amazon.com supply chain for some products is longer than that of a bookstore chain such as Borders or Barnes and Noble because of the presence of an additional intermediary—the distributor. Unlike the PC industry where e-business facilitates direct sales by manufacturers, e-business has resulted in longer

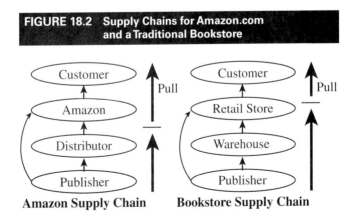

FIGURE 18.2   Supply Chains for Amazon.com and a Traditional Bookstore

supply chains in the book industry. Given distributor margins, this leaves lower margins for Amazon.

As is the case with Dell, customers wanting a book quickly cannot shop at Amazon.com. Thus Amazon.com can only attract customers that are willing to wait a few days to get the book. Amazon.com also cannot attract customers that value the ability to leaf through books. The company tries to counter this problem by providing reviews and other information on books to allow customers to get a feel for the book online.

To counter these drawbacks, Amazon.com has exploited several opportunities on the Internet to attract customers and increase revenues. Amazon.com attracts many customers by offering a wide selection of millions of books. Customers can search for hard to find books or those of special interest. A large physical bookstore, in contrast, can carry less than a hundred thousand titles. Amazon.com also uses the Internet to recommend books to customers based on their purchase history. E-mails are sent out to customers informing them of new titles that match their interests. New titles are quickly introduced and made available online whereas in a brick-and-mortar book-store chain, all retail stores have to be stocked.

Amazon.com uses the Internet to allow customers to order a book any time of the day from the comfort of their own home. If customers know the books they want, they can place the order online and the books will be delivered to their door. There is no need to leave the house and spend the hour or two that going to a physical book-store would take. This fact allows Amazon.com to attract customers that value this convenience and are willing to wait for delivery.

Cost Impact of E-business on the Book Industry

Amazon.com also uses e-business to lower its inventory and some of its facility costs. Processing costs at facilities and transportation costs, however, increase as a result of selling books online.

Inventory Costs Amazon.com is able to decrease inventories by geographically aggregating the inventories in a few locations (see Chapter 11). A bookstore chain, in contrast, has higher inventories because titles are carried at every store. The reduction of inventories from aggregation is most significant for low-demand books with high demand uncertainty. The benefit is less significant for best-sellers with demand that is more predictable. Amazon.com carries high-demand titles in inventory while it purchases low-demand titles from the distributor in response to a customer order. This allows the Amazon.com supply chain to further reduce inventories of low-demand titles because distributors are able to aggregate across other booksellers in addition to Amazon.

Facility Costs E-business allows Amazon.com to lower facility costs because it does not need the retail infrastructure that a bookstore chain like Borders or Barnes and Noble must have. Initially, Amazon.com did not have a warehouse and purchased all books from distributors. When demand volumes were low, the distributor was a better location to carry inventories because they could aggregate demand across other book-sellers besides Amazon.com. As demand has grown, however, Amazon.com has opened its own warehouses where it stocks high-demand books. Amazon.com now purchases the high-demand books directly from publishers and only goes to distributors for the lower demand books. Thus, facility costs at Amazon.com are growing though they are still much lower than the facility costs for a bookstore chain because Amazon.com has no retail sites.

Amazon.com, however, incurs higher order processing costs than a bookstore chain. At a bookstore, the customer selects the books and only cashiers are needed to receive payment. At Amazon.com, no cashiers are needed but every order is picked off the warehouse shelves and packed for delivery. For books that are received from distributors, additional handling at Amazon.com adds to the cost of processing the order.

Transportation Costs   The Amazon.com supply chain incurs higher transportation costs than a bookstore chain selling through retail stores. Local bookstores do not have the cost of individually shipping books to customers. Amazon.com, in contrast, incurs the cost of shipping books to its customers from warehouses. The shipping cost from an Amazon.com warehouse represents a significant fraction of the cost of a book (could be as high as 100 percent for an inexpensive book). As demand has grown, Amazon.com has opened several warehouses in an effort to get closer to customers, decrease its transportation costs, and improve response time.

Information Costs   As with Dell, setting up an e-business takes some additional investment in IT, but this is not incrementally significant compared with the IT that is required to run a brick-and-mortar business. Therefore, IT costs for e-business are somewhat higher, but not prohibitively so.

E-business Impact on Performance at Amazon

Amazon's e-business scorecard is summarized in Table 18.3.

A comparison of Tables 18.2 and 18.3 shows that e-business offers far greater advantages when selling PCs than when selling books. Some key differences between the two products are (a) product differentiation in PCs can be postponed until after the customer has placed an order, whereas books are currently published well in advance

TABLE 18.3 Impact of E-Business on Amazon.com Performance			
Area	*Impact*	*Area*	*Impact*
Direct sales	=	Convenience/automated processes	=
24-hour access	+		
Wider product portfolio	++	Inventory	+
Personalization/ customization	+	Facilities	+
Faster time to market	+	Transportation	—
Flexible pricing, portfolio, promotions	+	Information	–
Price discrimination	=		
Efficient funds transfer	=		
Lower stockouts	+		

++ Very Positive; + Positive; = Neutral; – Negative; — Very Negative

of a sale and (b) the relative fraction of the price that the increase in transportation costs represents is much higher for books than for PCs. If books become downloadable, Amazon.com will be able to exploit all the advantages that Dell currently exploits, along with being able to ship the product over the Internet. As a result, many of Amazon's current disadvantages would disappear.

Other potentially downloadable products that Amazon.com currently sells include software and music. In both instances, Amazon.com can increase the benefit of e-business if it either creates compact discs in response to a customer order or allows customers to download these products. For other products like toys and hand tools, limited possibilities exist for postponement. The advantages of e-business for Amazon.com in those product categories will continue to be small compared to physical retail outlets.

Value of E-Business for a Traditional Bookstore Chain

Traditional bookstore chains have a lot to gain by setting up an e-business to complement their retail stores. Going online allows a bookstore chain to offer the same convenience and variety as a brick-and-mortar store and exploit all the other revenue advantages that e-business provides Amazon.

Bookstore chains can also use the fact that the benefits of aggregation are most significant for low-demand books whose demand is hard to forecast. The chains should structure themselves such that retail outlets carry many copies of best-sellers for customer purchase and one copy of low-demand books to encourage customers to browse and make impulse purchases. Terminals or Internet kiosks should be provided so that customers wanting to order any low-demand books can place their orders online. The presence of kiosks increases the variety of books that the bookstore can offer. This approach would allow bookstore chains to reduce inventories by aggregating low-demand books sold online. The chains would also be able to incur low transportation costs for best-sellers sold at retails stores.

Once new printing technology is implemented, bookstore chains can also reduce inventory costs by using printers that allow a book to be produced in a few minutes on demand rather than carrying that book in inventory.

A traditional bookstore chain can integrate e-business into its retail stores to take advantage of the strengths of each and provide an effective ordering and delivery network.

Using E-Business to Sell Groceries: Peapod

The grocery industry saw a spurt in new e-businesses in 1998 and 1999, although virtually all have gone out of business. Peapod, one of the oldest online grocers, is one of the few left. Given this industry's poor track record, one could surmise that this is an industry not well suited for e-business. Let us take a look with our scorecard to see whether this is the case.

Peapod started by supplying orders using workers at grocery stores to pick and deliver orders. The company has now moved to supplying orders from centralized fulfillment centers and also some large supermarkets. Each fulfillment center is much larger than a supermarket and is comparable to a warehouse. As shown in Figure 18.3, the Peapod and supermarket supply chains are comparable except that with a

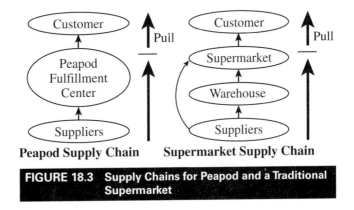

FIGURE 18.3 Supply Chains for Peapod and a Traditional Supermarket

supermarket, some products come from a warehouse while the rest come directly from suppliers.

Revenue Impact of E-Business on the Grocery Industry

Peapod and other online groceries have tried to sell convenience and the time savings they offer customers. For most people, grocery shopping is a chore that is time consuming and rarely enjoyable. Peapod allows customers to place orders at any time and have them delivered at home, eliminating a trip to the supermarket. This can be a significant convenience especially in urban areas where customers have to walk to a supermarket and carry all their groceries home. In a suburban area, the benefit is smaller because people can drive to supermarkets with relative ease. The convenience of saving time, however, remains quite valuable.

The convenience factor related to access is even more significant if a specialty food provider goes online. For example, ethnic food stores are not as accessible as supermarkets and people often drive long distances to reach them. Offering ethnic foods on the Internet provides easy access to customers and saves a long drive. An example of this is Ethnicgrocer.com, an e-business that specializes in, as the name suggests, ethnic groceries. Peapod, however, does not offer significantly more variety than a typical supermarket.

Peapod is able to increase revenues by creating a personalized shopping experience for customers and delivering customized, one-to-one advertising and promotions. This is done using extensive member profiles that Peapod creates based on online shopping behavior, purchase histories, and surveys. Unlike a supermarket where the store does not know what customers have selected until they check out, Peapod can guide online customers based on what they purchase. For example, if a customer buys some pasta, Peapod can suggest a type of pasta sauce or some Parmesan cheese. Over longer periods, Peapod can collect shopping patterns and suggest products that match a customer's preferences. Such suggestions enhance revenues by increasing customers' impulse purchases.

Peapod also adds to its revenues by giving consumer goods companies a forum for targeted interactive advertising and electronic coupons. Peapod increases revenues by selling data on consumer choices to product manufacturers. Consumer choice data available to an online grocer is more valuable than scanner data from a supermarket because scanner data only reveals the customer's final purchases. An online grocer, in contrast, can record the customer's decision process. For example, an online grocer can record a customer's substitution patterns for items that are out of stock. With scanner data, a supermarket cannot record substitutions because it has no way of finding out if the customer looked for something that is out of stock.

Cost Impact of E-Business on the Grocery Industry

Peapod and other online grocers use e-business to lower some facility costs and, to an extent, inventory costs. Processing costs at facilities and transportation costs, however, are much higher than for traditional supermarkets.

Inventory Costs   Compared to a supermarket chain, an online grocer like Peapod can lower inventories by aggregating the inventory in a few large replenishment centers. The degree of aggregation, however, is less than that achieved by Amazon.com or Dell because Peapod needs fulfillment centers in every urban area it serves to get food to the customer in an acceptable condition.

The benefits of aggregation are further diminished by the fact that the majority of products sold at a supermarket are staple items with steady demand. Thus, aggregation provides a marginal benefit in terms of improved forecast accuracy and reduced inventories (see Chapter 11). The benefits of aggregation are higher for specialty, low-demand items with high demand uncertainty. These products constitute a small fraction of overall sales at a supermarket. Thus, aggregation allows e-grocers to lower their inventory costs only marginally compared to a typical supermarket. If online grocers focused primarily on specialty items like ethnic foods, the inventory benefits of aggregation would be larger.

Facility Costs   E-business allows Peapod to lower facility costs because it only needs warehouse facilities and can save on the cost of retail outlets such as supermarkets. Processing costs at Peapod to fulfill an order, however, are significantly higher than those for a supermarket, and overwhelm the savings from fewer facilities. Peapod saves on checkout clerks compared to a supermarket but must pick the customer order, a task the customer performs at a supermarket and one that is much more time consuming than checkout. Thus, e-business results in a loss of customer participation compared to a supermarket and raises overall facility costs.

Transportation   An online grocer like Peapod has significantly higher transportation costs than a supermarket. Supermarkets have the advantage of having to bear only inbound transportation cost for products, with customers providing transportation from the supermarket to their homes. Inbound transportation costs tend to be low because supermarkets have large deliveries that enable them to exploit economies of scale in transportation. Peapod, in contrast, has to bear inbound transportation cost to its fulfillment centers and then outbound delivery costs from the fulfillment centers to customer homes. Outbound delivery costs are high because individual orders must be delivered to each customer's home. The task becomes all the more problematic given the different temperature requirements for different types of food.

Compared to computers and even books, groceries have a low value to weight/volume ratio. For example, paper towels and bathroom tissues have very low value but occupy a lot of space in the truck. Thus, transportation costs are a significant fraction of the cost incurred by online grocers. This makes it very difficult for an online grocer to compete with a supermarket on prices.

Information Costs   Again, the IT infrastructure required for an e-business increases costs. In the case of an e-grocer, this is somewhat more significant than with the other e-businesses we have been discussing as there is a wider range of functions taken on by the e-business that the shopper usually does themselves. Therefore, IT costs are higher for an e-grocer. As in the other examples, however, IT costs are not a deal breaker for this business model.

E-Business Impact on Performance at Peapod

E-business offers some revenue enhancement opportunities in the grocery indus-try. Costs, however, are significantly higher for an online grocer than a supermarket, as we can see from Table 18.4.

A comparison of Tables 18.2, 18.3, and 18.4 shows that e-business offers few ben-efits when selling groceries compared to books and PCs. Supermarkets are large enough to enjoy most of the inventory benefits that aggregation has to offer without having to incur the additional delivery cost that an online grocer incurs. Online grocers cannot compete with supermarkets on price, and online profits from the sale of groceries are likely to be small. Online grocers will succeed only if there are enough people willing to pay a significant additional price for the convenience of home delivery.

Value of E-Business to a Traditional Grocery Chain

Traditional supermarket chains can benefit by using an e-business to complement the strengths of their existing network. The e-business can be used to offer convenience to customers that value it and are willing to pay for it. Supermarkets can be used to tar-get the customers that value the lower prices offered.

TABLE 18.4   Impact of E-Business on Peapod Performance

Area	*Impact*	*Area*	*Impact*
Direct sales	=	Efficient funds transfer	=
24-hour access	+	Lower stockouts	=
Wider product portfolio	=	Convenience/automated processes	++
Personalization/ customization	+	Inventory	=
Faster time to market	=	Facilities	–
Flexible pricing, portfolio, promotions	+	Transportation	—
Price discrimination	=	Information	–

++ Very Positive; + Positive; = Neutral; – Negative; — Very Negative

A supermarket chain with an e-business has the opportunity to offer an entire array of services at differing prices based on the amount of work the customer does. The cheapest service involves customers walking into the supermarket and shopping for the products they want. In this case the customer picks the order from the shelves and provides outbound transportation for it. For an additional charge, a supermarket could allow customers to place orders online to be picked up at a later time. In this case the supermarket personnel pick the order from the shelf but the customer provides outbound transportation. The most expensive service is when the customer places orders online for home delivery. In this case the supermarket chain is responsible for both picking the order from the shelf and delivering it to the customer's home. The varying services and prices would allow supermarket chains to efficiently satisfy the needs of a variety of customers.

Among the supermarket chains, Alberston's has taken the lead in combining e-business with physical supermarkets. They have renamed some of their stores Albertsons.com. Half the store remains a traditional supermarket while the other half is used to fulfill online grocery orders. This allows the firm to exploit economies of scale on inbound transportation while keeping delivery distances to customers short on the outbound side. Customers are allowed to pick up their orders at the store or have the order delivered to their home. Based on our analysis, the Alberston's model is likely to be the most effective method for combining e-business with existing super-markets in the grocery industry and pure online grocers are likely to be less effective.

Using E-Business to Sell MRO supplies: Grainger.com

W. W. Grainger is a B2B distributor of MRO supplies. W. W. Grainger sells over 200,000 different products ranging from consumables like machine lubricants to hardware items like nuts and bolts. W. W. Grainger has traditionally sold its products using a paper catalog. Customers place orders on the phone or walk up to one of about 400 branches (similar to a large retail store) in the United States. Orders placed over the phone are either picked up at a branch or shipped to the customer using a package carrier. In 1995, W. W. Grainger established an e-business when it set up Grainger.com, allowing customers to place orders online. E-business has grown rapidly in the MRO supplies industry and competitors like McMaster Carr have also built e-businesses.

Revenue Impact of E-Business for W. W. Grainger

W. W. Grainger is in a position to exploit several of the revenue enhancing opportunities offered by the Internet. Grainger.com allows a customer access to all the 220,000 products that W. W. Grainger sells whereas the catalog only offers about 80,000 products. Compared to a catalog, searching for a product is simpler on the Internet using search engines that W. W. Grainger has developed. The increased variety allows W. W. Grainger to attract more customers and satisfy more needs of existing customers. The Internet allows W. W. Grainger to enhance revenues by introducing a new product as soon as it becomes available. With direct mail marketing, W. W. Grainger had to wait for a new catalog to be shipped before customers were informed about new products. An e-business also allows W. W. Grainger to offer promotions and easily change prices without having to send out new catalogs.

Grainger.com allows customers to place orders and check their status at any time of the day. This is a significant benefit to customers who can use this ability to improve their MRO purchase process. For example, a customer's night shift personnel can use the Internet to place and check on orders for supplies they need. They no longer have to wait for people from the day shift to place their order. This improves the accuracy of orders and reduces the time needed to process them. A study by the Aberdeen Group indicates that online purchases decrease the duration of the order and fulfillment cycle from an average of 7.3 days to an average of two days. The decreased order fulfillment times allow W. W. Grainger to attract more orders through its e-business. A study by W. W. Grainger Consulting estimates that MRO distributors could see incremental sales gains of 10 to 20 percent by selling online.

Product margins, however, are likely to drop as a result of e-business in the MRO supply industry. With customers able to compare prices easily over the Internet, the growth in e-business has put pressure on MRO supply companies to lower price.

Cost Impact of E-Business at W. W. Grainger

W. W. Grainger uses e-business to lower its order processing costs and to some extent its facility costs. Notably, W. W. Grainger customers will also see a significant reduction in order processing costs as a result of e-business.

Inventory Costs   As Internet orders that are shipped by package carrier grow, W. W. Grainger will be able to aggregate more of it inventories, resulting in some inventory reduction. W. W. Grainger will achieve further inventory reduction if online sales grow large enough to enable the company to close some of its branches. The inventory benefits, however, are likely to be small because W. W. Grainger's existing supply chain network is well suited to online sales. Customers also save on inventory costs as a result of e-business because replenishment lead times over the Internet are lower than with traditional procurement methods.

Facility Costs   W. W. Grainger's facility costs will come down to some extent if more Internet sales are shipped using package carriers and some branches are closed. W. W. Grainger will see a bigger reduction in processing costs from online sales. Customers placing orders over the Internet perform all order placement activities. This allows W. W. Grainger to decrease the number of customer service representatives in its call centers.

Customers also save on order processing costs as a result of e-business. E-business is a convenient way for corporations to place content-rich catalogs in the hands of end users of MRO supplies. As a result, companies no longer require people to process MRO purchase orders. E-business offers many companies a quick and convenient chance to get away from inefficient manual methods of procurement. The Aberdeen Group estimates that online purchase of MRO supplies saves about $30 per order in administrative costs.

Transportation Costs   Transportation costs in the W. W. Grainger supply chain are unlikely to change significantly as a result of e-business. Transportation costs may increase if more Internet orders are shipped using package carriers rather than being picked up at branches. Overall, however, the costs are likely to remain unchanged as the method of ordering should not have a large impact on how a customer wants an order delivered.

Information Costs Information costs will increase to fund the creation of the Grainger.com storefront but beyond that there will be little additional cost.

E-Business Impact on Performance at W. W. Grainger

MRO distributors like W. W. Grainger are likely to find e-business a somewhat attractive proposition as summarized in Table 18.5. Most of the gains from e-business come from a decrease in their order processing costs. The structure of the MRO supply chain will not be significantly different for online orders compared to the current phone orders. Thus, there are few significant supply chain gains for MRO distributors.

18.3 THE B2B ADDITION TO THE E-BUSINESS FRAMEWORK

The e-business framework presented earlier is useful for analyzing all types of e-business opportunities. As we have shown, it can be applied to both B2C (Dell, Amazon.com, Peapod) and B2B (Dell again and W. W. Grainger) relationships. The framework covers a wide variety of factors, each listed in the scorecard, that may or may not be particularly important to customers or sellers in the e-business transaction.

With B2B transactions, however, this wide variety of factors can be greatly simplified into a much smaller list of motivations for pursuing e-business. Understanding these areas where e-business can add value helps businesses target their e-business efforts. It is for this reason that we have included an additional B2B framework to be used when analyzing e-business in a B2B context. A more detailed discussion of this framework can be found in the article "B2B E-Commerce Opportunities" by Chopra, Dougan, and Taylor.

For a business engaged in transactions with other businesses, the motivation for engaging in e-business can be broken down into value coming from three sources:

TABLE 18.5   Impact of E-Business on W. W. Grainger Performance

Area	Impact	Area	Impact
Direct sales	=	Efficient funds transfer	=
24-hour access	+	Lower stockouts	=
Wider product portfolio	++	Convenience/automated processes	+
Personalization/ customization	+	Inventory	=
Faster time to market	+	Facilities	+
Flexible pricing, portfolio, promotions	+	Transportation	=
Price discrimination	=	Information	–

++ Very Positive; + Positive; = Neutral; – Negative; — Very Negative

- Reduced transaction costs
- Improved market efficiencies
- Supply chain benefits

Transaction costs are incurred to execute a transaction and include the cost of handling proposals and quotations, processing orders, procurement staff, call centers, and so forth. Transaction costs are reduced by automating processes, eliminating duplication of work, reducing error rates, and decreasing cycle time during the order placement process.

Market efficiencies offer two avenues for a firm to extract value—the price paid to suppliers and the ability of the firm to match surplus capacity in its supply chain with unmet demand. The price paid may decrease either because of better aggregation of orders or because of increased competition between suppliers.

Supply chain benefits result from better coordination and collaboration across different stages of a supply chain. Better coordination improves utilization of available assets and matching of supply and demand. Improved collaboration allows different stages of a supply chain to use common information to make product design and introduction, pricing, production, and distribution decisions in a manner that allows profits for each party in the supply chain to increase.

Before making any investment in B2B e-business, a firm must quantify the value created under each of the three categories. The relative position of the three categories will not be the same for all firms but will vary based on their industry and position in the supply chain. A firm must focus its e-business implementation to support categories where the value created is high relative to the cost of implementation.

What is the Magnitude of the Value?

To identify the magnitude of the value from B2B e-business, firms need to consider the strengths and weaknesses of their current supply chain interactions. Significant value can be extracted from each of the three categories only if the current supply chain structure has inefficiencies that can be corrected using the Internet. A firm must identify these inefficiencies to focus its e-business efforts.

Transaction Costs

E-business is likely to reduce transaction costs by a significant amount if the following conditions hold:

- Transactions are frequent and small in size
- Phone and fax are the current mode of transmitting orders
- A lot of effort is spent reconciling product and financial flows

The purchase of MRO items is a perfect setting for using e-business to reduce transaction costs. Typical customer orders are small and significant effort is spent placing and receiving the order and reconciling payments. To reduce transaction charges, e-business efforts can eliminate duplication of work, reduce error rates, and decrease the cycle time by providing customers the ability to:

- Search for products
- Identify product availability and pricing
- Identify substitutes

- Perform credit checks and financing
- Place and track the order until delivery
- Process payment

British Telecom claims to have reduced transaction costs associated with procurement by 90 percent using e-business. For firms with well-established EDI systems in place, however, the Internet is unlikely to reduce transaction charges by a significant amount. For example, in Australia two retail chains, Coles Meyer and Woolworths, dominate the consumer packaged goods industry. Given that they are already linked via EDI to their major suppliers, they are unlikely to reduce their transaction costs significantly by moving to the Internet. Similarly, the automotive industry in the United States is unlikely to reduce transaction costs by a significant amount simply by moving from EDI to an Internet platform. Moving to the Internet will offer some advantage with smaller suppliers that are currently not on EDI. The Internet also provides a less expensive infrastructure than EDI with lower ongoing maintenance cost.

Improved Market Efficiencies

B2B e-business can provide significant value by reducing prices if the following conditions exist:

- Limited buyer/seller qualification is required
- A fragmented market exists with many competing players either on the buy or sell side
- A large numbers of buyers/sellers can be attracted to the online site

B2B e-business can provide significant value by improving the matching of supply surplus and unmet demand in industries where capacity is expensive and mismatches of surplus supply and unmet demand are common.

If significant buyer/seller qualification is required, the ability of the Internet channel to provide market efficiencies by decreasing prices is diminished. For example, in the purchase of most direct materials, all bidders have to be pre-qualified. As a result, an online auction simply serves as a dynamic tendering process. Some companies have reported up to a 20 percent decrease in prices paid using auction mechanisms, even in heavy manufacturing. These reductions, however, are not because of identifying a lower cost supplier. In most cases, the contract was awarded to the incumbent supplier who felt pressured into lowering their prices. These price reductions are unlikely to be repeated in the future because no fundamental reduction in cost has occurred; margin has simply been passed from one party to another. Moreover, a worsening of supplier relationships is likely, hurting potential value from supply chain improvements that require collaboration.

Market efficiencies are much more likely to decrease prices if buyer/seller qualification is not important and the market is highly fragmented. In such a situation, a truly lower cost supplier is likely to be identified providing real supply chain value. Of course, this can only happen if many suppliers are willing and able to participate in the online bidding process. A suitable example would be the MRO industry in the United States, where even large players like W. W. Grainger have a relatively small share of the market. Use of the Internet for MRO buying has resulted in downward price pressure, with observed savings of up to 30 percent on selected indirect materials.

Market efficiencies are also likely to decrease prices when many small buyers use the Internet as an infrastructure for aggregating orders. An example is FleetXchange.com, which aggregates buying for small truck fleets. These price reductions are likely to be sustainable because the supplier benefits from having a relatively steady aggregated demand compared to the highly variable demand from each small fleet.

In most supply chains, the major value from market efficiencies will derive from matching surplus supply with unmet demand. Cisco has done this effectively by moving demand to suppliers with available capacity. The value from matching surplus supply and unmet demand is likely to be the largest in industries that face highly uncertain demand and where flexible supply exists that can be diverted to satisfy unmet demand from any source. For example, General Mills was able to save 7 percent of its transportation costs by implementing a back-haul transportation exchange with its business partners to take advantage of unutilized transportation capacity. Unused fleet capacity was matched with partner freight requirements that resulted in higher asset utilization, reduced cost, and improved cycle times. The Internet also provides an ideal channel to dispose of surplus supply as shown by the airline, rental car, and hotel industry.

Supply Chain Benefits

The value of supply chain benefits is likely to be highest in industries with the following characteristics:

- The bull-whip effect is quite significant due to information distortion in the supply chain
- The supply chain as a whole achieves low inventory turns and poor product availability
- Each stage has little visibility into either the customer or supplier stage
- There is little collaboration in the supply chain in terms of promotions and new product introduction
- Product life cycles are short

At the most basic level, the Internet allows increased visibility across a supply chain. This visibility offers value if all stages can plan to anticipate consumer demand. The value of visibility increases with the number of stages in the supply chain. The full value of visibility, however, is only achieved when different stages of the supply chain plan their activities collaboratively based on a common forecast of customer demand. A good example of the value from improved visibility and collaborative planning is the relationship between Wal-Mart and P&G. The benefits of collaboration can also be significant if the Internet is used to coordinate new product design and introduction throughout the supply chain. The automotive industry has put a significant effort in this direction.

Achieving visibility is often difficult but collaboration in planning and new product introduction is even harder because it requires significant changes in organizational structure along with the implementation of technology. In fact, a case can be made that the organizational changes play a more important role than technology when implementing collaboration. Potential benefits from collaboration, however, will far exceed the benefits obtained from simple visibility. Companies that are implementing industry initiatives like Efficient Consumer Response (ECR), VMI, and CPFR are

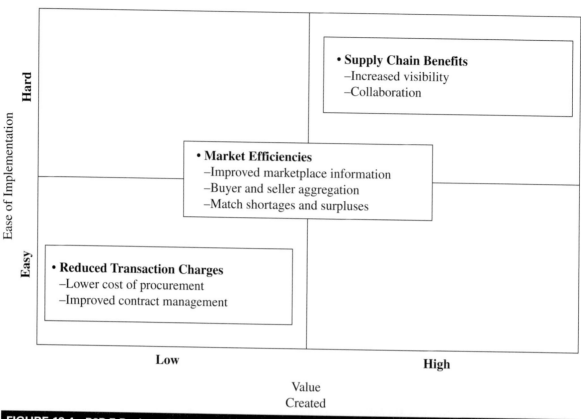

FIGURE 18.4 B2B E-Business Value Proposition

Source: Adapted from Chopra, Sunil, Darren Dougan, and Gareth Taylor. 2001. "B2B E-Commerce Opportunities." *Supply Chain Management Review* (May–June): 50–58.

putting into place organizational changes that can be coupled with B2B technology to achieve the benefits of collaboration.

As shown in Figure 18.4, the magnitude of the benefits increase as a firm moves from reducing transaction costs to increasing market efficiency to improving supply chain coordination. Unfortunately, so does the difficulty in achieving these benefits. Reducing transaction costs is relatively simple, as much of this work can be done internal to the company—and the cooperation needed from the firm's supply chain partners is relatively minimal. On the other end of the spectrum, supply chain coordination requires a large degree of interaction and trust between different supply chain partners. Although there is lots of work to be done internally, most of the work involves close interaction with partners. This makes coordination more difficult to achieve.

The B2B addition to the e-business framework attempts to determine how large an opportunity exists for a particular company in each of these value areas. The framework consists of a decision tree a company should analyze to determine the value bucket to target with e-business, the magnitude of the value of e-business, and ultimately, whether it is worth it to pursue e-business at all. The decision tree is shown in Figure 18.5.

We now apply this decision tree to show how it can be used by an automotive manufacturer like General Motors weighing a range of e-business options. They begin with the decision tree by looking at reducing transaction costs through e-business. The company is already connected to their major suppliers via EDI. Switching to the Internet will create an infrastructure that is cheaper to maintain but will also require additional investment. The company, however, could streamline operations with their minor suppliers of direct materials and their suppliers of indirect materials using e-business. Thus, a firm like General Motors would find limited opportunity for transaction cost reduction.

Next, General Motors should look at increasing market efficiency through e-business. General Motors should start by considering various categories of products

FIGURE 18.5   B2B Addition to the E-Business Framework

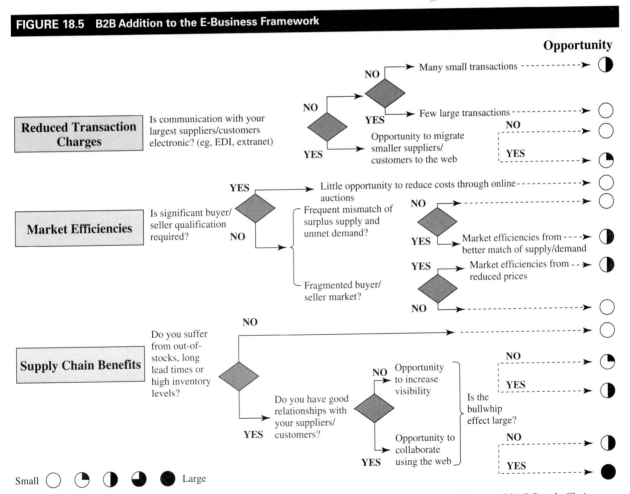

Source: Adapted from Chopra, Sunil, Darren Dougan and Gareth Taylor. 2001. "B2B E-Commerce Opportunities." *Supply Chain Management Review* (May–June): 50–58.

that are sourced (see Chapter 13). For critical and strategic items, General Motors qualifies most of its suppliers and the supply base is not fragmented. Thus, there is little opportunity for price reduction through market efficiencies. For critical and strategic items with multiple sources, General Motors can use e-business to better match component shortages at its plants with available supply/capacity at its vendors. For general and bulk purchase items, however, online auctions could be used to obtain lower prices. General items would include MRO supplies, whereas bulk items include transportation.

The biggest opportunity at General Motors is likely to lie in the use of e-business to improve supply chain visibility and coordination for critical and strategic items. Critical and strategic items form a large fraction of the spending at General Motors and there are several tiers of suppliers for these products resulting in long supply lead times. The long supply chain leads to a significant bullwhip effect. Thus, improved visibility and coordination would have high value. E-business can also help improve visibility and coordination with dealers. Coordination with dealers can help General Motors improve the matching of supply and demand and avoid the expensive buildup of finished goods inventory. General Motors would be best served by developing good relationships with major suppliers and dealers so they can use e-business to improve visibility and coordination throughout the supply chain. While the effort involved is significant, the value from this effort will also be large.

Exploring all three value buckets in the decision tree, supply chain coordination offers the highest value for General Motors and could be a prime target for the use of e-business if it can justify the cost.

It is worthwhile noting that Dell has achieved its success by realizing that for a company in the PC industry, e-business's greatest opportunity is to increase supply chain coordination. Dell was one of the first companies to use the Internet to improve visibility and coordination in their supply chain.

Other companies in different industries will have different results. For instance, a company like W. W. Grainger that we studied earlier in the chapter will find that using e-business to decrease the costs of transactions offers the greatest opportunity from e-business. Given this variability, it is important for companies in B2B to use such a framework to make sure their e-business efforts are targeted at providing the maximum payback for their investment.

18.4   E-BUSINESS IN PRACTICE

A firm can be successful with e-business only if it can integrate the Internet with existing channels of distribution in a way that uses the strengths of each appropriately. The Internet's ability to provide access to many customers must be coupled with a suitable supply chain network to fulfill those orders. Managers should consider the following ideas when setting up an e-business in practice.

1. *Integrate the Internet with the existing physical network.* To extract maximum benefit from e-business, firms should integrate it with their existing supply chain networks. This coupling of e-business with the existing physical network has been referred to as clicks and mortar. The success of an e-business is closely linked to the distribution capabilities of the existing supply chain network. Separating them will add to inefficiencies within the supply chain.

Alberston's use of its physical assets to satisfy both online orders and people that want to shop in a supermarket is an effective integration of e-business within a supply chain network. Another example of an effective clicks-and-mortar strategy is The Gap, which allows customers to place online orders through computers placed in the stores and also return items purchased online at retail stores. The Internet is used to expand the variety available to customers at a Gap store. Gap stores stock popular items while customers can order online the colors or sizes that may not be available in the store. This allows the Gap to centralize low-demand items while increasing the variety available to customers and extract the maximum benefit from integrating its e-business with its physical network.

2. *Devise shipment pricing strategies that reflect costs.* Incomplete consideration of shipping costs has played a significant role in the losses incurred by e-businesses to date. Forrester reports that less than half the companies they surveyed make a profit on each shipped package. Companies must be aware of the cost to fulfill an order and reflect this cost in the prices they charge. Charging standard fees regardless of size or weight adds to losses that firms incur. As long as carriers charge based on weight, size, and destination, e-businesses must account for these factors when charging customers for shipping. Some firms have eliminated shipping charges in the beginning to attract customers. Over time, however, they must have a plan to recover these costs. An example of the potential problems is Ethnicgrocer.com, based in the Chicago area. By offering free shipping, Ethnicgrocer.com has attracted customers who live in suburban or rural areas that are far from ethnic grocery stores. Ethnicgrocer.com cannot make money by shipping ten-pound bags of rice for free. Without a plan for charging customers for shipping or getting out of the business of selling ten-pound bags of rice, Ethnicgrocer.com will have difficulty becoming profitable.

3. *Optimize e-business logistics to handle packages not pallets.* The growth of e-business increases the amount shipped in small packages to customers. For example, whereas Borders and Barnes and Noble send all their merchandise in large quantities to replenish their stores, online booksellers must send packages containing one or two books to each customer. With smaller packages, it becomes critical for companies to exploit every possible opportunity to consolidate shipments to lower costs. This may involve partnering with other firms to consolidate shipments. To increase consolidation and reduce transportation costs, e-businesses must try to bundle an entire customer order into a single package.

4. *Design the e-business supply chain to efficiently handle returns.* Customers purchasing products online are likely to have a higher rate of return than customers purchasing from a physical store. Regardless of how good a Web site is, it cannot match the customer experience of touching and seeing the product at a retail store. As a result, the product purchased online is often different from the customer's expectation. E-businesses have had a lot of difficulty handling returns and this has contributed to customers having a bad experience. E-businesses like Gap.com that are integrated with retail stores have handled returns by allowing customers to return unwanted merchandise at a store. Pure e-businesses, however, have no other choice at this stage but to allow customers to mail back the unwanted merchandise. This adds to supply chain costs and tarnishes the customer's experience. The problem is magnified when an

e-business allows a customer to place a single order across several suppliers. Ideally the returns should be sent to a single location as well. Some e-businesses, however, are not structured to allow a customer to do this. In many instances, customers must return the product to the supplier that it came from. The problem is magnified when different suppliers have different return policies.

5. *Keep customers informed throughout the order fulfillment cycle.* E-businesses must keep customers involved as their orders proceed through fulfillment. Customers must be allowed to check the status of their order online or be informed proactively by e-mail about the order's status. Online customers are more likely to check on the status of their order than customers ordering through other channels. An e-business can lose its cost advantage in order placement if a customer has to call back to check on the status of the order. E-businesses should inform customers about the total fulfillment cycle time rather than just the shipping time. This will set customer expectations in line with reality and reduce the number of customers calling back to ask why their order did not arrive when it was promised.

18.5 SUMMARY OF LEARNING OBJECTIVES

1. Identify the role of e-business in a supply chain.

E-business is the execution of business transactions over the Internet. Firms use e-business to provide information across the supply chain, negotiate prices and contracts, allow customers to place and track orders, allow customers to download orders, and receive payment from customers. E-business's role is to make these processes both more responsive and more efficient.

2. Understand the impact e-business can have on supply chain performance.

Supply chains have used e-business to enhance responsiveness (and therefore revenues) by selling direct to customers, providing twenty-four-hour access, widening the product portfolio, providing customers with a personalized and customized shopping experience, reducing the time taken to bring new products to market, changing prices based on product availability and services provided, enabling price discrimination, using the Internet for efficient funds transfer, lowering stockouts, and making the experience convenient for the purchaser. The revenue enhancement achieved has varied with the extent to which

an e-business has been able to exploit these opportunities. Supply chains have used e-business in a variety of ways to impact costs in each of the four supply chain drivers—inventory (by lowering inventory levels), facilities (by reducing the number of facilities and the operating costs within those facilities), transportation (in general, by increasing outbound transportation costs), and information (by requiring some additional IT investment). In a B2B setting, it is beneficial to analyze three categories of these benefits, namely reduced transaction costs, increased market efficiency, and increased supply chain coordination, to determine where to target e-business efforts.

3. Utilize the e-business frameworks to evaluate whether a company is a good candidate for e-business and where they should target their e-business efforts.

The e-business scorecard rates the impact of e-business on each category that impacts revenues or costs. The magnitude of the impact of e-business in each category will vary depending on the industry the company is in as well as the strategy they are taking. After rating a particular company on the e-business scorecard, one can gauge whether or not this business is a good fit for e-business. If a company is in a B2B environment, the B2B addition to the framework can be used to channel one's e-business efforts toward those areas that will provide the greatest return.

DISCUSSION QUESTIONS

1. Discuss how a catalog retailer like L. L. Bean can use e-business to its advantage.
2. Consider the sale of home improvement products at Amazon.com, Home Depot, or a chain of hardware stores like Tru-Value. Who can extract the greatest benefit from going online? Why?
3. Amazon.com sells books, music, electronics, software, toys, and home improvement products online. In which product category does e-business offer the greatest advantage compared to a retail store chain? In which product category does e-business offer the smallest advantage (or a potential cost disadvantage) compared to a retail store chain? Why?
4. Why should an e-business like Amazon.com build more warehouses as its sales volume grows?
5. The Gap has integrated its e-business with its retail stores. What potential advantages does this strategy offer compared to having a separate e-business?
6. Why is the benefit from e-business larger in the PC industry than in the book or grocery industry?
7. Why is it difficult for an e-business in the grocery industry to compete against supermarkets on the basis of price?

BIBLIOGRAPHY

Business Trade & Technology Strategies, The Forrester Report (August 1998).

Chopra, Sunil, and Jan Van Mieghem. 2000. "Which E-Business Is Right for Your Supply Chain?" *Supply Chain Management Review* (July–August): 32–40.

Chopra, Sunil, Darren Dougan, and Gareth Taylor. 2001. "B2B E-Commerce Opportunities." *Supply Chain Management Review* (May–June): 50–58.

Evans, Philip, and Thomas S. Wurster. 1999. "Getting Real about Virtual Commerce." *Harvard Business Review* (November–December): 84–94.

Goller, Albert, and Herbert Heinzel. 2002. "Siemens—the E-Company." *Supply Chain Management Review* (March–April): 58–65.

Handfield, Robert B. 2001. "Before You Build Your B2B Network, Redesign Your Supply Chain." *Supply Chain Management Review* (July–August): 18–26.

Hanson, Ward. 2000. *Principles of Internet Marketing.* Cincinnati, Ohio: South-West College Publishing.

Lee, Hau L., and Seungjin Whang. 2001. "Winning the Last Mile of E-Commerce." *Sloan Management Review* (Summer): 54–62.

Mastering Commerce Logistics, The Forrester Report (August 1999).

Poirier, Charles C. 1999. "The Convergence of Business & Technology." *Supply Chain Management Review* (Fall): 52–58.

Retail's Growth Spiral, The Forrester Report (November 1998).

Ricker, Fred R., and Ravi Kalakota. 1999. "Order Fulfillment: The Hidden Key to E-Commerce Success." *Supply Chain Management Review* (Fall): 60–70.

Salcedo, Simon, and Ann Grackin. 2000. "The E-Value Chain." *Supply Chain Management Review* (Winter): 63–70.

Sengupta, Sumantra. 2001. "B2B Exchanges Anyone? New Paths to Success." *Supply Chain Management Review* (November–December): 68–73.

Shapiro, Carl, and Hal R. Varian. 1999. *Information Rules: A Strategic Guide to the Network Economy*. Boston: Harvard Business School Press.

"The E-Enabled Supply Chain." Global Supplement, *Supply Chain Management Review* (Fall 1999).

Turban, Efraim, Jae Lee, David King, and H. Michael Chung. 2000. *Electronic Commerce: A Managerial Perspective*. Upper Saddle River, N.J.: Prentice Hall.

Willcocks, Leslie P., and Robert Plant. 2001. "Pathways to E-Business Leadership: Getting from Bricks to Clicks." *Sloan Management Review* (Spring): 50–59.

Name Index

Subject Index